BEHAVIOR INTERVENTION MANUAL

Goals, Objectives, and Intervention Strategies

Edited by Samm N. House

Copyright © 2002 by Hawthorne Educational Services, Inc.

Printed in the
United States of America.
1/04

H A W T H O R N E
Educational Services, Inc.
800 Gray Oak Drive
Columbia, MO 65201
Telephone: (573) 874-1710
FAX: (800) 442-9509
www.hes-inc.com

Table of Contents

B. Emotional or Physical Well-Being

Behavior
Number

C. Group Behavior

Behavior
Number

D. Hyperactive-Impulsive

Behavior
Number

E. Inappropriate Behavior

Behavior
Number

F. Interpersonal Relationships

Behavior
Number

G. Listening

**Behavior
Number**

H. Motivation

**Behavior
Number**

I. Organization

**Behavior
Number**

J. Personal Hygiene

**Behavior
Number**

K. Rules and Expectations

**Behavior
Number**

L. Social Interactions

**Behavior
Number**

I. *Behavior Intervention Manual*

The *Behavior Intervention Manual* (BIM) is a compilation of goals, objectives, and intervention strategies for 253 behaviors grouped by categories. It is designed to respond to the most typical behavior problems exhibited by students in educational settings. The interventions are appropriate for any student engaging in the selected behaviors. The student need not be identified as behaviorally disordered/emotionally disturbed or handicapped in anyway. The appropriateness of the interventions relates directly to the behavior problem and not to classification labels. The interventions selected reflect positive teacher behavior, contribute to a positive classroom atmosphere, and have been proven to contribute to student success in the educational environment. All interventions included have been found to be successful by administrators, teachers, aides, counselors, parents, and other persons intent on helping students.

The interventions contained in this manual represent solutions which are both preventive and reactive. Preventive interventions are environmental modifications used to reduce variables (e.g., noise, movement, another student, etc.) which may stimulate problem behavior. Reactive interventions "teach" the student more appropriate ways to deal with his/her behavior. These strategies include increased self-control, problem-solving skills, etc.

Some interventions in this manual apply to most students and should be implemented first to provide a more general approach to problem reduction. Other interventions are more specific and should be individually selected for a student based on the appropriateness of the intervention for that student and the situation.

Professional judgment should guide the choice of interventions for any particular student. The student's age, gender, grade level, local community standards, and handicap, if one exists, are all to be considered in selecting appropriate intervention strategies.

For any behavior problem exhibited by students, it will be of value to assess the extent to which institutional variables influence the behavior and possibly contribute to the problem. Limited supervision in play areas, hallways, and during extracurricular activities, as well as arbitrary groups and seating arrangements are examples of factors which are inherent in the educational setting and often contribute to problem behavior. As a first step in improving unsuccessful or inappropriate behavior, institutional variables should be evaluated and reduced. To appropriately respond to individual situations, all related variables in the educational setting which influence student behavior problems should be identified and considered when choosing appropriate interventions to facilitate a student's success. In order not to overlook any historical or contemporary determinants of behavior, other variables to consider are vision, hearing, general health, nutrition, and family case history.

The goals and objectives in this manual were developed to serve as examples which may be used in writing IEPs. Criteria for measuring the success of the student's attainment of the goals and objectives must be determined by those professional educators and parents who are aware of the student's current abilities and program recommendations.

Interventions may be chosen by a team of professionals, a special educator in a self-contained class or functioning in a resource or consultant capacity, or by a regular education teacher. The interventions have been found appropriate for special education, as well as regular education classroom environments.

Use of the same interventions in all settings by all teachers and instructional personnel working with the student facilitates the likelihood of student success in the educational environment. The interventions included in this manual are appropriate for all educational environments and lend themselves particularly well to creating continuity across all the educational settings in which the student functions.

II. Goals, Objectives, and Interventions

1 Has difficulty asking for assistance or clarification, when necessary, after receiving directions and/or attempting work independently

Goals:
1. The student will ask for assistance when appropriate.

Objectives:
1. The student will determine when assistance is required in ____ out of ____ trials.
2. The student will ask questions in order to obtain additional information during structured classroom activities in ____ out of ____ trials.
3. The student will ask questions in order to obtain additional information during everyday activities in ____ out of ____ trials.
4. The student will demonstrate the ability to determine if the answer he/she received to a question is adequate with ____% accuracy.
5. The student will demonstrate the ability to ask a question on ____ out of ____ trials.
6. The student will ask for assistance during structured classroom time ____ out of ____ trials.
7. The student will ask for assistance during everyday activities on ____ out of ____ trials.
8. The student will ask for assistance only when necessary when performing tasks on ____ out of ____ trials.

Interventions:

1. Reinforce the student for seeking assistance rather than remaining inactive: (a) give the student a tangible reward (e.g., classroom privileges, line leading, passing out materials, five minutes free time, etc.) or (b) give the student an intangible reward (e.g., praise, handshake, smile, etc.).

2. Reinforce the student for performing assignments independently.

3. Speak to the student to explain (a) what he/she is doing wrong (e.g., sitting and waiting, doing nothing, etc.) and (b) what he/she should be doing (e.g., beginning an activity, asking for assistance if necessary, etc.).

4. Establish classroom rules:
- Work on-task.
- Work quietly.
- Request assistance when needed.
- Remain in your seat.
- Finish task.
- Meet task expectations.

Review rules often. Reinforce students for following rules.

5. Reinforce those students in the classroom who find things to do, remain active, ask for assistance, etc.

6. Reinforce the student for seeking assistance when appropriate based on the number of times he/she can be successful. As the student demonstrates success, gradually increase the number of times required for reinforcement.

7. Write a contract with the student specifying what behavior is expected (e.g., seeking assistance when needed, etc.) and what reinforcement will be made available when the terms of the contract have been met.

8. Communicate with the parents (e.g., notes home, phone calls, etc.) to share information concerning the student's progress. The parents may reinforce the student at home for remaining active and seeking assistance at school.

9. Choose a peer to model seeking assistance when appropriate for the student.

10. Encourage the student to question any directions, explanations or instructions he/she does not understand.

11. Be a model for seeking assistance in the community (e.g., asking for directions, asking for help in a department store, etc.).

12. Offer the student assistance frequently throughout the day.

13. Make certain that directions, explanations, and instructions are delivered on the student's ability level.

14. Structure the environment so the student is not required to rely on others for information about assignments (e.g., make certain the student's tasks are on his/her ability level, make certain instructions are clear, and maintain frequent interactions with the student in order to ensure his/her success).

15. Communicate with the student as often as opportunities permit to detect the student's needs.

16. Demonstrate accepting behavior (e.g., willingness to help others, making criticisms constructive and positive, demonstrating confidentiality in personal matters, etc.).

17. Communicate to the student an interest in his/her needs.

18. Communicate to the student that he/she is a worthwhile individual.

19. Call on the student often to encourage communication.

20. Teach the student communication skills to be used in the classroom (e.g., hand-raising, expressing needs in written and/or verbal forms, etc.).

21. Encourage communication skills in the classroom and community.

22. Encourage conversational interchange in the classroom on a daily basis with particular emphasis on giving and receiving information.

23. Maintain mobility throughout the classroom in order to determine the student's needs.

24. Teach the student appropriate communication skills to be used in the community (e.g., locating a security guard when lost in a mall, asking a clerk for assistance in a retail store, etc.).

25. Encourage the student to communicate his/her needs to other personnel in the educational environment (e.g., school counselor, school psychologist, principal, etc.).

26. Communicate with parents, agencies, or the appropriate parties to inform them of the problem, determine the cause of the problem, and consider possible solutions to the problem.

27. Teach the student to communicate his/her needs in an appropriate manner (e.g., raise hand, use a normal tone of voice when speaking, verbally express problems, etc.).

28. Recognize the student's attempts to communicate his/her needs (e.g., facial expressions, gestures, inactivity, self-depreciating comments, etc.).

29. Have the student interact with a peer to encourage him/her to communicate his/her needs to others. As the student demonstrates success in communicating his/her needs to others, gradually increase peer interaction.

30. Pair the student with a non-threatening peer, a peer with similar interests and ability level, etc.

31. Give the student responsibilities in the classroom to increase the probability of more involvement and activity (e.g., passing out materials, collecting lunch money, collecting schoolwork, etc.).

32. Give the student responsibilities in the classroom that require communication (e.g., peer tutor, group leader, teacher assistant, etc.).

33. Present the task in the most interesting manner possible.

34. Assess the degree of task difficulty in comparison with the student's ability to perform the task.

35. Reduce distracting stimuli (e.g., place the student in the front row, provide a carrel or quiet place away from distractions, etc.). This is to be used as a means of reducing distracting stimuli and not as a form of punishment.

36. Encourage the student to ask for clarification of directions for assignments.

37. Provide the student with step-by-step written directions for performing assignments.

38. Choose a peer from whom the student may seek assistance.

39. Explain to the student that work not done during work time will have to be done during other times (e.g., break time, recreational time, after school, etc.).

40. Maintain consistency of expectations while keeping expectations within the ability level of the student.

41. Maintain consistency in the daily routine.

42. Work a few problems with the student on an assignment in order to serve as a model and help the student begin a task.

43. Reinforce the student for beginning, working on, asking for assistance, and completing assignments.

44. Attempt to provide assistance immediately. Gradually increase the length of time the student must wait for assistance when the teacher is helping another student, instructing, etc.

45. Encourage the student to go to the next problem, go to another part of the assignment, begin a new assignment, etc., when waiting for assistance from an instructor.

46. Allow the student to perform alternative assignments. Gradually introduce more components of the regular assignments until those assignments are routinely performed.

47. Establish alternative activities for the student to perform when waiting for assistance from an instructor (e.g., check work already completed, color, look at a magazine, organize work area, begin another task, etc.).

48. Explain the importance of understanding directions and/or carrying out instructions as well as the importance of asking for assistance.

49. Discuss with the student what behavior is expected (e.g., following directions, asking for assistance when needed, etc.).

50. Teach the student to recognize key words and phrases related to directions/instructions in order to increase his/her ability to follow directions accurately and to ask for assistance.

2 Fails to perform tasks or assignments independently

Goal:

1. The student will independently perform assignments.

Objectives:

1. The student will attempt to perform a given assignment before asking for teacher assistance on _____ out of _____ trials.
2. The student will read necessary directions, instructions, explanations, etc., before asking for teacher assistance on _____ out of _____ trials.
3. The student will independently complete _____ out of _____ assignments per school day.
4. The student will ask for teacher assistance only when necessary when performing assignments on _____ out of _____ trials.
5. The student will work for _____ minutes without requiring assistance from the teacher on _____ out of _____ trials.

Interventions:

1. Establish classroom rules:
   - Stay on-task.
   - Work quietly.
   - Request assistance when needed.
   - Remain in your seat.
   - Finish task.
   - Meet task expectations.

Review rules often. Reinforce students for following the rules.

2. Set time limits for completing assignments.

3. Reinforce the student for performing assignments independently.

4. Have the student prioritize tasks by importance (e.g., task A must be done today, task B can be done today, and task C can wait until tomorrow).

5. Structure the environment to facilitate task completion (i.e. make certain the student's tasks are on his/her ability level, be sure that instructions are clear, and maintain frequent interactions with the student in order to facilitate success).

6. Encourage parents to set aside and enforce a consistent time period at home for the student to complete homework. All family members should work on tasks (e.g., correspondence, balancing accounts, reading, etc.) during this time.

7. Provide the student with structure for all academic activities (e.g., specific directions, routine format for tasks, time limits, etc.).

8. Reinforce the student for beginning, working on, and completing assignments.

9. Make certain that directions, explanations, and instructions are delivered on the student's ability level.

10. Allow the student additional time to complete assignments when working independently.

11. Provide the student with a selection of assignments and require him/her to choose a minimum number of assignments to perform independently (e.g., present the student with 10 academic tasks from which six must be completed that day).

12. Assess the appropriateness of giving the student assignments which require copying if the student's ability level makes it impossible for him/her to complete the assignment.

13. Communicate your expectations to the student for the successful completion of assignments.

14. Provide a written list of directions for a long-term assignment.

15. Schedule recreational activities at the end of the day. Make participation in these activities dependent upon completion of assignments.

16. Communicate with the student's parents (e.g., notes home, phone calls, etc.) in order to share information concerning their child's progress. The parents may reinforce the student at home for completing assignments independently.

17. Assess the degree of task difficulty in relation to the student's ability to perform the task.

18. Be consistent in expecting the student to complete assignments. Do not allow the student to fail to complete assigned tasks one time and expect tasks to be completed the next time.

19. Reinforce those students in the classroom who complete assignments independently.

20. Encourage the student to follow a less desirable task with a more desirable task. Make completion of the first necessary to perform the second.

21. Assess the degree of task difficulty to determine whether or not the student will require additional information, time, assistance, etc., before beginning a task.

22. Instruct the student in thinking through instructions/directions before beginning a task.

23. Instruct the student on ways to reduce distracting activities which interfere with his/her responsibilities (e.g., turn off the TV when it is time to complete tasks, do not allow friends to come over when it is time to do homework, etc.).

24. Explain to the student that work not done during work time will have to be done during other times (e.g., break time, recreational time, after school, etc.).

25. Assist the student in writing a contract for himself/herself designating a time to complete an assignment and avoid procrastination.

26. Encourage the student to reward himself/ herself (e.g., take a ten minute break, speak briefly with a relative, telephone a friend, etc.) for concentrating on an assignment for a specific length of time.

27. Provide the student with step-by-step written directions for assignments.

28. Specify exactly what is to be done for the completion of an assignment (e.g., indicate definite starting and stopping points, indicate the minimum requirements, etc.).

29. Do not give directions to the student from across the room. Go to student, get his/her undivided attention, and tell him/her what to do.

30. Reinforce the student for completing assignments independently: (a) give the student a tangible reward (e.g., classroom privileges, free homework pass, five minutes free time, etc.) or (b) give the student an intangible reward (e.g., praise, handshake, smile, etc.).

31. Allow the student to perform alternative assignments. Gradually introduce more components of the regular assignments until those assignments are routinely performed.

32. Have the student keep a chart/graph representing the number of assignments performed independently.

33. Have the student review and update his/her assignment calendar daily. Encourage the student to prepare in advance for assignments, due dates, etc.

34. Communicate with parents, agencies, or the appropriate parties, to inform them of the problem, determine the cause of the problem, and consider possible solutions to the problem.

35. Reduce distracting stimuli (e.g., place the student in the front row, provide a carrel or quiet place away from distractions, etc.). This is to be used as a means of reducing stimuli and not as a form of punishment.

36. Communicate to the student an interest in his/ her success.

37. Allow the student to set a timer in order to complete assignments in a reasonable period of time.

38. Create challenges in assignments to increase interest and motivation (e.g., stress problem solving and creative/critical thinking rather than drill/repetition, etc.).

39. Communicate to the student that he/she is a worthwhile individual.

40. Present assignments in the most interesting manner possible.

41. Communicate clearly with the student the length of time he/she has to complete an assignment and when the assignment is due. The student may want to use a timer in order to complete the tasks within the given period of time.

42. Reinforce the student for completing assignments independently based on the number of times he/she can be successful. Gradually increase the number of times required for reinforcement as the student demonstrates success.

43. Encourage the student to ask for clarification of any directions, explanations, and instructions before beginning a task to reinforce comprehension.

44. Have the student assemble all materials necessary to work on a project, assignment, etc., to reduce the need to search for materials.

45. Make certain that the student understands the relationship between inappropriate behavior and the consequences which follow (e.g., failure to complete assignments independently results in lower grades, less responsibility, etc.).

46. Make certain that assignments given to the student are appropriate for his/her level of development and ability.

47. Establish an environmental setting for the classroom that promotes optimal individual performance (e.g., quiet room, background music, fresh air, etc.).

48. Maintain consistent expectations within the ability level of the student.

49. Choose a peer, friend, etc., who displays the ability to organize an assignment prior to beginning it. Have the student observe that person and try to model the behaviors which allow him/her to organize assignments.

50. Discuss with the student the expectation at the beginning of each period so he/she knows what is required.

51. Work a few problems of the assignment with the student to serve as a model and start the student on the assignment.

52. Assign the student shorter tasks. As the student demonstrates success, gradually increase the length of the tasks.

53. Organize assignments by breaking them into small segments. Set deadlines and provide the student with a reward after completing each segment of the assignment.

54. Develop a checklist/chart for daily assignments to be completed by the student.

55. Teach the student time-management skills. Have the student make a daily plan and follow it. Encourage the student to avoid becoming distracted by events, impulses, and moods.

56. Enlist the help of a peer, paraprofessional, parent, etc., to remind the student of assignments.

57. Maintain mobility throughout the classroom in order to determine the student's attention to task.

58. Call on the student often in order to encourage communication.

59. Have the student use a daily calendar to write down assignments, projects, due dates, etc. Use the calendar to develop the student's time-management skills.

60. Have the student schedule independent working times when he/she is most likely to maintain attention (e.g., one hour after medication, 45 minutes after dinner, first thing in the morning, etc.).

61. Allow the student more decision-making opportunities relative to class activities and assignments.

62. Have the student use electronic reminders to assist him/her in completion of assignments (e.g., programmable watch, computer programs, voice mail, etc.).

63. Speak to the student to explain (a) what he/she is doing wrong (e.g., off-task, failing to complete assignments) and (b) what he/she should be doing (e.g., attending to task, completing assignments sequentially, completing tasks).

64. Write a contract with the student specifying what behavior is expected (e.g., complete assigned project by due date) and what reinforcement will be made available when the terms of the contract have been met.

65. Have the student develop a checklist/chart to follow which will allow him/her to complete all assignments.

66. Make sure the student is paying attention when he/she is told to do something. Have the student make eye contact and repeat the information to check for understanding.

67. Encourage the student to take a break while working on monotonous assignments to relieve restlessness and improve concentration. Set a definite time limit for breaks.

68. Develop an environment that is quiet and uncluttered (e.g., clean, well-lighted, fresh-smelling, and at a comfortable temperature).

3 Does not demonstrate the ability to follow a routine

Goals:

1. The student will demonstrate the ability to follow a routine.

Objectives:

1. The student will follow a routine, with physical assistance, on _____ out of _____ trials.
2. The student will follow a routine, with verbal reminders, on _____ out of _____ trials.
3. The student will independently follow a routine on _____ out of _____ trials.
4. The student will rely on environmental cues to follow a routine (e.g., class schedule, school schedule, bells, lights turned off and on, clock) on _____ out of _____ trials.

Interventions:

1. Communicate with the student's parents (e.g., notes home, phone calls, etc.) to share information concerning their child's progress. The parents may reinforce the student at home for demonstrating the ability to follow a routine at school.

2. Encourage the student to establish a schedule to follow consistently at home (e.g., make the bed before eating breakfast, load the dishwasher before going to school, perform daily chores right after school, clean the kitchen before sitting down to watch TV, etc.). Have the student post the schedule on the refrigerator as a reminder.

3. Encourage the student to develop a 30 second definition of his/her goal to help him/her stay on-task and follow a routine (e.g., "I will complete this task to the best of my ability. The better I focus and stay on-task, the better job I will do.").

4. Have the student rely on a predetermined signal in order to enhance his/her ability to follow a routine (e.g., bells, lights, etc.).

5. Consider carefully the student's age and maturity level before expecting him/her to follow a routine.

6. Choose a classmate to model the ability to follow a routine for the student.

7. Have the student question any directions, explanations, or instructions he/she does not understand about a routine.

8. Have the student work near a peer in order to follow the same routine that the peer follows.

9. Make certain that the student consistently follows his/her daily routine.

10. Provide the student with a schedule of daily events which identifies the daily activities and the times at which they occur.

11. Provide the student with a schedule of daily events to be attached to the student's desk and/or carried with the student at all times.

12. Try to give the student as much structure and "sameness" in his/her school day as possible.

13. Have the student develop an awareness of the consequences of his/her behavior on the job site by writing down or talking through problems which may occur due to his/her inability to follow a routine (e.g., if you do not establish a routine, you will not finish all your responsibilities then you may not get the raise you want or you could lose your job).

14. Establish a routine to follow before changing activities (e.g., put away materials, assemble materials for the next activity, make a list of what materials need to be replenished, etc.).

15. Reduce distracting stimuli which might cause the student to be unable to follow a routine (e.g., peers, physical activity, etc.).

16. Monitor the student's performance in activities or tasks to make certain the student begins, works on, and completes an assignment in order to be ready to move to the next activity in his/her routine.

17. Have the student develop a checklist/chart to follow which will allow him/her to follow a specific routine.

18. Maintain consistency in the classroom's daily routine.

19. Allow the student to help decide what his/her routine responsibilities will be.

20. Have the student rely on environmental events to remind him/her when to change activities in his/her routine (e.g., other students changing activities, bells, etc.).

21. Provide the student with structure for all academic activities (e.g., specific directions, routine format for tasks, time limits, etc.).

22. Have the student define his/her goals. Assist the student in developing specific strategies to achieve his/her goals and follow through on those strategies.

23. Have the student ask himself/herself questions (e.g., "What's next?") to keep himself/herself focused on the daily classroom routine.

24. Discuss the student's routine with him/her at the beginning of each day and make certain that he/she knows the expectations.

25. Allow the student to participate in deciding when changes in his/her routine will occur.

26. Limit the number of changes in the student's established routine. As the student demonstrates success, gradually increase the number of changes in the routine.

27. Remind the student when it is time to change activities in order to enhance his/her ability to follow a routine.

28. Make certain that the activities in the student's routine are on his/her ability level.

29. Make certain that the teacher is a model for following a routine.

30. Explain to the student the need to maintain flexibility in following a routine when changes in the routine are required.

31. Make sure the student does not have a lot of unstructured time.

32. Have the student identify a peer who has the ability to follow a routine. Encourage the student to observe that person and try to model the behaviors which allow him/her to follow a routine without becoming distracted.

33. Make it a habit to periodically review the classroom/school routines with the student.

34. Establish classroom routines (e.g., materials ready when class begins, homework turned in before the end of class, etc.).

35. Have the student use electronic reminders to assist him/her in following a routine (e.g., a programmable watch, computer programs, electronic calendar, etc.).

36. Have the student maintain written reminders of task sequences.

37. Have the student establish a routine for himself/herself. Assist the student in developing a weekly schedule and weekend schedule.

38. Have the student imagine the steps required to complete a routine before beginning it.

39. Establish rules for working:
- Work on the task at hand.
- Work quietly.
- Remain in your seat.
- Complete the task.
- Meet task expectations.

Review rules often. Reinforce students for following the rules.

40. Limit interruptions in the student's routine by persons or events in the school (e.g., cancellation of classes or activities such as art, music, physical education; testing; special services; delays; etc.).

41. Provide the student with a limited routine to follow. As the student demonstrates success, gradually increase the activities in the routine as the student experiences success.

42. Provide the student with an alternative routine to follow if he/she encounters difficulty following his/her regular routine.

43. Provide the student with a schedule of daily events in order that he/she will know which activity comes next and can prepare for it.

44. Enlist different people (e.g., parent, school counselor, peer, etc.) to help the student follow a daily routine.

45. Have a peer accompany the student to other locations in the building which are part of the student's routine.

46. Allow the student to contribute to the development of his/her routine in order to enhance his/her ability to follow the routine (e.g., have the student determine the order of activities).

47. Have a peer remind the student when to change activities according to his/her routine.

48. Be consistent in expecting the student to follow a routine. Do not allow the student to not follow a routine one time and expect him/her to follow a routine the next time.

49. Be personally available for assistance when the student is dealing with changes in his/her routine (e.g., switching semester classes, attending school assembly, etc.).

50. Limit the student's responsibilities to increase his/her ability to focus on a routine (e.g., extracurricular activities, part-time job, etc.).

51. Have the student anticipate future tasks/assignments and develop plans for addressing them.

52. Post the classroom routine throughout the classroom (e.g., on the student's desk, chalkboard, bulletin board, etc.).

53. Have the student perform the same responsibilities each day, week, etc.

54. Provide the student with a revised schedule of daily events when there is a change in routine which identifies the activities for the day and the times when they will occur (e.g., special assembly schedule, half day schedule, etc.).

55. Discuss any necessary changes in the student's routine well in advance of the occurrence of the changes.

56. Make certain the student is able to tell time in order to enhance his/her ability to follow a routine.

57. Reinforce the student for demonstrating the ability to follow a routine: (a) give the student a tangible reward (e.g., classroom privileges, passing out materials, five minutes free time, etc.) or (b) give the student an intangible reward (e.g., praise, handshake, smile, etc.).

58. Speak to the student to explain (a) what he/she is doing wrong (e.g., failing to come to class on time, failing to follow the schedule of activities, etc.) and (b) what he/she should be doing (e.g., coming to class on time, following the schedule of activities, etc.).

59. Establish classroom rules:
- Stay on-task.
- Work quietly.
- Remain in your seat.
- Finish task.
- Meet task expectations.

Review rules often. Reinforce students for following the rules.

60. Reinforce those students in the classroom who demonstrate the ability to follow a routine.

61. Reinforce the student for demonstrating the ability to follow a routine based on the length of time the student can be successful. As the student demonstrates success, gradually increase the length of time required for reinforcement.

62. Allow the student to contribute to the development of his/her routine in order to enhance his/her ability to follow the routine (e.g., have the student determine the order of activities).

63. Provide the student with a verbal reminder of changes in his/her routine.

64. Have the student use a timer to indicate when to change activities in his/her routine.

65. Determine an expected length of time for each individual activity in order to help the student follow his/her routine (i.e., make certain the student can finish an activity in an established length of time in order to help him/her stay within the time restrictions of the routine).

66. Teach the student to tell time in order to enhance his/her ability to follow a routine.

67. Communicate with the student's parents to establish a routine for the student to follow for getting ready for school, doing chores, completing homework, etc. This will help the student remember what is expected.

68. Write a contract with the student specifying what behavior is expected (e.g., following the schedule of activities) and what reinforcement will be made available when the terms of the contract have been met.

69. Evaluate the appropriateness of the routine to determine (a) if the routine is too easy, (b) if the routine is too difficult, and (c) if the length of time scheduled to complete the routine is adequate.

70. Communicate with the student's cooperative work experience/vocational education teacher to choose an appropriate job site for the student. Reinforce the student for following a routine on the job.

71. Teach problem-solving skills:
- Identify the problem.
- Identify the goals and objectives.
- Develop a strategy/plan for action.
- Carry out the plan.
- Evaluate the results.

72. Make certain that the student's daily routine is consistent.

4 Does not demonstrate appropriate behavior in an academic group setting

Goals:

1. The student will demonstrate appropriate behavior in an academic group setting.

Objectives:

1. The student will work quietly in a small academic group setting on _____ out of _____ trials.
2. The student will raise his/her hand in a small academic group setting on _____ out of _____ trials.
3. The student will remain seated in a small academic group setting on _____ out of _____ trials.
4. The student will verbally participate in a small academic group setting on _____ out of _____ trials.
5. The student will physically participate in a small academic group setting on _____ out of _____ trials.
6. The student will follow directions in a small academic group setting on _____ out of _____ trials.
7. The student will begin working on a task in a small academic group setting on _____ out of _____ trials.
8. The student will work continuously on a task in a small academic group setting on _____ out of _____ trials.
9. The student will complete assignments in a small academic group setting on _____ out of _____ trials.
10. The student will ask for assistance when necessary in a small academic group setting on _____ out of _____ trials.
11. The student will work independently in a small academic group setting on _____ out of _____ trials.
12. The student will talk in a quiet voice in a small academic group setting on _____ out of _____ trials.
13. The student will share materials in a small academic group setting on _____ out of _____ trials.
14. The student will wait his/her turn in a small academic group setting on _____ out of _____ trials.

Interventions:

1. DO NOT FORCE the student to participate in a small academic group setting.

2. Choose a peer to sit/work directly with the student (e.g., in different settings such as art, music, P.E.; or different activities such as tutoring; group projects; etc.).

3. Ask the student questions that cannot be answered simply by "yes" or "no."

4. Call on the student when he/she is most likely to be able to respond successfully (e.g., when discussing something in which the student is interested, when you are certain the student knows the answer, etc.).

5. Try various groupings in order to determine the situation in which the student is most comfortable.

6. Have peers invite the student to participate in school or extracurricular activities.

7. Request that the student be the leader of a small group activity if he/she possesses mastery or an interest in the activity.

8. Allow the student to be present during small group activities without requiring active participation. As the student demonstrates success, require more involvement.

9. Have the student work with one or two other group members. As the student becomes more comfortable, gradually increase the group size.

10. Demonstrate respect for the student's opinions, responses, suggestions, etc.

11. Review group rules/expectations at the beginning of each group activity.

12. Give the student the opportunity to pick a topic or activity for the group to work on together.

13. Give the student the opportunity to choose a group activity and choose the group members (e.g., along with the teacher decide what the activity will be, what individual group members will do, etc.).

14. Assign the student a role to perform in the group activity that he/she can perform successfully (e.g., secretary, researcher, group behavior monitor, etc.).

15. Make certain the student is productive and accurate in performing individual assignments before placing him/her in small group activities.

16. Make certain that the student can follow classroom rules/expectations independently before placing him/her in small group activities.

17. Reduce the emphasis on competition. Fear of failure may cause the student to refuse to work in small group activities.

18. Help the student learn to be satisfied with personal best effort rather than some arbitrary measure of success. Success is measured individually according to ability level, and progress of any kind is a measure of success.

19. Place the student with peers who will be appropriate role models and are likely to facilitate his/her academic and behavioral success.

20. Place the student with group members who are least likely to be threatening to the student (e.g., younger students, students just learning a skill he/she has mastered, etc.).

21. Remove the student from the group if he/she behaves inappropriately.

22. Make certain that the student understands instructions/directions for the group activity (e.g., give instructions in a variety of ways; make certain that the student understands his/her role; review the rules for group behavior before the activity begins; etc.).

23. Make certain that the student has all needed materials to perform his/her role in the group (e.g., paper, pencil, art supplies, reference materials, etc.).

24. Make certain that the student has enough room to work successfully (e.g., consider distance from other students, room for all materials, etc.).

25. Make certain the student is actively involved in the group (e.g., call on the student frequently; assign the student a responsibility such as teacher assistant; have the student be group leader; etc.).

26. Make certain the academic and social demands of the group situation are within the student's ability level.

27. Help the student get to know group members before requiring group participation (e.g., introduce the students to one another; allow the students unstructured free time together; etc.).

28. Reduce distracting stimuli which could interfere with the student's success in a group activity (e.g., provide enough room to move without physical contact; keep noise level to a minimum; keep movement in the environment to a minimum; etc.).

29. Schedule activities so your time can be spent uninterrupted with the group.

30. Schedule small group activities as part of the student's daily routine (i.e., small group activities should occur on a regularly scheduled basis so that the student will be prepared and know what to expect).

31. Place the student in group activities he/she prefers. Gradually include less desirable activities over time.

32. Provide the student with alternative ways to perform a group assignment and allow him/her to choose the most desirable (e.g., a written paragraph assignment may be accomplished by writing a note to a friend, writing about a recent experience, describing a favorite pastime, etc.).

33. Allow the student to participate in the one small group activity he/she prefers. As the student experiences success, require him/her to participate in more small group activities.

34. Schedule small group activities when the student is most likely to be successful (e.g., before break time rather than immediately after break time, after the first individual assignment of the day has been completed in order to establish productive behavior, etc.).

35. Program alternative individual activities if the student is unlikely to be successful (e.g., if the schedule has been changed; if holidays or special events have stimulated the student, making successful group interactions unlikely; etc.).

36. Speak to the student to explain (a) what the student is doing wrong (e.g., failing to participate) and (b) what the student should be doing (e.g., talking, taking turns, sharing, etc.).

37. Position the student's desk or work so that he/she works near other students but is not visually distracted by them (e.g., turn the student's desk away from other students).

38. Allow the student to leave a small group activity and return to independent work when the student can no longer be successful in the group activity (e.g., he/she is disrupting the group, fighting, etc.).

39. Have the student question any directions, explanations, or instructions not understood.

40. Evaluate the appropriateness of the task to determine (a) if the task is too easy, (b) if the task is too difficult, and (c) if the length of time scheduled to complete the task is adequate.

41. Communicate with parents (e.g., notes home, phone calls, etc.) to share information concerning the student's progress. The parents may reinforce the student at home for demonstrating appropriate behavior in small academic group settings at school.

42. Write a contract with the student specifying what behavior is expected (e.g., working appropriately with peers) and what reinforcement will be made available when the terms of the contract have been met.

43. Reinforce the student for demonstrating appropriate behavior in a small academic group setting based on the length of time the student can be successful. As the student demonstrates success, gradually increase the length of time required for reinforcement.

44. Reinforce those students in the classroom who demonstrate appropriate behavior in a small academic group setting.

45. Allow the student to join the group after the activity has begun if he/she is unable to participate appropriately at the beginning of the activity.

46. Establish classroom rules:
- Work on-task.
- Remain in your seat.
- Finish task.
- Meet task expectations.
- Raise your hand.

Review rules often. Reinforce students for following rules.

47. Reinforce the student for demonstrating appropriate behavior in a small academic group setting: (a) give the student a tangible reward (e.g., classroom privileges, line leading, passing out materials, five minutes free time, etc.) or (b) give the student an intangible reward (e.g., praise, handshake, smile, etc.).

48. Teach the student to think before acting (e.g., ask himself/herself: "What is happening?" "What am I doing?" "What should I do?" "What will be best for me?").

5   Is reluctant to attempt new assignments or tasks

Goals:
1. The student will attempt new assignments.
2. The student will attempt new tasks.

Objectives:
1. The student will attempt new assignments/tasks with physical assistance on _____ out of _____ trials.
2. The student will attempt new assignments/tasks with verbal prompts on _____ out of _____ trials.
3. The student will attempt new assignments/tasks with peer assistance on _____ out of _____ trials.
4. The student will independently attempt new assignments/tasks on _____ out of _____ trials.
5. The student will attempt new assignments/tasks within _____ (indicate a given time period).

Interventions:

1. Present the task in the most interesting and attractive manner possible.

2. Maintain mobility to provide assistance for the student.

3. Structure time units so that the student knows exactly how long he/she has to work and when the work must be finished.

4. Provide the student with more than enough time to finish an activity. As the student demonstrates success, gradually decrease the amount of time provided.

5. Give directions in a variety of ways to increase the probability of understanding (e.g., if the student fails to understand verbal directions, present them in written form).

6. Have the student repeat the directions verbally to the teacher.

7. Give a signal (e.g., clapping hands, turning lights off and on, etc.) before giving verbal directions.

8. Provide the student with a predetermined signal when he/she is not beginning a task (e.g., verbal cue, hand signal, etc.).

9. Tell the student that directions will only be given once.

10. Rewrite directions at a lower reading level.

11. Deliver verbal directions in a simple concrete manner.

12. Help the student with the first few items on a task and gradually reduce the amount of help over time.

13. Follow a less desirable task with a highly desirable task, making the completion of the first necessary to perform the second.

14. Provide the student with shorter tasks given more frequently.

15. Provide the student with a schedule of daily events so that he/she knows exactly what and how much there is to do in a day.

16. Prevent the student from becoming overstimulated by an activity (e.g., frustrated, angry, etc.).

17. Specify exactly what is to be done for the completion of a task (e.g., make definite starting and stopping points, a minimum requirement, etc.).

18. Require the student to begin each assignment within a specified period of time (e.g., three minutes, five minutes, etc.).

19. Provide the student with a selection of assignments, requiring him/her to choose a minimum number from the total (e.g., present the student with ten academic tasks from which six must be finished that day).

20. Start with a single problem and add more problems to the task over time.

21. Reduce emphasis on competition (e.g., academic or social). Fear of failure may cause the student to refuse to attempt new assignments or tasks.

22. Provide the student with self-checking materials so he/she may check work privately, thus reducing the fear of public failure.

23. Have the student attempt the new assignment/task in a private place (e.g., carrel, "office," quiet study area, etc.).

24. Have the student practice a new skill (e.g., jumping rope, dribbling a basketball, etc.) alone or with a peer or the teacher before the entire group attempts the activity.

25. Provide the student with the opportunity to perform the assignment/task in a variety of ways (e.g., on tape, with a calculator, verbally, etc.).

26. Allow the student to perform a new assignment/task in a variety of places in the building (e.g., resource room, library, learning center, etc.).

27. Provide the student with a sample of the assignment/task which has been partially completed by a peer or teacher (e.g., book report, project, etc.).

28. Have the student maintain a record (e.g., chart or graph) of his/her performance in attempting new assignments/tasks.

29. Allow the student the option of performing the assignment/task at another time (e.g., earlier in the day, later, on another day, etc.).

30. Make certain that the student has all the materials needed to perform the assignment/task.

31. Have the student paraphrase to the teacher what should be done to perform the assignment/task.

32. Explain to the student that work not done during work time will have to be made up at other times (e.g., at break time, before school, after school, during lunch time, etc.).

33. Teach the student direction-following skills: (a) listen carefully, (b) ask questions, (c) use environmental cues, (d) rely on examples provided, and (e) wait until directions are given before beginning.

34. Provide the student with optional courses of action to prevent total refusal to obey teacher directives.

35. Allow the student to perform alternative versions of a new assignment. Gradually introduce more components of the regular assignments until they can be performed successfully.

36. Have the student act as a peer tutor to teach another student a concept he/she has mastered. This can serve as reinforcement for the student.

37. Provide practice in new assignments or tasks using a computer software program that gives the student immediate feedback.

38. Make certain the student has mastery of concepts at each level before introducing a new skill level.

39. Have the student time activities to monitor his/her own behavior and accept time limits.

40. Communicate clearly to the student when it is time to begin.

41. Do not require the student to complete the assignment/task in one sitting.

42. Reduce distracting stimuli (e.g., place the student on the front row, provide a carrel or "office" space away from distractions, etc.). This is used as a means of reducing distracting stimuli and not as punishment.

43. Structure the environment to provide the student with increased opportunity for help or assistance.

44. Choose a peer or volunteer to help the student begin a task.

45. Assess the quality and clarity of directions, explanations, and instructions given to the student.

46. Have the student question any directions, explanations, or instructions not understood.

47. Speak with the student to explain (a) what the student is doing wrong (e.g., not attempting a new task) and (b) what the student should be doing (e.g., asking for assistance or clarification, following directions, starting on time, etc.).

48. Reinforce the student for attempting a new assignment/task: (a) give the student a tangible reward (e.g., classroom privileges, line leading, passing out materials, five minutes free time, etc.) or (b) give the student an intangible reward (e.g., praise, handshake, smile, etc.).

49. Write a contract with the student specifying what behavior is expected (e.g., attempting a new assignment/task) and what reinforcement will be made available when the terms of the contract have been met.

50. Reinforce the student for attempting a new assignment/task within the length of time he/she can be successful. As the student demonstrates success, gradually decrease the amount of time to begin the task in order to be reinforced.

51. Reinforce those students in the classroom who attempt a new assignment/task.

52. Evaluate the appropriateness of the task to determine (a) if the task is too easy, (b) if the task is too difficult and (b) if the length of time scheduled to complete the task is adequate.

53. Communicate with parents (e.g., notes home, phone calls, etc.) to share information concerning the student's progress. The parents may reinforce the student at home for attempting a new assignment/task at school.

6   Begins an assignment or activity before receiving or reading complete directions or instructions or fails to follow directions or instructions

Goals:

1. The student will begin assignments or activities after receiving directions or instructions.
2. The student will follow directions.
3. The student will follow instructions.

Objectives:

1. The student will begin assignments or activities after receiving directions, instructions, etc., with physical assistance on _____ out of _____ occasions.
2. The student will begin assignments or activities after receiving directions, instructions, etc., with verbal prompts on _____ out of _____ occasions.
3. The student will independently begin assignments or activities after receiving directions, instructions, etc., on _____ out of _____ occasions.
4. The student will begin assignments or activities after receiving directions, instructions, etc., within _____ (indicate a given time period).
5. The student will begin assignments or activities with peer assistance after receiving directions, instructions, etc., on _____ out of _____ occasions.

Interventions:

1. Practice direction-following skills on nonacademic tasks.

2. Establish classroom rules:
- Stay on-task.
- Work quietly.
- Remain in your seat.
- Finish task.
- Meet task expectations.

Review rules often. Reinforce students for following the rules.

3. Speak with the student to explain (a) what he/she is doing wrong (e.g., not following directions when performing academic tasks) and (b) what he/she should be doing (e.g., listening to directions, asking for clarification if not understood, taking notes, following one step at a time, etc.).

4. Follow a less desirable task with a highly desirable task. Make the completion of the first task necessary to perform the second task.

5. Rewrite directions for the student at a lower reading level.

6. Clarify instructions/directions/expectations before assigning a task.

7. Have the student maintain a record (e.g., chart or graph) of performance in attempting new assignments/activities.

8. Post needed information in a readily accessible location (e.g., bulletin board, desktop, dictation slide, etc.).

9. Reduce the emphasis on competition. Competitive activities may cause the student to hurry to begin the assignment without following the directions.

10. Have the student time his/her activities to monitor personal behavior and accept time limits.

11. Start with a single problem and add more problems to the task over time.

12. Reinforce the student for beginning assignments after receiving directions or instructions: (a) give the student a tangible reward (e.g., classroom privileges, passing out materials, five minutes free time, etc.) or (b) give the student an intangible reward (e.g., praise, handshake, smile, etc.).

13. Reinforce the student for beginning assignments after receiving directions, instructions, etc., based on the length of time the student can be successful. Gradually decrease the amount of time to begin the task in order for the student to be reinforced.

14. Relate the importance of waiting for and following directions as skills required for success on the job site.

15. Assess the quality and clarity of directions, explanations, and instructions given to the student.

16. Require that assignments done incorrectly, for any reason, be redone.

17. Require the student to begin each assignment within a specified period of time (e.g., three minutes, five minutes, etc.).

18. Have the student attempt the new assignment/activity in a private place (e.g., carrel, "office," quiet study area, etc.) to reduce the fear of public failure.

19. Allow the student to perform new assignments/activities in a variety of places in the building (e.g., resource room, library, learning center, etc.).

20. Maintain mobility in order to provide assistance to the student.

21. Reduce the number of directions given at one time (i.e., give the student each additional step after completion of the previous step).

22. Make instructions meaningful to the student. Attempt to relate instructions to future experiences on the job site.

23. Establish assignment rules (e.g., listen to directions, wait until all verbal directions have been given, ask questions about anything not understood, make certain you have all of the necessary materials, and begin the assignment when you are certain about what you are supposed to do, etc.).

24. Make certain that the student is attending to the teacher (e.g., making eye contact, hands free of writing materials, looking at assignment, etc.) before directions are given.

25. Encourage the student to develop an awareness of the consequences of his/her behavior by writing down or talking through problems which may occur due to his/her failure to receive/read directions (e.g., if you don't read the directions before beginning the assignment, you will waste time and possibly have to redo the assignment).

26. Provide directions/instructions on a one-to-one basis before assigning a task.

27. Tell the student that directions will be given only once.

28. Reinforce those students who receive directions before beginning a new task.

29. Try to prevent the student from beginning something before being given directions or instructions (e.g., sit next to him/her, give out materials when it is time to begin the task, etc.).

30. Prevent the student from becoming overstimulated by an activity (e.g., frustrated, angry, etc.).

31. Have the student develop a flow chart of the steps necessary to complete a task.

32. Teach the student to follow graphic charts and diagrams closely when reading directions.

33. Do not require the student to complete the assignment/activity in one sitting.

34. Encourage the student to understand the consequences of impulsive behavior (e.g., if you begin a work assignment before all directions are given, you may do things incorrectly).

35. Make certain that the student has all materials needed to perform the assignment/activity.

36. Specify exactly what is to be done for the completion of the task (e.g., make definite starting and stopping points, identify a minimum requirement, etc.).

37. Explain to the student that work done incorrectly during class time will have to be made up at other times (e.g., during homeroom, before/after school, during lunch time, etc.).

38. Provide the student with more than enough time to finish an activity. As the student demonstrates success, gradually decrease the amount of time provided.

39. Communicate with the student's cooperative work experience/vocational education teacher to consistently reinforce receiving directions prior to beginning a task.

40. Have the student question any directions, explanations, or instructions not understood before beginning a task to reinforce comprehension.

41. Have the student verbally repeat directions, explanations, or instructions after they have been given to reinforce retention.

42. Help the student with the first few items on a task and gradually reduce the amount of help over time.

43. Provide alternatives to the traditional format for directions (e.g., tape record directions, summarize directions, peers give directions, etc.).

44. Enlist different people (e.g., peer, paraprofessional, friend, etc.) to reinforce the student when he/she receives/reads instructions before beginning a task.

45. Require the student to ask permission from the teacher to begin an assignment.

46. Provide the student with shorter tasks given more frequently.

47. Teach the student direction-following skills (e.g., listen carefully, write down important points, ask for clarification, wait until all directions are received before beginning).

48. Stand next to the student when giving directions.

49. Teach the student to recognize when he/she is becoming overanxious and beginning things before receiving directions or instructions.

50. Choose a peer or volunteer to help the student begin a task.

51. Encourage the student to manage his/her daily performance as if he/she were self-employed. This should increase his/her motivation to successfully complete projects.

52. Have the student outline, underline, or highlight important information in printed materials.

53. Have the student proofread all of his/her work before submitting it.

54. Have the student highlight important information in written directions prior to beginning an assignment.

55. Present assignments in the most interesting and attractive manner possible.

56. Provide the student with self-checking materials in order to check work privately, reducing the fear of public failure.

57. Set a positive example by dealing in a socially-acceptable way with situations which require you to sit through directions or instructions.

58. Along with a directive, provide an incentive statement (e.g., "If you wait to begin your work, I will come around to help you with the first problem." etc.).

59. Communicate clearly to the student when it is time to begin.

60. Teach and have the student practice listening for key information when he/she is being given directions or receiving information (e.g., write down main points, ideas, step-by-step instructions, etc.).

61. Structure time units so the student knows exactly how long to work and when to be finished.

62. Provide clearly-stated directions, written or verbal. Make the directions as simple and concrete as possible.

63. Communicate with the student's parents (e.g., notes home, phone calls, etc.) to share information concerning their child's progress. The parents may reinforce the student at home for beginning assignments after receiving directions at school.

64. Provide the student with a selection of assignments, requiring him/her to choose a minimum number from the total (e.g., present the student with 10 academic tasks from which 6 must be finished that day).

65. Provide the student with a schedule of activities so he/she will know exactly what and how much there is to do in a day.

66. Provide the student with a sample of the assignment/activity which has been partially completed by a peer or teacher (e.g., book reports, projects).

67. Interact frequently with the student in order to help him/her follow directions for the activity.

68. Deliver directions and instructions before handing out materials.

69. Do not allow the student to participate in a situation unless he/she can demonstrate self-control and listen to directions or instructions before beginning.

70. Allow the student access to pencils, pens, etc., only after directions have been given.

71. Reduce distracting stimuli (e.g., place the student in the front row, provide a carrel or "office" space away from distractions, etc.). This is used as a means of reducing distracting stimuli and not as a form of punishment.

72. Write a contract with the student specifying what behavior is expected (e.g., beginning assignments after listening to directions) and what reinforcement will be made available when the terms of the contract have been met.

73. Provide the student the opportunity to perform the assignment/activity in a variety of ways (e.g., on tape, with a calculator, orally, etc.).

74. Allow the student the option of performing the assignment at another time (e.g., earlier in the day, later, on another day).

75. Provide directions/instructions in the student's preferred learning style (e.g., visual, auditory, etc.).

76. Have a peer, paraprofessional, friend, etc., quiz the student on directions/instructions before he/she begins a task.

77. Have the student imagine the steps required to complete a task before beginning that task.

78. Provide the student with a predetermined signal when he/she is not beginning a task (e.g., turning lights off and on, hand signals, etc.).

79. Immediately remove the student from a situation when he/she begins doing things before receiving directions or instructions.

80. Organize assignments by breaking them into small segments. Set deadlines and provide the student with a reward after completing each segment of the assignment.

81. Seat the student close to the source of information to maintain attention (e.g., in the front row or near the speaker in a group activity).

82. Require the student to wait until other students begin the task.

83. Have the student practice a new skill (e.g., jumping rope, dribbling a basketball) alone, with a peer, or with the teacher before the entire group attempts the activity.

84. Structure the environment to provide the student with increased opportunities for help or assistance (e.g., peer tutoring, directions for work sent home, frequent interactions, etc.).

85. Maintain visibility to and from the student to keep his/her attention when oral questions/directions are being delivered. The teacher should be able to see the student and the student should be able to see the teacher. Make eye contact possible at all times.

86. Write down verbal directions. Instruct the student to cross each step off as it is completed.

87. Have the student explain to the teacher what is to be done in order to perform the assignment.

88. Have the student demonstrate attention to the source of information by maintaining eye contact, keeping hands free from other materials, and practicing attending posture.

89. Require the student to wait until the teacher gives a signal to begin (e.g., hand signal, ringing of bell, etc.).

90. Inform individuals who will be spending time with the student (e.g., substitute teachers, coaches, activity sponsors, etc.) about his/her tendency to begin things before receiving directions or instructions.

91. Assess the degree of task difficulty to determine whether or not the student will require additional information, time, assistance, etc., before beginning a task.

92. Make necessary adjustments in the environment to prevent the student from becoming overly excited or anxious (e.g., give out materials after delivering directions or instructions).

93. Have the student read directions aloud to ensure directions/instructions are read prior to beginning a task.

94. Evaluate the appropriateness of the task to determine (a) if the task is too difficult and (b) if the length of time scheduled to complete the task is adequate.

95. Give a signal (e.g., clapping hands, turning lights off and on, etc.) before giving verbal directions.

96. Give directions in a variety of ways to increase the probability of understanding (i.e., if the student fails to understand verbal directions, present them in written form).

97. Make certain the student achieves success when following directions.

7   Blurts out answers without being called on

Goals:
1. The student will answer only when called on.
2. The student will communicate with others in an acceptable manner in the classroom.
3. The student will work quietly in the classroom.

Objectives:
1. The student will gain permission from the teacher to speak, by raising his/her hand, when he/she has an answer on _____ out of _____ trials.
2. The student will contribute his/her opinion/answer after being recognized by the teacher on _____ out of _____ trials.
3. The student will wait his/her turn to talk when engaged, or attempting to engage, in interactions with others on _____ out of _____ trials.
4. The student will refrain from making sounds which are inappropriate for the situation on _____ out of _____ trials.

Interventions:

1. Establish classroom rules:
   - Stay on-task.
   - Remain in your seat.
   - Finish task.
   - Meet task expectations.
   - Raise your hand.

   Review rules often. Reinforce students for following the rules.

2. Communicate with parents (e.g., notes home, phone calls, etc.) to share information concerning the student's appropriate behavior. The parents may reinforce the student at home for waiting to be called on before speaking.

3. Call on the student frequently to prevent the student from becoming impatient and blurting out answers.

4. Do not criticize when correcting the student; be honest yet supportive. Never cause the student to feel negatively about himself/herself.

5. Do not allow the student to interrupt you by letting him/her talk to you at the time he/she blurts out answers. Tell the student that he/she will need to wait until you are finished talking. Allowing the student to talk after interrupting reinforces the behavior and may increase the number of times he/she blurts out answers.

6. Provide the student with many social and academic successes.

7. Do not allow the student to use ADHD as an excuse. Hold the student responsible for his/her actions. However, understand and accept problems that ADHD brings into the student's life while he/she is learning to make accommodations.

8. Call on the student when he/she is most likely to be able to respond correctly.

9. Attempt to provide equal attention to all students in the classroom.

10. Deliver directions, explanations, and instructions in a clear, concise manner to reduce the student's need to ask questions.

11. Reduce activities which might threaten the student (e.g., reduce peer pressure, academic failure, teasing, etc.).

12. Give the student responsibilities in the classroom (e.g., running errands, opportunities to help the teacher, etc.).

13. Have the student be the leader of a small group activity if he/she possesses mastery of a skill or has an interest in that area.

14. Remove the student from the group or activity until he/she can demonstrate appropriate behavior and self-control.

15. Treat the student with respect. Talk in an objective manner at all times.

16. Teach the student to use techniques such as crossing his/her arms and legs, clinching his/her fists, and webbing his/her hands when he/she feels the urge to blurt out answers without being called on.

17. Explain to the student the reasons why blurting out answers without being called on is inappropriate (e.g., impolite, hurts others' feelings, etc.).

18. Reinforce the student for waiting to be called on before speaking: (a) give the student a tangible reward (e.g., classroom privileges, line leading, passing out materials, five minutes free time, etc.) or (b) give the student an intangible reward (e.g., praise, handshake, smile, etc.).

19. Reinforce the student for waiting to be called on before speaking based on the number of times the student can be successful. As the student demonstrates success, gradually increase the number of times required for reinforcement.

20. Make certain that the student's feelings are considered when it is necessary to deal with inappropriate comments (i.e., handle comments in such a way as to not diminish the student's enthusiasm for participation).

21. Make certain that reinforcement is not inadvertently given for inappropriate behavior (e.g., attending to the student only when he/she blurts out answers without being called on).

22. Reinforce the student for raising his/her hand to be recognized.

23. Explain to the student, after telling him/her to stop talking, the reason why he/she should not be talking.

24. Provide the student with a predetermined signal if he/she begins to blurt out answers without being called on.

25. Provide constant, positive reinforcement for appropriate behavior. Ignore as many inappropriate behaviors as possible.

26. Encourage the student to self-monitor his/her impulsivity. Awareness should reduce impulsive behaviors.

27. Have the student work in small groups in which there are frequent opportunities to speak. As the student learns to wait longer for a turn to speak, gradually increase the size of the group.

28. Assess the appropriateness of the social situation in relation to the student's ability to function successfully.

29. Structure the environment to limit opportunities for inappropriate behaviors (e.g., keep the student engaged in activities, have the student seated near the teacher, allow multiple responses when appropriate, etc.).

30. Educate yourself and others about ADHD to increase understanding and accommodation of impatient behavior.

31. Provide the student with a clearly understood list of consequences for inappropriate behavior.

32. Help the student improve concentration skills (e.g., listening to the speaker, taking notes, preparing comments in advance, making comments in the appropriate context, etc.).

33. Reduce the emphasis on competition. Competitive activities may cause the student to become overexcited and blurt out answers without being called on.

34. Educate the student about ADHD and the need for developing skills to self-monitor behavior.

35. Encourage the student to develop an awareness of himself/herself and those around him/her. Have the student periodically step back and ask himself/herself, "Am I blurting out answers and dominating the conversation?"

36. Encourage the student to develop an awareness of the consequences of his/her behavior by writing down or talking through problems which may occur due to his/her impulsivity (e.g., perceived as unmannerly, avoided, etc.).

37. Make the student aware of the number of times he/she blurts out answers without being called on.

38. Instruct the student to carry a notepad with him/her at all times and to write information down to help him/her remember.

39. Make certain the student does not become overstimulated by an activity.

40. Have the student practice waiting for short periods of time for a turn to speak. Gradually increase the length of time required for a turn to speak.

41. Give adequate opportunities to respond (i.e., enthusiastic students need many opportunities to contribute).

42. Provide academic and leisure activities which allow the student to be highly active and talkative.

43. Interact frequently with the student to reduce the need to blurt out answers without being called on.

44. Try various groupings to determine the situation in which the student is most comfortable.

45. Have a peer, paraprofessional, friend, etc., cue the student when he/she blurts out responses (e.g., the person can touch the student on his/her arm or desk as a signal that he/she is blurting out responses).

46. Teach the student to recognize the appropriate time to speak (e.g., when the teacher has finished speaking, after raising his/her hand, to make comments within the context of the situation, to make comments that are a follow-up to what has just been said, etc.).

47. Make the necessary adjustments in the environment to prevent the student from experiencing stress, frustration or anger (e.g., reduce peer pressure, academic failure, teasing, etc.).

48. Encourage the student to remind himself/herself to wait when he/she feels the urge to blurt out responses/answers (e.g., "Stop. Count to ten.").

49. Maintain visibility to and from the student to keep his/her attention when oral questions/directions are being delivered. The teacher should be able to see the student and the student should be able to see the teacher. Make eye contact possible at all times.

50. Establish rules for conversing with others (e.g., wait your turn to talk, stand quietly by the person with whom you want to talk until you are noticed, excuse yourself when you interrupt others, etc.). These rules should be consistent and followed by everyone in the class. Talk about the rules often.

51. Reinforce those students in the classroom who wait to be called on before speaking.

52. Speak with the student to explain (a) what the student is doing wrong (e.g., blurting out answers) and (b) what the student should be doing (e.g., waiting until it is appropriate to speak, waiting to be called on before speaking, etc.).

53. Write a contract with the student specifying what behavior is expected (e.g., waiting to be called on before speaking) and what reinforcement will be made available when the terms of the contract have been met.

54. Encourage the student to model the behavior of peers who successfully wait to answer questions.

8   Cheats

Goals:

1. The student will independently perform his/her assignments.
2. The student will not cheat.

Objectives:

1. The student will independently perform his/her assignments on ___ out of ___ trials.
2. The student will refrain from cheating on ___ out of ___ tasks.
3. The student will independently perform ___ out of ___ tasks.
4. The student will refrain from copying other students' work on ___ out of ___ trials.
5. The student will refrain from using notes during ___ out of ___ quizzes.
6. The student will independently perform ___ out of ___ homework assignments.
7. The student will ask for teacher assistance when necessary on ___ out of ___ trials.

Interventions:

1. Have the student question any directions, explanations, or instructions not understood.

2. Review prior to administering tests and quizzes to better prepare the student.

3. Reduce the emphasis on test and quiz scores by grading the student's daily performances.

4. Maintain mobility to frequently be near the student when he/she takes tests or quizzes or performs daily assignments.

5. Reduce the emphasis on competition. Fear of failure may cause the student to resort to cheating or copying others' work in order to be successful.

6. Seat the student away from others if he/she is prone to cheating and/or copying others' work.

7. Seat the student near the teacher when taking tests or quizzes.

8. Make certain that other students do not allow the student to look at their work during tests and quizzes and while performing assignments.

9. Make certain the student is aware of the consequences for cheating and/or copying others' work (e.g., assignments will be taken away, failing grades will be recorded, etc.).

10. Arrange to have a peer help the student study for tests and quizzes and perform daily assignments.

11. Evaluate the level of difficulty in relation to the student's ability to perform the task.

12. Make certain the student understands all directions, explanations, and instructions prior to taking tests or quizzes and performing assignments.

13. Make certain the student knows that questions can be asked when taking tests and quizzes or performing assigned activities.

14. Communicate with parents or guardians so they may help the student study for tests and quizzes (e.g., send home directions, explanations, instructions relating to content covered on tests and quizzes, material to review, etc.).

15. Have the student take tests and quizzes elsewhere in the building under the individual supervision of an instructor (e.g., library, resource room, counselor's office, etc.).

16. Check the student for obvious attempts to cheat prior to taking a test or quiz (e.g., "cheat sheet," answers written on hands or cuffs, etc.).

17. Help the student accept the fact that self-improvement is more important than getting the highest grade in the class, making all A's, being the first one done with an assignment, etc., by reinforcing and grading on the basis of self-improvement.

18. Teach the student to ask for help, stop playing, etc., when he/she feels like cheating.

19. Help the student improve skills in activities in which he/she has cheated in order to reduce the need to cheat.

20. Do not put an emphasis on perfection or winning. If the student feels that perfection or winning is the most important thing, he/she may resort to cheating in order to reach perfection or win.

21. Limit the student's participation in competitive activities.

22. Teach the student appropriate ways in which to deal with anger, frustration, etc., so the student does not feel the need to cheat.

23. Help the student accept the fact that self-improvement is more important than being the best, "winning," "beating" someone else, etc., (e.g., improving his/her own best time in swimming is better than always trying to "beat" someone else, etc.).

24. Before beginning a game or assignment, make sure the student knows the rules, is familiar with the game, understands directions, etc.

25. Encourage the student to engage in less competitive activities (e.g., reading, clubs, scouts, student council, etc.).

26. Help the student to have self-confidence and satisfaction in personal self-worth and successes by pointing out strengths, emphasizing positive aspects, etc.

27. Deal with the student's behavior consistently each time there is a problem with cheating (e.g., when the student cheats remove him/her from the situation and do not allow him/her to return, etc.).

28. Deal with the student's cheating privately rather than in public.

29. Do not take action unless you are certain that the student is cheating.

30. Choose a peer to model performing his/her own work for the student.

31. Evaluate the appropriateness of the task to determine (a) if the task is too difficult and (b) if the length of time scheduled to complete the task is adequate.

32. Communicate with parents (e.g., notes home, phone calls, etc.) to share information concerning the student's progress. The parents may reinforce the student at home for doing his/her own work at school.

33. Write a contract with the student specifying what behavior is expected (e.g., doing his/her own work) and what reinforcement will be made available when the terms of the contract have been met.

34. Reinforce the student for doing his/her own work based on the length of time the student can be successful. As the student demonstrates success, gradually increase the length of time required for reinforcement.

35. Reinforce those students in the classroom who do their own work.

36. Establish classroom rules:
- Stay on-task.
- Remain in your seat.
- Finish task.
- Meet task expectations.
- Raise your hand.

Review rules often. Reinforce students for following the rules.

37. Speak to the student to explain (a) what the student is doing wrong (e.g., cheating, copying, etc.) and (b) what the student should be doing (i.e., his/her own work).

38. Reinforce the student for doing his/her own work: (a) give the student a tangible reward (e.g., classroom privileges, line leading, passing out materials, five minutes free time, etc.) or (b) give the student an intangible reward (e.g., praise, handshake, smile, etc.).

9   Does not complete assignments or tasks during the time provided

Goals:

1. The student will complete classroom assignments or tasks during class time.
2. The student will improve his/her task-related behavior.
3. The student will improve his/her academic performance.
4. The student will complete assignments or tasks during the time provided.

Objectives:

1. The student will complete a task before going on to the next task on _____ out of _____ trials.
2. The student will complete _____ out of _____ assigned tasks per day.
3. The student will remain on-task for _____ out of _____ minutes per class period.
4. The student will use the time provided to work on assigned tasks in order to complete _____ tasks per day.
5. The student will begin assignments after receiving directions or instructions on ____ out of ____ occasions.
6. The student will work on assignments in a given period of time on ____ out of ____ occasions.
7. The student will complete assignments with assistance in a given period of time on ____ out of ____ occasions.
8. The student will independently complete assignments in a given period of time on ____ out of ____ occasions.
9. The student will ask for clarification of directions or instructions not understood on ____ out of ____ occasions.
10. The student will begin the required task after receiving directions or instructions on ____ out of ____ occasions.
11. The student will work on-task during a given time period on ____ out of ____ occasions.
12. The student will complete a task with assistance in a given time period on ____ out of ____ occasions.
13. The student will independently complete a task in a given time period on ____ out of ____ occasions.

Interventions:

1. Teach the student direction-following skills (e.g., listen carefully, write down important points, ask for clarification, wait until all directions are received before beginning, etc.).

2. Practice direction-following skills on nonacademic tasks.

3. Establish assignment rules:
- Listen to directions.
- Wait until all directions have been given.
- Ask questions about anything you do not understand.
- Begin the assignment only when you are certain about what you are supposed to do.
- Make certain you have all necessary materials, etc.

4. Deliver directions/instructions before handing out materials.

5. Maintain consistency in the classroom's daily routine.

6. Allow natural consequences to occur (e.g., may not participate in extra-curricular sports, may not earn graduation credit, etc.) due to the student's failure to complete classwork.

7. Assign the student shorter tasks (e.g., modify a 20-problem math activity to 4 activities of 5 problems each to be done at various times during the day). As the student demonstrates success, gradually increase the length of each task and decrease the number of tasks.

8. Communicate with the student's parents (e.g., notes home, phone calls, etc.) to share information concerning their child's progress. The parents may reinforce the student at home for completing assignments at school.

9. Assign one task/assignment at a time. Give the student ample time to complete it.

10. Assist the student in writing a contract for himself/herself designating a time to complete an assignment and avoid procrastination.

11. Establish a timeline for completing a project. Expect the student to meet each deadline in order to complete the project on time.

12. Maintain consistent expectations within the ability level of the student.

13. Deliver reinforcement for any and all measures of improvement.

14. Encourage the student to develop an awareness of the consequences of his/her behavior by writing down or talking through problems which may occur due to his/her failure to complete assignments (e.g., if the student does not focus on assignments in class, he/she may not pass the class. If he/she does not pass the class, he/she will not earn a credit, etc.).

15. Encourage the student to develop an awareness of himself/herself and the environment. Instruct the student to step back and ask himself/ herself, "Am I on-task and completing my assignments?" "What should I be doing now?"

16. Choose a peer to model appropriate completion of the assignments or tasks during the time provided for the student.

17. Supervise the student during class assignments to maintain on-task behavior.

18. Reinforce the student for completing assignments or tasks based on the amount of work he/she can successfully complete in a given period of time. Gradually increase the duration of assignments or tasks.

19. Provide the student with shorter assignments or tasks given more frequently.

20. Reinforce the student for completing assignments or tasks during the time provided based on the length of time the student can be successful (e.g., every 5 minutes, 10 minutes, etc.). As the student demonstrates success, gradually increase the length of time required for reinforcement.

21. Schedule important activities/assignments/ meetings at times when the student is most likely to maintain attention (e.g., one hour after medication, 45 minutes after lunch, first thing in the morning, etc.).

22. Specify exactly what is to be done for the completion of an assignment or task (e.g., indicate definite starting and stopping points, indicate the minimum requirements, etc.).

23. Have the student keep a chart/graph representing the number of class assignments completed.

24. Have the student develop a checklist/chart to follow which will allow him/her to complete all assignments.

25. Have the student and a classmate who has the same assignment do their classwork together.

26. Reinforce those students in the classroom who complete assignments or tasks during the time provided.

27. Set time limits for completing classroom assignments so that the student knows exactly how long he/she has to work and when to be finished. Encourage the student to be aware of time constraints when working on projects.

28. Allow some free time between classwork assignments if the student appears to need a break.

29. Assess the degree of task difficulty to determine whether or not the student will require additional information, time, assistance, etc., before beginning a task.

30. Assess the degree of task difficulty in comparison with the student's ability to perform the task.

31. Establish classroom rules:
- Stay on-task.
- Work quietly.
- Remain in your seat.
- Finish task.
- Meet task requirements.

Review rules often. Reinforce students for following the rules.

32. Have the student question any directions, explanations, and instructions he/she does not understand.

33. Have the student repeat the directions verbally to the teacher.

34. Require the student to begin each assignment or task within a specified period of time (e.g., three minutes, five minutes, etc.).

35. Speak with the student to explain (a) what he/she is doing wrong (e.g., not completing assignments) and (b) what he/she should be doing (e.g., completing assignments during class).

36. Provide the student with structure for all academic activities (e.g., specific directions, routine format for tasks, time limits, etc.).

37. Make it pleasant and positive for the student to ask questions about things he/she does not understand. Reinforce the student by assisting, congratulating, praising, etc.

38. Encourage the student to ask for clarification of directions for classroom assignments.

39. Provide alternatives to the traditional format of directions (e.g., tape record directions, summarize directions, peers give directions, etc.).

40. Reduce directions to steps (e.g., give the student each additional step after completion of the previous step).

41. Teach the student time management skills. Have the student make a daily plan and follow it. Encourage the student to avoid becoming distracted by events, impulses, and moods.

42. Interact frequently with the student in order to help him/her follow directions for the assignments.

43. Explain to the student, when he/she does not complete an assignment exactly, what he/she is doing wrong, what he/she is supposed to be doing, and why.

44. Have the student ask for help when he/she needs it.

45. Have the student schedule his/her own time for assignments or tasks (e.g., 20 minutes for each of 3 assignments, 15 minutes for each of 4 assignments, etc.) in order to pace himself/herself.

46. Encourage the student to manage his/her daily performance as if he/she were self-employed. This should increase his/her motivation to successfully complete assignments.

47. Assist the student in performing his/her classwork. Gradually decrease the assistance and require the student to independently assume more responsibility as he/she demonstrates success.

48. Interact frequently with the student to maintain involvement with class assignments (e.g., ask the student questions, ask the student's opinion, stand close to the student, seat the student near the teacher's desk, etc.).

49. Provide simple, concrete, clearly-stated directions in written or verbal form.

50. Present the assignment or task in the most attractive and interesting manner possible.

51. Have the student complete assignments in a private place (e.g., carrel, "office," quiet study area, etc.) in order to reduce the anxiety of public failure.

52. Repeat directions to increase the probability of the student's understanding.

53. Organize assignments by breaking them into small segments. Set deadlines and provide the student with a reward after completing each segment of the assignment.

54. Make certain that the student is attending to the teacher when directions are given (e.g., making eye contact, hands free of writing materials, looking at assignment, etc.).

55. Remind the student when it is time to do classwork.

56. Consider carefully the student's ability level and experience before assigning tasks to him/her.

57. Provide the student with quality material to perform the assignment (e.g., pencil with eraser, paper, dictionary, handwriting sample, etc.). Be certain that the student has only the necessary material on his/her desk.

58. Make certain the student is not required to learn more information than he/she is capable of learning at any one time.

59. Complete the first few items of an assignment or task with the student to serve as a model and start the student on the assignment or task.

60. Assess the quality and clarity of directions, explanations, and instructions given to the student.

61. Allow the student the option of performing the assignment or task at another time (e.g., earlier in the day, later, on another day, or at home).

62. Give directions in a variety of ways to increase the probability of understanding (e.g., if the student fails to understand verbal directions, present them in written form).

63. Reward the student for concentrating on an assignment for a specific length of time (e.g., smile, verbal praise, a note acknowledging his/her effort, etc.).

64. Reduce the amount of information on a page if it is visually distracting for the student (e.g., less print to read, fewer problems, isolate information that is presented to the student, etc.).

65. Reduce emphasis on academic and social competition. Fear of failure may cause the student to not want to complete assignments or tasks during the time provided.

66. Reinforce the student for the steps of beginning, working on, and completing each individual assignment or task during the time provided.

67. Provide the student with the opportunity to perform assignments/activities in a variety of ways (e.g., on tape, with a calculator, verbally, etc.).

68. Have the student time assignments or tasks to monitor his/her own behavior and accept time limits.

69. Maintain consistency in the assignments or tasks to be completed within the time provided.

70. Prevent the student from becoming over-stimulated by an activity (e.g., frustrated, angry, excited, etc.).

71. Have the student identify a peer who has the ability to complete work assignments. Instruct the student to observe that person and try to model the behaviors which allow him/her to complete assignments.

72. Allow the student access to pencils, pens, etc., only after directions have been given.

73. Encourage the parents to make positive comments about school and the importance of completing classwork.

74. Provide the student with a schedule of activities so that he/she knows exactly what and how much there is to do in a given period of time.

75. Provide the student with a selection of assignments and require him/her to choose a minimum number from the total (e.g., present the student with 10 academic tasks from which 6 must be completed that day).

76. Ask the student why he/she is not completing assignments or tasks in the time provided. The student may have the most accurate perception as to why he/she is not completing the required assignments or tasks during the time provided.

77. Allow the student more decision-making opportunities relative to class activities and assignments.

78. Provide the student with increased opportunities for help or assistance on academic assignments or tasks (e.g., peer tutoring, directions for work sent home, frequent interactions, etc.).

79. Evaluate the visual and auditory stimuli in the classroom. Determine the amount of stimuli the student can tolerate. Remove the extraneous stimuli from the environment.

80. Write a contract with the student specifying what behavior is expected (e.g., completing assignments or tasks during the time provided) and what reinforcement will be made available when the terms of the contract have been met.

81. Structure time units so the student knows exactly how long he/she has to work and when to be finished.

82. Make certain the student achieves success when following directions.

83. Prioritize tasks by importance (e.g., task A must be done today, task B can be done today, and task C can wait until tomorrow).

84. Teach the student organizational and task completion skills (e.g., begin with a clean desk, read directions carefully, collect all necessary materials, ask for assistance if needed, look for the main idea, follow examples provided, answer questions you know first and leave those you are unsure of for last, etc.).

85. Evaluate the appropriateness of the task to determine (a) if the task is too easy, (b) if the task is too difficult, and (c) if the length of time scheduled to complete the task is adequate.

86. Provide the student with more than enough time to finish an activity. As the student demonstrates success, gradually decrease the amount of time provided.

87. Make certain the student understands that classwork not completed and turned in on time must still be completed and turned in at a later time.

88. Encourage the student to realize that all behavior has negative or positive consequences. Encourage the student to practice behaviors that will lead to positive consequences.

89. Have the student explain to the teacher what he/she should do in order to perform the assignment or task.

90. Communicate clearly with the student the length of time he/she has to complete an assignment and when the assignment is due. The student may want to use a timer in order to complete the tasks within the given period of time.

91. Reinforce the student for completing the assignments or tasks during the time provided: (a) give the student a tangible reward (e.g., classroom privileges, line leading, passing out materials, five minutes free time, etc.) or (b) give the student an intangible reward (e.g., praise, handshake, smile, etc.).

92. Deliver directions verbally to increase the probability of the student's understanding of class assignments.

93. Make certain the student understands the natural consequences for failing to complete assignments or tasks during the time provided (e.g., students who do not finish their work are not allowed to do more desirable activities).

94. Discuss the student's responsibilities at the beginning of each class period so he/she knows what is expected.

95. Maintain visibility to and from the student. The teacher should be able to see the student and the student should be able to see the teacher. Make eye contact possible at all times.

96. Reduce distracting stimuli (e.g., place the student on the front row, provide a carrel or "office" space away from distractions, etc.). This is used as a means of reducing stimuli and not as a form of punishment.

97. Have the student assemble all the materials necessary to work on a project, assignment, etc., to reduce the need to search for materials and unnecessary distractions.

98. Have the student verbally repeat the directions to the teacher.

99. Work a few problems of the assignment with the student to serve as a model and start the student on the assignment.

100. Choose a peer to help the student with class assignments or tasks.

101. Structure the environment to provide the student with increased opportunity for help or assistance on assignments (e.g., peer tutoring, directions for work sent home, frequent interactions, etc.).

102. Along with the student, chart those assignments that have been completed within the time provided.

103. Have the student record the time it took him/her to complete each assignment or task in order to accurately determine how much time is spent on each assignment or task.

104. Present one assignment at a time. As each assignment is completed, deliver reinforcement along with the presentation of the next assignment.

105. Have the student use a timer in order to complete tasks within a given period of time.

106. Create challenges in assigned tasks to increase interest and motivation (e.g., cooperative learning strategies, etc.).

107. Provide an incentive statement along with a directive (e.g., "When you finish your classwork, you may go to lunch.").

108. Establish assignment rules (e.g., listen to directions, wait until all verbal directions have been given, ask questions about anything not understood, make certain you have all of the necessary materials, and begin the assignment when you are certain about what you are supposed to do, etc.).

109. Make certain that the student understands the relationship between inappropriate behavior and the consequences which follow (e.g., failure to perform or complete classroom assignments will result in a low grade).

110. Check over the student's classwork when he/she is finished so you can be certain that everything is completed.

111. Follow a less desirable assignment with a highly desirable assignment, requiring the student to complete the first in order to begin the second.

112. Take proactive steps to deal with a student's refusal to perform an assignment in order to prevent contagion in the classroom (e.g., refrain from arguing with the student, place the student at a carrel or other quiet place to work, remove the student from the group or classroom, etc.).

113. Allow the student additional time to complete class assignments or homework.

114. Explain to the student that work not done during class\work time will have to be done during other times (e.g., recess, break time, recreational time, before\after school, lunch time, etc.).

115. Reinforce the student for beginning, working on, and completing assignments.

116. Provide the student with step-by-step written directions for completing class assignments or tasks.

10 Does not complete assignments with at least minimal accuracy

Goals:

1. The student will improve his/her academic task-related behavior.
2. The student will improve his/her academic performance.
3. The student will complete assignments with at least minimal accuracy.

Objectives:

1. The student will complete classroom tests and quizzes with a ____% level of minimal accuracy (indicate a level of performance).
2. The student will complete homework assignments with a ____% level of minimal accuracy (indicate a level of performance).
3. The student will complete classroom assignments with a _____ percent level of minimal accuracy (indicate a level of performance).

Interventions:

1. Give shorter assignments, but more frequently. Increase the length of the assignments over time.

2. Reduce distracting stimuli (e.g., place the student on the front row, provide a carrel or "office" space away from distractions, etc.). This is used as a means of reducing distracting stimuli and not as a form of punishment.

3. Teach the student study skills.

4. Establish a level of minimal accuracy which will be accepted as a level of mastery.

5. Provide adequate repetition and drill to assure minimal accuracy of assignments presented (e.g., require mastery/minimal accuracy before moving to the next skill level).

6. Have assignments read to the student.

7. Make certain the assignments assess knowledge of content and not related skills such as writing or reading.

8. Establish classroom rules:
- Work on-task.
- Work quietly.
- Remain in your seat.
- Finish task.
- Meet task expectations.

Review rules often. Reinforce students for following rules.

9. Maintain consistency in assignment format and expectations so as not to confuse the student.

10. Deliver reinforcement for any measure of improvement.

11. Provide frequent interactions and encouragement to support the student's confidence and optimism for success (e.g., make statements such as, "You're doing great" "Keep up the good work" "I'm really proud of you" etc.).

12. Have the student maintain a performance record.

13. Modify instruction to include more concrete examples to facilitate student learning.

14. Monitor student performance to detect errors and determine where learning problems exist.

15. Identify resource personnel from whom the student may receive additional assistance (e.g., librarian, special education teacher, other personnel with expertise or time to help, etc.).

16. Provide multiple opportunities for the student to learn the information covered by assignments (e.g., films, visitors, community resources, etc.).

17. Teach the student direction-following skills.

18. Provide parents with information on homework assignment content (e.g., what material will be covered by the assignment, format, types of questions, etc.).

19. Assess quality and clarity of directions, explanations, and instructions given to the student.

20. Speak to the student to explain (a) what he/she is doing wrong (e.g., not completing assignments, failing assignments, etc.) and (b) what the student should be doing (e.g., completing assignments on time with passing grades).

21. Provide instruction and task format in a variety of ways (e.g., verbal instructions, written instructions, demonstrations, simulations, manipulatives, audio-visual presentations, drill activities with peers, etc.).

22. Choose a peer to model appropriate completion of assignments with an acceptable level of accuracy for the student.

23. Have the assignments tape recorded and allow the student to listen to questions as often as necessary.

24. Allow the student to respond to alternative assignment questions (e.g., more generalized questions that represent global understanding.).

25. Provide the student with self-checking materials and require correction before completing assignments.

26. Write a contract with the student and his/her parents so that reinforcement may be delivered at home for academic accuracy at school.

27. Allow the student to put an assignment away and return to it at a later time if he/she could be more successful at a later time.

28. Provide the student with feedback for assignments completed (e.g., identify what the student did successfully, what errors were made, and what should be done to correct the errors).

29. Have the student answer assignment problems verbally.

30. Build varying degrees of difficulty into assignments to assure the student's self-confidence and at the same time provide a challenge (e.g., easier problems are included with problems designed to measure knowledge gained).

31. Should the student consistently fail to complete assignments with an acceptable level of accuracy, evaluate the appropriateness of tasks assigned.

32. Provide time at school for the completion of homework if assigned homework has not been completed or has resulted in failure.

33. It is not necessary to grade every assignment completed by the student. Assignments may be used to evaluate student ability or knowledge and provide feedback. Grades need not be given until mastery/minimal accuracy has been attained.

34. Have the student question any directions, explanations, instructions he/she does not understand.

35. Reinforce the student for completing his/her assignments with an acceptable level of accuracy: (a) give the student a tangible reward (e.g., classroom privileges, line leading, passing out materials, five minutes free time, etc.) or (b) give the student an intangible reward (e.g., praise, handshake, smile, etc.).

36. If the student has difficulty completing homework assignments with an acceptable level of accuracy, provide a time during the day when he/she can receive assistance.

37. Interact frequently with the student to monitor task performance.

38. Assess student performance in a variety of ways (e.g., have the student give verbal explanations, simulations, physical demonstration of skills, etc.).

39. Monitor the first problem or part of an assignment to make certain the student knows what is expected of him/her (e.g., provide the student with feedback which will assure accuracy).

40. Provide the student with opportunities for review prior to grading assignments.

41. Provide the student with a selection of assignments and require him/her to choose a minimum number from the total amount (e.g., present the student with 10 academic tasks from which he/she must finish 6 that day).

42. Teach the student note-taking skills.

43. Communicate with parents (e.g., notes home, phone calls, etc.) to share information concerning the student's progress. The parents may reinforce the student at home for completing his/her assignments with minimal accuracy at school.

44. Have the student maintain a chart representing the number of tasks and homework assignments completed and the accuracy rate.

45. Provide the student with opportunities for review prior to grading assignments.

46. Mastery should not be expected too soon after introducing new information, skills, etc.

47. Write a contract with the student specifying what behavior is expected (e.g., completing an assignment with 50 percent accuracy) and what reinforcement will be made available when the terms of the contract have been met.

48. Structure the environment to provide the student with increased opportunity for help or assistance on academic or homework tasks.

49. Remove the threat of publicizing the student's failure. Assignment results should not be read aloud or posted.

50. Teach the student to practice basic study skills (e.g., reading for the main point, note-taking, summarizing, highlighting, studying in a good environment, using time wisely, etc.).

51. Arrange a time for the student to study with a peer tutor before completing a graded assignment.

52. Evaluate the appropriateness of the task to determine (a) if the task is too easy, (b) if the task is too difficult, and (c) if the length of time scheduled to complete the task is adequate.

53. Provide the opportunity for the student to work with a peer tutor or other person who can provide individual help.

54. Provide the opportunity for the student to study assignments with a peer.

55. Have the student perform assignments with which he/she experiences difficulty in the resource room where the resource teacher can answer questions.

56. Reduce the emphasis on competition. Students who compete academically and fail to win may cease to try to succeed and do far less than they are able. Academic performance need not be made public and students need not compete in order to encourage academic success.

57. Allow/require the student to make corrections after assignments have been checked the first time.

58. Reinforce those students in the classroom who complete their assignments with an acceptable level of accuracy.

59. Have the student practice an assignment with the teacher, aide, or peer before performing the assignment for a grade.

60. Provide the student with clearly stated written directions for homework so that someone at home may be able to provide assistance.

11 Rushes through activities or assignments with little or no regard to accuracy, quality, or neatness

Goals:
1. The student will improve the accuracy of school assignments.
2. The student will improve the quality of school assignments.
3. The student will perform assignments neatly.

Objectives:
1. The student will perform school assignments with _____% accuracy.
2. The student will check school assignments to correct errors on _____ out of _____ trials.
3. The student will turn in school assignments for the teacher to proofread and provide feedback for corrections and improvement on _____ out of _____ trials.
4. The student will re-do corrected school assignments with _____% accuracy.
5. The student will have a peer check his/her school assignments and correct errors found on _____ out of _____ trials.
6. The student will perform written tasks in a legible manner on _____ out of _____ trials.
7. The student will take his/her time when performing a written task to make it legible on _____ out of _____ tasks.
8. The student will turn in written work which is legible on _____ out of _____ trials.
9. The student will turn in written assignments that are clean, free of tears, neat, etc., on _____ out of _____ trials.
10. The student will re-copy his/her written assignments before turning them in on _____ out of _____ trials.

Interventions:

1. Communicate with parents (e.g., notes home, phone calls, etc.) to share information concerning the student's progress. The parents may reinforce the student at home for improving the quality of his/her handwriting at school.

2. Provide the student with self-checking materials, requiring correction before turning in assignments.

3. Assess the appropriateness of assigning homework to the student.

4. Maintain consistency in assignment format and expectations.

5. Make certain the assignments measure knowledge of content and not related skills such as reading or writing.

6. Teach the student note-taking skills.

7. Have the student practice an assignment with the teacher, an aide, or a peer before performing the assignment for a grade.

8. Reinforce conscientiousness in improving handwriting (e.g., double checking spelling, proper positioning of letters, spacing, etc.): (a) give the student a tangible reward (e.g., classroom privileges, line leading, passing out materials, five minutes free time, etc.) or (b) give the student an intangible reward (e.g., praise, handshake, smile, etc.).

9. Teach the student direction-following skills: (a) listen carefully, (b) ask questions, (c) use environmental cues, (d) rely on examples provided, etc.

10. Provide parents with information regarding appropriate ways in which to help their child with homework (e.g., read directions with the student, work a few problems together, answer questions, check the completed assignment, etc.).

11. Provide frequent interactions and encouragement to support the student's confidence and optimism for success (e.g., make statements such as, "You're doing great." "Keep up the good work." "I'm really proud of you." etc.).

12. Establish classroom rules:
- Work on-task.
- Work quietly.
- Remain in your seat.
- Finish task.
- Meet task expectations.

Review rules often. Reinforce students for following rules.

13. Reinforce conscientiousness in improving accuracy and quality of assignments (e.g., double checking spelling, proper positioning of letters, adequate spacing, etc.): (a) give the student a tangible reward (e.g., classroom privileges, line leading, passing out materials, five minutes free time, etc.) or (b) give the student an intangible reward (e.g., praise, handshake, smile, etc.).

14. Make certain the student has a number line and alphabet strip on his/her desk to use as a reference for the correct form of letters and numbers to reduce errors.

15. Establish levels of expectations for accuracy and quality of performance and require the student to correct or repeat assignments until the expectations are met.

16. Deliver reinforcement for any and all measures of improvement.

17. Have the assignments tape recorded allowing the student to listen to questions as often as necessary.

18. Use lined paper that is also vertically lined (e.g., | | | | |) to teach the student appropriate spacing skills (e.g., K | a | t | h | y).

19. Ask parents to set aside an established length of time each evening (e.g., 45 minutes, one hour, etc.) for homework rather than allowing the student to watch TV or play "as soon as the homework is finished."

20. Allow the student to put an assignment away and return to it at a later time if this helps the student be more successful.

21. Along with a directive, provide an incentive statement (e.g., "When you finish your work neatly, you may have free time." etc.).

22. Provide the student with an appropriate model of handwriting (e.g., other students' work, teacher samples, commercial samples, etc.) to use at his/her desk.

23. Teach the student to practice basic study skills (e.g., reading for the main idea, note taking, summarizing, highlighting, studying in a good environment, using time wisely, etc.).

24. Have the student maintain a chart representing the number of tasks completed and the accuracy rate of each task.

25. Reinforce those students in the classroom who turn in assignments which are legible.

26. Reinforce those students in the classroom who turn in assignments which are accurate and of high quality.

27. Reduce the emphasis on competition. Competitive activities may cause the student to rush through work. Students who compete academically and fail to succeed may cease to try to do well and do far less than they are able.

28. If the student does not complete his/her work according to teacher directions and expectations, it must be completed during recreational or break time.

29. If the student has difficulty completing homework assignments with minimal accuracy, provide a time during the day when assistance can be given at school.

30. Modify instructions to include more concrete examples to enhance student learning.

31. Assess quality and clarity of directions, explanations, and instructions given to the student.

32. Have the student question any directions, explanations, and instructions not understood.

33. Recognize accuracy and quality (e.g., display the student's work, congratulate the student, etc.).

34. Use adhesive material (e.g., tape, Dycem material, etc.) to keep paper positioned appropriately for handwriting.

35. Monitor student performance to detect errors and determine where learning problems exist.

36. Speak with the student to explain (a) what the student is doing wrong (e.g., turning in work which has spelling errors or spacing errors, work that is illegible, etc.) and (b) what he/she should be doing (e.g., taking time to check for spelling, spacing errors, etc.).

37. Provide the student with evaluative feedback for assignments completed (i.e., identify what the student did successfully, what errors were made, and what should be done to correct the errors).

38. Provide the student with opportunities for review prior to grading assignments.

39. It is not necessary to grade every assignment performed by the student. Assignments may be used to evaluate student ability or knowledge and provide feedback. Grades may not need to be assigned until mastery/minimal accuracy has been attained.

40. Provide older students with functional handwriting opportunities (e.g., job application forms, reinforcer surveys, order forms, check writing, etc.).

41. Teach the student procedures for improving accuracy and quality of work (e.g., listen to directions, make certain directions are understood, work at an acceptable pace, check for errors, correct for neatness, copy the work over, etc.).

42. Provide instruction and task format in a variety of ways (e.g., verbal instructions, written instructions, demonstrations, simulations, manipulative, drill activities with peers, etc.).

43. Monitor the first problem or part of the assignment to make certain the student knows what is expected.

44. Modify academic tasks (e.g., format, requirements, length, etc.).

45. Gradually reduce the space between lines as the student's handwriting improves.

46. Allow/require the student to make corrections after assignments have been checked the first time.

47. Provide the student with quality materials to perform assignments (e.g., pencil with eraser, paper, dictionary, handwriting sample, etc.).

48. Have the student trace handwriting models and fade the model as the student develops the skill.

49. Have the student chart the number of times his/her handwriting is acceptable during a given week.

50. Provide the student with samples of work which may serve as models for acceptable levels of accuracy and quality (e.g., the student is to match the quality of the sample before turning in the assignment).

51. Work the first few problems of an assignment with the student to make certain that he/she knows what to do, how to perform the assignment, etc.

52. Provide a multitude of handwriting opportunities for the student to practice handwriting skills (e.g., writing letters to sports and entertainment figures, relatives, friends; writing for free information on a topic in which the student is interested, etc.).

53. Provide the student with ample opportunity to master handwriting skills (e.g., instruction in letter positioning, direction, spacing, etc.).

54. Have the student read/go over school work with the teacher so the student can become aware of the quality of his/her work.

55. Build varying degrees of difficulty into assignments to ensure the student's self-confidence and at the same time provide a challenge (e.g., easier problems are intermingled with problems designed to measure knowledge gained).

56. Establish levels of expectations for quality handwriting performance, and require the student to correct or repeat assignments until the expectations are met.

57. Allow the student to perform school work in a quiet place (e.g., study carrel, library, resource room, etc.) to reduce distractions.

58. Provide the student with a selection of assignments and require him/her to choose a minimum number from the total amount (e.g., present the student with 10 academic tasks from which 6 must be finished that day).

59. Supervise the student while he/she is performing school work to monitor accuracy and quality.

60. Provide the student with clearly stated step-by-step directions for homework so someone at home may be able to provide assistance.

61. Provide the student with clearly stated criteria for acceptable work.

62. Provide multiple opportunities for the student to learn information covered by assignments (e.g., films, visitors, community resources, etc.).

63. Arrange a time for the student to study with a peer tutor before completing a graded assignment.

64. Write a contract with the student specifying what behavior is expected (e.g., improving the accuracy and quality of assignments) and what reinforcement will be made available when the terms of the contract have been met.

65. Make certain that your comments take the form of constructive criticism rather than criticism that can be perceived as personal, threatening, etc., (e.g., instead of saying, "You always make the same mistake." say, "A better way to do that might be . . .").

66. Evaluate the appropriateness of the task to determine (a) if the task is too easy, (b) if the task is too difficult, and (c) if the length of time scheduled to complete the task is adequate.

67. Provide the student with shorter tasks, but more of them throughout the day (e.g., 4 assignments of 5 problems each rather than one assignment of 20 problems).

68. Have the student respond to tasks verbally.

69. Make certain the student understands that work not done neatly must be redone until it is neat.

70. Use handwriting models with arrows that indicate the direction in which the student should correctly form the letters.

71. Check the student's grip on the pencil to make certain that he/she is holding the pencil correctly.

72. Reduce distracting stimuli (e.g., place the student in the front row, provide a carrel or "office" space away from distractions, etc.). This is to be used as a means of reducing distracting stimuli and not as a form of punishment.

73. Conduct a preliminary evaluation of the work, requiring the student to make necessary corrections before final grading.

74. Provide time at school for the completion of homework if homework assigned has not been completed or has resulted in failure. (The student's failure to complete homework assignments may be the result of variables in the home over which he/she has no control.)

75. Reinforce the student for improving the accuracy and quality of his/her work based on ability. As the student demonstrates success, gradually increase the amount of improvement expected for reinforcement.

76. Identify resource personnel from whom the student may receive additional assistance (e.g., librarian, special education teacher, other personnel with expertise or time to help, etc.).

77. Use primary paper to assist the student in sizing upper-case and lower-case letters. Use standard lined paper when the student's skills improve.

78. Make certain that homework relates to concepts already taught rather than introducing a new concept.

79. Give shorter assignments, but give them more frequently. Increase the length of assignments as the student demonstrates success.

80. Use a pencil grip (e.g., three-sided, foam rubber, etc.) to provide the student assistance in appropriate positioning of the pencil or pen.

81. Provide the student with additional time to perform school work to achieve increased accuracy and quality.

82. Model appropriate handwriting at all times.

83. Should the student consistently fail to complete assignments with minimal accuracy, evaluate the appropriateness of tasks assigned.

84. Allow the student to respond to alternative assignment questions (e.g., more generalized questions that represent global understanding).

85. Interact frequently with the student to monitor task performance.

86. Structure the environment to provide the student with increased opportunities for help or assistance on academic or homework tasks (e.g., peer tutors, seat the student near the teacher or aide, etc.).

87. Provide adequate repetition and drill to assure minimal accuracy of assignments presented (i.e., require mastery/minimal accuracy before moving to the next skill level).

88. Mastery should not be expected too soon after introducing new information, skills, etc.

89. Assess student performance in a variety of ways (e.g., have the student give verbal explanations, simulations, physical demonstrations, etc.).

90. Assign the student shorter tasks while increasing accuracy and quality expectations.

91. Make certain that all educators who work with the student maintain consistent expectations of accuracy and quality.

92. Choose a peer to work with the student to provide an acceptable model for the student.

12 Does not complete assignments within a specified time period

Goals:

1. The student will complete assignments within a specified time period.

Objectives:

1. The student will begin assignments after receiving directions or instructions on _____ out of _____ trials.
2. The student will work on assignments within a specified time period (indicate length of time).
3. The student will complete assignments with assistance within a specified time period (indicate length of time).
4. The student will independently complete assignments within a specified time period (indicate length of time).
5. The student will ask for clarification of directions or instructions not understood within a specified time period (indicate length of time) on _____ out of _____ trials.

Interventions

1. Reinforce the student for completing the required number of assignments in a given time period: (a) give the student a tangible reward (e.g., classroom privileges, line leading, passing out materials, five minutes free time, etc.) or (b) give the student an intangible reward (e.g., praise, handshake, smile, etc.).

2. Speak to the student to explain (a) what he/she is doing wrong (e.g., not working during work time) and (b) what the student should be doing (e.g., working during work time).

3. Have the student use a timer in order to complete tasks within a given period of time.

4. Reinforce those students in the classroom who complete the required number of assignments in a given period of time.

5. Reinforce the student for completing the required number of assignments in a given period of time based on the length of time the student can be successful (e.g., every 5 minutes, 10 minutes, etc.). As the student demonstrates success, gradually increase the length of time required for reinforcement.

6. Evaluate the appropriateness of the task to determine (a) if the task is too easy, (b) if the task is too difficult, and (c) if the length of time scheduled to complete the task is adequate.

7. Communicate with parents (e.g., notes home, phone calls, etc.) to share information concerning the student's progress. The parents may reinforce the student at home for completing the required number of assignments in a given period of time at school.

8. Write a contract with the student specifying what behavior is expected (e.g., completing four assignments in one period of time) and what reinforcement will be made available when the terms of the contract have been met.

9. Choose a peer to model appropriate completion of the required number of assignments in a given period of time for the student.

10. Have the student question any directions, explanations, instructions he/she does not understand.

11. Assign the student shorter tasks (e.g., modify a 20-problem math activity to four activities of five problems each to be done at various times during the day). Gradually increase the number of problems over time.

12. Reinforce the student for completing assignments based on the amount of work he/she can successfully complete in a given period of time. Gradually increase the number of assignments required in a given period of time.

13. Along with the student, chart those assignments that have been completed in a given period of time.

14. Present one assignment at a time. As each assignment is completed, deliver reinforcement along with the presentation of the next assignment.

15. Establish classroom rules:
- Work on-task.
- Work quietly.
- Remain in your seat.
- Finish task.
- Meet task expectations.

Review rules often. Reinforce students for following rules.

16. Provide the student with a schedule of activities so that he/she knows exactly what and how much there is to do in a given period of time.

17. Prevent the student from becoming overstimulated by an activity (e.g., frustrated, angry, etc.).

18. Specify exactly what is to be done for the completion of the task (e.g., make definite starting and stopping points, establish a minimum requirement, etc.).

19. Require the student to begin each assignment within a specified period of time (e.g., three minutes, five minutes, etc.).

20. Provide the student with a selection of assignments, requiring him/her to choose a minimum number from the total (e.g., present the student with 10 academic tasks from which he/she must finish 6 in a given time period).

21. Reduce the emphasis on academic and social competition. Fear of failure may cause the student to not want to complete the required number of assignments in a given period of time.

22. Have the student complete his/her assignments in a private place (e.g., carrel, "office," quiet study area, etc.) to reduce the anxiety of public failure.

23. Make certain the student achieves success when following directions.

24. Make certain that the student is attending to the teacher when directions are given (e.g., making eye contact, hands free of writing materials, looking at assignment, etc.).

25. Make certain that the student has all the materials he/she needs in order to perform the assignments.

26. Have the student explain to the teacher what he/she should do in order to perform the assignments.

27. Explain to the student that work not done during work time will have to be made up at other times (e.g., break time, before school, after school, lunch time, etc.).

28. Teach the student direction-following skills (e.g., listen carefully, write down important points, ask for clarification, wait until all directions are received before beginning).

29. Provide clearly stated directions in written or verbal form (e.g., make the directions as simple and concrete as possible).

30. Interact frequently with the student in order to help him/her follow directions for the assignments.

31. Structure the environment to provide the student with increased opportunity for help or assistance on assignments (e.g., peer tutoring, directions for work sent home, frequent interactions, etc.).

32. Provide alternatives for the traditional format of directions (e.g., tape record directions, summarize directions, directions given by peers, etc.).

33. Practice direction-following skills on non-academic tasks.

34. Reduce directions to steps (e.g., give the student each additional step after completion of the previous step).

35. Provide the student with the opportunity to perform assignments/activities in a variety of ways (e.g., on tape, with a calculator, verbally, etc.).

36. Reduce the emphasis on early completion. Hurrying to complete assignments may cause the student to fail to follow directions.

37. Establish assignment rules (e.g., listen to directions; wait until all directions have been given; ask questions about anything you do not understand; begin assignment only when you are certain about what you are supposed to do; make certain you have all necessary materials; etc.).

38. Allow the student access to pencils, pens, etc., only after directions have been given.

39. Deliver directions/instructions before handing out materials.

40. Maintain visibility to and from the student to make certain the student is attending. The teacher should be able to see the student and the student should be able to see the teacher. Make eye contact possible at all times.

41. Present the assignment in the most attractive, interesting manner possible.

42. Reduce distracting stimuli (e.g., place the student on the front row, provide a carrel or "office" space away from distractions, etc.). This is used as a means of reducing distracting stimuli and not as a form of punishment.

43. Interact frequently with the student to maintain involvement with class assignments (e.g., ask the student questions; ask the student's opinion; stand close to the student; seat the student near the teacher's desk, etc.).

44. Reinforce the student for the steps of beginning, working on, and completing each individual assignment.

45. Supervise the student during class assignments to maintain on-task behavior.

46. Follow a less desirable assignment with a highly desirable assignment, requiring the student to complete the first in order to begin the second.

47. Allow natural consequences to occur when the required number of assignments are not completed within a given period of time (e.g., students who do not complete the required number of assignments do not get to perform more desirable activities).

48. Allow the student to perform alternative assignments. Gradually introduce more components of the assignment until those assignments are routinely performed.

49. Maintain consistency in the number of assignments required to be completed in a given period of time.

50. Work the first few problems with the student in order to serve as a model and start the student on the assignment.

51. Allow the student additional time to complete class assignments or homework.

52. Teach the student organizational and assignment completion skills (e.g., begin with a clean desk, read directions carefully, collect all necessary materials, ask for assistance if needed, look for the main idea, follow examples provided, answer questions you know first and leave those you are unsure of for last, etc.).

53. Have the student schedule his/her own time for assignments (e.g., 20 minutes for each of three assignments, 15 minutes for each of four assignments, etc.) in order to pace himself/herself.

54. Have the student record the time it took him/her to complete each assignment in order to accurately determine how much time is spent on each assignment.

55. Ask the student why he/she is not completing the required number of assignments in a given period of time. The student may have the most accurate perception as to why he/she is not completing the required number of assignments in a given period of time.

13 Demonstrates difficulty or reluctance in beginning tasks

Goals:

1. The student will attempt new tasks.

Objectives:

1. The student will attempt new tasks with teacher assistance on ___ out of ___ trials.
2. The student will independently attempt new tasks on ___ out of ___ trials.
3. The student will read the directions when attempting a new task on ___ out of ___ trials.
4. The student will perform a new task along with a peer on ___ out of ___ trials.
5. The student will attempt ___ out of ___ new tasks per day.
6. The student will begin a new task within ___ minutes.
7. The student will listen to directions prior to attempting a new task on ___ out of ___ trials.
8. The student will attempt to perform a new task before asking for teacher assistance on ___ out of ___ trials.
9. The student will work for ___ minutes without requiring teacher assistance on ___ out of ___ trials.

Interventions:

1. Structure the environment to provide the student with increased opportunities for help or assistance.

2. Reduce distracting stimuli (e.g., place the student on the front row, provide a carrel or "office" space away from distractions, etc.). This is used as a means of reducing distracting stimuli and not as a form of punishment.

3. Have the student maintain a record (e.g., chart or graph) of his/her performance in attempting new assignments/activities.

4. Communicate clearly to the student when it is time to begin.

5. Have the student time activities to monitor personal behavior and accept time limits.

6. Present the task in the most interesting and attractive manner possible.

7. Maintain mobility to provide assistance to the student.

8. Structure time units so the student knows exactly how long he/she has to work and when the work must be finished.

9. Provide the student with more than enough time to finish an activity. As the student demonstrates success, decrease the amount of time provided.

10. Give directions in a variety of ways to increase the probability of understanding (i.e., if the student fails to understand verbal directions, present them in written form to ensure understanding).

11. Have the student repeat the directions verbally to the teacher.

12. Give a signal (e.g., clapping hands, turning lights off and on, etc.) before giving verbal directions.

13. Provide the student with a predetermined signal when he/she is not beginning a task (e.g., turning lights off and on, hand signals, etc.).

14. Tell the student that directions will only be given once.

15. Rewrite directions at a lower reading level.

16. Help the student with the first few items on a task and gradually reduce the amount of help over time.

17. Reinforce the student for beginning assignments after receiving directions, instructions, etc., based on the length of time the student can be successful. Gradually decrease the amount of time to begin the task in order to be reinforced.

18. Follow a less desirable task with a highly desirable task. Make completion of the first task necessary to perform the second.

19. Provide the student with a schedule of activities so that he/she knows exactly what and how much there is to do in a day.

20. Prevent the student from becoming overstimulated by an activity (e.g., frustrated, angry, etc.).

21. Specify exactly what is to be done for the completion of the task (e.g., make definite starting and stopping points, identify a minimum requirement, etc.).

22. Require the student to begin each assignment within a specified period of time (e.g., three minutes, five minutes, etc.).

23. Provide the student with shorter tasks given more frequently.

24. Provide the student with a selection of assignments, requiring the student to choose a minimum number from the total (e.g., present the student with ten academic tasks from which six must be finished).

25. Start with a single problem and add more problems to the task over time.

26. Reduce emphasis on competition (e.g., academic or social). Fear of failure may cause the student to refuse to attempt new assignments/activities.

27. Provide the student with self-checking materials so that he/she may check work privately, reducing the fear of public failure.

28. Have the student attempt a new assignment/activity in a private place (e.g., carrel, "office," quiet study area, etc.) to reduce the fear of public failure.

29. Have the student practice a new skill (e.g., jumping rope, dribbling a basketball, etc.) alone, with a peer, or with the teacher before the entire group attempts the activity.

30. Provide the student with the opportunity to perform the assignment/activity in a variety of ways (e.g., on tape, with a calculator, verbally, etc.).

31. Allow the student to perform new assignments/activities in a variety of places in the building (e.g., resource room, library, learning center, etc.).

32. Provide the student with a sample of the assignment/activity which has been partially completed by a peer or teacher (e.g., book reports, projects, etc.).

33. Do not require the student to complete the assignment/activity in one sitting.

34. Allow the student the option of performing the assignment at another time (e.g., earlier in the day, later, on another day, etc.).

35. Deliver directions/instructions before handing out materials.

36. Make certain the student achieves success when following directions.

37. Have the student explain to the teacher what he/she thinks should be done to perform the assignment/activity.

38. Explain to the student that work not done during work time will have to be made up at other times (e.g., at recess, before school, after school, during lunch time, break time, etc.).

39. Teach the student direction-following skills (e.g., listen carefully, write down important points, ask for clarification, and wait until all directions are received before beginning).

40. Provide clearly stated directions, written or verbal (e.g., make the directions as simple and concrete as possible).

41. Interact frequently with the student to help him/her follow directions for the activity.

42. Structure the environment to provide the student with increased opportunity for help or assistance on academic tasks (e.g., peer tutoring, directions for work sent home, frequent interactions, etc.).

43. Provide alternatives to the traditional format for directions (e.g., tape record directions, summarize directions, directions given by peers, etc.).

44. Practice direction-following skills on nonacademic tasks.

45. Evaluate the appropriateness of the task to determine (a) if the task is too easy, (b) if the task is too difficult, and (c) if the length of time scheduled to complete the task is adequate.

46. Deliver directions and instructions before handing out materials.

47. Require that assignments done incorrectly, for any reason, be redone.

48. Make certain that the student has all the materials needed to perform the assignment/task.

49. Reduce the emphasis on competition. Competitive academic activities may cause the student to hurry into the assignment without following the directions.

50. Establish assignment rules (e.g., listen to directions, wait until all directions have been given, ask questions about anything you do not understand, begin assignments only when you are certain about what is required, make certain you have all necessary materials, etc.).

51. Make certain that the student is attending to the teacher (e.g., making eye contact, hands free of writing materials, looking at assignments, etc.) before directions are given.

52. Stand next to the student when giving directions.

53. Require the student to ask permission from the teacher to begin.

54. Maintain visibility to and from the student. The teacher should be able to see the student and the student should be able to see the teacher. Make eye contact possible at all times to make certain the student is attending.

55. Along with a directive, provide an incentive statement (e.g., "When you begin your work, I will come around to see if you have questions." etc.).

56. Use a timer to help the student know how much time he/she has to follow through with directions.

57. Choose a peer or volunteer to help the student begin a task.

58. Assess the quality and clarity of directions, explanations, and instructions given to the student.

59. Have the student question any directions, explanations, and instructions not understood.

60. Reduce the number of directions given at one time (i.e., give the student each additional step after completion of the previous step).

61. Communicate with the parents (e.g., notes home, phone calls, etc.) to share information concerning the student's progress. The parents may reinforce the student at home for beginning assignments after receiving directions, instructions, etc., at school.

62. Write a contract with the student specifying what behavior is expected (e.g., begin assignments after listening to directions) and what reinforcement will be made available when the terms of the contract have been met.

63. Establish classroom rules:
- Work on-task.
- Remain in your seat.
- Finish task.
- Meet task expectations.
- Raise your hand.

Review rules often. Reinforce students for following rules.

64. Speak to the student to explain (a) what the student is doing wrong (e.g., not beginning assignments after receiving directions, instructions, etc.) and (b) what the student should be doing (e.g., listening to directions, asking for clarification if directions are not understood, taking notes, following one step at a time, etc.).

65. Reinforce the student for beginning assignments after receiving directions, instructions, etc.: (a) give the student a tangible reward (e.g., classroom privileges, line leading, passing out materials, five minutes free time, etc.) or (b) give the student an intangible reward (e.g., praise, handshake, smile, etc.).

14 Does not follow directions, written or verbal, related to academic tasks

Goals:
1. The student will follow written directions.
2. The student will follow verbal directions.

Objectives:
1. The student will read all directions before beginning tasks and activities on _____ out of _____ trials.
2. The student will verbally state written directions on _____ out of _____ trials.
3. The student will follow one-step directions on _____ out of _____ trials.
4. The student will follow two-step directions on _____ out of _____ trials.
5. The student will follow multi-step directions on _____ out of _____ trials.
6. The student will ask for clarification of written directions not understood on _____ out of _____ trials.
7. The student will follow written directions with assistance on _____ out of _____ trials.
8. The student will independently follow written directions on _____ out of _____ trials.
9. The student will follow verbal directions in correct sequential order on _____ out of _____ trials.
10. The student will follow _____ out of _____ verbal directions on _____ out of _____ trials.
11. The student will demonstrate the ability to follow verbal directions by listening carefully and completing the task with _____% accuracy on _____ out of _____ trials.
12. The student will follow verbal directions with teacher assistance on _____ out of _____ trials.
13. The student will independently follow verbal directions on _____ out of _____ trials.
14. The student will listen to verbal directions on his/her ability level and follow them in correct sequential order on _____ out of _____ trials.
15. The student will complete one step of the verbal direction before going on to the next step on _____ out of _____ trials.
16. The student will follow one-step verbal directions on _____ out of _____ trials. (As the student demonstrates success, gradually increase expectations.)

Interventions:

1. Work the first problem or problems with the student to make certain that he/she follows the written or verbal directions accurately.

2. Write a contract with the student specifying what behavior is expected (e.g., following written or verbal directions) and what reinforcement will be made available when the terms of the contract have been met.

3. Communicate with parents (e.g., notes home, phone calls, etc.) to share information concerning the student's progress. The parents may reinforce the student at home for following written or verbal directions at school.

4. Work through the steps of the written or verbal directions as they are delivered in order to make certain the student follows the directions accurately.

5. Make certain that written directions are presented on the student's reading level.

6. Make certain that verbal directions are delivered in a supportive rather than threatening manner (e.g., "Will you please. . . ." or "You need. . . ." rather than "You better. . . ." or "If you don't. . . .").

7. Transfer directions from texts and workbooks when pictures or other stimuli make it difficult to attend to or follow written directions.

8. Establish classroom rules:
   - Work on-task.
   - Work quietly.
   - Remain in your seat.
   - Finish task.
   - Meet task expectations.

Review rules often. Reinforce students for following rules.

9. Make certain that all directions, questions, explanations, and instructions are delivered in a clear and concise manner and at an appropriate pace for the student.

10. Have the student repeat written directions verbally to the teacher.

11. Follow a less desirable task with a highly desirable task; make the completion of the first task necessary to perform the second.

12. Give written or verbal directions before handing out materials.

13. Have the student practice following written or verbal directions on nonacademic tasks (e.g., recipes, games, etc.).

14. Have the student maintain a record (e.g., chart or graph) of his/her performance in following written or verbal directions.

15. Choose a peer to model appropriate following of written or verbal directions for the student.

16. Make certain that directions are given at the level at which the student can be successful (e.g., two-step or three-step directions should not be given to students who can only successfully follow one-step directions).

17. Give the student one task to perform at a time. Introduce the next task only when the student has successfully completed the previous task.

18. Make certain that the student is attending to the teacher (e.g., eye contact, hands free of writing materials, looking at assignment, etc.) before giving written or verbal directions.

19. Have the student repeat or paraphrase directions after receiving verbal directions.

20. Use visual cues such as green dot to start, red dot to stop, arrows, etc., in written directions.

21. Interact frequently with the student to help him/her follow written or verbal directions.

22. Have the student repeat to himself/herself information just read to help remember the important facts.

23. Highlight, circle, or underline key words in written directions (e.g., key words such as match, circle, underline, etc.).

24. Make certain that verbal directions are delivered in a nonthreatening manner (e.g., positive voice, facial expression, language used, etc.).

25. As the student becomes more successful in following directions, gradually increase the degree of difficulty or complexity of written or verbal directions.

26. Have a designated person be the only individual to deliver verbal directions to the student.

27. Maintain a consistent format for written or verbal directions.

28. Have the student question any written or verbal directions, explanations, or instructions he/she does not understand.

29. Have the student carry out written or verbal directions one step at a time, checking with the teacher to make certain that each step is successfully followed before attempting the next.

30. Maintain visibility to and from the student. The teacher should be able to see the student and the student should be able to see the teacher. Make eye contact possible at all times.

31. Teach the student skills for following verbal directions (e.g., listen carefully, write down important points, use environmental cues, wait until all directions are received before beginning, etc.).

32. Make certain that the print is bold and large enough to increase the likelihood of following written directions.

33. Give directions in a variety of ways in order to increase the probability of understanding (e.g., if the student fails to understand verbal directions, present them in written form).

34. Have a peer help the student with any written or verbal directions not understood.

35. Teach the student written direction-following skills (e.g., read carefully, write down important points, ask for clarification, wait until all directions are received before beginning, etc.).

36. Make certain the student achieves success when following written or verbal directions.

37. Make certain the student has all the materials needed to perform the assignment or activity.

38. Present directions in both written and verbal form.

39. Prevent the student from becoming over stimulated by an activity (e.g., frustrated, angry, etc.).

40. Provide alternatives for the traditional format of presenting verbal directions (e.g., tape record directions, summarize directions, directions given by peers, etc.).

41. Structure the environment to provide the student with increased opportunity for help or assistance on academic tasks (e.g., peer tutoring, directions for work sent home, frequent interactions, etc.).

42. Provide clearly stated written or verbal directions (i.e., make the directions as simple and concrete as possible).

43. Provide the student a quiet place (e.g., carrel, study booth, etc.) where he/she may go to participate in activities which require following directions.

44. Reinforce the student for following written or verbal directions based on the length of time the student can be successful. As the student demonstrates success, gradually increase the length of time required for reinforcement.

45. Seat the student close to the source of the written or verbal directions (e.g., teacher, aide, peer, chalkboard, projector, etc.).

46. Reinforce those students in the classroom who follow written or verbal directions.

47. Tape record directions for the student to listen to individually and repeat as necessary.

48. Reinforce the student for following written or verbal directions: (a) give the student a tangible reward (e.g., classroom privileges, line leading, passing out materials, five minutes free time, etc.) or (b) give the student an intangible reward (e.g., praise, handshake, smile, etc.).

49. When delivering directions, explanations, and information, be certain to use vocabulary that is within the student's level of comprehension.

50. Reduce the emphasis on competition. Competitive activities may cause the student to hurry to begin the task without following written or verbal directions.

51. Require that assignments done incorrectly, for any reason, be redone.

52. Provide the student with a copy of written directions at his/her desk rather than the chalkboard, posted in the classroom, etc.

53. Speak to the student to explain (a) what he/she is doing wrong (e.g., ignoring written or verbal directions) and (b) what he/she should be doing (e.g., following written or verbal directions).

54. Provide the student with a written copy of verbal directions.

55. Seat the student far enough away from peers to facilitate attending to written or verbal directions.

56. Reduce written or verbal directions to individual steps (e.g., give the student each additional step after completion of the previous step).

57. Provide the student with a predetermined signal when he/she is not following verbal directions (e.g., lights turned off and on, hand signals, etc.).

58. Reduce distracting stimuli to increase the student's ability to follow written or verbal directions (e.g., place the student on the front row, provide a carrel or "office" space away from distractions, etc.). This is used as a means of reducing distracting stimuli and not as a form of punishment.

59. Require the student to wait until the teacher gives him/her a signal to begin the task (e.g., hand signal, ring bell, etc.).

60. Teach the student direction following skills (e.g., read all directions, identify key words, ask for an explanation of any directions not understood, follow directions by steps).

61. Choose a peer to work with the student to help him/her follow written or verbal directions.

62. Evaluate the appropriateness of the task to determine (a) if the task is too difficult and (b) if the length of time scheduled to complete the task is adequate.

63. Develop assignments/activities for the following of written or verbal directions (e.g., informal activities designed to have the student carry out directions in steps, increasing the degree of difficulty).

64. Deliver written or verbal directions before handing out materials.

65. Deliver a predetermined signal (e.g., clapping hands, turning lights off and on, etc.) before giving written or verbal directions.

66. Communicate clearly to the student when it is time to listen to verbal directions.

67. Stand next to the student when giving verbal directions.

68. Assess the quality and clarity of written or verbal directions, explanations, and instructions given to the student.

15 Does not remain on-task for the required length of time

Goals:

1. The student will remain on-task.

Objectives:

1. The student will remain on-task until the task is completed on _____ out of _____ trials.
2. The student will remain on-task for the required length of time with supervision on _____ out of _____ trials.
3. The student will independently remain on-task for the required length of time on _____ out of _____ trials.
4. The student will rely on environmental cues (e.g., timers, clocks, bells, other students) to remain on-task for the required length of time on _____ out of _____ trials..
5. The student will ask for clarification of directions or instructions not understood on _____ out of _____ trials.
6. The student will demonstrate on-task behavior by sitting quietly at his/her seat, looking at his/her materials, and performing the task for _____ minutes at a time. (Gradually increase expectations as the student demonstrates success.)
7. The student will remain on-task for _____ minutes at a time. (Gradually increase expectations as the student demonstrates success.)
8. The student will remain on-task long enough to complete the task on _____ out of _____ tasks.
9. The student will maintain eye contact with the teacher for _____ minutes at a time.

Interventions:

1. Establish classroom rules:
- Work on-task.
- Work quietly.
- Remain in your seat.
- Finish task.
- Meet task expectations.

Review rules often. Reinforce students for following rules.

2. Set time limits for completing assignments.

3. Speak to the student to explain (a) what the student is doing wrong (e.g., failing to attend to tasks) and (b) what the student should be doing (e.g., attending to tasks).

4. Choose a peer to model on-task behavior for the student.

5. Encourage the student to develop a 30 second definition of his/her goal to help him/her stay on-task and focused (e.g., "I will complete ten math problems without a reminder from the teacher to stay on-task. The better I focus and stay on-task, the better I will perform.").

6. Move objects used for tactile stimulation (e.g., pens, paper clips, loose change, etc.) away from the student's reach.

7. Follow a less desirable task with a more desirable task. Make completion of the first necessary to perform the second.

8. Reinforce the student for attending to a task based on the length of time he/she can be successful. As the student demonstrates success, gradually increase the length of time required for reinforcement.

9. Provide an incentive statement along with a directive (e.g., "When you complete this assignment, you may earn a pass to the water fountain.").

10. Reduce auditory and visual stimuli to a level at which the student can successfully function. As the student demonstrates that he/she can successfully tolerate increased levels of stimuli, gradually allow auditory and visual stimuli to increase.

11. Present tasks in the most attractive and interesting manner possible.

12. Reward the student for concentrating on an assignment for a specific length of time (e.g., take a break, get a drink of water, converse briefly with a peer, etc.).

13. Position the student's desk or work area in such a way that he/she is not visually distracted by others (e.g., turn the student's desk away from other students, etc.).

14. Use more interesting or stimulating activities as a reward for completing less interesting activities (e.g., after completing a rough draft on paper, the student can choose graphics available on the computer).

15. Reward the student for completing an assignment within the amount of time allotted.

16. Assist the student in completing class assignments. As the student demonstrates success, gradually decrease assistance and require the student to independently remain on-task.

17. Have the student define a goal. Assist the student in developing specific strategies to achieve his/ her goal and following through on those strategies.

18. Encourage the student to develop an awareness of himself/herself and the environment. Have the student periodically, step back and ask himself/herself, "Am I on-task and paying attention?" "What should I be doing now?"

19. Help the student develop attention-maintaining behaviors (e.g., maintain eye contact, take notes on the subject, ask questions related to the subject, etc.).

20. Allow the student to take a break while working on monotonous assignments to relieve restlessness and improve concentration.

21. Have the student organize assignments by breaking them into small segments. Set deadlines and provide the student with a reward after completing each segment of the assignment.

22. Reduce the number of current assignments by adding new assignments when previous assignments have been completed.

23. Allow the student to close the classroom door or windows in order to reduce auditory and visual distractions from outside of the classroom.

24. Create a quiet area in the classroom where absolute silence must be observed.

25. Schedule a fun educational activity (e.g., computer games) during the day in order to provide incentive for the student to stay on-task and behave appropriately.

26. Assist the student in writing a contract for himself/herself designating a time to complete an assignment and avoid procrastination.

27. Be proactive. Work with the school counselor to design a schedule conducive to the student's success (e.g., physical education scheduled the last period of the day, intersperse electives which allow greater freedom of movement with classes requiring extended periods of concentration, etc.).

28. Make participation in extra-curricular activities dependent upon completion of class assignments.

29. Specify exactly what is to be done for the completion of the task (e.g., indicate definite starting and stopping points, indicate the minimum requirements, etc.).

30. Remove any peer from the immediate environment who may be interfering with the student's ability to remain on-task.

31. Have the student question any directions, explanations, and instructions not understood.

32. Reduce the emphasis on competition. Repeated failure may cause the student to remove himself/herself from competition by not remaining on-task.

33. Provide the student with increased opportunities for help or assistance on academic tasks (e.g., peer tutoring, directions for work, frequent interactions, etc.).

34. Provide activities which increase the opportunities for "active participation."

35. Make certain only those materials necessary for performing the task are on the student's desk (i.e., pencil, textbook, paper, etc.). Additional materials may distract the student (e.g., crayons, library book, etc.).

36. Have the student participate in small group activities (e.g., free time, math, reading, etc.). As the student demonstrates success, gradually increase group size.

37. Position the student's seat so that he/she experiences the least amount of auditory and visual distractions.

38. Assess the degree of task difficulty in relation to the student's ability to successfully perform the task.

39. Evaluate the auditory and visual stimuli in the classroom to determine what level of stimuli the student can respond to in an appropriate manner.

40. Model for the student appropriate behavior in the presence of auditory and visual stimuli in the classroom (e.g., continuing to work, asking for quiet, moving to a quieter part of the classroom, etc.).

41. Set aside time at the end of each class period to complete unfinished assignments.

42. Set clear expectations for the completion of tasks. Consistently deliver reinforcement and consequences to all students.

43. Provide the student with a selection of assignments and require him/her to choose a minimum number from the total (e.g., present the student with 10 academic tasks from which he/she must finish 6 that day).

44. Communicate clearly with the student the length of time he/she has to complete an assignment and when the assignment is due. The student may want to use a timer in order to complete the tasks within the given period of time.

45. Encourage the student to manage his/her class performance as if he/she were self-employed. This should increase his/her motivation to be organized and fulfill his/her responsibilities.

46. Deliver reinforcement for any and all measures of improvement.

47. Identify the student's most efficient learning mode and use it consistently to increase the probability of understanding and remaining on-task for longer periods of time.

48. Assign the student shorter tasks but more of them (e.g., modify a 20-problem math activity to 4 activities of 5 problems each, to be performed at various times during the day). As the student demonstrates success, gradually increase the number of problems for each activity.

49. Make certain the student has all necessary materials to perform assignments.

50. Have the student assemble all materials needed prior to beginning a task to reduce interruptions.

51. Require the student to be productive in the presence of auditory and visual stimuli for short periods of time. As the student demonstrates success, gradually increase the length of time the student is required to be productive.

52. Make certain the student understands the instructions/directions for the task (e.g., present instructions in a variety of ways; have the student verbalize what he/she is to do in order to perform the activity; etc.).

53. Provide the student with a list of assignments for the day and allow the student to choose the order of the activities. The student may be in the best position to identify the order of tasks he/she will be able to perform successfully.

54. Provide a routine that will minimize off-task behavior which may result in negative consequences.

55. Structure the environment to reduce the opportunity for off-task behavior. Reduce lag time by providing the student with enough activities to maintain productivity.

56. Monitor the student's performance in activities or tasks to make certain the student begins, works on, and completes an assignment to be ready to move to the next activity in his/her routine.

57. Provide the student with a carrel or divider at his/her desk to reduce auditory and visual distractions.

58. Have the student time activities in order to monitor personal behavior and accept time limits.

59. Interact frequently with the student in order to maintain involvement in the activity (e.g., ask the student questions, ask the student's opinion, stand close to the student, seat the student near the teacher's desk, etc.).

60. Have the student chart his/her own record of on-task behavior. Reinforce the student for increasing the amount of time spent on-task.

61. Have the student work with a peer tutor to maintain attention to tasks.

62. Have the student work with a peer who manages time well.

63. Position the student away from those peers who create the most auditory and visual stimulation in the classroom.

64. Give the student one task to perform at a time. Introduce the next task only when the student has successfully completed the previous task.

65. Allow the student some movement while performing tasks. Monitor and limit the amount of movement.

66. Have the student communicate with appropriate personnel (e.g., counselor, nurse, administrator, etc.) about concerns (e.g., home, peer, personal problems, etc.) which interfere with his/her ability to stay on-task.

67. Communicate with parents (e.g., notes home, phone calls, etc.) to share information concerning the student's progress. The parents may reinforce the student at home for staying on-task in the classroom.

68. Provide the student with a quiet place in which to work where auditory and visual stimuli are reduced. This is used to reduce distracting stimuli and not as punishment.

69. Have the student ask himself/herself questions (e.g., "What's next?") to keep himself/herself focused on assignments/projects.

70. Develop a classroom environment that is quiet and uncluttered (e.g., clean, well-lighted, fresh-smelling, and at a comfortable temperature).

71. Have the student maintain a chart representing the amount of time spent on-task.

72. Teach the student appropriate ways to respond to visual and auditory stimuli in the classroom (e.g., moving to another part of the room, asking others to be quiet, leaving the group, etc.).

73. Help the student learn to be satisfied with his/her own best effort rather than some arbitrary measure of success. Success is measured individually according to ability levels and progress of any kind is a measure of success.

74. Seat the student so that he/she experiences the least amount of auditory and visual stimuli.

75. Provide the student with a predetermined signal (e.g., hand signal, verbal cue, etc.) when he/she begins to display off-task behaviors.

76. Write a contract with the student specifying what behavior is expected (establish a reasonable length of time to stay on-task) and what reinforcement will be made available when the terms of the contract have been met.

77. Schedule highly desirable activities contingent upon staying on-task a required amount of time (i.e., staying on-task for a required amount of time earns the student the opportunity to participate in a desirable activity).

78. Provide flexibility in scheduling so the student may perform alternative activities which result in more successful on-task behavior.

79. Maintain visibility to and from the student. The teacher should be able to see the student and the student should be able to see the teacher, making eye contact possible at all times.

80. Minimize stimulation which interferes with the student's ability to remain on-task (e.g., maintain a routine schedule of events, schedule special activities for the end of the day, etc.).

81. Allow the student to leave the task and return to it at a later time when he/she can be more successful remaining on-task.

82. Reinforce the student for staying on-task in the classroom: (a) give the student a tangible reward (e.g., classroom privileges, line leading, passing out materials, five minutes free time, etc.) or (b) give the student an intangible reward (e.g., praise, handshake, smile, etc.).

83. Allow the student to take assignments/tasks to other areas of the school where he/she is most likely to be able to demonstrate on-task behavior (e.g., library, study hall, learning center, etc.).

84. Provide the student with alternative ways to perform an assignment and allow the student to choose the most desirable.

85. Use multiple modalities to accommodate more than one learning style (e.g., visual, auditory, tactile, etc.) when presenting directions/instructions, explanations, and instructional content.

86. Have a peer, paraprofessional, etc., cue the student when he/she is off-task (e.g., the person can touch the student's arm as a signal that he/she is not remaining on-task).

87. Make certain that the student understands the relationship between inappropriate behavior and the consequences which follow (e.g., failure to remain on-task will result in incomplete assignments).

88. Provide the student with assistance for those activities which he/she has the most difficulty attending to for the required amount of time.

89. Provide the student with adequate transition time between activities in order to increase on-task behavior after activities have begun (e.g., after break time, lunch, special activities, etc.).

90. Teach the student how to manage time until the teacher can provide assistance (e.g., try the problem again, go on to the next problem, wait quietly, etc.).

91. Provide the student with a timer to be used to increase the amount of time during which he/she maintains attention (e.g., have the student work on the activity until the timer goes off).

92. Provide assignments that involve immediate, short-term tasks.

93. Make certain the student knows what to do when he/she cannot successfully perform assignments (e.g., raise hand, ask for assistance, go to the teacher, etc.).

94. Provide the student with the opportunity to move to a quiet place in the classroom when auditory and visual distractions interfere with his/her ability to function successfully.

95. Assess the degree of task difficulty to determine whether or not the student will require additional information, time, assistance, etc., before beginning a task.

96. Remove the student from an activity until he/she can demonstrate appropriate on-task behavior.

97. Make certain that all auditory and visual stimuli in the classroom are reduced as much as possible for all learners.

98. Have the student's cooperative work experience/vocational education teacher provide him/her with interventions to assist in remaining on-task at his/her job.

99. Provide the student with earphones to wear if auditory stimuli interfere with his/her ability to function. As the student functions more successfully in the presence of auditory stimuli, gradually reduce the amount of time the earphones are worn.

100. Designate a specific period of time when it is permissible for the student to converse with his/her peers (e.g., each hour on the hour, last five minutes of class, after completing a task, etc.).

101. Have the student ask for help when he/she needs it.

102. Make certain to recognize the student when his/her hand is raised in order to convey that assistance will be provided as soon as possible.

103. Make certain the student has enough work area to perform the task.

104. Provide the student with shorter tasks which do not require extended attention to be successful. As the student demonstrates success, gradually increase the length of the tasks.

105. Reinforce those students in the classroom who demonstrate on-task behavior.

106. Place the student with peers who will be appropriate role models and likely to facilitate his/her academic and behavioral success.

107. Reduce distracting stimuli which could interfere with the student's ability to remain on-task (e.g., provide enough room to move without physical contact; keep noise level to a minimum; keep movement in the environment to a minimum; etc.).

108. Consider individual needs of the student which may be interfering with his/her on-task behavior (e.g., hunger, need for rest, comfort level, etc.). Intervene to correct the situation or change the expectations.

109. Make certain the student understands that work not done during work time must be completed at other times (e.g., lunch, during assemblies, after school, etc.).

16 Fails to complete homework assignments and return them to school

Goals:

1. The student will complete homework assignments and return them to school.

Objectives:

1. The student will take homework assignments home on _____ out of _____ occasions.
2. The student will complete homework assignments at home on _____ out of _____ occasions.
3. The student will return completed homework assignments to school on _____ out of _____ occasions.
4. The student will complete homework assignments at school when he/she cannot complete the assignments at home on _____ out of _____ occasions.
5. The student will receive help at home when completing homework assignments on _____ out of _____ occasions.
6. The student will complete ___ out of ___ homework assignments each day.
7. The student will complete ___ out of ___ homework assignments each week.
8. The student will bring ___ out of ___ of his/her completed homework assignments to school and turn them in each day.
9. The student will bring ___ out of ___ of his/her completed homework assignments to school and turn them in each week.
10. The student will carry his/her homework assignments to and from school in a book bag/backpack in order to prevent loss on ___ out of ___ trials.
11. The student will perform ___ out of ___ homework assignments at home and return them to school each day.
12. The student will perform ___ out of ___ homework assignments at home and return them to school each week.

Interventions:

1. Chart homework assignments completed.

2. Speak to the student to explain (a) what the student is doing wrong (e.g., not turning in homework assignments) and (b) what the student should be doing (i.e., completing homework assignments and returning them to school).

3. Encourage the student to reduce distractions (e.g., turn off the radio and/or TV, have people talk quietly, etc.) in order to complete homework.

4. Take proactive steps to deal with a student's refusal to perform a homework assignment to prevent contagion in the classroom (e.g., refrain from arguing with the student, place the student at a carrel or other quiet place to work, remove the student from the group or classroom, etc.).

5. Choose a peer to model completing homework assignments and returning them to school for the student.

6. Encourage the student to realize that all behavior has negative or positive consequences. Encourage the student to practice behaviors that will lead to positive consequences.

7. Encourage the student to set up an "office" where homework can be completed.

8. Have the student evaluate the visual and auditory stimuli in his/her designated work space at home to determine the amount of stimuli he/she can tolerate.

9. Develop a contract with the student and his/her parents requiring that homework be done before more desirable activities take place at home (e.g., playing, watching television, going out for the evening, etc.).

10. Make certain that homework provides drill and practice rather than introducing new concepts or information.

11. Assign small amounts of homework initially. As the student demonstrates success, gradually increase the amount of homework (e.g., one or two problems to perform may be sufficient to begin the homework process).

12. Maintain consistency in assigning homework (i.e., assign the same amount of homework each day).

13. Make sure the amount of homework assigned is not excessive and can be completed within a reasonable amount of time. Remember, secondary students may have six or seven teachers assigning homework each day.

14. Evaluate the appropriateness of the homework assignment to determine (a) if the task is too easy, (b) if the task is too difficult and (c) if the length of time scheduled to complete the task is adequate.

15. Reinforce the student for completing homework assignments and returning them to school: (a) give the student a tangible reward (e.g., classroom privileges, five minutes free time, etc.) or (b) give the student an intangible reward (e.g., praise, handshake, smile, etc.).

16. Reinforce the student for completing homework assignments based on the number of assignments the student can successfully complete. As the student demonstrates success, gradually increase the number of assignments required for reinforcement.

17. Reinforce those students who complete their assignments at school during the time provided.

18. Send home only one homework assignment at a time. As the student demonstrates success completing assignments at home, gradually increase the number of homework assignments sent home.

19. Present the tasks in the most attractive and interesting manner possible.

20. Identify the materials the student consistently fails to take home. Provide a set of those materials for the student to keep at home.

21. Encourage the student to develop an awareness of the consequences of his/her behavior by writing down or talking through problems which may occur due to his/her inability to complete homework assignments (e.g., if he/she does not complete the homework assignment, his/her grade may drop then he/she may not be able to participate in extra-curricular activities).

22. Provide the student with a book bag, back pack, etc., to take homework assignments and materials to and from home.

23. Provide a reinforcing activity at the beginning of the day/class period, contingent upon the completion and return of homework assignments.

24. Have the student organize assignments by breaking them into small segments. Have the student set deadlines and provide himself/herself with a reward after completing each segment of the assignment.

25. Have the student develop a checklist/chart to follow which will allow him/her to complete all assignments.

26. Establish an environmental setting for the classroom that promotes optimal individual performance (e.g., quiet room, background music, fresh air, etc.).

27. Encourage the parents to make positive comments about school and the importance of completing homework.

28. Provide time at school for homework completion when the student cannot be successful in performing assignments at home.

29. Specify exactly what is to be done for the completion of the homework task (e.g., indicate definite starting and stopping points, indicate the minimum requirements, etc.).

30. Have the student question any directions, explanations, or instructions not understood.

31. Allow natural consequences to occur for failure to complete homework assignments (e.g., students who do not finish their homework do not get to engage in more desirable activities).

32. Provide the student with written directions for doing homework assignments.

33. Provide the parents with information necessary for them to help the student with homework (e.g., what the assignments are and how to help with the assignments).

34. Encourage the student to reward himself/herself (e.g., take a ten minute break, speak briefly with a relative, telephone a friend, etc.) for concentrating on an assignment for a specific length of time.

35. Allow the student to perform a highly desirable task when homework has been turned in to the teacher.

36. Have the student place notes in highly visible areas (e.g., refrigerator door, bathroom door, front door, etc.) to remind the student to take homework assignments to school.

37. Allow the student to perform alternative homework assignments. Gradually introduce more components of the regular homework assignment until the assignments are routinely performed and returned to school.

38. Make certain the student understands that homework assignments not completed and turned in to the teacher will have to be completed during other times (e.g., break time, recreational time, before/after school, etc.).

39. Work a few problems of the homework assignment with the student to serve as a model and start the student on the assignment.

40. Have the student enlist the help of a relative, friend, etc., to remind him/her of homework assignments.

41. Make certain the student understands that homework not completed and turned in on time must still be completed and turned in.

42. Have the student verbally repeat the homework assignment in order to reinforce the student's awareness of the assignment.

43. Have the student prioritize tasks by importance (e.g., task A must be done today, task B can be done today, and task C can wait until tomorrow).

44. Find a tutor (e.g., a volunteer in the community, one of the student's classmates, etc.) to help the student complete homework.

45. Have the student set a timer in order to complete assignments in a reasonable period of time.

46. Deliver directions verbally in order to increase the probability of the student's understanding of homework assignments.

47. Encourage the student to follow a less desirable task with a more desirable task. Make completion of the first necessary to perform the second.

48. Maintain consistent expectations within the ability level of the student.

49. Encourage the student to set time limits for completing homework assignments. Encourage the student to be aware of time constraints when working on projects.

50. Encourage the student to recite a mantra to himself/herself when he/she brings work home (e.g., I will finish, I will finish, I will finish).

51. Deliver reinforcement for any and all measures of improvement.

52. Communicate with the student's parents the need to establish homework rules at home (e.g., start homework upon arriving home from school, finish homework before watching TV or talking on the phone, ask for help when necessary, etc.).

53. Encourage the student to reduce the number of visual distractions around him/her (e.g., move his/her work area away from windows, doors, kitchen, TV, etc.).

54. Encourage the student to put completed homework assignments in a designated place to be taken to school (e.g., in front of the door, at the bottom of the stairs, etc.).

55. Establish homework assignment rules:
- Stay on-task.
- Finish task.
- Meet task expectations.

Review rules often. Reinforce students for following the rules.

56. Encourage the student to choose interesting or stimulating activities as a reward for completing less interesting activities (e.g., complete homework before going to the mall).

57. Have the student keep a chart or graph representing the number of homework assignments completed and returned to school.

58. Encourage the student's parents to check over their child's homework when he/she is finished so the student can be certain that everything is complete.

59. Introduce the student to other resource persons who may be of help in performing homework assignments (e.g., librarian, special education teacher, other personnel with expertise or time to help, etc.).

60. Communicate with parents (e.g., notes home, phone calls, etc.) in order to share information concerning the student's progress. The parents may reinforce the student at home for returning completed homework to school.

61. Arrange with the student's parents to pick up homework each day if the student has difficulty "remembering" to take it home.

62. Establish a timeline for completing a project. Expect the student to meet each deadline in order to complete the project on time.

63. Do not use homework as a punishment (i.e., additional work should not be assigned as a consequence for inappropriate behavior at school or as a consequence for not preparing for school assignments).

64. Encourage the parents to set aside quiet time each night when the family turns off the TV, radio, etc., to read, do homework, write letters, etc.

65. Have the student maintain sample letters, reports, forms, etc., as references for completing homework assignments.

66. Encourage the student to establish a routine for himself/herself. Have the student develop a weekly schedule and a weekend schedule. Have the student develop a checklist/chart for daily homework assignments to be completed.

67. Communicate with the student's parents by sending home explanations of how to help their child with homework if it is necessary for the student to receive help.

68. Have the student develop problem-solving skills:
- Identify the problem (e.g., not completing homework, not returning completed homework to school).
- Identify the goals and objectives.
- Develop a strategy/plan for action.
- Carry out the plan.
- Evaluate the results.

69. Schedule the student's time at school so that homework will not be absolutely necessary if he/she takes advantage of the school time provided to complete assignments.

70. Write a contract with the student specifying what behavior is expected (e.g., completing homework assignments and returning them to school) and what reinforcement will be made available when the terms of the contract have been met.

71. Assess the appropriateness of giving the student assignments which require copying if the student's ability level makes it impossible for him/her to complete the assignment.

72. Encourage the parents to provide the student with a quiet, comfortable place and adequate time to do homework.

73. Encourage the parents to reward the student for following homework rules. Possible rewards include verbal praise (e.g., "Thank you for finishing your homework before going to the mall."), a kiss on the cheek, a hug, staying up late, watching a favorite TV show, renting a video, etc.

74. Choose a peer to help the student with homework.

75. Assess the appropriateness of assigning the student homework if his/her ability level or circumstances at home make it impossible for him/her to complete and return the assignments.

76. Develop an assignment sheet for the student. Talk with the student's parents so they are aware of the assignment sheet and the work that should be completed each night. Ask the parents to sign the assignment sheet so the teacher is aware that the parents reviewed it.

77. Ask the parents to review the student's homework responsibilities after school so the student knows what he/she is expected to do that evening.

78. Make sure the student has all the materials necessary prior to beginning an assignment to reduce unnecessary distractions.

79. Meet with parents to discuss appropriate ways to help the student with homework.

80. Have the student ask for help when he/she needs it.

81. Set up a homework system for the student (e.g., 2 days a week work with drill flash cards, 3 days a week work on book work sent home, etc.). This will add some variety to the student's homework.

82. Make certain that the student understands the relationship between inappropriate behavior and the consequences which follow (e.g., forgetting to complete homework will result in a low grade).

83. Make certain the student has mastered the concepts presented at school. Homework should be a form of practice for what has been learned at school.

84. Repeat directions in order to increase the student's probability of understanding.

85. Have the student establish a specific time each evening to work on homework assignments.

86. Assess the degree of task difficulty to determine whether or not the student will require additional information, time, assistance, etc., in order to complete a task at home.

87. Have the student ask a friend to call him/her at night or in the morning to remind him/her to bring assignments to school.

88. Allow the student additional time to turn in homework assignments.

89. Give directions in a variety of ways to increase the probability of understanding (e.g., if the student fails to understand verbal directions, present them in written form).

90. Teach the student time-management skills. Have the student make a daily plan and follow it. Encourage the student to avoid becoming distracted by events, impulses, and moods.

91. Create a learning center at school where professional educators are available to help with homework assignments before school begins, the last hour of each school day, etc.

92. Have the student and a classmate who has the same assignment do their homework together (e.g., right after school at one home or the other, during study hall, etc.).

93. Reinforce those students in the classroom who complete their homework assignments and return them to school.

94. Send homework assignments and materials home with someone other than the student (e.g., brother, sister, neighbor, etc.).

95. Make certain to provide the student with a selection of assignments, requiring him/her to choose a minimum number from the total (e.g., present the student with 10 academic tasks from which he/she must finish 6 that day).

17 Refuses or fails to complete class assignments or homework

Goals:

1. The student will complete classroom assignments during class time.
2. The student will turn in homework assignments.

Objectives:

1. The student will complete a task before going on to the next task on ___ out of ___ trials.
2. The student will complete ___ out of ___ assigned tasks per day.
3. The student will attempt ___ out of ___ assigned tasks per day.
4. The student will remain on task for ___ out of ___ minutes per class period.
5. The student will use the time provided to work on assigned tasks in order to complete ___ tasks per day.
6. The student will complete ___ out of ___ homework assignments each day.
7. The student will complete ___ out of ___ homework assignments each week.
8. The student will bring ___ out of ___ of his/her completed homework assignments to school and turn them in each day.
9. The student will bring ___ out of ___ of his/her completed homework assignments to school and turn them in each week.
10. The student will carry his/her homework assignments to and from school in a bookbag/backpack in order to prevent loss on ___ out of ___ trials.
11. The student will perform ___ out of ___ homework assignments at home and return them to school each day.
12. The student will perform ___ out of ___ homework assignments at home and return them to school each week.

Interventions:

1. Structure the environment to provide the student with increased opportunities for help or assistance.

2. Have the student maintain a record (e.g., chart or graph) of his/her performance in completing assignments.

3. Communicate clearly to the student the length of time he/she has to complete an assignment.

4. Have the student time assignments in order to monitor personal behavior and accept time limits.

5. Present tasks in the most interesting and attractive manner possible.

6. Provide the student with more than enough time to finish an activity and decrease the amount of time as the student demonstrates success.

7. Choose a peer to model appropriate completion of class assignments for the student.

8. Give directions in a variety of ways to increase the probability of understanding (e.g., if the student fails to understand verbal directions, present them in written form).

9. Have the student repeat the directions orally to the teacher.

10. Rewrite directions at a lower reading level.

11. Make directions as simple and concrete as possible.

12. Provide the student with shorter tasks given more frequently.

13. Specify exactly what is to be done for the completion of the task (e.g., indicate definite starting and stopping points, indicate a minimum requirement, etc.).

14. Provide the student with written directions for doing class/homework assignments.

15. Provide the student with a selection of assignments, requiring the student to choose a minimum number from the total (e.g., present the student with ten academic tasks from which six must be finished).

16. Provide the student with a certain number of problems to do on an assignment, requiring the student to choose a minimum number from the total (e.g., present the student with ten math problems from which six must be completed).

17. Write a contract with the student specifying what behavior is expected (e.g., completing class assignments) and what reinforcement will be made available when the terms of the contract have been met.

18. Reinforce those students in the classroom who complete assignments during time provided at school.

19. Assess the quality and clarity of directions, explanations, and instructions the student does not understand.

20. Have the student questions any directions, explanations, and instructions not understood.

21. Evaluate the appropriateness of the task to determine (a) if the task is too difficult, and (b) if the length of time scheduled to complete the task is adequate.

22. Communicate with the parents (e.g., notes home, phone calls, etc.) to share information concerning the student's progress. The parents may reinforce the student at home for completing class assignments/homework.

23. Choose a peer to work with the student and aid him/her in completing class assignments/homework.

24. Reinforce the student for completing classroom assignments/homework. As the student demonstrates success, gradually increase the number of times required for reinforcement.

25. Assess the appropriateness of assigning the student homework if his/her ability or circumstances at home make it impossible to complete and return the assignments.

26. Allow the student additional time to turn in class/homework assignments.

27. Deliver directions verbally in order to increase the probability of the student's understanding of class/homework assignments.

28. Chart class/homework assignments completed.

29. Along with a directive, provide an incentive statement (e.g., "After your work is finished, you may play a game." etc.).

30. Repeat directions in order to increase the student's probability of understanding.

31. Allow the student to perform a highly desirable task when the class assignment/homework has been turned in.

32. Allow natural consequences to occur for failure to complete class/homework assignments (e.g., students who do not finish their assignments do not get to engage in more desirable activities).

33. Introduce the student to other resource persons who may be of help in doing class/ homework assignments (e.g., other teachers, the librarian, etc.).

34. Maintain consistency of expectations and keep the expectations within the ability level of the student.

35. Take proactive steps to deal with student refusal to perform a class/homework assignment to prevent contagion (e.g., refrain from arguing with the student, place the student in a carrel or other quiet place to work, remove the student from the group or classroom, etc.).

36. Allow the student to perform alternative homework assignments. Gradually introduce more components of the regular class/homework assignment until the assignments are routinely performed and returned to school.

37. Work a few problems with the student on class/homework assignments to serve as a model and start the student on task.

38. Assign small amounts of classwork/homework initially. One or two problems may be sufficient to begin the work process. As the student demonstrates success, gradually increase the number or problems.

39. Reinforce those students in the classroom who turn in their class/homework assignments.

40. Establish class/homework assignment rules:
- Work on-task.
- Finish task.
- Meet task expectations.
- Turn in task.

Review rules often. Reinforce students for following rules.

41. Speak to the student to explain (a) what the student is doing wrong (e.g., not turning in class/homework assignments) and (b) what the student should be doing (e.g., completing class/homework assignments and turning them in).

42. Reinforce the student for turning in class/homework assignments: (a) give the student a tangible reward (e.g., classroom privileges, line leading, passing out materials, five minutes free time, etc.) or (b) give the student an intangible reward (e.g., praise, handshake, smile, etc.).

43. Reduce distracting stimuli (e.g., place the student on the front row, provide a carrel or "office" space away from distractions, etc.). This is used as a means of reducing distracting stimuli and not as a form of punishment.

44. Maintain mobility in order to provide assistance to the student when completing class assignments.

45. Structure time units so the student knows exactly how long he/she has to work and when the work must be finished.

46. Provide the student with a schedule of activities so he/she knows exactly what and how much there is to do in a day.

47. Prevent the student from becoming overstimulated by an activity (e.g., frustrated, angry, etc.).

48. Require the student to begin each assignment within a specified period of time (e.g., three minutes, five minutes, etc.).

49. Use a timer to help the student know how much time he/she has to finish as assignment.

50. Meet with parents to instruct them in appropriate ways to help the student with homework.

51. Encourage the parents to provide the student with a quiet, comfortable place and adequate time to do homework.

52. Make certain that homework is designed to provide drill activities rather than introduce new information.

53. Develop a contract with the student and his/her parents requiring that homework be done before more desirable activities take place at home (e.g., playing, watching television, going out for the evening, etc.).

54. Provide a set of necessary materials to be kept at home and send directions for homework home with the student.

55. Find a tutor (e.g., peer, volunteer, etc.) to work with the student at home.

56. Maintain consistency in assigning homework (i.e., assign the same amount of homework each day).

57. Provide time at school for homework completion when the student cannot be successful in performing assignments at home.

58. Provide the student with a book bag, backpack, etc., to take homework assignments and materials to and from home.

59. Arrange with the student's parents to pick up homework each day if the student has difficulty "remembering" to take it home.

60. Set up a homework system for the student (e.g., 2 days a week work with drill flash cards, 3 days a week work on book work sent home, etc.). This will add some variety to homework.

61. Make certain the student has mastered the concepts presented at school. All homework should be a form of practice for what has been learned at school.

62. Do not use homework as a punishment (i.e., homework should not be assigned as a consequence for inappropriate behavior at school).

63. Send homework assignments and materials directly to the home with someone other than the student (e.g., brother or sister, neighbor, bus driver, etc.).

64. Schedule the student's time at school so that homework will not be absolutely necessary if he/she takes advantage of the school time provided to complete assignments.

65. Create a learning center at school where professional educators are available to help with homework assignments before school begins, the last hour of each school day, etc.

18 Does not wait appropriately for assistance from an instructor

Goals:

1. The student will wait appropriately for assistance from an instructor.

Objectives:

1. The student will wait quietly for assistance from an instructor on _____ out of _____ occasions.
2. The student will continue working on parts of the assignment while waiting for assistance from the instructor on _____ out of _____ occasions.
3. The student will remain seated while waiting for assistance from an instructor on _____ out of _____ occasions.

Interventions:

1. Communicate with the student's parents (e.g., notes home, phone calls, etc.) to share information concerning their child's progress. They may reinforce the student at home for waiting appropriately for assistance from an instructor at school.

2. Evaluate the appropriateness of the task to determine (a) if the task is too easy, (b) if the task is too difficult, and (c) if the length of time scheduled to complete the task is adequate.

3. Tell the student that you will assist him/her as soon as possible (e.g., "Stephen, I'll be with you shortly.") to increase the probability that the student will wait appropriately for assistance.

4. Choose a peer from whom the student may seek assistance.

5. Attempt to provide assistance immediately. Gradually increase the length of time the student must wait for assistance when the instructor is helping another student, instructing, etc.

6. Have the student ask for clarification if he/she does not understand directions that are given verbally or in writing.

7. Reinforce the student for waiting appropriately for assistance from an instructor: (a) give the student a tangible reward (e.g., classroom privileges, passing out materials, five minutes free time, etc.) or (b) give the student an intangible reward (e.g., praise, handshake, smile, etc.).

8. Speak to the student to explain (a) what he/she is doing wrong (e.g., leaving his/her seat, talking to other students, etc.) and (b) what he/she should be doing (e.g., waiting quietly for assistance, remaining seated, etc.).

9. Establish classroom rules:
- Stay on-task.
- Work quietly.
- Remain in your seat.
- Finish task.
- Meet task expectations.

Review rules often. Reinforce students for following the rules.

10. Reinforce those students in the classroom who remain seated in assigned areas and remain quiet while waiting for assistance from the instructor.

11. Reinforce the student for waiting appropriately for assistance from an instructor based on the length of time he/she can be successful. As the student demonstrates success, gradually increase the length of time required for reinforcement.

12. Choose a classmate to model appropriate behavior (e.g., remaining in seat or assigned area, remaining quiet, etc.) when waiting for assistance from an instructor for the student.

13. Encourage the student to go to the next problem, go to another part of the assignment, begin a new assignment, etc., when waiting for assistance from an instructor.

14. Provide constant, positive reinforcement for appropriate behavior. Ignore as many inappropriate behaviors as possible.

15. Provide the student with a clearly understood list of consequences for inappropriate behavior.

16. Increase supervision (e.g., by teacher, peer, etc.) of the student to allow intervention to occur before the student exhibits disruptive behavior.

17. Have the student question any directions, explanations, or instructions he/she does not understand prior to beginning an assignment.

18. Have the student question any directions, explanations, or instructions before beginning a task to reinforce comprehension.

19. Reduce the emphasis on competition. Highly competitive activities may cause the student to feel anxious and have difficulty waiting for assistance from the teacher.

20. Discuss the student's behavior with him/her in private rather than in front of others.

21. Make certain that the activities in which the student engages are not too difficult for him/her.

22. Do not place an emphasis on perfection. If the student feels he/she must live up to your expectations and cannot, it may cause him/her to become impatient while waiting for assistance.

23. Closely supervise the student to monitor his/her behavior at all times.

24. Assess the degree of task difficulty to determine whether or not the student will require additional information, time, assistance, etc., before beginning a task.

25. Post needed information in a readily accessible location (e.g., bulletin board, desktop, etc.), to decrease the student's need for assistance from the instructor.

26. Establish alternative activities for the student to perform when waiting for assistance from an instructor (e.g., check work already completed, look at a magazine, organize work area, begin another task, etc.).

27. Maintain visibility to and from the student while he/she waits until assistance can be provided. The instructor should be able to see the student and the student should be able to see the instructor. Make eye contact possible at all times.

28. Maintain verbal communication with the student until assistance can be provided (e.g., "Thank you for waiting quietly. I'll be there shortly.").

29. Teach the student to use techniques which limit the need for teacher assistance (e.g., refer to previous math problems for models, use reference materials as a source for answers, etc.).

19 Performs classroom tests, quizzes, or tasks at a failing level

Goals:

1. The student will improve his/her performance on classroom tests.
2. The student will improve his/her performance on classroom quizzes.

Objectives:

1. The student will perform classroom tests with ___% accuracy. (Gradually increase expectations as the student demonstrates success.)
2. The student will perform classroom quizzes with ___% accuracy. (Gradually increase expectations as the student demonstrates success.)
3. The student will meet a ___% level of mastery on classroom tests. (Gradually increase expectations as the student demonstrates success.)
4. The student will meet a ___% level of mastery on classroom quizzes. (Gradually increase expectations as the student demonstrates success.)

Interventions:

1. Teach and encourage the student to practice basic study skills (e.g., reading for the main point, note taking, summarizing, highlighting, studying in an appropriate environment, using time wisely, etc.) before taking tests or quizzes.

2. Assess student performance in a variety of ways (e.g., have the student give verbal explanations, simulations, physical demonstrations of a skill, etc.).

3. Give shorter tests or quizzes, but give them more frequently. As the student demonstrates success, gradually increase the length of tests or quizzes over time.

4. Have tests or quizzes read to the student.

5. Have the student answer tests or quizzes verbally.

6. Have the tests or quizzes tape recorded and allow the student to listen to questions as often as necessary.

7. Arrange a time for the student to study with a peer tutor before taking tests or quizzes.

8. Have the student take tests or quizzes in the resource room where the resource teacher can clarify questions, offer explanations, etc.

9. Provide the student with opportunities for review before taking tests or quizzes.

10. Have the student question anything he/she does not understand while taking tests or quizzes.

11. Make certain that the tests or quizzes measure knowledge of content and not related skills, such as reading or writing.

12. Teach the student test-taking strategies (e.g., answer questions you are sure of first, learn to summarize, check each answer, etc.).

13. Have the student maintain a performance record for each subject in which he/she is experiencing difficulty.

14. Allow the student to take tests or quizzes in a quiet place in order to reduce distractions (e.g., study carrel, library, etc.).

15. Provide a variety of opportunities for the student to learn the information covered by tests or quizzes (e.g., films, visitors, community resources, etc.).

16. Allow the student to respond to alternative test or quiz questions (e.g., more generalized questions which represent global understanding).

17. Provide the opportunity for the student to study daily assignments with a peer.

18. Have the student take a sample test or quiz before the actual test.

19. Remove the threat of public knowledge of failure (e.g., test or quiz results are not read aloud or posted, test ranges are not made public, etc.).

20. Reduce the emphasis on formal testing by grading the student on daily performance.

21. Provide parents with information on test or quiz content (e.g., which material will be covered by the test or quiz, format, types of questions, etc.).

22. Modify instructions to include more concrete examples in order to enhance student learning.

23. Monitor student performance to detect errors and determine where learning problems exist.

24. Reduce the emphasis on competition. Students who compete academically and fail may cease to try to succeed and do far less than they are capable of achieving.

25. Only give tests and quizzes to the student when he/she is certain to succeed (e.g., after determining that the student has learned the information).

26. Make certain the student has mastery of skills at each level before testing a concept.

27. Make certain that all directions, questions, explanations, and instructions are delivered in a clear, concise manner and at an appropriate pace for the student.

28. Provide the student with increased opportunities for help or assistance on academic tasks (e.g., peer tutoring, directions for work sent home, frequent interactions, etc.).

29. Identify the student's most efficient learning mode and use it when giving tests or quizzes to increase the probability of understanding.

30. Evaluate the appropriateness of the task to determine (a) if the task is too easy, (b) if the task is too difficult, and (c) if the length of time scheduled for the task is adequate.

31. Communicate with the parents (e.g., notes home, phone calls, etc.) to share information concerning the student's progress. The parents may reinforce the student at home for improved test or quiz scores.

32. Write a contract with the student specifying what behavior is expected (e.g., improved test or quiz scores) and what reinforcement will be made available when the terms of the contract have been met.

33. Reinforce those students who demonstrate improved test or quiz scores. (It may be best to reinforce privately rather than publicly.)

34. Establish classroom rules:
- Work on-task.
- Work quietly.
- Remain in your seat.
- Finish task.
- Meet task expectations.

Review rules often. Reinforce students for following rules.

35. Speak with the student to explain (a) what the student is doing wrong (e.g., not attending during class, not using study time, etc.) and (b) what the student should be doing (e.g., attending during class, asking questions, using study time, etc.).

36. Reinforce improved test or quiz scores: (a) give the student a tangible reward (e.g., classroom privileges, line leading, passing out materials, five minutes free time, etc.) or (b) give the student an intangible reward (e.g., praise, handshake, smile, etc.).

20 Performs daily academic tasks or homework at a failing level

Goals:

1. The student will improve his/her performance on daily academic tasks.
2. The student will improve his/her performance on homework assignments.

Objectives:

1. The student will perform classroom assignments with ___% accuracy. (Gradually increase expectations as the student demonstrates success.)
2. The student will perform homework assignments with ___% accuracy. (Gradually increase expectations as the student demonstrates success.)

Interventions:

1. Assess student performance in a variety of ways (e.g., have the student give verbal explanations, simulations, physical demonstrations, etc.).

2. Give shorter assignments, but give them more frequently. As the student demonstrates success, increase the length of the assignments.

3. Structure the environment to provide the student with increased opportunity for help or assistance on academic or homework tasks (e.g., provide peer tutors, seat the student near the teacher or aide, etc.).

4. Provide the student with self-checking materials, requiring correction before turning in assignments.

5. Interact frequently with the student to monitor task performance.

6. Have the student maintain a chart representing the number of tasks completed and the accuracy rate of each task.

7. Provide time at school for the completion of homework if homework assigned has not been completed or has resulted in failure. (The student's failure to complete homework assignments may be the result of variables in the home over which he/she has no control.)

8. Assess the quality and clarity of directions, explanations, and instructions given to the student.

9. Teach the student note-taking skills.

10. Assess the appropriateness of assigning homework to the student.

11. Teach the student direction-following skills: (a) listen carefully, (b) ask questions, (c) use environmental cues, (d) rely on examples provided, etc.

12. Identify resource personnel from whom the student may receive additional assistance (e.g., librarian, special education teacher, other personnel with expertise or time to help, etc.).

13. Establish a level of minimum accuracy which will be accepted as a level of mastery.

14. Deliver reinforcement for any and all measures of improvement.

15. Mastery should not be expected too soon after introducing new information, skills, etc.

16. Reduce distracting stimuli (e.g., place the student in the front row, provide a carrel or "office" space away from distractions, etc.). This is used as a means of reducing distracting stimuli and not as a form of punishment.

17. Should the student consistently fail to complete assignments with minimal accuracy, evaluate the appropriateness of tasks assigned.

18. Provide instruction and task format in a variety of ways (e.g., verbal instructions, written instructions, demonstrations, simulations, manipulatives, drill activities with peers, etc.).

19. If the student has difficulty completing homework assignments with minimal accuracy, provide a time during the day when he/she can receive assistance at school.

20. Make certain the assignments measure knowledge of content and not related skills such as reading or writing.

21. Have assignments read to the student.

22. Have the student respond to tasks verbally.

23. Have the assignments tape recorded and allow the student to listen to questions as often as necessary.

24. Provide the student with opportunities for review prior to grading assignments.

25. Arrange a time for the student to study with a peer tutor before completing a graded assignment.

26. Provide multiple opportunities for the student to learn the information covered by assignments (e.g., films, visitors, community resources, etc.).

27. Allow the student to respond to alternative assignment questions (e.g., more generalized questions that represent global understanding).

28. Provide parents with information regarding appropriate ways in which to help their child with homework (e.g., read directions with the student, work a few problems together, answer questions, check the completed assignment, etc.).

29. Monitor the student's performance of the first problem or part of the assignment in order to make certain the student knows what is expected.

30. Monitor student performance in order to detect errors and determine where learning problems exist.

31. Allow/require the student to make corrections after assignments have been checked the first time.

32. Maintain consistency in assignment format and expectations so as not to confuse the student.

33. Provide the student with evaluative feedback for assignments completed (i.e., identify what the student did successfully, what errors were made, and what should be done to correct the errors).

34. Provide adequate repetition and drill to assure minimal accuracy of tasks assigned (i.e., require mastery/minimal accuracy before moving to the next skill level).

35. It is not necessary to grade every assignment performed by the student. Assignments may be used to evaluate student ability or knowledge and provide feedback. Grades may not need to be assigned until mastery/minimal accuracy has been attained.

36. Allow the student to put an assignment away and return to it at a later time if he/she could be more successful.

37. Have the student practice an assignment with the teacher, aide, or peer before performing the assignment for a grade.

38. Modify instruction to include more concrete examples in order to enhance student learning.

39. Provide frequent interactions and encouragement to support the student's confidence and optimism for success (e.g., make statements such as "You're doing great." "Keep up the good work." "I'm really proud of you." etc.).

40. Build varying degrees of difficulty into assignments in order to insure the student's self-confidence and at the same time provide a challenge (e.g., easier problems are intermingled with problems designed to measure knowledge gained).

41. Work the first few problems of an assignment with the student in order to make certain that he/she knows what to do, how to perform the assignment, etc.

42. Modify academic tasks (e.g., format, requirements, length, etc.).

43. Provide the student with clearly stated step-by-step directions for homework so that someone at home may be able to provide assistance.

44. Make certain that homework relates to concepts already taught rather than introducing a new concept.

45. Allow the student to perform alternative versions of the assignments. Gradually introduce more components of the regular assignments until those can be performed successfully.

46. Communicate clearly with the student the length of time he/she has to complete the assignment and when the assignment should be completed. The student may want to use a timer in order to complete tasks within a given period of time.

47. Have the student act as a peer tutor to teach another student a concept he/she has mastered. This can serve as reinforcement for the student.

48. Make certain the student has mastery of concepts at each level before introducing a new skill level.

49. Make certain the student is not required to learn more information than he/she is capable of at any one time.

50. Identify the student's most efficient learning mode and use it consistently to increase the probability of understanding.

51. Evaluate the appropriateness of the task to determine (a) if the task is too easy, (b) if the task is too difficult and (c) if the length of time scheduled to complete the task is adequate.

52. Communicate with the parents (e.g., notes home, phone calls, etc.) to share information concerning the student's progress. The parents may reinforce the student at home for improving his/her academic task and homework performance.

53. Write a contract with the student specifying what behavior is expected (e.g., completing an assignment with ___% accuracy) and what reinforcement will be made available when the terms of the contract have been met.

54. Reinforce those students in the classroom who show improvement on academic task and homework performance.

55. Give directions in a variety of ways to increase the probability of understanding (e.g., if the student fails to understand verbal directions, present them in written form).

56. Meet with parents to discuss with them appropriate ways to help the student with homework.

57. Choose a peer to help the student with academic tasks/homework.

58. Present the tasks in the most attractive and interesting manner possible.

59. Allow the student additional time to turn in homework assignments.

60. Deliver directions verbally in order to increase the probability of the student's understanding of academic tasks/homework assignments.

61. Repeat directions in order to increase the student's probability of understanding.

62. Establish classroom rules:
- Work on-task.
- Work quietly.
- Remain in your seat.
- Finish task.
- Meet task expectations.

Review rules often. Reinforce students for following rules.

63. Have the student question any directions, explanations, and instructions not understood.

64. Speak to the student to explain (a) what the student is doing wrong (e.g., performing below his/her ability level, failing assignments, etc.) and (b) what the student should be doing (e.g., improving his/her academic task and homework performance).

65. Reinforce the student for improving academic tasks and homework performance: (a) give the student a tangible reward (e.g., classroom privileges, line leading, passing out materials, five minutes free time, etc.) or (b) give the student an intangible reward (e.g., praise, handshake, smile, etc.).

66. Encourage the parents to provide the student with a quiet, comfortable place and adequate time to do homework.

67. Maintain consistency of expectations and keep the expectations within the ability level of the student.

68. Find a tutor (e.g., peer, volunteer, etc.) to work with the student at home.

69. Maintain consistency in assigning homework (i.e., assign the same amount of homework each day).

70. Create a learning center at school, open the last hour of each school day, where professional educators are available to help with homework.

71. Have tests or quizzes read to the student.

72. Have the student complete academic tasks in the resource room where the resource teacher can clarify questions, offer explanations, etc.

73. Teach and encourage the student to practice basic study skills (e.g., reading for the main point, note taking, summarizing, highlighting, studying in an appropriate environment, using time wisely, etc.) before taking tests or quizzes.

74. Provide the opportunity for the student to study daily assignments with a peer.

75. Remove the threat of public knowledge of failure (e.g., test or quiz results are not read aloud or posted, test ranges are not made public, etc.).

76. Reduce the emphasis on competition. Students who compete academically and fail may cease to try to succeed and do far less than they are capable of achieving.

77. Only give academic tasks/homework assignments to the student when he/she is certain to succeed (e.g., after determining that the student has learned the information).

78. Make certain that all directions, questions, explanations, and instructions are delivered in the most clear and concise manner and at an appropriate pace for the student.

Please Note: If the student continues to fail in spite of the above interventions and is not being served by special education personnel, he/she should be referred for consideration for special education services.

21 Does not make the most appropriate decisions or choices based on information available and a consideration of probable outcomes

Goal:

1. The student will make appropriate/realistic choices for the situation.
2. The student will develop short-term goals to pursue.
3. The student will develop long-term goals to pursue.
4. The student will develop effective planning skills in reaching his/her desired goals.
5. The student will demonstrate appropriate decision-making skills through leadership roles.

Objectives:

1. The student will make appropriate/realistic decisions with assistance in ____% of situations.
2. The student will independently make appropriate/realistic decisions in ____% situations.
3. The student will solve problems with assistance in ____% of situations.
4. The student will independently solve problems in ____% of situations.
5. The student will make correct inferences with assistance in ____% of situations.
6. The student will independently make correct inferences in ____% of situations.
7. The student will make appropriate/realistic choices which demonstrate that he/she has considered the consequences of his/her choice on ____ out of ____ trials.
8. The student will solve problems by reasoning in conflict situations on ____ out of ____ occasions.
9. The student will be allowed ____ hours of class time per week to explore materials and resources in preparation for setting goals.
10. The student will designate, in a pre-planned written assessment, the long-term goal(s) he/she wishes to pursue.
11. The student will designate, in a pre-planned written assessment, the short-term goal(s) he/she wishes to pursue.
12. The student will assume responsibility for decisions made by completing all assignments with ____% accuracy.
13. The student will assume responsibility for decisions made by completing all assignments within a mutually agreed upon time frame.
14. The student will improve his/her ability to make appropriate decisions by independently engaging in evaluative thinking techniques ____ times per week.
15. The student will engage in forecasting activities ____ times per week.
16. The student will engage in simulated problem-solving activities requiring decision-making skills ____ times per week.
17. The student will participate in training activities that provide opportunities for leadership ____ times per week.

Interventions

1. Show an interest in the student (e.g., acknowledge the student, ask the student's opinion, spend time working one-on-one with the student, etc.).

2. Have the student answer analogy situations (e.g., A garage is to a car as a house is to a____ ?).

3. Have the student read stories involving a moral (e.g., *The Tortoise and the Hare, The Boy Who Cried Wolf*, etc.) and explain the reason for the outcome of the story.

4. Set aside time each day for a problem-solving activity, analogies, decision-making activities, assigned responsibilities, etc.

5. Have the student keep a journal about all of his/her leadership experiences.

6. Teach the student to "think" before acting (e.g., ask himself/herself, "What is happening?" "What am I doing?" "What should I do?" "What will be best for me?").

7. Give the student fill-in-the-blank statements requiring an appropriate response from multiple choice possibilities (e.g., The boy's dog was dirty, so the boy decided to give his dog a ___[dog biscuit, bath, toy].).

8. Teach the student to list pros and cons of choices available to him/her in making decisions.

9. Have the student answer such questions as, "Why do we have rules?" "Why do you have to be a certain age before you can drive a car?" etc.

10. Allow the student to develop an awareness of leadership qualities by reading about the lives of famous leaders (e.g., George Washington, Abraham Lincoln, Napoleon, Eleanor Roosevelt, etc.).

11. Ask the student to evaluate the behavior of a group of people (e.g., "What makes children afraid of the principal?" etc.). Have the student choose what his/her own behavior might be under similar circumstances. Encourage the student to evaluate what his/her predicted behavior tells about himself/herself (e.g., beliefs, values, etc.).

12. Give the student responsibilities in the classroom (e.g., teacher assistant, peer tutor, group leader, etc.).

13. Make certain the student experiences the consequences of his/her behavior (e.g., appropriate behavior results in positive consequences while inappropriate behavior results in negative consequences).

14. Provide the student with natural consequences for inappropriate/unrealistic choices (e.g., not being allowed to complete an assignment during classtime if he/she chose to go to a basketball game the night before).

15. Have the student identify appropriate consequences for rules (e.g., consequences for following rules and consequences for not following rules). Have the student explain the choice of consequences he/she identified.

16. Require the student to design a criteria matrix chart for evaluation goals.

17. Present the student with a simulated creative problem to solve (e.g., a problem with several acceptable solutions, fuzzy situations, etc.):
- Have the student work individually or in a small group to determine the main problem to solve.
- Allow the student(s) time to discuss the nature of the problem and all of its parameters (e.g., "Juvenile crime is on the rise chiefly because of a lack of positive parental support and supervision on planet K in the year 2050." etc.).
- After completing research, ask the student(s) to decide which alternative solutions are available.
- Have the student(s) debate several criteria by which to judge the alternative solutions (e.g., time involved in implementation, cost, acceptability of solution, etc.).
- Ask the student(s) to evaluate each alternative solution by the criteria and place them in order by rank.
- Permit the student(s) to discuss the highest ranked alternative solution and its anticipated results as it might be implemented in the situation.

18. When faced with a social decision, encourage the student to interpret the feelings of a participant in a given situation (e.g., in a scene from a play, story episode, classroom event, etc.); allow the student to determine why the participant should feel that way.

19. Require the student to determine the end result of a goal accomplishment (e.g., product, place in competition, personal/intrinsic motivation, newspaper recognition, reward, etc.).

20. Have the student question any directions, explanations, and instructions he/she does not understand.

21. Ask the student to choose relevant facts of a presented situation or problem (e.g., pertinent information in a math question, relevant evidence in a witness's deposition, etc.)

22. Give the student situations/pictures and have him/her explain what variables are related (e.g., Snow is falling, the wind is blowing. Is the temperature hot or cold? What should you wear outdoors?).

23. When something is broken, lost, etc., have the student identify what could have been done to prevent the situation. When materials are properly organized, maintained, and serviceable, have the student discuss the value of such practices.

24. Have the student make up rules. Have him/her explain why each is necessary.

25. Teach the student to budget his/her money so the student is able to make realistic choices regarding purchases.

26. Encourage the student to list his/her goal options and indicate which goals are of primary importance and which are secondary.

27. Communicate with the parents (e.g., notes home, phone calls, etc.) in order to share information concerning the student's progress. The parents may reinforce the student at home for making appropriate/realistic choices at school.

28. Teach the student problem-solving skills: (a) identify the problem; (b) identify goals and objectives; (c) develop strategies; (d) develop a plan for action; and (e) carry out the plan.

29. Have the student investigate, individually or in a group, necessary training for various vocations of interest to help him/her make appropriate/realistic choices.

30. Provide the student with all necessary information when making decisions (e.g., guest speaker from a vocational school, field trip to the high school, books regarding careers, etc.).

31. Make certain that parental/guardian input is available in situations regarding education.

32. Encourage the student to participate in leadership roles through in-school and out-of-school situations (e.g., student council, Scouts, debate club, service organizations, etc.).

33. Give the student responsibilities that require logical thinking (e.g., assign the student to water plants and provide him/her with a watering can and a glass, telling him/her to use the most appropriate container; etc.).

34. When the classroom encounters a situation necessitating active decision-making, have the student describe the situation (e.g., interpersonal problem-solving, etc.):
- Ask the student to respond with what he/she feels a person should do in that situation.
- As the student to judge his/her own past actions in similar situations.
- Require the student to state reasons for acting that way in the past.
- Have the student suggest alternative behaviors.
- Ask the student to predict his/her behavior in future situations.

35. Lead and direct the student. Do not lecture and make demands.

36. Provide the student with a list of questions, involving logic, which he/she answers verbally (e.g., "Why do we post *wet paint signs*?" "Why do we have *Stop* signs at intersections?" "Why do we wear seatbelts?"; etc.).

37. Encourage the student to follow a pre-designed plan of procedural steps to achieve his/her goals.

38. Each day provide the student with problem-solving situations which require logical thinking (e.g., "A stranger takes you by the arm in a department store. What do you do?" "You see smoke coming out of a neighbor's house and no one is home. What do you do?" etc.).

39. Reinforce the student for making appropriate/realistic choices for the situation: (a) give the student a tangible reward (e.g., classroom privileges, line leading, passing out materials, five minutes free time, etc.) or (b) give the student an intangible reward (e.g., smile, praise, handshake, etc.).

40. Allow the student more decision-making opportunities relative to class activities and assignments.

41. Allow time for the student to role-play leadership characteristics in class simulations of group dynamics (e.g., stabilizer, organizer, dissention-maker, etc.).

42. Provide opportunities for the student to serve as a group leader in class situations (e.g., discussions, decision-making, organizing activities, etc.).

43. Show the student pictures of dangerous situations and have him/her explain why it is dangerous (e.g., a child running into the street between parked cars, a child riding a bicycle without using his/her hands, etc.).

44. When deciding upon goals, encourage the student to list possible problems associated with each optional goal (e.g., availability of resources, feasibility of goal achievement, etc.).

45. When deciding upon goals, have the student rank by order his/her primary optional goals based on probable outcomes (i.e., feasibility of goal achievement).

46. After deciding upon goals, require the student to decide which goal will be pursued first.

47. Point out the consequences of other student choices as they occur (e.g., take the opportunity to point out that consequences occur for all choices and for all persons).

48. When deciding upon goals, have the student rank by order his/her primary optional goals based on information available.

49. Provide a learning experience which emphasizes the cause-and-effect relationship between choices made and the inevitability of some form of consequence (e.g., both negative and positive choices and consequences).

50. Have the student list steps in the plan for beginning the pursuit of a goal (e.g., letter writing, interviewing, physical or mental skill work, visiting specific locations, etc.).

51. Avoid competition. Competitive situations may cause the student to make inappropriate/unrealistic choices.

52. Have the student read short stories without endings. Require the student to develop logical endings for the stories.

53. Teach the student decision-making steps: (a) think about how others may be influenced; (b) think about consequences; (c) carefully consider the unique situation; (d) think of different courses of action which are possible; (e) think about what is ultimately best for him/her, etc.

54. Ask the student to develop a time frame schedule within which to complete each step of a goal.

55. Ask the student to list resources to be utilized in his/her pursuit of a goal (e.g., specific persons, books, equipment, films, practice sites, etc.).

56. Conduct a simulation activity requiring students to pay for living expenses with a given income to create an awareness of reasonable purchases for a set income (e.g., it is not reasonable to purchase an expensive sports car if earning minimum wage).

57. Use cause-and-effect relationships as they apply to nature and people. Discuss what led up to a specific situation in a story or picture, what could happen next, etc.

58. Make certain that the student can verbalize the reason for real-life outcomes of behavior (e.g., why the student had to leave the class line on the way to recess, why he/she earned the privilege of being line leader, etc.).

59. Supervise the student closely in situations where he/she is likely to make an inappropriate/unrealistic choice (e.g., maintain close physical proximity, communicate frequently with the student, etc.).

60. Provide the student with positive feedback which indicates that he/she is successful, important, respected, etc.

61. Reinforce those students in the classroom who demonstrate logical thinking (e.g., making appropriate decisions, solving problems, making inferences, etc.).

62. Reinforce those students in the classroom who make appropriate/realistic choices.

22 Fails to make a decision or come to a conclusion regarding choices, opportunities, courses of action, etc.

Goals:

1. The student will make positive, informed decisions (e.g., representative of the student's best interests without causing others harm) for himself/herself.

Objectives:

1. The student will make positive, informed decisions on _____ out of _____ trials.
2. The student will decrease indecisiveness on _____ out of _____ trials.

Interventions:

1. Reinforce the student for making positive decisions: (a) give the student a tangible reward (e.g., classroom privileges, line leading, passing out materials, five minutes free time, etc.) or (b) give the student an intangible reward (e.g., praise, handshake, smile, etc.).

2. Provide the student time and encouragement to establish rapport. Make certain the student receives options of other support such as counseling when there are other concerns.

3. Do not force the student to make decisions or choose a course of action. It is more important to offer opportunities for reinforcement for making positive decisions and choosing positive courses of action.

4. The student needs careful attention as to what constitutes positive reinforcement. Social praise from an instructor may decrease a student's desire to repeat that choice in the future due to embarrassment. Through a reinforcer survey; interviews with the student, and parents; and observations, develop a list of positive reinforcers specific to that student.

5. Speak with the student to explain (a) what he/she has done correctly (e.g., being present in the room, attempting to interact, etc.) and (b) what he/she might be doing to improve response (e.g., expressing a choice, participating in chosen activities, etc.).

6. Establish classroom rules that delineate participation expectations. Review rules often. Reinforce students for following rules or guidelines.

7. Communicate with parents (e.g., notes home, phone calls, etc.) to share information concerning the student's progress. The parents may reinforce the student at home for making positive decisions at school.

8. Evaluate the appropriateness of the task to determine (a) if the task is too easy, (b) if the task is too difficult, and (c) if the length of time the student is expected to passively and/or actively socially participate is reasonable.

9. Choose a peer to sit/work directly with the student (e.g., in different settings or activities such as art, music, P.E., on the bus, tutoring, group projects, running errands in the building, recess, etc.). Periodically reinforce the peer for making positive decisions. Reinforce the student when he/she models the peer's positive response.

10. The student who expresses difficulty in making positive decisions may need additional assistance to develop goals and objectives. The following may be helpful:
- Help the student identify a short-term (e.g., within three to five days) goal related to class work to be completed.
- Help the student develop a few objectives to attain the short-term goal.
- Provide the student with assistance to follow through with the plans to achieve the goal.
- Provide the student with positive reinforcement for his/her attempts at goal attainment.
- Use the success experienced by the student in this situation to help him/her build toward other successes to replace indecisive behavior.

11. Write a contract with the student specifying what behavior is expected and what reinforcement will be available when the terms of the contract have been met.

12. When the student expresses indecisive behavior, establish with him/her those positive steps he/she may choose immediately. Provide positive comments and reinforcement for those times when the student chooses positive action.

13. Teach the student to identify antecedents to anxious behavior. For example, the student may learn to recognize the stress he/she experiences in testing situations. Once the problem situation is recognized by the student, work with him/her to develop positive coping strategies for use during those times (e.g., the student could set aside time to prepare for tests, gain the skills required for true-false, multiple choice, essay tests, etc.).

14. When the student's inability to choose pervasively affects his/her ability to respond to situations, modifying expectations may be necessary. The student may respond more effectively if he/she knows an opportunity to make corrective responses (e.g., turning in additional work on the topic) will be possible. Encourage the student to focus upon such positive recourse when indecisiveness is evident.

15. Teach the student to ask questions and actively engage in other information-gathering activities before he/she is expected to make decisions.

16. Involve the class in student government by seeking and employing student involvement in rule-making. Identify key government functions for daily classroom affairs (e.g., class representative, student activity coordinator, entertainment coordinator, etc.), and delegate students to these roles for defined periods of time (e.g., four to six weeks). Make certain students who perform these government services represent class interests and work together in a special small group. Encourage involvement, but make certain that students who have difficulty making decisions do not feel forced to fill these government posts.

17. Encourage the student to organize information gathered about potential activities in a file for future decisions.

18. Help the student develop a likes and dislikes list to reference for making choices. Encourage the student to weigh participation based upon priorities (e.g., a student may decide to shop at a busy mall during a holiday season even though he/she dislikes crowds because giving a gift to a loved one is a high priority).

19. Demonstrate respect for the student's opinions, responses, suggestions, etc.

20. Provide the student with a variety of activity choices throughout the day. Reinforce the student for making activity choices for himself/herself.

21. Modify or adjust situations that make the student reluctant to participate (e.g., degree of difficulty, competition, fear of failure, threat of embarrassment, etc.).

22. Give the student ample time to think through thoughts and feelings at a specific time of day (e.g., at the end of the day when all work is completed). Ask the student to include positive and negative thoughts, and help him/her identify accomplishments of that day. Use the successes to build toward positive, goal-directed behavior for ensuing days.

23. Help the student develop a way of charting his/her progress toward goals he/she develops.

24. When a student hesitates about involvement in an activity, encourage him/her to participate. When participation occurs, reinforce the student for the effort and reflect with him/her on the accomplishment. When participation is not chosen by the student, assure he/she is involved in an alternate activity. Help the student reflect upon this choice based upon benefit and loss when activities are completed.

25. Encourage or reinforce others for choosing to participate in group or special activities.

26. Give the student the responsibility of helping a peer make choices in the course of group activities.

27. Request the student lead a small-group activity if he/she expresses an interest and/or mastery of the subject.

28. Encourage friendship building in the classroom (e.g., students may wish to attend extra-curricular activities in small groups, etc.). The opportunity to work with friends on projects may help the student overcome his/her inability to make positive, informed decisions.

29. Allow passive participation as a choice across learning activities and environments.

30. Reduce the emphasis on competition. Frequent or continuous failure may result in an increase in the student's indecisiveness.

31. Provide the student with positive feedback to indicate he/she is successful at making choices.

32. Allow the student to choose a special event or activity for the class. When the student is extremely anxious about making a decision and/or easily embarrassed, minimize the amount of group attention the student could receive from making such a choice. It may be most helpful to thank the student for his/her input following a successful activity if this attention would not be too embarrassing for the student.

33. Provide the student with success-oriented special events or activities (e.g., opportunity to be a charter member of a reading or hobby club, etc.) to develop the student's interests and afford him/her the opportunity for meaningful participation choices without unwarranted fears.

34. When a student experiences dissatisfaction, frustration, anger, etc., concerning a choice he/she has made, reassure him/her. Remind him/her that best effort is always more important than perfection. After the student has had the opportunity to calm, review the situation with him/her and determine a modified approach for future reference.

35. Emphasize individual success or progress over winning or "beating" others.

36. Do not expect the student to confront his/her "worst nightmare" (e.g., activities in which the student has voiced unwarranted or extreme concerns such as dances, athletic games, etc.). Help the student build toward a desired goal in small, nonthreatening steps (e.g., small-group work interactions might build toward a class party, then a picnic involving two classes, etc.).

37. Provide the student with many social and academic opportunities to experience success at making positive, informed decisions.

38. Allow the student a choice of peers when forming small groups for activities.

39. Provide the student with opportunity and encouragement to question directions, explanations, and/or instructions he/she does not understand so he/she has the information needed for choices during the course of activities.

40. Structure the environment so the student has many opportunities to make successful choices.

41. Help the student identify the benefits of choosing to participate in scheduled activities.

42. Supervise classroom activities closely so peers with whom the student interacts do not stimulate inappropriate behavior or ridicule. The student may be easily intimidated or influenced by others.

43. Teach the student problem-solving skills so he/she is better equipped to make positive decisions in stressful situations (e.g., talking, walking away, calling upon an arbitrator, compromising, etc.).

44. Minimize concerns for the student by not placing him/her in humiliating situations (e.g., expecting him/her to choose active participation in class discussions after he/she has just experienced failure, etc.).

45. Prior to activities, make certain the student is able to successfully participate (e.g., understands the rules, is familiar with the activity, will be compatible with peers engaged in the activity, etc.).

46. Make certain the student has necessary materials for the classroom activity he/she has chosen.

47. Make certain the student knows how to use all materials for the classroom activity he/she has chosen.

48. Teach the student to incorporate self-reinforcement systems (e.g., a student may decide to follow his/her choice of a required activity with a favorite recreational or hobby activity).

49. Provide the student with a variety of ways to develop rapport with instructor(s) (e.g., writing notes, talking about concerns privately, etc.).

50. Through observation and interaction with the student, identify when the student will most likely experience the inability to make decisions. With the student, develop coping mechanisms and other choices he/she may opt for in these situations (e.g., going to a restroom if the need to cry is experienced during a meeting in which the student has chosen to participate, etc.). Always provide the student with positive reinforcement for his/her attempts at using such coping mechanisms.

51. Build positive self-concept among students by including the following approaches:
  (a) Offer opportunities for students to work together noncompetitively on class projects;
  (b) identify and compliment each student's unique contribution to group work when this will be perceived by the student as positive reinforcement; and
  (c) set aside time to speak with students individually.

52. The student who experiences difficulty with decision making may benefit from the following:
  (a) Frequent opportunities to rehearse coping mechanisms the student and instructor have developed;
  (b) frequent opportunities for making choices successfully; and
  (c) gradual increases in activity participation expectations (e.g., passive, then active participation).

53. Avoid forcing a student to participate when he/she is experiencing difficulty with making a decision. Give the student encouragement to develop and work toward his/her goals to self-manage. Provide the student with frequent opportunities to attempt correct responses. Reinforce the student for attempts to participate.

54. The student will probably experience negative natural consequences for not participating (e.g., isolation from others, nonparticipation in activities the student might actually like if the fears were overcome, etc.). It is important to realize the student needs positive experiences which occur incidentally throughout the day for skill development.

55. The student may benefit from the additional focus of a daily and weekly activity schedule. Involve the student as much as possible throughout schedule development to enhance student participation in making choices.

56. Help the student to review his/her schedule to assure needed instructions and materials are on hand before each activity. The student may benefit from a brief review of the procedures he/she needs to use to successfully complete the activity.

57. The student who experiences indecisiveness may be extremely self-critical. Encourage the student to critique himself/herself by
  (a) providing the student with a concise, structured set of review questions for self-evaluation of performance (e.g., What went OK? What things need to change?);
  (b) providing the student with structured activity choices in which his/her failure rate is minimal; and
  (c) providing the student with the support he/she needs to experience self-choice rather than relying upon others.

58. The student may be afraid of making a mistake. Provide the student with examples of how people can learn from mistakes (e.g., trial-and-error learning, evaluating experiences to problem solve for similar situations in the future, etc.).

59. Provide structured opportunities for success. Raise task expectations based upon student success.

60. The student may appreciate constructive remarks and verbal praise in conversations away from the group and/or in a nonintrusive delivery style typical for an entire group. Loud, open remarks do more harm than good.

61. Provide the student with opportunities to role-play making choices in various situations.

62. Provide the student with a routine to be followed when making decisions (e.g., place a list of decision-making strategies on the student's desk).

63. Encourage the student to timeline information-gathering objectives for making choices based upon the subject (e.g., a student may choose to give himself/herself two weeks to gather information about two to three different subjects before deciding to pursue one topic for a special report). Decrease instructor involvement based upon student success at determining and achieving goals within timelines.

64. Allow the student more decision-making opportunities relative to class activities and assignments.

65. Teach the student decision-making steps: (a) think about how others may be influenced, (b) think about consequences, (c) carefully consider the unique situation, (d) think of different courses of action which are possible, (e) think about what is ultimately best, etc.

66. Encourage the student to think through potential choices in terms of benefits and consequences. Teach the student to list benefits and consequences before making a decision.

23 Forgets

Goals:

1. The student will remember to return materials to their proper places.
2. The student will remember to follow classroom routines.

Objectives:

1. The student will return materials to their proper places with reminders on ____out of ____trials.
2. The student will return materials to their proper places with no reminders on ___out of ___trials. (Gradually increase expectations as the student demonstrates success).
3. The student will follow classroom routines with reminders for ____minutes at a time.
4. The student will follow classroom routines without reminders for ____minutes at a time.

Interventions:

1. Reinforce the student for remembering: (a) give the student a tangible reward (e.g., classroom privileges, line leading, passing out materials, etc.) or (b) give the student an intangible reward (e.g., praise, smile, pat on the back, etc.).

2. Speak with the student to explain (a) what he/she is doing wrong (e.g., forgetting to put materials away, etc.), and (b) what he/she should be doing (e.g., putting materials where they belong when he/she is finished using them, etc.).

3. Establish classroom rules (e.g., put materials away when you are done with them, ask to use others' property before you touch it, etc.). Review rules often. Reinforce students for following the rules.

4. Reinforce students in the classroom who remember to put materials away, ask before touching others' property, get needed materials gathered for an activity, etc.

5. Reinforce the student for remembering based upon the length of time he/she can be successful. As the student demonstrates success, gradually increase the length of time required for reinforcement.

6. Remove the student from an activity until he/she can demonstrate responsibility for caring for classroom materials.

7. Communicate with parents (e.g., notes home, telephone calls, etc.) in order to share information concerning the student's appropriate behavior. The parents may reinforce the student at home for remembering.

8. Evaluate the appropriateness of the task to determine (a) if the task is too easy, (b) if the task is too difficult, (c) if the length of time scheduled for the task is adequate.

9. Interact frequently with the student to enable him/her to remember more readily.

10. Reduce stimuli which would contribute to the student's forgetting.

11. Modify or eliminate situations which cause the student to forget.

12. Establish a regular daily routine: (a) discuss the routine, (b) provide an illustrated list, and (c) refer to this list frequently throughout the class day.

13. Make certain that reinforcement is not inadvertently given for inappropriate behavior (e.g., attending to the student only when he/she is forgetful, etc.).

14. Provide the student with a calm, quiet environment in which to work.

15. Have the student question any directions, explanations, and instructions he/she does not understand prior to beginning an activity.

16. Have the student work near the teacher.

17. Reinforce students in the classroom for remembering.

18. Maintain consistency in expectations for students concerning remembering in the classroom.

19. Provide the student with a cubby or other special place for him/her to keep his/her materials.

20. Model organizational skills for the student (e.g., have materials ready for each activity, have the classroom well organized, keep the supply area organized and clean, etc.).

21. Provide the student with a well organized classroom (e.g., low shelves with materials well labeled with words and pictures, particular areas to keep specific materials, etc.).

22. Have the student perform the "forgotten" chore before moving on to a new activity.

23. Limit the student's freedom to take property from school if he/she is unable to remember to return the items.

24. Allow natural consequences to occur due to the students "forgetting" (e.g., losing privileges with materials because he/she did not care for them appropriately, not participating in an activity because he/she is not ready, etc.).

25. Give the student responsibility for a number of activities. As the student demonstrates success, gradually increase the number of activities for which the student is responsible.

26. Establish a daily classroom schedule and adhere to this schedule as closely as possible to aid the student's memory of the sequence of events or activities.

27. Have the student repeat to himself/herself information just heard to help remember the information.

28. Make certain that the student sees the connection between behavior and consequences (e.g., forgotten chores will have to be done before moving to new activities, lack of preparation may result in not being able to participate in an activity, etc.).

29. Assess the meaningfulness of the material to the student. Remembering is more likely to occur when the material is meaningful and the student can relate to the real experience.

24 Has difficulty concentrating

Goals:

1. The student will improve his/her ability to concentrate.

Objectives:

1. The student will work on a task for ____minutes.
2. The student will work on a task until completed on ____out of ____trials.
3. The student will attend to an activity for ____minutes.
4. The student will attend to an activity until it is completed on ____out of ____trials.
5. The student will attend to a lecture, conversation, or discussion for ____minutes.
6. The student will attend to a lecture, conversation, or discussion until it is completed on ____out of ____ trials.

Interventions:

1. Demonstrate when teaching new skills. Allow the student to practice hands-on learning of new skills to enhance concentration.

2. Use pictures, diagrams, chalkboard, and gestures when delivering information to maintain the student's attention.

3. Use multiple modalities (e.g., auditory, visual, tactile, etc.) when presenting directions, explanations, and instructional content. By using multiple modalities, the information may hold the student's interest for a longer period of time.

4. Schedule important activities/assignments/ meetings at times when the student is most likely to maintain attention (e.g., one hour after medication, 45 minutes after lunch, first thing in the morning, etc.).

5. Give an assignment that involves immediate, short-term tasks.

6. Highlight or underline important information the student reads (e.g., directions, reading assignments, math word problems, etc.).

7. Allow natural consequences to occur (e.g., work not done or completed inaccurately must be made up during recreational time, not concentrating while people are talking results in not knowing what to do, etc.) as a result of the student's inability to concentrate.

8. Teach time-management skills. Provide a daily plan and have the student follow it.

9. Establish classroom rules:
- Stay on-task.
- Work quietly.
- Remain in your seat.
- Finish task.
- Meet task expectations.

Review rules often. Reinforce students for following the rules.

10. Organize assignments by breaking them into small segments. Set deadlines and provide the student with a reward after completing each segment of the assignment.

11. Present assignments in small amounts (e.g., assign 10 problems, use pages removed from workbooks, etc.).

12. Teach and practice information-gathering skills (e.g., listen carefully, write down important points, ask for clarification, wait until all information is presented before beginning a task, etc.).

13. Reinforce the student for beginning, staying on, and completing assignments.

14. Structure the environment to reduce distracting stimuli (e.g., place the student on the front row; provide a carrel or quiet place away from distractions; etc.). This is used as a means of reducing stimuli and not as a form of punishment.

15. Set time limits for completing assignments. Prompt the student as a reminder of time constraints when working on projects.

16. Use more interesting or stimulating activities as a reward for completing less interesting activities (e.g., the student must complete drill and practice before working on the computer).

17. Reinforce the student for concentrating: (a) give the student a tangible reward (e.g., classroom privileges, passing out materials, five minutes free time, etc.) or (b) give the student an intangible reward (e.g., praise, handshake, smile, etc.).

18. Communicate clearly with the student the length of time he/she has to complete an assignment and when the assignment is due. The student may want to use a timer to complete the tasks within the given period of time.

19. Maintain physical contact with the student while talking to him/her (e.g., touch the student's hand or shoulder).

20. Provide clearly-stated directions, written or verbal. Make directions as simple and concrete as possible.

21. Establish an environmental setting for the classroom that promotes optimal individual performance (e.g., quiet room, background music, fresh air, etc.).

22. Provide clearly stated directions, written or verbal (e.g., make directions as simple and concrete as possible).

23. Enlist different people (e.g., peer, counselor, paraprofessional, etc.) to help the student remain on-task.

24. Have the student listen and take "Who, What, Where, When, How, and Why" notes when information is presented.

25. Present directions following the outline of (1) What, (2) How, (3) Materials, and (4) When.

26. Move objects used for tactile stimulation (e.g., pens, paper clips, loose change, etc.) away from the student's reach.

27. Provide the student with an individual assignment when the group setting is overly distracting.

28. Encourage the student to develop a 30 second definition of his/her goal to help him/her stay on-task and focused (e.g., "I will listen carefully. The better I focus and stay on-task, the better I will perform.").

29. Deliver information to the student on a one-to-one basis or use a peer tutor.

30. Provide an incentive statement along with a directive (e.g., "You can go to lunch after you complete 15 math problems.").

31. Reinforce the student for concentrating on a task for the length of time the student can be successful. As the student demonstrates success, gradually increase the length of time required for reinforcement.

32. Reduce the amount of information on a page if it is visually distracting for the student (e.g., less print to read, fewer problems, isolate information that is presented to the student, etc.).

33. Follow a less desirable task with a more desirable task. Make completion of the first necessary to perform the second.

34. Match the assignments with the student's activity level. When the student is feeling highly active, provide assignments which require a great degree of movement. When the student is most likely to maintain attention, provide assignments that require less movement and more sitting.

35. Reward the student for concentrating on an assignment for a specific length of time (e.g., take a break, visit briefly with a peer, etc.).

36. Encourage the student to avoid ingesting any substance (e.g., drugs, alcohol, cold remedies, etc.) that might further alter his/her ability to concentrate.

37. Assist the student in staying on-task. As the student demonstrates success, gradually reduce the amount of assistance provided and require the student to independently remain on-task.

38. Develop an environment that is quiet and uncluttered (e.g., clean, well-lighted, fresh-smelling, and at a comfortable temperature).

39. Allow the student to occasionally take assignments home when the work setting is overly distracting.

40. Reward the student for completing an assignment within the amount of time allotted.

41. Encourage the student to develop an awareness of himself/herself and the environment. Instruct the student to periodically step back and ask himself/herself, "Am I on-task and paying attention?" "What should I be doing now?"

42. Encourage the student to develop an awareness of the consequences of his/her behavior by writing down or talking through problems which may occur due to his/her inability to concentrate (e.g., not focusing on directions may cause misunderstanding of an assignment which could lead to a lower grade and losing a place on the soccer team).

43. Encourage the student to eat a balanced diet and get plenty of rest to enhance his/her ability to concentrate.

44. Allow the student to take a break to regroup when he/she is no longer on-task.

45. Have the student develop a checklist/chart to follow which will allow him/her to record all assignments.

46. Encourage the student to ask for clarification of any directions, explanations, and instructions before beginning a task to enhance comprehension.

47. Teach the student to use basic concentration and study skills (e.g., reading for the main idea, note-taking, highlighting, outlining, summarizing, studying in an appropriate environment, etc.).

48. Require the student to make eye contact while delivering information to him/her.

49. Teach the student note-taking skills (e.g., copy main ideas from the chalkboard, identify main ideas from lectures, condense statements into a few key words, etc.).

50. Have a peer, paraprofessional, friend, etc., cue the student when he/she is off-task (e.g., the person can touch the student's arm as a signal that he/she is not remaining on-task).

51. Have the student take notes when directions are being given following the "What, How, Materials, and When" format.

52. Make certain the student knows that directions will only be given once.

53. Tell the student what to listen for when being given directions or receiving information, etc.

54. Assign one task at a time. Give the student a specific amount of time to complete it.

55. Have the student repeat to himself/herself information just heard to help the student remember the important facts.

56. Instruct the student to ask himself/herself questions (e.g., "What's next?") to keep himself/herself focused on assignments/projects.

57. Allow the student to underline or highlight important information he/she reads (e.g., directions, reading assignments, etc.) to enhance concentration.

58. Evaluate the visual and auditory stimuli in the classroom. Determine the amount of stimuli the student can tolerate. Remove extraneous stimuli from the student's environment.

59. Set a timer for the student indicating a limited amount of time to finish a task or assignment.

60. Present concepts following the outline of (1) Who, (2) What, (3) Where, (4) When, (5) How, and (6) Why.

61. Have the student listen for key information when being given directions or receiving information (e.g., write down main points, ideas, step-by-step instructions, etc.).

62. Allow the student to tape record information from lectures and assemblies and make notes from these tapes.

63. Write a contract with the student. It should be written within his/her ability level and focus on only one behavior at a time. Specify what behavior is expected (e.g., concentrating on a task) and what reinforcement will be made available when the terms of the contract have been met.

64. Provide the student with appropriate time limits for the completion of assignments.

65. Encourage the student to recite a mantra to himself/herself when entering a situation where he/she has to sit for an extended period of time (e.g., concentrate, concentrate, concentrate).

66. Do not assign the student too many things to do at once; provide more than enough time to complete tasks; and do not expect perfection.

67. Have the student assemble all the materials necessary to work on a project, assignment, etc., to reduce the need to search for materials.

68. Use a variety of high interest means to communicate with the student (e.g., auditory, visual, manipulatives, etc.).

69. Instruct the student to imagine the necessary steps required to complete a task before beginning that task.

70. Have the student maintain a list of things to do to organize and focus on what needs to be accomplished for a specific task, day, etc.

71. Have the student work with a peer who is calm and capable of concentrating on an assignment for an extended period of time.

72. Allow the student some movement while performing tasks. Monitor and limit the amount of movement.

73. Give the student one task to perform at a time. Introduce the next task after the student has successfully completed the previous task.

74. Stop at various points during a presentation of information to check the student's comprehension.

75. Establish a timeline for completing a project. Expect the student to meet each deadline in order to complete the project on time.

76. Make the subject matter meaningful to the student (e.g., explain the purpose of an assignment, relate the subject matter to the student's environment, etc.).

77. Make it a habit to periodically review with the student notes, the daily calendar of events, or tasks that need to be completed.

78. Assess the quality and clarity of directions, explanations, and instructions given to the student.

79. Explain to the student when he/she does not stay on-task, attend to a conversation, etc., exactly what he/she did wrong, what should have been done, and why.

80. Seat the student close to the source of information to enhance his/her ability to maintain attention.

81. Teach the student listening skills (e.g., stop working, clear desk of nonessential materials, attend to the source of information, write down important points, ask for clarification, and wait until all directions are received before beginning).

82. While concepts are presented, have the student listen and take notes for "Who, What, Where, When, How, and Why."

83. Maintain visibility to and from the student at all times to monitor the student's concentration.

84. Reduce directions to steps. Give the student each additional step after the previous step has been completed.

85. Break down large tasks into smaller tasks (e.g., assign the student to write an outline for a book report, then the first rough draft, etc.).

86. Make certain that the student's academic tasks are on his/her ability level.

87. Avoid placing the student in situations that require listening for an extended period of time such as lectures, assemblies, seminars, etc. Provide the information for the student through a tape recording or lecture notes.

88. Reduce distracting stimuli in and around the student's desk (e.g., materials in/on the desk, etc.).

89. Have the student participate in games requiring varying degrees of concentration (e.g., tic-tac-toe, checkers, chess, etc.).

90. Make certain the tasks required of the student are appropriate for his/her level of development and ability.

91. Make certain that the student understands the relationship between inappropriate behavior and the consequences which follow (e.g., failing to concentrate on schoolwork could result in low grades or incomplete work).

92. Assign the student fewer tasks. As the student demonstrates success, gradually increase the number of tasks over time.

93. Tell the student when it is time to begin an assignment, listen to others, etc.

94. Deliver one-, two-, and three-step directions to the student. As the student demonstrates success in concentrating, gradually increase the number of steps.

95. Assess the degree of task difficulty to determine whether or not the student will require additional information, time, assistance, etc., before beginning a task.

96. Make certain the student knows what to look for when reading (e.g., main characters, main ideas, sequence of events, etc.).

97. Choose a peer tutor to work with the student to model appropriate work habits.

98. Avoid seating the student near people with whom he/she may be tempted to converse during lectures, assemblies, group projects, etc.

99. Allow the student the option of working on the assignment at another time (e.g., earlier/later in the day, on another day, or at home) when he/she will be able to concentrate better.

100. Give directions in a variety of ways to increase the probability of understanding (e.g., if the student fails to understand verbal directions, present them in written form).

101. Provide simple, concrete directions.

102. Assign short-term projects that can be quickly completed.

103. Designate a specific period of time when it is permissible for the student to converse with peers (e.g., the last five minutes of each hour, transitioning from one task to another, after completing a task, etc.).

104. Provide the student with a prompt when the student is off-task (e.g., move close to the student, speak to the student, etc.).

105. Have the student identify a peer who has the ability to remain on-task. Instruct the student to observe that person and try to model the behaviors which allow him/her to maintain attention.

106. Separate the student from the peers who may be encouraging or stimulating the inappropriate behavior.

107. Make certain the student is attending to the source of information (e.g., eye contact is being made, hands are free of materials, student is looking at the assignment, etc.).

108. Instruct the student to maintain attention to the source of information by maintaining eye contact, keeping hands free from other materials, and reducing other distractions.

109. Try various groupings in the classroom to determine the situation in which the student is most successful concentrating.

25 Is overly critical of self in school-related performance, abilities, personal appearance, etc.

Goals:

1. The student will demonstrate realistic, objective self-appraisal.
2. The student will improve his/her self-perception.

Objectives:

1. The student will make an accurate appraisal of his/her performance at the end of each activity on ___ out of ___ trials.
2. The student will discuss his/her abilities in a realistic manner on ___ out of ___ trials.
3. The student will make ___ positive comment(s) about himself/herself per day.
4. The student will refrain from making self-depreciating remarks such as "I'm stupid," "I'm dumb," "I'm ugly," etc., on ___ out of ___ trials.
5. The student will attempt ___ out of ___ assigned tasks per day.
6. The student will ask for teacher assistance only when necessary on ___ out of ___ trials.
7. The student will work for ___ minutes without requiring teacher assistance.

Interventions:

1. Explain to the student that he/she should be happy with personal best effort rather than expecting perfection.

2. Reinforce the student for accepting errors that he/she makes.

3. Speak with the student to explain (a) what the student is doing wrong (i.e., being overly critical of himself/herself) and (b) what the student should be doing (i.e., being more constructive in self-criticism when evaluating himself/herself).

4. Reward others for accepting errors they make.

5. Write a contract with the student specifying what behavior is expected (e.g., accepting personal best effort) and what reinforcement will be made available when the terms of the contract have been met.

6. Evaluate the appropriateness of the task to determine (a) if the task is too easy, (b) if the task is too difficult, and (c) if the length of time scheduled to complete the task is adequate.

7. Reinforce the student for improvement rather than expecting excellence.

8. Recognize the student often and in various settings (e.g., hallways, cafeteria, etc.).

9. Provide the student with positive feedback which indicates he/she is successful, competent, important, valuable, etc.

10. Provide the student with success-oriented tasks. The expectation is that success will result in more positive attitudes and perceptions toward self and environment.

11. Provide the student with as many social and academic successes as possible.

12. Make the necessary adjustments in the environment to prevent the student from experiencing stress, frustration, etc.

13. Choose a peer to help the student with class assignments, homework, etc.

14. Emphasize individual differences and that everyone has strengths and weaknesses.

15. Reduce emphasis on competition and perfection. Repeated failure may result in unwarranted self-blame or self-criticism.

16. Encourage the student to refrain from comparing personal performance to other students' performance, and emphasize attention to personal improvement (e.g., maintain records of own progress rather than comparing work to others).

17. Provide the student with evidence of his/her ability so that he/she might better understand that self-blame/criticism is unwarranted.

18. Have the student regularly record his/her own progress in order to have tangible evidence of success.

19. Deliver praise and constructive criticism consistently to all students.

20. Make cleaning up accidents a group responsibility in order to convey the idea that we all make mistakes and accidents are common to all of us.

21. Call on the student when he/she will most likely be able to answer correctly.

22. Encourage the student to act as a peer tutor in order to recognize his/her own strengths and abilities.

23. Reduce activities which might threaten the student (e.g., announcing test score ranges or test scores aloud, making students read aloud in class, emphasizing the success of a particular student or students, etc.).

24. Help the student learn those skills necessary to improve his/her personal appearance and hygiene.

25. Make certain that your comments take the form of constructive criticism rather than criticism that can be perceived as personal, threatening, etc., (e.g., instead of saying, "You always make that same mistake." say, "A better way to do that might be . . .").

26. Deliver a predetermined signal when the student begins to be overly critical of self.

27. Assess the appropriateness of the social situation and place the student in the group in which he/she will be most successful.

28. Pair the student with a younger or less capable peer to enhance his/her feelings of success or accomplishment.

29. Deliver praise and recognition privately so that the student is not aware of the performance of others.

30. Encourage all students to be complimentary of each other's performance.

31. Do not criticize when correcting the student, be honest yet supportive. Never cause the student to feel badly about himself/herself.

32. Talk with the student about individual differences and discuss strengths and weaknesses of individuals the student knows. Stress that the student does not have to do the same things everyone else does.

33. Encourage the student to refrain from comparing himself/herself to others.

26 Does not make realistic decisions regarding the spending of money

Goals:
1. The student will develop a budget to meet needs and wants within his/her means.
2. The student will consistently manage his/her finances by adhering to his/her budget.

Objectives:
1. With instruction and assistance, the student will develop a budget to meet needs and wants within his/her means on all occasions for _____ consecutive weeks/months.
2. Independently, the student will develop his/her budget as needed to meet expectations/needs on _____ out of _____ occasions.
3. With instruction and assistance, the student will manage his/her expenses within the parameters of a budget on _____ out of _____ occasions.
4. Independently, the student will manage his/her expenses within the parameters of a budget on _____ out of _____ occasions.

Interventions:

1. Reinforce the student for making realistic decisions regarding the spending of money: (a) give the student a tangible reward (e.g., classroom privileges, line leading, passing out materials, five minutes free time, etc.) or (b) give the student an intangible reward (e.g., praise, handshake, smile, etc.).

2. Explain to the student what he/she has done correctly, what is expected for total correct response, and what he/she can be doing to improve toward or reach total correct response.

3. Reinforce the student for adjusting his/her behavior to different situations in the community based on the length of time the student can be successful. As the student demonstrates success, gradually increase the length of time required for reinforcement.

4. Communicate with parents (e.g., notes home, phone calls, etc.) to share information concerning the student's progress. The parents may reinforce the student at home for his/her positive attempts at budgeting and consumer-related skills at school and in the community.

5. Encourage parents of older students to establish a dual signature checking account with the student after he/she has demonstrated the ability to save money.

6. Be certain the student is involved in planning and purchasing items he/she not only wants, but needs as well.

7. Expose the student to his/her community so information can be gathered and reviewed about employment and consumerism.

8. As much as possible, involve students in all aspects of budgeting and of following a budget on a daily basis.

9. Reinforce those students who are responding to activity and behavior expectations.

10. Write a contract with the student specifying consumer behavior and activity expectations and what reinforcement will be available when the terms of the contract have been met.

11. Encourage the parents' input in developing behavioral and activity expectations in community sites to encourage consistency between home and school.

12. Evaluate the appropriateness of the tasks to be taught in the community to determine (a) if the task is too easy; (b) if the task is too hard; (c) if the length of time scheduled to complete the task is adequate.

13. Explain to the student that his/her best effort is more important than perfection to help decrease frustration with the task.

14. Choose a peer to model learning consumer-related and budgeting skills in community and classroom settings for the student .

15. Establish exactly what is to be done to complete a consumer-related task in school or in the community (e.g., establish definite starting and stopping points, a minimum requirement, etc.).

16. Have the student explain what he/she thinks should be done to correctly perform the task.

17. Identify the expectations of different environments and help the student develop skills needed for success in those environments.

18. Assign the student shorter activities in the community and gradually increase the length of activities based on student success.

19. Maintain consistency of expectations and keep these expectations within the ability of the students.

20. Give directions in a variety of different ways to increase the probability of understanding (e.g., if the student does not understand verbal instructions, present these in writing).

21. Help the student on the first few items of a task and gradually reduce the amount of help over time.

22. Encourage development and use of a shopping list before the student goes shopping. This will help the student think through his/her impulses.

23. When a student desires to impulsively purchase an item not on his/her list, encourage the student to record the item and its cost for future shopping excursions.

24. When possible, afford the student opportunities to learn skills across different community environments.

25. Use role-play to rehearse new skills and alternatives to be used in community settings.

26. Students who are impulsive about shopping may feel that the desired item will not be available at a later time. Let the student know of positive alternatives to impulse buying (e.g., he/she may locate the item at a later time in various stores, he/she may later decide to call and order the item, he/she could take a little more time to do some comparative shopping, etc.).

27. Socially reinforce the student when he/she chooses a positive alternative to impulse buying.

28. Provide the student multiple opportunities to learn and develop his/her consumer preferences.

29. Incorporate student and family preferences into the list of community stores to be accessed for teaching and training consumer skills. This may encourage parental and student involvement, and may increase the likelihood that the skills you are teaching will be used by the student.

30. Some students may benefit from saving money in coin banks which show a visible increase in the amount of money saved from one day/week to the next.

31. Money skills may be most meaningfully taught when (a) the student is earning real money for real work; (b) the student invests with his/her instructor and other supportive persons in developing employment and consumer goals and objectives, and in determining how these goals/objectives can be met; (c) the student is provided supports and materials necessary to goal/objective attainment which are natural to the environment and best meet the student's strengths and needs.

32. Incidentally teach, rehearse, and reinforce functional academics as students locate community stores for consumer skills.

33. Reinforce the student for only purchasing items on his/her shopping list instead of impulse shopping.

34. As much as possible, gather baseline information about the student's strengths and needs in community settings to assist in individualizing student lesson plans.

35. Teach the student to reinforce himself/herself for staying within his/her budget on a weekly basis or on another interval of time within this student's needs and abilities. Reinforcement may be most meaningful when it occurs within the natural context of the community (e.g., going out to a movie with a friend instead of earning food items).

36. Be certain the student has incidental opportunities to appreciate the value of his/her budgeting by (a) reinforcing the student; (b) providing the student activities contingent upon his/her ability to stick with a budget; (c) helping the student positively define budgeting, and (d) making informed consumer related decisions.

37. Tailor budgeting and consumer-related activity materials to the student's needs, abilities, and learning style(s). As much as possible, use materials accessible to anyone (e.g., a calculator, a checkbook, savings account, etc.). Be certain the student can use these materials and has the monitoring and support he/she needs to manage money responsibly (e.g., requiring two signatures on checks, etc.).

38. Help the student modify his/her approach toward goal attainment and/or modify goals/objectives when the student is frustrated, and when consumer-related goals remain unmet for sustained periods of time.

39. Give the student monitored, natural consequences for choosing not to budget money or practice positive consumer-related skills.

40. Provide the student opportunity to gather information about budgeting and consumer-related skills in his/her community. Activities which might prove helpful include (a) visiting banks and other money management resources in the community; (b) providing the student exposure to stores and banks and gathering information about these resources so informed decisions can be made; (c) providing the student positive role models specific to his/her community (e.g., successful business persons, etc.).

41. Observe the student's present abilities, noting strengths and weaknesses, before developing a budgeting and consumer-related skill teaching plan.

42. The student's schedule should include time to plan: (a) keeping purchases for wants/needs within means; (b) balancing checkbook; (c) planning future expenditures by developing inventories, shopping lists, etc.; and (d) scheduling and meeting any payment dates (e.g., for rent, utilities, etc.).

27 Does not respond appropriately to redirection in academic situations

Goals:

1. The student will respond appropriately to redirection in academic situations.

Objectives:

1. The student will correct errors when instructed to do so on _____ out of _____ trials.
2. The student will return to task when instructed to do so on _____ out of _____ trials.
3. The student will be quiet when instructed to do so on _____ out of _____ trials.
4. The student will cease interaction with others when instructed to do so on _____ out of _____ trials.
5. The student will respond immediately to redirection in academic situations on _____ out of _____ trials.

Interventions:

1. Allow natural consequences to occur when the student fails to respond appropriately to redirection in academic situations (i.e., make highly reinforcing activities contingent upon responding appropriately to redirection in academic situations).

2. Remove the student from the activity if he/she fails to respond appropriately to redirection in academic situations.

3. Be consistent in expectations when redirecting the student in academic situations (e.g., require the student to immediately correct errors after work has been checked, require the student to return to his/her seat within three minutes, etc.).

4. Provide adequate time for the student to respond appropriately to redirection in academic situations.

5. Make certain that redirection in academic situations is delivered in the most positive manner.

6. Deliver redirection to the student as privately as possible.

7. Deliver instructions in a clear and concise manner.

8. Assist the student in responding appropriately to redirection in academic situations (e.g., help the student correct one or two items to get started).

9. Develop subsequent tasks based on errors the student makes rather than requiring an immediate correction of work done incorrectly.

10. Make certain the student understands the assignment or activity by having him/her rephrase the directions.

11. Determine the reason for errors made by the student.

12. Make certain the student understands the communication regarding redirection by having the student rephrase the direction.

13. Evaluate the demands made on the student in academic situations to make certain that all expectations are within the student's ability level.

14. In order to reduce the need for redirection in academic situations, require the student to check all work for errors prior to handing in assignments.

15. When redirection is delivered to the student in academic situations, make certain that an explanation for the redirection is also given (e.g., "You need to return to your seat because we are ready to begin a new activity.").

16. Make certain that an activity does not overstimulate and result in the student's inability to respond appropriately to redirection in academic situations.

17. Make certain that attention is not inadvertently given to the student for failing to respond appropriately to redirection in academic situations (e.g., remove attention from the student in those instances when attention is reinforcing the inappropriate behavior).

18. Monitor the student's behavior to provide redirection before the student's errors or inappropriate behavior exceed his/her ability to respond appropriately.

19. Base expectations for student response to redirection in academic situations on ability level (e.g., one student may be expected to return to his/her seat immediately upon redirection while another student may be given three minutes to respond appropriately).

20. Do not allow redirection to become a necessary part of every academic situation in which the student participates.

21. Avoid those circumstances where the student demonstrates difficulty in responding appropriately to redirection in academic situations (e.g., highly competitive situations, situations in which the student is embarrassed by his/her errors, etc.).

22. Make certain that the student understands that redirection is designed to help him/her succeed rather than as a form of punishment (e.g., use statements such as, "This sentence would be much easier to read if it were written with correct capitalization and punctuation. Please write it again and I'll check it for you.").

23. Make certain that communications with the student regarding redirection are appropriate to that student's ability to respond (e.g., match the form in which redirection is delivered to the student's most likely successful response, such as "Would you please go to your seat" rather than "You need to go to your seat immediately.").

24. Do not criticize when correcting the student; be honest yet supportive. Never cause the student to feel badly about himself/herself.

25. Choose a peer to model appropriate response to redirection in academic situations for the student.

26. Write a contract with the student specifying what behavior is expected (e.g., returning to seat when told to do so) and what reinforcement will be made available when the terms of the contract have been met.

27. Communicate with parents (e.g., notes home, phone calls, etc.) to share information concerning the student's progress. The parents may reinforce the student at home for responding appropriately to redirection in academic situations at school.

28. Evaluate the appropriateness of the task to determine (a) if the task is too easy, (b) if the task is too difficult, and (c) if the length of time scheduled to complete the task is adequate.

29. Reinforce the student for responding appropriately to redirection within a given period of time based on the number of times the student can be successful. As the student demonstrates success, gradually increase the number of times required for reinforcement.

30. Reinforce those students in the classroom who respond appropriately to redirection in academic and social situations.

31. Establish classroom rules:
- Work on-task.
- Work quietly.
- Remain in your seat.
- Finish task.
- Meet task expectations.

Review rules often. Reinforce students for following rules.

32. Speak to the student to explain (a) what the student is doing wrong (e.g., not correcting errors on an assignment, failing to return to seat when told to do so, etc.) and (b) what the student should be doing (e.g., correcting errors on an assignment, returning to seat when told to do so, etc.).

33. Reinforce the student for responding appropriately to redirection in academic situations: (a) give the student a tangible reward (e.g., classroom privileges, line leading, passing out materials, five minutes free time, etc.) or (b) give the student an intangible reward (e.g., praise, handshake, smile, etc.).

34. Have the student question any directions, explanations, instructions not understood.

28 Responds too quickly and impulsively to questions about academic material

Goals:
1. The student will answer only when called on.
2. The student will communicate with others in an acceptable manner in the classroom.
3. The student will work quietly in the classroom.

Objectives:
1. The student will gain permission from the teacher to speak, by raising his/her hand, when he/she has an answer on ___ out of ___ trials.
2. The student will contribute his/her opinion/answer after being recognized by the teacher on ___ out of ___ trials.
3. The student will await his/her turn to talk when engaged, or attempting to engage, in interactions with others on ___ out of ___ trials.
4. The student will refrain from making sounds which are inappropriate for the situation on ___ out of ___ trials.

Interventions:

1. Reinforce the student for waiting to be called on before speaking: (a) give the student a tangible reward (e.g., classroom privileges, line leading, passing out materials, five minutes free time, etc.) or (b) give the student an intangible reward (e.g., praise, handshake, smile, etc.).

2. Speak with the student to explain (a) what he/she is doing wrong (e.g., blurting out answers) and (b) what he/she should be doing (e.g., waiting until it is appropriate to speak, waiting to be called on before speaking, etc).

3. Establish classroom rules:
- Work on-task.
- Work quietly.
- Remain in your seat.
- Finish task.
- Meet task expectations.
- Raise your hand.

Review rules often. Reinforce students for following rules.

4. Make certain that reinforcement is not inadvertently given for inappropriate behavior (e.g., blurting out answers without being called on).

5. Reinforce the student for waiting to be called on before speaking based on the number of times he/she can be successful. As the student demonstrates success, gradually increase the number of times required for reinforcement.

6. Remove the student from the group or activity until he/she can demonstrate appropriate behavior and self-control.

7. Write a contract with the student specifying what behavior is expected (e.g., waiting to be called on before speaking) and what reinforcement will be made available when the terms of the contract have been met.

8. Communicate with the parents (e.g., notes home, phone calls, etc.) to share information concerning the student's appropriate behavior. They may reinforce the student at home for waiting to be called on before speaking.

9. Evaluate the appropriateness of tasks to determine (a) if the tasks are too easy, (b) if the tasks are too difficult, and (c) if the length of time scheduled for tasks is adequate.

10. Reinforce those students in the classroom who wait to be called on before speaking.

11. Give adequate opportunities to respond (i.e., enthusiastic students need many opportunities to contribute).

12. Have the student be the leader of a small group activity if he/she possesses mastery of skills or an interest in that area.

13. Provide the student with a predetermined signal if he/she begins to blurt out answers without being called on.

14. Structure the environment to limit opportunities for inappropriate behaviors (e.g., keep the student engaged in activities, have the student seated near the teacher, etc.).

15. Give the student responsibilities in the classroom (e.g., running errands, opportunities to help the teacher, etc.).

16. Reduce activities which might threaten the student (e.g., announcing test score ranges or test scores aloud, making students read aloud in class, emphasizing the success of a particular student or students, etc.).

17. Provide the student with many social and academic successes.

18. Make the necessary adjustments in the environment to prevent the student from experiencing stress, frustration or anger (e.g., reduce peer pressure, academic failure, teasing, etc.).

19. Maintain visibility to and from the student. The teacher should be able to see the student and the student should be able to see the teacher. Make eye contact possible at all times.

20. Interact frequently with the student to reduce his/her need to blurt out answers without being called on.

21. Assess the appropriateness of the social situation in relation to the student's ability to function successfully.

22. Try various groupings to determine the situation in which the student is most comfortable.

23. Make the student aware of the number of times he/she blurts out answers without being called on.

24. Call on the student when he/she is most likely to be able to respond correctly.

25. Have the student work in small groups in which he/she will have frequent opportunities to speak. As the student learns to wait longer for his/her turn to speak, gradually increase the size of the group.

26. Make certain that the student's feelings are considered when it is necessary to deal with his/her inappropriate comments (i.e., do not diminish the student's enthusiasm for participation).

27. Encourage the student to model the behavior of peers who are successful.

28. Help the student improve concentration skills (e.g., listening to the speaker, taking notes, preparing comments in advance, making comments in the appropriate context, etc.).

29. Have the student question any directions, explanations, instructions he/she does not understand.

30. Deliver directions, explanations, and instructions in a clear and concise manner to reduce the student's need to ask questions.

31. Have the student practice waiting for short periods of time for his/her turn to speak. As the student demonstrates success, gradually increase the length of time required for reinforcement.

32. Explain to the student the reasons why blurting out answers without being called on is inappropriate (e.g., is impolite, hurts others' feelings, etc.).

33. Attempt to provide equal attention to all students in the classroom.

34. Reinforce the student for raising his/her hand to be recognized.

29 Physically runs away from personal or school experiences

Goals:
1. The student will accept responsibility for his/her problems.
2. The student will attempt to resolve his/her problems.

Objectives:
1. The student will accept responsibility for his/her problems on ___ out of ___ trials.
2. The student will attempt to resolve his/her problems by talking, cooperating, etc., on ___ out of ___ trials.
3. The student will attempt new tasks on ___ out of ___ trials.
4. The student will ask for teacher assistance when necessary to help resolve his/her problems on ___ out of ___ trials.

Interventions:

1. Structure the environment to reduce opportunities to run away from the school/classroom (e.g., change seating, increase supervision, reduce stimuli which contribute to running away, etc.).

2. Maintain supervision of the student at all times and in all parts of the school.

3. Maintain visibility to and from the student. The teacher should be able to see the student and the student should be able to see the teacher. Make eye contact possible at all times.

4. Provide the student with as many academic and social successes as possible.

5. Record or chart attendance with the student.

6. Give the student a preferred responsibility to be performed at various times throughout the day.

7. Present tasks in the most attractive and interesting manner possible.

8. Interact frequently with the student to maintain involvement in the activity (e.g., ask the student questions, ask the student's opinion, stand close to the student, seat the student near your desk, etc.).

9. Make the necessary adjustments in the environment to prevent the student from experiencing stress, frustration, anger, etc., as much as possible.

10. Make certain all school personnel are aware of the student's tendency to run away.

11. Limit the student's independent movement in the school environment.

12. Discuss with the student ways to deal with unpleasant experiences which would typically cause him/her to run away (e.g., talk to a teacher, visit with a counselor, go to a quiet area in the school, etc.).

13. Identify variables in the environment which cause the student to become upset, and reduce or remove those variables.

14. Do not provide the student with additional opportunities to run away by seating the student in the hallway, sending him from class, etc.

15. Consider alternative forms of negative consequences if current consequences cause the student to run away. Do not use negative consequences which contribute to a worsening of the situation.

16. Intervene early to prevent the student from becoming upset enough to run away.

17. Provide the student with a quiet place as an alternative to running away. This can be a place where the student elects to go as a form of self-control instead of running away.

18. Identify the student's favorite activities and provide as many of these as possible throughout the day.

19. Do not criticize when correcting the student; be honest yet supportive. Never cause the student to feel badly about himself/herself.

20. Intervene early when there is a problem to prevent more serious problems from occurring.

21. Make certain there will be adult supervision at all times for the student (e.g., during P.E., recess, lunch, etc.).

22. Treat the student with respect. Talk in an objective manner at all times.

23. Be careful to avoid embarrassing the student by giving him/her orders, demands, etc., in front of others.

24. Teach the student acceptable ways to communicate displeasure, anger, frustration, etc.

25. Remove the student from the group or activity until he/she can demonstrate appropriate behavior and self-control.

26. Teach the student to "think" before acting (e.g., ask himself/herself, "What is happening?" "What am I doing?" "What should I do?" "What will be best for me?").

27. Make certain the student is allowed to voice an opinion in a situation to avoid becoming angry or upset.

28. Talk to the student about ways of handling situations successfully without conflict (e.g., walk away from a situation, change to another activity, ask for help, etc.).

29. Evaluate the appropriateness of the task to determine (a) if the task is too easy, (b) if the task is too difficult, or (c) if the length of time scheduled to complete the task is adequate.

30. Communicate with the parents (e.g., notes home, phone calls, etc.) to share information concerning the student's progress. The parents may reinforce the student at home for dealing with problems in appropriate ways at school.

31. Write a contract with the student specifying what behavior is expected (e.g., asking for help) and what reinforcement will be made available when the terms of the contract have been met.

32. Encourage the student to use problem-solving skills: (a) identify the problem, (b) identify goals and objectives, (c) develop strategies, (d) develop a plan for action, and (e) carry out the plan.

33. Reinforce the student for dealing with problems in appropriate ways based on the length of time the student can be successful. As the student demonstrates success, gradually increase the length of time required for reinforcement.

34. Reinforce those students in the classroom who deal with problems in appropriate ways.

35. Establish classroom rules:
- Work on-task.
- Remain in your seat.
- Finish task.
- Meet task expectations.
- Raise your hand.

Review rules often. Reinforce students for following rules.

36. Speak with the student to explain (a) what the student is doing wrong (e.g., running away from situations, running out of the room, running away from school, etc.) and (b) what the student should be doing (e.g., asking for help, calling attention to the problem, practicing problem- solving skills, using self-control, etc.).

37. Reinforce the student for dealing with problems in appropriate ways: (a) give the student a tangible reward (e.g., classroom privileges, line leading, passing out materials, five minutes free time, etc.) or (b) give the student an intangible reward (e.g., praise, handshake, smile, etc.).

30 Does not participate in social situations for fear that he/she would say or do the wrong thing

Goal:

1. The student will voluntarily, actively participate in social situations.

Objectives:

1. The student will passively participate in his/her choice of social situations on ___out of ___trials.
2. The student will actively participate in his/her choice of social situations on ___out of ___trials.

Interventions:

1. Reinforce the student for participating in group activities or special events: (a) give the student a tangible reward (e.g., classroom privileges, line leading, passing out materials, five minutes free time, etc.) or (b) give the student an intangible reward (e.g., praise, handshake, smile, etc.).

2. Provide the student with time and encouragement to establish rapport regardless of his/her lack of verbal response. Make certain the student receives options of other supports, such as counseling when there are concerns about withdrawn behavior. Any vast change in behavior, such as a student's total withdrawal after displaying acceptable and typical age appropriate social behaviors, may warrant the need of additional supports.

3. Do not force the student to socialize. It is more important to offer opportunities for positive reinforcement from socialization than to demand display of socialization skills.

4. The student needs your careful attention to the issue of what constitutes positive reinforcement. Social praise from an instructor or an authority source may decrease socializing behavior due to fear of embarrassment. Through a reinforcer survey and interviews with the student, and parents, and observations, develop a list of positive reinforcers specific to that student.

5. Speak with the student to explain (a) what he/she has done correctly (e.g., being present in the room, attempting to interact, etc.) and (b) what he/she might be doing to improve response (e.g., talking, taking turns, playing, sharing, etc.).

6. Reinforce others for participating in the group or special activities.

7. Establish classroom rules that indicate times when it is appropriate to socialize (e.g., at recess, during class parties, lunch time, after work is completed at the end of the day, at the beginning of each day, etc.). Review rules often. Reinforce student for following rules.

8. Write a contract with the student specifying what behavior is expected (e.g., contributing in group activities) and what reinforcement will be available when the terms of the contract have been met.

9. Communicate with parents (e.g., notes home, phone calls, etc.) to share information concerning the student's progress. The parents may reinforce the student at home for participating in group activities or special events at school.

10. Evaluate the appropriateness of the task to determine (a) if the task is too easy, (b) if the task is too difficult, (c) if the length of time the student is expected to passively and/or actively socially participate is reasonable.

11. Choose a peer to sit/work directly with the student (e.g., in different settings or activities such as art, music, P.E., on the bus, tutoring, group projects, running errands in the building, recess, etc.). As the student becomes comfortable working with one person, gradually increase the size of the group.

12. Provide opportunities for small-group interchanges in social situations (e.g., recess, lunch time, school parties, dances, etc.).

13. Give the student the responsibility of helping another in the group.

14. Allow passive participation as a social choice across learning activities and environments.

15. Ask the student questions that cannot be answered with a yes or no. Provide the student with encouragement for his/her attempts at answering these open-ended questions.

16. Call on the student when he/she is more likely to respond successfully (e.g., something of interest to the student, when the teacher is certain the student knows the answer, etc.).

17. Try various groupings to determine the situation in which the student is most successful.

18. Encourage friendship building in the classroom (e.g., students may wish to attend extracurricular activities in small groups, etc.).

19. Request the student lead a small-group activity if he/she expresses an interest and/or mastering of the subject.

20. Reduce the emphasis on competition. Frequent or continuous failure may result in embarrassment which will cause reluctance to participate.

21. Demonstrate respect for the student's opinions, responses, suggestions, etc.

22. Provide the student with many social and academic successes.

23. Provide the student with positive feedback to indicate he/she is successful.

24. Present tasks in the most attractive, interesting manner possible.

25. Allow the student to choose a special event or activity for the class.

26. Provide the student with success oriented special events or activities (e.g., opportunity to be a charter member of a reading or hobby club, etc.) to develop the student's interests and provide him/her the opportunity for meaningful social interchanges.

27. Modify situations that cause the student to be reluctant to participate (e.g., degree of difficulty, competition, fear of failure, threat of embarrassment, etc.).

28. Emphasize individual success or progress over winning or "beating" others.

29. Do not expect the student who is fearful of social interchanges to attend large social events (e.g., activities such as dances, athletic games, etc.) where the student may feel threatened by social interchanges. Help the student build toward a desired social goal in small, nonthreatening steps (e.g., small-group work interchanges might build toward a class party, then a picnic involving two classes, etc.).

30. Provide the student with opportunities for small-group rather than large-group participation.

31. Encourage the student to share things of special interest with others in the class (e.g., special hobbies such as coin collecting, etc.).

32. Choose a peer to model appropriate interactions in classroom activities for the student.

33. Provide the student with opportunity and encouragement to question directions, explanations, or instructions he/she does not understand.

34. Allow the student's choice of peers with whom he/she feels comfortable.

35. Identify peers with whom the student would most prefer to interact and attempt to facilitate interaction.

36. Assign outgoing, nonthreatening peers to help the student participate in classroom activities.

37. Structure the environment so the student has many opportunities to interact with other peers in classroom activities.

38. Assign the student to classroom activities in which he/she is likely to interact successfully with peers.

39. Conduct a sociometric activity to identify peers who would most prefer to interact with the student in classroom activities.

40. Teach the student appropriate ways to interact with others (e.g., share materials, problem solve, take turns, converse, etc.).

41. Supervise classroom activities closely so peers with whom the student interacts do not stimulate inappropriate behavior.

42. Make certain classroom activities and the social atmosphere do not provoke difficulties with desired classroom interactions (e.g., a noisy classroom may overstimulate the student).

43. Teach the student problem-solving skills so he/she is better equipped to manage potential problems (e.g., talking, walking away, calling upon an arbitrator, compromising, etc.).

44. Minimize embarrassment for the student by not placing him/her in humiliating situations (e.g., expecting him/her to participate actively in class discussions after he/she has just experienced failure, etc.).

45. Provide the student with opportunities to learn how to interact in social situations by teaching such social mannerisms in role-play.

46. Make certain the student is aware that others make social mistakes, and provide him/her examples of what he/she might do in an awkward situation (e.g., if a glass spills in a role-play situation, a student actor might apologize or excuse himself/herself and clean the spill).

47. Select nonacademic opportunities that enhance appropriate social interaction during classroom activities for all students (e.g., coloring, board games, model building, etc.).

48. Use information gained from interviews with other students to identify skills and behaviors students feel important for successful interactions.

49. Have the student practice appropriate interactions with the teacher(s) in classroom activities (e.g., simulations, role-play, etc.).

50. Prior to activities, make certain the student is able to successfully participate (e.g., understands the rules, is familiar with the activity, will be compatible with peers engaged in the activity, etc.).

51. Make certain the student has necessary materials for the classroom activity.

52. Assign responsibilities related to activities (e.g., being a leader, passing out materials, acting as a peer tutor, etc.) which may enhance the student's opportunities for interaction.

53. Make certain the student knows how to use all materials for the classroom activity.

54. The student who feels fearful of social situations may appreciate constructive remarks and verbal praise in conversations away from the group and/or in a nonintrusive delivery style.

55. Encourage students to give each other positive feedback for small-group contributions and other forms of positive verbal exchange.

56. Provide the student with a variety of ways to develop rapport with instructor(s) (e.g., writing notes, talking about concerns privately, etc.).

57. When a student expresses concerns or fears, always make certain the student knows you value such sincere thoughts and feelings. The following might prove helpful throughout a problem-solving process:
- Provide the student with credibility for thoughts/feelings and avoid attempts at minimizing the feelings.
- With student input, develop objectives which gradually build upon the student's social successes.
- Periodically, assess the student's comfort as he/she is involved in social situations (e.g., read his/her nonverbal forms of communication such as facial expressions and outward signals of nervousness).
- Encourage the student to evaluate his/her progress and consider the highlights and benefits of his/her social experience.
- Help the student develop reinforcement following social successes (e.g., watching a favorite program on TV, playing a favorite game, etc.).

31 Is not independent

Goals:

1. The student will independently perform assignments.

Objectives:

1. The student will attempt to perform a given assignment before asking for teacher assistance on _____ out of _____ trials.
2. The student will read necessary directions, instructions, explanations, etc., before asking for teacher assistance on _____ out of _____ trials.
3. The student will independently complete _____ out of _____ assignments per school day.
4. The student will ask for teacher assistance only when necessary when performing assignments on _____ out of _____ trials.
5. The student will work for _____ minutes without requiring assistance from the teacher on _____ out of _____ trials.

Interventions:

1. Reinforce the student for functioning independently: (a) give the student a tangible reward (e.g., classroom privileges, line leading, passing out materials, five minute free time, etc.) or (b) give the student an intangible reward (e.g., praise, handshake, smile, etc.).

2. Reinforce the student for performing assignments independently.

3. Communicate with parents (e.g., notes home, phone calls, etc.) to share information concerning the student's progress. The parents may reinforce the student at home for functioning independently at school.

4. Establish classroom rules:
- Work on-task.
- Work quietly.
- Request assistance when needed.
- Remain in your seat.
- Finish task.
- Meet task expectations.

Review rules often. Reinforce students for following rules.

5. Reinforce those students in the classroom who function independently.

6. Reinforce the student for functioning independently based on the number of times he/she can be successful. As the student demonstrates success, gradually increase the number of times required for reinforcement.

7. Write a contract with the student specifying what behavior is expected (e.g., functioning independently, asking for teacher assistance only when necessary) and what reinforcement will be made available when the terms of the contract have been met.

8. Speak to the student to explain (a) what he/she is doing wrong (e.g., asking for teacher assistance when not necessary) and (b) what he/she should be doing (e.g., functioning independently).

9. Choose a peer to model functioning independently for the student.

10. Encourage the student to question any directions, explanations, instruction he/she does not understand.

11. Evaluate the appropriateness of expecting the student to function independently in performing assignments, etc.

12. Maintain mobility throughout the classroom to determine the student's needs.

13. Offer the student assistance frequently throughout the day to help him/her remain active and gradually increase his/her independent functioning.

14. Make certain directions, explanations, and instructions are delivered on the student's ability level.

15. Structure the environment so the student is not required to communicate all needs to others (e.g., make certain the student's tasks are on his/her ability level; make certain instructions are clear; maintain frequent interactions with the student to ensure his/her success).

16. Communicate with the student as often as opportunities permit, to detect the student's needs.

17. Demonstrate accepting behavior (e.g., willingness to help others, making criticisms constructive and positive, demonstrating confidentiality in personal matters, etc.).

18. Communicate to the student an interest in his/her needs.

19. Communicate to the student that he/she is a worthwhile individual.

20. Call on the student often to encourage communication.

21. Encourage communication skills in the classroom.

22. Communicate your own personal needs and feelings to the student.

23. Encourage the student to communicate his/her needs to other personnel in the educational environment (e.g., school counselor, school psychologist, principal, etc.).

24. Communicate with parents, agencies, or the appropriate parties to inform them of the problem, determine the cause of the problem, and consider possible solutions to the problem.

25. Teach the student to communicate his/her needs in an appropriate manner (e.g., raise hand, use a normal tone of voice when speaking, verbally express problems, etc.).

26. Recognize the student's attempts to communicate his/her needs (e.g., facial expressions, gestures, inactivity, self-deprecating comments, etc.).

27. Have the student interact with a peer to encourage communicating his/her needs to others. As the student demonstrates success in communicating his/her needs to others, gradually increase the number of peers with whom the student interacts.

28. Pair the student with a non-threatening peer, a peer with similar interests and ability level, etc.

29. Give the student responsibilities in the classroom to increase the probability of communication (e.g., passing out materials, collecting lunch money, collecting schoolwork, etc.).

30. Give the student responsibilities in the classroom that require communication (e.g., peer tutor, group leader, teacher assistant, etc.).

31. Have the student keep a chart or graph representing the number of assignments he/she completes independently.

32. Assess the degree of task difficulty in comparison with the student's ability to perform the task.

33. Assign the student shorter tasks (e.g., modify a 20-problem math activity to 4 activities of 5 problems each, to be done at various times during the day). As the student demonstrates success, gradually increase the number of problems.

34. Present the task in the most interesting manner possible.

35. Reduce distracting stimuli (e.g., place the student in the front row, provide a carrel or quiet place away from distractions, etc.). This is to be used as a means of reducing distracting stimuli and not as a form of punishment.

36. Allow the student additional time to complete assignments when working independently.

37. Encourage the student to ask for clarification of directions for assignments.

38. Provide the student with step-by-step written directions for performing assignments.

39. Allow the student to perform alternative assignments. Gradually introduce more components of the assignment until those assignments are routinely performed.

40. Reinforce the student for beginning, working on, and completing assignments.

41. Maintain consistent expectations. Keep expectations within the ability level of the student.

42. Maintain a consistent daily routine.

43. Work a few problems with the student on an assignment to serve as a model and help the student begin a task.

44. Explain to the student that work not done during work time will have to be done during other times (e.g., break time, recreational time, after school, etc.).

32 Does not change from one activity to another without difficulty

Goals:

1. The student will change from one activity to another without difficulty.

Objectives:

1. The student will change from one activity to another without difficulty with physical assistance on _____ out of _____ trials.
2. The student will change from one activity to another without difficulty with verbal prompts on _____ out of _____ trials.
3. The student will independently change from one activity to another without difficulty on _____ out of _____ trials.
4. The student will rely on environmental cues (e.g., bells, timers, clocks, other students) to change from one activity to another without difficulty on _____ out of _____ trials.
5. The student will adjust his/her behavior to the requirements of different activities (e.g., change in rules, expectations) on _____ out of _____ trials.
6. The student will immediately stop one activity and begin another when necessary on _____ out of _____ trials.
7. The student will immediately put materials away and get ready for another activity on _____ out of _____ trials.

Interventions:

1. Prevent the student from becoming over-stimulated by an activity. Supervise student behavior to limit overexcitement in physical activities, games, parties, etc.

2. Establish definite time limits and provide the student with this information before the activity begins.

3. Inform the student that work not completed in one sitting can be completed later. Provide the student with ample time to complete earlier assignments to guarantee closure.

4. Provide the student with more than enough time to finish an activity. As the student demonstrates success, decrease the amount of time provided to finish an activity.

5. Structure time limits so the student knows exactly the amount of time there is to work and when he/she must be finished.

6. Allow a transition period between activities so the student can make adjustments in his/her behavior.

7. Employ a signal technique (e.g., turning the lights off and on) to warn that the end of an activity is near.

8. Have the student time activities to monitor personal behavior and accept time limits.

9. Assign the student shorter activities. As the student demonstrates success, gradually increase the length of the activities.

10. Maintain a consistent daily routine.

11. Maintain consistent expectations; keep expectations within the ability level of the student.

12. Allow the student to finish an activity unless it will be disruptive to the schedule.

13. Provide the student with a list of materials needed for each activity (e.g., pencil, paper, textbook, workbook, etc.).

14. Present instructions/directions prior to handing out necessary materials.

15. Collect the student's materials (e.g., pencil, paper, textbook, workbook, etc.) when it is time to change from one activity to another.

16. Provide the student with clearly stated expectations for all situations.

17. Prevent the student from becoming so stimulated by an event or activity that the student cannot control his/her behavior.

18. Establish rules that are to be followed in various parts of the school building (e.g., lunchroom, music room, art room, gymnasium, library, etc.).

19. Identify the expectations of different environments and help the student develop the skills to be successful in those environments.

20. In conjunction with other school personnel, develop as much consistency as possible in the school environment (e.g., rules, criteria for success, behavioral expectations, consequences, etc.).

21. Reduce the student's involvement in activities which prove too stimulating for him/her.

22. Have the student participate in relaxing transitional activities designed to reduce the effects of stimulating activities (e.g., put head on desk; listen to the teacher read a story; put headphones on and listen to relaxing music; etc.).

23. Provide the student with more than enough time to adapt or modify his/her behavior to different situations (e.g., have the student stop free time activities five minutes prior to returning to class).

24. Schedule activities so the student has more than enough time to finish the activity if he/she works consistently.

25. Communicate clearly to the student when it is time to begin an activity.

26. Communicate clearly to the student when it is time to stop an activity.

27. Provide the student with a schedule of daily events so he/she will know which activity comes next and can prepare for it.

28. Reduce the emphasis on competition (e.g., academic or social). Fear of failure may cause the student to fail to adapt or modify his/her behavior to different situations.

29. Have the student begin an activity in a private place (e.g., carrel, "office," quiet study area, etc.) to reduce the difficulty in adapting or modifying his/her behavior to different situations.

30. Allow the student the option of performing the activity at another time (e.g., earlier in the day, later in the day, another day, etc.).

31. Do not allow the student to begin a new activity until he/she has gained self-control.

32. Evaluate the appropriateness of the situation in relation to the student's ability to successfully adapt or modify his/her behavior.

33. Let the student know in advance when changes in his/her schedule will occur (e.g., a change from class time to break time, when reading class will begin, etc.).

34. Explain to the student that he/she should be satisfied with personal best effort rather than insisting on perfection.

35. Choose a peer to work with the student to provide an appropriate model.

36. Have the student question any directions, explanations, or instructions not understood.

37. Evaluate the appropriateness of the task to determine (a) if the task is too easy, (b) if the task is too difficult, and (c) if the length of time scheduled to complete the task is adequate.

38. Communicate with parents (e.g., notes home, phone calls, etc.) to share information concerning the student's progress. The parents may reinforce the student at home for demonstrating acceptable behavior at school.

39. Write a contract with the student specifying what behavior is expected (e.g., putting materials away and getting ready for another activity) and what reinforcement will be made available when the terms of the contract have been met.

40. Reinforce the student for demonstrating acceptable behavior based on the length of time the student can be successful. As the student demonstrates success, gradually increase the length of time required for reinforcement.

41. Reinforce those students in the classroom who change their behavior from one situation to another without difficulty.

42. Establish classroom rules:
- Work on-task.
- Work quietly.
- Remain in your seat.
- Finish task.
- Meet task expectations.

Review rules often. Reinforce students for following rules.

43. Speak to the student to explain (a) what the student is doing wrong (e.g., failing to stop one activity and begin another) and (b) what the student should be doing (e.g., changing from one activity to another).

44. Reinforce the student for changing his/her behavior from one situation to another without difficulty: (a) give the student a tangible reward (e.g., classroom privileges, line leading, passing out materials, five minutes free time, etc.) or (b) give the student an intangible reward (e.g., praise, handshake, smile, etc.).

33 Seems to be upset by or afraid of new situations or changes in routine

Goals:

1. The student will accept changes in an established routine.
2. The student will adjust easily to new situations.
3. The student will demonstrate appropriate behavior when an established routine is temporarily altered.

Objectives:

1. The student will accept changes in an established routine on ___ out of ___ trials.
2. The student will demonstrate appropriate behavior when an established routine is temporarily altered on ___ out of ___ trials.
3. The student will maintain self-control when changes in his/her schedule have been made on ___ out of ___ trials.
4. The student will demonstrate flexibility in performing tasks in a variety of ways on ___ out of ___ trials.
5. The student will demonstrate appropriate behavior in the presence of a student teacher on ___ out of ___ trials.
6. The student will demonstrate appropriate behavior in the presence of a substitute teacher on ___ out of ___ trials.
7. The student will follow established rules and behavioral expectations when changes in an established routine occur on ___ out of ___ trials.
8. The student will follow teacher directives when given ___ cues. (Gradually increase expectations as the student demonstrates success.)
9. The student will immediately respond to redirection on ___ out of ___ trials.
10. The student will maintain self-control when redirected in an academic situation on ___ out of ___ trials.
11. The student will maintain self-control when redirected in a social situation on ___ out of ___ trials.
12. The student will stop an activity when told to do so by the teacher on ___ out of ___ trials.

Interventions:

1. Have the student work near a peer to follow changes in an established routine.

2. Provide the student with a schedule of revised daily events which identifies the activities for the day and the times when they will occur.

3. Revisions in the schedule for the day's events should be attached to the student's desk and/or carried with the student throughout the day.

4. Post the revised routine throughout the classroom (e.g., on the student's desk, chalkboard, bulletin board, etc.).

5. Have the student rely on a predetermined signal (e.g., lights turned off and on, hand signal, etc.) to enhance the ability to accept change in an established routine.

6. Attempt to limit the number of times that changes must occur in the student's routine.

7. Discuss any necessary changes in the student's routine well in advance of the occurrence of the changes.

8. Teach the student to tell time to enhance his/her ability to accept changes in an established routine.

9. Have the student use a timer to remind him/her of changes in an established routine.

10. Reduce distracting stimuli which might cause the student to be unable to accept changes in an established routine (e.g., movement, noise, peers, etc.).

11. Model acceptance of changes in an established routine.

12. Have a peer remind the student of changes in routine.

13. Have the student rely on environmental cues to remind the student when to change activities in his/her revised routine (e.g., other students changing activities, bells, lights, buses arriving, etc.).

14. Remind the student when it is time to change activities.

15. Have a peer accompany the student to other locations in the building when change in an established routine has occurred.

16. Allow the student an appropriate amount of time to accept changes in an established routine.

17. Explain changes in routine to the student personally.

18. Provide activities similar to those canceled in the student's routine (e.g., if an art activity is canceled due to the art teacher's absence, provide an art activity in the classroom for the student).

19. Make certain that the substitute teacher is familiar with the behavioral support system used in the classroom (e.g., rules, point system, reinforcers, etc.).

20. If change in the student's routine proves too difficult, have the student remain with the established routine (e.g., if an assembly is too overstimulating for the student, have the student continue to work in his/her established routine).

21. Initially limit the number/degree of changes in the student's established routine. As the student demonstrates success, gradually increase the number/degree of changes in the routine.

22. Implement environmental changes within the classroom to provide the student with experience in change (e.g., change in seating, instructional delivery, task format, etc.) to help the student accept change in an established routine.

23. Prepare a substitute teacher information packet that includes information pertaining to the classroom (e.g., student roster, class schedule, class rules, behavior management techniques, class helpers, etc.).

24. Make certain the student understands that classroom rules and consequences are in effect when a substitute teacher is in the classroom.

25. Indicate the names of several teachers and where they can be found in case the substitute teacher should need their assistance.

26. Inform the substitute teacher of the classroom rules and the consequences if the rules are not followed by the student.

27. Have the student work on practice work (e.g., work that has already been taught to the student and that the student knows how to do) when a substitute teacher is in the classroom to reduce frustration and feelings of failure.

28. Provide the student with highly desirable activities to perform when changes in his/her routine are necessary.

29. Provide the substitute teacher with detailed information on the activities and assignments.

30. Assign the student specific activities to perform on any day when a substitute teacher may be responsible for the classroom (e.g., assistant to the substitute teacher, errand runner, line leader, class monitor, etc.).

31. Make certain the substitute teacher follows all procedures indicated by the classroom teacher (e.g., academic activities, behavioral support system, etc.).

32. Choose a peer to work with the student to model appropriate behavior and provide information necessary for success when changes are made in an established routine.

33. If an aide works in the classroom, have the aide monitor the student's behavior, provide reinforcement, deliver instructions, etc., when a substitute teacher is in the classroom.

34. Provide a quiet place for the student to work.

35. Inform the students in advance when it will be necessary for a substitute teacher to be in the classroom, and establish expectations for behavior and academic performance.

36. Let the student know in advance when changes in his/her schedule will occur (e.g., going to P.E. at a different time, going on a field trip, etc.).

37. Teach the student acceptable ways to communicate displeasure, anger, frustration, etc.

38. Have the student question any directions, explanations, and instructions not understood concerning the change in an established routine.

39. Choose a peer to model appropriate acceptance of changes in an established routine for the student.

40. Evaluate the appropriateness of the change in routine to determine if the change is too difficult and if the length of time scheduled is adequate.

41. Reinforce the student for accepting changes in an established routine: (a) give the student a tangible reward (e.g., classroom privileges, line leading, passing out materials, five minutes free time, etc.) or (b) give the student an intangible reward (e.g., praise, handshake, smile, etc.).

42. Write a contract with the student specifying what behavior is expected (e.g., accepting a change in routine) and what reinforcement will be made available when the terms of the contract have been met.

43. Reinforce those students in the classroom who accept changes in an established routine.

44. Reinforce the student for accepting changes in an established routine based on the number of times the student can be successful. As the student demonstrates success, gradually increase the number of times required for reinforcement.

45. Establish classroom rules:
- Work on-task.
- Work quietly.
- Remain in your seat.
- Finish task.
- Meet task expectations.

Review rules often. Reinforce students for following rules.

46. Speak to the student to explain (a) what the student is doing wrong (e.g., having a tantrum, refusing to accept the change, etc.) and (b) what the student should be doing (e.g., accepting the change in routine).

47. Communicate with the parents (e.g., notes home, phone calls, etc.) to share information concerning the student's progress. The parents may reinforce the student at home for accepting changes in an established routine at school.

34 Fails to concentrate, eat, or sleep because of personal or school experiences

Goal:

1. The student will sleep despite problems or situations in the home or school.
2. The student will function successfully at school despite problems or situations in the home or school.

Objectives:

1. The student will attend ____ out of ____ school days per month. (Gradually increase expectations as the student demonstrates success.)
2. The student will attend ____ out of ____ school days per week. (Gradually increase expectations as the student demonstrates success).
3. The student will be on time to school on ____ out of ____ days per month. (Gradually increase expectations as the student demonstrates success.)
4. The student will be on time to school on ____ out of ____ days per week. (Gradually increase expectations as the student demonstrates success.)
5. The student will be on time to class or activities ____ times per day. (Gradually increase expectations as the student demonstrates success.)
6. The student will complete ____% of his/her assigned tasks each day. (Gradually increase expectations as the student demonstrates success.)
7. The student will not worry over situations he/she cannot control on ____ out of ____ trials.
8. The student will perform assigned tasks with ____% accuracy.
9. The student will perform tests or quizzes with ____% accuracy.
10. The student will practice problem-solving techniques when dealing with personal or school experiences on ____ out of ____ trials.
11. The student will socially interact in an appropriate manner during ____ out of ____ interactions.
12. The student will stay on-task for ____ minutes at a time. (Gradually increase expectations as the student demonstrates success.)

Interventions:

1. Call attention to the student's accomplishments (e.g., publicly or privately depending on which is more appropriate).

2. Encourage the student to tell you about problems that occur with other students at school.

3. Provide as many enjoyable and interesting activities as possible.

4. Encourage participation in school and extra-curricular activities.

5. Provide praise and recognition as often as possible.

6. Discuss concerns with other professionals to determine if further investigation is warranted (e.g., abuse or neglect).

7. Teach the student alternative ways to deal with demands, challenges, and pressures of the school-age experience (e.g., deal with problems when they arise, practice self-control at all times, share problems or concerns with others, etc.).

8. Choose a peer to sit/work directly with the student.

9. Make the necessary adjustments in the environment to prevent the student from experiencing stress, frustration, anxiety, etc.

10. Reduce the emphasis on competition. Repeated failure may heighten anxiety about performance.

11. Offer to provide extra academic help for the student when he/she experiences a problem that interferes with his/her academic performance.

12. Maintain trust and confidentiality with the student at all times.

13. Explain that concerns or worries, while legitimate, are not unusual for students (e.g., everyone worries about tests, grades, etc.).

14. Structure the environment so time does not permit opportunities for the student to dwell on concerns or worries.

15. Provide opportunities for tutoring from peers or teacher.

16. Have peers invite the student to participate in extracurricular activities.

17. Teach/demonstrate methods for dealing with problems early to prevent problems from becoming overwhelming.

18. Teach the student appropriate ways to react to personal or school experiences (e.g., calling attention to the problem, practicing problem solving, moving away from the situation if it is threatening, etc.).

19. Demonstrate respect for the student's opinions, responses, suggestions, etc.

20. Discuss ways in which to practice self-improvement.

21. Try various groupings to determine the situation in which the student is most successful.

22. Provide the student with opportunities for social and academic success.

23. Provide the student with opportunities for special project responsibilities, leadership, etc.

24. Provide parents with necessary information to help the student with homework and study activities at home.

25. Seek assistance from the school counselors, the principal, other teachers, etc., to help the student learn to deal with personal problems so he/she can concentrate at school.

26. Take the time to listen so the student realizes that your concern is genuine.

27. Avoid discussion of topics sensitive to the student (e.g., divorce, death, unemployment, alcoholism, etc.).

28. Record or chart the number of times the student expresses concerns or worries about school or home to make the student aware of the frequency of his/her behavior.

29. Help the student feel comfortable coming to you for assistance with a problem by listening and helping with a solution to the problem.

30. Provide the student with alternative approaches to testing (e.g., test the student verbally, make tests shorter, allow the student to respond verbally, allow the student to take the test in the resource room, etc.).

31. Separate the student from a peer who may be encouraging or stimulating the inappropriate behavior.

32. Identify persons the student may contact with his/her worries or concerns (e.g., guidance counselor, school nurse, social worker, school psychologist, etc.).

Reminder: Do not "force" the student to participate in any activity.

35 Indicates concern regarding problems or situations in the home or fails to deal with classroom requirements because of out-of-school situations

Goal:

1. The student will function successfully at school despite problems or situations in the home or out of school.

Objectives:

1. The student will stay on-task for ___ minutes at a time. (Gradually increase expectations as the student demonstrates success.)
2. The student will complete ___% of his/her assigned tasks each day. (Gradually increase expectations as the student demonstrates success.)
3. The student will attend ___ out of ___ school days per week. (Gradually increase expectations as the student demonstrates success.)
4. The student will attend ___ out of ___ school days per month. (Gradually increase expectations as the student demonstrates success.)
5. The student will be on time to school on ___ out of ___ days per week. (Gradually increase expectations as the student demonstrates success.)
6. The student will be on time to school on ___ out of ___ days per month. (Gradually increase expectations as the student demonstrates success.)
7. The student will be on time to class or activities ___ times per day. (Gradually increase expectations as the student demonstrates success.)
8. The student will perform assigned tasks with ___% accuracy.
9. The student will perform tests or quizzes with ___% accuracy.
10. The student will socially interact in an appropriate manner during ___ out of ___ interactions.

Interventions:

1. Discuss concerns with other professionals to determine if further investigation is warranted (e.g., abuse or neglect).

2. Record or chart the number of times the student expresses concerns or worries about school or home to make the student aware of the frequency of his/her behavior.

3. Evaluate the appropriateness of the task to determine (a) the task is too easy, (b) the task is too difficult, and (c) the length of time scheduled for the task is adequate.

4. Take the time to listen so the student realizes your concern is genuine.

5. Explain that the concerns or worries, while legitimate, are not unusual for students (e.g., everyone worries about tests, grades, etc.).

6. Identify persons the student may contact with his/her worries or concerns (e.g., guidance counselor, school nurse, social worker, school psychologist, etc.).

7. Discuss ways in which to practice self-improvement.

8. Provide the student with opportunities for social and academic success.

9. Separate the student from a peer who may be encouraging or stimulating the inappropriate behavior.

10. Provide praise and recognition as often as possible.

11. Encourage participation in school and extracurricular activities.

12. Reduce the emphasis on competition. Repeated failure may heighten anxiety about performance.

13. Provide opportunities for tutoring from peers or teacher.

14. Choose a peer to sit/work directly with the student.

15. Try various groupings to determine the situation in which the student is most successful.

16. Make the necessary adjustments in the environment to prevent the student from experiencing stress, frustration, anxiety, etc.

17. Structure the environment so time does not permit opportunities for the student to dwell on concerns or worries.

18. Have peers invite the student to participate in extracurricular activities.

19. Demonstrate respect for the student's opinions, responses, suggestions, etc.

20. Provide the student with alternative approaches to testing (e.g., test the student verbally, make tests shorter, allow the student to respond verbally, allow the student to take the test in the resource room, etc.).

21. Provide parents with necessary information to help the student with homework and study activities at home.

22. Call attention to the student's accomplishments (e.g., publicly or privately depending on which is more appropriate).

23. Avoid discussion of topics sensitive to the student (e.g., divorce, death, unemployment, alcoholism, etc.).

24. Provide the student with opportunities for special project responsibilities, leadership, etc.

25. Provide as many enjoyable and interesting activities as possible.

Reminder: Do not "force" the student to participate in any activity.

36 Reacts physically in response to excitement, disappointment, surprise, happiness, fear, etc.

Goals:

1. The student will demonstrate self-control in stimulating situations.
2. The student will control his/her physical response to stimulating situations.

Objectives:

1. The student will demonstrate self-control in ___ out of ___ stimulating situations.
2. The student will control his/her physical response to ___ out of ___ stimulating situations.
3. The student will refrain from flapping his/her hands in ___ out of ___ stimulating situations.
4. The student will refrain from shuddering or trembling in response to ___ out of ___ stimulating situations.
5. The student will refrain from stuttering or stammering in response to ___ out of ___ stimulating situations.
6. The student will temporarily remove himself/herself from a stimulating situation to avoid physically responding to the situation on ___ out of ___ trials.
7. The student will refrain from physically responding to stimulating situations when cued by the teacher on ___ out of ___ trials.

Interventions:

1. Make the necessary adjustments in the environment to prevent the student from experiencing stress, frustration, anger, etc., as much as possible.

2. Maintain visibility to and from the student. The teacher should be able to see the student and the student should be able to see the teacher. Make eye contact possible at all times.

3. Facilitate on-task behavior by providing a full schedule of activities. Prevent lag time from occurring when the student would be more likely to engage in involuntary physical behavior.

4. Seat the student close to the teacher.

5. Reduce stimuli that contributes to unnecessary or excessive behavior.

6. Interact frequently with the student to direct his/her attention to the activity (e.g., ask the student questions, ask the student's opinion, stand close to the student, seat the student near the teacher's desk, etc.).

7. Structure the environment so the student does not have time to dwell on problems that are either real or imagined.

8. Prevent the student from becoming overly stimulated by an activity (e.g., monitor or supervise student behavior to limit overexcitement in physical activities, games, parties, etc.).

9. Expose the student to increased stimuli in the environment on a gradual basis after success has been demonstrated.

10. Teach the student appropriate ways to react to personal or school experiences (e.g., calling attention to the problem, practicing problem solving, moving away from the situation if it is threatening, etc.).

11. Provide the student with as many social and academic successes as possible.

12. Present the task in the most attractive and interesting manner possible.

13. Identify individuals the student may contact with his/her worries or concerns (e.g., guidance counselor, school nurse, social worker, school psychologist, etc.).

14. Maintain supervision at all times and in all parts of the school environment.

15. Prevent frustrating or anxiety-producing situations from occurring (e.g., give the student tasks only on his/her ability level, give the student only the number of tasks that can be tolerated in one sitting, reduce social interactions which stimulate the student to demonstrate involuntary physical reactions, etc.).

16. Be mobile to be frequently near the student.

17. Teach and encourage the student to use problem-solving skills: (a) identify the problem, (b) identify goals and objectives, (c) develop strategies, (d) develop a plan of action, and (e) carry out the plan.

18. Provide an environment which is calm, consistent, and structured.

19. Provide the student with a predetermined signal if he/she begins to exhibit the inappropriate behavior.

20. Make certain that positive reinforcement is not inadvertently given for inappropriate behavior (e.g., responding to the student when errors are made, responding to the student when he/she feigns a need for help, etc.).

21. Encourage the student to practice self-control activities designed to allow the student to compose himself/herself before continuing an activity (e.g., placing hands on desk, sitting with feet flat on the floor, making eye contact with the instructor, etc.).

22. Provide the student with a quiet place to work when involuntary physical reactions occur. This is not meant as punishment but as a means of helping the student be more successful in the environment.

23. Remove the student from the group or activity until he/she can demonstrate appropriate behavior and self-control.

24. Make certain the student does not become involved in overstimulating activities.

25. Teach the student acceptable ways to communicate displeasure, anger, frustration, etc.

26. Do not force the student to interact with others.

27. Make sure you express your feelings in a socially acceptable way.

28. Make certain the student is allowed to voice an opinion in a situation to avoid becoming angry or upset.

29. Talk to the student about ways of handling situations successfully without conflict (e.g., walk away from a situation, change to another activity, ask for help, etc.).

30. Try various groupings to determine the situation in which the student is most comfortable.

31. Evaluate the appropriateness of the task to determine (a) if the task is too easy, (b) if the task is too difficult, and (c) if the length of time scheduled to complete the task is adequate.

32. Communicate with the parents (e.g., notes home, phone calls, etc.) to share information concerning the student's progress. The parents may reinforce the student at home for demonstrating physical self-control at school.

33. Intervene early when there is a problem to prevent more serious problems from occurring.

34. Write a contract with the student specifying what behavior is expected (e.g., demonstrating physical self-control) and what reinforcement will be made available when the terms of the contract have been met.

35. Reinforce the student for demonstrating physical self-control based on the length of time the student can be successful. As the student demonstrates success, gradually increase the amount of time required for reinforcement.

36. Reinforce those students in the classroom who demonstrate physical self-control.

37. Establish classroom rules:
- Work on-task.
- Work quietly.
- Remain in your seat.
- Finish task.
- Meet task expectations.

Review rules often. Reinforce students for following rules.

38. Speak with the student to explain (a) what the student is doing wrong (e.g., shaking, flapping hands, etc.) and (b) what the student should be doing (e.g., practicing self-control).

39. Do not allow the student to begin a new activity until he/she has gained self-control.

40. Reinforce the student for demonstrating physical self-control: (a) give the student a tangible reward (e.g., classroom privileges, line leading, passing out materials, five minutes free time, etc.) or (b) give the student an intangible reward (e.g., praise, handshake, smile, etc.).

41. Teach the student to recognize signs of becoming overexcited so he/she may deal with it appropriately.

42. Assess the appropriateness of the social situation in relation to the student's ability to function successfully.

37 Demonstrates involuntary physical reactions in response to personal or school experiences

Goals:

1. The student will demonstrate self-control in stimulating situations.
2. The student will control his/her physical response to stimulating situations.

Objectives:

1. The student will demonstrate self-control in ___ out of ___ stimulating situations.
2. The student will control his/her physical response to ___ out of ___ stimulating situations.
3. The student will refrain from flapping his/her hands in ___ out of ___ stimulating situations.
4. The student will refrain from shuddering or trembling in response to ___ out of ___ stimulating situations.
5. The student will refrain from stuttering or stammering in response to ___ out of ___ stimulating situations.
6. The student will temporarily remove himself/herself from a stimulating situation to avoid physically responding to the situation on ___ out of ___ trials.
7. The student will refrain from physically responding to stimulating situations when cued by the teacher on ___ out of ___ trials.

Interventions:

1. Make the necessary adjustments in the environment to prevent the student from experiencing stress, frustration, anger, etc., as much as possible.

2. Maintain visibility to and from the student. The teacher should be able to see the student and the student should be able to see the teacher. Make eye contact possible at all times.

3. Facilitate on-task behavior by providing a full schedule of activities. Prevent lag time from occurring when the student would be more likely to engage in involuntary physical behavior.

4. Seat the student close to the teacher.

5. Reduce stimuli that contributes to unnecessary or excessive behavior.

6. Interact frequently with the student to direct his/her attention to the activity (e.g., ask the student questions, ask the student's opinion, stand close to the student, seat the student near the teacher's desk, etc.).

7. Maintain supervision at all times and in all parts of the school environment.

8. Prevent the student from becoming overly stimulated by an activity (e.g., monitor or supervise student behavior to limit overexcitement in physical activities, games, parties, etc.).

9. Expose the student to increased stimuli in the environment on a gradual basis after success has been demonstrated.

10. Teach the student appropriate ways to react to personal or school experiences (e.g., calling attention to the problem, practicing problem-solving, moving away from the situation if it is threatening, etc.).

11. Provide the student with as many social and academic successes as possible.

12. Present the task in the most attractive and interesting manner possible.

13. Identify individuals the student may contact with his/her worries or concerns (e.g., guidance counselor, school nurse, social worker, school psychologist, etc.).

14. Prevent frustrating or anxiety-producing situations from occurring (e.g., give the student tasks only on his/her ability level, give the student only the number of tasks that can be tolerated in one sitting, reduce social interactions which stimulate the student to demonstrate involuntary physical reactions, etc.).

15. Be mobile to be frequently near the student.

16. Structure the environment so the student does not have time to dwell on problems that are either real or imagined.

17. Teach and encourage the student to use problem-solving skills: (a) identify the problem, (b) identify goals and objectives, (c) develop strategies, (d) develop a plan for action, and (e) carry out the plan.

18. Provide an environment which is calm, consistent, and structured.

19. Provide the student with a predetermined signal if he/she begins to exhibit the inappropriate behavior.

20. Make certain that positive reinforcement is not inadvertently given for inappropriate behavior (e.g., responding to the student when errors are made, responding to the student when he/she feigns a need for help, etc.).

21. Encourage the student to practice self-control activities designed to allow the student to compose himself/herself before continuing an activity (e.g., placing hands on desk, sitting with feet flat on the floor, making eye contact with the instructor, etc.).

22. Reinforce those students in the classroom who demonstrate physical self-control.

23. Intervene early when there is a problem to prevent more serious problems from occurring.

24. Make certain the student does not become involved in overstimulating activities.

25. Teach the student acceptable ways to communicate displeasure, anger, frustration, etc.

26. Do not force the student to interact with others.

27. Make sure you express your feelings in a socially acceptable way.

28. Speak with the student to explain (a) what the student is doing wrong (e.g., shaking, flapping hands, etc.) and (b) what the student should be doing (e.g., practicing self-control).

29. Make certain the student is allowed to voice an opinion in a situation to avoid becoming angry or upset.

30. Talk to the student about ways of handling situations successfully without conflict (e.g., walk away from a situation, change to another activity, ask for help, etc.).

31. Try various groupings to determine the situation in which the student is most comfortable.

32. Evaluate the appropriateness of the task to determine (a) if the task is too easy, (b) if the task is too difficult, and (c) if the length of time scheduled to complete the task is adequate.

33. Communicate with the parents (e.g., notes home, phone calls, etc.) to share information concerning the student's progress. The parents may reinforce the student at home for demonstrating physical self-control at school.

34. Remove the student from the group or activity until he/she can demonstrate appropriate behavior and self-control.

35. Write a contract with the student specifying what behavior is expected (e.g., demonstrating physical self-control) and what reinforcement will be made available when the terms of the contract have been met.

36. Reinforce the student for demonstrating physical self-control based on the length of time the student can be successful. As the student demonstrates success, gradually increase the amount of time required for reinforcement.

37. Provide the student with a quiet place to work when involuntary physical reactions occur. This is not meant as punishment but as a means of helping the student be more successful in the environment.

38. Establish classroom rules:

- Work on-task.
- Work quietly.
- Remain in your seat.
- Finish task.
- Meet task expectations.

Review rules often. Reinforce students for following rules.

39. Reinforce the student for demonstrating physical self-control: (a) give the student a tangible reward (e.g., classroom privileges, line leading, passing out materials, five minutes free time, etc.) or (b) give the student an intangible reward (e.g., praise, handshake, smile, etc.).

38 Does not interact with others because of fear of not being liked, accepted, etc.

Goals:

1. The student will interact with others.

Objectives:

1. The student will develop interaction skills and use them when interacting with a peer(s) during ___ out of ___ interactions.
2. The student will demonstrate acceptable physical contact such as a handshake, pat on the back, "high five," etc., when appropriate on ___ out of ___ trials.
3. The student will interact with other students in a physically appropriate manner on ___ out of ___ trials.
4. The student will develop hygiene skills and manners and use them when interacting with other students on ___ out of ___ trials.
5. The student will demonstrate consideration/regard for his/her peers on ___ out of ___ trials.
6. The student will demonstrate peer interaction skills by sharing materials, waiting his/her turn, and talking in an acceptable manner on ___ out of ___ trials.
7. The student will successfully interact with a peer ___ times per day.
8. The student will successfully interact with a peer ___ times per week.

Interventions:

1. Provide the student with as many academic and social successes as possible so peers may view him/her in a more positive way.

2. Make the necessary adjustments in the environment to prevent the student from experiencing stress, frustration, anger, etc.

3. Assign additional responsibilities to the student (e.g., chores, errands, etc.) to give him/her a feeling of success or accomplishment.

4. Structure the environment so the student does not have time to dwell on real or imagined problems.

5. Help the student identify things he/she wishes were in the environment, and work with the student toward those goals.

6. Try various groupings to determine the situation in which the student is most comfortable.

7. Encourage the student to participate in extracurricular activities that will help develop those skills necessary to interact appropriately with others at school.

8. Provide the student with alternative activities to perform in case some activities prove upsetting.

9. Reduce the emphasis on competition. Repeated failure may cause the student to feel that others do not like or care about him/her.

10. Encourage and help the student to make friends (e.g., pair the student with a peer; when that relationship is successful, introduce other students).

11. Provide the student with as many positive interactions as possible (e.g., recognize the student, greet the student, compliment attire, etc.).

12. Discourage the student from engaging in those activities that cause him/her unhappiness.

13. Take the time to listen so the student will realize your concern and interest.

14. Teach the student alternative ways to deal with unpleasant social interactions during the school-age experience (e.g., deal with problems when they arise, practice self-control at all times, share problems or concerns with others, etc.).

15. Speak with the student to explain that he/she may be trying too hard to fit in and that he/she should relax and allow friendships to develop naturally.

16. Reinforce those students in the classroom who appropriately interact with other students.

17. Have the student be the leader of a small-group activity if he/she possesses mastery of skills or an interest in that area.

18. Make certain the student is not demonstrating a lack of confidence to get the attention of others.

19. Maintain maximum supervision of the student's interactions and gradually decrease the amount of supervision over time.

20. Give the student responsibilities in group situations so peers may view the student in a more positive way.

21. Encourage the student to further develop any ability or skill he/she may have so peers may view the student in a more positive way.

22. Help the student to identify his/her inappropriate behaviors and teach the student ways to change those behaviors.

23. Ask the student to choose a peer to work with on a specific assignment. Encourage the student and peer to interact with each other in nonacademic areas (e.g., recess, lunch, break time, etc.).

24. Do not criticize. When correcting the student, be honest yet supportive. Never cause the student to feel badly about himself/herself.

25. Do not force the student to interact with students with whom he/she is not completely comfortable.

26. Treat the student with respect. Talk in an objective manner at all times.

27. Allow the student to attempt something new in private before doing so in front of others.

28. Do not assume that the student is being treated nicely by other students. Others may be stimulating inappropriate behavior on the part of the student.

29. Encourage the student to interact with others.

30. Provide the student with frequent opportunities to meet new people.

31. Do not force the student to interact with others.

32. Give the student the responsibility of tutoring a peer if he/she possesses the skills to be shared.

33. Teach the student problem-solving skills: (a) identify the problem, (b) identify goals and objectives, (c) develop strategies, (d) develop a plan of action, and (e) carry out the plan.

34. Communicate with parents (e.g., notes home, phone calls, etc.) to share information concerning the student's progress. The parents may reinforce the student at home for interacting appropriately with others at school.

35. Write a contract with the student specifying what behavior is expected (e.g., interacting appropriately with others) and what reinforcement will be made available when the terms of the contract have been met.

36. Reinforce the student for interacting with others based on the length of time the student can be successful. As the student demonstrates success, gradually increase the length of time required for reinforcement.

37. Reinforce those students in the classroom who make positive, supportive comments to the student.

38. Establish classroom rules:
- Work on-task.
- Work quietly.
- Remain in your seat.
- Finish task.
- Meet task expectations.

Review rules often. Reinforce students for following rules.

39. Reinforce the student for interacting with others: (a) give the student a tangible reward (e.g., classroom privileges, line leading, passing out materials, five minutes free time, etc.) or (b) give the student an intangible reward (e.g., praise, handshake, smile, etc.).

40. Have peers invite the student to participate in school or extracurricular activities.

41. Conduct a sociometric activity with the class to determine the peer who would most prefer to interact with the student.

Reminder: Do not "force" the student to interact with others with whom he/she is uncomfortable.

39 Demonstrates fear of becoming embarrassed in front of others

Goals:

1. The student will overcome his/her fears related to becoming embarrassed in front of other people.

Objectives:

1. The student will develop positive social skills to replace his/her fear of becoming embarrassed in front of others on ____ out of ____ trials.
2. The student will decrease fear of becoming embarrassed in front of others on ____ out of ____ trials.

Interventions:

1. Reinforce the student for participating in group activities or special events: (a) give the student a tangible reward (e.g., classroom privileges, line leading, passing out materials, five minutes free time, etc.) or (b) give the student an intangible reward (e.g., praise, handshake, smile, etc.).

2. Provide the student with time and encouragement to establish rapport regardless of his/her lack of verbal response. Any vast change in behavior, such as a student's total withdrawal after displaying acceptable and typical age appropriate social behaviors, may warrant the need of additional supports.

3. Do not force the student to socialize. It is more important to offer opportunities for positive reinforcement from socialization than to demand display of socialization skills.

4. The student who is fearful of embarrassment in front of others and/or withdraws from socializing needs your careful attention to the issue of what constitutes positive reinforcement. Social praise by his/her instructor or an authority source may decrease socializing behavior due to fear of embarrassment. Through a reinforcer survey and interviews with the student, and parents, and observations, develop a list of positive reinforcers specific to that student.

5. Speak with the student to explain (a) what he/she has done correctly (e.g., being present in the room, attempting to interact, etc.) and (b) what he/she might be doing to improve response (e.g., talking, taking turns, playing, sharing, etc.).

6. Encourage or reinforce others for participation in the group or special activities.

7. Establish classroom rules that indicate times when it is appropriate to socialize (e.g., at recess, during class parties, lunch-time, after work is completed at the end of the day, at the beginning of each day before attendance, etc.). Review rules often. Reinforce students for following rules.

8. Write a contract with the student specifying what behavior is expected (e.g., contributing in group activities) and what reinforcement will be available when the terms of the contract have been met.

9. Communicate with parents (e.g., notes home, phone calls, etc.) to share information concerning the student's progress. The parents may reinforce the student at home for participating in group activities or special events at school.

10. Evaluate the appropriateness of the task to determine (a) if the task is too easy, (b) if the task is too difficult, and (c) if the length of time the student is expected to passively and/or actively socially participate is reasonable.

11. Choose a peer to sit/work directly with the student (e.g., in different settings or activities such as art, music, P.E., on the bus, tutoring, group projects, running errands in the building, recess, etc.). When the student has become comfortable working with one person, gradually increase the size of the group.

12. Include opportunities for small-group interchanges in social situations (e.g., recess, lunchtime, school parties, dances, etc.).

13. Give the student the responsibility of helping another in the group.

14. Ask the student questions that cannot be answered with a yes or no. Provide the student with encouragement for his/her attempts at answering these open-ended questions.

15. Call on the student when he/she is more likely to respond successfully (e.g., something of interest to the student, when the teacher is certain the student knows the answer, etc.).

16. Try various groupings to determine the situation in which the student is most successful.

17. Encourage friendship building in the classroom (e.g., students may wish to attend extracurricular activities in small groups, etc.).

18. Request the student lead a small-group activity if he/she expresses an interest and/or mastery of the subject.

19. Allow passive participation as a social choice across learning activities and environments.

20. Reduce the emphasis on competition. Frequent or continuous failure may result in embarrassment which will cause reluctance to participate.

21. Demonstrate respect for the student's opinions, responses, suggestions, etc.

22. Provide the student with many social and academic successes.

23. Provide the student with positive feedback to indicate he/she is successful.

24. Present tasks in the most attractive, interesting manner possible.

25. Allow the student to choose a special event or activity for the class.

26. Provide the student with success-oriented special events or activities (e.g., opportunity to be a charter member of a reading or hobby club, etc.) to develop the student's interests and afford him/her the opportunity for meaningful social interchanges without embarrassment.

27. Modify situations that cause the student to be reluctant to participate (e.g., degree of difficulty, competition, fear of failure, threat of embarrassment, etc.).

28. Emphasize individual success or progress over winning or "beating" others.

29. Do not expect the student who is fearful of social interchanges to attend large social events (e.g., activities such as dances, athletic games, etc.) where the student may feel threatened by social interchanges. Help the student build toward a desired social goal in small, nonthreatening steps (e.g., small-group work interchanges might build toward a class party, then a picnic involving two classes, etc.).

30. Provide the student with opportunities for small-group rather than large-group participation.

31. Encourage the student to share things of special interest with others in the class (e.g., special hobbies such as coin collecting, etc.).

32. Choose a peer to model appropriate interactions in classroom activities for the student.

33. Provide the student with opportunity and encouragement to question directions, explanations, or instructions he/she does not understand.

34. Allow the student to choose to interact with peers with whom he/she feels comfortable.

35. Identify peers with whom the student would most prefer to interact and attempt to facilitate interaction.

36. Assign outgoing, nonthreatening peers to help the student participate in classroom activities.

37. Structure the environment so the student has many opportunities to interact with other peers in classroom activities.

38. Assign the student to classroom activities in which he/she is likely to interact successfully with peers.

39. Assign responsibilities related to activities (e.g., being a leader, passing out materials, acting as a peer tutor, etc.) which may facilitate the student's opportunities for interaction.

40. Teach the student appropriate ways to interact with others (e.g., share materials, problem solve, take turns, converse, etc.).

41. Supervise classroom activities closely so peers with whom the student interacts do not stimulate inappropriate behavior.

42. Make certain the classroom activities and social atmosphere do not provoke difficulties with desired classroom interactions (e.g., a noisy classroom may overstimulate the student).

43. Teach the student problem-solving skills so he/she is better equipped to manage potential problems (e.g., talking, walking away, calling upon an arbitrator, compromising, etc.).

44. Minimize embarrassment for the student by not placing him/her in humiliating situations (e.g., expecting him/her to participate actively in class discussions after he/she has just experienced failure, etc.).

45. Provide the student with opportunities to learn how to interact in social situations by teaching such social mannerisms in role-play.

46. Make certain the student is aware that others make social mistakes, and provide him/her with examples of what he/she might do in an awkward situation. For example, if a glass spills in a role-play situation, a student actor might apologize or excuse himself/herself and clean the spill.

47. Select nonacademic opportunities that enhance appropriate social interaction during classroom activities for all students (e.g., coloring, board games, model building, etc.).

48. Use information gained from interviews with other students to identify skills and behaviors students feel are important for successful interactions.

49. Have the student practice appropriate interactions with the teacher(s) in classroom activities (e.g., simulations, role-play, etc.).

50. Prior to activities, make certain the student is able to successfully participate (e.g., understands the rules, is familiar with the activity, will be compatible with peers engaged in the activity, etc.).

51. Make certain the student has necessary materials for the classroom activity.

52. Conduct a sociometric activity to identify peers who would most prefer to interact with the student in classroom activities.

53. Make certain the student knows how to use all materials for the classroom activity.

54. The student who feels fearful of social situations may appreciate constructive remarks and verbal praise in conversations away from the group and/or in a nonintrusive delivery style.

55. Encourage students to give each other positive feedback for small-group contributions and other forms of positive verbal exchange.

56. When a student expresses concerns and/or fears, always make certain the student knows you value such sincere thoughts and feelings. The following might prove helpful throughout a problem-solving process:

(a) Provide the student with credibility for thoughts/feelings and avoid attempts at minimizing the feelings;

(b) with student input, develop objectives which gradually build upon the student's social successes;

(c) periodically, assess the student's comfort as he/she is involved in social situations (e.g., read his/her nonverbal forms of communication such as facial expressions and outward signals of nervousness);

(d) encourage the student to evaluate his/her progress and consider the highlights and benefits of his/her social experience; and

(e) help the student develop self-reinforcement following social successes (e.g., watching a favorite program on TV, playing a favorite game, etc.).

57. Give the student frequent opportunities to use the positive social skills he/she is learning.

58. Be specific and positive when providing the student constructive criticism.

59. Provide the student with a variety of ways to develop rapport with instructor(s) (e.g., writing notes, talking about concerns privately, etc.).

60. Provide the student with frequent opportunities to attempt correct responses (e.g., attempts to self-manage in front of others) and make certain the student receives positive reinforcement for those attempts.

61. Through observation and interaction with the student, identify when the student will most likely experience blushing, crying, etc., (e.g., during oral reports, during meetings, etc.). Develop coping mechanisms and other choices he/she may choose in these situations (e.g., going to a restroom if the need to cry is experienced during a meeting in which the student has chosen to participate; developing concise, organized notes for public speaking for focus in the event of embarrassment; etc.). Reinforce the student for his/her attempts at using such coping mechanisms.

62. Do not aggressively confront student problems with embarrassment. Encourage the student to work with you on positive, nonthreatening approaches (e.g., using coping skills to manage difficult situations).

63. Build positive self-concept among students by including the following approaches:
(a) Offer opportunities for students to work together noncompetitively on class projects;
(b) identify and compliment each student's unique contribution to group work when this will be perceived by the student as positive reinforcement; and
(c) organize time to speak with students individually.

64. The student who experiences fear of embarrassment in front of others may benefit from
(a) frequent opportunities to rehearse coping mechanisms the student and instructor have developed;
(b) frequent opportunities for social success; and
(c) gradual increases in social expectations (e.g., increase in time, in numbers of persons, etc.).

65. The student will experience natural consequences for not participating socially (e.g., isolation from others, avoidance of activities the student might actually like if the fears were overcome, etc.). It is important to realize this student needs positive social experiences which occur incidentally throughout the day for social skills development.

40 Blames other persons or materials to avoid taking responsibility for his/her mistakes or failures

Goal:

1. The student will take responsibility for his/her mistakes.

Objectives:

1. The student will take responsibility for his/her mistakes on ___ out of ___ trials.
2. The student will correct his/her mistakes when asked to do so by the teacher on ___ out of ___ trials.
3. The student will immediately correct his/her mistakes when he/she becomes aware of them on ___ out of ___ trials.
4. The student will independently correct his/her mistakes when assignments are returned to him/her for corrections on ___ out of ___ trials.

Interventions:

1. Structure the environment for the student to reduce interference from peers (e.g., remove the opportunity to blame others).

2. Teach the student problem-solving skills: (a) identify the problem, (b) identify goals and objectives, (c) develop strategies, (d) develop a plan of action, and (e) carry out the plan.

3. Provide the student with as many social and academic successes as possible.

4. Make the necessary adjustments in the environment to prevent the student from experiencing stress, frustration, anger, etc.

5. Provide the student with positive feedback which indicates he/she is successful, competent, important, valuable, etc.

6. Make certain that excuses are not accepted in place of meeting responsibility.

7. Make certain that all materials are appropriate and in good working order.

8. Be certain to recognize the student when he/she indicates a need for help.

9. Provide the student with all necessary information prior to an activity to increase the likelihood of success.

10. Reduce stimuli in the environment which may contribute to the student's failures or difficulties.

11. Provide the student with a quiet place to work. This is used as a form of reducing distracting stimuli and not as a form of punishment.

12. Program assignments which will ensure initial success. As the student's ability and responsibility increases, gradually increase the degree of difficulty of assignments.

13. Make certain that instructions and expectations are clearly stated.

14. Reduce the emphasis on competition. Repeated failure may result in the student blaming someone or something for his/her own failure.

15. Encourage the student to begin assignments early to have time to deal with problems which may arise.

16. Provide the student with a schedule of daily events to plan his/her time accordingly.

17. When the student blames others for his/her behavior, calmly confront the student with the facts. Encourage an open and honest line of communication. Do not make the student fearful of telling the truth even though you may not be happy about the behavior.

18. Help the student to feel comfortable coming to you for assistance with a problem by listening and helping with a solution to the problem.

19. Be consistent with the student. Do not discipline for misbehavior one time and ignore misbehavior the next time.

20. The student must understand that, regardless of the reason, it is necessary to take responsibility for not turning in math papers, losing pencils, etc.

21. Do not put the student in a situation where the student feels that he/she must blame others for his/her mistakes.

22. Evaluate the appropriateness of the task to determine (a) if the task is too easy, (b) if the task is too difficult, and (c) if the length of time scheduled to complete the task is adequate.

23. Avoid arguing with the student concerning whether or not he/she is making excuses; simply explain that he/she is not being completely honest about a situation.

24. Make certain that consequences delivered for inappropriate behavior are not extreme and are directly related to the inappropriate behavior (e.g., things that are destroyed must be replaced, work not done during work time has to be made up during recreational time, etc.).

25. Avoid arguing with the student concerning whether or not he/she is telling the truth. If you do not have proof, it is better to avoid blaming someone who might be innocent.

26. Always determine the accuracy of the student's claim that someone or something caused him/her to have a problem or to fail. In some cases someone or something may legitimately be causing the student to experience problems or failure.

27. Make certain the student understands that not being honest when confronted will result in more negative consequences than telling the truth. Be certain to be very consistent in this approach.

28. Explain to the student that he/she should be satisfied with personal best effort rather than perfection.

29. Attempt to have an open, honest relationship with the student. Encourage the student to tell the truth, and do not use threats to make him/her tell the truth (e.g., "You had better tell the truth or else!").

30. Communicate with parents (e.g., notes home, phone calls, etc.) to share information concerning the student's progress. The parents may reinforce the student at home for accepting the responsibility for his/her behavior at school.

31. Remove the student from the group or activity until the student can accept responsibility for his/her behavior.

32. Write a contract with the student specifying what behavior is expected (e.g., accepting responsibility for his/her own mistakes) and what reinforcement will be made available when the terms of the contract have been met.

33. Reinforce the student for accepting responsibility for his/her own behavior based on the length of time the student can be successful. As the student demonstrates success, gradually increase the length of time required for reinforcement.

34. Reinforce those students in the classroom who accept responsibility for their own behavior.

35. Establish classroom rules:
- Work on-task.
- Work quietly.
- Remain in your seat.
- Finish task.
- Meet task expectations.

Review rules often. Reinforce students for following rules.

36. Speak with the student to explain (a) what the student is doing wrong (e.g., failing to take responsibility for his/her behavior, blaming other persons or materials, etc.) and (b) what the student should be doing (e.g., accepting responsibility for his/her own behavior, accepting outcomes, etc.).

37. Reinforce the student for accepting responsibility for his/her own behavior: (a) give the student a tangible reward (e.g., classroom privileges, line leading, passing out materials, five minutes free time, etc.) or (b) give the student an intangible reward (e.g., praise, handshake, smile, etc.).

41   Appears to be generally bored with or disinterested in daily activities

Goals:

1. The student will participate in classroom activities.
2. The student will demonstrate interest by participating in classroom activities.

Objectives:

1. The student will participate in ___ out of ___ classroom activities per day.
2. The student will participate in ___ out of ___ classroom activities per week.
3. The student will participate in ___ out of ___ classroom activities per month.
4. The student will demonstrate an interest in classroom activities by asking about the activities, talking about the activities, helping prepare for the activities, etc., in ___ out of ___ activities.
5. The student will passively participate in a classroom activity by sitting quietly, assisting the teacher, taking notes, etc., during ___ out of ___ activities.
6. The student will actively participate in a classroom activity by being the group leader or spokesperson, answering questions, providing his/her opinion, etc., during ___ out of ___ activities.
7. The student will interact with a peer for ___ minutes per day. (Gradually increase expectations as the student demonstrates success.)
8. The student will initiate ___ interactions with a peer per day. (Gradually increase expectations as the student demonstrates success.)
9. The student will interact with the teacher for ___ minutes per day. (Gradually increase expectations as the student demonstrates success.)
10. The student will initiate ___ interactions with the teacher per day. (Gradually increase expectations as the student demonstrates success.)
11. The student will perform academic tasks with ___% accuracy. (Gradually increase expectations as the student demonstrates success.)
12. The student will identify something he/she enjoys doing at school when asked by the teacher on ___ out of ___ occasions.
13. The student will identify a reinforcer he/she would like to earn for participating in classroom activities on ___ out of ___ trials.
14. The student will perform ___ out of ___ academic tasks per day. (Gradually increase expectations as the student demonstrates success.)

Interventions:

1. Call on the student when he/she can answer successfully.

2. Avoid competition. Failure may cause the student to lose interest or not participate in school activities.

3. Allow the student more decision-making opportunities relative to class activities and assignments.

4. Present tasks in the most attractive and interesting manner possible.

5. Give the student responsibilities in the classroom (e.g., teacher assistant, peer tutor, group leader, etc.).

6. Provide a full schedule of daily events to keep the student actively involved.

7. Provide the student with as many academic and social successes as possible.

8. Evaluate the appropriateness of the task in relation to the student's ability to perform the task successfully.

9. Determine the student's preferred activities, interests, etc., and incorporate them into the daily schedule, program, etc., at various points throughout the day.

10. Provide the student with "real-life" experiences from the environment. Have individuals from the work force (e.g., mechanic, draftsman, secretary, etc.) visit the class to relate the importance of school to work experiences that involve math, reading, writing, etc.

11. Show an interest in the student (e.g., acknowledge the student, ask the student's opinion, spend time working one-on-one with the student, etc.).

12. Investigate the possibility that the student is involved in the use of drugs or alcohol.

13. Provide the student with frequent opportunities to meet new people.

14. Be careful to avoid embarrassing the student by giving the student orders.

15. Treat the student with respect. Talk in an objective manner at all times.

16. Make positive comments about school and the importance of school.

17. Allow the student to attempt something new in private before doing it in front of others.

18. Evaluate the appropriateness of the task to determine (a) if the task is too easy, (b) if the task is too difficult, and (c) if the length of time scheduled to complete the task is adequate.

19. Communicate with parents, agencies, or the appropriate parties to inform them of the problem, determine the cause of the problem, and consider possible solutions to the problem.

20. Communicate with the parents (e.g., notes home, phone calls, etc.) to share information concerning the student's progress. The parents may reinforce the student at home for showing an interest in participating in school activities.

21. Do not criticize when correcting the student; be honest yet supportive. Never cause the student to feel badly about himself/herself.

22. Write a contract with the student specifying what behavior is expected (e.g., showing an interest and participating in school activities) and what reinforcement will be made available when the terms of the contract have been met.

23. Reinforce those students in the classroom who show an interest and participate in school activities.

24. Establish classroom rules:
- Work on-task.
- Remain in your seat.
- Finish task.
- Meet task expectations.
- Raise your hand.

Review rules often. Reinforce students for following rules.

25. Speak with the student to explain (a) what the student is doing wrong (e.g., failing to show an interest and participate in school activities) and (b) what the student should be doing (e.g., showing an interest and participating in school activities).

26. Reinforce the student for showing an interest and participating in school activities: (a) give the student a tangible reward (e.g., classroom privileges, line leading, passing out materials, five minutes free time, etc.) or (b) give the student an intangible reward (e.g., praise, handshake, smile, etc.).

27. Investigate the student's eating habits and the amount of rest he/she is getting outside of school.

28. Reinforce the student for showing an interest and participating in school activities based on the length of time he/she can be successful. As the student demonstrates success, gradually increase the length of time required for reinforcement.

42 Avoids or has difficulty discussing personal problems

Goals:

1. The student will discuss personal problems with teachers, guidance counselors, school psychologists, or social workers.

Objectives:

1. The student will verbally respond to ___ out of ___ questions asked by the teacher, guidance counselor, school psychologist, social worker, etc.
2. The student will interact with the teacher, guidance counselor, school psychologist, social worker, etc., ___ times per day. (Gradually increase expectations as the student demonstrates success.)
3. The student will initiate ___ interaction(s) with the teacher, guidance counselor, school psychologist, social worker, etc., per day. (Gradually increase expectations as the student demonstrates success.)
4. The student will interact for ___ minutes per day with the teacher, guidance counselor, school psychologist, social worker, etc. (Gradually increase expectations as the student demonstrates success.)

Interventions:

1. Speak with the student to explain what he/she should be doing to deal with personal problems (e.g., talking with teachers, etc.).

2. Write a contract with the student specifying what behavior is expected (e.g., asking to talk with the teacher, etc.) when faced with personal problems.

3. Provide the student with adequate opportunities (e.g., free time, scheduled conferences, etc.) to discuss personal problems with teacher, guidance counselor, school psychologist, or social worker.

4. Make certain the student understands the role of the counselor, school psychologist, or social worker in discussing personal problems with students.

5. Have the student join a group which meets to discuss personal problems.

6. Communicate with the student as often as opportunities permit, to detect the student's need to talk about personal problems.

7. Have the teacher, guidance counselor, school psychologist, or social worker interact with the student from a distance, gradually decreasing the distance until a close proximity is achieved (e.g., a degree of familiarity).

8. Arrange for one-to-one interactions with teacher, guidance counselor, school psychologist, or social worker.

9. Choose a peer to model discussing personal problems with a teacher, guidance counselor, school psychologist, or social worker for the student.

10. Evaluate the appropriateness of expecting the student to communicate his/her personal problems to teachers, guidance counselors, school psychologist, or social worker.

11. Maintain mobility throughout the classroom to determine the student's needs.

12. Have the student run errands which will require frequent interactions with teachers, etc., (e.g., delivering attendance reports, taking messages to other teachers, etc.).

13. Demonstrate accepting behavior and interest in the student's personal problems (e.g., willingness to help others, making criticisms constructive and positive, demonstrating confidentiality in personal matters, etc.).

14. Communicate to the student that he/she is a worthwhile individual.

15. Teach the student communication skills (e.g., requesting a conference with teacher, guidance counselor, school psychologist, or social worker, expressing personal problems in written and/or verbal form, etc.).

16. Direct the student to communicate his/her personal problems to other personnel in the educational environment (e.g., guidance counselor, school psychologist, social worker, etc.).

17. Communicate with the appropriate personnel (e.g., guidance counselor, school psychologist, social worker) to inform them of the problem, determine the cause of the problem, and consider possible solutions to the problem.

18. Recognize the student's need to communicate his/her personal problems (e.g., facial expressions, gestures, inactivity, self-deprecating comments, etc.).

19. Teach the student appropriate verbalization for problem resolution as an alternative (e.g., "Let's talk about it." "I have some questions." "I have this problem." "Is it normal to feel like...?").

20. Teach the student skills in maintaining conversations with a teacher, guidance counselor, school psychologist, or social worker (e.g., asking questions, listening while the other person speaks, making eye contact, head nodding, making comments which relate to what the other person has said, etc.).

21. Discuss your concerns about the student's behavior with other professionals to determine if further investigation is warranted (e.g., abuse or neglect).

22. Take the time to listen so the student realizes your concern is genuine.

23. Encourage those persons with whom the student has contact (teachers, guidance counselors, school psychologist, or social worker) to offer their help with the student's personal problems instead of expecting the student to approach them.

24. Encourage the student to keep a journal or diary of his/her personal problems which may or may not be shared with the appropriate professional depending on the student's preference.

25. Find a discussion group the student can join which would address sensitive topics (e.g., divorce, death, unemployment, alcohol or drug abuse, abuse, neglect, etc.).

26. Determine an individual(s) in the school environment with whom the student would most want to share personal problems (e.g., custodian, librarian, resource teacher, principal, etc.). Allow the student to spend time with the individual(s) each day.

27. Explain that the personal problems or worries, while legitimate, are not unusual for students (e.g., everyone worries about tests, grades, etc.).

28. Make the necessary adjustments in the environment to prevent the student from suffering from personal problems (e.g., make certain the student is getting enough to eat, is appropriately clothed, etc.).

29. Avoid discussion of topics sensitive to the student (e.g., divorce, death, unemployment, alcoholism, etc.).

30. Provide the student with opportunities for special project responsibilities, leadership, etc.

31. Provide as many enjoyable activities as possible.

43 Becomes pale, may vomit, or pass out when anxious or frightened

Goals:

1. The student will reduce the number of times he/she becomes pale, vomits, or passes out.
2. The student will react in an appropriate manner when anxious or frightened.
3. The student will deal with anxiety or fright in an appropriate manner.

Objectives:

1. The student will reduce the number of times he/she becomes pale, vomits, or passes out by ___% when anxious or frightened. (Gradually increase expectations as the student demonstrates success.)
2. The student will react in an appropriate manner when anxious or frightened on ___out of ___trials.
3. The student will deal with anxiety or fright in an appropriate manner on ___out of ___trials.
4. The student will temporarily remove himself/herself from anxiety or fright-provoking situations on ___ out of ___ trials.
5. The student will engage in relaxation activities when he/she is anxious or frightened on ___out of ___ trials.
6. The student will prepare for assignments, tests, or quizzes on ___out of ___trials.
7. The student will communicate his/her anxiety or fright to the teacher on ___out of ___trials.

Interventions:

1. Reinforce the student for eating a nutritional lunch at school.

2. Discuss concerns with other professionals to determine if further investigation is warranted.

3. Take the time to listen so the student realizes your concern and interest in him/her is genuine.

4. Identify individuals the student may contact if his/her symptoms persist (e.g., guidance counselor, school nurse, social worker, school psychologist, parents, etc.).

5. Provide the student with as many social and academic successes as possible.

6. Prevent frustrating or anxiety-producing situations from occurring (e.g., give the student tasks only on his/her ability level, give the student only those number of tasks which can be tolerated in one sitting, reduce social interactions which stimulate the student to become angry or upset, etc.).

7. Provide the student with success-oriented tasks. The expectation is that success will result in more positive attitudes and perceptions toward self and environment.

8. Provide the student with positive feedback which indicates that he/she is successful, competent, important, valuable, etc.

9. Teach the student problem-solving skills: (a) identify the problem, (b) identify goals and objectives, (c) develop strategies, (d) develop a plan for action, and (e) carry out the plan.

10. Determine which activities the student most enjoys and include those activities as much as possible in the daily routine.

11. Provide the student with opportunities to rest if necessary.

12. Have the parents reinforce the student at home for a balanced program of nutrition, rest, and exercise.

13. Arrange alternative lunches for the student at school (e.g., bring lunch from home, eat off campus, suggest an additional entree from the cafeteria, etc.).

14. Determine that the physical symptom is not the result of a medical problem, neglect, abuse, or drug use.

15. Reduce the emphasis on competition. High levels of competition or repeated failure may result in physical symptoms such as paleness, vomiting, etc.

16. Emphasize individual success or progress rather than comparing performance to other students.

17. Communicate with the parents (e.g., notes home, phone calls, etc.) to share information concerning the student's progress. The parents may reinforce the student at home for dealing with problems in appropriate ways at school.

18. Encourage the student to identify problems which result in paleness, vomiting, etc., and act on those problems to resolve their influence.

19. Encourage the student to take responsibility for assignments and obligations in an ongoing fashion rather than waiting until the night before or the day the assignment is due.

20. Help the student recognize problems that are within his/her ability to deal with and not to worry needlessly about situations over which the student has no control.

21. Explain, if appropriate, that some concerns or worries, while legitimate, are not unusual for students (e.g., everyone worries about tests, grades, etc.).

22. Offer to provide extra academic help for the student when he/she experiences a problem that interferes with his/her academic performance.

23. Do not force the student to do something that he/she is not completely comfortable doing.

24. Be careful to avoid embarrassing the student by giving him/her orders, demands, etc., in front of others.

25. Maintain trust and confidentiality with the student at all times.

26. Allow the student to attempt something new in private before doing so in front of others.

27. Go with the student or have someone else accompany the student to an activity the student may be trying to avoid. If something unpleasant is causing the student to pretend to be sick, do all you can to change the situation.

28. Teach the student appropriate ways to communicate displeasure, anger, frustration, etc.

29. Do not force the student to interact with others.

30. Make sure you express your feelings in a socially acceptable way.

44 Blames self for situations beyond his/her control

Goals:

1. The student will demonstrate realistic, objective self-appraisal.

Objectives:

1. The student will make _____ positive statement(s) about himself/herself per day. (Gradually increase expectations as the student demonstrates success.)
2. The student will demonstrate the ability to accept mistakes by refraining from crying, making negative self-statements, etc., on ___ out of ___ trials.
3. The student will demonstrate the ability to refrain from expecting perfection on his/her own part, by working on a specific task for a realistic amount of time on ___ out of ___ trials.
4. Given five situations over which the student has control and five situations over which he/she has no control, the student will correctly identify ___ of which he/she either has control or no control.
5. The student will make an accurate appraisal of his/her performance, at the end of each activity, on ___ out of ___ trials.

Interventions:

1. Explain to the student that he/she should be happy with his/her own best effort rather than perfection.

2. Reinforce the student for accepting errors that he/she makes.

3. Speak with the student to explain (a) what he/she is doing wrong (e.g., being overly critical of himself/herself) and (b) what he/she should be doing (e.g., being more constructive in self-criticism when evaluating himself/herself).

4. Reward others for accepting errors they make.

5. Write a contract with the student specifying what behavior is expected (e.g., accepting his/her own best effort) and what reinforcement will be made available when the terms of the contract have been met.

6. Evaluate the appropriateness of the task to determine (a) if the task is too easy, (b) if the task is too difficult, and (c) if the length of time scheduled for the task is adequate.

7. Reinforce the student for improvement rather than expecting excellence.

8. Recognize the student often and in various settings (e.g., hallways, cafeteria, etc.).

9. Provide the student with positive feedback which indicates he/she is successful, competent, important, valuable, etc.

10. Provide the student with success-oriented tasks (i.e., the expectation is that success will result in more positive attitudes and perceptions toward self and environment).

11. Provide the student with as many social and academic successes as possible.

12. Make the necessary adjustments in the environment to prevent the student from experiencing stress, frustration, etc.

13. Choose a peer to help the student with class assignments, homework, etc.

14. Emphasize individual differences and that everyone has strengths and weaknesses.

15. Reduce the emphasis on competition and perfection. Repeated failure may result in unwarranted self-blame or self-criticism.

16. Encourage the student to refrain from comparing his/her performance to other students' performances and emphasize personal improvement (e.g., maintain records of own progress rather than comparing work to others).

17. Provide the student with evidence of his/her ability in order that he/she might better understand that self-blame/criticism is unwarranted.

18. Deliver praise and constructive criticism consistently to all students.

19. Reduce activities which might threaten the student (e.g., announcing test score ranges or test scores aloud, making students read aloud in class, emphasizing the success of a particular student(s), etc.).

20. Call on the student when he/she will most likely be able to answer correctly.

21. Have the student regularly record his/her own progress to have tangible evidence of success.

22. Encourage the student to act as a peer tutor so he/she may recognize his/her own strengths and abilities.

23. When accidents occur, make "clean up" a group responsibility to convey the idea that we all make mistakes and accidents are common to all of us.

Reminder: Make certain that the self-blame or self-criticism is in fact unwarranted.

45 Complains of physical discomfort

Goal:

1. The student will complain of physical discomfort only when legitimate physical discomfort exists.

Objectives:

1. The student will complain of physical discomfort only when appropriate.
2. The student will complain of physical discomfort only when in need of assistance.

Interventions:

1. Determine that the physical discomfort is being used as an excuse to escape situations and is not the result of a medical problem, neglect, or abuse.

2. Reinforce the student for engaging in appropriate behavior: (a) give the student a tangible reward (e.g., classroom privileges, line leading, passing out materials, five minutes free time, etc.) or (b) give the student an intangible reward (e.g., praise, handshake, smile, etc.).

3. Speak with the student to explain (a) what he/she is doing wrong (e.g., frequently complaining) and (b) what he/she should be doing (e.g., reporting only legitimate discomfort).

4. Evaluate the appropriateness of tasks to determine (a) if the task is too easy, (b) if the task is too difficult, and (c) if the length of time scheduled for the task is adequate.

5. Provide the student with positive feedback that indicates that he/she is successful, competent, important, valuable, etc.

6. Structure the environment so time does not permit the student to dwell on real or imagined physical discomfort.

7. Give the student additional responsibilities (e.g., chores, errands, etc.) to keep him/her actively involved and to keep his/her mind off any physical discomfort, real or imagined.

8. Reinforce the student for the length of time between physical discomfort complaints; gradually increase the length of time between reinforcements.

9. Communicate with the parents (e.g., notes home, phone calls, etc.). The parents may reinforce the student at home for engaging in activities without complaints of physical discomfort at school.

10. Write a contract with the student specifying what behavior is expected (e.g., participating in classroom activities without complaining of physical discomfort) and what reinforcement will be made available when the terms of the contract have been met.

11. Communicate with parents, agencies, or the appropriate parties to inform them of the problem, determine the cause of the problem, and consider possible solutions to the problem.

12. Have the student record and chart his/her own appropriate behavior (e.g., for participating in classroom activities without complaints of physical discomfort).

13. Choose a peer to engage in recreational activities with the student to develop a friendship.

14. Provide the student with as many high-interest activities as possible to keep him/her from dwelling on physical discomfort, real or imagined.

15. Make certain that reinforcement is not inadvertently given for complaints of physical discomfort (e.g., allowing the student to leave the room, avoid assignments, leave school, etc.).

16. Seek student input in planning curriculum and extra-curricular activities, etc.

17. Reduce the emphasis on competition. Repeated failure may cause the student to use complaints of physical discomfort to avoid competitive situations.

18. Provide the student with a selection of assignments and require him/her to choose a minimum number from the total amount (e.g., present the student with ten academic tasks from which he/she must finish six that day).

19. Teach the student to be happy with his/her own best effort rather than perfection (e.g., reduce the emphasis on competition; help the student realize that success is individually defined).

20. Allow the student adequate time to prepare for activities (i.e., allow the student to ease into activities rather than require immediate performance).

21. Follow less desirable activities with more desirable activities.

22. Explain to the student that work not done during work time must be done during other times (e.g., recreational time, break time, after school, etc.).

23. Provide the student with as many success-oriented activities as possible.

46 Creates imaginary or fantasy situations in an attempt to escape from or avoid reality

Goals:

1. The student will deal with reality without relying on imaginary or fantasy situations as a means of escape.
2. The student will refer only to actual experiences.
3. The student will be in touch with the reality of his/her environment.

Objectives:

1. The student's statements will be realistic for the situation on ___ out of ___ trials.
2. The student will make statements that are factual on ___ out of ___ trials.
3. The student will make statements that are based on reality on ___ out of ___ trials.
4. The student will relate actual experiences on ___ out of ___ trials.
5. The student's statements will be socially appropriate for the situation on ___ out of ___ trials.
6. The student will engage in a conversation without making references to imaginary or fantasy situations on ___ out of ___ trials.

Interventions:

1. Reduce the emphasis on competition. Competitive activities may cause the student to create imaginary or fantasy situations to escape from or avoid reality.

2. Emphasize individual successes or progress rather than winning or "beating" other students.

3. Interact frequently with the student to decrease the opportunities for the student to engage in imaginary or fantasy situations.

4. Separate the student from peers who may stimulate him/her to become anxious or excited and cause him/her to feel the need to escape from or avoid reality.

5. Deliver a predetermined signal (e.g., touch on the shoulder, hand signal) when he/she is engaging in imaginary and fantasy situations.

6. Assess the situations in which the student creates fantasy or imaginary situations. Based on these observations, determine ways to prevent situations which stimulate the student to create fantasy or imaginary situations to avoid or escape from reality.

7. Try various groupings to determine the situation in which the student is most comfortable.

8. Provide the student with many social and academic successes.

9. Take time to talk with the student so the student realizes your interest in him/her is genuine.

10. Teach/demonstrate methods for dealing with problems early to prevent problems from becoming overwhelming.

11. Provide the student with as many positive interactions as possible (e.g., recognize the student, greet the student, compliment his/her attire, etc.).

12. Structure the situations in which the student relates actual experiences (e.g., who, what, when, where, why, and how).

13. Encourage the student to use problem-solving skills: (a) identify the problem, (b) identify goals and objectives, (c) develop strategies, (d) develop a plan for action, and (e) carry out the plan.

14. Make certain that reinforcement is not given for inappropriate behavior (e.g., attending to the student only when he/she is creating fantasy or imaginary situations).

15. Make certain consequences for both appropriate and inappropriate behavior are consistent.

16. Encourage and assist the student in joining extracurricular activities, clubs, etc.

17. Provide the student with positive feedback which indicates that he/she is successful, competent, important, respected, etc.

18. Identify individuals the student may contact concerning his/her need to escape from or avoid reality (e.g., guidance counselor, school nurse, social worker, school psychologist, etc.).

19. Assign additional responsibilities to the student (e.g., chores, errands, etc.) to give him/her a feeling of success or accomplishment.

20. Structure the environment so the student does not have time to dwell on real or imagined problems.

21. Help the student identify how he/she would like things in the environment and work with the student toward those goals.

22. Teach the student alternative ways to deal with demands, challenges, and pressures in his/her environment (e.g., deal with problems when they arise, practice self-control at all times, share problems or concerns with others, etc.).

23. Teach the student alternative ways to communicate his/her desire to escape from or avoid reality (communicate in writing, create a puppet show, etc.).

24. Avoid topics, situations, etc., which remind the student of unpleasant experiences or problems (e.g., divorce, death, unemployment, alcoholism, etc.).

25. Avoid putting the student in a situation where he/she might be stimulated to create fantasy or imaginary situations to escape from or avoid reality.

26. Give the student some decision-making power (e.g., seating assignment, order of tasks, daily schedule, etc.).

27. Help the student choose activities that do not cause anger, frustration, anxiety, etc. Encourage conversations/statements which are factual and based on reality.

28. Communicate with parents, agencies, or the appropriate parties to inform them of the problem, determine the cause of the problem, and consider possible solutions to the problem.

29. Communicate with the parents (e.g., notes home, phone calls, etc.) to share information concerning the student's progress. The parents may reinforce the student at home for dealing with reality without referring to fantasy or imaginary situations.

30. Reinforce the student for making realistic, factual statements based on the number of times he/she can be successful. As the student demonstrates success, gradually increase the number of times required for reinforcement.

31. Speak with the student to explain (a) that you recognize that he/she is frustrated, anxious, frightened, etc., and (b) appropriate ways to deal with frustration, anxiety, fear, etc.

32. Reinforce the student for dealing with reality in an appropriate manner (e.g., verbally stating his/her feelings, problem-solving, etc.): (a) give the student a tangible reward (e.g., classroom privileges, line leading, passing out materials, five minutes free time, etc.) or (b) give the student an intangible reward (e.g., praise, handshake, smile, etc.) for dealing with reality appropriately.

33. Provide the student with alternative activities to perform in case some activities cause unhappiness, anxiety, excitement, etc.

34. Make sure that the student understands that when statements are based on fantasy or imaginary situations, people may not believe him/her if it is ever necessary (e.g., *The Boy Who Cried Wolf*).

35. Communicate with the student to differentiate between factual information and the story that he/she related.

36. Provide satisfying real-life experiences for the student so he/she does not feel the need to create fantasy or imaginary situations to make up for a lack of satisfying experiences.

37. Following a satisfying real-life experience (e.g., field trip) have the student practice relating the actual experience.

38. Reduce stressful situations which may cause the student to feel the need to escape from or avoid reality.

39. Remove the student from the group or activity until he/she can deal with reality.

40. Explain to the student that creating fantasy or imaginary situations is natural but attempting to escape from or avoid reality will not change the problem.

41. Provide the student with preferred responsibilities throughout the school.

42. Provide an opportunity for the student to express fantasy and imaginary situations in creative ways (e.g., puppet shows, painting, drawing, creative writing, etc.).

43. Do not put the student in social situations that he/she is not able to handle (e.g., everyone else tells about their vacation, but he/she did not take a vacation).

44. Intervene early to interrupt trips into fantasy (e.g., hand signals, touch on the shoulder).

45. Speak to the student about why he/she creates fantasy or imaginary situations to escape from or avoid reality. The student may have the most accurate perception.

46. Deal with problems early to avoid allowing the student to become so stimulated that he/she begins to fantasize or imagine unrealistic situations.

47 Cries in response to personal or school situations

Goals:

1. The student will respond appropriately to personal experiences.
2. The student will respond appropriately to school experiences.

Objectives:

1. The student will respond appropriately to personal experiences on ___out of ___trials.
2. The student will respond appropriately to school experiences on ___out of ___trials.
3. The student will refrain from whining or crying in response to personal experiences on __out of __trials.
4. The student will refrain from whining or crying in response to school experiences on ___out of ___ trials.
5. The student will talk with the teacher when he/she has difficulty handling a personal experience on ___ out of ___ trials.
6. The student will talk with the teacher when he/she has difficulty handling a school experience on ___ out of ___ trials.
7. The student will continue to engage in an activity when he/she experiences difficulty on ___out of ___ trials.
8. The student will be actively involved in assigned activities for ___minutes at a time.

Interventions:

1. Modify the environment to reduce situations which cause the student to be unhappy (e.g., if the student is upset by losing in competitive activities, reduce the number of competitive activities).

2. Share concerns with the administration and seek referral to an agency for investigation of possible abuse or neglect.

3. Try various groupings to determine the situation in which the student is most comfortable.

4. Provide the student with many social and academic successes.

5. Take time to talk with the student so the student realizes your interest in him/her is genuine.

6. Teach/demonstrate methods for dealing with problems early to prevent problems from becoming overwhelming.

7. Explain to the student that feelings of unhappiness are natural, but that there is an appropriate length of time for public displays of that emotion.

8. Teach the student to be satisfied with his/her own best effort rather than perfection.

9. When natural consequences occur as the result of the student's display of unhappiness, point them out to the student (e.g., peers prefer not to interact with him/her).

10. Provide the student with as many positive interactions as possible (e.g., recognize the student, call the student by name, compliment his/her attire, etc.).

11. Make certain that positive reinforcement is not inadvertently given for inappropriate behavior.

12. Make certain that consequences for inappropriate behavior are consistent.

13. Encourage and assist the student in joining extracurricular activities, clubs, etc.

14. Remove the student from the peer(s) who is causing his/her unhappiness.

15. Discourage the student from engaging in those activities which cause his/her unhappiness.

16. Give the student additional responsibilities (e.g., chores, errands, etc.) to give him/her a feeling of success or accomplishment.

17. Encourage the student to use problem-solving skills: (a) identify the problem, (b) identify goals and objectives, (c) develop strategies, (d) develop a plan for action, and (e) carry out the plan.

18. Identify individuals the student may contact concerning his/her unhappiness (e.g., guidance counselor, school nurse, social worker, school psychologist, etc.).

19. Structure the environment so the student does not have time to dwell on real or imagined problems.

20. Maintain anecdotal records of the student's behavior to check for patterns or changes in behavior.

21. Teach the student alternative ways to express his/her unhappiness (e.g., talking, writing, creating, etc.).

22. Provide the student with a quiet place to relax when becoming upset. This is not to be used as a form of punishment but as an opportunity to function more successfully in the environment.

23. Do not criticize. When correcting the student, be honest yet supportive. Never cause the student to feel badly about himself/herself.

24. Treat the student with respect. Talk in an objective manner at all times.

25. Be careful to avoid embarrassing the student by giving orders, demands, etc., in front of other students.

26. Make positive comments about school and the student.

27. Teach the student acceptable ways to communicate displeasure, anger, frustration, etc.

28. Make certain you express your feelings in a socially acceptable way.

29. Make certain the student is allowed to voice an opinion in a situation to avoid becoming angry or upset.

30. Communicate with parents, agencies, or the appropriate parties to inform them of the problem, determine the cause of the problem, and consider possible solutions to the problem.

31. Evaluate the appropriateness of the task to determine (a) if the task is too easy, (b) if the task is too difficult, and (c) if the length of time scheduled to complete the task is adequate.

32. Communicate with the parents (e.g., notes home, phone calls, etc.) to share information concerning the student's progress. The parents may reinforce the student at home for dealing with unhappiness in an appropriate manner at school.

33. Write a contract with the student specifying what behavior is expected (e.g., dealing with unhappiness in an appropriate manner) and what reinforcement will be made available when the terms of the contract have been met.

34. Remove the student from the group or activity until he/she can demonstrate appropriate behavior and self-control.

35. Reinforce the student for dealing with unhappiness in an appropriate manner based on the length of time the student can be successful. As the student demonstrates success, gradually increase the amount of time required for reinforcement.

36. Reinforce those students in the classroom who deal with unhappiness in an appropriate manner.

37. Establish classroom rules:
- Work on-task.
- Remain in your seat.
- Finish task.
- Meet task expectations.
- Raise your hand.

Review rules often. Reinforce students for following rules.

38. Reinforce the student for demonstrating appropriate behavior in response to unpleasant situations (e.g., failure, peer pressure, disappointment, losing in competition, etc.): (a) give the student a tangible reward (e.g., classroom privileges, line leading, passing out materials, five minutes free time, etc.) or (b) give the student an intangible reward (e.g., praise, handshake, smile, etc.).

39. Speak with the student to explain (a) that you recognize he/she is unhappy and (b) appropriate ways for dealing with his/her unhappiness (e.g., by talking, problem solving, etc.).

48 Deliberately hurts self or damages own property or clothing

Goals:

1. The student will demonstrate self-regard.
2. The student does not demonstrate self-destructive behaviors.

Objectives:

1. The student will refrain from engaging in self-destructive behaviors when experiencing stress, anger, frustration, etc., during ___ out of ___ situations.
2. The student will care for his/her clothing in an appropriate manner when experiencing stress, anger, unhappiness, etc., during ___ out of ___ situations.
3. The student will care for personal property in an appropriate manner when experiencing stress, anger, anxiety, etc., during ___ out of ___ situations.
4. The student will walk away from stressful, anger-producing situations on ___ out of ___ trials.
5. The student will seek assistance from the teacher when experiencing anger, frustration, hopelessness, etc., during ___ out of ___ trials.
6. The student will refrain from tearing his/her clothing when angry, upset, frustrated, etc., on ___ out of ___ trials.
7. The student will refrain from damaging personal property when angry, upset, anxious, etc., on ___ out of ___ trials.
8. The student will refrain from demonstrating self-destructive behaviors upon receiving constructive criticism from the teacher on ___ out of ___ trials.

Interventions:

1. Remove the student from the group or activity until he/she can demonstrate appropriate behavior and self-control.

2. Write a contract with the student specifying what behavior is expected (e.g., not engaging in self-destructive behavior) and what reinforcement will be made available when the terms of the contract have been met.

3. Communicate with parents (e.g., notes home, phone calls, etc.) to share information concerning the student's progress. The parents may reinforce the student at home for appropriate behavior at school.

4. Interact frequently with the student to prevent self-destructive behavior by meeting the student's needs as they occur.

5. Prevent frustrating or anxiety-producing situations from occurring (e.g., give the student tasks on his/her ability level, give the student the number of tasks that can be tolerated in one sitting, stop social situations which stimulate the student to become self-destructive, etc.).

6. Evaluate the appropriateness of the task to determine (a) if the task is too easy, (b) if the task is too difficult, and (c) if the length of time scheduled to complete the task is adequate.

7. Maintain visibility to and from the student. The teacher should be able to see the student, and the student should be able to see the teach. Make eye contact possible at all times.

8. Facilitate on-task behavior by providing a full schedule of daily events. Prevent lag time from occurring when the student will be free to engage in self-destructive behavior.

9. Remove from the environment any object which the student may use to hurt himself/herself.

10. Provide the student with a quiet place to work (e.g., carrel or study area).

11. Provide the student with positive feedback which indicates he/she is successful, important, respected, etc.

12. Maintain a positive/calm environment (e.g., deliver positive comments, acknowledgment of successes, quiet communications, etc.).

13. Reduce the emphasis on competition. Repeated failure may result in anger and frustration which may cause the student to try to hurt himself/herself.

14. Maintain consistent expectations to reduce the likelihood of the student hurting himself/herself.

15. Allow the student to have an input relative to making decisions (e.g., changing activities, choosing activities, deciding length of activities, etc.).

16. Provide the student with a selection of optional activities to be performed (e.g., if an activity results in self-destructive behaviors, an optional activity can be substituted).

17. Teach the student appropriate ways to deal with anxiety, frustration, and anger (e.g., move away from the stimulus, verbalize unhappiness, choose another activity, etc.).

18. Teach the student problem-solving skills: (a) identify the problem, (b) identify goals and objectives, (c) develop strategies, (d) develop a plan for action, and (e) carry out the plan.

19. Maintain a consistent daily routine.

20. Avoid discussions or prevent stimuli in the environment which remind the student of unpleasant experiences/sensitive topics (e.g., divorce, death, unemployment, alcoholism, etc.).

21. Do not criticize. When correcting the student, be honest yet supportive. Never cause the student to feel badly about himself/herself.

22. Intervene early when there is a problem to prevent more serious problems from occurring.

23. Make certain the student does not become involved in overstimulating activities.

24. Treat the student with respect. Talk in an objective manner at all times.

25. Teach the student appropriate ways to communicate displeasure, anger, frustrations, etc.

26. Make sure you express your feelings in a socially acceptable way.

27. Teach the student to think before acting (e.g., ask himself/herself, "What is happening?" "What am I doing?" "What should I do?" "What will be best for me?").

28. Make certain the student is allowed to voice an opinion in a situation to avoid becoming angry or upset.

29. Talk to the student about ways of handling situations successfully without conflict (e.g., walk away from a situation, change to another activity, ask for help, etc.).

30. Reinforce the student for demonstrating appropriate behavior based on the length of time the student can be successful. As the student demonstrates success, gradually increase the amount of time required for reinforcement.

31. Reinforce those students in the classroom who engage in appropriate behaviors.

32. Establish classroom rules:
- Work on-task.
- Remain in your seat.
- Finish task.
- Meet task expectations.
- Raise your hand.

Review rules often. Reinforce students for following rules.

33. Speak with the student to explain (a) what the student is doing wrong (e.g., hurting self) and (b) what the student should be doing (e.g., talking about the situation, demonstrating self-control, problem-solving, etc.).

34. Reinforce the student for engaging in appropriate behavior: (a) give the student a tangible reward (e.g., classroom privileges, line leading, passing out materials, five minutes free time, etc.) or (b) give the student an intangible reward (e.g., praise, handshake, smile, etc.).

Note: Help the student accept the fact that self-improvement is more important than getting the highest grade in the class, making all A's, being the first one done with an assignment, etc., by reinforcing and grading on the basis of self-improvement.

49 Demonstrates an increase in appetite

Goals:

1. The student will govern food consumption based on medically recommended need rather than impulsivity.

Objectives:

1. The student will follow a balanced diet to meet his/her individual requirements and weight maintenance needs on ____ out of ____ trials.
2. The student will engage in exercises/physical activities to meet his/her own individual requirements and weight maintenance on ____ out of ____ trials.
3. The student will manage weight maintenance within his/her medically recommended range on ____ out of ____ trials.

Interventions:

1. Reinforce the student for positively managing an increase in appetite: (a) give the student a tangible reward (e.g., classroom privileges, line leading, passing out materials, five minutes free time, etc.) or (b) give the student an intangible reward (e.g., praise, handshake, smile, etc.).

2. Provide the student with time and encouragement to establish rapport. Any vast change in behavior, such as sudden, rapid weight gain or loss, withdrawn behavior, and/or other behavior changes may warrant the need of additional support.

3. Do not force the student to participate in weight-maintenance activities. It is more important to offer opportunities for positive reinforcement for participation.

4. Communicate with parents (e.g., notes home, phone calls, etc.) to share information concerning the student's progress with weight maintenance at school. The parents may reinforce the student at home.

5. Assist the student in the development of coping strategies for stress which do not include eating (e.g., exercising frequently, developing a hobby, finding means of self-expression through dance or writing, becoming involved in an individual or team sport, etc.).

6. Help the student develop a list of activities he/she finds enjoyable (e.g., purchasing new clothes, seeing a movie, going to a dance, etc.). The student may then refer to this list for reinforcement after he/she has correctly attempted weight-maintenance activities.

7. Encourage the student to weigh himself/herself throughout the week at a specified time of day. The student should not weigh himself/herself more than once in a given day.

8. Encourage the student to drink non-caloric, decaffeinated fluids (e.g., juices, water).

9. Encourage the development of positive self-concept in a classroom environment that is accepting of individual differences (e.g., overweight or underweight persons need not feel ostracized from the class).

10. Consult with medical professionals to determine if the student's increase in appetite is a result of a medical problem.

11. Provide the student with individually tailored ways of tracking progress with weight maintenance. This might include

(a) developing a daily/weekly schedule of activities the student could follow and check off (e.g., exercise, meals, snack times, etc.);
(b) helping the student develop a daily journal in which he/she logs meal and snack choices for his/her review; and
(c) assisting the student to develop a chart or graph of his/her weight gains/losses.

12. Encourage the student to drink eight ounces of water before eating a meal.

13. Encourage the student to eat healthy, non-caloric snacks such as fruit, air popped popcorn, etc. Snacks need to be tailored to individual dietetic need and should have medical approval.

14. The student may not have a realistic perception of himself/herself (e.g., he/she may view himself/herself as too fat, too thin, ugly, etc.). Encourage the student to find personal strengths and attributes (e.g., activities in which the student excels at school, a personal attribute such as hair or eye color, etc.).

15. When teaching the student strategies to control food consumption, teach and emphasize self-control rather than control by outside sources (e.g., teachers, parents, other sources of adult authority).

16. The student may feel failure from an inability to meet a hallmark of perfection. Encourage the student to view individual effort as more important by: (a) helping the student set and achieve meaningful, short-term goals (e.g., following his/her diet and exercise schedule for a week) and (b) making certain the student receives meaningful positive reinforcement following goal achievement.

17. The student may not feel he/she has been given an opportunity to make self-governing choices. Assist the student to identify choices he/she may make within realistic parameters (e.g., age, situation, etc.). Reinforce the student for making choices that benefit him/her without hurting others.

18. Help the student develop weight-management strategies that are based upon healthy eating habits (e.g., eating three balanced meals per day, eating healthy snacks, etc.) in lieu of unhealthy choices (e.g., fasting, going on unusual diets, etc.).

19. The student will need careful attention to what constitutes positive reinforcement. Social reinforcement that draws attention to the student in front of his/her classmates may actually punish (instead of promote) healthy weight maintenance if the student becomes embarrassed.

20. The student may not be able to view progress with behavioral changes and weight-maintenance skills in a short period of time. Assist the student to develop and reach short-term, behavioral objectives which progressively lead to long-term goal completion.

21. Make certain the student has the opportunity to learn how he/she is appreciated regardless of his/her weight.

22. When the student expresses concern about his/her weight, establish with him/her those positive steps he/she may choose right now.

23. Teach the student to identify his/her antecedents to overeating behavior. For example, the student may learn to recognize his/her tendency to eat when anxious (e.g., when watching a scary movie or when studying for a test). Once the problem situation is recognized by the student, work with him/her to develop positive coping strategies for use instead of continuous eating.

24. Encourage or reinforce others for participation in group weight-maintenance and exercise activities.

25. Demonstrate respect for the student's opinions, responses, suggestions, etc.

26. Provide the student with many social and academic successes.

27. Provide the student with positive feedback to indicate he/she is successful.

28. Present tasks in the most attractive, interesting manner possible.

29. Emphasize individual success or progress over winning or "beating" others.

30. Structure the environment so the student has many opportunities to succeed.

31. Supervise classroom activities closely so peers with whom the student interacts do not stimulate inappropriate behavior or ridicule.

32. Teach the student problem-solving skills so he/she is better equipped to manage potential problems (e.g., talking, walking away, calling upon an arbitrator, compromising, etc.). This may help the student feel better equipped to manage situations which provoke stress associated with overeating and/or undereating.

33. The student will appreciate constructive remarks and verbal praise in conversations away from the group and/or in a nonintrusive delivery style typical for an entire group. Loud, open remarks may do more harm than good regarding the promotion of any skills (especially social skills), for the student.

34. Provide the student with a variety of ways to develop rapport with instructor(s) (e.g., writing notes, talking about concerns privately, etc.).

35. Build positive self-concept among students by including the following approaches
  (a) offer opportunities for students to work together noncompetitively on class projects;
  (b) identify and sincerely compliment each student's unique contribution to group work when this will be perceived by the student as positive reinforcement; and
  (c) organize time to speak with students individually.

36. The student may benefit from (a) frequent opportunities to rehearse coping mechanisms the student and instructor have developed, (b) frequent opportunities for social success, and (c) gradual increases in activity participation expectations (e.g., passive, then active participation).

37. Encourage the student to develop and work toward his/her goals to self-manage his/her weight.

38. Give the student opportunities to use the positive replacement skills he/she is learning.

39. When developing a schedule, plan for highly reinforcing activities to follow less desirable activities.

40. Help the student identify the benefits of choosing to participate in scheduled weight- maintenance activities (e.g., diet, exercising).

41. The student may be overly self-critical when mistakes are made or progress is delayed. Help the student use problem-solving skills to address such concerns by identifying problems, developing solutions to try, and evaluating efforts.

42. Encourage the student to drink fluids while eating meals.

43. Encourage the student to chew each bite a prescribed number of times (e.g., 15 times) before swallowing to help slow eating pace.

50 Indicates that he/she is not happy through physical expression

Goals:
1. The student will handle anger, frustration, disappointment, anxiety, etc., in an appropriate manner.
2. The student will demonstrate self-control.
3. The student will not throw temper tantrums.

Objectives:
1. The student will handle anger, frustration, disappointment, anxiety, etc., in an appropriate manner on ___ out of ___ trials.
2. The student will demonstrate self-control when angry, frustrated, disappointed, anxious, etc., on ___ out of ___ trials.
3. The student will not throw temper tantrums when angry, frustrated, disappointed, anxious, etc., on ___ out of ___ trials.
4. The student will demonstrate appropriate ways in which to express his/her anger, frustration, disappointment, anxiety, etc., on ___ out of ___ trials.

Interventions:

1. Assess the situations in which the student throws temper tantrums. Based on these observations, determine ways to prevent situations which stimulate the student to throw temper tantrums.

2. Try various groupings to determine the situation in which the student is most comfortable.

3. Provide the student with many social and academic successes.

4. Take the time to talk with the student so the student realizes that your interest in him/her is genuine.

5. Teach/demonstrate methods for dealing with problems early to prevent problems from becoming overwhelming.

6. Encourage and help the student to make friends (e.g., pair the student with a peer and when that relationship is successful, introduce other peers).

7. Explain to the student that feelings of unhappiness are natural, but there is an appropriate length of time for public display of that emotion.

8. Make certain that consequences for both appropriate and inappropriate behavior are consistent.

9. When natural consequences occur as a result of the student's throwing temper tantrums, point them out to the student (e.g., peers prefer not to interact with him/her; property is damaged or destroyed, resulting in loss of use or costly replacement; etc.).

10. Provide the student with as many positive interactions as possible (e.g., recognize the student, greet the student, compliment his/her attire, etc.).

11. Encourage the student to use problem-solving skills: (a) identify the problem, (b) identify goals and objectives, (c) develop strategies, (d) develop a plan of action, and (e) carry out the plan.

12. Make certain that reinforcement is not inadvertently given for inappropriate behavior (e.g., attending to the student only when he/she throws a temper tantrum).

13. Provide the student with preferred responsibilities throughout the school environment.

14. Encourage and assist the student in joining extracurricular activities, clubs, etc.

15. Move the student away from the peer(s) who may be causing his/her unhappiness.

16. Discourage the student from engaging in those activities which cause him/her unhappiness.

17. Provide the student with positive feedback which indicates he/she is successful, competent, important, respected, etc.

18. Identify individuals the student may contact concerning his/her unhappiness (e.g., guidance counselor, school nurse, social worker, school psychologist, etc.).

19. Assign additional responsibilities to the student (e.g., chores, errands, etc.) to give him/ her a feeling of success or accomplishment.

20. Structure the environment so the student does not have time to dwell on real or imagined problems.

21. Help the student identify how he/she would like things in the environment and work with the student toward those goals.

22. Teach the student alternative ways to deal with demands, challenges, and pressures of the school-age experience (e.g., deal with problems when they arise, practice self-control at all times, share problems or concerns with others, etc.).

23. Help the student identify when he/she is getting upset so something can be done to help him/her calm down (e.g., walk away, talk about feelings in a socially acceptable way, seek help from an adult, etc.).

24. Teach the student alternative ways to communicate unhappiness (e.g., communicate in writing, verbally, etc.).

25. Avoid topics, situations, etc., which remind the student of unpleasant experiences or problems (e.g., divorce, death, unemployment, alcoholism, etc.).

26. Follow less desirable activities with more desirable activities.

27. Provide the student with alternative activities to perform in case some activities prove upsetting.

28. Give the student some decision-making power (e.g., seating assignment, order of tasks, daily schedule, etc.).

29. Reduce the emphasis on competition. Repeated failure may cause the student to throw a temper tantrum.

30. Help the student choose activities that do not cause anger, frustration, anxiety, etc.

31. Ignore the student's temper tantrums. Do not let the student have his/her way when crying.

32. Show the student how to control angry feelings when things do not go his/her way (e.g., count to ten, say the alphabet, etc.).

33. Make certain you do not give in to the student's temper tantrums because others are present. Maintain consistency at all times.

34. Write a contract with the student specifying what behavior is expected (e.g., dealing with unhappiness in an appropriate manner) and what reinforcement will be made available when the terms of the contract have been met.

35. Provide the student with alternative activities, games, etc., in case some activities prove upsetting.

36. Communicate with parents, agencies, or the appropriate parties to inform them of the problem, determine the cause of the problem, and consider possible solutions to the problem.

37. Evaluate the appropriateness of the task to determine (a) if the task is too easy, (b) if the task is too difficult, and (c) if the length of time scheduled to complete the task is adequate.

38. Communicate with the parents (e.g., notes home, phone calls, etc.) to share information concerning the student's progress. The parents may reinforce the student at home for dealing with unhappiness in an appropriate manner at school.

39. After telling the student that he/she cannot do or have something, explain the reason.

40. Remove the student from the group or activity until he/she can demonstrate appropriate behavior and self-control.

41. Reinforce the student for dealing with unhappiness in an appropriate manner based on the number of times he/she can be successful. As the student demonstrates success, gradually increase the number of times required for reinforcement.

42. Establish classroom rules:
- Work on-task.
- Remain in your seat.
- Finish task.
- Meet task expectations.
- Raise your hand.

Review rules often. Reinforce students for following rules.

43. Reinforce those students in the classroom who deal with unhappiness in an appropriate manner.

44. Speak with the student to explain (a) that you recognize that he/she is unhappy and (b) appropriate ways to deal with unhappiness.

45. Reinforce the student for dealing with unhappiness in an appropriate manner (e.g., verbally stating his/her unhappiness, problem solving, etc.): (a) give the student a tangible reward (e.g., classroom privileges, line leading, passing out materials, five minutes free time, etc.) or (b) give the student an intangible reward (e.g., praise, handshake, smile, etc.).

51 Demonstrates facial expression of sadness or displeasure

Goals:

1. The student will smile during typical classroom situations.
2. The student will demonstrate happiness during typical classroom situations.
3. The student will refrain from frowning, scowling, and looking unhappy during typical classroom situations.
4. The student will behave in a manner appropriate for the situation.

Objectives:

1. The student will smile when appropriate during ___ out of ___ typical classroom situations.
2. The student will demonstrate happiness during ___ out of ___ typical classroom situations.
3. The student will refrain from frowning, scowling, and looking unhappy during ___ out of ___ typical classroom situations.
4. The student will show emotion that is appropriate for the situation during ___ out of ___ occasions.
5. The student will demonstrate happiness by smiling, laughing, joking, etc., when appropriate during ___ out of ___ typical classroom situations.
6. The student will laugh or smile when humorous events or activities take place on ___ out of ___ trials.
7. The student will demonstrate emotion like that of his/her peers during ___ out of ___ typical classroom situations.

Interventions:

1. Share concerns with administration and seek referral to an agency for investigation of abuse or neglect.

2. Communicate your concern to the student.

3. Reinforce the student for engaging in appropriate behavior: (a) give the student a tangible reward (e.g., classroom privileges, line leading, passing out materials, five minutes free time, etc.) or (b) give the student an intangible reward (e.g., praise, handshake, smile, etc.).

4. Provide the student with success-oriented tasks (i.e., the expectation is that success will result in more positive attitudes and perceptions toward self and environment).

5. Choose a peer to engage in recreational activities with the student to develop a friendship.

6. Provide the student with positive feedback that indicates he/she is successful, competent, important, valuable, etc.

7. Give the student additional responsibilities (e.g., chores, errands, etc.) to give the student a feeling of success or accomplishment.

8. Identify individuals the student may contact with concerns or problems (e.g., guidance counselor, school nurse, social worker, school psychologist, etc.).

9. Create the most positive environment possible.

10. Seek the student's input in planning the curriculum and extracurricular activities, classes, etc., (i.e., attempt to include student preferences and favored activities).

11. Follow less desirable activities with more desirable activities throughout the day to maintain interest and variety.

12. Facilitate the development of friendships with peers (e.g., assign activities for the student involving peers, give the student and a peer joint responsibilities, etc.).

13. Do not punish the student for not participating in classroom activities.

14. Teach the student to be satisfied with personal best effort rather than insisting on perfection (e.g., reduce the emphasis on competition, help the student realize that success is individually defined).

15. De-emphasize arbitrary levels of success (i.e., rather than absolute excellence, progress of any amount should be considered a measure of success).

16. Respect the student's right to privacy when appropriate.

17. Take the time to listen so the student realizes that your concern/interest is genuine.

18. Maintain consistent interactions (e.g., do not provide extra attention when the student is demonstrating facial expressions of displeasure).

19. Ask the student why he/she frowns, scowls, or looks unhappy during typical classroom situations. The student may have the most accurate perception.

20. Communicate with parents, agencies, or the appropriate parties to inform them of the problem, determine the cause of the problem, and consider possible solutions to the problem.

21. Reduce emphasis on competition. Repeated failure will most likely contribute to the student's unhappiness.

22. Do not force the student to interact with individuals with whom he/she is not completely comfortable.

23. Treat the student with respect. Talk in an objective manner at all times.

24. Be careful to avoid embarrassing the student by giving him/her orders, demands, etc., in front of others.

25. Make positive comments about participating in school and special activities.

26. Go with the student or have someone else accompany the student to activities in which he/she may not want to participate. Gradually decrease the length of time you or someone else stays with the student.

27. Carefully consider those activities the student avoids. If something unpleasant is causing the student to not participate, try to change the situation.

28. Do not force the student to interact with others.

52 Seems unable or unwilling to communicate feelings or emotions to others

Goals:

1. The student will increase his/her interactions with peers.
2. The student will increase his/her interactions with teachers.

Objectives:

1. The student will verbally respond to ___ out of ___ questions asked by the teacher.
2. The student will interact with the teacher ___ times per day. (Gradually increase expectations as the student demonstrates success.)
3. The student will initiate ___ interaction(s) with the teacher per day. (Gradually increase expectations as the student demonstrates success.)
4. The student will interact for ___ minutes per day with the teacher. (Gradually increase expectations as the student demonstrates success.)
5. The student will interact with a peer for ___ minutes at a time.
6. The student will interact with a peer ___ times per day. (Gradually increase expectations as the student demonstrates success.)
7. The student will initiate ___ interaction(s) with a peer per day. (Gradually increase expectations as the student demonstrates success.)

Interventions:

1. Find a discussion group which the student could join to practice communication skills.

2. Teach the student appropriate positive verbal greetings (e.g., "Hi." "How are you doing?" "Good to see you." "Haven't seen you in a long time." etc.).

3. Teach the student appropriate positive verbal requests (e.g., "Please pass the paper." "May I be excused?" "Will you please help me?" etc.).

4. Teach the student appropriate positive ways to verbally indicate disagreement (e.g., "Excuse me." "I'm sorry, but I don't think that's correct." etc.).

5. Teach the student appropriate verbalization for problem resolution as an alternative (e.g., "Let's talk about it." "Let's compromise." "Let's see what would be fair for both of us." etc.).

6. Require the student to practice verbal communications with an identified number of teachers throughout the school day.

7. Provide the student with many social and academic successes.

8. Teach the student appropriate ways to communicate to teachers that a problem exists (e.g., "I do not understand the directions." "I was unable to complete my assignment." "I cannot find all of my materials." etc.).

9. Contact teachers with whom the student most often interacts to make certain that they model appropriate verbal communications for the student.

10. Determine an individual(s) in the school environment with whom the student would most want to converse (e.g., custodian, librarian, resource teacher, principal, older student, etc.). Allow the student to spend time with the individual(s) each day.

11. Spend some time each day talking with the student on an individual basis about his/her interests.

12. Use an alternative form of communication (e.g., puppet).

13. Make certain that all teachers interact with the student on a regular basis and use positive verbal communication when speaking to him/her.

14. Choose a peer to model communicating with teachers for the student.

15. Evaluate the appropriateness of expecting the student to communicate his/her feelings or emotions to teachers.

16. Maintain mobility throughout the classroom to determine the student's need to communicate.

17. Demonstrate accepting behavior and interest in the student (e.g., willingness to help others, making criticisms constructive and positive, demonstrating confidentiality in personal matters, etc.).

18. Communicate to the student that he/she is a worthwhile individual.

19. Call on the student often to encourage communication.

20. Teach the student communication skills (e.g., hand raising, expressing needs in written and/or verbal form, etc.).

21. Encourage the student to communicate with other personnel in the educational environment (e.g., school counselor, school psychologist, principal, etc.).

22. Communicate with parents to inform them of the problem, determine the cause of the problem, and solutions to the problem.

23. Recognize the student's attempts to communicate (e.g., facial expressions, gestures, inactivity, self-deprecating comments, etc.).

24. Speak with the student to explain that he/she should be communicating with the teacher.

25. Reinforce those students in the classroom who communicate with teachers.

26. Reinforce the student for communicating with teachers based on the length of time he/she can be successful. As the student demonstrates success, gradually increase the length of time required for reinforcement.

27. Write a contract with the student specifying what behavior is expected (e.g., sitting near the teacher, talking to the teacher, etc.).

28. Communicate with the parents (e.g., notes home, phone calls, etc.) to share information concerning the student's progress. The parents may reinforce the student at home for communicating with teachers at school.

29. Be certain to greet or recognize the student as often as possible (e.g., hallways, cafeteria, welcome to class, acknowledge a job well done, call the student by name, etc.).

30. Have the student run errands which will require communication with teachers (e.g., delivering attendance reports, taking messages to other teachers, etc.).

31. Interact with the student from a distance, gradually decreasing the distance until a close proximity is achieved (e.g., until a degree of familiarity is achieved).

32. Arrange for one-to-one, teacher/student interactions.

33. Speak with the student to explain that he/she should be communicating with peers.

34. Reinforce those students in the classroom who communicate with peers.

35. Reinforce the student for communicating with peers based on the length of time he/she can be successful. As the student demonstrates success, gradually increase the length of time required for reinforcement.

36. Write a contract with the student specifying what behavior is expected (e.g., sitting near another student, talking to another student, etc.) and what reinforcement will be made available when the terms of the contract have been met.

37. Communicate with the parents (e.g., notes home, phone calls, etc.) to share information concerning the student's progress. The parents may reinforce the student at home for communicating with peers at school.

38. Choose a peer to sit/work directly with the student (e.g., in different settings or activities such as art, music, P.E., on the bus, tutoring, group projects, running errands in the building, recess, etc.). When the student has become comfortable working with another student, gradually increase the size of the group.

39. Encourage or reward others for communicating with the student.

40. Give the student the responsibility of tutoring a peer.

41. Reduce the emphasis on competition. Failure may cause the student to be reluctant to communicate with peers.

42. Request that the student be the leader of a small group activity if he/she possesses mastery of skills or an interest in that area.

43. Try various groupings to determine the situation in which the student is most comfortable.

44. Assess the appropriateness of the social setting in relation to the student's ability to communicate with peers.

45. Assign the student to work with one or two peers on a long-term project (e.g., mural, bulletin board, report, etc.).

46. Create situations in which the student must communicate (e.g., returning completed assignments to students, proofreading other students' work, etc.).

47. Have the student work with a peer who is younger or smaller (e.g., choose a peer who would be the least threatening).

48. Choose a peer to model appropriate communication with peers for the student.

49. Determine the peer(s) the student would most prefer to communicate with and attempt to facilitate the communication.

50. Have the student run errands with a peer to facilitate communication.

51. Structure the environment so the student has many opportunities to communicate with peers (e.g., clustering desks, describing favorite movie).

52. Conduct a sociometric activity with the class to determine the peer who would most prefer to interact with the student.

53. Make certain that the student understands that interacting with a peer is contingent upon appropriate interactions.

54. Teach the student appropriate ways to communicate with another student (e.g., how to greet another student, suggest activities, share materials, problem solve, take turns, converse, etc.).

55. Ask the student to choose a peer to work with on a specific assignment. If the student has difficulty choosing someone, determine the student's preference by other means such as a class survey.

56. Find a peer with whom the student is most likely to be able to successfully communicate (e.g., a student with similar interests, background, classes, behavior patterns, nonacademic schedule, etc.).

57. Structure the communication to the needs/abilities of the student (e.g., establish rules, limit the stimulation of the activity, limit the length of the activity, consider time of day, etc.).

58. Select nonacademic activities designed to enhance appropriate communication of the student and a peer (e.g., board games, model building, coloring, etc.).

59. Through interviews with other students and observations, determine those characteristics of the student which interfere with successful communication to determine skills or behaviors the student needs to develop for successful communication.

60. Have the student communicate with a peer for short periods of time to enhance success. As the student experiences success, gradually increase the length of time.

Reminder: Do not force the student to interact with peers.

53 Does not demonstrate emotions

Goals:

1. The student will smile when appropriate.
2. The student will laugh when appropriate.
3. The student will demonstrate happiness when appropriate.
4. The student will demonstrate unhappiness when appropriate.

Objectives:

1. The student will smile when appropriate on ___ out of ___ trials.
2. The student will laugh when appropriate on ___ out of ___ trials.
3. The student will demonstrate happiness when appropriate on ___ out of ___ trials.
4. The student will demonstrate happiness by smiling, laughing, joking with peers, etc., on ___ out of ___ trials.
5. The student will laugh or smile when humorous events or activities take place on ___ out of ___ trials.
6. The student will demonstrate unhappiness when appropriate by frowning, complaining, etc., on ____ out of ___ trials.

Interventions:

1. Present tasks in the most attractive and interesting manner possible.

2. Determine those activities the student prefers and provide them often.

3. Reduce or discontinue competitive activities. Repeated failure reduces enjoyment of the activity.

4. Make every attempt to create a positive atmosphere in the classroom (e.g., cooperative group activities, positive motivation strategies, positive communications, etc.).

5. Provide the student with as many social and academic successes as possible.

6. Include the student in classroom/group activities (e.g., invite the student to join a group, assign the student a part or responsibility in an activity, etc.).

7. Make certain that interactions with the student are natural and not contrived.

8. Include fun and enjoyable activities as a part of the daily curriculum.

9. Have peers invite the student to participate in school and extracurricular activities.

10. Avoid discussions of topics sensitive to the student (e.g., divorce, death, unemployment, alcoholism, etc.).

11. Be certain to greet or recognize the student as often as possible (e.g., greet in hallways or in the cafeteria, welcome to class, acknowledge a job well done, etc.).

12. Call attention to the student's accomplishments (e.g., publicly or privately, depending on which is most appropriate).

13. Interact frequently with the student.

14. Try various groupings to determine the situation in which the student is most comfortable.

15. Indicate a need for the student's involvement in an activity (e.g., the student is a part of the class/activities, is valued and needed, etc.).

16. Help the student develop a friendship by assigning him/her to work with a peer on an activity, project, etc.

17. Have the student complete a reinforcer survey to determine his/her interests, his/her favorite activities, what is rewarding to the student, etc. Use the information obtained to create a pleasant atmosphere at school for the student.

18. Reinforce those students in the classroom who deal with emotions in an appropriate manner.

19. Take time to talk with the student so the student will realize that the teacher's interest in him/her is genuine.

20. Make certain that reinforcement is not inadvertently given when the student does not demonstrate emotion (e.g., attending to the student only when he/she shows no reaction to events that would normally evoke emotional responses).

21. Discourage the student from engaging in those activities which cause him/her to feel uncomfortable.

22. Give the student additional responsibilities (e.g., chores, errands, etc.) to give him/her a feeling of success or accomplishment.

23. Help the student identify things he/she wishes were in the environment and work with the student toward these goals.

24. Treat the student with respect. Talk in an objective manner at all times.

25. Allow the student to attempt something new in private before doing so in front of others.

26. Encourage the student to interact with others.

27. Provide the student with frequent opportunities to meet new people.

28. Do not force the student to interact with others.

29. Make sure you express your feelings in a socially acceptable way.

30. Evaluate the appropriateness of the task to determine (a) if the task is too easy, (b) if the task is too difficult, and (c) if the length of time scheduled to complete the task is adequate.

31. Communicate with parents, agencies, or the appropriate parties to inform them of the problem, determine the cause of the problem, and consider possible solutions to the problem.

32. Reinforce those students in the classroom who engage in classroom activities or special events.

33. Encourage the student to engage in classroom activities or special events.

34. Reinforce the student for demonstrating emotional responses when appropriate: (a) give the student a tangible reward (e.g., classroom privileges, line leading, passing out materials, five minutes free time, etc.) or (b) give the student an intangible reward (e.g., praise, handshake, smile, etc.).

35. Call on the student when he/she can answer successfully.

36. Investigate the possibility of the student being involved in the use of drugs or alcohol.

37. Investigate the student's eating habits and the amount of rest he/she is getting outside of school.

38. Choose a peer to model appropriate emotional responses for the student.

39. Identify variables in the environment which may cause the student to withdraw from situations which might elicit an emotional response.

40. Provide a consistent routine for the student to enhance stability.

41. Teach the student acceptable ways to communicate happiness, disappointment, anger, frustration, etc.

42. Acknowledge the student when he/she demonstrates an emotional response (e.g., "You really have a nice smile!" or "I can see that you are disappointed about the assembly being canceled.").

54 Demonstrates phobic reactions

Goals:

1. The student will demonstrate appropriate behavior in response to typical school experiences.
2. The student will not demonstrate phobic-type reactions.

Objectives:

1. The student will demonstrate appropriate behavior in response to typical school experiences on ___ out of ___ trials.
2. The student will demonstrate appropriate behavior in response to speaking in front of a group on ___ out of ___ trials.
3. The student will demonstrate appropriate behavior in response to changing clothes for physical education on ___ out of ___ trials.
4. The student will attend school ___ out of ___ days per week.
5. The student will attend school ___ out of ___ days per month.
6. The student will attend school ___ out of ___ days per semester.
7. The student will speak in front of a peer for ___ minutes at a time. (Gradually increase expectations as the student demonstrates success.)
8. The student will speak in front of a group for ___ minutes at a time. (Gradually increase expectations as the student demonstrates success.)
9. The student will change clothes for physical education in the presence of a peer on ___ out of ___ trials.
10. The student will change clothes for physical education in the presence of several peers on ___ out of ___ trials.
11. The student will remove himself/herself from a stressful situation on ___ out of ___ trials.
12. The student will attempt ___ out of ___ tasks per day.
13. The student will engage in relaxation activities when he/she begins to demonstrate phobic-type reactions on ___ out of ___ trials.

Interventions:

1. Reinforce the student for taking part in activities: (a) give the student a tangible reward (e.g., classroom privileges, line leading, passing out materials, five minutes free time, etc.) or (b) give the student an intangible reward (e.g., praise, handshake, smile, etc.).

2. Speak to the student to explain (a) what he/she is doing wrong (e.g., avoiding activities) and (b) what he/she should be doing (e.g., taking part in activities).

3. Evaluate the appropriateness of the expectations for taking part in activities based on the student's ability to perform the task.

4. Reinforce the student for taking part in activities based on the length of time he/she can do so comfortably. As the student demonstrates success, gradually increase the number of times required for reinforcement.

5. Write a contract with the student specifying what behavior is expected (e.g., changing clothing for physical education) and what reinforcement will be made available when the terms of the contract have been met.

6. Communicate with parents (e.g., notes home, phone calls, etc.) to share information concerning the student's progress. The parents may reinforce the student at home for taking part in activities at school.

7. Choose a peer to model taking part in activities for the student.

8. Have the student question any directions, explanations, instructions he/she does not understand.

9. Reinforce those students in the classroom who participate in activities.

10. If necessary, provide the student with a private place in which to change clothing for physical education.

11. Provide a pleasant/calm atmosphere.

12. To the extent necessary, provide assistance to the student for changing his/her clothing for physical education.

13. Have the student engage in activities which require minimal participation. As the student becomes more comfortable, gradually increase the student's participation

14. Make certain that the physical education clothing the student is expected to wear is appropriate.

15. If the student is reluctant to change clothing for physical education in the presence of others, allow the student to change clothing in private. Gradually increase the number of peers in whose presence the student changes clothing as he/she becomes more comfortable.

16. Be certain the student makes appropriate use of the time provided for activities.

17. If necessary, provide additional time for the student to change clothing for physical education. As the student demonstrates success, gradually reduce the additional time provided.

18. Make certain the student has the necessary clothing for physical education.

19. Prevent peers from making the student uncomfortable when he/she takes part in activities (i.e., prevent other students from making fun, teasing, etc.).

20. When requiring the student to engage in an activity in which he/she is uncomfortable, pair the student with a peer/friend to reduce his/her discomfort.

21. Evaluate the necessity of requiring the student to participate in activities in which he/she is uncomfortable.

22. Make certain the student has adequate time in which to perform activities.

23. Provide the student with alternatives to activities which make him/her uncomfortable (e.g., allow the student to write a poem instead of reciting it in front of a group).

24. Allow the student to be an observer of activities without requiring him/her to be an active participant.

25. Allow the student to perform functions or activities which require little participation (e.g., scorekeeper, note taker, etc.).

26. Ask the student to identify under what circumstances he/she would be willing to participate in activities (i.e., the student may be able to suggest acceptable conditions under which he/she would be comfortable participating in activities).

27. Provide a schedule whereby the student gradually increases the length of time spent at school each day, in the classroom, in a particular class or activity, etc.

28. Communicate with parents, agencies, or the appropriate parties to inform them of the problem, determine the cause of the problem, and consider possible solutions to the problem.

29. If the student is extremely uncomfortable at school, allow a parent, relative, or friend to stay with the student all day if necessary. As the student becomes more comfortable, gradually reduce the length of time the person remains with the student.

Reminder: Do not "force" the student to participate in any activity which makes him/her uncomfortable.

55 Demonstrates self-destructive behavior

Goals:

1. The student will demonstrate self-regard.
2. The student will not demonstrate self-destructive behaviors.

Objectives:

1. The student will refrain from engaging in self-destructive behaviors when experiencing stress, anger, frustration, etc., during ___ out of ___ situations.
2. The student will care for his/her clothing in an appropriate manner when experiencing stress, anger, unhappiness, etc., during ___ out of ___ situations.
3. The student will care for personal property in an appropriate manner when experiencing stress, anger, anxiety, etc., during ___ out of ___ situations.
4. The student will walk away from stressful, anger-producing situations on ___ out of ___ trials.
5. The student will seek assistance from the teacher when experiencing anger, frustration, hopelessness, etc., during ___ out of ___ trials.
6. The student will refrain from tearing his/her clothing when angry, upset, frustrated, etc., on ___ out of ___ trials.
7. The student will refrain from damaging personal property when angry, upset, anxious, etc., on ___ out of ___ trials.
8. The student will refrain from demonstrating self-destructive behaviors upon receiving constructive criticism from the teacher on ___ out of ___ trials.

Interventions:

1. Remove the student from the group or activity until he/she can demonstrate appropriate behavior and self-control.

2. Write a contract with the student specifying what behavior is expected (e.g., not engaging in self-destructive behavior) and what reinforcement will be made available when the terms of the contract have been met.

3. Communicate with parents (e.g., notes home, phone calls, etc.) to share information concerning the student's progress. The parents may reinforce the student at home for appropriate behavior at school.

4. Evaluate the appropriateness of the task to determine (a) if the task is too easy, (b) if the task is too difficult, and (c) if the length of time scheduled to complete the task is adequate.

5. Prevent frustrating or anxiety-producing situations from occurring (e.g., give the student tasks on his/her ability level, give the student the number of tasks that can be tolerated in one sitting, stop social situations which stimulate the student to become self-destructive, etc.).

6. Interact frequently with the student to prevent self-destructive behavior by meeting the student's needs as they occur.

7. Maintain visibility to and from the student. The teacher should be able to see the student, and the student should be able to see the teacher. Make eye contact possible at all times.

8. Facilitate on-task behavior by providing a full schedule of daily events. Prevent lag time from occurring when the student will be free to engage in self-destructive behavior.

9. Remove from the environment any object which the student may use to hurt himself/herself.

10. Provide the student with a quiet place to work (e.g., carrel or study area).

11. Provide the student with positive feedback which indicates he/she is successful, important, respected, etc.

12. Teach the student appropriate ways to communicate displeasure, anger, frustrations, etc.

13. Maintain a positive/calm environment (e.g., deliver positive comments, acknowledgment of successes, quiet communications, etc.).

14. Reduce the emphasis on competition. Repeated failure may result in anger and frustration which may cause the student to try to hurt himself/herself.

15. Talk to the student about ways of handling situations successfully without conflict (e.g., walk away from a situation, change to another activity, ask for help, etc.).

16. Allow the student to have an input relative to making decisions (e.g., changing activities, choosing activities, deciding length of activities, etc.).

17. Provide the student with a selection of optional activities to be performed (e.g., if an activity results in self-destructive behaviors, an optional activity can be substituted).

18. Teach the student appropriate ways to deal with anxiety, frustration, and anger (e.g., move away from the stimulus, verbalize unhappiness, choose another activity, etc.).

19. Teach the student problem-solving skills: (a) identify the problem, (b) identify goals and objectives, (c) develop strategies, (d) develop a plan for action, and (e) carry out the plan.

20. Maintain a consistent daily routine.

21. Avoid discussions or prevent stimuli in the environment which remind the student of unpleasant experiences/sensitive topics (e.g., divorce, death, unemployment, alcoholism, etc.).

22. Do not criticize. When correcting the student, be honest yet supportive. Never cause the student to feel badly about himself/herself.

23. Intervene early when there is a problem to prevent more serious problems from occurring.

24. Make certain the student does not become involved in overstimulating activities.

25. Treat the student with respect. Talk in an objective manner at all times.

26. Make sure you express your feelings in a socially acceptable way.

27. Teach the student to think before acting (e.g., ask himself/herself, "What is happening?" "What am I doing?" "What should I do?" "What will be best for me?").

28. Make certain the student is allowed to voice an opinion in a situation to avoid becoming angry or upset.

29. Maintain consistent expectations to reduce the likelihood of the student hurting himself/herself.

30. Reinforce the student for demonstrating appropriate behavior based on the length of time the student can be successful. As the student demonstrates success, gradually increase the amount of time required for reinforcement.

31. Reinforce those students in the classroom who engage in appropriate behaviors.

32. Establish classroom rules:
- Work on-task.
- Remain in your seat.
- Finish task.
- Meet task expectations.
- Raise your hand.

Review rules often. Reinforce students for following rules.

33. Speak with the student to explain (a) what the student is doing wrong (e.g., hurting self) and (b) what the student should be doing (e.g., talking about the situation, demonstrating self-control, problem-solving, etc.).

34. Reinforce the student for engaging in appropriate behavior: (a) give the student a tangible reward (e.g., classroom privileges, line leading, passing out materials, five minutes free time, etc.) or (b) give the student an intangible reward (e.g., praise, handshake, smile, etc.).

Note: Help the student accept the fact that self-improvement is more important than getting the highest grade in the class, making all A's, being the first one done with an assignment, etc., by reinforcing and grading on the basis of self-improvement.

56 Does not demonstrate stability

Goals:
1. The student will maintain consistency in behavior.
2. The student will demonstrate self-control.
3. The student will demonstrate behavior appropriate to the situation.

Objectives:
1. The student will wait quietly for assistance from an instructor on _____ out of _____ trials.
2. The student will wait his/her turn when engaged in activities with peers on _____ out of _____ trials.
3. The student will make decisions appropriate to the situation on _____ out of _____ trials.
4. The student will attempt a task before asking for assistance on _____ out of _____ trials.
5. The student will ask to use materials before taking them on _____ out of _____ trials.
6. The student will use materials appropriately and return them in the same or better condition on _____ out of _____ trials.
7. The student will stay in his/her seat for _____ minutes at a time. (Gradually increase expectations as the student demonstrates success.)
8. The student will raise his/her hand to leave his/her seat on _____ out of _____ trials.
9. The student will raise his/her hand to gain the teacher's attention on _____ out of _____ trials.
10. The student will listen to directions before beginning a task on _____ out of _____ trials.
11. The student will read directions before beginning a task on _____ out of _____ trials.
12. The student will refrain from touching others during _____ out of _____ interactions.
13. The student will demonstrate consideration/regard for others on _____ out of _____ trials.
14. The student will demonstrate behavior that is appropriate to the situation on _____ out of _____ trials.
15. The student will show emotion that is appropriate to the situation during _____ out of _____ situations.
16. The student will maintain consistency in his/her mood for _____ day(s) at a time.
17. The student will react in a consistent manner in similar situations on _____ out of _____ trials.
18. The student will recognize his/her mood changes on _____ out of _____ occasions.
19. The student will remove himself/herself from the group when he/she experiences difficulty behaving appropriately on _____ out of _____ trials.

Interventions:

1. Reinforce the student for acting in a deliberate and responsible manner: (a) give the student a tangible reward (e.g., classroom privileges, line leading, passing out materials, five minutes free time, etc.) or (b) give the student an intangible reward (e.g., praise, handshake, smile, etc.).

2. Speak with the student to explain (a) what he/she is doing wrong (e.g., taking action before thinking about what he/she is doing) and (b) what he/she should be doing (e.g., considering consequences, thinking about the correct response, considering others, etc.).

3. Remove the student from the group or activity until he/she can demonstrate appropriate behavior and self-control.

4. Establish classroom rules:
- Work on-task.
- Work quietly.
- Remain in your seat.
- Finish task.
- Meet task expectations.

Review rules often. Reinforce students for following rules.

5. Reinforce those students in the classroom who act in a deliberate and responsible manner.

6. Reinforce the student for demonstrating appropriate behavior based on the length of time he/she can be successful. As the student demonstrates success, gradually increase the length of time required for reinforcement.

7. Write a contract with the student specifying what behavior is expected (e.g., acting in a deliberate and responsible manner) and what reinforcement will be made available when the terms of the contract have been met.

8. Communicate with parents (e.g., notes home, phone calls, etc.) to share information concerning the student's progress. The parents may reinforce the student at home for acting in a deliberate and responsible manner at school.

9. Evaluate the appropriateness of the task to determine (a) if the task is too easy, (b) if the task is too difficult, and (c) if the length of time scheduled for the task is adequate.

10. Reduce the opportunity to act impulsively by limiting decision making. As the student demonstrates success, gradually increase opportunities for decision making.

11. Maintain supervision at all times and in all areas of the school environment.

12. Maintain visibility to and from the student. The teacher should be able to see the student; the student should be able to see the teacher. Make eye contact possible at all times.

13. Be mobile to be frequently near the student.

14. Emphasize individual success or progress rather than winning or "beating" other students.

15. Prevent the student from becoming overstimulated by an activity (e.g., monitor or supervise student behavior to limit overexcitement in physical activities, games, parties, etc.).

16. Provide the student with adequate time to perform activities to reduce his/her impulsive behavior.

17. Provide the student with a routine to be followed when making decisions (e.g., place a list of decision-making strategies on the student's desk).

18. Explain to the student that he/she should be satisfied with his/her own best effort rather than perfection.

19. Provide the student with clear, simply stated explanations, instructions, and directions so he/she knows exactly what is expected.

20. Assist the student in beginning each task to reduce impulsive responses.

21. Choose a peer to model deliberate and responsible behavior in academic and social settings for the student.

22. Reduce distracting stimuli (e.g., place the student on the front row, provide a carrel or quiet place away from distractions, etc.). This is used as a means of reducing distracting stimuli and not as a form of punishment.

23. Teach the student decision-making steps: (a) think about how other persons may be influenced; (b) think about consequences; (c) carefully consider the unique situation; (d) think of different courses of action which are possible; and (e) think about what is ultimately best for him/her.

24. Make the student aware of the reasons we all must practice responsibility (e.g., others' rights are not infringed upon, others are not hurt, order is not lost, property is not damaged or destroyed, etc.).

25. Reduce the emphasis on competition. Competition may result in impulsive behavior to win or be first.

26. Give the student additional responsibilities (e.g., chores, errands, etc.) to give him/her a feeling of success or accomplishment.

27. Make certain that all students get equal opportunities to participate in activities (e.g., students take turns; everyone has an equal opportunity to be first, etc.).

28. Allow natural consequences to occur so the student will learn that persons who take their turn and act in a deliberate fashion are more successful than those who act impulsively.

29. Deliver a predetermined signal (e.g., hand signal, verbal cue, etc.) when the student begins to demonstrate impulsive behaviors.

30. Make certain the student has an adequate amount or number of activities scheduled to prevent the likelihood of impulsively engaging in unplanned activities.

31. Assign the student to an area of the classroom where he/she is to remain during certain activities.

32. Maintain a consistent daily routine of activities.

33. Make certain the student knows which areas or activities in the classroom are "off limits" to him/her.

Reminder: Do not confuse impulsive behavior with enthusiasm. Impulsive behavior should be controlled while enthusiasm should be encouraged.

57 Exhibits sudden or extreme mood changes

Goals:

1. The student will demonstrate behavior appropriate to the situation.

Objectives:

1. The student will demonstrate behavior that is appropriate to the situation on ___out of ___trials.
2. The student will show emotion that is appropriate to the situation during ___out of ___situations.
3. The student will maintain consistency in his/her mood for ___day(s) at a time.
4. The student will react in a consistent manner in similar situations on ___out of ___trials.
5. The student will recognize his/her mood changes on ___out of ___occasions.
6. The student will remove himself/herself from the group when he/she experiences difficulty behaving appropriately on ___ out of ___ trials.

Interventions:

1. Provide the student with as many social and academic successes as possible.

2. Inform the student in advance when a change at school is going to occur (e.g., change in routine, special events, end of one activity and beginning of another, etc.).

3. Provide a consistent routine for the student to enhance stability.

4. Try various groupings to determine the situation in which the student is most comfortable.

5. Allow flexibility in meeting academic demands when the student demonstrates sudden or dramatic mood changes (e.g., allow more time, modify assignments, provide help with assignments, etc.).

6. Separate the student from the peer who stimulates the sudden or dramatic mood changes.

7. Teach the student problem-solving skills: (a) identify the problem, (b) identify goals and objectives, (c) develop strategies, (d) develop a plan for action, and (e) carry out the plan.

8. Teach the student to recognize a mood change so he/she may deal with it appropriately.

9. Provide a pleasant/calm atmosphere which would lessen the possibility of sudden or dramatic mood changes.

10. Make the necessary adjustments in the environment to prevent the student from experiencing stress, frustration, anger, etc.

11. Give the student adequate time to make adjustments to activity changes, situations, etc., (e.g., provide the student with several minutes to move from one activity to another).

12. Do not criticize. When correcting the student, be honest yet supportive. Never cause the student to feel badly about himself/herself.

13. Prevent the occurrence of specific stimuli that cause the student to demonstrate sudden or dramatic mood changes (e.g., demanding situations, interruptions, competition, announcing test scores, abrupt changes, etc.).

14. Avoid discussions or prevent stimuli in the environment that remind the student of unpleasant experiences/sensitive topics (e.g., divorce, death, unemployment, alcoholism, etc.).

15. Intervene early when there is a problem to prevent a more serious problem from occurring.

16. Make certain the student does not become involved in overstimulating activities that would cause him/her to have mood changes.

17. Be careful to avoid embarrassing the student by giving him/her orders, demands, etc., in front of others.

18. Teach the student appropriate ways to communicate displeasure, anger, frustration, etc.

19. Make sure you express your feelings in a socially acceptable way.

20. Teach the student to "think" before acting (e.g., ask himself/herself, "What is happening?" "What am I doing?" "What should I do?" "What will be best for me?").

21. Talk to the student about ways of handling situations successfully without conflict (e.g., walk away from a situation, change to another activity, ask for help, etc.).

22. Communicate with parents, agencies, or the appropriate parties to inform them of the problem, determine the cause of the problem, and consider possible solutions to the problem.

23. Evaluate the appropriateness of the task to determine (a) if the task is too easy, (b) if the task is too difficult, and (c) if the time scheduled to complete the task is adequate.

24. Reinforce the student for demonstrating consistent and appropriate behavior: (a) give the student a tangible reward (e.g., classroom privileges, line leading, passing out materials, five minutes free time, etc.) or (b) give the student an intangible reward (e.g., praise, handshake, smile, etc.).

25. Communicate with parents (e.g., notes home, phone calls, etc.) to share information concerning the student's progress. The parents may reinforce the student at home for demonstrating consistent and appropriate behavior at school.

26. Write a contract with the student specifying what behavior is expected (e.g., consistent and appropriate behavior) and what reinforcement will be made available when the terms of the contract have been met.

27. Establish classroom rules:
- Work on-task.
- Work quietly.
- Remain in your seat.
- Finish task.
- Meet task expectations.

Review rules often. Reinforce students for following rules.

28. Speak with the student to explain (a) what the student is doing wrong (e.g., becoming angry or upset easily, etc.) and (b) what the student should be doing (e.g., following rules, considering others, controlling impulsive behavior, etc.).

29. Reinforce the student for demonstrating appropriate behavior (academic or social) based on the length of time he/she can be successful. As the student demonstrates success, gradually increase the length of time required for reinforcement.

58 Does not develop close relationships with other males and/or females because of fear of rejection, disapproval, ridicule, etc.

Goal:

1. The student will develop close relationships with other males and/or females.

Objectives:

1. The student will develop interaction skills and use them when interacting with a peer(s) during ___ out of ___ interactions.
2. The student will demonstrate acceptable physical contact such as a handshake, pat on the back, "high five," etc., when appropriate on ___ out of ___ trials.
3. The student will interact with other students in a physically appropriate manner on ___ out of ___ trials.
4. The student will develop hygiene skills and manners and use them when interacting with other students on ___ out of ___ trials.
5. The student will talk to his/her peers in a socially acceptable manner during ___ out of ___ interactions.
6. The student will show emotion that is appropriate for the situation during ___ out of ___ situations.
7. The student will demonstrate consideration/regard for his/her peers on ___ out of ___ trials.
8. The student will demonstrate peer interaction skills by sharing materials, waiting his/her turn, and talking in an acceptable manner on ___ out of ___ trials.
9. The student will successfully interact with a peer ___ times per day.
10. The student will successfully interact with a peer ___ times per week.

Interventions:

1. Provide the student with as many academic and social successes as possible so peers may view him/her in a more positive way.

2. Make the necessary adjustments in the environment to prevent the student from experiencing stress, frustration, anger, etc.

3. Assign additional responsibilities to the student (e.g., chores, errands, etc.) to give him/her a feeling of success or accomplishment.

4. Structure the environment so the student does not have time to dwell on real or imagined problems.

5. Take the time to listen so the student realizes your concern and interest.

6. Try various groupings to determine the situation in which the student is most comfortable.

7. Encourage the student to participate in extracurricular activities that will help develop those skills necessary to interact appropriately with others at school.

8. Provide the student with alternative activities to perform in case some activities prove upsetting.

9. Reduce the emphasis on competition. Repeated failure may cause the student to feel that others do not like or care about him/her.

10. Encourage and help the student to make friends (e.g., pair the student with a peer; when that relationship is successful, introduce other students).

11. Provide the student with as many positive interactions as possible (e.g., recognize the student, greet the student, compliment attire, etc.).

12. Reinforce those students in the classroom who appropriately interact with other students.

13. Have the student be the leader of a small-group activity if he/she possesses mastery of skills or an interest in that area.

14. Give the student the responsibility of tutoring a peer if he/she possesses the skills to be shared.

15. Maintain maximum supervision of the student's interactions and gradually decrease the amount of supervision over time.

16. Give the student responsibilities in group situations so peers may view the student in a more positive way.

17. Encourage the student to further develop any ability or skill he/she may have so peers may view the student in a more positive way.

18. Help the student to identify his/her inappropriate behaviors and teach the student ways to change those behaviors.

19. Ask the student to choose a peer to work with on a specific assignment. Encourage the student and peer to interact with each other in nonacademic areas (e.g., recess, lunch, break time, etc.).

20. Do not criticize. When correcting the student, be honest yet supportive. Never cause the student to feel negatively about himself/herself.

21. Do not force the student to interact with students with whom he/she is not completely comfortable.

22. Treat the student with respect. Talk in an objective manner at all times.

23. Allow the student to attempt something new in private before doing so in front of others.

24. Choose a peer to engage in recreational activities with the student to develop a friendship.

25. Encourage the student to interact with others.

26. Provide the student with frequent opportunities to meet new people.

27. Do not force the student to interact with others.

28. Make certain the student is not demonstrating a lack of confidence to get the attention of others.

29. Communicate with parents (e.g., notes home, phone calls, etc.) to share information concerning the student's progress. The parents may reinforce the student at home for interacting appropriately with others at school.

30. Write a contract with the student specifying what behavior is expected (e.g., interacting appropriately with others) and what reinforcement will be made available when the terms of the contract have been met.

31. Reinforce the student for interacting with others based on the length of time the student can be successful. As the student demonstrates success, gradually increase the length of time required for reinforcement.

32. Reinforce those students in the classroom who make positive, supportive comments to the student.

33. Reinforce the student for interacting with others: (a) give the student a tangible reward (e.g., classroom privileges, line leading, passing out materials, five minutes free time, etc.) or (b) give the student an intangible reward (e.g., praise, handshake, smile, etc.).

34. Do not assume that the student is being treated nicely by other students. Others may be stimulating inappropriate behavior on the part of the student.

Reminder: Do not "force" the student to interact with others with whom he/she is uncomfortable.

59 Does not participate or demonstrate an interest in classroom activities or special events that are interesting to other students

Goals:

1. The student will participate in classroom activities or special events.

Objectives:

1. The student will participate in ___ out of ___ classroom activities each week.
2. The student will participate in ___ out of ___ special events per month.
3. The student will demonstrate an interest in classroom activities by asking about the activities, talking about the activities, helping prepare for the activities, etc., in ___ out of ___ activities.
4. The student will demonstrate an interest in special events by asking about the events, talking about the events, helping prepare for the events, etc., in ___ out of ___ special events.
5. The student will passively participate in a classroom activity by sitting quietly, assisting the teacher, taking notes, etc., during ___ out of ___ activities.
6. The student will actively participate in a classroom activity by being the group leader or spokesperson, answering questions, providing his/her opinion, etc., during ___ out of ___ activities.
7. The student will passively participate in a special event by sitting/standing quietly, walking with the group, watching others play games, etc., during ___ out of ___ events.
8. The student will actively participate in a special event by having a role in the play, producing the play, decorating the room, performing in the assembly, etc., during ___ out of ___ events.

Interventions:

1. Encourage or reward others for participation in group or special activities.

2. Give the student the responsibility of helping another student in the group.

3. Give the student responsibilities in a group so others might view him/her in a positive light.

4. Ask the student questions that cannot be answered yes or no.

5. Call on the student when he/she is most likely to be able to respond successfully (e.g., when discussing something in which the student is interested, when the teacher is certain the student knows the answer, etc.).

6. Try various groupings to determine the situation in which the student is most successful.

7. Have peers invite the student to participate in school or extracurricular activities.

8. Request that the student be the leader of a small group activity if he/she possesses mastery or an interest in the activity.

9. Allow the student to be present during group activities without requiring active participation.

10. Reduce the emphasis on competition. Frequent or continuous failure is likely to result in embarrassment which will cause reluctance to participate.

11. Demonstrate respect for the student's opinions, responses, suggestions, etc.

12. Provide the student with many social and academic successes.

13. Provide the student with positive feedback which indicates he/she is successful.

14. Present tasks in the most attractive and interesting manner possible.

15. Determine the student's interests so activities which require participation might be presented through his/her interests.

16. Allow the student to choose a special event or interesting activity for the class.

17. Provide the student with success-oriented special events or activities so he/she may develop an interest in them.

18. Modify or adjust situations that cause the student to be reluctant to participate (e.g., degree of difficulty, competition, fear of failure, threat of embarrassment, etc.).

19. Emphasize individual success or progress rather than winning or "beating" other students.

20. Provide the student with opportunities for small-group participation as opposed to large-group participation.

21. Encourage the student to participate in small groups. As the student demonstrates success, gradually increase the size of the group.

22. Encourage the student to share things of special interest with other members of the class.

23. Choose a peer to model appropriate interactions in classroom activities for the student.

24. Have the student question any directions, explanations, and instructions not understood.

25. Allow the student to choose a group of peers with whom he/she feels comfortable.

26. Determine the peers the student would most prefer to interact with in classroom activities and attempt to facilitate the interaction.

27. Choose outgoing, nonthreatening peers to help the student participate in classroom activities.

28. Structure the environment so the student has many opportunities to interact with other peers in classroom activities.

29. Assign the student to classroom activities in which he/she is likely to interact successfully with peers.

30. Conduct a sociometric activity with the class to determine those peers who would most prefer to interact with the student in classroom activities.

31. Teach the student appropriate ways to interact with peers in classroom activities (e.g., share materials, problem solve, take turns, converse, etc.).

32. Supervise classroom activities closely so peers with whom the student interacts do not stimulate inappropriate behavior.

33. Make certain that the classroom activity is not so stimulating as to make successful interactions with peers difficult.

34. Teach the student problem-solving skills to better deal with problems that may occur in interactions with peers in classroom activities (e.g., talking, walking away, calling upon an arbitrator, compromising, etc.).

35. Limit opportunities for interaction in classroom activities on those occasions when the student is not likely to be successful (e.g., when the student has experienced academic or social failure prior to the scheduled classroom activity).

36. Select nonacademic activities designed to enhance appropriate social interaction of the student and peers during classroom activities (e.g., board games, model building, coloring, etc.).

37. Treat the student with respect. Talk in an objective manner at all times.

38. Through interviews with other students and observations, determine those characteristics of the student which interfere with successful interactions during classroom activities. Use information gained to determine skills or behaviors the student needs to develop for successful interactions.

39. Have the student practice appropriate interactions with the teacher(s) in classroom activities (e.g., simulations, role-playing, etc.).

40. Make certain, beforehand, that the student is able to successfully engage in the classroom activity (e.g., the student understands the rules, is familiar with the activity, will be compatible with peers engaged in the activity, etc.).

41. Make certain the student has the necessary materials for the classroom activity.

42. Assign the student responsibilities to perform during classroom activities to enhance peer interaction (e.g., being a leader, passing out materials, acting as a peer tutor, etc.).

43. Make certain the student knows how to use all materials for the classroom activity.

44. Do not punish the student for not participating in classroom activities or special events.

45. Do not force the student to interact with someone with whom he/she is not completely comfortable.

46. Be careful to avoid embarrassing the student by giving him/her orders, demands, etc., in front of others.

47. Make positive comments about participating in school and special events.

48. Do not force the student to interact with others.

49. Go with the student or have someone else accompany the student to those activities in which he/she may not want to participate. Gradually decrease the length of time you or someone else stays with the student.

50. Carefully consider those activities the student avoids. If something unpleasant is causing the student not to participate, try to change the situation.

51. Reinforce other students in the classroom for participating in group activities or special events.

52. Choose a peer to sit/work directly with the student (e.g., in different settings or activities such as art, music, P.E., tutoring, group projects, recess, etc.). When the student has become comfortable working with one other student, gradually increase the size of the group.

53. Evaluate the appropriateness of the task to determine (a) if the task is too easy, (b) if the task is too difficult, and (c) if the length of time scheduled to complete the task is adequate.

54. Communicate with parents (e.g., notes home, phone calls, etc.) to share information concerning the student's progress. The parents may reinforce the student at home for participating in group activities or special events at school.

55. Write a contract with the student specifying what behavior is expected (e.g., taking part in group activities) and what reinforcement will be made available when the terms of the contract have been met.

56. Establish classroom rules:
- Work on-task.
- Work quietly.
- Remain in your seat.
- Finish task.
- Meet task expectations.

Review rules often. Reinforce students for following rules.

57. Speak with the student to explain (a) what the student is doing wrong (e.g., failing to take part) and (b) what the student should be doing (e.g., talking, taking turns, playing, sharing, etc.).

58. Reinforce the student for participating in group activities or special events: (a) give the student a tangible reward (e.g., classroom privileges, line leading, passing out materials, five minutes free time, etc.) or (b) give the student an intangible reward (e.g., praise, handshake, smile, etc.).

59. Give the student the opportunity to choose a group activity and the group members (e.g., along with the teacher decide what the activity will be, decide what individual group members will do, etc.).

60. Give the student the opportunity to pick a topic or activity for the group to work on together.

61. Have the student engage in activities which require minimal participation. As he/she becomes more comfortable, gradually increase the student's participation.

Reminder: Do not "force" the student to take part in any activity or special event.

60 Indicates that he/she no longer cares about special events, social activities, or fun things in which he/she was formerly involved, etc.

Goal:

1. The student will participate in social activities or special events.

Objectives:

1. The student will participate in ___ out of ___ social activities each week.
2. The student will participate in ___ out of ___ special events per month.
3. The student will demonstrate an interest in social activities by asking about the activities, talking about the activities, helping prepare for the activities, etc., in ___ out of ___ activities.
4. The student will demonstrate an interest in special events by asking about the events, talking about the events, helping prepare for the events, etc., in ___ out of ___ special events.
5. The student will passively participate in a social activity during ___ out of ___ activities.
6. The student will actively participate in a social activity during ___ out of ___ activities.
7. The student will passively participate in a special event by sitting/standing quietly, walking with the group, watching others play games, etc., during ___ out of ___ events.
8. The student will actively participate in a special event by having a role in the play, producing the play, decorating the room, performing in the assembly, etc., during ___ out of ___ events.

Interventions:

1. Encourage or reward others for participation in group or special activities.

2. Give the student the responsibility of helping another student in the group.

3. Give the student responsibilities in a group so others might view him/her in a positive light.

4. Ask the student questions that cannot be answered yes or no.

5. Call on the student when he/she is most likely to be able to respond successfully (e.g., when discussing something in which the student is interested, when the teacher is certain the student knows the answer, etc.).

6. Try various groupings to determine the situation in which the student is most successful.

7. Have peers invite the student to participate in school or extracurricular activities.

8. Request that the student be the leader of a small-group activity if he/she possesses mastery or an interest in the activity.

9. Allow the student to be present during group activities without requiring active participation.

10. Reduce the emphasis on competition. Frequent or continuous failure is likely to result in embarrassment which will cause reluctance to participate.

11. Demonstrate respect for the student's opinions, responses, suggestions, etc.

12. Provide the student with many social and academic successes.

13. Provide the student with positive feedback which indicates he/she is successful.

14. Present tasks in the most attractive and interesting manner possible.

15. Determine the student's interests so activities which require participation might be presented through his/her interests.

16. Allow the student to choose a special event or interesting activity for the class.

17. Provide the student with success-oriented special events or activities so he/she may develop an interest in them.

18. Modify or adjust situations that cause the student to be reluctant to participate (e.g., degree of difficulty, competition, fear of failure, threat of embarrassment, etc.).

19. Emphasize individual success or progress rather than winning or "beating" other students.

20. Provide the student with opportunities for small-group participation as opposed to large-group participation.

21. Encourage the student to participate in small groups. As the student demonstrates success, gradually increase the size of the group.

22. Encourage the student to share things of special interest with other members of the class.

23. Choose a peer to model appropriate interactions in classroom activities for the student.

24. Have the student question any directions, explanations, and instructions not understood.

25. Allow the student to choose a group of peers with whom he/she feels comfortable.

26. Determine the peers the student would most prefer to interact with in classroom activities and attempt to facilitate the interaction.

27. Choose outgoing, nonthreatening peers to help the student participate in classroom activities.

28. Structure the environment so the student has many opportunities to interact with other peers in classroom activities.

29. Assign the student to classroom activities in which he/she is likely to interact successfully with peers.

30. Conduct a sociometric activity with the class to determine those peers who would most prefer to interact with the student in classroom activities.

31. Teach the student appropriate ways to interact with peers in classroom activities (e.g., share materials, problem solve, take turns, converse, etc.).

32. Supervise classroom activities closely so peers with whom the student interacts do not stimulate inappropriate behavior.

33. Make certain that the classroom activity is not so stimulating as to make successful interactions with peers difficult.

34. Teach the student problem-solving skills to better deal with problems that may occur in interactions with peers in classroom activities (e.g., talking, walking away, calling upon an arbitrator, compromising, etc.).

35. Limit opportunities for interaction in classroom activities on those occasions when the student is not likely to be successful (e.g., when the student has experienced academic or social failure prior to the scheduled classroom activity).

36. Select nonacademic activities designed to enhance appropriate social interaction of the student and peers during classroom activities (e.g., board games, model building, coloring, etc.).

37. Treat the student with respect. Talk in an objective manner at all times.

38. Do not force the student to interact with others.

39. Through interviews with other students and observations, determine those characteristics of the student which interfere with successful interactions during classroom activities. Use information gained to determine skills or behaviors the student needs to develop for successful interactions.

40. Have the student practice appropriate interactions with the teacher(s) in classroom activities (e.g., simulations, role-playing, etc.).

41. Make certain, beforehand, that the student is able to successfully engage in the classroom activity (e.g., the student understands the rules, is familiar with the activity, will be compatible with peers engaged in the activity, etc.).

42. Make certain the student has the necessary materials for the classroom activity.

43. Assign the student responsibilities to perform during classroom activities to enhance peer interaction (e.g., being a leader, passing out materials, acting as a peer tutor, etc.).

44. Make certain the student knows how to use all materials for the classroom activity.

45. Do not punish the student for not participating in classroom activities or special events.

46. Do not force the student to interact with someone with whom he/she is not completely comfortable.

47. Be careful to avoid embarrassing the student by giving him/her orders, demands, etc., in front of others.

48. Make positive comments about participating in school and special events.

49. Go with the student or have someone else accompany the student to activities in which he/she may not want to participate. Gradually decrease the length of time you or someone else stays with the student.

50. Carefully consider those activities the student avoids. If something unpleasant is causing the student not to participate, try to change the situation.

51. Speak with the student to explain (a) what the student is doing wrong (e.g., failing to take part) and (b) what the student should be doing (e.g., talking, taking turns, playing, sharing, etc.).

52. Evaluate the appropriateness of the task to determine (a) if the task is too easy, (b) if the task is too difficult, and (c) if the length of time scheduled to complete the task is adequate.

53. Communicate with parents (e.g., notes home, phone calls, etc.) to share information concerning the student's progress. The parents may reinforce the student at home for participating in group activities or special events at school.

54. Write a contract with the student specifying what behavior is expected (e.g., taking part in group activities) and what reinforcement will be made available when the terms of the contract have been met.

55. Reinforce other students in the classroom for participating in group activities or special events.

56. Establish classroom rules:
- Work on-task.
- Work quietly.
- Remain in your seat.
- Finish task.
- Meet task expectations.

Review rules often. Reinforce students for following rules.

57. Choose a peer to sit/work directly with the student (e.g., in different settings or activities such as art, music, P.E., tutoring, group projects, recess, etc.). When the student has become comfortable working with one other student, gradually increase the size of the group.

58. Reinforce the student for participating in group activities or special events: (a) give the student a tangible reward (e.g., classroom privileges, line leading, passing out materials, five minutes free time, etc.) or (b) give the student an intangible reward (e.g., praise, handshake, smile, etc.).

59. Discuss concerns with other professionals to determine if further investigation is warranted (e.g., abuse or neglect).

Reminder: Do not "force" the student to take part in any activity or special event.

61 Does not smile, laugh, or demonstrate happiness

Goals:
1. The student will smile.
2. The student will laugh.
3. The student will demonstrate happiness.

Objectives:
1. The student will smile when appropriate on ___ out of ___ trials.
2. The student will laugh when appropriate on ___ out of ___ trials.
3. The student will demonstrate happiness when appropriate on ___ out of ___ trials.
4. The student will demonstrate happiness by smiling, laughing, joking with peers, etc., on ___ out of ___ trials.
5. The student will laugh or smile when humorous events or activities take place on ___ out of ___ trials.

Interventions:

1. Present tasks in the most attractive and interesting manner possible.

2. Determine those activities the student prefers and provide them often.

3. Reduce or discontinue competitive activities. Repeated failure reduces enjoyment of the activity.

4. Make every attempt to create a positive atmosphere in the classroom (e.g., cooperative group activities, positive motivation strategies, positive communications, etc.).

5. Provide the student with as many social and academic successes as possible.

6. Include the student in classroom/group activities (e.g., invite the student to join a group, assign the student a part or responsibility in an activity, etc.).

7. Indicate a need for the student's involvement in an activity (e.g., the student is a part of the class/activities, is valued and needed, etc.).

8. Include fun and enjoyable activities as a part of the daily curriculum.

9. Speak to the student to explain (a) that you recognize he/she is unhappy and (b) appropriate ways to deal with unhappiness.

10. Avoid discussions of topics sensitive to the student (e.g., divorce, death, unemployment, alcoholism, etc.).

11. Be certain to greet or recognize the student as often as possible (e.g., greet in hallways or the cafeteria, welcome to class, acknowledge a job well done, etc.).

12. Call attention to the student's accomplishments (e.g., publicly or privately, depending on which is most appropriate).

13. Interact frequently with the student.

14. Try various groupings to determine the situation in which the student is most comfortable.

15. Make certain that interactions with the student are natural and not contrived.

16. Help the student develop a friendship by assigning him/her to work with a peer on an activity, project, etc.

17. Have the student complete a reinforcer survey to determine his/her interests, favorite activities, what is rewarding to the student, etc., and use the information obtained to create a pleasant atmosphere at school for the student.

18. Have peers invite the student to participate in school and extracurricular activities.

19. Reinforce those students in the classroom who deal with unhappiness in an appropriate manner.

20. Take time to talk with the student so the student realizes that the teacher's interest in him/her is genuine.

21. Make certain that reinforcement is not inadvertently given when the student does not smile, laugh, or demonstrate happiness (e.g., attending to the student only when he/she demonstrates unhappiness).

22. Discourage the student from engaging in those activities which cause him/her unhappiness.

23. Give the student additional responsibilities (e.g., chores, errands, etc.) to give him/her a feeling of success or accomplishment.

24. Help the student identify things he/she wishes were in the environment and work with the student toward these goals.

25. Treat the student with respect. Talk in an objective manner at all times.

26. Allow the student to attempt something new in private before doing so in front of others.

27. Encourage the student to interact with others.

28. Provide the student with frequent opportunities to meet new people.

29. Do not force the student to interact with others.

30. Make sure you express your feelings in a socially acceptable way.

31. Evaluate the appropriateness of the task to determine (a) if the task is too difficult and (b) if the length of time scheduled to complete the task is appropriate.

32. Communicate with parents, agencies, or the appropriate parties to inform them of the problem, determine the cause of the problem, and consider possible solutions to the problem.

33. Reinforce those students in the classroom who engage in classroom activities or special events.

34. Encourage the student to engage in classroom activities or special events.

35. Reinforce the student for demonstrating happiness when appropriate: (a) give the student a tangible reward (e.g., classroom privileges, line leading, passing out materials, five minutes free time, etc.) or (b) give the student an intangible reward (e.g., praise, handshake, smile, etc.).

62 Expresses concerns or worries about school, home, or personal situations through words or pictures

Goals:

1. The student will function successfully at school despite problems or situations in the school environment.
2. The student will function successfully at school despite problems or situations in the home.
3. The student will function successfully at school despite personal problems.

Objectives:

1. The student will write accurate descriptions of situations at school on ___out of ___trials.
2. The student will write accurate descriptions of situations at home on ___out of ___trials.
3. The student will write accurate descriptions of personal problems on ___out of ___trials.
4. The student will write positive statements about school on ___out of ___trials.
5. The student will write positive statements about home on ___out of ___trials.
6. The student will write positive statements about personal situations on ___out of ___trials.
7. The student will demonstrate happiness by smiling, laughing, joking with peers, etc., on ___ out of ___ trials.
8. The student will smile or laugh when humorous events or activities take place on ___ out of ___ trials.
9. The student will demonstrate emotions like those of his/her peers during ___out of ___typical classroom situations.

Interventions:

1. Discuss concerns with other professionals to determine if further investigation is warranted (e.g., abuse or neglect).

2. Record or chart the number of times the student writes about fears or concerns regarding school, home, or personal situations to make the student aware of the frequency of his/her behavior.

3. Take the time to listen so the student realizes that your concern is genuine.

4. Explain that fears and concerns, while legitimate, are not unusual for students (e.g., everyone worries about tests, grades, etc.).

5. Identify persons the student may contact with his/her fears and concerns (e.g., guidance counselor, school nurse, social worker, school psychologist, etc.).

6. Discuss ways in which to practice self-improvement.

7. Provide the student with opportunities for social and academic success.

8. Separate the student from a peer who may be encouraging or stimulating fears or concerns about school, home, or personal situations.

9. Reduce the emphasis on competition. Repeated failure may result in anxiety about performance at school, home, and in personal situations.

10. Provide parents with necessary information to help the student with homework and study activities at home.

11. Make the necessary adjustments in the environment to prevent the student from experiencing stress, frustration, anxiety, etc.

12. Structure the environment so time does not permit opportunities for the student to dwell on fears or concerns.

13. Provide the student with alternative approaches to testing (e.g., test the student verbally, make the tests shorter, allow the student to respond verbally, allow the student to take the test in the resource room, etc.).

14. Have peers invite the student to participate in extracurricular activities.

15. Emphasize individual differences and that everybody has strengths and weaknesses.

16. Reduce activities which might threaten the student (e.g., announcing test score ranges or test scores aloud in class, emphasizing the success of a particular student(s), etc.).

17. Provide the student with positive feedback which indicates he/she is successful, competent, important, valuable, etc.

18. Seek assistance from the school counselor, the principal, other teachers, etc., to help the student deal with fears and concerns about school, home, and personal problems so he/she can concentrate at school.

19. Encourage the student to use problem solving skills: (a) identify the problem, (b) identify goals and objectives, (c) develop strategies, (d) develop a plan of action, and (e) carry out the plan.

20. Provide praise and recognition as often as possible.

21. Call attention to the student's accomplishments (e.g., publicly or privately depending on which is more appropriate).

22. Encourage participation in school and extracurricular activities.

23. Try various groupings to determine the situation in which the student is most successful.

24. Demonstrate respect for the student's opinions, responses, suggestions, etc.

25. Avoid discussion of topics sensitive to the student (e.g., divorce, death, unemployment, alcoholism, etc.).

26. Provide the student with opportunities for special project responsibilities, leadership, etc.

27. Provide the student with as many enjoyable and interesting activities as possible.

28. Reinforce the student for improvement rather than expecting excellence.

29. Treat the student with respect. Talk in an objective manner at all times.

30. Maintain trust and confidentiality with the student at all times.

31. Encourage participation in school and extracurricular activities.

32. Provide opportunities for tutoring from peers or a teacher.

33. Choose a peer to sit/work directly with the student.

Goals:

1. The student will participate in classroom activities.
2. The student will demonstrate interest by participating in classroom activities.

Objectives:

1. The student will participate in ___ out of ___ classroom activities per day.
2. The student will participate in ___ out of ___ classroom activities per week.
3. The student will participate in ___ out of ___ classroom activities per month.
4. The student will demonstrate an interest in classroom activities by asking about the activities, talking about the activities, helping prepare for the activities, etc., in ___ out of ___ activities.
5. The student will passively participate in a classroom activity by sitting quietly, assisting the teacher, taking notes, etc., during ___ out of ___ activities.
6. The student will actively participate in a classroom activity by being the group leader or spokesperson, answering questions, providing his/her opinion, etc., during ___ out of ___ activities.
7. The student will interact with a peer for ___ minutes per day. (Gradually increase expectations as the student demonstrates success.)
8. The student will initiate ___ interactions with a peer per day. (Gradually increase expectations as the student demonstrates success.)
9. The student will interact with the teacher for ___ minutes per day. (Gradually increase expectations as the student demonstrates success.)
10. The student will initiate ___ interactions with the teacher per day. (Gradually increase expectations as the student demonstrates success.)
11. The student will perform academic tasks with ___% accuracy. (Gradually increase expectations as the student demonstrates success.)
12. The student will identify something he/she enjoys doing at school when asked by the teacher on ___ out of ___ occasions.
13. The student will identify a reinforcer he/she would like to earn for participating in classroom activities on ___ out of ___ trials.
14. The student will perform ___ out of ___ academic tasks per day. (Gradually increase expectations as the student demonstrates success.)

Interventions:

1. Call on the student when he/she can answer successfully.

2. Provide the student with as many academic and social successes as possible.

3. Allow the student more decision-making opportunities relative to class activities and assignments.

4. Present tasks in the most attractive and interesting manner possible.

5. Give the student responsibilities in the classroom (e.g., teacher assistant, peer tutor, group leader, etc.).

6. Provide a full schedule of daily events to keep the student actively involved.

7. Avoid competition. Failure may cause the student to lose interest or not participate in school activities.

8. Evaluate the appropriateness of the task in relation to the student's ability to perform the task successfully.

9. Determine the student's preferred activities, interests, etc., and incorporate them into the daily schedule, program, etc., at various points throughout the day.

10. Provide the student with "real-life" experiences from the environment. Have individuals from the work force (e.g., mechanic, draftsman, secretary, etc.) visit the class to relate the importance of school to work experiences that involve math, reading, writing, etc.

11. Show an interest in the student (e.g., acknowledge the student, ask the student's opinion, spend time working one-on-one with the student, etc.).

12. Investigate the possibility of the student being involved in the use of drugs or alcohol.

13. Be careful to avoid embarrassing the student by giving the student orders.

14. Treat the student with respect. Talk in an objective manner at all times.

15. Make positive comments about school and the importance of school.

16. Allow the student to attempt something new in private before doing it in front of others.

17. Provide the student with frequent opportunities to meet new people.

18. Evaluate the appropriateness of the task to determine (a) if the task is too easy, (b) if the task is too difficult, and (c) if the length of time scheduled to complete the task is adequate.

19. Communicate with parents, agencies, or the appropriate parties to inform them of the problem, determine the cause of the problem, and consider possible solutions to the problem.

20. Communicate with the parents (e.g., notes home, phone calls, etc.) to share information concerning the student's progress. The parents may reinforce the student at home for showing an interest in participating in school activities.

21. Do not criticize when correcting the student; be honest yet supportive. Never cause the student to feel badly about himself/herself.

22. Write a contract with the student specifying what behavior is expected (e.g., showing an interest and participating in school activities) and what reinforcement will be made available when the terms of the contract have been met.

23. Reinforce the student for showing an interest and participating in school activities based on the length of time he/she can be successful. As the student demonstrates success, gradually increase the length of time required for reinforcement.

24. Reinforce those students in the classroom who show an interest and participate in school activities.

25. Establish classroom rules:
- Work on-task.
- Remain in your seat.
- Finish task.
- Meet task expectations.
- Raise your hand.

Review rules often. Reinforce students for following rules.

26. Investigate the student's eating habits and the amount of rest he/she is getting outside of school.

27. Reinforce the student for showing an interest and participating in school activities: (a) give the student a tangible reward (e.g., classroom privileges, line leading, passing out materials, five minutes free time, etc.) or (b) give the student an intangible reward (e.g., praise, handshake, smile, etc.).

28. Speak with the student to explain (a) what the student is doing wrong (e.g., failing to show an interest and participate in school activities) and (b) what the student should be doing (e.g., showing an interest and participating in school activities).

64 Exhibits loss of appetite

Goals:

1. The student will consume an appropriate amount of food for his/her body type.

Objectives:

1. The student will consume an appropriate amount of food for his/her body type on ___out of ___days per week.

Interventions:

1. Make certain that appropriate foods the student enjoys are available to him/her.

2. Try various groupings to determine the situation in which the student is most comfortable.

3. Choose a peer to work directly with the student to prevent stress, frustration, anxiety, etc.

4. Reduce situations which may contribute to loss of appetite (e.g., testing situations, timed activities, competition, etc.).

5. Remove the student from activities or experiences which contribute to loss of appetite. As the student demonstrates success, gradually introduce these activities into the student's schedule.

6. Prevent the student from experiencing situational stress or anxiety.

7. Inform the appropriate personnel or agencies of the student's problem so intervention can take place in other areas of the student's environment in addition to school.

8. Arrange for the student to eat meals with an adult (i.e., teacher, counselor, volunteer, principal, etc.) so the quantity and type of food consumed by the student can be monitored and supervised.

9. Assist the student in making appropriate food choices.

10. Ask the student why he/she is having a loss of appetite. The student may have the most accurate perception as to why he/she is having a loss of appetite.

11. Reinforce the student for practicing appropriate eating habits.

12. Provide the student with a high-interest activity which he/she prefers.

13. Avoid the discussion of topics that are sensitive to the student (e.g., death, divorce, unemployment, alcoholism, etc.).

14. Help the student to be satisfied with his/her own effort rather than insisting on perfection.

15. Provide the student with as many social and academic successes as possible.

16. Separate the student from a peer who may be encouraging or stimulating eating problems.

17. Reduce the emphasis on competition and perfection. Repeated failure and frustration may cause the student's loss of appetite.

18. Involve the student in extracurricular activities to provide opportunities for success. Eating problems may diminish as he/she experiences success.

19. Identify a support system (e.g., guidance counselor, school nurse, school psychologist, teen hotline, support group, etc.) the student may contact with worries or concerns.

20. Communicate with the parents (e.g., notes home, phone calls, etc.) to share information concerning the student's eating problem. The parents may reinforce the student at home for making suitable food choices.

21. Consult with parents to determine whether the student's loss of appetite could be a reaction to a medical treatment and determine whether a modification should be made (i.e., take medication after a meal rather than before, eat small quantities of food throughout the day).

22. Make certain the student understands why it is important to eat appropriate quantities of nutritional food (e.g., maintaining appropriate weight, growth and development, etc.).

23. Allow the student to eat in alternative settings if being in the cafeteria causes anxiety resulting in loss of appetite.

24. Structure the environment so time does not permit opportunities for the student to dwell on concerns or worries.

25. Provide the student with "real life" experiences from the environment. Have individuals in food/nutrition related fields (i.e., dietitian, psychologist specializing in eating disorders, university extension department personnel, chef, etc.) visit the class to relate information about eating disorders, nutrition, food preparation, etc.

26. Help the student recognize problems that are within his/her ability to deal with and not to worry needlessly about situations over which the student has no control.

27. Investigate the possibility of the student being involved in the use of drugs or alcohol.

Note: Serious eating disorders must be brought to the attention of a physician.

65 Is pessimistic

Goals:

1. The student will become more optimistic.
2. The student will improve his/her perception of school-related activities.

Objectives:

1. The student will make optimistic statements regarding expected outcomes on ___ out of ___ trials.
2. The student will improve his/her perception of school-related activities on ___ out of ___ trials.
3. The student will attempt ___ out of ___ tasks. (Gradually increase expectations as the student demonstrates success.)
4. The student will passively participate in a classroom activity by sitting quietly, assisting the teacher, taking notes, etc., during ___ out of ___ activities.
5. The student will actively participate in a classroom activity by being the group leader or spokesperson, answering questions, providing his/her opinion, etc., during ___ out of ___ activities.
6. The student will interact with others for ___ minutes at a time. (Gradually increase expectations as the student demonstrates success.)
7. The student will work on ___ short-term projects per month.
8. The student will work on ___ long-term projects per semester.
9. The student will voluntarily participate in competitive activities on ___ out of ___ trials.
10. The student will participate in one or more extracurricular activities per semester.

Interventions:

1. Communicate with parents, agencies, or the appropriate parties to inform them of the problem, determine the cause of the problem, and consider possible solutions to the problem.

2. Evaluate the appropriateness of the task to determine (a) if the task is too easy, (b) if the task is too difficult, or (c) if the length of time scheduled to complete the task is adequate.

3. Choose a peer to model positive reactions to situations for the student.

4. Have the student question any directions, explanations, or instructions not understood.

5. Remove the student from the group or activity until he/she can be more positive.

6. Provide the student with many social and academic successes.

7. Modify the environment to reduce situations which cause the student to be pessimistic (e.g., determine those activities the student dislikes and avoid forcing the student to engage in those activities).

8. Encourage the student to participate in those activities in which he/she is successful.

9. Provide the student with positive feedback which indicates he/she is successful, competent, important, respected, etc.

10. Identify individuals the student may contact concerning his/her unhappiness (e.g., guidance counselor, school nurse, social worker, school psychologist, etc.).

11. Encourage and help the student to make friends (e.g., pair the student with a peer; when that relationship is successful introduce other peers).

12. Explain to the student that feelings of pessimism are natural, but public display of that emotion should be limited.

13. Make the student aware of natural consequences that occur due to the student's displays of pessimism (e.g., others prefer not to interact with the student, he/she will not be chosen by peers to join in activities, etc.).

14. Provide the student with as many positive interactions as possible (e.g., recognize the student, greet the student, compliment his/her attire, etc.).

15. Require the student to make at least one positive comment about himself/herself on a daily basis. As the student demonstrates success, gradually increase the number of positive comments required.

16. Encourage and assist the student in joining extracurricular activities, clubs, etc.

17. Give the student additional responsibilities (e.g., chores, errands, etc.) to give him/her a feeling of success or accomplishment.

18. Help the student identify how he/she wishes things were in the environment and work with the student toward those goals.

19. Take time to talk with the student so the student realizes your interest in him/her is genuine.

20. Conduct a reinforcer survey with the student to determine his/her reinforcer preferences.

21. Communicate with parents to determine what the student finds reinforcing at home.

22. Help the student to be satisfied with personal best effort rather than insisting on perfection.

23. Identify the words or phrases the student uses to indicate his/her pessimism. Help the student recognize and in turn limit the statements.

24. Give the student a predetermined signal when he/she begins to be pessimistic.

25. Along with a directive, provide an incentive statement (e.g., "When you finish your math, you may have free time." "You may play a game when your desk is cleaned up." etc.).

26. Do not criticize when correcting the student, be honest yet supportive. Never cause the student to feel negatively about himself/herself.

27. Teach the student to respect others by respecting the student.

28. Treat the student with respect. Talk in an objective manner at all times.

29. Make positive comments about school and the student.

30. Teach the student appropriate ways to communicate displeasure, anger, frustration, etc.

31. Teach the student to "think" before acting (e.g., ask himself/herself, "What is happening?" "What am I doing?" "What should I do?" "What will be best for me?").

32. Make certain the student is allowed to voice an opinion in a situation to avoid becoming angry or upset.

33. Communicate with parents (e.g., notes home, phone calls, etc.) to share information concerning the student's progress. The parents may reinforce the student at home for being more positive at school.

34. Write a contract with the student specifying what behavior is expected (e.g., making positive comments) and what reinforcement will be made available when the terms of the contract have been met.

35. Reinforce the student for being more positive based on the length of time the student can be successful. As the student demonstrates success, gradually increase the length of time required for reinforcement.

36. Reinforce those students in the classroom who are positive in reacting to situations.

37. Establish classroom rules:
- Work on-task.
- Work quietly.
- Remain in your seat.
- Finish task.
- Meet task expectations.

Review rules often. Reinforce students for following rules.

38. Reinforce the student for being more positive in reacting to situations (e.g., attempting a task, making a positive comment about an activity, etc.): (a) give the student a tangible reward (e.g., classroom privileges, line leading, passing out materials, five minutes free time, etc.) or (b) give the student an intangible reward (e.g., praise, handshake, smile, etc.)

39. Speak to the student to explain (a) what the student is doing wrong (e.g., complaining, not taking part, reacting negatively, etc.) and (b) what the student should be doing (e.g., taking part, being enthusiastic, etc.).

66 Exhibits physical problems related to eating

Goals:
1. The student will consume only edible food items.
2. The student will consume an appropriate amount of food for his/her body type.

Objectives:
1. The student will consume an appropriate amount of food for his/her body type on ___out of ___ days per week.
2. The student will consume only edible food on ___ out of ___days per week.

Interventions:

1. Have the student develop his/her own healthy menu for a day, week, month.

2. Make certain that appropriate foods the student enjoys are available to him/her.

3. Make certain the student can consume only an appropriate amount of food while on the school grounds.

4. Assign an adult or peer to accompany the student throughout the school day to prevent self-induced vomiting.

5. Have the student study the nutritional value of the foods available to him/her.

6. Try various groupings to determine the situation in which the student is most comfortable.

7. Choose a peer to work directly with the student to prevent stress, frustration, anxiety, etc.

8. Reduce situations which may contribute to eating problems (e.g., testing situations, timed activities, competition, etc.).

9. Remove the student from activities or experiences which contribute to eating problems. As he/she demonstrates success, gradually introduce such activities into the student's schedule.

10. Monitor the student closely to make certain he/she only eats edible foods.

11. Make certain the student knows which objects/items in the environment are edible foods.

12. Prevent the student from experiencing situational stress or anxiety which result in his/her eating inedible objects/items.

13. Inform the appropriate personnel or agencies of the student's problem so intervention can take place in other areas of the student's environment in addition to school.

14. Arrange for the student to eat meals with an adult (i.e., teacher, counselor, volunteer, principal, etc.) so the quantity and type of food consumed by the student can be monitored and supervised.

15. Assist the student in making appropriate food choices.

16. Arrange for the student to eat small quantities throughout the day rather than eating only at mealtime.

17. Communicate with the parents (e.g., notes home, phone calls, etc.) to share information concerning the student's eating problem. The parents may reinforce the student at home for making suitable food choices.

18. Reinforce the student for practicing appropriate eating habits.

19. Provide the student with a high-interest activity which he/she prefers.

20. Avoid the discussion of topics that are sensitive to the student (e.g., death, divorce, unemployment, alcoholism, etc.).

21. Help the student to be satisfied with his/her own effort rather than insisting on perfection.

22. Provide the student with as many social and academic successes as possible.

23. Separate the student from a peer who may be encouraging or stimulating eating problems.

24. Make certain the student understands why it is important to eat appropriate quantities of nutritional food (e.g., maintaining appropriate weight, growth and development, etc.).

25. Involve the student in extracurricular activities to provide opportunities for success. Eating problems may diminish as he/she experiences success.

26. Help the student identify a support system (e.g., teen hotline, support group, etc.) that he/she can communicate with to help understand and control his/her eating problems.

27. Ask the student why he/she is having eating problems. The student may have the most accurate perception as to why he/she is having eating problems.

28. Consult with parents to determine whether the eating problems could be a reaction to a medical treatment and determine whether a modification should be made (i.e., take medication after a meal rather than before, eat small quantities of food throughout the day).

29. Investigate the possibility of the student being involved in the use of drugs or alcohol.

30. Allow the student to eat in alternative settings if being in the cafeteria causes anxiety resulting in eating problems.

31. Reduce the emphasis on competition and perfection. Repeated failure and frustration may cause the student to have eating problems.

32. Provide the student with "real life" experiences from the environment. Have individuals in food/nutrition related fields (e.g., dietitian, psychologist specializing in eating disorders, university extension department personnel, chef, etc.) visit the class to relate information about eating disorders, nutrition, food preparation, etc.

Note: Serious eating disorders must be brought to the attention of a physician.

67 Exhibits unwarranted self-blame or self-criticism

Goals:

1. The student will demonstrate realistic, objective self-appraisal.

Objectives:

1. The student will make ___ positive statement(s) about himself/herself per day. (Gradually increase expectations as the student demonstrates success.)
2. The student will demonstrate the ability to accept mistakes by refraining from crying, making negative self-statements, etc., on ___ out of ___ trials.
3. The student will demonstrate the ability to refrain from expecting perfection on his/her own part, by working on a specific task for a realistic amount of time on ___ out of ___ trials.
4. Given five situations over which the student has control and five situations over which he/she has no control, the student will correctly identify ___ of which he/she either has control or no control.
5. The student will make an accurate appraisal of his/her performance, at the end of each activity, on ___ out of ___ trials.

Interventions:

1. Reinforce the student for improvement rather than expecting excellence.

2. Recognize the student often and in various settings (e.g., hallways, cafeteria, etc.).

3. Provide the student with positive feedback which indicates he/she is successful, competent, important, valuable, etc.

4. Deliver praise and constructive criticism consistently to all students.

5. Have the student regularly record his/her own progress to have tangible evidence of success.

6. Make the necessary adjustments in the environment to prevent the student from experiencing stress, frustration, etc.

7. Choose a peer to help the student with class assignments, homework, etc.

8. Emphasize individual differences and the fact that everyone has strengths and weaknesses.

9. Reduce emphasis on competition and perfection. Repeated failure may result in unwarranted self-blame or self-criticism.

10. Encourage the student to refrain from comparing his/her performance to other students' performances, and emphasize personal improvement (e.g., maintain records of own progress rather than comparing work to others).

11. Provide the student with evidence of his/her ability so the student might better understand that self-blame/self-criticism is unwarranted.

12. Provide the student with success-oriented tasks (i.e., the expectation is that success will result in more positive attitudes and perceptions toward self and environment).

13. Provide the student with as many social and academic successes as possible.

14. When accidents occur, make "cleanup" a group responsibility to convey the idea that we all make mistakes and accidents are common to all of us.

15. Call on the student when he/she will most likely be able to answer correctly.

16. Encourage the student to act as a peer tutor so the student may recognize his/her own strengths and abilities.

17. Reduce activities which might threaten the student (e.g., announcing test score ranges or test scores aloud, making students read aloud in class, emphasizing the success of a particular student(s), etc.).

18. Intervene early when there is a problem to prevent more serious problems from occurring.

19. Reduce or remove punishment for accidents, and situations with inadequate evidence. Placing too much emphasis on uncontrollable situations may cause the student to feel guilty.

20. Encourage the student to use problem-solving skills: (a) identify the problem, (b) identify goals and objectives, (c) develop strategies, (d) develop a plan of action, and (e) carry out the plan.

21. Speak with the student to explain (a) what the student is doing wrong (e.g., being overly critical of himself/herself) and (b) what the student should be doing (e.g., being more constructive in self-criticism when evaluating himself/herself).

22. Write a contract with the student specifying what behavior is expected (e.g., accepting his/her own best effort) and what reinforcement will be made available when the terms of the contract have been met.

23. Reward others for accepting errors they make.

24. Reinforce the student for accepting errors that he/she makes.

25. Evaluate the appropriateness of the task to determine (a) if the task is too easy, (b) if the task is too difficult, and (c) if the length of time scheduled to complete the task is adequate.

26. Explain to the student that he/she should be happy with personal best effort rather than expecting perfection.

Reminder: Make certain that the self-blame or self-criticism is in fact unwarranted.

68   Expresses thoughts of death

Goals:

1. The student will not threaten to hurt self.
2. The student will not threaten to commit suicide.

Objectives:

1. The student will express his/her feelings in an appropriate manner on ___out of ___trials.
2. The student will talk to the teacher when he/she is feeling depressed, anxious, upset, hopeless, etc., on ___ out of ___ occasions.

Interventions:

1. Remove the student from the group or activity until he/she can demonstrate appropriate behavior and self-control.

2. Communicate with parents (e.g., notes home, phone calls, etc.) to share information concerning the student's progress. The parents may reinforce reinforce the student at home for appropriate behavior at school.

3. Evaluate the appropriateness of the task to determine (a) if the task is too easy, (b) if the task is too difficult, and (c) if the length of time scheduled to complete the task is adequate.

4. Prevent frustrating or anxiety-producing situations from occurring (e.g., give the student tasks on his/her ability level, give the student only the number of tasks that can be tolerated in one sitting, stop social interactions that stimulate the student to threaten self-harm, etc.).

5. Interact frequently with the student to prevent self-abusive behavior by meeting the student's needs as they occur.

6. Maintain visibility to and from the student. The teacher should be able to see the student and the student should be able to see the teacher. Make eye contact possible at all times.

7. Facilitate on-task behavior by providing a full schedule of daily events. Prevent lag time from occurring when the student will be free to engage in self-abusive behavior.

8. Remove from the environment any object that the student may use to hurt himself/herself.

9. Provide the student with positive feedback that indicates he/she is successful, important, respected, etc.

10. Maintain a positive/calm environment (e.g., positive comments, acknowledgment of successes, quiet communications, etc.).

11. Provide the student with a quiet place to work (e.g., carrel, study area).

12. Reduce the emphasis on competition. Repeated failure may result in anger and frustration that may cause the student to try to hurt himself/ herself.

13. Maintain consistent expectations.

14. Allow the student to have input relative to making decisions (e.g., changing activities, choosing activities, deciding length of activities, etc.).

15. Provide the student with a selection of optional activities to be performed (e.g., if an activity results in harmful behaviors, an optional activity can be substituted).

16. Teach the student appropriate ways to deal with anxiety, frustration, and anger (e.g., move away from the stimulus, verbalize unhappiness, choose another activity, etc.).

17. Teach the student problem-solving skills: (a) identify the problem, (b) identify goals and objectives, (c) develop strategies, (d) develop a plan of action, and (e) carry out the plan.

18. Maintain a consistent daily routine.

19. Do not allow the student to be unsupervised anywhere in the school environment.

20. Avoid discussions or prevent stimuli in the environment that remind the student of unpleasant experiences/sensitive topics (e.g., divorce, death, unemployment, alcoholism, etc.).

21. Do not criticize. When correcting the student, be honest yet supportive. Never cause the student to feel badly about himself/herself.

22. Intervene early when there is a problem to prevent more serious problems from occurring.

23. Treat the student with respect. Talk in an objective manner at all times.

24. Maintain trust and confidentiality with the student at all times.

25. Make certain the student is allowed to voice an opinion in a situation to avoid becoming angry or upset.

26. Talk to the student about ways of handling situations successfully without conflict (e.g., walk away from a situation, change to another activity, ask for help, etc.).

27. Reinforce the student for demonstrating appropriate behavior based on the length of time the student can be successful. As the student demonstrates success, gradually increase the amount of time required for reinforcement.

28. Reinforce those students in the classroom who engage in appropriate behavior.

29. Establish classroom rules:
- Work on-task.
- Work quietly.
- Remain in your seat.
- Finish task.
- Meet task expectations.

Review rules often. Reinforce students for following rules.

30. Speak with the student to explain (a) what the student is doing wrong (e.g., threatening to hurt self) and (b) what the student should be doing (e.g., talking about the situation, demonstrating self-control, problem solving, etc.).

31. Reinforce the student for engaging in appropriate behavior: (a) give the student a tangible reward (e.g., classroom privileges, line leading, passing out materials, five minutes free time, etc.) or (b) give the student an intangible reward (e.g., praise, handshake, smile, etc.).

32. Discuss concerns with other professionals to determine if further investigation is warranted (e.g., abuse or neglect).

33. Structure the environment so the student does not have time to dwell on real or imagined problems.

Note: All references to suicide should be considered serious, and steps should be taken to respond to the situation.

69 Frowns, scowls, looks unhappy during typical classroom situations

Goals:

1. The student will smile during typical classroom situations.
2. The student will demonstrate happiness during typical classroom situations.
3. The student will refrain from frowning, scowling, and looking unhappy during typical classroom situations.
4. The student will behave in a manner appropriate for the situation.

Objectives:

1. The student will smile when appropriate during ___ out of ___ typical classroom situations.
2. The student will demonstrate happiness during ___ out of ___ typical classroom situations.
3. The student will refrain from frowning, scowling, and looking unhappy during ___ out of ___ typical classroom situations.
4. The student will show emotion that is appropriate for the situation during ___ out of ___ occasions.
5. The student will demonstrate happiness by smiling, laughing, joking, etc., when appropriate during ___ out of ___ typical classroom situations.
6. The student will laugh or smile when humorous events or activities take place on ___ out of ___ trials.
7. The student will demonstrate emotion like that of his/her peers during ___ out of ___ typical classroom situations.

Interventions:

1. Share concerns with administration and seek referral to an agency for investigation of abuse or neglect.

2. Communicate your concern to the student.

3. Reinforce the student for engaging in appropriate behavior: (a) give the student a tangible reward (e.g., classroom privileges, line leading, passing out materials, five minutes free time, etc.) or (b) give the student an intangible reward (e.g., praise, handshake, smile, etc.).

4. Follow less desirable activities with more desirable activities throughout the day to maintain interest and variety.

5. Choose a peer to engage in recreational activities with the student to develop a friendship.

6. Provide the student with positive feedback that indicates that he/she is successful, competent, important, valuable, etc.

7. Give the student additional responsibilities (e.g., chores, errands, etc.) to give him/her a feeling of success or accomplishment.

8. Identify individuals the student may contact with his/her concerns or problems (e.g., guidance counselor, school nurse, social worker, school psychologist, etc.).

9. Create the most positive environment possible.

10. Seek the student's input in planning the curriculum and extracurricular activities, classes, etc., (i.e., attempt to include student preferences and favored activities).

11. Provide the student with success-oriented tasks (i.e., the expectation is that success will result in more positive attitudes and perceptions toward self and environment).

12. Facilitate the development of friendships with peers (e.g., assign activities for the student involving peers, give the student and a peer joint responsibilities, etc.).

13. Reduce the emphasis on competition. Repeated failure will most likely contribute to the student's unhappiness.

14. Teach the student to be satisfied with his/her own best effort rather than insisting on perfection (e.g., reduce the emphasis on competition, help the student realize that success is individually defined).

15. De-emphasize arbitrary levels of success (i.e., rather than absolute excellence, progress of any amount should be considered a measure of success).

16. Respect the student's right to privacy when appropriate.

17. Take the time to listen so the student realizes your concern/interest is genuine.

18. Maintain consistent interactions (e.g., do not provide extra attention when the student is demonstrating facial expressions of displeasure).

19. Make certain that reinforcement is not inadvertently given when the student does not smile, laugh or demonstrate happiness (e.g., attending to the student only when he/she demonstrates unhappiness).

20. Communicate with parents, agencies, or the appropriate parties to inform them of the problem, determine the cause of the problem, and consider possible solutions to the problem.

21. Speak to the student to explain (a) that you recognize he/she is unhappy and (b) appropriate ways to deal with unhappiness.

22. Explain to the student that feelings of unhappiness are natural, but there is an appropriate length of time for public display of that emotion.

23. Teach the student alternative ways to communicate unhappiness (e.g., in writing, by talking, etc.).

24. Remove the student from the group or activity until he/she can be more positive.

25. Ask the student why he/she frowns, scowls, looks unhappy during typical classroom situations. The student may have the most accurate perception.

70 Has attempted suicide

Goals:

1. The student will not attempt to hurt self.
2. The student will not attempt to commit suicide.

Objectives:

1. The student will express his/her feelings in an appropriate manner on ___ out of ___ trials.
2. The student will talk to the teacher when he/she is feeling depressed, anxious, upset, hopeless, etc., on ___ out of ___ occasions.

Interventions:

1. Remove the student from the group or activity until he/she can demonstrate appropriate behavior and self-control.

2. Communicate with parents (e.g., notes home, phone calls, etc.) to share information concerning the student's progress. The parents may reinforce the student at home for appropriate behavior at school.

3. Evaluate the appropriateness of the task to determine (a) if the task is too easy, (b) if the task is too difficult, and (c) if the length of time scheduled to complete the task is adequate.

4. Prevent frustrating or anxiety-producing situations from occurring (e.g., give the student tasks on his/her ability level, give the student only the number of tasks that can be tolerated in one sitting, stop social interactions that stimulate the student to threaten self-harm, etc.).

5. Interact frequently with the student to prevent self-abusive behavior by meeting the student's needs as they occur.

6. Maintain visibility to and from the student. The teacher should be able to see the student and the student should be able to see the teacher. Make eye contact possible at all times.

7. Facilitate on-task behavior by providing a full schedule of daily events. Prevent lag time from occurring when the student will be free to engage in self-abusive behavior.

8. Remove from the environment any object that the student may use to hurt himself/herself.

9. Provide the student with positive feedback that indicates he/she is successful, important, respected, etc.

10. Maintain a positive/calm environment (e.g., positive comments, acknowledgment of successes, quiet communications, etc.).

11. Provide the student with a quiet place to work (e.g., carrel, study area).

12. Reduce the emphasis on competition. Repeated failure may result in anger and frustration that may cause the student to try to hurt himself/herself.

13. Maintain consistent expectations.

14. Allow the student to have input relative to making decisions (e.g., changing activities, choosing activities, deciding length of activities, etc.).

15. Provide the student with a selection of optional activities to be performed (e.g., if an activity results in harmful behaviors, an optional activity can be substituted).

16. Teach the student appropriate ways to deal with anxiety, frustration, and anger (e.g., move away from the stimulus, verbalize unhappiness, choose another activity, etc.).

17. Teach the student problem-solving skills: (a) identify the problem, (b) identify goals and objectives, (c) develop strategies, (d) develop a plan of action, and (e) carry out the plan.

18. Maintain a consistent daily routine.

19. Do not allow the student to be unsupervised anywhere in the school environment.

20. Avoid discussions or prevent stimuli in the environment that remind the student of unpleasant experiences/sensitive topics (e.g., divorce, death, unemployment, alcoholism, etc.).

21. Do not criticize. When correcting the student, be honest yet supportive. Never cause the student to feel badly about himself/herself.

22. Intervene early when there is a problem to prevent more serious problems from occurring.

23. Treat the student with respect. Talk in an objective manner at all times.

24. Maintain trust and confidentiality with the student at all times.

25. Make certain the student is allowed to voice an opinion in a situation to avoid becoming angry or upset.

26. Talk to the student about ways of handling situations successfully without conflict (e.g., walk away from a situation, change to another activity, ask for help, etc.).

27. Reinforce the student for demonstrating appropriate behavior based on the length of time the student can be successful. As the student demonstrates success, gradually increase the amount of time required for reinforcement.

28. Structure the environment so the student does not have time to dwell on real or imagined problems.

29. Establish classroom rules:
- Work on-task.
- Work quietly.
- Remain in your seat.
- Finish task.
- Meet task expectations.

Review rules often. Reinforce students for following rules.

30. Speak with the student to explain (a) what the student is doing wrong (e.g., threatening to hurt self) and (b) what the student should be doing (e.g., talking about the situation, demonstrating self-control, problem solving, etc.).

31. Reinforce the student for engaging in appropriate behavior: (a) give the student a tangible reward (e.g., classroom privileges, line leading, passing out materials, five minutes free time, etc.) or (b) give the student an intangible reward (e.g., praise, handshake, smile, etc.).

32. Share concerns with administration and seek referral to an agency for investigation of abuse or neglect.

33. Investigate the possibility of the student being involved in the use of drugs or alcohol.

34. Act as a resource for parents by providing information on agencies, counseling programs, etc.

35. Reinforce those students in the classroom who engage in appropriate behavior.

Note: All references to suicide should be considered serious, and steps should be taken to respond to the situation.

71   Has experienced weight gain

Goals:
1. The student will consume an appropriate amount of food for his/her body type.
2. The student will maintain weight within the range medically recommended for him/her.

Objectives:
1. The student will consume an appropriate amount of food for his/her body type on ___ out of ___ days per week.
2. The student will follow a balanced diet to meet his/her individual requirements and weight maintenance needs on ____ out of ____ trials.
3. The student will engage in exercises/physical activities to meet his/her individual requirements and weight maintenance on ____ out of ____ trials.
4. The student will manage weight maintenance with his/her medically recommended range on ___ out of ____ trials.

Interventions:

1. Reinforce the student for positively participating in weight-maintenance activities: (a) give the student a tangible reward (e.g., classroom privileges, line leading, passing out materials, five minutes free time, etc.) or (b) give the student an intangible reward (e.g., praise, handshake, smile, etc.).

2. Provide the student with time and encouragement to establish rapport. Any vast change in behavior, such as sudden, rapid weight gain or loss, withdrawn behavior, and/or other behavior changes may warrant the need of additional support.

3. Encourage the student to weigh himself/herself throughout the week at a specified time of day. The student should not weigh himself/herself more than once in a given day.

4. Write a contract with the student specifying what behavior is expected (e.g., participating in weight maintenance activities) and what reinforcement will be available when the terms of the contract have been met.

5. Communicate with parents (e.g., notes home, phone calls, etc.) to share information concerning the student's progress with weight maintenance at school. The parents may reinforce the student at home.

6. Encourage the student who experiences weight fluctuations to drink non-caloric, decaffeinated fluids (e.g., juices, water).

7. Assist the student in the development of coping strategies for stress which do not include eating (e.g., exercising regularly, developing a hobby, finding means of self-expression through dance or writing, becoming involved in an individual or team sport, etc.).

8. Help the student develop a list of activities he/she finds enjoyable (e.g., purchasing new clothes, seeing a movie, going to a dance, etc.). The student may then refer to this list for reinforcement after he/she has correctly attempted weight maintenance activities.

9. The student who experiences weight fluctuations need not feel forced to participate in weight maintenance activities. It is more important to offer opportunities for positive reinforcement for participation.

10. Encourage the development of positive self-concept in a classroom environment that is accepting of individual differences (e.g., overweight or underweight persons need not feel ostracized from the class).

11. The student may not have a realistic perception of himself/herself (e.g., he/she may view himself/herself as too fat, too thin, ugly, etc.). Encourage the student to find genuine personal strengths and attributes (e.g., activities in which the student excels at school, a personal attribute such as hair or eye color, etc.).

12. Provide the student with individually tailored ways of tracking progress with weight. This might include

   (a) developing a daily/weekly schedule of activities the student could follow and check off (e.g., exercise, meals, snack times, etc.);

   (b) helping the student develop a daily journal in which he/she logs meal and snack choices for his/her review; and

   (c) assisting the student to develop a chart or graph of his/her weight gains/losses.

13. The student may feel failure from an inability to meet a hallmark of perfection. Encourage the student to view individual effort as more important by (a) helping the student set and achieve meaningful, short term goals (e.g., following his/her diet and exercise schedule for a week) and (b) assuring the student receives meaningful positive reinforcement following goal achievement.

14. The student may not feel he/she has been given an opportunity to make self-governing choices. Assist the student to identify choices he/she may make within realistic parameters (e.g., age, situation, etc.). Reinforce the student for making choices that benefit him/her without hurting others.

15. Help the student develop weight-management strategies that are based upon healthy eating habits (e.g., eating three balanced meals per day, eating healthy snacks, etc.) in lieu of unhealthy choices (e.g., fasting, going on unusual diets, etc.).

16. The student will need careful attention to what constitutes positive reinforcement. Social reinforcement that draws attention to the student in front of his/her classmates may actually punish (instead of promote) healthy weight maintenance if the student becomes embarrassed.

17. The student may not be able to view progress with behavioral changes and weight-maintenance skills in a short period of time. Assist the student to develop and reach short-term, behavioral objectives which progressively lead to long-term goal completion.

18. Make certain the student has the opportunity to learn how he/she is appreciated regardless of his/her weight.

19. When the student expresses concern about his/her weight, establish with him/her those positive steps he/she may choose right now. Provide positive comments and reinforcement for those times when the student chooses positive action.

20. Teach the student to identify his/her antecedents to overeating or undereating behavior. For example, the student may learn to recognize his/her tendency to eat when anxious (e.g., when watching a scary movie or when studying for a test). Once the problem situation is recognized by the student, work with him/her to develop positive coping strategies for use instead of continuous eating.

21. Encourage or reinforce others for participation in group weight-maintenance and exercise activities.

22. Give the student the responsibility of helping another in the group.

23. Demonstrate respect for the student's opinions, responses, suggestions, etc.

24. Encourage friendship building in the classroom (e.g., students may wish to attend extracurricular activities in small groups, etc.). The opportunity to work with friends on projects may help the student overcome his/her unwarranted fears or concerns.

25. Request the student lead a small-group activity when these are areas of interest and/or mastery for the student.

26. Provide the student with many social and academic successes.

27. Provide the student with positive feedback to indicate he/she is successful.

28. Emphasize individual success or progress over winning or "beating" others.

29. Structure the environment so the student has many opportunities to succeed.

30. Supervise classroom activities closely so peers with whom the student interacts do not stimulate inappropriate behavior or ridicule.

31. Teach the student problem-solving skills so he/she is better equipped to manage potential problems (e.g., talking, walking away, calling upon an arbitrator, compromising, etc.). This may help the student feel better equipped to manage situations which provoke stress associated with overeating and/or undereating.

32. The student will appreciate constructive remarks and verbal praise in conversations away from the group and/or in a nonintrusive delivery style typical for an entire group. Loud, open remarks may do more harm than good regarding the promotion of any skills (especially social skills) for the student.

33. Provide the student with a variety of ways to develop rapport with instructor(s) (e.g., writing notes, talking about concerns privately, etc.).

34. Be specific and positive when providing the student constructive criticism.

35. Help the student identify the benefits of choosing to participate in scheduled weight- maintenance activities (e.g., diet, exercising).

36. The student may be overly self-critical when mistakes are made or progress is delayed. Help the student use problem-solving skills to address such concerns by identifying problems, developing solutions to try, and evaluating efforts.

37. Consult with medical professionals to determine if the student's weight fluctuations are the result of a medical problem.

38. The student who experiences weight fluctuations may benefit from (a) frequent opportunities to rehearse coping mechanisms the student and instructor have developed, (b) frequent opportunities for social success, (c) gradual increases in activity participation expectations (e.g., passive, then active participation).

39. The student will probably experience natural consequences for not participating socially (e.g., isolation from others, avoidance of activities the student might actually like if the fears were overcome, etc.). It is important to realize the student needs positive experiences which occur incidentally throughout the day for skills development.

40. Give the student opportunities to use the positive replacement skills he/she is learning.

41. When developing a schedule, plan for highly reinforcing activities to follow less desirable activities.

42. Build positive self-concept among students by including the following approaches:
(a) Offer opportunities for students to work together noncompetitively on class projects;
(b) identify and sincerely compliment each student's unique contribution to group work when this will be perceived by the student as positive reinforcement; and
(c) organize time to speak with students individually.

72 Has experienced weight loss

Goals:

   1. The student will consume an appropriate amount of food for his/her body type.

Objectives:

   1. The student will consume an appropriate amount of food for his/her body type on ___out of ___days per week.

Interventions:

1. Discuss concerns with other professionals to determine if further investigation is warranted (e.g., abuse or neglect).

2. Take the time to listen so the student realizes your concern is genuine.

3. Identify persons the student may contact with his/her worries or concerns (e.g., guidance counselor, school nurse, social worker, school psychologist, etc.).

4. Provide the student with opportunities for social and academic success.

5. Provide praise and recognition as often as possible.

6. Encourage participation in school and extracurricular activities.

7. Reduce the emphasis on competition. Repeated failure may cause the student to have eating problems.

8. Try various groupings to determine the situation in which the student is most successful.

9. Make the necessary adjustments in the environment to prevent the student from experiencing stress, frustration, anxiety, etc.

10. Structure the environment so time does not permit opportunities for the student to dwell on concerns or worries.

11. Have peers invite the student to participate in extracurricular activities.

12. Demonstrate respect for the student's opinions, responses, suggestions, etc.

13. Call attention to the student's accomplishments (e.g., publicly or privately depending on which is more appropriate).

14. Avoid discussion of topics sensitive to the student (e.g., divorce, death, unemployment, alcoholism, etc.).

15. Provide the student with opportunities for special project responsibilities, leadership, etc.

16. Provide as many enjoyable and interesting activities as possible.

17. Help the student recognize problems that are within his/her ability to deal with and not to worry needlessly about situations over which the student has no control.

18. Allow the student to eat in alternative settings if being in the cafeteria causes anxiety resulting in weight loss.

19. Consult with parents to determine whether the student's weight loss could be a reaction to a medical treatment and determine whether a modification could be made (e.g., take medication after a meal rather than before, eat small quantities of food throughout the day, etc.).

20. Make certain the student understands why it is important to eat appropriate quantities of nutritional food (e.g., maintaining appropriate weight, growth and development, etc.).

Reminder: Do not "force" the student to participate in any activity.

73 Threatens to hurt self or commit suicide

Goals:

1. The student will not threaten to hurt self.
2. The student will not threaten to commit suicide.

Objectives:

1. The student will express his/her feelings in an appropriate manner on ___ out of ___ trials.
2. The student will talk to the teacher when he/she is feeling depressed, anxious, upset, hopeless, etc., on ___ out of ___ occasions.

Interventions:

1. Remove the student from the group or activity until he/she can demonstrate appropriate behavior and self-control.

2. Communicate with parents (e.g., notes home, phone calls, etc.) to share information concerning the student's progress. The parents may reinforce the student at home for appropriate behavior at school.

3. Evaluate the appropriateness of the task to determine (a) if the task is too easy, (b) if the task is too difficult, and (c) if the length of time scheduled to complete the task is adequate.

4. Prevent frustrating or anxiety-producing situations from occurring (e.g., give the student tasks on his/her ability level, give the student only the number of tasks that can be tolerated in one sitting, stop social interactions that stimulate the student to threaten self-harm, etc.).

5. Interact frequently with the student to prevent self-abusive behavior by meeting the student's needs as they occur.

6. Maintain visibility to and from the student. The teacher should be able to see the student and the student should be able to see the teacher. Make eye contact possible at all times.

7. Facilitate on-task behavior by providing a full schedule of daily events. Prevent lag time from occurring when the student will be free to engage in self-abusive behavior.

8. Remove from the environment any object that the student may use to hurt himself/herself.

9. Provide the student with positive feedback that indicates he/she is successful, important, respected, etc.

10. Maintain a positive/calm environment (e.g., positive comments, acknowledgment of successes, quiet communications, etc.).

11. Provide the student with a quiet place to work (e.g., carrel, study area).

12. Reduce the emphasis on competition. Repeated failure may result in anger and frustration that may cause the student to try to hurt himself/herself.

13. Maintain consistent expectations.

14. Allow the student to have input relative to making decisions (e.g., changing activities, choosing activities, deciding length of activities, etc.).

15. Provide the student with a selection of optional activities to be performed (e.g., if an activity results in harmful behaviors, an optional activity can be substituted).

16. Teach the student appropriate ways to deal with anxiety, frustration, and anger (e.g., move away from the stimulus, verbalize unhappiness, choose another activity, etc.).

17. Teach the student problem-solving skills: (a) identify the problem, (b) identify goals and objectives, (c) develop strategies, (d) develop a plan of action, and (e) carry out the plan.

18. Maintain a consistent daily routine.

19. Do not allow the student to be unsupervised anywhere in the school environment.

20. Avoid discussions or prevent stimuli in the environment that remind the student of unpleasant experiences/sensitive topics (e.g., divorce, death, unemployment, alcoholism, etc.).

21. Do not criticize. When correcting the student, be honest yet supportive. Never cause the student to feel badly about himself/herself.

22. Intervene early when there is a problem to prevent more serious problems from occurring.

23. Treat the student with respect. Talk in an objective manner at all times.

24. Maintain trust and confidentiality with the student at all times.

25. Make certain the student is allowed to voice an opinion in a situation to avoid becoming angry or upset.

26. Talk to the student about ways of handling situations successfully without conflict (e.g., walk away from a situation, change to another activity, ask for help, etc.).

27. Reinforce the student for demonstrating appropriate behavior based on the length of time the student can be successful. As the student demonstrates success, gradually increase the amount of time required for reinforcement.

28. Reinforce those students in the classroom who engage in appropriate behavior.

29. Establish classroom rules:
- Work on-task.
- Work quietly.
- Remain in your seat.
- Finish task.
- Meet task expectations.

Review rules often. Reinforce students for following rules.

30. Speak with the student to explain (a) what the student is doing wrong (e.g., threatening to hurt self) and (b) what the student should be doing (e.g., talking about the situation, demonstrating self-control, problem solving, etc.).

31. Reinforce the student for engaging in appropriate behavior: (a) give the student a tangible reward (e.g., classroom privileges, line leading, passing out materials, five minutes free time, etc.) or (b) give the student an intangible reward (e.g., praise, handshake, smile, etc.).

32. Share concerns with administration and seek referral to an agency for investigation of abuse or neglect.

33. Investigate the possibility of the student being involved in the use of drugs or alcohol.

34. Act as a resource for parents by providing information on agencies, counseling programs, etc.

35. Structure the environment so the student does not have time to dwell on real or imagined problems.

Note: All references to suicide should be considered serious, and steps should be taken to respond to the situation.

74 Indicates that he/she is not happy through verbal expression

Goals:

1. The student will indicate unhappiness with acceptable verbal expressions.
2. The student will become more optimistic.
3. The student will improve his/her perception of school-related experiences.

Objectives:

1. The student will use appropriate verbal expressions to indicate unhappiness on ___ out of ___ situations.
2. The student will demonstrate emotions that are appropriate to the situation on ___ out of ___ trials.
3. The student will talk about situations in a realistic manner on ___ out of ___ trials.
4. The student will make optimistic statements regarding expected outcomes on ___ out of ___ trials.
5. The student will improve his/her perception of school-related activities on ___ out of ___ trials.
6. The student will smile when appropriate during ___ out of ___ typical classroom situations.
7. The student will demonstrate happiness during ___ out of ___ typical classroom situations.
8. The student will demonstrate happiness by smiling, laughing, joking, etc., when appropriate during ___ out of ___ typical classroom situations.
9. The student will laugh or smile when humorous events or activities take place on ___ out of ___ trials.
10. The student will demonstrate emotion like that of his/her peers during ___ out of ___ typical classroom situations.

Interventions:

1. Reinforce the student for displaying appropriate moods for a situation: (a) give the student a tangible reward (e.g., classroom privileges, line leading, passing out materials, five minutes free time, etc.) or (b) give the student an intangible reward (e.g., praise, handshake, smile, etc.).

2. Establish classroom rules:
- Work on-task.
- Work quietly.
- Remain in your seat.
- Finish task.
- Meet task expectations.

Review rules often. Reinforce students for following rules.

3. Reinforce those students in the classroom who make positive, supportive comments.

4. Reinforce the student for making positive, supportive comments based on the length of time the student can be successful. Gradually increase the length of time required for reinforcement.

5. Remove the student from the group until he/she can demonstrate appropriate behavior and self-control.

6. Write a contract with the student specifying what behavior is expected (e.g., making positive, supportive comments) and what reinforcement will be made available when the terms of the contract have been met.

7. Communicate with the parents (e.g., notes home, phone calls, etc.) The parents may reinforce the student at home for appropriate behavior at school.

8. Evaluate the appropriateness of a task to determine (a) if the task is too easy, (b) if the task is too difficult, and (c) if the length of time scheduled for the task is adequate.

9. Record or chart the number of times the student verbally expresses that he/she is not happy to make the student aware of the frequency.

10. Explain, if appropriate, that there are many things a student must do which might make him/her unhappy, but complaining is not a solution.

11. Provide the student with as many academic and social successes as possible.

12. Identify persons the student may contact about his/her unhappiness (e.g., guidance counselor, school nurse, social worker, school psychologist, etc.).

13. Teach the student problem-solving skills: (a) identify the problem, (b) identify goals and objectives, (c) develop strategies, (d) develop a plan for action, and (e) carry out the plan.

14. Make the necessary adjustments in the environment to prevent the student from experiencing stress, frustration, anger, etc.

15. Give the student additional responsibilities (e.g., chores, errands, etc.) to give the student a feeling of success or accomplishment.

16. Structure the environment so the student does not have time to dwell on real or imagined problems.

17. Take the time to listen so the student realizes the teacher's concerns and interest in him/her.

18. Determine which activities the student most enjoys and include them as much as possible in the daily routine.

19. Reduce the emphasis on competition. Repeated failure may result in unhappiness for the student.

20. Reduce stimuli which contribute to the student's verbal expressions of unhappiness (e.g., seek input from the student as to what upsets him/her).

21. Separate the student from the peer who stimulates the verbal expressions of unhappiness.

22. Try various groupings to determine the situation in which the student is most comfortable.

23. Follow less desirable activities with more desirable activities.

24. Encourage the student to participate in extra-curricular activities.

25. Make certain that reinforcement (e.g., attention, getting his/her way, etc.) is not inadvertently given for verbal expressions of unhappiness.

26. Provide the student with alternative activities to perform in case some activities prove upsetting.

27. Give the student some decision-making power (e.g., seating assignment, order of tasks, daily schedule, etc.).

28. Identify for the student more appropriate ways to express his/her feelings.

75 Indicates that no one likes him/her, no one cares about him/her, etc.

Goals:

1. The student will improve his/her self-esteem.
2. The student will develop a friendship.

Objectives:

1. The student will make ___ positive self-statement(s) per day.
2. The student will interact with a peer(s) when asked on ___ out of ___ trials.
3. The student will initiate an interaction with a peer(s) ___ times per day.
4. The student will participate in assigned activities on ___ out of ___ trials.
5. The student will demonstrate emotions that are appropriate to the situation on ___ out of ___ trials.
6. The student will talk about situations in a realistic manner on ___ out of ___ trials.
7. The student will develop ___ friendship(s) in a month's period.
8. The student will indicate that he/she is liked by others on ___ out of ___ trials.
9. The student will indicate that others care about him/her on ___ out of ___ trials.

Interventions:

1. Provide the student with as many academic and social successes as possible so peers may view him/her in a more positive way.

2. Make the necessary adjustments in the environment to prevent the student from experiencing stress, frustration, anger, etc.

3. Give the student additional responsibilities (e.g., chores, errands, etc.) to give him/her a feeling of success or accomplishment.

4. Structure the environment so the student does not have time to dwell on real or imagined problems.

5. Take the time to listen so the student realizes your concern and interest.

6. Identify for the student more appropriate ways to express his/her feelings.

7. Reduce stimuli that contribute to the student's verbal expression of unhappiness (e.g., seek input from the student as to what upsets him/her).

8. Separate the student from the peer(s) who stimulates the verbal expression of unhappiness.

9. Reinforce those students in the classroom who deal with unhappiness in an appropriate manner.

10. Try various groupings to determine the situation in which the student is most comfortable.

11. Encourage the student to participate in extracurricular activities that will help develop those skills necessary to interact appropriately with others at school.

12. Make certain that reinforcement (e.g., attention, getting his/her way, etc.) is not inadvertently given for verbal expressions of unhappiness.

13. Provide the student with alternative activities to perform in case some activities prove upsetting.

14. Reduce the emphasis on competition. Repeated failure may cause the student to feel that others do not like or care about him/her.

15. Encourage and help the student to make friends (e.g., pair the student with a peer; when that relationship is successful, introduce other students).

16. When natural consequences occur as a result of the student's displays of unhappiness, point them out to him/her (e.g., peers prefer not to interact with the student).

17. Provide the student with as many positive interactions as possible (e.g., recognize the student, greet the student, compliment attire, etc.).

18. Discourage the student from engaging in those activities that cause him/her unhappiness.

19. Help the student identify things he/she wishes were in the environment and work with the student toward those goals.

20. Teach the student alternative ways to deal with unpleasant social interactions during the school-age experience (e.g., deal with problems when they arise, practice self-control at all times, share problems or concerns with others, etc.).

21. Teach the student alternative ways to communicate unhappiness (e.g., written, spoken, etc.).

22. Speak with the student to explain that he/she may be trying too hard to fit in and that he/she should relax and allow friendships to develop naturally.

23. Reinforce those students in the classroom who appropriately interact with other students.

24. Have the student be the leader of a small-group activity if he/she possesses mastery of skills or an interest in that area.

25. Give the student the responsibility of tutoring a peer if he/she possesses the skills to be shared.

26. Provide the student with a predetermined signal (e.g., verbal cue, hand signal, etc.) when he/she begins to demonstrate inappropriate behaviors when interacting with others (e.g., whining, fighting, throwing objects, refusing to share, etc.).

27. Maintain maximum supervision of the student's interaction and gradually decrease the amount of supervision over time.

28. Give the student responsibilities in group situations so peers may view the student in a more positive way.

29. Encourage the student to further develop any ability or skill he/she may have so peers may view the student in a more positive way.

30. Help the student to identify his/her inappropriate behaviors and teach the student ways to change those behaviors.

31. Ask the student to choose a peer to work with on a specific assignment. Encourage the student and peer to interact with each other in nonacademic areas (e.g., recess, lunch, break time, etc.).

32. Do not criticize. When correcting the student, be honest yet supportive. Never cause the student to feel badly about himself/herself.

33. Do not force the student to interact with students with whom he/she is not completely comfortable.

34. Treat the student with respect. Talk in an objective manner at all times.

35. Allow the student to attempt something new in private before doing so in front of others.

36. Do not assume that the student is being treated nicely by other students. Others may be stimulating inappropriate behavior on the part of the student.

37. Encourage the student to interact with others.

38. Provide the student with frequent opportunities to meet new people.

39. Do not force the student to interact with others.

40. Make certain the student is not demonstrating a lack of confidence to get the attention of others.

41. Teach the student problem-solving skills: (a) identify the problem, (b) identify goals and objectives, (c) develop strategies, (d) develop a plan for action, and (e) carry out the plan.

42. Record or chart the number of times the student verbally expresses that others do not like or care about him/her to make the student aware of the frequency.

43. Communicate with parents (e.g., notes home, phone calls, etc.) to share information concerning the student's progress. The parents may reinforce the student at home for interacting appropriately with others at school.

44. Write a contract with the student specifying what behavior is expected (e.g., interacting appropriately with others) and what reinforcement will be made available when the terms of the contract have been met.

45. Remove the student from the group until he/she can interact appropriately with others.

46. Communicate to the student that he/she is a worthwhile individual.

47. Establish classroom rules:
- Work on-task.
- Work quietly.
- Remain in your seat.
- Finish task.
- Meet task expectations.

Review rules often. Reinforce students for following rules.

48. Reinforce those students in the classroom who make positive, supportive comments to the student.

49. Reinforce the student for interacting with others: (a) give the student a tangible reward (e.g., classroom privileges, line leading, passing out materials, five minutes free time, etc.) or (b) give the student an intangible reward (e.g., praise, handshake, smile, etc.).

50. Identify individuals the student may contact with his/her concerns (e.g., guidance counselor, school nurse, social worker, school psychologist, etc.).

51. Reinforce the student for interacting with others based on the length of time the student can be successful. As the student demonstrates success, gradually increase the length of time required for reinforcement.

Reminder: Do not "force" the student to interact with others with whom he/she is uncomfortable.

76 Is tired, listless, apathetic, unmotivated, not interested in school

Goals:

1. The student will participate in classroom activities.
2. The student will demonstrate interest by participating in classroom activities.

Objectives:

1. The student will participate in ___ out of ___ classroom activities per day.
2. The student will participate in ___ out of ___ classroom activities per week.
3. The student will participate in ___ out of ___ classroom activities per month.
4. The student will demonstrate an interest in classroom activities by asking about the activities, talking about the activities, helping prepare for the activities, etc., in ___ out of ___ activities.
5. The student will passively participate in a classroom activity by sitting quietly, assisting the teacher, taking notes, etc., during ___ out of ___ activities.
6. The student will actively participate in a classroom activity by being the group leader or spokesperson, answering questions, providing his/her opinion, etc., during ___ out of ___ activities.
7. The student will interact with a peer for ___ minutes per day. (Gradually increase expectations as the student demonstrates success.)
8. The student will initiate ___ interactions with a peer per day. (Gradually increase expectations as the student demonstrates success.)
9. The student will interact with the teacher for ___ minutes per day. (Gradually increase expectations as the student demonstrates success.)
10. The student will initiate ___ interactions with the teacher per day. (Gradually increase expectations as the student demonstrates success.)
11. The student will perform academic tasks with ___% accuracy. (Gradually increase expectations as the student demonstrates success.)
12. The student will identify something he/she enjoys doing at school when asked by the teacher on ___ out of ___ occasions.
13. The student will identify a reinforcer he/she would like to earn for participating in classroom activities on ___ out of ___ trials.
14. The student will perform ___ out of ___ academic tasks per day. (Gradually increase expectations as the student demonstrates success.)

Interventions:

1. Call on the student when he/she can answer successfully.

2. Provide a full schedule of daily events to keep the student actively involved.

3. Allow the student more decision-making opportunities relative to class activities and assignments.

4. Present tasks in the most attractive and interesting manner possible.

5. Give the student responsibilities in the classroom (e.g., teacher assistant, peer tutor, group leader, etc.).

6. Avoid competition. Failure may cause the student to lose interest or not participate in school activities.

7. Provide the student with as many academic and social successes as possible.

8. Evaluate the appropriateness of the task in relation to the student's ability to perform the task successfully.

9. Determine the student's preferred activities, interests, etc., and incorporate them into the daily schedule, program, etc., at various points throughout the day.

10. Provide the student with "real-life" experiences from the environment. Have individuals from the work force (e.g., mechanic, draftsman, secretary, etc.) visit the class to relate the importance of school to work experiences that involve math, reading, writing, etc.

11. Write a contract with the student specifying what behavior is expected (e.g., showing an interest and participating in school activities) and what reinforcement will be made available when the terms of the contract have been met.

12. Investigate the possibility of the student being involved in the use of drugs or alcohol.

13. Do not criticize when correcting the student, be honest yet supportive. Never cause the student to feel badly about himself/herself.

14. Be careful to avoid embarrassing the student by giving the student orders.

15. Treat the student with respect. Talk in an objective manner at all times.

16. Make positive comments about school and the importance of school.

17. Allow the student to attempt something new in private before doing it in front of others.

18. Provide the student with frequent opportunities to meet new people.

19. Evaluate the appropriateness of the task to determine (a) if the task is too easy, (b) if the task is too difficult, and (c) if the length of time scheduled for the task is adequate.

20. Communicate with parents, agencies, or the appropriate parties to inform them of the problem, determine the cause of the problem, and consider possible solutions to the problem.

21. Communicate with parents (e.g., notes home, phone calls, etc.) to share information concerning the student's progress. The parents may reinforce the student at home for showing an interest in participating in school activities.

22. Show an interest in the student (e.g., acknowledge the student, ask the student's opinion, spend time working one-on-one with the student, etc.).

23. Reinforce the student for showing an interest and participating in school activities based on the length of time he/she can be successful. As the student demonstrates success, gradually increase the length of time required for reinforcement.

24. Reinforce those students in the classroom who show an interest and participate in school activities.

25. Establish classroom rules:
- Work on-task.
- Work quietly.
- Remain in your seat.
- Finish task.
- Meet task expectations.

Review rules often. Reinforce students for following rules.

26. Speak with the student to explain (a) what the student is doing wrong (e.g., failing to show an interest and participate in school activities) and (b) what the student should be doing (e.g., showing an interest and participating in school activities).

27. Reinforce the student for showing an interest and participating in school activities: (a) give the student a tangible reward (e.g., classroom privileges, line leading, passing out materials, five minutes free time, etc.) or (b) give the student an intangible reward (e.g., praise, handshake, smile, etc.)

28. Investigate the student's eating habits and the amount of rest he/she is getting outside of school.

77 Makes comments that others are disappointed in him/her

Goals:

1. The student will improve his/her self-esteem.
2. The student will develop a friendship.

Objectives:

1. The student will make ___ positive self-statement(s) per day.
2. The student will interact with a peer(s) when asked on ___ out of ___ trials.
3. The student will initiate an interaction with a peer(s) ___ times per day.
4. The student will participate in assigned activities on ___ out of ___ trials.
5. The student will demonstrate emotions that are appropriate to the situation on ___ out of ___ trials.
6. The student will talk about situations in a realistic manner on ___ out of ___ trials.
7. The student will develop ___ friendship(s) in a month period.
8. The student will indicate that he/she is liked by others on ___ out of ___ trials.
9. The student will indicate that others care about him/her on ___ out of ___ trials.

Interventions:

1. Provide the student with as many academic and social successes as possible so peers may view him/her in a more positive way.

2. Make the necessary adjustments in the environment to prevent the student from experiencing stress, frustration, anger, etc.

3. Assign additional responsibilities to the student (e.g., chores, errands, etc.) to give him/her a feeling of success or accomplishment.

4. Structure the environment so the student does not have time to dwell on real or imagined problems.

5. Take the time to listen so the student realizes your concern and interest.

6. Identify for the student more appropriate ways to express his/her feelings.

7. Reduce stimuli that contribute to the student's verbal expression of unhappiness (e.g., seek input from the student as to what upsets him/her).

8. Separate the student from the peer(s) who stimulates the verbal expression of unhappiness.

9. Try various groupings to determine the situation in which the student is most comfortable.

10. Encourage the student to participate in extracurricular activities that will help develop those skills necessary to interact appropriately with others at school.

11. Make certain that reinforcement (e.g., getting attention, getting his/her way, etc.) is not inadvertently given for verbal expressions of unhappiness.

12. Provide the student with alternative activities to perform in case some activities prove upsetting.

13. Reduce the emphasis on competition. Repeated failure may cause the student to feel that others do not like or care about him/her.

14. Reinforce those students in the classroom who deal with unhappiness in an appropriate manner.

15. Encourage and help the student to make friends (e.g., pair the student with a peer; when that relationship is successful, introduce other students).

16. When natural consequences occur as a result of the student's displays of unhappiness, point them out to him/her (e.g., peers prefer not to interact with the student).

17. Provide the student with as many positive interactions as possible (e.g., recognize the student, greet the student, compliment attire, etc.).

18. Discourage the student from engaging in those activities that cause him/her unhappiness.

19. Help the student identify things he/she wishes were in the environment, and work with the student toward those goals.

20. Teach the student alternative ways to deal with unpleasant social interactions during the school-age experience (e.g., deal with problems when they arise, practice self-control at all times, share problems or concerns with others, etc.).

21. Teach the student alternative ways to communicate unhappiness (e.g., in writing, by talking, etc.).

22. Speak with the student to explain that he/she may be trying too hard to fit in and that he/she should relax and allow friendships to develop naturally.

23. Reinforce those students in the classroom who appropriately interact with other students.

24. Have the student be the leader of a small-group activity if he/she possesses mastery of skills or an interest in that area.

25. Give the student the responsibility of tutoring a peer if he/she possesses the skills to be shared.

26. Provide the student with a predetermined signal (e.g., verbal cue, hand signal, etc.) when he/she begins to demonstrate inappropriate behaviors when interacting with others (e.g., whining, fighting, throwing objects, refusing to share, etc.).

27. Maintain maximum supervision of the student's interactions and gradually decrease the amount of supervision over time.

28. Teach the student problem-solving skills: (a) identify the problem, (b) identify goals and objectives, (c) develop strategies, (d) develop a plan of action, and (e) carry out the plan.

29. Encourage the student to further develop any ability or skill he/she may have so peers may view the student in a more positive way.

30. Help the student to identify his/her inappropriate behaviors and teach the student ways to change those behaviors.

31. Ask the student to choose a peer to work with on a specific assignment. Encourage the student and peer to interact with each other in nonacademic areas (e.g., recess, lunch, break time, etc.).

32. Do not criticize. When correcting the student, be honest yet supportive. Never cause the student to feel badly about himself/herself.

33. Do not force the student to interact with students with whom he/she is not completely comfortable.

34. Treat the student with respect. Talk in an objective manner at all times.

35. Allow the student to attempt something new in private before doing so in front of others.

36. Do not assume that the student is being treated nicely by other students. Others may be stimulating inappropriate behavior on the part of the student.

37. Encourage the student to interact with others.

38. Provide the student with frequent opportunities to meet new people.

39. Do not force the student to interact with others.

40. Make certain the student is not demonstrating a lack of confidence to get the attention of others.

41. Give the student responsibilities in group situations so peers may view the student in a more positive way.

42. Record or chart the number of times the student verbally expresses that others do not like or care about him/her to make the student aware of the frequency.

43. Communicate with the parents (e.g., notes home, phone calls, etc.) to share information concerning the student's progress. The parents may reinforce the student at home for interacting appropriately with others at school.

44. Write a contract with the student specifying what behavior is expected (e.g., interacting appropriately with others) and what reinforcement will be made available when the terms of the contract have been met.

45. Remove the student from the group until he/she can interact appropriately with others.

46. Reinforce the student for interacting with others based on the length of time the student can be successful. As the student demonstrates success, gradually increase the length of time required for reinforcement.

47. Reinforce those students in the classroom who make positive, supportive comments to the student.

48. Establish classroom rules:
- Work on-task.
- Work quietly.
- Remain in your seat.
- Finish task.
- Meet task expectations.

Review rules often. Reinforce students for following rules.

49. Reinforce the student for interacting with others: (a) give the student a tangible reward (e.g., classroom privileges, line leading, passing out materials, five minutes free time, etc.) or (b) give the student an intangible reward (e.g., praise, handshake, smile, etc.).

50. Discuss concerns with other professionals to determine if further investigation is warranted (e.g., abuse, neglect).

51. Make positive comments about school and the student.

52. Have the student make a list of his/her strong points or things done well to improve the student's overall level of confidence.

53. Communicate to the student that he/she is a worthwhile individual.

54. Provide the student with positive feedback which indicates he/she is successful, important, respected, etc.

55. Encourage others to compliment the student.

56. Show an interest in the student (e.g., acknowledge the student, ask the student's opinion, spend time working one-on-one with the student, etc.).

Reminder: Do not "force" the student to interact with others with whom he/she is uncomfortable.

78 Makes statements, written or verbal, that he/she feels worthless or helpless

Goals:

1. The student will demonstrate realistic, objective self-appraisal.
2. The student will improve his/her perception of self.
3. The student will improve his/her self-esteem.

Objectives:

1. The student will discuss his/her abilities in a realistic manner on ___out of ___trials.
2. The student will make ___positive comment(s) about himself/herself per day. (Gradually increase expectations as the student demonstrates success.)
3. The student will make optimistic statements regarding expected outcomes on ___out of ___trials.

Interventions:

1. Help the student find activities (e.g., reading, creating, peer tutoring, etc.) in which he/she can achieve personal satisfaction and success.

2. The expectations (academic, physical, social, etc.) established for the student may need to be reviewed and changes implemented.

3. Investigate the existence of abusiveness in the school or home environment (e.g., parents, extended family, other students).

4. Help the student with a problem-solving approach to his/her situation (e.g., identify the problem, identify options available to resolve the problem, choose an option likely to provide success, implement the problem-solving option).

5. Allow the student to have control over as many variables in the day's activities as possible (e.g., where he/she sits, the order in which activities will be performed, choosing another student to work with, etc.).

6. Make certain the student has adequate support for academic classwork (e.g., tutoring from retired individuals, service organizations, etc.).

7. Reinforce those students in the classroom who accept their own best effort rather than insisting on perfection.

8. Make certain that other school personnel are aware of the student's feelings of worthlessness so they can facilitate the student's success, feelings of accomplishment, etc.

9. Investigate other areas of the school environment to determine if the student is being intimidated by other teachers, students, or unrealistic requirements.

10. Speak with the student to explain (a) what the student is doing wrong (e.g., being overly critical of himself/herself) and (b) what the student should be doing (e.g., being satisfied with improvement rather than insisting on perfection).

11. Reinforce the student for accepting his/her own best effort: (a) give the student a tangible reward (e.g., classroom privileges, line leading, passing out materials, five minutes free time, etc.) or (b) give the student an intangible reward (e.g., praise, handshake, smile, etc.).

12. Reinforce the student for making positive comments about himself/herself based on the length of time he/she can be successful. As the student demonstrates success, gradually increase the length of time required for reinforcement.

13. Communicate with parents (e.g., notes home, phone calls, etc.) to share information concerning the student's progress. The parents may reinforce the student at home for making positive comments about himself/herself at school.

14. Communicate with parents, agencies, or the appropriate parties to inform them of the problem, determine the cause of the problem, and consider possible solutions to the problem.

15. Evaluate the apropriateness of the task the student is expected to perform to determine (a) if the task is too easy, (b) if the task is too difficult, and (c) if the length of time scheduled for the task is adequate.

16. Call on the student when he/she can respond successfully.

17. Avoid competition. Failure may cause the student to feel worthless.

18. Allow the student to choose from a selection of activities so he/she can choose an activity with which he/she will be successful.

19. Give the student responsibilities in the classroom with which he/she can expect success (e.g., teacher assistant, peer tutor, group leader, etc.).

20. Provide the student with as many academic and social successes as possible.

21. Determine the student's preferred activities, interests, etc., and incorporate them into his/her daily schedule, program, etc., at various points throughout the day.

22. Show an interest in the student (e.g., acknowledge the student, ask the student's opinion, spend time working one-on-one with the student, etc.).

23. Reinforce the student for accepting errors that he/she makes.

24. Reward others for accepting errors they make.

25. Reinforce the student for improvement rather than expecting excellence.

26. Provide the student with success-oriented tasks. The expectation is that success will result in more positive attitudes and perceptions toward self and environment.

27. Choose a peer to help the student with class assignments, homework, etc.

28. Encourage the student to refrain from comparing his/her performance to other students' performance and emphasize attention to personal improvement (e.g., maintain records of own progress rather than comparing work to others).

29. Have the student regularly record his/her own progress to have tangible evidence of success.

30. Reduce activities which might cause the student to feel worthless (e.g., announcing test score ranges or test scores aloud, making students read aloud in class, emphasizing the success of a particular student or students, etc.).

31. Make certain that your comments take the form of constructive criticism rather than criticism that can be perceived as personal, threatening, etc., (e.g., instead of saying "You always make that same mistake." say "A better way to do that might be ...").

32. Assess the appropriateness of the social situation and place the student in the group in which he/she would be most successful.

33. Pair the student with a younger or less capable peer to enhance his/her feelings of success or accomplishment.

34. Deliver praise and recognition privately so the student is not aware of the performance of others.

35. Encourage all students to be complimentary of each other's performance.

36. Have the student question any directions, explanations, or instructions, he/she does not understand.

37. Provide the student with positive feedback which indicates he/she is successful, competent, important, respected, etc.

38. Modify the environment to reduce situations which cause the student to feel worthless.

39. Identify individuals the student may contact concerning his/her feelings of worthlessness (e.g., guidance counselor, school nurse, social worker, school psychologist, teen hotline, etc.).

40. Encourage and help the student make friends (e.g., pair the student with a peer; when that relationship is successful, introduce other peers).

41. Explain to the student that feelings of worthlessness are natural and happen to everyone at some time.

42. Require the student to make at least one positive comment about himself/herself on a daily basis. As the student demonstrates success, gradually increase the number of positive comments required.

43. Help the student identify how he/she wishes things were in the environment and work with the student toward those goals.

44. Conduct a reinforcer survey with the student to determine his/her reinforcer preferences.

45. Communicate with parents to determine what the student finds reinforcing at home.

46. Help the student to be satisfied with his/her best effort rather than insisting on perfection.

47. Make positive comments about school and the student.

48. Have the student make a list of his/her strong points or things done well to improve the student's overall level of confidence.

49. Communicate to the student that he/she is a worthwhile individual.

50. Provide frequent interactions and encouragement to support the student's confidence and optimism for success (e.g., make statements such as "You're doing great." "Keep up the good work." "I'm really proud of you." etc.).

51. Do not criticize when correcting the student; be honest yet supportive. Never cause the student to feel badly about himself/herself.

52. Help the student to develop self-confidence and satisfaction in personal self-worth and successes by pointing out strengths, emphasizing positive aspects, etc.

53. Avoid discussions or prevent stimuli in the environment that remind the student of unpleasant experiences/sensitive topics (e.g., divorce, death, unemployment, alcoholism, etc.).

Note: The teacher needs to find an activity in which the student will be successful (e.g., extracurricular activity, clubs, etc.).

79 Says he/she would be better off dead

Goals:

1. The student will not threaten to hurt self.
2. The student will not threaten to commit suicide.

Objectives:

1. The student will express his/her feelings in an appropriate manner on ___out of ___trials.
2. The student will talk to the teacher when he/she is feeling depressed, anxious, upset, hopeless, etc., on ___ out of ___ occasions.

Interventions:

1. Remove the student from the group or activity until he/she can demonstrate appropriate behavior and self-control.

2. Communicate with parents (e.g., notes home, phone calls, etc.) to share information concerning the student's progress. The parents may reinforce the student at home for appropriate behavior at school.

3. Evaluate the appropriateness of the task to determine (a) if the task is too easy, (b) if the task is too difficult, and (c) if the length of time scheduled for the task is adequate.

4. Prevent frustrating or anxiety-producing situations from occurring (e.g., give the student tasks on his/her ability level; give the student only the number of tasks that can be tolerated in one sitting, stop social interactions that stimulate the student to threaten self-harm, etc.).

5. Interact frequently with the student to prevent self-abusive behavior by meeting the student's needs as they occur.

6. Maintain visibility to and from the student. The teacher should be able to see the student and the student should be able to see the teacher. Make eye contact possible at all times.

7. Facilitate on-task behavior by providing a full schedule of daily events. Prevent lag time from occurring when the student will be free to engage in self-abusive behavior.

8. Remove from the environment any object that the student may use to hurt himself/herself.

9. Provide the student with positive feedback that indicates he/she is successful, important, respected, etc.

10. Maintain a positive/calm environment (e.g., positive comments, acknowledgment of successes, quiet communications, etc.).

11. Provide the student with a quiet place to work (e.g., carrel, study area).

12. Reduce the emphasis on competition. Repeated failure may result in anger and frustration that may cause the student to try to hurt himself/herself.

13. Maintain consistent expectations.

14. Allow the student to have input relative to making decisions (e.g., changing activities, choosing activities, deciding length of activities, etc.).

15. Provide the student with a selection of optional activities to be performed (e.g., if an activity results in harmful behaviors, an optional activity can be substituted).

16. Teach the student appropriate ways to deal with anxiety, frustration, and anger (e.g., move away from the stimulus, verbalize unhappiness, choose another activity, etc.).

17. Teach the student problem-solving skills: (a) identify the problem, (b) identify goals and objectives, (c) develop strategies, (d) develop a plan of action, and (e) carry out the plan.

18. Maintain a consistent daily routine.

19. Do not allow the student to be unsupervised anywhere in the school environment.

20. Avoid discussions or prevent stimuli in the environment that remind the student of unpleasant experiences/sensitive topics (e.g., divorce, death, unemployment, alcoholism, etc.).

21. Do not criticize. When correcting the student, be honest yet supportive. Never cause the student to feel badly about himself/herself.

22. Intervene early when there is a problem to prevent more serious problems from occurring.

23. Treat the student with respect. Talk in an objective manner at all times.

24. Maintain trust and confidentiality with the student at all times.

25. Make certain the student is allowed to voice an opinion in a situation to avoid becoming angry or upset.

26. Talk to the student about ways of handling situations successfully without conflict (e.g., walk away from a situation, change to another activity, ask for help, etc.).

27. Reinforce the student for demonstrating appropriate behavior based on the length of time the student can be successful. As the student demonstrates success, gradually increase the amount of time required for reinforcement.

28. Reinforce those students in the classroom who engage in appropriate behavior.

29. Establish classroom rules:
- Work on-task.
- Work quietly.
- Remain in your seat.
- Finish task.
- Meet task expectations.

Review rules often. Reinforce students for following rules.

30. Speak with the student to explain (a) what the student is doing wrong (e.g., threatening to hurt self) and (b) what the student should be doing (e.g., talking about the situation, demonstrating self-control, problem solving, etc.).

31. Reinforce the student for engaging in appropriate behavior: (a) give the student a tangible reward (e.g., classroom privileges, line leading, passing out materials, five minutes free time, etc.), or (b) give the student an intangible reward (e.g., praise, handshake, smile, etc.).

32. Share concerns with administration and seek referral to an agency for investigation of abuse or neglect.

33. Structure the environment so the student does not have time to dwell on real or imagined problems.

Note: All references to suicide should be considered serious, and steps should be taken to respond to the situation.

80 Verbalizes fears or concerns about school, home, or personal situations

Goals:

1. The student will function successfully at school despite problems or situations in the school environment.
2. The student will function successfully at school despite problems or situations in the home.
3. The student will function successfully at school despite personal problems.

Objectives:

1. The student will use verbalizations which accurately describe situations at school on ___out of ___ trials.
2. The student will use verbalizations which accurately describe situations at home on ___out of ___ trials.
3. The student will use verbalizations which accurately describe personal problems on ___out of ___ trials.
4. The student will make positive comments about school on ___out of ___trials.
5. The student will make positive comments about home on ___out of ___trials.
6. The student will make positive comments about personal situations on ___out of ___trials.
7. The student will demonstrate happiness by smiling, laughing, joking with peers, etc., on ___out of ___ trials.
8. The student will laugh or smile when humorous events or activities take place on ___out of ___ trials.
9. The student will demonstrate emotions like those of his/her peers during ___out of ___typical classroom activities.

Interventions:

1. Discuss concerns with other professionals to determine if further investigation is warranted (e.g., abuse or neglect).

2. Record or chart the number of times the student expresses fears or concerns about school, home, or personal situations to make the student aware of the frequently of his/her behavior.

3. Take the time to listen so the student realizes that your concern is genuine.

4. Explain that fears and concerns, while legitimate, are not unusual for students (e.g., everyone worries about tests, grades, etc.).

5. Identify persons the student may contact with his/her fears and concerns (e.g., guidance counselor, school nurse, social worker, school psychologist, etc.).

6. Discuss ways in which to practice self-improvement.

7. Provide the student with opportunities for social and academic success.

8. Separate the student from a peer who may be encouraging or stimulating fears or concerns about school, home, or personal situations.

9. Reduce the emphasis on competition. Repeated failure may result in anxiety about performance at school, home, and in personal situations.

10. Provide parents with necessary information to help the student with homework and study activities at home.

11. Make the necessary adjustments in the environment to prevent the student from experiencing stress, frustration, anxiety, etc.

12. Structure the environment so time does not permit opportunities for the student to dwell on fears or concerns.

13. Provide the student with alternative approaches to testing (e.g., test the student verbally, make the tests shorter, allow the student to respond verbally, allow the student to take the test in the resource room, etc.).

14. Call attention to the student's accomplishments (e.g., publicly or privately depending on which is more appropriate).

15. Emphasize individual differences and that everybody has strengths and weaknesses.

16. Maintain trust and confidentiality with the student at all times.

17. Provide the student with positive feedback which indicates he/she is successful, competent, important, valuable, etc.

18. Seek assistance from the school counselor, the principal, other teachers, etc., to help the student deal with fears and concerns about school, home, and personal problems so he/she can concentrate at school.

19. Encourage the student to use problem solving skills: (a) identify the problem, (b) identify goals and objectives, (c) develop strategies, (d) develop a plan of action, and (e) carry out the plan.

20. Provide praise and recognition as often as possible.

21. Encourage participation in school and extracurricular activities.

22. Try various groupings to determine the situation in which the student is most successful.

23. Have peers invite the student to participate in extracurricular activities.

24. Demonstrate respect for the student's opinions, responses, suggestions, etc.

25. Avoid discussion of topics sensitive to the student (e.g., divorce, death, unemployment, alcoholism, etc.).

26. Provide the student with opportunities for special project responsibilities, leadership, etc.

27. Provide the student with as many enjoyable and interesting activities as possible.

28. Reinforce the student for improvement rather than expecting excellence.

29. Treat the student with respect. Talk in an objective manner at all times.

30. Reduce activities which might threaten the student (e.g., announcing test score ranges or test scores aloud in class, emphasizing the success of a particular student(s), etc.).

81 Does not assist others

Goals:

1. The student will provide assistance to others when asked.
2. The student will provide assistance to others independently.

Objectives:

1. The student will give directions to others on ____ out of ____ trials.
2. The student will share materials with others on ____ out of ____ trials.
3. The student will work quietly with others on ____ out of ____ trials.
4. The student will take turns with others on ____ out of ____ trials.
5. The student will take a leadership role with others on ____ out of ____ trials.
6. The student will verbally participate with others on ____ out of ____ trials.
7. The student will physically participate with others on ____ out of trials.
8. The student will attempt extra activities/assignments on ____ out of ____ trials.
9. The student will help a friend perform assignments on ____ out of ____ trials.
10. The student will take an active role in chores, work-related activities, etc., on ____ out of ____ trials.
11. The student will take responsibility for a classroom activity on ____ out of ____ trials.
12. The student will help others with physical tasks on ____ out of ____ occasions.

Interventions:

1. Reinforce the student for assisting others: (a) give the student a tangible reward (e.g., classroom privileges, line leading, passing out materials, five minutes free time, etc.) or (b) give the student an intangible reward (e.g., praise, handshake, smile, etc.).

2. Speak to the student to explain (a) what he/she is doing wrong (e.g., failing to assist others) and (b) what he/she should be doing (e.g., contributing information, providing assistance, sharing, etc.).

3. Reinforce those students in the classroom who assist others.

4. Reinforce the student for assisting others based on the length of time the student can be successful. As the student demonstrates success, gradually increase the length of time required for reinforcement.

5. Write a contract with the student specifying what behavior is expected (e.g., working appropriately with peers) and what reinforcement will be made available when the terms of the contract have been met.

6. Evaluate the appropriateness of the expectations for the student to provide assistance to others.

7. Communicate with the parents (e.g., notes home, phone calls, etc.) to share information concerning the student's progress. The parents may reinforce the student at home for providing assistance to others at school.

8. Have the student question any directions, explanations, instructions he/she does not understand.

9. DO NOT FORCE the student to assist others.

10. Try various groupings to determine the situation in which the student is most comfortable.

11. Have peers invite the student to participate in school or extracurricular activities.

12. Request that the student be the leader of a small group activity if he/she possesses mastery or an interest in the activity.

13. Have the student work with one or two other group members. As the student becomes more comfortable, gradually increase the size of the group.

14. Demonstrate respect for the student's opinions, responses, suggestions, etc.

15. Give the student the opportunity to pick a topic or activity for the group to work on together.

16. Give the student the opportunity to choose a group activity and choose the group members (e.g., along with the teacher, decide what the activity will be, decide what individual group members will do, etc.).

17. Assign the student a role to perform in the group activity which he/she can perform successfully (e.g., secretary, researcher, group behavior monitor, etc.).

18. Reduce the emphasis on competition. Competitive situations may cause the student to refuse to provide assistance to others.

19. Place the student with peers who will be appropriate role models for providing assistance to others.

20. Place the student with group members who are least likely to be threatening to him/her (e.g., younger students, students just learning a skill he/she has mastered, etc.).

21. Create and reinforce activities in which the student and others work together for a common goal (e.g., mural, wildlife garden, etc.) rather than individual success or recognition. Point out that larger accomplishments are realized through group effort rather than individual effort, thus making assistance to one another necessary.

22. Make certain the academic and social demands of the situation are within the student's ability level.

23. Help the student get to know group members before requiring group participation (e.g., introduce the students to one another, allow the students unstructured free time together, etc.).

24. Reinforce the student for assuming extra responsibilities, tasks, etc.: (a) give the student a tangible reward (e.g., classroom privileges, line leading, passing out materials, five minutes free time, etc.) or (b) give the student an intangible reward (e.g., praise, handshake, smile, etc.).

25. Teach the student a variety of ways to provide assistance to others.

26. Structure the environment to provide the student with increased opportunity to assist others.

27. Have the student maintain a record (e.g., chart or graph) of his/her performance in assuming new responsibilities/tasks.

28. Give the student the responsibility of helping a peer in group situations.

29. Provide a role model for the student by assisting others (e.g., other teachers, parents, janitor, principal, students, etc.) when appropriate.

30. Provide an atmosphere where everyone works together to get things done (e.g., cleaning the classroom, passing out materials, etc.).

31. Help the student see the natural rewards of assisting others (e.g., others helping in return, personal satisfaction, friendships, etc.).

32. Make certain the student understands instructions/directions for the group activity (e.g., give instructions in a variety of ways, make certain that the student understands his/her role, go over the rules for group behavior before the activity begins, etc.).

33. Make certain the student understands that providing assistance to others is contingent upon completion of his/her own responsibilities.

82   Requires excessive assistance from others

Goal:

1. The student will independently perform assignments.

Objectives:

1. The student will attempt to perform a given assignment before asking for teacher assistance on ___ out of ___ trials.
2. The student will read necessary directions, instructions, explanations, etc., before asking for teacher assistance on ___ out of ___ trials.
3. The student will independently complete ___ out of ___ assignments per school day.
4. The student will ask for teacher assistance only when necessary when performing assignments on ___ out of ___ trials.
5. The student will work for ___ minutes without requiring assistance from the teacher on ___ out of ___ trials.

Interventions:

1. Establish classroom rules:

- Work on-task.
- Work quietly.
- Request assistance when needed.
- Remain in your seat.
- Finish task.
- Meet task expectations.

Review rules often. Reinforce students for following rules.

2. Reinforce those students in the classroom who communicate needs to others when necessary.

3. Reinforce the student for communicating needs to others based on the number of times he/she can be successful. As the student demonstrates success, gradually increase the number of times required for reinforcement.

4. Write a contract with the student specifying what behavior is expected (e.g., asking for teacher assistance when necessary) and what reinforcement will be made available when the terms of the contract have been met.

5. Communicate with the parents (e.g., notes home, phone calls, etc.) to share information concerning the student's progress. The parents may reinforce the student at home for providing assistance to others at school.

6. Choose a peer to model communication of needs to others for the student.

7. Encourage the student to question any directions, explanations, and instructions not understood.

8. Evaluate the appropriateness of expecting the student to communicate needs to others when necessary.

9. Maintain mobility throughout the classroom to determine the student's needs.

10. Offer the student assistance frequently throughout the day.

11. Make certain that directions, explanations, and instructions are delivered on the student's ability level.

12. Structure the environment so the student is not required to communicate all needs to others (i.e., make certain the student's tasks are on his/her ability level, be sure that instructions are clear, and maintain frequent interactions with the student to ensure success).

13. Communicate with the student as often as opportunities permit to detect the student's needs.

14. Demonstrate accepting behavior (e.g., willingness to help others, making criticisms constructive and positive, demonstrating confidentiality in personal matters, etc.).

15. Communicate to the student an interest in his/her needs.

16. Communicate to the student that he/she is a worthwhile individual.

17. Call on the student often to encourage communication.

18. Teach the student communication skills (e.g., hand raising, expressing needs in written and/or verbal forms, etc.).

19. Encourage communication skills in the classroom.

20. Communicate your own personal needs and feelings to the student.

21. Encourage the student to communicate needs to other personnel in the educational environment (e.g., school counselor, school psychologist, principal, etc.).

22. Communicate with parents, agencies, or the appropriate parties to inform them of the problem, determine the cause of the problem, and consider possible solutions to the problem.

23. Teach the student to communicate needs in an appropriate manner (e.g., raise hand, use a normal tone of voice when speaking, verbally express problems, etc.).

24. Recognize the student's attempts to communicate needs (e.g., facial expressions, gestures, inactivity, self-deprecating comments, etc.).

25. Have the student interact with a peer to encourage him/her to communicate needs to others. As he/she demonstrates success in communicating needs to others, gradually increase the number of peers.

26. Pair the student with a nonthreatening peer, a peer with similar interests and ability level, etc.

27. Give the student responsibilities in the classroom to increase the probability of communication (e.g., passing out materials, collecting lunch money, collecting schoolwork, etc.).

28. Give the student responsibilities in the classroom that require communication (e.g., peer tutor, group leader, teacher assistant, etc.).

29. Have the student keep a chart or graph representing the number of assignments performed independently.

30. Assess the degree of task difficulty in comparison with the student's ability to perform the task.

31. Assign the student shorter tasks (e.g., modifying a twenty-problem math activity to four activities of five problems each, to be done at various times during the day). As the student demonstrates success, gradually increase the number of problems.

32. Present the task in the most interesting manner possible.

33. Reduce distracting stimuli (e.g., place the student in the front row, provide a carrel or quiet place away from distractions, etc.). This is to be used as a means of reducing stimuli and not as a form of punishment.

34. Allow the student additional time to complete assignments when working independently.

35. Encourage the student to ask for clarification of directions for assignments.

36. Provide the student with step-by-step written directions for assignments.

37. Allow the student to perform alternative assignments. Gradually introduce more components of the regular assignments until those assignments are routinely performed.

38. Explain to the student that work not done during work time will have to be done during other times (e.g., break time, recreational time, after school, etc.).

39. Maintain consistent expectations within the ability level of the student.

40. Maintain a consistent daily routine.

41. Work a few problems with the student on an assignment to serve as a model and help the student begin a task.

42. Reinforce the student for beginning, working on, and completing assignments.

43. Provide the student with a selection of assignments and require him/her to choose a minimum number of assignments to perform independently (e.g., present the student with ten academic tasks from which six must be finished that day).

44. Reinforce the student for communicating needs to others when necessary: (a) give the student a tangible reward (e.g., classroom privileges, line leading, passing out materials, five minutes free time, etc.) or (b) give the student an intangible reward (e.g., praise, handshake, smile, etc.).

45. Specify exactly what is to be done for the completion of the task (e.g., indicate definite starting and stopping points, indicate the minimum requirements, etc.).

46. Reinforce the student for performing assignments independently.

47. Speak to the student to explain (a) what the student is doing wrong (e.g., asking for teacher assistance when not necessary) and (b) what the student should be doing (e.g., asking for teacher assistance when necessary).

48. Communicate clearly with the student the length of time he/she has to complete the assignment and when the assignment should be completed. The student may want to use a timer to complete tasks within a given period of time.

83　Interrupts the teacher or other students

Goals:

1. The student will answer only when called upon.
2. The student will communicate with others in an acceptable manner in the classroom.
3. The student will work quietly in the classroom.

Objectives:

1. The student will gain permission from the teacher, by raising his/her hand, when he/she needs to talk with a peer on _____ out of _____ trials.
2. The student will contribute his/her opinion/answer after being recognized by the teacher on _____ out of _____ trials.
3. The student will await his/her turn to talk when engaged, or attempting to engage, in interactions with the teacher on _____ out of _____ trials.
4. The student will make comments to the teacher which are relevant to the situation on _____ out of _____ trials.
5. The student will refrain from making sounds which are inappropriate for the situation on _____ out of _____ trials.

Interventions:

1. Communicate with the parents (e.g., notes home, phone calls, etc.) to share information concerning their child's appropriate behavior. The parents may reinforce the student at home for waiting his/her turn to speak at school.

2. Give adequate opportunities to respond (i.e., enthusiastic students need many opportunities to contribute).

3. Structure the environment to limit opportunities for interrupting the teacher (e.g., keep the student engaged in activities, have the student seated near the teacher, etc.).

4. Instruct the student to carry a notepad with him/her at all times and to write information down to help him/her remember.

5. Maintain a full schedule of activities. Keeping the student occupied should prevent interruptive behavior from occurring.

6. Educate yourself and others about ADHD to increase understanding and accommodation of interruptive behavior.

7. Encourage the student to develop an awareness of himself/herself and those around him/her. Have the student periodically step back and ask himself/herself, "Am I interrupting others?"

8. Educate the student about ADHD and the need for developing skills to self-monitor behavior.

9. Provide constant, positive reinforcement for appropriate behavior. Ignore as many inappropriate behaviors as possible.

10. Teach the student to use techniques such as crossing his/her arms and legs, clinching his/her fists, and webbing his/her hands when he/she feels the urge to interrupt.

11. Explain to the student when he/she interrupts that you are talking now and he/she may talk to you in a few moments.

12. Talk to the student before beginning an activity and remind him/her of the importance of listening and not interrupting.

13. Reinforce those students in the classroom who wait their turn to speak.

14. Provide the student with a clearly understood list of consequences for inappropriate behavior.

15. Reduce the emphasis on competition. Competitive activities may cause the student to become overexcited and interrupt others.

16. Have a peer, paraprofessional, friend, etc., cue the student when he/she interrupts others (e.g., the person can touch the student's arm as a signal that he/she is interrupting).

17. Speak with the student to explain (a) what he/she is doing wrong (e.g., interrupting the teacher) and (b) what he/she should be doing (e.g., waiting until it is appropriate to speak, waiting to be called on, etc.).

18. Make certain that the student's feelings are considered when it is necessary to deal with his/her interruptions (i.e., use comments that do not diminish the student's enthusiasm for participation).

19. Reinforce the student for waiting for a turn to speak based on the length of time the student can be successful. As the student demonstrates success, gradually increase the length of time required for reinforcement.

20. Reinforce the student for waiting for a turn to speak: (a) give the student a tangible reward (e.g., classroom privileges, passing out materials, five minutes free time, etc.) or (b) give the student an intangible reward (e.g., praise, handshake, smile, etc.).

21. Have the student practice waiting for short periods of time for a turn to speak. Gradually increase the length of time required for a turn to speak.

22. Remove the student from the group or activity until he/she can demonstrate appropriate behavior and self-control.

23. Call on the student when he/she is most likely to be able to respond correctly.

24. Encourage the student to remind himself/herself to wait when he/she feels the need to interrupt (e.g., "Stop. Count to ten.").

25. Teach appropriate social rituals (e.g., say, "Excuse me," before interrupting; wait until someone stops speaking to begin talking, etc.).

26. Deliver directions, explanations, and instructions in a clear, concise manner to reduce the student's need to ask questions.

27. Instruct the student on how to interrupt for an emergency. Make certain he/she does it in a way which conveys the urgency (e.g., "I'm sorry for interrupting." "May I stop you for a minute?" etc.).

28. Explain to the student why it is inappropriate to interrupt the teacher (e.g., impolite, unfair to other students, others cannot hear what the teacher is saying, etc.).

29. Have the student make a list of consequences associated with frequently occurring behaviors (e.g., by disrupting others, I will be perceived as unmannerly; by behaving aggressively, people will avoid me.).

30. Make certain that reinforcement is not inadvertently given for inappropriate behavior (e.g., the teacher responds to the student after he/she has interrupted).

31. Make sure that you do not interrupt others. If you interrupt others, the student will continue to do so.

32. Acknowledge the student's presence and/or need to talk with you (e.g., by saying, "Just a minute"; putting your arm around the student; smiling and nodding your head; etc.).

33. Establish rules for conversing with others (e.g., wait your turn to talk, stand quietly by the person with whom you want to talk until you are noticed, excuse yourself when you interrupt others, etc.). These rules should be consistent and followed by everyone in the class. Talk about the rules often.

34. Provide the student with a predetermined signal if he/she begins to interrupt.

35. Reinforce the student for raising his/her hand to be recognized.

36. Have the student identify the situations in which he/she is most likely to interrupt. After he/she has identified these situations, have him/her think of ways to minimize their occurrences.

37. Help the student improve concentration skills (e.g., listening to the speaker, taking notes, preparing comments in advance, making comments in the appropriate context, etc.).

38. Be consistent in expecting the student to behave appropriately during class lectures. Do not allow the student to interrupt one time and expect him/her not to interrupt the next time.

39. Write a contract with the student specifying what behavior is expected (e.g., waiting for a turn to speak) and what reinforcement will be made available when the terms of the contract have been met.

40. Treat the student with respect. Talk in an objective manner at all times.

41. Encourage the student to realize that all behavior has negative or positive consequences. Encourage the student to practice behaviors that will lead to positive consequences.

42. Maintain visibility to and from the student to keep his/her attention when verbal questions/directions are being delivered. The teacher should be able to see the student and the student should be able to see the teacher. Make eye contact possible at all times.

43. Reduce activities which might cause the student to interrupt or talk out (e.g., announcing test score ranges or test scores aloud, emphasizing the success of a particular student or students, etc.).

44. Teach the student to recognize the appropriate time to speak (e.g., when the teacher has finished speaking, after raising his/her hand, to make comments within the context of the situation, to make comments that are a follow-up to what has just been said, etc.).

45. Do not criticize when correcting the student; be honest yet supportive. Never cause the student to feel negatively about himself/herself.

46. Make the student aware of the number of times he/she interrupts the teacher.

47. Make the necessary adjustments in the environment to prevent the student from experiencing stress, frustration, or anger (e.g., reduce peer pressure, academic failure, teasing, etc.).

48. Encourage the student to model the behavior of peers who are successful at not interrupting the teacher.

49. Do not allow the student to use ADHD as an excuse. Hold the student responsible for his/her actions. However, understand and accept problems ADHD brings into the student's life while he/she is learning to make accommodations.

50. Give the student frequent opportunities to join in conversations with others by allowing him/her time to talk, asking him/her to restate an experience, etc.

51. Interact frequently with the student to reduce the need for him/her to interrupt.

52. Attempt to provide equal attention to all students in the classroom.

53. Do not allow the student to interrupt you by letting him/her talk to you at the time he/she interrupts. Tell the student that he/she will need to wait until you are finished talking. Allowing the student to talk after interrupting reinforces the behavior and may increase the number of times he/she interrupts others.

54. Make certain that the student understands the relationship between inappropriate behavior and the consequences which follow (e.g., others ignoring him/her, hurting others' feelings, etc.).

55. Show the student the appropriate way to get someone's attention without interrupting.

56. Do not interrupt the student when he/she is doing something, talking to someone, etc.

57. Make certain the student knows when it is acceptable to interrupt others (e.g., in an emergency).

84   Has difficulty working effectively in a group situation

Goals:
1. The student will be productive when working in a group situation.
2. The student will communicate with others in an acceptable manner in the classroom.
3. The student will talk quietly in the classroom.

Objectives:
1. The student will participate verbally in a group situation on _____ out of _____ occasions.
2. The student will take turns while working in a group situation on _____ out of _____ occasions.
3. The student will share materials while working in a group situation on _____ out of _____ occasions.
4. The student will work with one other student in a group situation on _____ out of _____ occasions.
5. The student will work with all the members of a group on _____ out of _____ occasions.
6. The student will participate physically in a group situation on _____ out of _____ occasions.
7. The student will work independently in a group situation on _____ out of _____ occasions.
8. The student will work in a group situation with supervision on _____ out of _____ occasions.
9. The student will be productive in a group situation on _____ out of _____ occasions.
10. The student's work in a group situation will be done with _____% accuracy.
11. The student will gain permission from the teacher, by raising his/her hand, when he/she needs to speak on _____ out of _____ trials.
12. The student will contribute his/her opinion/answer after being recognized by the teacher on _____ out of _____ trials.
13. The student will wait his/her turn to talk when engaged, or attempting to engage, in interactions with others on _____ out of _____ trials.
14. The student will make comments which are relevant to the situation on _____ out of _____ trials.

Interventions:

1. Reinforce the student for working in a group situation: (a) give the student a tangible reward (e.g., classroom privileges, line leading, passing out materials, five minutes free time, etc.) or (b) give the student an intangible reward (e.g., praise, handshake, smile, etc.).

2. Speak with the student to explain (a) what the student is doing wrong (e.g., failing to take part) and (b) what the student should be doing (e.g., talking, taking turns, playing, sharing, etc.).

3. Establish classroom rules:
- Work on-task.
- Remain in your seat.
- Finish task.
- Meet task expectations.
- Raise your hand.

Review rules often. Reinforce students for following rules.

4. Reinforce other students in the classroom for working appropriately in a group situation.

5. Write a contract with the student specifying what behavior is expected (e.g., working appropriately with peers) and what reinforcement will be made available when the terms of the contract have been met.

6. Communicate with parents (e.g., notes home, phone calls, etc.) to share information concerning the student's progress. The parents may reinforce the student at home for participating in group situations at school.

7. Do not force the student to participate in group situations until he/she can be successful.

8. Choose a peer to sit/work directly with the student (e.g., in different settings such as art, music, P.E., on the bus; or different activities such as tutoring, group projects, running errands in the building, recess, etc.).

9. Reward or encourage other students for participation in group situations.

10. Give the student the responsibility of helping a peer in group situations.

11. Go over group rules and expectations at the beginning of each group activity.

12. Call on the student when he/she is most likely to be able to respond successfully (e.g., when discussing a topic in which the student is interested, when the teacher is certain the student knows the answer, etc.).

13. Try various groupings to determine the situation in which the student is most comfortable.

14. Have peers invite the student to participate in school or extracurricular activities.

15. Have the student lead a small group activity when he/she possesses mastery or an interest in the activity.

16. Allow the student to be present during group activities without requiring active participation. Require more involvement over time as the student becomes more active in group situations.

17. Reduce the emphasis on competition. Fear of failure may cause the student to be reluctant to participate in group situations.

18. Have the student work with one or two other group members. As the student becomes more comfortable, gradually increase the size of the group.

19. Demonstrate respect for the student's opinions, responses, suggestions, etc.

20. Give the student the opportunity to pick a topic or activity for the group to work on together.

21. Give the student the opportunity to choose a group activity and the group members (e.g., along with the teacher decide what the activity will be, decide what individual group members will do, etc.).

22. Assign the student a role to perform in the group activity which he/she can perform successfully (e.g., secretary, researcher, group behavior monitor, etc.).

23. Make certain the student is productive and accurate in performing individual assignments before placing him/her in a group activity.

24. Give the student responsibilities in group situations so others might view the student in a positive light.

25. Make certain that the student can follow classroom rules and expectations independently before placing him/her in a group activity.

26. Help the student learn to be satisfied with his/her own best effort rather than some arbitrary measure of success. Success is measured individually according to ability level, and progress of any kind is a measure of success.

27. Group the student with peers who will be appropriate role models and are likely to facilitate the student's academic and behavioral successes.

28. Group the student with group members who are least likely to be threatening (e.g., younger students, students just learning a skill he/she has mastered, etc.).

29. Make certain the student understands instructions/directions for the group activity (e.g., give instructions in a variety of ways, make certain that the student understands his/her role, go over the rules for group behavior before the activity begins, etc.).

30. Make certain the student has all needed materials to perform his/her role in the group (e.g., paper, pencil, art supplies, reference materials, etc.).

31. Make certain the student has enough room to work successfully (e.g., distance from other students, room for all materials, etc.).

32. Make certain the academic and social demands of the group situation are within the student's ability level.

33. Remove the student from the group if his/her behavior is inappropriate.

34. Make certain the student is actively involved in the group situation (e.g., call on the student frequently, assign the student a responsibility such as teacher assistant, have him/her be the group leader, etc.).

35. Allow the student to join the group after the activity has begun if he/she is unable to participate appropriately at the beginning of the group activity.

36. Help the student get to know group members before requiring group participation (e.g., introduce the students to one another, allow the students unstructured free time together, etc.).

37. Reduce distracting stimuli which could interfere with the student's success in a group activity (e.g., provide enough room to move without physical contact, keep noise level at a minimum, keep movement in the environment to a minimum, etc.).

38. Schedule group activities so the teacher's time can be spent uninterrupted with the group.

39. Schedule group activities as part of the student's daily routine (i.e., group activities should occur on a regularly scheduled basis so the student will be prepared and know what to expect).

40. Place the student in those group activities he/she prefers. Gradually require the student to participate in less desirable activities.

41. Provide the student with alternative ways to perform a group assignment and allow the student to choose the most desirable (e.g., a written paragraph assignment may be accomplished by writing a note to a friend, writing about a recent experience, describing a favorite pastime, etc.).

42. Allow the student to participate in one group activity he/she prefers. Require the student to participate in more group activities as he/she experiences success.

43. Schedule group activities when the student is most likely to be successful (e.g., before recess rather than immediately after recess, after the first individual assignment of the day has been completed to establish productive behavior, etc.).

44. Program alternative individual activities if the student is unlikely to be successful (e.g., if the schedule has been changed, if holidays or special events have stimulated the student and make successful group interaction unlikely, etc.).

45. Evaluate the appropriateness of the assigned task to determine (a) if the task is too easy, (b) if the task is too difficult, and (c) if the length of time scheduled is adequate.

46. Position the student's desk or work area so he/she works near other students but is not visually distracted by them (e.g., turn the student's desk away from other students, etc.).

47. Allow the student to leave a group activity and return to independent work when he/she can no longer be successful in the group activity (e.g., as an alternative to disrupting the group, fighting, etc.).

48. Carefully consider the student's age and experience before expecting him/her to get along in a group.

49. Intervene early when there is a problem to prevent more serious problems from occurring.

50. Do not force the student to interact with people with whom he/she is not completely comfortable.

51. Teach the student acceptable ways to communicate displeasure, anger, frustration, etc.

52. Teach the student to "think" before acting (e.g., ask himself/herself "What is happening?" "What am I doing?" "What should I do?" "What will be best for me?").

53. Encourage the student to use problem-solving skills: (a) identify the problem, (b) identify goals and objectives, (c) develop strategies, (d) develop a plan for action, (e) carry out the plan.

54. Make certain the student is allowed to voice an opinion in a situation to avoid becoming angry or upset.

55. Talk to the student about ways of handling situations successfully without conflict (e.g.,walk away from the situation, change to another activity, ask for help, etc.).

56. Reinforce the student for talking an appropriate length of time and at appropriate times in the classroom: (a) give the student a tangible reward (e.g., classroom privileges, line leading, passing out materials, five minutes free time, etc.) or (b) give the student an intangible reward (e.g., praise, handshake, smile, etc.).

57. Speak with the student to explain (a) what he/she is doing wrong (e.g., talking more than is necessary or at inappropriate times) and (b) what he/she should be doing (e.g., keeping comments brief, waiting until it is appropriate to speak, thinking of comments which relate to the situation, etc.).

58. Reinforce those students in the classroom who make their comments brief or speak at appropriate times.

59. Reinforce the student for making appropriate comments or speaking at the appropriate time based on the length of time he/she can be successful. As the student demonstrates success, gradually increase the length of time required for reinforcement.

60. Write a contract with the student specifying what behavior is expected (e.g., making short, appropriate comments and speaking at appropriate times) and what reinforcement will be made available when the terms of the contract have been met.

61. Communicate with parents (e.g., notes home, phone calls, etc.) to share information concerning the student's appropriate behavior. The parents may reinforce the student at home for making appropriate comments at school.

62. Evaluate the appropriateness of the task to determine (a) if the task is too easy, (b) if the task is too difficult, and (c) if the length of time scheduled for the task is adequate.

63. Make certain that reinforcement is not inadvertently given for inappropriate behavior (e.g., talking beyond what is expected or at inappropriate times).

64. Give adequate opportunities to respond (i.e., enthusiastic students need many opportunities to contribute).

65. Provide the student with a predetermined signal if he/she begins to talk beyond what is expected or at inappropriate times.

66. Explain to the student that he/she may be trying too hard to fit in and he/she should relax, talk less and at appropriate times.

67. Provide the student with many social and academic successes.

68. Make the necessary adjustments in the environment to prevent the student from experiencing stress, frustration, or anger (e.g., reduce peer pressure, academic failure, teasing, etc.).

69. Maintain visibility to and from the student. The teacher should be able to see the student and the student should be able to see the teacher. Make eye contact possible at all times.

70. Interact frequently with the student to reduce the need to talk beyond what is expected or at inappropriate times.

71. Assess the appropriateness of the social situation in relation to the student's ability to function successfully.

72. Reinforce the student for raising his/her hand to be recognized.

73. Teach the student to recognize when to speak, to know how much to say and to make appropriate comments (e.g., brief comments, comments within the context of the situation, comments that are a follow-up to what has just been said, etc.).

74. Have the student work in small groups in which he/she would have frequent opportunities to speak. As the student learns to wait longer for his/her turn to speak, gradually increase the size of the group.

75. Make certain that the student's feelings are considered when it is necessary to deal with his/her inappropriate comments (i.e., use comments that do not diminish the student's enthusiasm for participation).

76. Encourage the student to model the behavior of peers who are successful.

77. Create and reinforce activities (e.g., school bulletin board, class project, bake sale, etc.) in which students work together for a common goal rather than individual success or recognition. Point out that larger accomplishments are realized through group effort rather than by individual effort.

78. Deliver directions, explanations, and instructions in a clear and concise manner to reduce the student's need to ask questions.

79. Have the student practice waiting for short periods of time for his/her turn to speak. As the student demonstrates success, gradually increase the length of time required for reinforcement.

80. Explain to the student the reasons why talking beyond what is expected and at inappropriate times is unacceptable (e.g., is impolite, interrupts others, etc.).

81. Attempt to provide equal attention to all students in the classroom.

82. Make the student aware of the number of times he/she talks beyond what is expected and at inappropriate times.

83. Write group contracts which encourage students to work together for group success.

84. After telling the student why he/she should not be talking, explain the reason.

85. Have the student engage in small group activities (e.g., free time, math, reading, etc.) to reduce the level of auditory and visual stimuli in the group. As the student can function successfully, gradually increase the size of the group.

86. Help the student improve concentration skills (e.g., listening to the speaker, taking notes, preparing comments in advance, making comments in the appropriate context, etc.).

87. Have the student question any directions, explanations, or instructions he/she does not understand.

85 Does not demonstrate appropriate behavior in competitive activities

Goals:
1. The student will demonstrate appropriate behavior in competitive activities.

Objectives:
1. The student will take turns in group games on _____ out of _____ trials.
2. The student will interact appropriately with peers in group games with supervision on _____ out of _____ trials.
3. The student will interact appropriately with peers in group games without supervision on _____ out of _____ trials.
4. The student will follow existing rules of group games with verbal prompts on _____ out of _____ trials.
5. The student will independently follow existing rules of group games on _____ out of _____ trials.
6. The student will share materials in group games on _____ out of _____ trials.
7. The student will communicate verbally in group games on _____ out of _____ trials.
8. The student will demonstrate good sportsmanship in group games on _____ out of _____ trials.

Interventions:

1. Reinforce the student for interacting appropriately with one other student in nonacademic situations: (a) give the student a tangible reward (e.g., classroom privileges, line leading, passing out materials, five minutes free time, etc.) or (b) give the student an intangible reward (e.g., praise, handshake, smile, etc.).

2. Speak to the student to explain (a) what he/she is doing wrong (e.g., failing to follow rules, cheating, etc.) and (b) what he/she should be doing (e.g., following rules, playing fairly, etc.).

3. Establish classroom rules:
- Work on-task.
- Remain in your seat.
- Finish task.
- Meet task expectations.
- Raise your hand.

Review rules often. Reinforce students for following rules.

4. Reinforce those students in the classroom who demonstrate appropriate behavior in competitive activities.

5. Reinforce the student for demonstrating appropriate behavior in competitive activities based on the length of time the student can be successful. As the student demonstrates success, gradually increase the length of time required for reinforcement.

6. Choose a peer to model appropriate behavior in competitive activities for the student.

7. Write a contract with the student specifying what behavior is expected (e.g., following rules) and what reinforcement will be made available when the terms of the contract have been met.

8. Communicate with parents (e.g., notes home, phone calls, etc.) to share information concerning the student's progress. The parents may reinforce the student at home for demonstrating appropriate behavior in competitive activities at school.

9. Evaluate the appropriateness of the competitive activity to determine if the game is too difficult and if the length of time scheduled to complete the game is adequate.

10. Have the student question any directions, explanations, instructions he/she does not understand.

11. Evaluate the expectations for participation in competitive activities to determine if the student can be successful in the interaction and for the expected length of time.

12. Allow the student to choose a group of peers with whom he/she feels comfortable.

13. Have the student participate in a game activity with one peer. As the student demonstrates success, gradually increase the size of the group.

14. Determine the peers with whom the student would most prefer to interact in competitive activities and attempt to facilitate the interaction.

15. Assign outgoing, nonthreatening peers to interact with younger peers in competitive activities.

16. Structure the environment so the student has many opportunities to interact with peers in competitive activities.

17. Assign the student to interact with younger peers in competitive activities.

18. Assign the student to competitive activities in which he/she is likely to interact successfully with peers.

19. Conduct a sociometric activity with the class to determine those peers who would most prefer to interact with the student in competitive activities.

20. Make certain that the student demonstrates appropriate behavior in nonacademic situations prior to placing him/her with peers for competitive activities.

21. Make certain that the student understands that interacting with peers in competitive activities is contingent upon appropriate behavior.

22. Teach the student appropriate ways to interact with peers in competitive activities (e.g., suggest activities, share materials, problem solve, take turns, follow game rules, etc.).

23. Supervise competitive activities closely so peers with whom the student interacts do not stimulate inappropriate behavior.

24. Make certain that competitive activities are not so stimulating as to make successful interactions with peers difficult.

25. Choose older peers with positive social skills to interact with the student in competitive activities.

26. Involve the student in extracurricular activities to encourage interactions with peers in competitive activities.

27. Reduce the emphasis on competition. Failure may stimulate inappropriate behavior in competitive activities.

28. Teach the student problem-solving skills so he/she may better handle problems that may occur in interactions with peers in competitive activities (e.g., talking, walking away, calling upon an arbitrator, compromising, etc.).

29. Find the peer with whom the student is most likely to be able to successfully interact in competitive activities (e.g., a student with similar interests, background, classes; similar behavior patterns; nonacademic schedule; etc.).

30. Structure the competitive activities according to the needs/ability of the student (e.g., establish rules; limit the stimulation of the activities; limit the length of the game; consider the time of day; etc.).

31. Limit opportunities for interaction in competitive activities on those occasions in which the student is not likely to be successful (e.g., the student has experienced academic or social failure prior to the scheduled group game).

32. Select competitive activities designed to facilitate appropriate interaction between the student and peers.

33. Through interviews with other students and observations, determine those characteristics of the student which interfere with successful interactions during group games. Determine the skills or behaviors the student needs to develop for successful interactions.

34. Have the student practice appropriate interactions with the teacher(s) in competitive activities.

35. Make certain beforehand that the student is able to successfully participate in the competitive activity (e.g., the student understands the rules; the student is familiar with the game; the student will be compatible with the other students playing the game; etc.).

36. Allow the student to choose the competitive activity which he/she will play with peers.

37. Have the student interact with peers for short periods of time to facilitate success. As the student demonstrates success, gradually increase the length of interactions.

38. Have the student study, practice, simulate, etc., the rules for competitive activities before participating.

39. Establish a set of standard behavior rules for competitive activities (e.g., follow rules of the game; take turns; make positive comments; work as a team member; be a good sport; etc.).

40. Have the student participate in competitive activities of short duration. As the student demonstrates success, gradually increase the length of activities.

41. Remove the student from competitive activities if he/she is unable to demonstrate appropriate behavior.

42. Play the game with the student before he/she participates in the game with peers to model appropriate behavior, determine the student's ability to play the game, determine the student's ability to follow behavior rules, etc.

43. Make certain that the student understands that failing to interact appropriately with peers during competive activities may result in termination of the game and/or loss of future opportunities to participate.

44. Teach the student the skills necessary to successfully participate in particular competitive activities (e.g., volleyball, basketball, football, baseball, etc.).

86 Does not demonstrate appropriate behavior in group games

Goals:

1. The student will improve his/her interpersonal behavior.
2. The student will improve his/her interpersonal behavior in academic settings.
3. The student will improve his/her interpersonal behavior in nonacademic settings.

Objectives:

1. The student will take turns in group games on ____out of ____occasions.
2. The student will interact with peers in group games with supervision on ____out of ____occasions.
3. The student will interact with peers in group games without supervision on ____out of ____occasions.
4. The student will follow existing rules of group games with verbal prompts on ____out of ____ occasions.
5. The student will independently follow existing rules of group games on ____out of ____occasions.
6. The student will share materials in group games on ____out of ____occasions.
7. The student will communicate verbally in group games on ____out of ____occasions.
8. The student will demonstrate good sportsmanship in group games on ____out of ____occasions.

Interventions:

1. Reinforce the student for demonstrating appropriate behavior in group games: (a) give the student a tangible reward (e.g., classroom privileges, line leading, passing out materials, five minutes free time, etc.) or (b) give the student an intangible reward (e.g., praise, handshake, smile, etc.).

2. Speak to the student to explain (a) what he/she is doing wrong (e.g., failing to follow rules, cheating, etc.) and (b) what he/she should be doing (e.g., following rules, playing fairly, etc.).

3. Establish classroom rules:
- Work on-task.
- Remain in your seat.
- Finish task.
- Meet task expectations.
- Raise your hand.

Review rules often. Reinforce students for following rules.

4. Reinforce those students in the classroom who demonstrate appropriate behavior in group games.

5. Reinforce the student for demonstrating appropriate behavior in group games based on the length of time the student can be successful. As the student demonstrates success, gradually increase the length of time required for reinforcement.

6. Write a contract with the student specifying what behavior is expected (e.g., following rules) and what reinforcement will be made available when the terms of the contract have been met.

7. Communicate with parents (e.g., notes home, phone calls, etc.) to share information concerning the student's progress. The parents may reinforce the student at home for demonstrating appropriate behavior in group games at school.

8. Evaluate the appropriateness of the group game to determine if the game is too difficult and if the length of time scheduled to complete the game is adequate.

9. Choose a peer to model appropriate behavior in group games for the student.

10. Have the student question any directions, explanations, or instructions he/she does not understand.

11. Evaluate the expectations for participation in group games to determine if the student can be successful in the interaction and for the expected length of time.

12. Allow the student to choose a group of peers with whom he/she feels comfortable to play group games.

13. Have the student engage in a game activity with one peer. As the student demonstrates success, gradually increase the size of the group.

14. Determine the peers with whom the student would most prefer to interact in group games and attempt to facilitate the interaction.

15. Assign outgoing, nonthreatening peers to interact with the student in group games.

16. Structure the environment so the student has many opportunities to interact with peers in group games.

17. Assign the student to interact with younger peers in group games.

18. Assign the student to group games in which he/she is likely to interact successfully with peers.

19. Conduct a sociometric activity with the class to determine those peers who would most prefer to interact with the student in group games.

20. Make certain that the student demonstrates appropriate behavior in nonacademic situations prior to placing him/her with peers for group games.

21. Make certain that the student understands that interacting with peers in group games is contingent upon appropriate behavior.

22. Have the student practice appropriate interactions with the teacher(s) in group games.

23. Teach the student appropriate ways to interact with peers in group games (e.g., suggest activities, share materials, problem-solve, take turns, follow game rules, etc.).

24. Supervise group games closely so peers with whom the student interacts do not stimulate inappropriate behavior.

25. Make certain that group games are not so stimulating as to make successful interactions with peers difficult.

26. Assign older peers with desirable social skills to interact with the student in group games.

27. Involve the student in extracurricular activities to encourage interaction with peers in group games.

28. Reduce the emphasis on competition. Failure may stimulate inappropriate behavior in group games.

29. Teach the student problem-solving skills so he/she may better deal with problems that may occur in interactions with peers in group games (e.g., talking, walking away, calling upon an arbitrator, compromising, etc.).

30. Find the peer with whom the student is most likely to be able to successfully interact in group games (e.g., a student with similar interests, background, classes, behavior patterns, nonacademic schedule, etc.).

31. Structure the group games according to the needs/abilities of the student (e.g., establish rules, limit the stimulation of the activities, limit the length of the game, consider the time of day, etc.).

32. Limit opportunities for interaction in group games on those occasions when the student is not likely to be successful (e.g., if the student has experienced academic or social failure prior to the scheduled group game).

33. Select group games designed to enhance appropriate interaction of the student and peers.

34. Through interviews with other students and observations, determine those characteristics of the student which interfere with successful interactions during group games to determine skills or behaviors the student needs to develop for successful interactions.

35. Make certain beforehand that the student is able to successfully engage in the group game (e.g., the student understands the rules, the student is familiar with the game, the student will be compatible with the other students playing the game, etc.).

36. Make certain the student understands that failing to interact appropriately with peers during group games may result in termination of the game and/or loss of future opportunities to engage in group games.

37. Have the student interact with peers for short periods of time to facilitate success. As the student demonstrates success, gradually increase the length of time.

38. Have the student study, practice, simulate, etc., the rules for group games before participating.

39. Establish a set of standard behavior rules for group games (e.g., follow rules of the game, take turns, make positive comments, work as a team member, be a good sport, etc.).

40. Remove the student from group games if he/she is unable to demonstrate appropriate behavior.

41. Play the game with the student before he/she engages in the game with peers to model appropriate behavior, determine the student's ability to play the game, determine the student's ability to follow behavior rules, etc.

42. Have the student engage in group games of short duration. As the student demonstrates success, gradually increase the duration of group games.

43. Teach the student necessary skills needed to successfully participate in particular group games (e.g., volleyball, basketball, football, baseball, etc.).

44. Allow the student to choose the group games which he/she will play with peers.

45. Carefully consider the student's age and experience before expecting him/her to get along with others when playing group games.

46. Make certain the student sees the relationship between his/her behavior and the consequences which may follow (e.g., failing to get along when playing a group game will result in others not wanting to play with him/her).

47. Intervene early when there is a problem to prevent more serious problems from occurring.

48. Do not force the student to play games with someone with whom he/she is not completely comfortable.

49. Find a peer to play with the student who will be a good influence (e.g., someone younger, older, of the same gender, of the opposite gender, etc.).

50. Teach the student acceptable ways to communicate displeasure, anger, frustration, etc.

51. Teach the student to "think" before acting (e.g., ask himself/herself "What is happening?" "What am I doing?" "What should I do?" "What will be best for me?").

52. Encourage the student to use problem-solving skills: (a) identify the problem; (b) identify goals and objectives; (c) develop strategies; (d) develop a plan for action; and (e) carry out the plan.

53. Make certain the student is allowed to voice an opinion in a situation to avoid becoming angry or upset.

54. Talk to the student about ways of handling situations successfully without conflict (e.g., walk away from a situation, change to another activity, ask for help, etc.).

87 Demonstrates inappropriate behavior when moving with a group

Goals:

1. The student will demonstrate appropriate behavior when moving with a group.

Objectives:

1. The student will demonstrate appropriate behavior when moving with a group on _____ out of _____ trials.
2. The student will stay in line when moving with a group on _____ out of _____ trials.
3. The student will walk quietly when moving with a group on _____ out of _____ trials.
4. The student will keep his/her hands to his/her sides when moving with a group on _____ out of _____ trials.
5. The student will demonstrate appropriate behavior for _____ minutes at a time when moving with a group.
6. The student will walk quietly by the teacher when moving with a group on _____ out of _____ trials.
7. The student will walk quietly by a peer when moving with a group on _____ out of _____ trials.

Interventions:

1. Communicate with parents (e.g., notes home, phone calls, etc.) to share information concerning their child's progress. The parents may reinforce the student at home for moving appropriately with a group at school.

2. Allow natural consequences to occur as a result of the student's inappropriate behavior (e.g., excessive physical contact may cause people to stay away from the student or may result in pushing, shoving, etc.).

3. Have the student be a line leader, line monitor, etc., when moving with a group.

4. State clearly the expectations for appropriate behavior when moving with a group.

5. Choose a classmate to model appropriate movement with a group for the student.

6. Reinforce the student for demonstrating appropriate behavior when moving with a group: (a) give the student a tangible reward (e.g., classroom privileges, line leading, passing out materials, etc.) or (b) give the student an intangible reward (e.g., praise, handshake, smile, etc.).

7. Reinforce those students who demonstrate appropriate behavior when moving with a group.

8. Reinforce the student for moving appropriately with a group based on the length of time the student can be successful. As the student demonstrates success, gradually increase the length of time required for reinforcement.

9. Have the student walk with arms crossed, arms against his/her side, hands in pockets, etc., if touching others is a problem.

10. Provide constant, positive reinforcement for appropriate behavior. Ignore as many inappropriate behaviors as possible.

11. Reinforce the student for walking at the same pace as other students when moving with a group.

12. Have the student walk alone, behind the group, beside the teacher, etc., when he/she displays inappropriate behavior when moving with a group.

13. Provide the student with a clearly understood list of consequences for inappropriate behavior when moving with a group.

14. Demonstrate/model for the student moving appropriately with a group.

15. Evaluate the appropriateness of the expectation of moving with a group to determine (a) if the task is too easy, (b) if the task is too difficult, and (c) if the length of time scheduled to complete the task is adequate.

16. Speak to the student to explain (a) what he/she is doing wrong (e.g., running, pushing peers, etc.) and (b) what he/she should be doing (e.g., walking without touching peers).

17. Establish rules for moving appropriately with a group:
- Walk in the halls.
- Go directly from one area to another.
- Talk quietly in the halls.
- Walk on the right side of the hall.
- Use the appropriate stairway.

Review rules often. Reinforce students for following the rules.

18. State clearly the manner in which you expect the student to act before going out in public or to a place where he/she has never been before.

19. Stop the line frequently to facilitate the student's success when moving with a group.

20. Have the students walk in pairs when moving as a group.

21. Separate the student from the peer that stimulates his/her inappropriate behavior.

22. Write a contract with the student specifying what behavior is expected (e.g., walking appropriately in a group) and what reinforcement will be made available when the terms of the contract have been met.

23. Remind the student before leaving the classroom of the rules for walking in a group (e.g., walk behind the person in front of you, keep hands to yourself, walk quietly, etc.).

24. Form a second line or group for those students who move at a slower pace.

88 Does not wait his/her turn in activities or games

Goals:

1. The student will allow others to take their turns.
2. The student will allow others to participate in activities and games.
3. The student will demonstrate appropriate interaction skills.

Objectives:

1. The student will allow others to take their turns on _____ out of _____ trials.
2. The student will demonstrate the ability to wait his/her turn by allowing others to take their turns on _____ out of _____ trials.
3. The student will take turns with a peer for _____ minutes at a time. (Gradually increase expectations as the student demonstrates success.)
4. The student will take turns with two peers for _____ minutes at a time. (Gradually increase expectations as the student demonstrates success.)
5. The student will take turns with four to six peers for _____ minutes at a time. (Gradually increase expectations as the student demonstrates success.)
6. The student will allow others to participate in activities and games on _____ out of _____ trials.
7. The student will demonstrate the ability to appropriately interact with others by allowing them to participate in activities and games on _____ out of _____ trials.
8. The student will participate with a peer in an activity or game for _____ minutes at a time. (Gradually increase expectations as the student demonstrates success.)
9. The student will participate with two peers in an activity or game for _____ minutes at a time. (Gradually increase expectations as the student demonstrates success.)
10. The student will participate with four to six peers in an activity or game for _____ minutes at a time. (Gradually increase expectations as the student demonstrates success.)
11. The student will demonstrate appropriate interaction skills during _____ out of _____ activities or games.
12. The student will demonstrate appropriate interaction skills when engaged in highly structured/ supervised activities or games on _____ out of _____ trials.
13. The student will demonstrate appropriate interaction skills when engaged in structured activities and games with minimal supervision on _____ out of _____ trials.
14. The student will demonstrate appropriate interaction skills when engaged in unstructured activities such as free time, lunch, recess, etc., on _____ out of _____ trials.

Interventions:

1. Reinforce the student for taking turns: (a) give the student a tangible reward (e.g., classroom privileges, line leading, passing out materials, five minutes free time, etc.) or (b) give the student an intangible reward (e.g., praise, handshake, smile, etc.).

2. Speak with the student to explain (a) what he/she is doing wrong (e.g., failing to give others opportunities to have a turn) and (b) what he/she should be doing (e.g., allowing others to have a turn).

3. Write a contract with the student specifying what behavior is expected (e.g., taking turns) and what reinforcement will be made available when the terms of the contract have been met.

4. Reinforce those students in the classroom who take turns.

5. Communicate with the parents (e.g., notes home, phone calls, etc.) to share information concerning the student's progress. The parents may reinforce the student at home for taking turns at school.

6. Assess the appropriateness of the task or social situation in relation to the student's ability to perform successfully.

7. Encourage group participation by giving students assignments which require working together to complete the activity (e.g., making murals, bulletin boards, maps, art projects, etc.).

8. Encourage peers to take turns with the student.

9. Have the student work directly with a peer to model taking turns, and gradually increase the size of the group over time.

10. Reduce competitiveness in the school environment (e.g., avoid situations where refusing to take turns contributes to winning; avoid situations where winning or "beating" someone else becomes the primary objective of a game, activity, or academic exercise; etc.).

11. Create and reinforce activities (e.g., school bulletin board, class project, bake sale, etc.) in which students work together for a common goal rather than individual success or recognition. Point out that larger accomplishments are realized through group effort rather than by individuals.

12. Allow the student to have many turns and enough materials to satisfy immediate needs, and gradually require sharing and taking turns.

13. Provide special activities for the entire class at the end of the day, which are contingent upon taking turns throughout the day.

14. Structure the classroom environment to take advantage of natural opportunities to take turns (e.g., allow more group activities, point out natural consequences when a student takes turns, etc.).

15. Capitalize on opportunities to work together (e.g., when there is a spill, assign students different responsibilities for cleaning it up; when a new student enters the classroom, assign different students responsibilities for orientation; etc.).

16. Discourage students from bringing personal possessions to school which others desire. Encourage the use of communal school property.

17. Require the student to practice taking turns if he/she is unable to willingly do so.

18. Provide enough materials, activities, etc., so taking turns will not always be necessary.

19. Provide the student with many opportunities to take turns to help him/her learn the concept of taking turns.

20. Make certain that every student gets to use materials, take a turn, etc., and that there is no opportunity for selfishness.

21. Point out to the student the natural rewards of taking turns (e.g., personal satisfaction, friendships, companionship, etc.).

22. Make certain that those students who are willing to take turns are not taken advantage of by their peers.

23. Make certain that other students are taking turns with the student so a reciprocal relationship can be expected.

24. Maintain a realistic level of expectation for taking turns.

25. Have the student engage in an activity with one peer and gradually increase the size of the group as the student demonstrates success.

26. Determine the peers with whom the student would most prefer to interact and attempt to facilitate the interaction.

27. Assign an outgoing, nonthreatening peer to interact with the student.

28. Assign the student to interact with younger peers.

29. Assign the student to engage in activities in which he/she is likely to interact successfully with peers.

30. Make certain that the student understands that interacting with peers is contingent upon appropriate behavior.

31. Teach the student appropriate ways to interact with peers in group games (e.g., suggest activities, share materials, problem solve, take turns, follow game rules, etc.).

32. Supervise activities closely so the peer(s) with whom the student interacts does not stimulate his/her inappropriate behavior.

33. Make certain that activities are not so stimulating as to make successful interactions with peers difficult.

34. Involve the student in extracurricular activities to encourage appropriate interaction with peers.

35. Do not force the student to interact with someone with whom he/she is not completely comfortable.

36. Make certain, beforehand, that the student is able to successfully engage in the activity (e.g., the student understands the rules, the student is familiar with the game, the student will be compatible with the other students playing the game, etc.).

37. Make certain that the student understands that failing to interact appropriately with peers during activities may result in termination of the game and/or loss of future opportunities to engage in activities.

38. Establish a set of standard behavior rules for group games (e.g., follow the rules of the game, take turns, make positive comments, work as a team member, be a good sport). Review rules often. Reinforce students for following the rules.

39. Talk to the student before playing a game and remind the student of the importance of taking turns.

40. Design activities in which each student takes short turns. As the student demonstrates success at taking turns, increase the length of each student's turn.

41. Allow natural consequences to occur when the student fails to take turns (e.g., other students will not want to interact with him/her, other students will not be willing to take turns, etc.).

42. Intervene early when there is a problem to prevent more serious problems from occurring.

43. Make certain there is adult supervision when the student is playing games with others.

44. Find the peer with whom the student is most likely to be able to successfully interact (e.g., a student with similar interests, background, classes, behavior patterns, nonacademic schedule, etc.).

45. Make certain the student does not become involved in overstimulating activities in which he/she gets excited and cannot settle down.

46. Treat the student with respect. Talk in an objective manner at all times.

47. Provide the student with a predetermined signal when he/she begins to display inappropriate behavior.

48. Teach the student to "take turns" (e.g., each student may use the colored pencils for 15 minutes, each student may have three turns, etc.).

89 Does not allow others to take their turn or participate in activities or games, etc.

Goals:

1. The student will allow others to take their turns.
2. The student will allow others to participate in activities and games.
3. The student will demonstrate appropriate interaction skills.

Objectives:

1. The student will allow others to take their turns on ____ out of ____ trials.
2. The student will demonstrate the ability to wait his/her turn by allowing others to take their turns on ____ out of ____ trials.
3. The student will take turns with a peer for ____ minutes at a time. (Gradually increase expectations as the student demonstrates success.)
4. The student will take turns with two peers for ____ minutes at a time. (Gradually increase expectations as the student demonstrates success.)
5. The student will take turns with four to six peers for ____ minutes at a time. (Gradually increase expectations as the student demonstrates success.)
6. The student will allow others to participate in activities and games on ____ out of ____ trials.
7. The student will demonstrate the ability to appropriately interact with others by allowing them to participate in activities and games on ____ out of ____ trials.
8. The student will participate with a peer in an activity or game for ____ minutes at a time. (Gradually increase expectations as the student demonstrates success.)
9. The student will participate with two peers in an activity or game for ____ minutes at a time. (Gradually increase expectations as the student demonstrates success.)
10. The student will participate with four to six peers in an activity or game for ____ minutes at a time. (Gradually increase expectations as the student demonstrates success.)
11. The student will demonstrate appropriate interaction skills during ____ out of ____ games.
12. The student will demonstrate appropriate interaction skills when engaged in highly structured/supervised activities or games on ____ out of ____ trials.
13. The student will demonstrate appropriate interaction skills when engaged in structured activities and games with minimal supervision on ____ out of ____ trials.
14. The student will demonstrate appropriate interaction skills when engaged in unstructured activities such as free time, lunch, recess, etc., on ____ out of ____ trials.

Interventions:

1. Assess the appropriateness of the task or social situation in relation to the student's ability to perform successfully.

2. Encourage group participation by giving students assignments which require working together to complete the activity (e.g., making murals, bulletin boards, maps, art projects, etc.).

3. Encourage peers to take turns with the student.

4. Have the student work directly with a peer to model taking turns. Gradually increase the size of the group over time.

5. Reduce competitiveness in the school environment (e.g., avoid situations where refusing to take turns contributes to winning; situations where winning or "beating" someone else becomes the primary objective of a game, activity, or academic exercise; etc.).

6. Create and reinforce activities in which students work together for a common goal rather than individual success or recognition (e.g., school bulletin board, class project, bake sale, etc.). Point out that larger accomplishments are realized through group effort than by individual effort.

7. Assign an outgoing, nonthreatening peer to interact with the student.

8. Provide special activities for the entire class at the end of the day which are contingent upon taking turns throughout the day.

9. Structure the classroom environment to take advantage of natural opportunities to take turns (e.g., allow more group activities, point out natural consequences when a student takes turns, etc.).

10. Capitalize on opportunities to work together (e.g., when there is a spill, assign students different responsibilities for cleaning it up; when a new student enters the classroom, assign different students responsibilities for his/her orientation; etc.).

11. Require the student to practice taking turns if he/she is unable to willingly do so.

12. Provide enough materials, activities, etc., so taking turns will not always be necessary.

13. Provide the student with many opportunities to take turns to help the student learn the concept of taking turns.

14. Make certain that every student gets to use materials, take a turn, etc., and that there is no opportunity for selfishness.

15. Point out to the student the natural rewards of taking turns (e.g., personal satisfaction, friendships, companionship, etc.).

16. Make certain that those students who are willing to take turns are not taken advantage of by their peers.

17. Make certain that other students are taking turns with the student so a reciprocal relationship can be achieved.

18. Maintain a realistic level of expectation for taking turns.

19. Have the student engage in an activity with one peer. As the student demonstrates success, gradually increase the size of the group.

20. Determine the peers with whom the student would most prefer to interact and attempt to facilitate the interaction.

21. Allow the student to have many turns and enough materials to satisfy immediate needs, and gradually require sharing and taking turns.

22. Assign the student to interact with younger peers.

23. Assign the student to engage in activities in which he/she is likely to interact successfully with peers.

24. Make certain the student understands that interacting with peers is contingent upon appropriate behavior.

25. Teach the student appropriate ways to interact with peers in group games (e.g., suggest activities, share materials, problem-solve, take turns, follow game rules, etc.).

26. Supervise activities closely so the peer(s) with whom the student interacts does not stimulate inappropriate behavior.

27. Make certain that activities are not so stimulating as to make successful interactions with peers difficult.

28. Involve the student in extracurricular activities to encourage appropriate interaction with peers.

29. Find the peer with whom the student is most likely to be able to successfully interact (e.g., a student with similar interests, background, classes, behavior patterns, nonacademic schedule, etc.).

30. Make certain, beforehand, that the student is able to successfully engage in the activity (e.g., the student understands the rules, the student is familiar with the game, the student will be compatible with the other students playing the game, etc.).

31. Make certain the student understands that failing to interact appropriately with peers during activities may result in termination of the game and/or loss of future opportunities to engage in activities.

32. Design activities in which each student takes short turns. Increase the length of each student's turn as the student demonstrates success at taking turns.

33. Establish a set of standard behavior rules for group games:
- Follow rules of the game.
- Take turns.
- Make positive comments.
- Work as a team member.
- Be a good sport.

Review rules often. Reinforce students for following rules.

34. Allow natural consequences to occur when the student fails to take turns (e.g., other students will not want to interact with him/her, other students will not be willing to take turns, etc.).

35. Talk to the student before playing a game and remind the student of the importance of taking turns.

36. Provide the student with a predetermined signal when he/she begins to display inappropriate behaviors.

37. Make certain there is adult supervision when the student is playing games with others.

38. Do not force the student to interact with someone with whom he/she is not completely comfortable.

39. Make certain the student does not become involved in overstimulating activities in which he/she gets excited and cannot settle down.

40. Treat the student with respect. Talk in an objective manner at all times.

41. Intervene early when there is a problem to prevent more serious problems from occurring.

42. Teach the student to take turns (e.g., each student may use the colored pencils for 15 minutes, each student may have three turns, etc.).

43. Communicate with the parents (e.g., note home, phone calls, etc.) to share information concerning the student's progress. The parents may reinforce the student at home for taking turns at school.

44. Write a contract with the student specifying what behavior is expected (e.g., taking turns) and what reinforcement will be made available when the terms of the contract have been met.

45. Reinforce those students in the classroom who take turns.

46. Speak with the student to explain (a) what the student is doing wrong (e.g., failing to give others opportunities to have a turn) and (b) what the student should be doing (e.g., allowing others to have a turn).

47. Reinforce the student for taking turns: (a) give the student a tangible reward (e.g., classroom privileges, line leading, passing out materials, five minutes free time, etc.) or (b) give the student an intangible reward (e.g., praise, handshake, smile, etc.).

90 Refuses to share possessions or materials or allow others to participate

Goals:

1. The student will share possessions.
2. The student will share materials.

Objectives:

1. The student will share possessions on ___ out of ___ trials.
2. The student will share materials on ___ out of ___ trials.
3. The student will share possessions without being asked to do so on ___ out of ___ trials.
4. The student will share materials when directed by the teacher on ___ out of ___ trials.
5. The student will share materials without being asked to do so on ___ out of ___ trials.
6. The student will allow a peer to play with his/her possessions for ___ minutes at a time.
7. The student will allow a peer to use materials for ___ minutes at a time.
8. The student will ask permission to use materials before taking them on ___ out of ___ trials.
9. The student will not bring possessions to school that he/she does not want to share on ___ out of ___ trials.

Interventions:

1. Assess the appropriateness of the task or social situation in relation to the student's ability to perform successfully.

2. Encourage sharing by giving assignments which require sharing to complete the activity (e.g., making murals, bulletin boards, maps, art projects, etc.).

3. Encourage peers to share with the student.

4. Teach the student the concept of sharing by having the student borrow from others or loan things to others.

5. Have the student work directly with a peer to model sharing. As the student demonstrates success, gradually increase the size of the group.

6. Reduce competitiveness in the school environment (e..g, avoid situations where refusing to share contributes to winning; situations where winning or "beating" someone else becomes the primary objective of a game, activity, or academic exercise; etc.).

7. Create and reinforce activities (e.g., school bulletin board, class project, bake sale, etc.) in which students work together for a common goal rather than individual success or recognition. Point out that larger accomplishments are realized through group effort rather than by individual effort.

8. Put the student in charge of communal school items (e.g., rulers, pencils, crayons, etc.) to experience sharing.

9. Allow the student to have many turns and enough materials to satisfy his/her immediate needs. As the student demonstrates success, gradually require sharing and taking turns.

10. Provide special activities for the entire class at the end of the day which are contingent upon sharing throughout the day.

11. Provide enough materials, activities, etc., so sharing will not always be necessary.

12. Structure the classroom environment to take advantage of natural sharing opportunities (e.g., allowing more group activities, pointing out natural consequences when a student shares, etc.).

13. Capitalize on opportunities to share and help (e.g., when there is a spill, assign students different responsibilities for cleaning it up; when a new student enters the classroom, assign students responsibilities for his/her orientation; etc.).

14. Discourage students from bringing personal possessions to school which others might desire. Encourage the use of communal school property.

15. Model sharing behavior by allowing students to use your materials contingent upon return of the items.

16. Provide the student with many opportunities to both borrow and lend to help the student learn the concept of sharing.

17. Make certain that every student gets to use materials, take a turn, etc., and that there is no opportunity for selfishness.

18. Point out to the student the natural rewards of sharing (e.g., personal satisfaction, friendships, having people share in return, etc.).

19. Make certain that those students who are willing to share are not taken advantage of by their peers.

20. Make certain that other students are sharing with the student so a reciprocal relationship can be achieved.

21. Maintain a realistic level of expectation for sharing.

22. Practice sharing by having each student work with a particular school material for an established length of time. At the end of the time period (e.g., ten minutes), have each student pass his/her material to another student.

23. Provide students with adequate time to complete activities requiring sharing, so the selfish use of school materials is not necessary for success. Students are less likely to share if sharing reduces the likelihood of finishing on time, being successful, etc.

24. Reduce the demands for the student to make verbal exchanges when sharing (e.g., shyness may inhibit sharing if the student is required to verbally communicate with others). Materials should be placed in a central location when not in use so they can be obtained by the students. This will enhance the aspect of sharing which makes materials available to others when not in use.

25. Do not force the student to interact with other students with whom he/she is not completely comfortable.

26. Establish rules for sharing school materials:
- Ask for materials you wish to use.
- Exchange materials carefully.
- Return materials when not in use.
- Offer to share materials with others.
- Take care of shared materials.
- Call attention to materials that need repair.

Review rules often. Reinforce students for following rules.

27. Intervene early when there is a problem to prevent more serious problems from occurring.

28. Teach the student to respect others' belongings by respecting the student's belongings.

29. Be a model for sharing (e.g., by loaning pencils, paper, etc.).

30. Teach the student to "take turns" sharing materials (e..g, each student may use the colored pencils for 15 minutes, one student cuts while the other student uses the glue, etc.).

31. Do not allow the student to bring items to school that he/she is not willing to share (e.g., games, toys, etc.).

32. Make certain the student is not expected to share everything (e.g., do not punish the student for not sharing a hat, gloves, personal items, etc.). Everyone has things they would prefer not to share with others.

33. Communicate with parents (e.g., notes home, phone calls, etc.) to share information concerning the student's progress. The parents may reinforce the student at home for sharing at school.

34. Write a contract with the student specifying what behavior is expected (e.g., sharing) and what reinforcement will be made available when the terms of the contract have been met.

35. Reinforce those students in the classroom who share.

36. Speak with the student to explain (a) what the student is doing wrong (e.g., failing to give others opportunities to use things) and (b) what the student should be doing (e.g., sharing materials).

37. Provide the student with enough materials to satisfy immediate needs (e.g., one of everything). Gradually reduce the number of materials over time, requiring the student to share the available materials as he/she becomes more successful.

38. Make certain that shared materials are returned to the student so he/she will develop a positive concept of sharing.

39. Students who cannot share with one another because of their personal dislike for each other should not be placed in the same group when sharing is required. If a student prefers not to share with one specific person, it does not mean that he/she does not have the ability to share.

40. Provide the student with many experiences to share with others and have materials returned. When the student learns that shared materials will be returned, the student will be more likely to share in the future.

41. Make certain the student understands that if shared materials are used up, worn out, broken under normal use, etc., they will be replaced.

42. In group situations, provide the student with necessary materials for the activity so sharing problems do not disrupt the learning experience.

43. Do not expect the student to share all materials. Students need to "own" some materials (e.g., jewelry, clothing, etc.).

44. Maintain a realistic level of expectation for sharing school materials based on the student's age level and ability to share.

45. Reinforce the student for sharing: (a) give the student a tangible reward (e.g., classroom privileges, line leading, passing out materials, five minutes free time, etc.) or (b) give the student an intangible reward (e.g., praise, handshake, smile, etc.).

91 Fails to participate verbally or physically in group situations

Goals:

1. The student will participate in classroom activities or group situations.

Objectives:

1. The student will participate in ___ out of ___ classroom activities each week.
2. The student will participate in ___ out of ___ group situations per month.
3. The student will demonstrate an interest in classroom activities by asking about the activities, talking about the activities, helping prepare for the activities, etc., in ___ out of ___ activities.
4. The student will passively participate in a classroom activity by sitting quietly, assisting the teacher, taking notes, etc., during ___ out of ___ activities.
5. The student will actively participate in a classroom activity by being the group leader or spokesperson, answering questions, providing his/her opinion, etc., during ___ out of ___ activities.
6. The student will passively participate in group situations by sitting/standing quietly, walking with the group, watching others play games, etc., during ___ out of ___ events.
7. The student will actively participate in group situations by having a role in the play, producing the play, decorating the room, performing in the assembly, etc., during ___ out of ___ events.

Interventions:

1. Reinforce the student for participating in group situations or classroom activities: (a) give the student a tangible reward (e.g., classroom privileges, line leading, passing out materials, five minutes free time, etc.) or (b) give the student an intangible reward (e.g., praise, handshake, smile, etc.).

2. Speak to the student to explain (a) what he/she is doing wrong (e.g., failing to take part), and (b) what he/she should be doing (e.g., talking, taking turns, playing, sharing, etc.).

3. Establish classroom rules:
- Work on-task.
- Remain in your seat.
- Finish task.
- Meet task expectations.
- Raise your hand.

Review rules often. Reinforce students for following rules.

4. Reinforce those students in the classroom who participate in group situations or classroom activities.

5. Write a contract with the student specifying what behavior is expected (e.g., taking part in group activities) and what reinforcement will be made available when the terms of the contract have been met.

6. Communicate with the parents (e.g., notes home, phone calls, etc.) to share information concerning the student's progress. The parents may reinforce the student at home for participating in group situations or classroom activities at school.

7. Evaluate the appropriateness of the task to determine (a) if the task is too easy, (b) if the task is too difficult, and (c) if the length of time scheduled to complete the task is adequate.

8. Choose a peer to sit/work directly with the student (e.g., in different settings or activities such as art, music, P.E., on the bus, tutoring, group projects, running errands in the building, recess, etc.). When the student has become comfortable working with one other student, gradually increase the size of the group.

9. Encourage or reward others for participation in the group situations or classroom activities.

10. Give the student the responsibility of helping another student in the group.

11. Give the student responsibilities in a group so others might view him/her in a positive light.

12. Ask the student questions that cannot be answered yes or no.

13. Call on the student when he/she is most likely to be able to respond successfully (e.g., something in which the student is interested, when the teacher is certain the student knows the answer, etc.).

14. Try various groups to determine the situation in which the student is most successful.

15. Have peers invite the student to participate in school or extracurricular activities.

16. Request that the student be the leader of a small group activity if he/she possesses mastery or an interest in the activity.

17. Allow the student to be present during group activities without requiring active participation.

18. Reduce the emphasis on competition. Frequent or continuous failure is likely to result in embarrassment which will cause reluctance to participate.

19. Demonstrate respect for the student's opinions, responses, suggestions, etc.

20. Provide the student with many social and academic successes.

21. Provide the student with positive feedback which indicates he/she is successful.

22. Present tasks in the most attractive and interesting manner possible.

23. Determine the student's interests so activities which require participation might be presented through his/her interests.

24. Allow the student to choose a special event or interesting activity for the class.

25. Provide the student with success-oriented special events or activities so he/she may develop an interest in them.

26. Modify or adjust situations that cause the student to be reluctant to participate (e.g., degree of difficulty, competition, fear of failure, threat of embarrassment, etc.).

27. Emphasize individual success or progress rather than winning or "beating" other students.

28. Provide the student with opportunities for small group participation as opposed to large group participation.

29. Encourage the student to participate in small groups. As the student demonstrates success, gradually increase the size of the group.

30. Encourage the student to share things of special interest with other members of the class.

31. Choose a peer to model appropriate interactions in classroom activities for the student.

32. Have the student question any directions, explanations, and instructions he/she does not understand.

33. Allow the student to choose a group of peers with whom he/she feels comfortable.

34. Determine the peers with whom the student would most prefer to interact in classroom activities and attempt to facilitate the interaction.

35. Assign outgoing, nonthreatening peers to help the student participate in classroom activities.

36. Structure the environment so the student has many opportunities to interact with other peers in classroom activities.

37. Assign the student to classroom activities in which he/she is likely to interact successfully with peers.

38. Conduct a sociometric activity with the class to determine those peers who would most prefer to interact with the student in classroom activities.

39. Make certain that the student understands that interacting with peers in classroom activities is contingent upon appropriate behavior.

40. Teach the student appropriate ways to interact with peers in classroom activities (e.g., share materials, problem solve, take turns, converse, etc.).

41. Supervise classroom activities closely so peers with whom the student interacts do not stimulate inappropriate behavior.

42. Make certain that the classroom activity is not so stimulating as to make successful interactions with peers difficult.

43. Teach the student problem-solving skills so he/she may better deal with problems that may occur in interactions with peers in classroom activities (e.g., talking, walking away, calling upon an arbitrator, compromising, etc.).

44. Limit opportunities for interaction in classroom activities on those occasions in which the student is not likely to be successful (e.g., the student has experienced academic or social failure prior to the scheduled classroom activity).

45. Select nonacademic activities designed to enhance appropriate social interaction of the student and peers during classroom activities (e.g., board games, model building, coloring, etc.).

46. Have the student practice appropriate interactions with the teacher(s) in classroom activities (e.g., simulations, role playing, etc.).

47. Through interviews with other students and observations, determine those characteristics the student exhibits which interfere with successful interactions during classroom activities. Use information gained to determine skills or behaviors the student needs to develop for successful interactions.

48. Make certain, beforehand, that the student is able to successfully engage in the classroom activity (e.g., the student understands the rules, is familiar with the activity, will be compatible with peers engaged in the activity, etc.).

49. Make certain the student has the necessary materials for the classroom activity.

50. Assign the student responsibilities to perform during classroom activities to enhance peer interaction (e.g., being a leader, passing out materials, acting as a peer tutor, etc.).

51. Make certain the student knows how to use all materials for the classroom activity.

Reminder: Do not "force" the student to take part in any activity or special event.

92 Does not interact appropriately in a group situation

Goals:

1. The student will improve his/her interpersonal behavior.
2. The student will improve his/her interpersonal behavior in academic settings.
3. The student will improve his/her interpersonal behavior in nonacademic settings.

Objectives:

1. The student will participate verbally in a group situation on ____ out of ____ occasions.
2. The student will take turns while working in a group situation on ____ out of ____ occasions.
3. The student will share materials while working in a group situation on ____ out of ____ occasions.
4. The student will successfully work with one other student in a group situation on ____ out of ____ occasions.
5. The student will successfully work with all the members of a group on ____ out of ____ occasions.
6. The student will successfully participate physically in a group situation on ____ out of ____ occasions.
7. The student will successfully work independently in a group situation on ____ out of ____ occasions.
8. The student will successfully work in a group situation with supervision on ____ out of ____ occasions.

Interventions:

1. Reinforce the student for interacting appropriately in a group situation: (a) give the student a tangible reward (e.g., classroom privileges, line leading, passing out materials, five minutes free time, etc.) or (b) give the student an intangible reward (e.g., praise, handshake, smile, etc.).

2. Speak to the student to explain (a) what he/she is doing wrong (e.g., failing to interact with others) and (b) what he/she should be doing (e.g., talking, taking turns, playing, sharing, etc.).

3. Establish classroom rules:
- Work on-task.
- Remain in your seat.
- Finish task.
- Meet task expectations.
- Raise your hand.

Review rules often. Reinforce students for following rules.

4. Reinforce those students in the classroom who interact appropriately in group situations.

5. Give the student responsibilities in a group so others might view him/her in a positive light.

6. Ask the student questions that cannot be answered yes or no.

7. Communicate with the parents (e.g., notes home, phone calls, etc.) to share information concerning the student's progress. The parents may reinforce the student at home for interacting appropriately in group situations at school.

8. Evaluate the appropriateness of the task to determine (a) if the task is too easy, (b) if the task is too difficult, and (c) if the length of time scheduled to complete the task is adequate.

9. Choose a peer to sit/work directly with the student (e.g., in different settings or activities such as art, music, P.E., on the bus, tutoring, group projects, running errands in the building, recess, etc.). When the student has become comfortable working with one other student, gradually increase the size of the group.

10. Encourage or reward others for interacting in the group situation.

11. Give the student the responsibility of helping another student in the group.

12. Write a contract with the student specifying what behavior is expected (e.g., interacting appropriately with peers) and what reinforcement will be made available when the terms of the contract have been met.

13. Call on the student when he/she is most likely to be able to respond successfully (e.g., something in which the student is interested, when the teacher is certain the student knows the answer, etc.).

14. Try various groups to determine the situation in which the student is most successful.

15. Have peers invite the student to participate in school or extracurricular activities.

16. Request that the student be the leader of a small group activity if he/she possesses mastery or an interest in the activity.

17. Allow the student to be present during group activities without requiring active participation.

18. Reduce the emphasis on competition. Frequent or continuous failure is likely to result in embarrassment which will cause reluctance to interact in group situations.

19. Demonstrate respect for the student's opinions, responses, suggestions, etc.

20. Provide the student with many social and academic successes.

21. Provide the student with positive feedback which indicates he/she is successful.

22. Present tasks in the most attractive and interesting manner possible.

23. Determine the student's interests so activities which require participation might be presented through his/her interests.

24. Allow the student to choose a special event or interesting activity for the class.

25. Provide the student with success-oriented special events or activities so he/she may develop an interest in them.

26. Modify or adjust situations that cause the student to be reluctant to interact (e.g., degree of difficulty, competition, fear of failure, threat of embarrassment, etc.).

27. Emphasize individual success or progress rather that "winning" or "beating" other students.

28. Provide the student with opportunities for small group participation as opposed to large group participation.

29. Encourage the student to participate in small groups. As the student demonstrates success, gradually increase the size of the group.

30. Encourage the student to share things of special interest with other members of the class.

31. Choose a peer to model appropriate interactions in group situations for the student.

32. Have the student question any directions, explanations, or instructions he/she does not understand.

33. Allow the student to choose a group of peers with whom he/she feels comfortable.

34. Determine the peers with whom the student would most prefer to interact in group situations and attempt to facilitate the interaction.

35. Assign outgoing, nonthreatening peers to help the student interact in group situations.

36. Structure the environment so the student has many opportunities to interact with other peers in group situations.

37. Assign the student to classroom activities in which he/she is likely to interact successfully with peers.

38. Conduct a sociometric activity with the class to determine those peers who would most prefer to interact with the student in group situations.

39. Make certain the student understands that interacting with peers in classroom activities is contingent upon appropriate behavior.

40. Teach the student appropriate ways to interact with peers in group situations (e.g., share materials, problem-solve, take turns, converse, etc.).

41. Supervise classroom activities closely so peers with whom the student interacts do not stimulate inappropriate behavior.

42. Make certain that the classroom activity is not so stimulating as to make successful interaction with peers difficult.

43. Make certain the student has the necessary materials for the group activity.

44. Limit opportunities for interaction in classroom activities on those occasions in which the student is not likely to be successful (e.g., the student has experienced academic or social failure prior to the scheduled classroom activity).

45. Have the student practice appropriate interactions with the teacher(s) in classroom activities (e.g., simulations, role-playing, etc.).

46. Through interviews with other students and observations, determine those characteristics the student exhibits which interfere with successful interactions during group situations. Use information gained to determine skills or behaviors the student needs to develop for successful interactions.

47. Select nonacademic activities designed to facilitate appropriate social interaction of the student and peers during group situations (e.g., board games, model building, coloring, etc.).

48. Make certain, beforehand, that the student is able to successfully engage in the group situation (e.g., the student understands the rules, is familiar with the activity, will be compatible with peers engaged in the activity, etc.).

49. Teach the student problem-solving skills so he/she may better deal with problems that may occur in interactions with peers in classroom activities (e.g., talking, walking away, calling upon an arbitrator, compromising, etc.).

50. Assign the student responsibilities to perform during group activities to enhance peer interaction (e.g., being a leader, passing out materials, acting as a peer tutor, etc.).

51. Make certain the student knows how to use all materials for the classroom activity.

Reminder: Do not "force" the student to take part in any activity or special event.

93 Becomes overexcited

Goals:

1. The student will maintain self-control in stimulating activities.

Objectives:

1. The student will temporarily remove himself/herself from an activity when he/she begins to become overexcited on _____ out of _____ trials.
2. The student will ask for teacher assistance when he/she becomes overexcited on _____ out of _____ trials.
3. The student will use a tone of voice appropriate to the situation on _____ out of _____ trials.
4. The student will maintain self-control when involved in _____ out of _____ stimulating activities.
5. The student will walk away from a stimulating situation and return when he/she has gained control of his/her behavior on _____ out of _____ trials.
6. The student will stop an activity when told to do so by the teacher on _____ out of _____ trials.
7. The student will physically interact with others in an appropriate manner on _____ out of _____ trials.
8. The student will refrain from reacting impulsively in _____ out of _____ stimulating activities.
9. The student will remain on-task in the presence of stimuli in the classroom on _____ out of _____ trials.
10. The student will remain quietly seated in the presence of stimuli on _____ out of _____ trials.
11. The student will follow rules in the presence of stimuli on _____ out of _____ trials.

Interventions:

1. Communicate with parents (e.g., notes home, phone calls, etc.) to share information concerning their child's progress. The parents may reinforce the student at home for demonstrating self-control in the presence of visual and auditory stimuli at school.

2. Intervene early when there is a problem to prevent a more serious problem from occurring.

3. Remove the student from an activity in the classroom if he/she is unable to demonstrate self-control in the presence of visual and auditory stimuli involved with the activity.

4. Educate yourself and others about ADHD to increase understanding and accommodation of over-excited behavior.

5. Remove the student immediately from an activity when he/she becomes too excited and cannot calm down.

6. Encourage the student to develop an awareness of himself/herself and those around him/her. Have the student periodically step back and ask himself/herself "Am I too excited?"

7. Educate the student about ADHD and the need to self-monitor behavior.

8. Encourage the student to develop an awareness of the consequences of his/her behavior by writing down or talking through problems which may occur due to his/her becoming overexcited (e.g., perceived as unmannerly, avoided, etc.).

9. Make certain that all visual and auditory stimuli in the classroom are reduced as much as possible for all learners.

10. Teach behaviors that promote self-control. Allow the student to gain his/her composure before continuing an activity (e.g., placing hands on desk, sitting with feet on the floor, making eye contact with the person who is talking, etc.).

11. Encourage the student to pause and consider his/her actions when becoming overexcited.

12. Have the student engage in another activity until he/she can settle down and gain control of his/her behavior.

13. Provide constant, positive reinforcement for appropriate behavior. Ignore as many inappropriate behaviors as possible.

14. Have the student take a break to regroup when he/she is becoming overexcited.

15. Choose a classmate to model demonstrating self-control in the presence of visual and auditory stimuli in the classroom for the student.

16. Remain calm when the student becomes over-excited. Calm behavior should have a calming effect on the student.

17. Teach the student to "think" before acting (e.g., ask himself/herself "What is happening?" "What am I doing?" "What should I do?" "What will be best for me?").

18. Model for the student appropriate behavior in the presence of visual and auditory stimuli in the classroom (e.g., continuing to work, asking for quiet, moving to a quieter part of the classroom, etc.).

19. Encourage the student to play games, sports, etc., with friends who do not stimulate him/her to become overexcited.

20. Reinforce those students in the classroom who demonstrate self-control.

21. Provide the student with a clearly under-stood list of consequences for inappropriate behavior.

22. Reduce the emphasis on competition. Competitive activities may cause the student to become overexcited.

23. Allow flexibility in meeting academic demands when the student becomes overexcited (e.g., allow more time, modify assignments, provide help with assignments, etc.).

24. Establish classroom rules:
- Work on-task.
- Work quietly.
- Remain in your seat.
- Finish task.
- Meet task expectations.

Review rules often. Reinforce students for following the rules.

25. Assess the degree of task difficulty to determine whether or not the student will require additional information, time, assistance, etc., to avoid becoming overexcited.

26. Explain to the student when he/she cannot calm down exactly what he/she is doing wrong, what he/she is supposed to be doing, and why.

27. Do not let the student engage in exciting activities for long periods of time.

28. Speak to the student to explain (a) what he/she is doing wrong (e.g., becoming overexcited or upset) and (b) what he/she should be doing (e.g., following rules, considering others, controlling impulsive behavior, etc.).

29. Provide the student with a carrel or divider at his/her desk to reduce visual and auditory stimuli.

30. Avoid discussion or prevent stimuli in the environment which reminds the student of unpleasant experiences/sensitive topics (e.g., divorce, death, unemployment, alcoholism, etc.) which might cause the student to become overexcited.

31. Encourage the student to engage in quiet, calming activities (e.g., listen to music, read, etc.) when feeling overexcited.

32. Encourage the student to avoid ingesting any substance (e.g., drugs, alcohol, cold remedies, etc.) that might further alter his/her ability to maintain self-control.

33. Have the student make a list of consequences associated with overexcitement (e.g., break something, hurt someone, embarrass self or others, etc.).

34. Make certain the student does not become involved in overstimulating activities.

35. Provide the student with the opportunity to move to a quiet place in the classroom whenever visual and auditory stimuli interfere with his/her ability to function successfully.

36. Increase supervision (e.g., by teacher, peer, paraprofessional, etc.) of the student when he/she is involved in activities that tend to overexcite him/her.

37. Separate the student from the peer that stimulates his/her inappropriate behavior.

38. Provide the student with a predetermined signal when he/she begins to display inappropriate behavior.

39. Provide the student with a quiet place in which to work where visual and auditory stimuli are reduced. This is used to reduce distracting stimuli and not as a form of punishment.

40. Reinforce the student for demonstrating self-control: (a) give the student a tangible reward (e.g., classroom privileges, passing out materials, five minutes free time, etc.) or (b) give the student an intangible reward (e.g., praise, handshake, smile, etc.).

41. Allow the student to close the classroom door or windows to reduce visual and auditory stimuli from outside of the classroom.

42. Give the student a special signal when he/she is becoming excited (e.g., a secret word, a hand signal, etc.).

43. Help the student recognize the signs of becoming overexcited. Teach the student appropriate actions to gain self-control.

44. Have the student engage in small group activities (e.g., free time, math, reading, etc.) to reduce the level of visual and auditory stimuli in the group. As the student successfully functions in the presence of visual and auditory stimuli, gradually increase the size of the group.

45. Prevent the student from becoming so stimulated by an event or activity that he/she cannot control his/her behavior.

46. Evaluate the visual and auditory stimuli in the classroom. Determine the level of stimuli to which the student can respond in an appropriate manner. Remove the extraneous stimuli from the environment.

47. Be consistent in expecting the student to settle down after becoming excited. Do not allow the student to participate until he/she has regained self-control.

48. Be consistent in expecting the student to leave a situation when he/she becomes overexcited (e.g., send the student to the counselor's office, make him/her sit in a chair for 5 minutes, etc.).

49. Designate a specific location the student can go to in order to regain control after becoming overexcited.

50. Provide a consistent routine for the student to enhance self-control.

51. Encourage the student to consider the consequences of his/her behavior before engaging in any activity.

52. Identify the situations in which the student is most likely to become overexcited. After you have identified these situations, think of ways to minimize their occurrences.

53. Reinforce the student for demonstrating self-control. As the student demonstrates success, gradually increase the length of time required for reinforcement.

54. Teach the student appropriate ways to gain self-control after becoming overexcited (e.g., take slow deep breaths, leave the activity, walk down the hallway to the water fountain, etc.).

55. Do not allow the student to participate in activities that cause him/her to become so excited that he/she cannot settle down.

56. Reduce visual and auditory stimuli to a level at which the student can successfully function. As the student demonstrates that he/she can successfully tolerate the increased levels without becoming overexcited, gradually allow visual and auditory stimuli to increase.

57. Make certain that the student understands the relationship between inappropriate behavior and the consequences which follow (e.g., missing out on special activities, being avoided by peers, etc.).

58. Provide a pleasant/calm atmosphere which will lessen the likelihood of the student becoming overexcited.

59. Write a contract with the student specifying what behavior is expected (e.g., maintaining self-control in the presence of visual and auditory stimuli in the classroom) and what reinforcement will be made available when the terms of the contract have been met.

Goals:

1. The student will respond appropriately to environmental cues.

Objectives:

1. The student will respond appropriately to environmental cues when given verbal reminders on _____ out of _____ trials.
2. The student will independently respond to environmental cues on _____ out of _____ trials.
3. The student will use environmental cues to move throughout the building, when appropriate, on _____ out of _____ trials.
4. The student will use environmental cues to find locations in the building on _____ out of _____ trials.

Interventions:

1. Match the environmental cues to the student's ability to respond (e.g., visual cues are used for students who cannot hear, symbols or auditory cues are used for students who cannot read, etc.).

2. Have the student question any environmental cues not understood.

3. Choose a peer to model appropriate responses to environmental cues for the student.

4. Provide supportive information to assist the student in responding appropriately to environmental cues (e.g., "When the bell rings, it is time for lunch.").

5. Provide repeated practice in responding appropriately to environmental cues.

6. Make the student responsible for identifying environmental cues for peers (e.g., bells, rules, reminders, etc.).

7. Provide the student with universal environmental cues (e.g., symbols for male and female, arrows, exit signs, danger symbols, etc.).

8. Pair environmental cues with verbal explanations and immediate reinforcement for appropriate responses.

9. Prepare the student in advance of the delivery of environmental cues to increase successful responding.

10. Make certain the same environmental cues are used throughout all locations in and outside of the building.

11. Establish environmental cues that the student is expected to follow (e.g., bells, rules, point cards, reminders, etc.).

12. Evaluate the appropriateness of the environmental cues the student is expected to follow to determine (a) if the cue is too difficult and (b) if the length of time required to respond to the cue is adequate.

13. Model appropriate responses to environmental cues for the student to imitate.

14. Have the student master appropriate responses to one environmental cue at a time, prioritizing environmental cues in order of importance for mastery, before introducing additional cues.

15. Have the student observe and imitate the responses of peers to environmental cues (e.g., as the student is learning to respond appropriately to doors identified as "In" and "Out," the student can imitate the behavior of peers who use the appropriate doors to enter and leave areas of the educational environment) to increase success in learning environmental cues.

16. Reinforce the student for asking the meaning of environmental cues not understood (e.g., bells, signs, etc.).

17. Provide the student with simulation activities in the classroom to teach successful responses to environmental cues (e.g., responses to words, symbols, directions, etc.).

18. Choose a peer to accompany the student and act as a model in teaching appropriate responses to environmental cues as the student moves throughout the building.

19. Stop at various points throughout the day (e.g., when the lunch bell rings, when walking by restroom signs, etc.) to point out the different cues to the students.

20. Provide the student with verbal reminders or prompts when he/she misses an environmental cue.

21. Review daily the environmental cues that are important to the student (e.g., bells, signs, etc.).

22. When delivering directions, explanations, and information, be certain to use vocabulary that is within the student's level of comprehension.

23. Communicate with parents (e.g., notes home, phone calls, etc.) to share information concerning the student's progress. The parents may reinforce the student at home for responding appropriately to environmental cues at school.

24. Write a contract with the student specifying what behavior is expected (e.g., responding appropriately to bells, rules, point cards, reminders, etc.) and what reinforcement will be made available when the terms of the contract have been met.

25. Reinforce the student for responding appropriately to environmental cues based on the number of environmental cues the student can successfully follow. As the student demonstrates success, gradually increase the number of appropriate responses to environmental cues required for reinforcement.

26. Reinforce those students in the classroom who respond appropriately to environmental cues.

27. Speak to the student to explain (a) what the student is doing wrong (e.g., failing to respond appropriately to bells, signs indicating restroom directions, etc.) and (b) what the student should be doing (e.g., responding appropriately to bells, signs indicating restroom directions, etc.).

28. Reinforce the student for responding appropriately to environmental cues: (a) give the student a tangible reward (e.g., classroom privileges, line leading, passing out materials, five minutes free time, etc.) or (b) give the student an intangible reward (e.g., praise, handshake, smile, etc.).

95 Acts impulsively without apparent self-control

Goal:

1. The student will demonstrate self-control.

Objectives:

1. The student will wait quietly for assistance from an instructor on ___ out of ___ trials.
2. The student will wait his/her turn when engaged in activities with peers on ___ out of ___ trials.
3. The student will make decisions appropriate to the situation on ___ out of ___ trials.
4. The student will attempt a task before asking for assistance on ___ out of ___ trials.
5. The student will ask to use materials before taking them on ___ out of ___ trials.
6. The student will use materials appropriately and return them in the same or better condition on ___ out of ___ trials.
7. The student will stay in his/her seat for ___ minutes at a time. (Gradually increase expectations as the student demonstrates success.)
8. The student will raise his/her hand to leave his/her seat on ___ out of ___ trials.
9. The student will raise his/her hand to gain the teacher's attention on ___ out of ___ trials.
10. The student will listen to directions before beginning a task on ___ out of ___ trials.
11. The student will read directions before beginning a task on ___ out of ___ trials.
12. The student will refrain from touching others during ___ out of ___ interactions.
13. The student will demonstrate consideration/regard for others on ___ out of ___ trials.

Interventions:

1. Reduce the opportunity to act impulsively by limiting decision making. As the student demonstrates success, gradually increase opportunities for decision making.

2. Provide the student with a routine to be followed when making decisions (e.g., place a list of decision making strategies on the student's desk).

3. Maintain visibility to and from the student. The teacher should be able to see the student and the student should be able to see the teacher. Make eye contact possible at all times.

4. Be mobile to be frequently near the student.

5. Assign additional responsibilities to the student (e.g., chores, errands, etc.) to give him/her a feeling of success or accomplishment.

6. Prevent the student from becoming overstimulated by an activity (e.g., monitor or supervise student behavior to limit overexcitement in physical activities, games, parties, etc.).

7. Provide the student with adequate time to perform activities to reduce his/her impulsive behavior.

8. Maintain supervision at all times and in all areas of the school environment.

9. Explain to the student that he/she should be satisfied with personal best effort rather than expecting perfection.

10. Provide the student with clear, simply stated explanations, instructions, and directions so that he/she knows exactly what is expected.

11. Assist the student in beginning each task to reduce impulsive responses.

12. Have a peer work with the student to model deliberate and responsible behavior in academic and social settings.

13. Reduce distracting stimuli (e.g., place the student on the front row, provide a carrel or quiet place away from distractions, etc.). This is used as a means of reducing distracting stimuli and not as a form of punishment.

14. Reduce the emphasis on competition. Competition may result in impulsive behavior to win or be first.

15. Teach the student decision-making steps: (a) think about how other persons may be influenced, (b) think about consequences, (c) carefully consider the unique situation, (d) think of different courses of action which are possible, and (e) think about what is ultimately best for him/her.

16. Make the student aware of the reasons we all must practice responsibility (e.g., others' rights are not infringed upon, others are not hurt, order is not lost, property is not damaged or destroyed, etc.).

17. Emphasize individual success or progress rather than winning or "beating" other students.

18. In order to determine if the student heard a direction, have the student repeat it.

19. Allow natural consequences to occur so the student can learn that persons who take turns and act in a deliberate fashion are more successful than those who act impulsively (e.g., if you begin an activity before understanding the directions, you will finish early; but you may perform the assignment incorrectly and receive a failing grade; you may have to repeat the assignment, etc.).

20. Deliver a predetermined signal (e.g., hand signal, verbal cue, etc.) when the student begins to demonstrate impulsive behaviors.

21. Make certain the student does not become involved in overstimulating activities on the playground, during P.E., during lunch, etc.

22. Make certain the student has an adequate amount or number of activities scheduled to prevent the likelihood of impulsively engaging in unplanned activities.

23. Assign the student to an area of the classroom where he/she is to remain at any one time.

24. Maintain a consistent daily routine of activities.

25. Make certain the student knows which areas in the classroom are "off limits" to him/her.

26. Make certain that all students get equal opportunities to participate in activities (e.g., students take turns, everyone has an equal opportunity to be first, etc.).

27. Do not criticize the student. When correcting the student, be honest yet supportive. Never cause the student to feel negatively about himself/herself.

28. Intervene early when there is a problem to prevent a more serious problem from occurring.

29. Do not leave a lot of unstructured time for the student.

30. Teach the student to "think" before acting (e.g., ask himself/herself "What is happening?" "What am I doing?" "What should I do?" "What is best for me?").

31. Evaluate the appropriateness of the task to determine (a) if the task is too easy, (b) if the task is too difficult, and (c) if the length of time scheduled to complete the task is adequate.

32. Communicate with parents (e.g., notes home, phone calls, etc.) to share information concerning the student's progress. The parents may reinforce the student at home for acting in a deliberate and responsible manner at school.

33. Write a contract with the student specifying what behavior is expected (e.g., acting in a deliberate and responsible manner) and what reinforcement will be made available when the terms of the contract have been met.

34. Remove the student from the group or activity until he/she can demonstrate appropriate behavior and self-control.

35. Reinforce the student for demonstrating appropriate behavior based on the length of time the student can be successful. As the student demonstrates success, gradually increase the length of time required for reinforcement.

36. Reinforce those students in the classroom who act in a deliberate and responsible manner.

37. Reinforce the student for acting in a deliberate and responsible manner: (a) give the student a tangible reward (e.g., classroom privileges, line leading, passing out materials, five minutes free time, etc.) or (b) give the student an intangible reward (e.g., praise, handshake, smile, etc.).

38. Speak with the student to explain (a) what the student is doing wrong (e.g., taking action before thinking about what he/she is doing) and (b) what the student should be doing (e.g., considering consequences, thinking about the correct response, considering others, etc.).

39. Establish classroom rules:
- Work on-task.
- Work quietly.
- Remain in your seat.
- Finish task.
- Meet task expectations.

Review rules often. Reinforce students for following the rules.

Reminder: Do not confuse impulsive behavior with enthusiasm. Impulsive behavior should be controlled while enthusiasm should be encouraged.

96 Reacts immediately to situations without thinking, is impatient, fails to wait for a turn or for assistance from a teacher, etc.

Goals:

1. The student will demonstrate appropriate interaction skills.
2. The student will demonstrate self-control.
3. The student will wait appropriately for assistance from an instructor.

Objectives:

1. The student will wait quietly for assistance from an instructor on _____ out of _____ trials.
2. The student will await his/her turn when engaged in activities with peers on _____ out of _____ trials.
3. The student will make decisions appropriate to the situation on _____ out of _____ trials.
4. The student will attempt a task before asking for assistance on _____ out of _____ trials.
5. The student will ask to use materials before taking them on _____ out of _____ trials.
6. The student will use materials appropriately and return them in the same or better condition on _____ out of _____ trials.
7. The student will stay in his/her seat for _____ minutes at a time. (Gradually increase expectations as the student demonstrates success.)
8. The student will raise his/her hand to leave his/her seat on _____ out of _____ trials.
9. The student will raise his/her hand to gain the teacher's attention on _____ out of _____ trials.
10. The student will listen to directions before beginning a task on _____ out of _____ trials.
11. The student will read directions before beginning a task on _____ out of _____ trials.
12. The student will refrain from touching others during _____ out of _____ interactions.
13. The student will demonstrate consideration/regard for others during _____ out of _____ trials.
14. The student will wait quietly for assistance from an instructor on _____ out of _____ occasions.
15. The student will continue working on parts of the assignment while waiting for assistance from the instructor on _____ out of _____ occasions.
16. The student will remain seated while waiting for assistance from an instructor on _____ out of _____ occasions.

Interventions:

1. Reduce the opportunity to act impulsively by limiting decision making. As the student demonstrates success, gradually increase opportunities for decision making.

2. Maintain supervision at all times and in all areas of the school environment.

3. Provide the student with adequate time to perform activities to reduce his/her impulsive behavior.

4. Be mobile to be frequently near the student.

5. Assign additional responsibilities to the student (e.g., chores, errands, etc.) to give him/her a feeling of success or accomplishment.

6. Prevent the student from becoming over-stimulated by an activity (e.g., monitor or supervise student behavior to limit overexcitement in physical activities, games, parties, etc.).

7. Maintain visibility to and from the student. The teacher should be able to see the student and the student should be able to see the teacher. Make eye contact possible at all times.

8. Provide the student with a routine to be followed when making decisions (e.g., place a list of decision making strategies on the student's desk).

9. Explain to the student that he/she should be satisfied with personal best effort rather than expecting perfection.

10. Provide the student with clear, simply stated explanations, instructions, and directions so that he/she knows exactly what is expected.

11. Assist the student in beginning each task to reduce impulsive responses.

12. Have a peer work with the student to model deliberate and responsible behavior in academic and social settings.

13. Reduce distracting stimuli (e.g., place the student on the front row, provide a carrel or quiet place away from distractions, etc.). This is used as a means of reducing distracting stimuli and not as a form of punishment.

14. Teach the student decision-making steps: (a) think about how other persons may be influenced, (b) think about consequences, (c) carefully consider the unique situation, (d) think of different courses of action which are possible, and (e) think about what is ultimately best for him/her.

15. Make the student aware of the reasons we all must practice responsibility (e.g., others' rights are not infringed upon, others are not hurt, order is not lost, property is not damaged or destroyed, etc.).

16. Reduce the emphasis on competition. Competition may result in impulsive behavior to win or be first.

17. Emphasize individual success or progress rather than winning or "beating" other students.

18. Make certain that all students get equal opportunities to participate in activities (e.g., students take turns, everyone has an equal opportunity to be first, etc.).

19. Allow natural consequences to occur so the student can learn that persons who take turns and act in a deliberate fashion are more successful than those who act impulsively (e.g., if you begin an activity before understanding the directions, you will finish early; but you may perform the assignment incorrectly and receive a failing grade; you may have to repeat the assignment, etc.).

20. Deliver a predetermined signal (e.g., hand signal, verbal cue, etc.) when the student begins to demonstrate impulsive behaviors.

21. Make certain the student does not become involved in overstimulating activities on the playground, during P.E., during lunch, etc.

22. Make certain the student has an adequate amount or number of activities scheduled to prevent the likelihood of impulsively engaging in unplanned activities.

23. Assign the student to an area of the classroom where he/she is to remain at any one time.

24. Maintain a consistent daily routine of activities.

25. Make certain the student knows which areas in the classroom are "off limits" to him/her.

26. In order to determine if the student heard a direction, have the student repeat it.

27. Do not criticize the student. When correcting the student, be honest yet supportive. Never cause the student to feel negatively about himself/herself.

28. Intervene early when there is a problem to prevent a more serious problem from occurring.

29. Do not leave a lot of unstructured time for the student.

30. Teach the student to "think" before acting (e.g., ask himself/herself "What is happening?" "What am I doing?" "What should I do?" "What is best for me?").

31. Evaluate the appropriateness of the task to determine (a) if the task is too easy, (b) if the task is too difficult, and (c) if the length of time scheduled to complete the task is adequate.

32. Communicate with parents (e.g., notes home, phone calls, etc.) to share information concerning the student's progress. The parents may reinforce the student at home for acting in a deliberate and responsible manner at school.

33. Write a contract with the student specifying what behavior is expected (e.g., acting in a deliberate and responsible manner) and what reinforcement will be made available when the terms of the contract have been met.

34. Remove the student from the group or activity until he/she can demonstrate appropriate behavior and self-control.

35. Reinforce the student for demonstrating appropriate behavior based on the length of time the student can be successful. As the student demonstrates success, gradually increase the length of time required for reinforcement.

36. Reinforce those students in the classroom who act in a deliberate and responsible manner.

37. Establish classroom rules:
- Work on-task.
- Work quietly.
- Remain in your seat.
- Finish task.
- Meet task expectations.

Review rules often. Reinforce students for following the rules.

38. Speak with the student to explain (a) what the student is doing wrong (e.g., taking action before thinking about what he/she is doing) and (b) what the student should be doing (e.g., considering consequences, thinking about the correct response, considering others, etc.).

39. Reinforce the student for acting in a deliberate and responsible manner: (a) give the student a tangible reward (e.g., classroom privileges, line leading, passing out materials, five minutes free time, etc.) or (b) give the student an intangible reward (e.g., praise, handshake, smile, etc.).

40. Reinforce the student for waiting appropriately for assistance from an instructor: (a) give the student a tangible reward (e.g., classroom privileges, line leading, passing out materials, five minutes free time, etc.) or (b) give the student an intangible reward (e.g., praise, handshake, smile, etc.).

41. Speak to the student to explain (a) what he/she is doing wrong (e.g., leaving his/her seat, talking to other students, etc.) and (b) what he/she should be doing (e.g., remaining in seat or assigned area, remaining quiet, etc.).

42. Reinforce those students in the classroom who remain seated in assigned areas and remain quiet.

43. Reinforce the student for waiting appropriately for assistance from an instructor based on the length of time he/she can be successful. As the student demonstrates success, gradually increase the length of time required for reinforcement.

44. Write a contract with the student specifying what behavior is expected (e.g., remaining in seat or assigned area, remaining quiet, etc.) and what reinforcement will be made available when the terms of the contract have been met.

45. Choose a peer to model appropriate behavior (e.g., remaining in seat or assigned area, remaining quiet, etc.) when waiting for assistance from an instructor for the student.

46. Have the student question any directions, explanations, or instructions he/she does not understand.

47. Communicate with parents (e.g., notes home, phone calls, etc.) to share information concerning the student's progress. The parents may reinforce the student at home for waiting appropriately for assistance from an instructor at school.

48. Tell the student that you will assist him/her as soon as possible (e.g., "Stephen, I'll be with you shortly.") to increase the probability that the student will wait appropriately for assistance.

49. Identify a peer from whom the student may seek assistance.

50. Attempt to provide assistance immediately. Gradually increase the length of time the student must wait for assistance when the teacher is helping another student, instructing, etc.

51. Encourage the student to go to the next problem, go to another part of the assignment, begin a new assignment, etc., when waiting for assistance from an instructor.

52. Establish alternative activities for the student to perform when waiting for assistance from an instructor (e.g., check work already completed, color, look at a magazine, organize work area, begin another task, etc.).

53. Position yourself so visibility to and from the student may be maintained until assistance can be provided.

54. Maintain verbal communication with the student until assistance can be provided (e.g., "Thank you for waiting quietly. I'll be there shortly.").

55. Make certain to recognize the student when his/her hand is raised to convey that assistance will be provided as soon as possible.

56. Supervise the student closely in situations in which he/she is likely to act impulsively (e.g., maintain close physical proximity, maintain eye contact, communicate frequently with the student, etc.).

Reminder: Do not confuse impulsive behavior with enthusiasm. Impulsive behavior should be controlled while enthusiasm should be encouraged.

97 Appears restless

Goals:
1. The student will sit in his/her seat without moving about.
2. The student will wait for assistance without moving about.
3. The student will wait his/her turn without moving about.
4. The student will demonstrate body movements appropriate to the situation.

Objectives:
1. The student will demonstrate body movements appropriate to the situation on _____ out of _____ trials.
2. The student will refrain from making unnecessary body movements for _____ minutes at a time. (Gradually increase expectations as the student demonstrates success.)
3. The student will stop unnecessary body movements when cued by the teacher on _____ out of _____ trials.
4. The student will ask to have a break from the activity, go to a specific location in the classroom, etc., when he/she begins to feel anxious, upset, frustrated, etc., on _____ out of _____ trials.
5. The student will demonstrate appropriate in-seat behavior by sitting quietly with his/her feet on the floor under the desk, keeping all four legs of the chair in contact with the floor, for _____ minutes at a time. (Gradually increase expectations as the student demonstrates success.)
6. The student will keep his/her feet on the floor while seated for _____ minutes at a time. (Gradually increase expectations as the student demonstrates success.)
7. The student will sit quietly for _____ minutes at a time. (Gradually increase expectations as the student demonstrates success.)

Interventions:

1. Communicate with parents (e.g., notes home, phone calls, etc.) to share information concerning their child's progress. The parents may reinforce the student at home for demonstrating physical self-control at school.

2. Encourage the student to develop a 30 second definition of his/her goal to help him/her stay on-task and focused (e.g., "I will listen carefully. The better I focus and stay on-task, the better job I will do.").

3. Give the student additional responsibilities (e.g., chores, errands, etc.) to keep him/her actively involved and give him/her a feeling of success or accomplishment.

4. Encourage the student to keep a small object in his/her pocket that is appropriate to handle at all times and would not disturb others (e.g., foam, rubber, or fabric ball; buckeye; worry stone; etc.).

5. Encourage the student to recite a mantra to himself/herself when entering a situation where he/she has to sit for an extended period of time (e.g., be still, be still, be still).

6. Maintain supervision at all times and in all parts of the school environment.

7. Match assignments with the student's activity level. When he/she is highly active, provide assignments which require a great degree of movement. When he/she is most likely to maintain attention, assign more sedentary assignments.

8. Make certain the student has all the necessary materials at his/her desk to reduce the need to leave his/her seat.

9. Teach behaviors that promote self-control. Allow the student to gain his/her composure before continuing an activity (e.g., placing hands on desk, sitting with feet on the floor, making eye contact with the person who is talking, etc.).

10. Encourage the student to develop an awareness of himself/herself and those around him/her. Have the student periodically step back and ask himself/herself "Am I restless and disturbing others?"

11. Maintain a full schedule of activities. Keeping the student occupied should prevent unnecessary movement.

12. Consider carefully the student's age and ability level when expecting him/her to attend to an activity and not act restless.

13. Reinforce the student for demonstrating appropriate behavior based on the length of time he/she can be successful. As the student demonstrates success, gradually increase the length of time required for reinforcement.

14. Teach the student to use techniques such as crossing his/her arms and legs, clinching his/her fists, and webbing his/her hands when he/she becomes restless.

15. Allow the student to occasionally take assignments home when the class setting is overly distracting.

16. Instruct the student to maintain attention to the source of information by maintaining eye contact, keeping hands free from other materials, and reducing other distractions.

17. Have the student develop an awareness of the consequences of his/her behavior by writing down or talking through problems which may occur due to his/her nervous habits (e.g., perceived as unmannerly, avoided, etc.).

18. Assign short-term projects that can be quickly completed.

19. Provide the student with a calm, quiet environment in which to work.

20. Reinforce those students in the classroom who demonstrate physical self-control.

21. Reduce the emphasis on competition. Competitive activities may cause the student to become anxious and restless.

22. Supervise the student through the completion of responsibilities to help him/her stay on-task and complete the responsibilities.

23. Assess the degree of task difficulty to determine whether or not the student will require additional information, time, assistance, etc., to avoid becoming frustrated and engaging in nervous habits.

24. Encourage the student to avoid ingesting any substance (e.g., drugs, alcohol, cold remedies, etc.) that might further alter his/her ability to maintain self-control.

25. Speak with the student to explain (a) what he/she is doing wrong (e.g., moving in seat, moving about the room, running, etc.) and (b) what he/she should be doing (e.g., practicing self-control, following rules, etc.).

26. Encourage the student to ask for your assistance instead of moving on to something else, giving up, etc.

27. Remove the student from the group or activity until he/she can demonstrate appropriate behavior and self-control.

28. Teach the student to verbalize his/her feelings before losing control (e.g., "I need a short break to regroup." "I'm having a bad day so please be patient.").

29. Encourage the student to self-monitor his/her behavior and limit distracting movements or overactivity.

30. Encourage the student to participate in high energy activities after school that allow him/her to release excess energy (e.g., racquetball, pinball, etc.).

31. Allow the student to engage in mild exercise such as walking up/downstairs, taking a message to the office, etc., when he/she is feeling restless.

32. Do not place the student in situations or places where he/she will have difficulty settling down and demonstrating acceptable behavior.

33. Require the student to engage in activities for only brief periods of time. Gradually increase the length of time required for the student to engage in activities.

34. Interact frequently with the student to maintain his/her attention to the activity (e.g., ask the student questions, ask the student's opinions, stand close to the student, seat the student near the teacher's desk, etc.).

35. Have the student question any directions, explanations, or instructions he/she does not understand.

36. Break the student's responsibilities down into smaller tasks.

37. Instruct the student to do isometric exercises (e.g., tighten and release muscles in his/her arms, legs, buttocks, etc.) to relieve restlessness.

38. Have the student chart the length of time he/she is able to remain in his/her seat.

39. Provide the student with the most attractive and interesting activities possible.

40. Allow the student some movement while performing tasks. Monitor and limit the amount of movement.

41. Make certain that reinforcement is not inadvertently given for inappropriate behavior (e.g., attending to the student only when he/she engages in excessive/unnecessary body movements).

42. Give the student the option of working on the assignment at another time (e.g., earlier/later in the day, on another day, or at home) when he/she will be able to concentrate better.

43. Establish classroom rules:
- Work on-task.
- Work quietly.
- Remain in your seat.
- Finish task.
- Meet task expectations.

Review rules often. Reinforce students for following the rules.

44. Instruct the student to flex or curl his/her toes instead of shaking his/her foot/leg.

45. Move objects used for tactile stimulation (e.g., pens, paper clips, loose change, etc.) away from the student's reach.

46. Prevent the student from becoming overly stimulated by an activity (e.g., frustrated, angry, excited, etc.).

47. Have the student identify a peer who has self-control. Encourage the student to observe that person and try to model the behaviors which contribute to self-control.

48. Separate the student from the peer who stimulates his/her inappropriate behavior.

49. Increase supervision (e.g., by teacher, peer, paraprofessional, etc.) of the student when he/she is involved in activities that tend to overexcite him/her and cause him/her to become restless.

50. Provide active learning opportunities whenever possible.

51. Deliver a predetermined signal (e.g., hand signal, bell ringing, etc.) when the student exhibits inappropriate behavior.

52. Facilitate on-task behavior by providing a full schedule of class activities. Prevent lag time when the student would be free to engage in excessive or unnecessary body movements.

53. Provide the student with a quiet place in the environment where he/she may go when he/she becomes overly restless. This is not meant as punishment, but as a means of helping the student be able to function successfully in his/her environment.

54. Reinforce the student for self-monitoring restless behavior: (a) give the student a tangible reward (e.g., classroom privileges, passing out materials, five minutes free time, etc.) or (b) give the student an intangible reward (e.g., praise, handshake, smile, etc.).

55. Remove the student from the situation when he/she becomes restless.

56. Avoid placing the student in situations that require sitting for an extended period of time such as lectures, seminars, etc. Provide the information for the student through a tape recording or lecture notes.

57. Evaluate the student's responsibilities to determine if they are too complicated for him/her to complete successfully and are causing him/her to act restless.

58. Evaluate the visual and auditory stimuli in the classroom. Determine the amount of stimuli the student can tolerate. Remove extraneous stimuli from the environment.

59. Schedule short activities for the student to perform while seated. As the student demonstrates a decrease in restless behavior, gradually increase the length of the activities.

60. Write a contract with the student specifying what behavior is expected (e.g., demonstrating physical self-control) and what reinforcement will be made available when the terms of the contract have been met.

61. Provide a break while the student is working on monotonous assignments to relieve restlessness and improve concentration.

62. Have a peer cue the student when he/she becomes restless (e.g., the person can touch the student on the arm as a signal that he/she is restless).

63. Be consistent in expecting the student to finish assignments without becoming restless. Do not allow him/her to fail to complete assignments one time and expect him/her to complete assignments the next time.

64. Provide activities which allow the student to be highly active and talkative.

65. Discuss your concerns regarding the student's attention span with the family, a school official, etc., if it is interfering with his/her progress at school.

66. Evaluate the appropriateness of the task to determine (a) if the task is too easy, (b) if the task is too difficult, and (c) if the length of time scheduled to complete the task is adequate.

67. Seat the student near the teacher.

68. Maintain visibility to and from the student to keep his/her attention when verbal questions/ directions are being delivered. The teacher should be able to see the student and the student should be able to see the teacher. Make eye contact possible at all times.

69. Establish an environmental setting for the classroom that promotes optimal individual performance (e.g., quiet room, background music, fresh air, etc.).

70. Make the necessary adjustments in the environment to prevent the student from experiencing stress, frustration, anger, etc., as much as possible.

71. Seat the student close to the source of information to maintain his/her attention (e.g., in the front row or near the speaker in an assembly).

72. Have the student assemble all the materials necessary to work on a project, assignment, etc., to reduce the need to search for materials.

73. Do not allow the student to participate in activities that cause him/her to become too restless.

74. Give the student frequent opportunities to leave his/her seat for appropriate reasons (e.g., getting materials, running errands, assisting the teacher, etc.).

75. Provide the student frequent opportunities to participate, take a turn, etc., to keep him/her involved in the activity.

76. Interact frequently with the student to prevent excessive or unnecessary body movements.

77. Try various groupings in the classroom to determine the situation in which the student is most successful in self-monitoring restlessness.

78. Reduce stimuli which contributes to unnecessary or excessive movement.

79. Allow the student to stand up and move about his/her desk instead of sitting down.

80. Allow the student to work with a peer who is calm and capable of concentrating on an assignment for an extended period of time.

81. Follow a less desirable task with a more desirable task. Make completion of the first task necessary to perform the second task.

82. Communicate with the student's cooperative work experience/vocational education teacher to select appropriate job sites that allow for a high degree of movement (e.g., jobs that allow the student to be on his/her feet, move from place to place, etc.).

83. Allow the student some movement while he/she is listening to class lectures. Monitor and limit the amount of movement.

98 Changes from one activity to another without finishing the first, without putting things away, before it is time to move on, etc.

Goals:

1. The student will be able to change from one activity to another without difficulty.

Objectives:

1. The student will change from one activity to another after finishing the first on _____ out of _____ occasions.
2. The student will change from one activity to another after putting things away on _____ out of _____ occasions.
3. The student will stop one activity and begin another when necessary on _____ out of _____ occasions.

Interventions:

1. Communicate with parents (e.g., notes home, phone calls, etc.) to share information concerning their child's progress. The parents may reinforce the student at home for appropriately changing from one activity to another at school.

2. Allow natural consequences to occur due to the student's failure to finish a task (e.g., failing to finish an assignment will result in having to give up a recreational activity to complete an unfinished task).

3. Establish rules for changing activities (e.g., finish one activity before moving on to another, put things away where they belong, return borrowed items in the same or better condition, complete cleanup on time, etc.). These rules should be consistent and followed by everyone in the class. Talk about the rules often.

4. Have the student develop a checklist/chart to follow which will allow him/her to complete all assignments.

5. Reinforce the student for demonstrating acceptable behavior based on the length of time the student can be successful. As the student demonstrates success, gradually increase the length of time required for reinforcement.

6. Use more interesting or stimulating activities as a reward for completing less interesting activities (e.g., complete paperwork before working on the computer).

7. Reduce the student's involvement in activities which prove too stimulating for him/her.

8. Require the student to put all materials away before moving on to a new activity.

9. Establish a timeline for completing an assignment.

10. Require the student to finish an activity unless it will be disruptive to the schedule.

11. Assign the student shorter activities. As the student demonstrates success, gradually increase the length of the activities.

12. Assign short-term projects that can be quickly completed.

13. Establish rules that are to be followed in various parts of the school building (e.g., lunchroom, music room, art room, gymnasium, library, playground, etc.) relating to appropriate transition between activities.

14. Maintain consistent expectations within the ability level of the student.

15. Reinforce those students in the classroom who change from one activity to another without difficulty.

16. Provide the student with a clearly understood list of consequences for inappropriate behavior.

17. Reduce the emphasis on competition. Competitive activities may cause the student to become impatient and leave activities incomplete.

18. Maintain consistency in the classroom's daily routines.

19. Make certain there is a designated place for all items in the classroom.

20. Assess the degree of task difficulty to determine whether or not the student will require additional information, time, assistance, etc., before beginning a task.

21. Schedule recreational activities at the end of the day. Make participation in these activities dependent upon completion of class responsibilities.

22. Set aside time at the end of each class period to complete unfinished assignments.

23. Inform the student that work not completed in one sitting can be completed later. Provide the student with ample time to complete earlier assignments to guarantee closure.

24. Provide the student with clearly stated expectations for all situations.

25. Speak to the student to explain (a) what he/she is doing wrong (e.g., failing to complete an activity before beginning another) and (b) what he/she should be doing (e.g., completing an activity before changing to another).

26. Show the student how to finish one activity before moving on to another (e.g., return things to their proper places, return borrowed items in the same or better condition, etc.) before expecting the student to perform the responsibilities on his/her own.

27. Establish classroom routines and procedures for transitioning from one activity to the next.

28. Establish rules for organization (i.e., everything has a place and everything should be in its place). Enforce these rules consistently in the classroom.

29. Reinforce the student for changing from one activity to another without difficulty: (a) give the student a tangible reward (e.g., classroom privileges, passing out materials, five minutes free time, etc.) or (b) give the student an intangible reward (e.g., praise, handshake, smile, etc.).

30. Schedule activities so the student has more than enough time to finish an activity if he/she works consistently.

31. Have the student ask for help when he/she needs it.

32. Encourage the student to manage his/her daily performance as if he/she were self-employed. This should increase his/her motivation to successfully complete projects.

33. Assign an activity that involves immediate, short-term tasks.

34. Have the student time activities to monitor personal behavior and accept time limits.

35. Identify the expectations of different environments and help the student develop the skills to be successful in those environments.

36. Establish classroom rules:
- Work on-task.
- Work quietly.
- Remain in your seat.
- Finish task.
- Meet task expectations.

Review rules often. Reinforce students for following the rules.

37. Collect the student's materials (e.g., pencil, paper, textbook, workbook, etc.) when it is time to change from one activity to another.

38. Designate a time during each class period to put away materials.

39. Develop, in conjunction with other school personnel, as much consistency across the various environments as possible (e.g., rules, criteria for success, behavioral expectations, consequences, etc.).

40. Provide the student with established time limits before an activity begins.

41. Assist the student in performing his/her responsibilities. As the student demonstrates success in performing responsibilities, gradually decrease assistance and require the student to independently assume more responsibility.

42. Be clear when giving directions to transition from one activity to the next.

43. Write a contract with the student specifying what behavior is expected (e.g., putting materials away and getting ready for another activity) and what reinforcement will be made available when the terms of the contract have been met.

44. Evaluate the appropriateness of the task to determine (a) if the task is too easy, (b) if the task is too difficult, and (c) if the length of time scheduled to complete the task is adequate.

45. Provide the student with more than enough time to finish an activity. Decrease the amount of time provided as the student demonstrates success.

46. Set time limits so that the student knows exactly how long he/she has to work and when he/she must be finished.

47. Provide adequate transition time for the student to finish an activity and get ready for the next activity.

48. Use a timer to help the student know when it is time to change to a new activity.

49. Teach time-management skills. Have the student make a daily plan and follow it. Encourage the student to avoid becoming distracted by events, impulses, and moods.

50. Discuss the student's responsibilities at the beginning of each class period so he/she knows what is expected.

51. Limit the student's use of those things he/she has been irresponsible in putting away, returning, etc.

52. Explain to the student when he/she does not put things away, exactly what he/she is doing wrong, what he/she is supposed to be doing, and why.

53. Make certain that responsibilities given to the student are appropriate for his/her level of development and ability.

54. Employ a signal technique (e.g., turning the lights off and on) to warn that the end of an activity is near and it is time to finish and put materials away.

55. Be consistent in expecting the student to change from one activity to another (e.g., do not allow the student to change activities without putting materials away one time and not the next).

56. Provide an incentive statement along with a directive (e.g., "You may listen to your CD player after you finish your assignment and put away all materials.").

57. Follow a less desirable task with a more desirable task. Make completion of the first task necessary to perform the second task.

58. Choose a peer to model finishing an activity and putting materials away for the student.

99 Moves about while seated

Goals:

1. The student will engage in appropriate behaviors while seated.
2. The student will sit appropriately in his/her seat.

Objectives:

1. The student will demonstrate appropriate in-seat behavior by sitting quietly with his/her feet on the floor under the desk, keeping all four legs of the chair in contact with the floor, for _____ minutes at a time. (Gradually increase expectations as the student demonstrates success.)
2. The student will refrain from tipping his/her chair for _____ minutes at a time. (Gradually increase expectations as the student demonstrates success.)
3. The student will refrain from tipping his/her desk while seated for _____ minutes at a time. (Gradually increase expectations as the student demonstrates success.)
4. The student will keep his/her feet on the floor while seated for _____ minutes at a time. (Gradually increase expectations as the student demonstrates success.)
5. The student will sit quietly for _____ minutes at a time. (Gradually increase expectations as the student demonstrates success.)
6. The student will refrain from touching others as they walk by on _____ out of _____ trials.
7. The student will refrain from tapping objects such as a pencil, paper clip, eraser, ruler, etc., for _____ minutes at a time. (Gradually increase expectations as the student demonstrates success.)

Interventions:

1. Communicate with parents (e.g., notes home, phone calls, etc.) to share information concerning their child's progress. The parents may reinforce the student at home for sitting appropriately in his/her seat at school.

2. Evaluate the appropriateness of the task to determine (a) if the task is too easy, (b) if the task is too difficult, and (c) if the length of time scheduled to complete the task is adequate.

3. Remove the student immediately from an activity when he/she becomes too excited and cannot sit still.

4. Encourage the student to keep a small object in his/her pocket that is appropriate to handle at all times and would not disturb others (e.g., foam, rubber, or fabric ball; buckeye; worry stone; etc.).

5. Use more interesting or stimulating activities as a reward for completing less interesting activities (e.g., complete paperwork before working on the computer).

6. Maintain a full schedule of activities. Keeping the student occupied should prevent unnecessary movement.

7. Teach behaviors that promote self-control. Allow the the student to gain his/her composure before continuing an activity (e.g., placing hands on desk, sitting with feet on the floor, making eye contact with the person who is talking, etc.).

8. Choose a classmate to model appropriate ways in which to sit in his/her seat for the student.

9. Encourage the student to develop an awareness of the consequences of his/her behavior by writing down or talking through problems which may occur due to his/her nervous habits (e.g., perceived as unmannerly, avoided, etc.).

10. Encourage the student to develop an awareness of himself/herself and those around him/her. Have the student periodically step back and ask himself/herself "Am I fidgeting and being overactive?"

11. Consider carefully the student's age and experience before expecting him/her to sit quietly without fidgeting and squirming.

12. Seat the student next to a peer who sits appropriately in his/her seat.

13. Reinforce the student for sitting appropriately in his/her seat: (a) give the student a tangible reward (e.g., classroom privileges, passing out materials, five minutes free time, etc.) or (b) give the student an intangible reward (e.g., praise, handshake, smile, etc.).

14. Teach the student to use techniques such as crossing his/her arms and legs, clinching his/her fists, and webbing his/her hands when moving about while seated is inappropriate.

15. Place the student in a carrel to reduce distracting stimuli which may cause him/her to inappropriately move about in his/her seat.

16. Deliver a predetermined signal (e.g., hand signal, verbal cue, etc.) when the student begins to move about inappropriately while seated.

17. Reduce the emphasis on competition. Competitive activities may cause the student to become anxious and move about unnecessarily.

18. Have the student flex or curl his/her toes instead of shaking his/her foot/leg.

19. Maintain consistency in the classroom's daily routine.

20. Assess the degree of task difficulty to determine whether or not the student will require additional information, time, assistance, etc., to avoid becoming frustrated and engaging in nervous movement.

21. Have the student do isometric exercises when seated (e.g., tighten and release his/her arms, legs, buttocks, etc.) to relieve restlessness.

22. Communicate with the student's cooperative work experience/vocational education teacher to provide an appropriate job site for the student.

23. Speak to the student to explain (a) what he/she is doing wrong (e.g., tipping chair) and (b) what he/she should be doing (e.g., sitting appropriately in his/her chair).

24. Reinforce those students in the classroom who sit appropriately in their seats.

25. Establish classroom rules:
- Work on-task.
- Work quietly.
- Remain in your seat.
- Finish task.
- Meet task expectations.

Review rules often. Reinforce students for following the rules.

26. Reinforce the student for sitting appropriately in his/her seat based on the length of time he/she can be successful. As the student demonstrates success, gradually increase the length of time required for reinforcement.

27. Write a contract with the student specifying what behavior is expected (e.g., sitting appropriately in his/her seat) and what reinforcement will be made available when the terms of the contract have been met.

28. Encourage the student to ask himself/herself questions to avoid impulsive behavior (e.g., "What should I be doing?" "How do I want to be perceived?").

29. Encourage the student to monitor his/her behavior and limit distracting movements or over-activity.

30. Allow the student to engage in mild exercise such as walking up/downstairs, carry a message to the office, etc., when he/she is feeling restless.

31. Encourage the student to participate in high energy activities after school that allow him/her to release excess energy (e.g., racquetball, soccer, etc.).

32. Encourage the student to avoid ingesting any substance (e.g., drugs, alcohol, cold remedies, etc.) that might further alter his/her ability to maintain self-control.

33. Have the student make a list of consequences associated with frequently occurring behaviors (e.g., by disrupting others, I will be perceived as unmannerly. By behaving aggressively, people will avoid me.).

34. Have the student recite a mantra to himself/herself when entering a situation where he/she has to sit for an extended period of time (e.g., be still, be still, be still).

35. Have a peer cue the student when he/she moves about unnecessarily (e.g., the person can touch the student's arm as a signal that he/she is moving about unnecessarily).

36. Increase supervision (e.g., by teacher, peer, paraprofessional, etc.) of the student when he/she is involved in activities that tend to overexcite him/her.

37. Establish times when it is permissible for the student to be out of his/her seat (e.g., leave his/her seat only to get a book, a drink of water, or use the pencil sharpener, etc.).

38. Be proactive. Work with the school counselor to schedule the student's classes to alternate classes requiring extensive seatwork with classes allowing higher levels of activity.

39. Allow the student some movement during assigned seatwork. Monitor and limit the amount of movement.

40. Present assignments that involve immediate, short-term tasks.

41. Give the student a special signal when he/she is fidgeting, squirming, etc., (e.g., a secret word, a hand signal, etc.).

42. Have the student identify the situations in which he/she is most likely to engage in inappropriate behavior while seated. After he/she has identified these situations, have him/her think of ways to minimize their occurrences.

43. Avoid placing the student in situations that require sitting for an extended period of time such as lectures, seminars, assemblies, etc. Provide the information for the student through tape recordings or lecture notes.

44. Evaluate the visual and auditory stimuli in the classroom. Determine the amount of stimuli the student can tolerate. Remove extraneous stimuli from the environment.

45. Allow some movement between assignments if the student appears to need a break.

46. Provide a break while the student is working on monotonous assignments to relieve restlessness and improve concentration.

47. Be consistent in expecting the student to settle down and sit quietly. Do not allow the student unlimited movement one day and expect him/her to sit quietly the next day.

48. Allow the student some movement while performing tasks. Monitor and limit the amount of movement.

49. Have desks and/or chairs that can be fastened to the floor or which are designed to prevent tipping.

50. Provide the student with a specific description of appropriate in-seat behavior (e.g., face forward, feet on floor, back straight, etc.).

51. Implement logical consequences for students who fail to sit appropriately in their seats (e.g., the student would have to sit on the floor, stand next to his/her desk to work, sit in a chair without a desk, etc.).

52. Establish an environmental setting for the classroom that promotes optimal individual performance (e.g., quiet room, background music, fresh air, etc.).

53. Evaluate the necessity of having the student sit facing forward, feet on floor, back straight, etc.

54. Make certain that the chair or desk to which the student is assigned is appropriate and/or comfortable for him/her (e.g., the desk is not too high, the chair is not too small, etc.).

55. Maintain consistent expectations for the student to sit appropriately in his/her seat.

56. Make certain the student is aware of the natural consequences that may occur from sitting inappropriately in his/her seat (e.g., injury, damaging property, hurting others, etc.).

57. Do not give the student too many tasks to do at one time.

58. Communicate clearly to the student the activity level expected during classtime.

59. Encourage the student to recognize the signs of becoming overexcited so he/she can independently take appropriate action to gain self-control.

60. Arrange for individual assignments when the group setting is overly distracting.

61. Have the student assemble all the materials necessary to work on a project, assignment, etc., to reduce the need to search for materials.

62. Do not allow the student to participate in activities that cause him/her to become so excited that he/she cannot settle down.

63. Provide activities which are interesting to the student to keep him/her on-task and sitting appropriately in his/her seat.

64. Seat the student near the teacher.

65. Seat the student away from peers to reduce the likelihood that he/she will sit inappropriately in his/her seat.

66. Teach the student to attend to the source of information by maintaining eye contact, keeping hands free from other materials, and reducing other distractions.

67. Seat the student close to the source of information to maintain his/her attention (e.g., in the front row or near the speaker in an assembly).

68. Reduce stimuli which contributes to unnecessary or excessive movement.

69. Move objects used for tactile stimulation (e.g., pens, paper clips, loose change, etc.) away from the student's reach.

70. Remove any materials the student uses to make noise while seated.

71. Require the student to engage in activities for only brief periods of time. Gradually increase the length of time required for the student to engage in activities.

72. Model for the student appropriate ways to sit in a chair or at a desk.

73. Provide activities for the student which allow him/her some degree of activity.

100   Engages in nervous habits

Goals:
1. The student will maintain self-control in stimulating activities.
2. The student will not engage in nervous habits.

Objectives:
1. The student will discontinue engaging in the nervous habit when cued by the teacher on _____ out of _____ trials.
2. The student will temporarily remove himself/herself from a stimulating activity on _____ out of _____ trials.
3. The student will maintain self-control when engaged in _____ out of _____ stimulating activities.
4. The student will refrain from biting his/her fingernails during _____ out of _____ stimulating activities.
5. The student will refrain from twirling his/her hair during _____ out of _____ stimulating activities.
6. The student will refrain from chewing the inside of his/her cheek during _____ out of _____ stimulating activities.
7. The student will refrain from chewing pencils or pens during _____ out of _____ stimulating activities.
8. The student will refrain from spinning/twirling objects during _____ out of _____ stimulating activities.

Interventions:

1. Communicate with parents (e.g., notes home, phone calls, etc.) to share information concerning their child's progress. The parents may reinforce the student at home for not engaging in nervous habits at school.

2. Provide a calm/pleasant atmosphere.

3. Allow the student to squeeze a tennis ball or rolled up towel to decrease engaging in nervous habits.

4. Allow the student to take a break to regroup when he/she is becoming nervous.

5. Avoid discussion of topics that are sensitive to the student (e.g., divorce, death, unemployment, alcoholism, etc.).

6. Maintain a full schedule of activities. Keeping the student occupied should prevent the student from engaging in nervous habits.

7. Allow the student some physical activity while performing tasks.

8. Provide the student with an alternate activity designed to result in productive behavior (e.g., drawing, cutting, using a calculator, working with a peer, etc.).

9. Encourage the student to develop an awareness of himself/herself and those around him/her. Encourage the student to periodically step back and ask himself/herself "Am I fidgeting and being overactive?"

10. Teach behaviors that promote self-control. Allow the student to gain his/her composure before continuing an activity (e.g., placing hands on desk, sitting with feet on the floor, making eye contact with the person who is talking, etc.).

11. Reinforce the student for demonstrating appropriate behavior: (a) give the student a tangible reward (e.g., classroom privileges, passing out materials, five minutes free time, etc.) or (b) give the student an intangible reward (e.g., praise, handshake, smile, etc.).

12. Reinforce the student for demonstrating appropriate academic/social behavior based on the length of time he/she can be successful. As the student demonstrates success, gradually increase the length of time required for reinforcement.

13. Allow the student to keep a small object in his/her pocket that is appropriate to handle at all times and would not disturb others (e.g., foam, rubber, or fabric ball; buckeye; worry stone; etc.).

14. Have the student develop an awareness of the consequences of his/her behavior by writing down or talking through problems which may occur due to his/her nervous habits (e.g., perceived as unmannerly, avoided, etc.).

15. Try various groupings in the classroom to determine the situation in which the student is most comfortable.

16. Reinforce those students in the classroom who demonstrate appropriate behavior.

17. Prevent situations in which peers contribute to the student's nervous behaviors.

18. Assess the degree of task difficulty to determine whether or not the student will require additional information, time, assistance, etc., to avoid becoming frustrated and engaging in nervous habits.

19. Speak with the student to explain (a) what he/she is doing wrong (e.g., chewing on pencil, nail biting, twirling objects, etc.) and (b) what he/she should be doing (e.g., practicing self-control, working on assignment, performing responsibilities, etc.).

20. Teach the student ways to gain self-control (e.g., count to ten, walk away, talk with someone, etc.).

21. Remove the student from the group or activity when he/she engages in nervous habits.

22. Provide the student with a high-interest activity he/she prefers.

23. Interact frequently with the student to maintain his/her involvement in class assignments.

24. Encourage the student to engage in quiet, calming activities (e.g., listen to music, read, etc.) when feeling restless and engaging in nervous behaviors.

25. Encourage the student to avoid ingesting any substance (e.g., drugs, alcohol, cold remedies, etc.) that might further alter his/her ability to maintain self-control.

26. Provide the student with as many social and academic successes as possible.

27. Explain to the student the need to develop self-monitoring skills to decrease nervous habits.

28. Encourage the student to reduce nervous behaviors such as nail biting, knuckle cracking, or chewing his/her lip/cheek by replacing them with a competing behavior (e.g., clinch his/her fists together to avoid cracking his/her knuckles, suck on hard candy instead of chewing his/her lip/cheek, etc.).

29. Remove from the environment any object which may be used by the student to engage in nervous habits (e.g., pencils, pens, rubberbands, paperclips, etc.).

30. Provide the student with a predetermined signal when he/she engages in nervous habits.

31. Reduce the emphasis on competition. Repeated failure and frustration may cause the student to engage in nervous habits.

32. Encourage the student to practice self-control activities designed to allow him/her to gain composure before continuing an activity (e.g., placing hands on desk, sitting with feet on the floor, making eye contact with the instructor, etc.).

33. Move objects used for tactile stimulation (e.g., pens, paper clips, loose change, etc.) away from the student's reach.

34. Write a contract with the student specifying what behavior is expected (e.g., not engaging in nervous habits) and what reinforcement will be made available when the terms of the contract have been met.

35. Evaluate the appropriateness of the task to determine (a) if the task is too easy, (b) if the task is too difficult, and (c) if the length of time scheduled to complete the task is adequate.

36. Teach the student to use techniques such as crossing his/her arms and legs, clinching his/her fists, and webbing his/her hands when he/she is engaging in nervous habits.

37. Structure the environment so time does not allow the student the opportunity to engage in nervous habits.

38. Reduce stimuli which may cause the student to engage in nervous habits (e.g., noise, movement, etc.).

39. Make the necessary adjustments in the environment to prevent the student from experiencing stress, frustration, nervousness, etc.

40. Identify the situations in which the student is likely to engage in nervous habits. After you have identified these situations, think of ways to minimize their occurrences.

41. Teach the student to attend to the source of information by maintaining eye contact, keeping hands free from other materials, and reducing other nervous habits.

42. Reduce situations which may contribute to nervous behavior (e.g., testing situations, timed activities, competition, etc.).

43. Interact frequently with the student to reduce nervous behavior.

44. Choose a peer tutor to work directly with the student to prevent stress, frustration, anxiety, etc.

101   Exhibits off-task behaviors

Goals:
1. The student will remain on task.

Objectives:
1. The student will demonstrate on-task behavior by sitting quietly at his/her seat, looking at his/her materials, and performing the task for ___minutes at a time. (Gradually increase expectations as the student demonstrates success.)
2. The student will remain on-task for ___minutes at a time. (Gradually increase expectations as the student demonstrates success.)
3. The student will remain on-task long enough to complete the task on ___out of ___tasks.
4. The student will remain on-task through its completion on ___out of ___tasks.
5. The student will maintain eye contact with the teacher for ___minutes at a time.

Interventions:

1. Evaluate the auditory and visual stimuli in the classroom to determine the level of stimuli to which the student can respond in an appropriate manner.

2. Reduce auditory and visual stimuli to a level at which the student can successfully function. As the student demonstrates that he/she can successfully tolerate the increased levels, gradually allow auditory and visual stimuli to increase.

3. Seat the student so that he/she experiences the least amount of auditory and visual stimuli.

4. Provide the student with a quiet place in which to work where auditory and visual stimuli are reduced. This is used to reduce distracting stimuli and not as a form of punishment.

5. Seat the student away from those peers who create the most auditory and visual stimulation in the classroom.

6. Provide the student with a carrel or divider at his/her desk to reduce auditory and visual stimuli.

7. Make certain that all auditory and visual stimuli in the classroom are reduced as much as possible for all learners.

8. Provide the student with the opportunity to move to a quiet place in the classroom any time that auditory and visual stimuli interfere with the ability to function successfully.

9. Provide the student with earphones to wear if auditory stimuli interfere with the ability to function. As the student can more successfully function in the presence of auditory stimuli, gradually remove the earphones.

10. Allow the student to close the door or windows to reduce auditory and visual stimuli from outside of the classroom.

11. Remove the student from an activity until he/she can demonstrate appropriate on-task behavior.

12. Require the student to be productive in the presence of auditory and visual stimuli for short periods of time. As the student becomes more successful, gradually increase the length of time the student is required to be productive.

13. Provide the student with shorter tasks which do not require extended attention to be successful. As the student demonstrates success, gradually increase the length of the tasks.

14. Have the student engage in small group activities (e.g., free time, math, reading, etc.) to reduce the level of auditory and visual stimuli in the group. As the student can function successfully, gradually increase the size of the group.

15. Model for the student appropriate behavior in the presence of auditory and visual stimuli in the classroom (e.g., continuing to work, asking for quiet, moving to a quieter part of the classroom, etc.).

16. Assign the student shorter tasks but more of them (e.g., modify a 20-problem math activity to 4 activities of 5 problems each, to be performed at various times during the day). As the student demonstrates success, gradually increase the number of problems for each activity.

17. Present tasks in the most attractive and interesting manner possible.

18. Assess the degree of task difficulty in relation to the student's ability to successfully perform the task.

19. Interact frequently with the student to maintain involvement in the activity (e.g., ask the student questions, ask the student's opinion, stand close to the student, seat the student near the teacher's desk, etc.).

20. Provide the student with a timer to be used to increase the amount of time during which he/she maintains attention (e.g., have the student work on the activity until the timer goes off).

21. Deliver a predetermined signal (e.g., hand signal, verbal cue, etc.) when the student begins to display off-task behaviors.

22. Structure the environment to reduce the opportunity for off-task behavior. Reduce lag time by providing the student with enough activities to maintain productivity.

23. Have the student work with a peer tutor to maintain attention to task.

24. Make certain the student has all necessary materials to perform assignments.

25. Make certain the student knows what to do when he/she cannot successfully perform assignments (e.g., raise hand, ask for assistance, go to the teacher, etc.).

26. Communicate with parents (e.g., notes home, phone calls, etc.) to share information concerning the student's progress. The parents may reinforce the student at home for staying on task in the classroom.

27. Make certain to recognize the student when his/her hand is raised to convey that assistance will be provided as soon as possible.

28. Teach the student how to manage time until the teacher can provide assistance (e.g., try the problem again, go on to the next problem, wait quietly, etc.).

29. Communicate clearly with the student the length of time he/she has to complete the assignment and when the assignment should be completed. The student may want to use a timer to complete tasks within a given period of time.

30. Specify exactly what is to be done for the completion of the task (e.g., indicate definite starting and stopping points, indicate the minimum requirements, etc.).

31. Make certain the student understands that work not done during work time must be completed at other times such as recess, free time, after school, etc.

32. Provide the student with increased opportunities for help or assistance on academic tasks (e.g., peer tutoring, directions for work, frequent interactions, etc.).

33. Identify the student's most efficient learning mode and use it consistently to increase the probability of understanding and remaining on task for longer periods of time.

34. Give the student one task to perform at a time. Introduce the next task only when the student has successfully completed the previous task.

35. Have the student question any directions, explanations, and instructions not understood.

36. Choose a peer to model on-task behavior for the student.

37. Maintain visibility to and from the student. The teacher should be able to see the student and the student should be able to see the teacher. Make eye contact possible at all times.

38. Write a contract with the student specifying what behavior is expected (e.g., establish a reasonable length of time to stay on task) and what reinforcement will be made available when the terms of the contract have been met.

39. Reinforce the student for staying on task in the classroom: (a) give the student a tangible reward (e.g., classroom privileges, line leading, passing out materials, five minutes free time, etc.) or (b) give the student an intangible reward (e.g., praise, handshake, smile, etc.).

40. Speak to the student to explain (a) what the student is doing wrong (e.g., failing to attend to tasks) and (b) what the student should be doing (e.g., attending to tasks).

41. Reinforce those students in the classroom who demonstrate on-task behavior.

42. Establish classroom rules:
- Work on-task.
- Work quietly.
- Remain in your seat.
- Finish task.
- Meet task expectations.

Review rules often. Reinforce students for following the rules.

43. Reinforce the student for attending to task based on the length of time he/she can be successful. As the student demonstrates success, gradually increase the length of time required for reinforcement.

102 Does not function appropriately in the presence of verbal and physical stimuli in the classroom

Goals:

1. The student will improve his/her independent behavior.
2. The student will improve his/her independent behavior in academic settings.
3. The student will improve his/her independent behavior in the classroom.

Objectives:

1. The student will stay on-task in the presence of verbal and physical stimuli in the classroom on ____out of ____ occasions.
2. The student will remain seated in the presence of verbal and physical stimuli in the classroom on ____ out of ____ occasions.
3. The student will follow rules in the presence of verbal and physical stimuli in the classroom on ____out of ____ occasions.
4. The student will maintain self-control in the presence of verbal and physical stimuli in the classroom on ____ out of ____ occasions.
5. The student will remain actively involved in activities in the presence of verbal and physical stimuli in the classroom on ____ out of ____ occasions.

Interventions:

1. Reinforce the student for functioning appropriately in the presence of verbal and physical stimuli in the classroom: (a) give the student a tangible reward (e.g., classroom privileges, line leading, passing out materials, five minutes free time, etc.) or (b) give the student an intangible reward (e.g., praise, handshake, smile, etc.).

2. Speak to the student to explain (a) what he/she is doing wrong (e.g., failing to attend, getting out of seat, fighting with a peer, talking, etc.) and (b) what he/she should be doing (e.g., maintaining self-control in the presence of verbal and physical stimuli in the classroom).

3. Have the student question any directions, explanations, instructions he/she does not understand.

4. Reinforce those students in the classroom who function appropriately in the presence of verbal and physical stimuli in the classroom.

5. Reinforce the student for functioning appropriately in the presence of verbal and physical stimuli in the classroom based on the length of time the student can be successful. As the student demonstrates success, gradually increase the length of time required for reinforcement.

6. Write a contract with the student specifying what behavior is expected (e.g., maintaining self-control in the presence of verbal and physical stimuli in the classroom) and what reinforcement will be made available when the terms of the contract have been met.

7. Communicate with parents (e.g., notes home, phone calls, etc.) to share information concerning the student's progress. The parents may reinforce the student at home for functioning appropriately in the presence of verbal and physical stimuli in the classroom.

8. Choose a peer to model functioning appropriately in the presence of verbal and physical stimuli in the classroom for the student.

9. Establish classroom rules:
- Work on-task.
- Work quietly.
- Remain in your seat.
- Finish task.
- Meet task expectations.

Review rules often. Reinforce students for following the rules.

10. Evaluate the verbal and physical stimuli in the classroom to determine the level of stimuli the student can respond to appropriately.

11. Reduce verbal and physical stimuli to a level at which the student can successfully function. As the student demonstrates that he/she can successfully tolerate the increased levels, gradually allow verbal and physical stimuli to increase.

12. Seat the student so that he/she experiences the least amount of verbal and physical stimuli possible.

13. Provide the student with a quiet place in which to work, where verbal and physical stimuli are reduced. This is used to reduce distracting stimuli and not as a form of punishment.

14. Place the student away from those peers in the classroom who create the most verbal and physical stimuli.

15. Provide the student with a carrel or divider at his/her desk to reduce verbal and physical stimuli.

16. Make certain that all verbal and physical stimuli in the classroom are reduced as much as possible for all learners.

17. Provide the student with the opportunity to move to a quiet place in the classroom any time verbal and physical stimuli interfere with his/her ability to function successfully.

18. Have the student practice a new skill or assignment alone, with an aide, the teacher, or a peer before the entire group attempts the activity or before performing for a grade.

19. Remove the student from an activity in the classroom if he/she is unable to function appropriately in the presence of the verbal and physical stimuli involved in the activity.

20. Require the student to be productive in the presence of verbal and physical stimuli for short periods of time. As he/she becomes successful, gradually increase the length of time the student is required to be productive.

21. Provide the student with shorter tasks which do not require extended attention to be successful. As the student demonstrates he/she can be successful in the presence of verbal and physical stimuli, gradually increase the length of the tasks.

22. Have the student engage in small-group activities (e.g., free time, math, reading, etc.) to reduce the level of verbal and physical stimuli in the group. As the student can function successfully in the presence of verbal and physical stimuli, gradually increase the size of the group.

23. Teach the student appropriate ways to respond to verbal and physical stimuli in the classroom (e.g., moving to another part of the room, asking others to be quiet, leaving the group, etc.).

24. Model for the student appropriate behavior in the presence of verbal and physical stimuli in the classroom (e.g., continuing to work, asking for quiet, moving to a quieter part of the classroom, etc.).

25. Allow the student to close the door or windows to reduce verbal and physical stimuli from outside of the classroom.

26. Provide the student with earphones to wear if verbal stimuli interfere with his/her ability to function. As the student can function more successfully in the presence of verbal stimuli, gradually remove the earphones.

103 Handles objects excessively

Goals:

1. The student will engage in appropriate behaviors while seated.
2. The student will sit appropriately in his/her seat.
3. The student will demonstrate body movements appropriate to the situation.

Objectives:

1. The student will have in his/her possession only those materials necessary on _____ out of _____ occasions.
2. The student will use only those materials necessary on _____ out of _____ occasions.
3. The student will handle only those materials necessary on _____ out of _____ occasions.
4. The student will engage only in those behaviors necessary for an activity or assignment on _____ out of _____ occasions.

Interventions:

1. Communicate with parents (e.g., notes home, phone calls, etc.) to share information concerning their child's appropriate behavior. The parents may reinforce the student at home for working and sitting without handling objects at school.

2. Have a peer cue the student when he/she handles an object excessively (e.g., the person can touch the student on the arm as a signal that he/she is handling an object excessively).

3. Allow the student to keep a small object in his/her pocket that is appropriate to handle at all times and would not disturb others (e.g., foam, rubber, or fabric ball; buckeye; worry stone; etc.).

4. Allow the student to squeeze a tennis ball or rolled up towel to reduce unnecessary handling of objects.

5. Maintain a full schedule of activities. Keeping the student occupied should prevent the student from handling objects excessively.

6. Reinforce the student for sitting and working quietly in his/her seat without handling objects: (a) give the student a tangible reward (e.g., classroom privileges, passing out materials, five minutes free time, etc.) or (b) give the student an intangible reward (e.g., praise, handshake, smile, etc.).

7. Choose a classmate to model appropriate ways in which to work and sit in his/her seat without handling objects for the student.

8. Speak to the student to explain (a) what he/she is doing wrong (e.g., twirling pencil, playing with things in desk, spinning ruler on pencil, clicking ballpoint pen, repeatedly sharpening pencils, etc.) and (b) what he/she should be doing (e.g., sitting and working quietly in his/her chair).

9. Establish classroom rules:
- Work on-task.
- Work quietly.
- Remain in your seat.
- Finish task.
- Meet task expectations.

Review rules often. Reinforce students for following the rules.

10. Reinforce those students in the classroom who work and sit appropriately in their seats.

11. Reinforce the student for working and sitting appropriately in his/her seat without unnecessary handling of objects based on the length of time he/she can be successful. As the student demonstrates success, gradually increase the length of time required for reinforcement.

12. Write a contract with the student specifying what behavior is expected (e.g., working and sitting appropriately in his/her seat) and what reinforcement will be made available when the terms of the contract have been met.

13. Provide the student with a specific description of appropriate in-seat behavior (e.g., face forward, feet on floor, back straight, hands free of objects, etc.).

14. Reduce the emphasis on competition. Competitive activities may cause the student to become anxious and handle objects excessively.

15. Prevent unnecessary objects, toys, materials, etc., from being available to the student or kept in his/her desk.

16. Maintain consistent expectations for the student to work and sit appropriately in his/her seat.

17. Place the student in a carrel to keep objects from his/her reach.

18. Seat the student next to a peer who works and sits appropriately in his/her seat.

19. Deliver a predetermined signal (e.g., hand signal, bell ringing, etc.) when the student fails to work or sit appropriately in his/her seat without handling objects.

20. Provide activities which are interesting to the student to keep him/her on-task and sitting appropriately in his/her seat without unnecessary handling of objects.

21. Seat the student near the teacher.

22. Have the student identify a peer who does not handle objects excessively. Encourage the student to observe that person and try to model the behaviors which keep him/her from handling objects excessively.

23. Move objects used for tactile stimulation (e.g., pens, paper clips, loose change, etc.) away from the student's reach.

24. Remove hazardous objects from the student's immediate work area to prevent accidents (e.g., paper cutter, lab chemicals, etc.).

25. Remove any materials the student uses to make noise while seated.

26. Teach the student to use techniques such as crossing his/her arms and legs, clinching his/her fists, and webbing his/her hands when he/she is acting impulsively.

27. Reduce the occurrence of situations that may contribute to the student handling objects (e.g., cluttered work environments, competition, long lectures, etc.).

28. Identify the situations in which the student is likely to engage in nervous habits or handle objects. After you have identified these situations, think of ways to minimize their occurrences.

29. Communicate with the student's cooperative work experience/vocational education teacher to provide appropriate interventions at the student's job site.

30. Make certain the student has only those materials necessary for him/her at any given time.

104 Has a short attention span unless the topic or task is interesting to him/her

Goals:

1. The student will increase attention to task behavior.

Objectives:

1. The student will display on-task behavior with cues on ____ out of ____ trials.
2. The student will display on-task behavior on ____ out of ____ trials.
3. The student will remain on task with cues for ____ minutes at a time.
4. The student will remain on task without cues for ____ minutes at a time.

Interventions:

1. Reinforce the student for remaining on task: (a) give the student a tangible reward (e.g., classroom privileges, line leading, passing out materials, etc.) or (b) give the student an intangible reward (e.g., praise, pat on the back, smile, etc.).

2. Speak with the student to explain (a) what he/she is doing wrong (e.g., wiggling during the story, not finishing a task, etc.) and (b) what he/she should be doing (e.g., listening to the story, working with materials until the task is completed, etc.).

3. Establish classroom rules:
- Work on-task.
- Work quietly.
- Remain in your seat.
- Finish task.
- Meet task expectations.

Review rules often. Reinforce students for following the rules.

4. Reinforce those students who remain on-task.

5. Reinforce the student for staying on-task based on the length of time he/she can be successful. As the student demonstrates success, gradually increase the length of time required for reinforcement.

6. Remove the student from the group or activity until he/she can demonstrate on-task behavior.

7. Communicate with parents (e.g., notes home, telephone calls, etc.) to share information concerning the student's appropriate behavior. The parents may reinforce the student at home for increased attention to tasks.

8. Try various groupings to determine the situation in which the student is most comfortable.

9. Make the necessary adjustments in the environment to prevent the student from experiencing stress, frustration, anger, etc., as much as possible.

10. Interact frequently with the student to prevent the student from getting off task.

11. Maintain visibility to and from the student. The teacher should be able to see the student and the student should be able to see the teacher. Make eye contact possible at all times.

12. Modify or eliminate situations which cause the student to experience off-task behaviors.

13. Provide the student with a predetermined signal when he/she begins to get off task.

14. Make certain that reinforcement is not inadvertently given for inappropriate behavior (e.g., attending to the student only when he/she is off task, etc.).

15. Remove the student from peers who stimulate the inappropriate behavior.

16. Have the student question any directions, explanations, and instructions he/she does not understand prior to beginning activities.

17. Choose a peer to model appropriate behavior (e.g., sitting still during a lecture, staying with a task until it is completed, etc.) for the student.

18. Model for the student the appropriate way to stay on-task (e.g., listening quietly as a student shares information, finishing a task in class, etc.).

19. Reduce distracting stimuli in the classroom which would contribute to the student not attending to task.

20. Work alongside the student during a task to encourage his/her attending to the task.

21. Make certain that the student sees the relationship between behavior and the consequences that follow (e.g., inattention will cause the student to be removed from the activity, tasks not completed during the given time will have to be completed before the student can begin a new activity, etc.).

22. Allow natural consequences to occur as a result of the student not attending to the task (e.g., being removed from a group activity because behavior is distracting to others, etc.).

23. Make certain that the student has all the materials necessary to complete the task (e.g., pencils, crayons, paper, scissors, etc.).

24. Allow the student to choose activities. Intrinsic motivation will keep the student on-task.

25. Assist the student in performing certain activities. As he/she demonstrates success, gradually reduce the amount of assistance provided.

26. Break down steps in tasks into smaller parts. Have the student move to the next step only when he/she has successfully completed the preceding step.

27. Give the student short tasks he/she can accomplish.

28. Make certain to give directions in a simple, concrete manner.

29. Be consistent when expecting the student to remain on-task. Do not allow the student to fail to attend to a task one time, and expect him/her to attend to a task the next time.

30. Allow natural consequences to occur as a result of the student's inability to concentrate (e.g., work not done or completed inaccurately must be made up during recreational time, not concentrating while people are talking results in not knowing what to do, etc.).

31. Help the student develop attention-maintaining behaviors (e.g., maintain eye contact, ask questions related to the subject, etc.).

105 Has accidents which are a result of impulsive or careless behavior

Goals:
1. The student will demonstrate self-control.

Objectives:
1. The student will wait quietly for assistance from an instructor on _____ out of _____ trials.
2. The student will await his/her turn when engaged in activities with peers on _____ out of _____ trials.
3. The student will make decisions appropriate to the situation on _____ out of _____ trials.
4. The student will attempt a task before asking for assistance on _____ out of _____ trials.
5. The student will ask to use materials before taking them on _____ out of _____ trials.
6. The student will use materials appropriately and return them in the same or better condition on _____ out of _____ trials.
7. The student will stay in his/her seat for _____ minutes at a time. (Gradually increase expectations as the student demonstrates success.)
8. The student will raise his/her hand to leave his/her seat on _____ out of _____ trials.
9. The student will raise his/her hand to gain the teacher's attention on _____ out of _____ trials.
10. The student will listen to directions before beginning a task on _____ out of _____ trials.
11. The student will read directions before beginning a task on _____ out of _____ trials.
12. The student will refrain from touching others during _____ out of _____ interactions.
13. The student will demonstrate consideration/regard for others during _____ out of _____ trials.

Interventions:

1. Reduce the opportunity to act impulsively by limiting decision making. As the student demonstrates success, gradually increase opportunities for decision making.

2. Maintain supervision at all times and in all areas of the school environment.

3. Maintain visibility to and from the student. The teacher should be able to see the student and the student should be able to see the teacher. Make eye contact possible at all times.

4. Be mobile to be frequently near the student.

5. Assign additional responsibilities to the student (e.g., chores, errands, etc.) to give him/her a feeling of success or accomplishment.

6. Prevent the student from becoming overstimulated by an activity (e.g., monitor or supervise student behavior to limit overexcitement in physical activities, games, parties, etc.).

7. Provide the student with adequate time to perform activities to reduce his/her impulsive behavior.

8. Provide the student with a routine to be followed when making decisions (e.g., place a list of decision making strategies on the student's desk).

9. Explain to the student that he/she should be satisfied with personal best effort rather than expecting perfection.

10. Provide the student with clear, simply stated explanations, instructions, and directions so that he/she knows exactly what is expected.

11. Assist the student in beginning each task to reduce impulsive responses.

12. Have a peer work with the student to model deliberate and responsible behavior in academic and social settings.

13. Reduce distracting stimuli (e.g., place the student on the front row, provide a carrel or quiet place away from distractions, etc.). This is used as a means of reducing distracting stimuli and not as a form of punishment.

14. Emphasize individual success or progress rather than winning or "beating" other students.

15. Teach the student decision making steps: (a) think about how other persons may be influenced, (b) think about consequences, (c) carefully consider the unique situation, (d) think of different courses of action which are possible, and (e) think about what is ultimately best for him/her.

16. Make the student aware of the reasons we all must practice responsibility (e.g., others' rights are not infringed upon, others are not hurt, order is not lost, property is not damaged or destroyed, etc.).

17. Reduce the emphasis on competition. Competition may result in impulsive behavior to win or be first.

18. Make certain that all students get equal opportunities to participate in activities (e.g., students take turns, everyone has an equal opportunity to be first, etc.).

19. Allow natural consequences to occur so the student can learn that persons who take turns and act in a deliberate fashion are more successful than those who act impulsively (e.g., if you begin an activity before understanding the directions, you will finish early; but you may perform the assignment incorrectly and receive a failing grade; you may have to repeat the assignment, etc.).

20. Deliver a predetermined signal (e.g., hand signal, verbal cue, etc.) when the student begins to demonstrate impulsive behaviors.

21. Make certain the student does not become involved in overstimulating activities on the playground, during P.E., during lunch, etc.

22. Make certain the student has an adequate amount or number of activities scheduled to prevent the likelihood of impulsively engaging in unplanned activities.

23. Assign the student to an area of the classroom where he/she is to remain at any one time.

24. Maintain a consistent daily routine of activities.

25. Make certain the student knows which areas in the classroom are "off limits" to him/her.

26. In order to determine if the student heard a direction, have the student repeat it.

27. Do not criticize the student. When correcting the student, be honest yet supportive. Never cause the student to feel negatively about himself/herself.

28. Intervene early when there is a problem to prevent a more serious problem from occurring.

29. Do not leave a lot of unstructured time for the student.

30. Teach the student to "think" before acting (e.g., ask himself/herself "What is happening?" "What am I doing?" "What should I do?" "What is best for me?").

31. Evaluate the appropriateness of the task to determine (a) if the task is too easy, (b) if the task is too difficult, and (c) if the length of time scheduled to complete the task is adequate.

32. Communicate with parents (e.g., notes home, phone calls, etc.) to share information concerning the student's progress. The parents may reinforce the student at home for acting in a deliberate and responsible manner at school.

33. Write a contract with the student specifying what behavior is expected (e.g., acting in a deliberate and responsible manner) and what reinforcement will be made available when the terms of the contract have been met.

34. Remove the student from the group or activity until he/she can demonstrate appropriate behavior and self-control.

35. Reinforce the student for demonstrating appropriate behavior based on the length of time the student can be successful. As the student demonstrates success, gradually increase the length of time required for reinforcement.

36. Reinforce those students in the classroom who act in a deliberate and responsible manner.

37. Establish classroom rules:
- Work on-task.
- Work quietly.
- Remain in your seat.
- Finish task.
- Meet task expectations.

Review rules often. Reinforce students for following the rules.

38. Speak with the student to explain (a) what the student is doing wrong (e.g., taking action before thinking about what he/she is doing) and (b) what the student should be doing (e.g., considering consequences, thinking about the correct response, considering others, etc.).

39. Reinforce the student for acting in a deliberate and responsible manner: (a) give the student a tangible reward (e.g., classroom privileges, line leading, passing out materials, five minutes free time, etc.) or (b) give the student an intangible reward (e.g., praise, handshake, smile, etc.).

40. Make certain that consequences are delivered consistently for behavior demonstrated (e.g., appropriate behavior results in positive consequences and inappropriate behavior results in negative consequences).

41. Provide the student with many social and academic successes.

42. Structure the environment to limit opportunities for inappropriate behavior (e.g., keep the student engaged in activities, have the student seated near the teacher, maintain visibility to and from the student, etc.).

43. Prevent the student from becoming overstimulated by an activity (e.g., monitor or supervise student behavior to limit overexcitement in physical activities, games, parties, etc.).

44. Provide the student with a clearly identified list of consequences for inappropriate behavior.

45. Teach the student problem-solving skills: (a) identify the problem, (b) identify goals and objectives, (c) develop strategies, (d) develop a plan of action, and (e) carry out the plan.

46. Clarify for the student that it is his/her behavior which determines consequences (e.g., positive or negative).

47. Provide a learning experience which emphasizes the cause-and-effect relationship between behavior and the inevitability of some form of consequence (e.g., both negative and positive behaviors and consequences).

48. Point out the consequences of other students' behavior as they occur (e.g., take the opportunity to point out that consequences occur for all behavior and for all persons).

49. Supervise the student closely in situations in which he/she is likely to act impulsively (e.g., maintain close physical proximity, maintain eye contact, communicate frequently with the student, etc.).

50. Prevent peers from engaging in those behaviors which would cause the student to fail to consider or regard the consequences of his/her behavior (e.g., keep other students from upsetting the student).

51. Make the consequence of a behavior obvious by identifying the consequence as it occurs and discussing alternative behavior which would have prevented the particular consequence.

52. Avoid competition. Failure may cause the student to ignore consequences of his/her behavior.

53. Allow the student more decision making opportunities relative to class activities and assignments.

54. Give the student responsibilities in the classroom (e.g., teacher assistant, peer tutor, group leader, etc.).

55. Evaluate the appropriateness of the task in relation to the student's ability to perform the task successfully.

56. Show an interest in the student (e.g., acknowledge the student, ask the student's opinion, spend time working one-on-one with the student, etc.).

57. Intervene early when there is a problem to prevent more serious problems from occurring.

58. Inform others who will be working with the student (e.g., teachers, the principal, clerks, etc.) about the student's tendency to ignore consequences of his/her behaviors.

59. Teach the student to "think" before acting (e.g., ask himself/herself "What is happening?" "What am I doing?" "What should I do?" "What will be best for me?").

60. Speak with the student to explain (a) what the student is doing wrong (e.g., taking action before thinking about what he/she is doing) and (b) what the student should be doing (e.g., considering consequences, thinking about the correct response, considering other persons, etc.).

61. Assist the student in beginning each task to reduce impulsive behavior.

62. Limit the use of those things which the student is careless in using.

63. Teach the student safety rules in the handling of personal property and materials (e.g., pencils, scissors, compass; science, industrial arts, and home economics materials; etc.).

64. Teach the student the appropriate use of personal property and materials (e.g., scissors, pencils, compass; science, industrial arts, and home economic materials; etc.).

65. Require that lost or damaged property be replaced by the student. If the student cannot replace the property, restitution can be made by working at school.

66. Make certain that the student is not inadvertently reinforced for losing or damaging property. Provide the student with used or damaged materials, copies of materials, etc., rather than new materials.

67. Provide the student with structure for all academic activities (e.g., specified directions, routine format for tasks, time units, etc.).

Reminder: Do not confuse impulsive behavior with enthusiasm. Impulsive behavior should be controlled while enthusiasm should be encouraged.

106　Is distracted by other activities in the classroom, other students, the teacher, etc.

Goal:

1. The student will remain on-task.

Objectives:

1. The student will demonstrate on-task behavior by sitting quietly at his/her seat, looking at his/her materials, and performing the task for _____ minutes at a time. (Gradually increase expectations as the student demonstrates success.)
2. The student will remain on-task for _____ minutes at a time. (Gradually increase expectations as the student demonstrates success.)
3. The student will remain on-task through task completion on _____ out of _____ tasks.
4. The student will maintain eye contact with the teacher for _____ minutes at a time.

Interventions:

1. Have the student tape-record information from lectures and seminars and make notes from those tapes.

2. Maintain a consistent daily routine in the classroom.

3. Provide a classroom atmosphere in which everyone works.

4. Have the student ask himself/herself questions (e.g., "What's next?") to keep himself/herself focused on assignments/projects.

5. Deliver a predetermined signal (e.g., hand signal, verbal cue, etc.) when the student begins to display off-task behaviors.

6. Use more interesting or stimulating activities as a reward for completing less interesting activities (e.g., independent seatwork completed prior to participating in lab or group activity, etc.).

7. Teach the student time-management skills. Have the student make a daily plan and follow it. Encourage the student to avoid becoming distracted by events, impulses, and moods.

8. Have the student engage in small group activities (e.g., free time, math, reading, etc.) to reduce the level of auditory and visual distractions in the group. As the student is able to function successfully, gradually increase the size of the group.

9. Alternate assignments of differing activity levels.

10. Have the student perform one task or assignment at a time.

11. Communicate with parents (e.g., notes home, phone calls, etc.) to share information concerning their child's progress. The parents may reinforce the student at home for staying on-task in the classroom.

12. Play environmental-background music (e.g., ocean waves, rainfall, crackling fire, etc.) to reduce auditory distractions.

13. Reinforce those students in the classroom who demonstrate on-task behavior.

14. Assess the degree of task difficulty to determine whether or not the student will require additional information, time, assistance, etc., before assigning a task.

15. Anticipate which assigned tasks may present attention difficulties for the student. Modify or substitute assignments to provide the opportunity for success.

16. Provide an incentive statement along with a directive (e.g., "After your assignment is completed, you may listen to the CD player or receive a pass to the library/restroom.").

17. Provide the student with a carrel or divider at his/her desk to reduce auditory and visual distractions.

18. Make certain the student knows what to do when he/she cannot successfully perform an assignment (e.g., raise hand, ask for assistance, go to the teacher, etc.).

19. Explain to the student that assignments not completed on time will have to be completed at other times (e.g., lunch, after school, study hall, etc.).

20. Seat the student so that he/she experiences the least amount of auditory and visual distractions possible.

21. Allow natural consequences to occur (e.g., miss extra-curricular activity, athletic practice, assembly, lunch, etc.) due to the student becoming distracted and not completing tasks.

22. Structure the environment to reduce the opportunity for off-task behavior. Reduce lag time by providing the student with enough activities to maintain productivity.

23. List five qualities of a productive student. Have the student choose one of those qualities to work on each week for five weeks.

24. Remove the student from an activity until he/she can demonstrate appropriate on-task behavior.

25. Provide the student with a timer which he/she may use to monitor the amount of time during which he/she maintains attention (i.e., have the student work on the activity until the timer goes off).

26. Teach the student how to manage his/her time until the teacher can provide assistance (e.g., try the problem again, go on to the next problem, wait quietly, etc.).

27. Make certain to acknowledge the student when his/her hand is raised and convey that assistance will be provided as soon as possible.

28. Arrange for the student to take assignments home occasionally when the classroom setting is overly distracting. Assist the student in identifying a study area in his/her home.

29. Provide the student with earphones to wear if auditory stimuli interfere with his/her ability to function. As the student functions more successfully in the presence of auditory stimuli, gradually reduce the amount of time the earphones are worn.

30. Provide the student with a quiet place in which to work where auditory and visual distractions are reduced. This is used to reduce distracting stimuli and not as a form of punishment.

31. Have the student question any directions, explanations, or instructions he/she does not understand.

32. Present assignments in the most attractive and interesting manner possible.

33. Designate a specific period of time when it is permissible for the student to converse with peers (e.g., last 5 minutes of class, after completing a task, transitioning from one activity to the next, etc.).

34. Reduce auditory and visual distractions to a level at which the student can successfully function. As the student demonstrates that he/she can successfully tolerate the increased levels, gradually allow auditory and visual distractions to increase.

35. Choose a peer to model on-task behavior for the student.

36. Follow a less desirable task with a more desirable task. Make completion of the first necessary to perform the second.

37. Provide the student with the opportunity to move to a quiet place in the classroom whenever auditory and visual distractions interfere with his/her ability to function successfully.

38. Prioritize tasks by importance (e.g., task A must be done today, task B can be done today, and task C can wait until tomorrow).

39. Make certain the student has all the materials necessary to perform assignments.

40. Encourage the student to develop an awareness of the consequences of his/her behavior by writing down or talking through problems which may occur due to the student's inability to maintain attention (e.g., not focusing on directions may cause misunderstanding of an assignment which could lead to a lower grade and losing a place on the soccer team).

41. Have the student ask for immediate clarification of directions.

42. Encourage the student to develop an awareness of himself/herself and the environment. Instruct the student to periodically step back and ask himself/herself "Am I on-task and paying attention?" "What should I be doing now?"

43. Assign the student shorter tasks but more of them (e.g., modify a 20 problem math activity to 4 activities of 5 problems each to be performed at various times during the day). As the student demonstrates success, gradually increase the length of each task and decrease the number of tasks.

44. Consider carefully if the student is capable of the sustained attention necessary to complete a specific task, project, or assignment.

45. Allow the student to close the classroom door or windows to reduce auditory and visual distractions outside of the classroom.

46. Have the student ask for help when he/she needs it.

47. Move objects used for tactile stimulation (e.g., pens, paper clips, loose change, etc.) away from the student's reach.

48. Have the student manage his/her daily performance as if he/she were self-employed. This should increase the student's motivation to successfully complete projects.

49. Make certain that the student understands the relationship between on-task behavior and the consequences which follow (e.g., less teacher intervention, greater quality of work, positive classroom environment, etc.).

50. Establish classroom rules:
- Work on-task.
- Work quietly.
- Remain in your seat.
- Finish task.
- Meet task expectations.

Review rules often. Reinforce students for following the rules.

51. Assess the degree of task difficulty in relation to the student's ability to successfully perform the task.

52. Enlist different people (e.g., teacher, paraprofessional, classmate seated nearby, etc.) to help the student remain on-task.

53. Organize assignments by breaking them into small segments. Set deadlines and provide the student with a reward after completing each segment of the assignment.

54. Instruct the student to maintain attention to the source of information by maintaining eye contact, keeping hands free from other materials, and reducing other distractions.

55. Make certain that all auditory and visual distractions in the classroom are reduced as much as possible for all learners

56. Reduce distracting activities which interfere with the student's completion of assignments (e.g., other students maintain quiet atmosphere when assignments are completed, limit movement in classroom, etc.).

57. Reinforce the student for attending to a task based on the length of time he/she can be successful. As the student demonstrates success, gradually increase the length of time required for reinforcement.

58. Require the student to be productive in the presence of auditory and visual distractions for short periods of time. As he/she becomes more successful, gradually increase the length of time the student is required to be productive.

59. Model for the student appropriate behavior in the presence of auditory and visual distractions in the classroom (e.g., continuing to work, asking for quiet, moving to a quieter part of the classroom, etc.).

60. Have the student work with a peer tutor to maintain attention to task.

61. Reduce the number of visual distractions around the student (e.g., move the student away from windows, doors, etc.).

62. Set aside time at the end of the period for the student to complete unfinished assignments.

63. Schedule recreational activities at the end of the day. Make participation in these activities dependent upon completion of daily assignments.

64. Make it a habit to periodically review the student's improvement of on-task behaviors.

65. Make certain that the assignments given to the student are appropriate for his/her level of development and ability.

66. Evaluate the auditory and visual distractions in the classroom. Determine the level of stimuli to which the student can respond in an appropriate manner.

67. Reinforce the student for staying on-task in the classroom: (a) give the student a tangible reward (e.g., classroom privileges, hall pass, five minutes free time, etc.) or (b) give the student an intangible reward (e.g., praise, handshake, smile, etc.).

68. Maintain visibility to and from the student. The teacher should be able to see the student and the student should be able to see the teacher. Make eye contact possible at all times.

69. Have the student do isometric exercises (e.g., tighten and release muscles in his/her arms, legs, buttocks, etc.) to relieve restlessness.

70. Develop a checklist/chart for the student to follow which will allow him/her to complete all assignments.

71. Provide the student with shorter tasks which do not require sustained attention to be successful. As the student demonstrates success, gradually increase the length of the tasks.

72. Identify a student who has the ability to remain on-task. Have the student observe that person and try to model the behaviors which allow him/her to maintain attention.

73. Have the student assemble all materials necessary to work on a project, assignment, etc., to reduce the need to search for materials.

74. Help the student begin a task (e.g., turn to beginning page, complete one problem, begin writing, etc.) to get the student started on the assignment.

75. Speak to the student to explain (a) what he/she is doing wrong (e.g., failing to attend to tasks) and (b) what he/she should be doing (e.g., attending to tasks).

76. Write a contract with the student specifying what behavior is expected, a reasonable length of time to stay on-task, and what reinforcement will be made available when the terms of the contract have been met.

77. Allow the student to take a break while working on monotonous assignments to relieve restlessness, increase concentration, and improve accuracy/quality.

78. Have the student work with a peer who is calm and capable of concentrating on an assignment for a sustained period of time.

79. Position the student away from those peers who create the most auditory and visual distractions in the classroom.

80. Avoid seating the student by peers with whom he/she may be tempted to converse during lectures and class assignments.

81. Reward the student for completing an assignment within the amount of time allotted.

82. Interact frequently with the student to maintain his/her involvement in the activity (e.g., ask the student questions, ask the student's opinions, stand close to the student, seat the student near the teacher's desk, etc.).

Goals:

1. The student will demonstrate self-control.

Objectives:

1. The student will wait quietly for assistance from an instructor on _____ out of _____ trials.
2. The student will await his/her turn when engaged in activities with peers on _____ out of _____ trials.
3. The student will make decisions appropriate to the situation on _____ out of _____ trials.
4. The student will attempt a task before asking for assistance on _____ out of _____ trials.
5. The student will ask to use materials before taking them on _____ out of _____ trials.
6. The student will use materials appropriately and return them in the same or better condition on _____ out of _____ trials.
7. The student will stay in his/her seat for _____ minutes at a time. (Gradually increase expectations as the student demonstrates success.)
8. The student will raise his/her hand to leave his/her seat on _____ out of _____ trials.
9. The student will raise his/her hand to gain the teacher's attention on _____ out of _____ trials.
10. The student will listen to directions before beginning a task on _____ out of _____ trials.
11. The student will read directions before beginning a task on _____ out of _____ trials.
12. The student will refrain from touching others during _____ out of _____ interactions.
13. The student will demonstrate consideration/regard for others during _____ out of _____ trials.

Interventions:

1. Communicate with parents (e.g., notes home, phone calls, etc.) to share information concerning their child's progress. The parents may reinforce the student at home for acting in a deliberate and responsible manner at school.

2. Allow natural consequences to occur so the student can learn that persons who take turns and act in a deliberate fashion are more successful than those who act impulsively (e.g., if you begin an activity before understanding the directions, you will finish early; but you may perform the assignment incorrectly and receive a failing grade then you may have to repeat the assignment, etc.).

3. Look for the warning signs (e.g., arguing, loud voices, etc.) that the student is getting upset or angry. Intervene to change the activity to prevent more serious problems from occurring.

4. Allow the student to take a break to regroup when he/she is acting impulsively.

5. Teach behaviors that promote self-control. Allow the student to gain his/her composure before continuing an activity (e.g., placing hands on desk, sitting with feet on the floor, making eye contact with the person who is talking, etc.).

6. Talk with the student's family, a school official, a social worker, a mental health worker, etc., about the student's failure to consider the consequences of his/her behavior.

7. Structure the environment to reduce distracting stimuli (e.g., place the student on or near the front row, provide a carrel or quiet place away from distractions, etc.). This is to be used as a means of reducing distracting stimuli and not as a form of punishment.

8. Encourage the student to recite a mantra to himself/herself when entering a situation where he/she may be inclined to act impulsively (e.g., be patient, be patient, be patient).

9. Maintain, as much as possible, a routine for the student to follow to decrease impulsive behavior.

10. Educate yourself and others about ADHD to increase understanding and accommodation of impulsive behavior.

11. Encourage the student to develop an awareness of himself/herself and those around him/her. Have the student periodically step back and ask himself/herself "Am I behaving impulsively?"

12. Make certain the student has an adequate amount or number of activities scheduled to prevent the student from impulsively engaging in unplanned activities.

13. Maintain supervision at all times and in all areas of the school environment.

14. Encourage the student to pause and consider his/ her thoughts before acting on them.

15. Encourage the student to pause and consider his/her thoughts before speaking.

16. Remind the student to "stop and think" when he/she begins to do something without thinking first.

17. Educate the student about ADHD and the need to self-monitor behavior.

18. Establish a rule (e.g., stop and think before acting). This rule should be consistent and followed by everyone in the class. Talk about the rule often.

19. Reinforce the student for demonstrating appropriate behavior based on the length of time the student can be successful. As the student demonstrates success, gradually increase the length of time required for reinforcement.

20. Provide constant, positive reinforcement for appropriate behavior. Ignore as many inappropriate behaviors as possible.

21. Allow natural consequences to occur as a result of the student's failure to think before acting.

22. Have the student develop an awareness of the consequences of his/her behavior by writing down or talking through problems which may occur due to his/her impulsivity (e.g., perceived as unmannerly, avoided, etc.).

23. Be mobile to be frequently near the student.

24. Teach the student to "think" before acting (e.g., ask himself/herself "What is happening?" "What am I doing?" "What should I do?" "What is best for me?").

25. Discuss consequences with the student before he/she begins an activity (e.g., acting impulsively in a game will result in the game ending and people not playing again).

26. Consider carefully the student's age before expecting him/her to always think before acting.

27. Reinforce those students in the classroom who act in a deliberate and responsible manner.

28. Provide the student with a clearly understood list of consequences for inappropriate behavior.

29. Reduce the emphasis on competition. Competitive activities may cause the student to act impulsively to win or be first.

30. Discuss with the student the consequences of engaging in daring or risky behavior (e.g., if he/she drives too fast or carelessly, he/she may get a ticket or be involved in an accident).

31. Have the student review the consequences of his/her behavior with someone he/she trusts. Have the student consider different choices he/she could have made and the different outcomes.

32. Maintain a consistent daily routine in the classroom.

33. Teach the student ways to deal with conflict situations (e.g., talking, reasoning, asking an adult to intervene, walking away, etc.).

34. Each time a consequence is delivered, whether it is positive or negative, have the student explain to you why he/she thinks it happened.

35. Assist the student in beginning each task to reduce impulsive responses.

36. Speak with the student to explain (a) what he/ she is doing wrong (e.g., taking action before thinking about what he/she is doing) and (b) what he/she should be doing (e.g., considering consequences, thinking about the correct response, considering others, etc.).

37. Prepare the student in advance for changes in the daily routine which will occur (e.g., guests, visitors, special events, highly stimulating outings, etc.).

38. Teach the student ways to gain self-control (e.g., count to ten, walk away, talk with someone, etc.).

39. Establish classroom rules:
- Work on-task.
- Work quietly.
- Remain in your seat.
- Finish task.
- Meet task expectations.

Review rules often. Reinforce students for following the rules.

40. Remove the student from the group or activity until he/she can demonstrate appropriate behavior and self-control.

41. Deliver a predetermined signal (e.g., hand signal, verbal cue, etc.) when the student begins to demonstrate impulsive behaviors.

42. Have the student ask for help when he/she needs it.

43. Encourage the student to remind himself/herself to wait when he/she feels impulsive (e.g., "Stop. Count to ten.").

44. Have the student put himself/herself in someone else's place (e.g., "How would you feel if someone called you dumb or stupid?").

45. Encourage the student to ask himself/herself questions to avoid impulsive behavior (e.g., "What should I be doing?" "How do I want to be perceived?").

46. Encourage the student to remove himself/herself from a situation when he/she needs to gain self-control.

47. Teach the student to self-monitor his/her impulsivity. Awareness should reduce impulsive behaviors.

48. Teach the student to verbalize his/her feelings before losing control (e.g., "I'm starting to act impulsively. I need to walk away from this situation.").

49. Point out natural consequences of impulsive behavior to help the student learn that persons who act in a more deliberate fashion are more successful than those who act impulsively (e.g., if he/she begins before understanding directions or what is needed, he/she may finish first; but he/she may do things wrong, things may be broken or destroyed, etc.)

50. Reduce the opportunity to act impulsively by limiting decision making. As the student demonstrates success, gradually increase opportunities for decision making.

51. Reinforce the student for acting in a deliberate and responsible manner: (a) give the student a tangible reward (e.g., classroom privileges, passing out materials, five minutes free time, etc.) or (b) give the student an intangible reward (e.g., praise, handshake, smile, etc.).

52. Encourage the student to participate in high energy activities after school that allow him/her to release excess energy (e.g., racquetball, soccer, etc.).

53. Encourage the student to engage in quiet, calming activities (e.g., listen to music, read, etc.) when he/she begins to feel impulsive.

54. Encourage the student to avoid ingesting any substance (e.g., drugs, alcohol, cold remedies, etc.) that might further alter his/her ability to maintain self-control.

55. Have the student make a list of consequences associated with impulsive behavior (e.g., break something, hurt someone, embarrass self or others, etc.).

56. Maintain a routine that will minimize erratic or impulsive behavior which may result in negative consequences.

57. Explain to the student the need to reduce impulsivity to increase work productivity and general happiness.

58. Discuss with the student the need to consider the consequences of his/her behavior before engaging in any activity.

59. Make certain the student does not become involved in overstimulating activities in the classroom, during physical education, during lunch, etc.

60. Help the student become aware of the times when he/she is most impulsive (e.g., in a large group of people, when he/she is hungry, when he/she is angry, etc.) and limit his/her interactions with others during these times.

61. Make sure the student does not have a lot of unstructured time.

62. Prevent the student from becoming overstimulated by an activity (e.g., frustrated, angry, excited, etc.).

63. Encourage the student to choose peer groups that do not engage in risky activities.

64. Have the student identify a peer who has self-control. Have the student observe that person and try to model the behaviors which contribute to self-control.

65. Provide the student with a place to go when he/she becomes overly excited (e.g., a quiet corner, counselor's office, etc.).

66. Emphasize individual success or progress rather than winning or "beating" other students.

67. Have the student complete the same chores and responsibilities each day, week, etc.

68. Teach the student ways to settle down (e.g., counting to 10, reciting lyrics to a favorite song, walking away, etc.) when he/she needs to slow down and think about what he/she is doing.

69. Provide the student with clear, simply stated explanations, instructions, and directions so that he/she knows exactly what is expected.

70. Help the student identify the situations in which he/she is likely to act impulsively. After he/she has identified these situations, have him/her think of ways to minimize their occurrences.

71. Supervise the student closely in situations in which he/she is likely to act impulsively (e.g., maintain close physical proximity, maintain eye contact, etc.).

72. Prevent the student from becoming so stimulated that he/she reacts with impulsive behavior (i.e., intervene when the student is becoming over-excited to prevent him/her from losing self-control).

73. Write a contract with the student specifying what behavior is expected (e.g., acting in a deliberate and responsible manner) and what reinforcement will be made available when the terms of the contract have been met.

74. Evaluate the appropriateness of the task to determine (a) if the task is too easy, (b) if the task is too difficult, and (c) if the length of time scheduled to complete the task is adequate.

75. Teach the student to use techniques such as crossing his/her arms and legs, clinching his/her fists, and webbing his/her hands when he/she is acting impulsively.

76. Make certain the student understands that consequences naturally follow behavior, whether it is his/hers, yours, or someone else's. It is his/her own behavior that makes the consequences occur in his/her life.

77. Review the rules with the student before he/she engages in activities to reduce the likelihood of impulsive behavior.

78. Make the student aware of the reasons we all must practice responsibility (e.g., others' rights are not infringed upon, others are not hurt, order is not lost, property is not damaged or destroyed, etc.).

79. Do not allow the student to use ADHD as an excuse. Hold the student responsible for his/her actions. However, understand and accept problems that ADHD brings into the student's life while he/she is learning to make accommodations.

80. Make sure the student understands the consequences of impulsive behavior (e.g., if he/she begins a work assignment before all directions are given, he/she may do things incorrectly).

81. Encourage the student to reduce the occurrence of activities that he/she knows will stimulate impulsive or careless behavior (e.g., limit the number of people in his/her room at one time; drive with only one other person in the car, etc.).

82. Choose a peer to model deliberate and responsible behavior in academic and social settings for the student.

83. Maintain visibility to and from the student to keep his/her attention when oral questions/directions are being delivered. The teacher should be able to see the student and the student should be able to see the teacher. Make eye contact possible at all times.

84. Remove the student immediately from the situation until he/she can demonstrate acceptable behavior and self-control.

85. Make certain that the student understands the relationship between inappropriate behavior and the consequences which follow (e.g., hurting others' feelings, not being allowed to participate in special activities, being avoided by others, etc.).

86. Teach the student decision-making steps: think about how other persons may be influenced, think about consequences, consider carefully the unique situation, think of different courses of action which are possible, think about what is ultimately best for him/her.

87. Supervise the student to make sure he/she thinks before acting.

88. Have the student identify a peer who is able to control impulsivity. Have the student observe that person and try to model the behaviors which allow him/her to be patient.

89. Teach the student to attend to the source of information by maintaining eye contact, keeping hands free from other materials, and reducing other distractions.

90. Allow the student some room to be impatient, but monitor and limit the occurrences of his/her impulsive behavior.

91. Explain to the student when he/she acts without thinking exactly what he/she is doing wrong, what should have been done, and why.

92. Remind the student to wait when he/she begins to lose control (e.g., by saying, "You need to count to ten." "Calm down." etc.).

93. Do not criticize when correcting the student; be honest yet supportive. Never cause the student to feel negatively about himself/herself.

94. Make certain the student knows which areas in the classroom are "off limits" to him/her.

95. Communicate with the student's cooperative work experience/vocational education teacher to reinforce impulse control on the student's job site.

96. Provide the student with adequate time to perform activities to reduce his/her impulsive behavior.

108 Moves about unnecessarily

Goals:

1. The student will move about the classroom only when necessary.
2. The student will demonstrate body movements appropriate to the situation.

Objectives:

1. The student will leave his/her seat only when given permission by the teacher on _____ out of _____ trials.
2. The student will move about the classroom only when given permission by the teacher on _____ out of _____ trials.
3. The student will go directly to a specific location and immediately return to his/her seat when given permission by the teacher on _____ out of _____ trials.
4. The student will demonstrate body movements appropriate to the situation on _____ out of _____ trials.
5. The student will refrain from making unnecessary body movements for _____ minutes at a time. (Gradually increase expectations as the student demonstrates success.)
6. The student will stop unnecessary body movements when cued by the teacher on _____ out of _____ trials.
7. The student will ask to have a break from the activity, go to a specific location in the classroom, etc., when he/she begins to feel anxious, upset, frustrated, etc., on _____ out of _____ trials.

Interventions:

1. Communicate with parents (e.g., notes home, phone calls, etc.) to share information concerning their child's progress. The parents may reinforce the student at home for demonstrating physical self-control at school.

2. Give the student additional responsibilities (e.g., chores, errands, etc.) to keep him/her actively involved and give him/her a feeling of success or accomplishment.

3. Facilitate on-task behavior by providing a full schedule of daily events. Prevent lag time when the student would be free to engage in excessive and unnecessary body movements.

4. Intervene early when there is a problem to prevent a more serious problem from occurring.

5. Maintain a full schedule of activities. Keeping the student occupied should prevent unnecessary movement.

6. Make certain the student has all the materials necessary to perform a task to reduce the need to leave his/her seat.

7. Remove the student immediately from an activity when he/she is moving about unnecessarily until he/she can participate appropriately.

8. Maintain supervision at all times and in all parts of the school environment.

9. Encourage the student to develop an awareness of himself/herself and those around him/her. Have the student periodically step back and ask himself/herself "Am I fidgeting and being overactive?"

10. Provide constant, positive reinforcement for appropriate behavior. Ignore as many inappropriate behaviors as possible.

11. Reinforce the student for demonstrating appropriate behavior based on the length of time the student can be successful. As the student demonstrates success, gradually increase the length of time required for reinforcement.

12. Choose a peer to model staying in his/her seat for the student.

13. Consider carefully the student's age before expecting him/her to sit quietly for a period of time. Middle school students need frequent opportunities for movement.

14. Provide the student with a calm, quiet environment in which to work.

15. Reinforce those students in the classroom who demonstrate physical self-control.

16. Provide the student with a clearly understood list of consequences for inappropriate behavior.

17. Reduce the emphasis on competition. Competitive activities may cause the student to become anxious and move about unnecessarily.

18. Schedule recreational activities at the end of the day. Make participation in these activities dependent upon completion of daily responsibilities and appropriate behavior.

19. Speak with the student to explain (a) what he/she is doing wrong (e.g., moving in seat, moving about the room, running, etc.) and (b) what he/she should be doing (e.g., practicing self-control, following rules, etc.).

20. Remove the student from the group or activity until he/she can demonstrate appropriate behavior and refrain from moving about unnecessarily.

21. Encourage the student to participate in high energy activities after school that allow him/her to release excess energy (e.g., racquetball, soccer, etc.).

22. Interact frequently with the student to maintain his/her attention to the activity (e.g., ask the student questions, ask the student's opinion, stand close to the student, seat the student near the teacher's desk, etc.).

23. Encourage the student to avoid ingesting any substance (e.g., drugs, alcohol, cold remedies, etc.) that might further alter his/her ability to maintain self-control.

24. Have the student chart the length of time he/she is able to remain in his/her seat without moving about unnecessarily.

25. Establish classroom rules:
- Work on-task.
- Work quietly.
- Remain in your seat.
- Finish task.
- Meet task expectations.

Review rules often. Reinforce students for following the rules.

26. Establish times when it is permissible for the student to be out of his/her seat (e.g., leave his/her seat only to get a book, a drink of water, etc.).

27. Provide the student with the most attractive and interesting activities possible.

28. Remain calm when the student moves about unnecessarily. Calm behavior should have a calming effect on the student.

29. Make certain the student does not become involved in activities which may be overstimulating and cause the student to move about unnecessarily.

30. Make certain that reinforcement is not inadvertently given for inappropriate behavior (e.g., attending to the student only when he/she engages in excessive/unnecessary body movements).

31. Make sure the student does not have a lot of unstructured time.

32. Provide the student with frequent opportunities to participate, take turns, etc., to keep him/her involved in the activity.

33. Separate the student from the peer who stimulates his/her inappropriate behavior.

34. Increase supervision (e.g., by teacher, peer, paraprofessional, etc.) of the student when he/she is involved in activities that tend to cause him/her to move about unnecessarily.

35. Reinforce the student for demonstrating physical self-control: (a) give the student a tangible reward (e.g., classroom privileges, passing out materials, five minutes free time, etc.) or (b) give the student an intangible reward (e.g., praise, handshake, smile, etc.).

36. Provide the student with a predetermined signal when he/she begins to leave his/her seat without permission.

37. Be proactive. Work with the school counselor to design a schedule conducive to the student's success (e.g., physical education scheduled the last period of the day, intersperse electives which allow greater freedom of movement with classes requiring extended periods of concentration, etc.).

38. Modify or eliminate situations at school which cause the student to experience stress or frustration and may contribute to the student moving about unnecessarily.

39. Give the student a special signal when he/she is moving about unnecessarily (e.g., a secret word, a hand signal, etc.).

40. Avoid placing the student in situations that require sitting for an extended period of time such as lectures, seminars, etc. Provide the information for the student through a tape recording or lecture notes.

41. Evaluate the appropriateness of the task to determine (a) if the task is too easy, (b) if the task is too difficult, and (c) if the length of time scheduled to complete the task is adequate.

42. Evaluate the visual and auditory stimuli in the classroom. Determine the amount of stimuli the student can tolerate. Remove extraneous stimuli which contributes to the student's unnecessary or excessive movement from the classroom environment.

43. Be consistent in expecting the student to sit quietly without moving about unnecessarily. Do not allow the student to move about unnecessarily one day and expect him/her to sit quietly the next day.

44. Schedule short activities for the student to perform while seated. As the student demonstrates success staying in his/her seat, gradually increase the length of the activities.

45. Write a contract with the student specifying what behavior is expected (e.g., demonstrating physical self-control) and what reinforcement will be made available when the terms of the contract have been met.

46. Have a peer cue the student when he/she moves about unnecessarily (e.g., the person can touch the student's arm as a signal that he/she is moving about unnecessarily).

47. Be consistent in having the student leave a situation when he/she begins to move about unnecessarily (e.g., send the student to a study carrel for 10 minutes, make him/her sit in a chair for 5 minutes, etc.).

48. Move objects used for tactile stimulation (e.g., pens, paper clips, loose change, etc.) away from the student's reach.

49. Seat the student near the teacher.

50. Make the necessary adjustments in the environment to prevent the student from experiencing stress, frustration, anger, etc., as much as possible.

51. Arrange for individual assignments when the group setting is overly distracting.

52. Maintain visibility to and from the student to keep his/her attention when verbal questions/directions are being delivered. The teacher should be able to see the student and the student should be able to see the teacher. Make eye contact possible at all times.

53. Have the student assemble all the materials necessary to work on a project, assignment, etc., to reduce the need to search for materials.

54. Establish an environmental setting for the classroom that promotes optimal individual performance (e.g., quiet room, background music, fresh air, etc.).

55. Interact frequently with the student to prevent excessive or unnecessary body movements.

56. Do not allow the student to participate in activities that cause him/her to become so excited that he/she moves about unnecessarily.

57. Supervise the student to prevent him/her from not sitting quietly and moving around unnecessarily.

58. Teach the student to use techniques to gain self-control when he/she is moving about unnecessarily (e.g., count to ten, say the alphabet, sit in a chair, leave the situation, etc.).

59. Give the student frequent opportunities to leave his/her seat for appropriate reasons (e.g., getting materials, running errands, assisting the teacher, etc.).

60. Allow the student some movement while performing tasks. Monitor and limit the amount of movement.

61. Communicate with the student's cooperative work experience/vocational education teacher to choose a job that allows for a high degree of physical movement (e.g., jobs which allow the student to be on his/her feet, move from room to room, have frequent contact with people, and travel from one job site to another, etc.).

109 Does not demonstrate appropriate behavior in the presence of a substitute authority figure

Goals:

1. The student will demonstrate appropriate behavior in the presence of a substitute authority figure.

Objectives:

1. The student will follow directions given by a substitute authority figure on _____ out of _____ trials.
2. The student will follow classroom rules in the presence of a substitute authority figure on _____ out of _____ trials.
3. The student will follow the daily schedule in the presence of a substitute authority figure on _____ out of _____ trials.
4. The student will stay on-task in the presence of a substitute authority figure on _____ out of _____ trials.
5. The student will follow building rules in the presence of a substitute authority figure (in the library, cafeteria, restrooms) on _____ out of _____ trials.
6. The student will work on and complete assignments given by the substitute authority figure on _____ out of _____ trials.
7. The student will respond accurately to questions concerning the classroom routine asked by the substitute authority figure on _____ out of _____ trials.

Interventions:

1. Prepare an information packet for a substitute authority figure that includes all information pertaining to the classroom (e.g., student roster, class schedule, class rules, behavior management techniques, class helpers, etc.).

2. Make certain that the student understands that classroom rules and behavioral consequences are in effect when a substitute authority figure is in the classroom.

3. Indicate where all needed materials are located to maintain structure in the classroom.

4. Indicate various activities in which the student can participate after completing his/her work for the day.

5. Indicate the names of several personnel and where they can be located in case the substitute authority figure should need some assistance.

6. Inform the substitute authority figure of the classroom rules and the consequences if the rules are not followed by the student.

7. Express the need for the substitute authority figure to maintain consistent discipline while in and outside of the classroom.

8. Inform the substitute authority figure of all privileges the students have both in and outside of the classroom.

9. Have the student work on practice work (e.g., work that has already been taught to the student and that he/she knows how to do) to reduce frustration and feelings of failure.

10. Set aside 10 minutes at the beginning of the day for the substitute authority figure to develop rapport with the students (e.g., introduce himself/herself to the class, learn the students' names, talk about things the students enjoy doing, etc.).

11. Indicate to the student that the substitute authority figure is in charge of the classroom at all times.

12. Schedule a fun educational activity (e.g., computer games) during the day to provide an incentive for the student to stay on-task and behave appropriately.

13. Assign a "special job" for the student to perform when there is a substitute authority figure in the classroom (e.g., substitute teacher's assistant, line leader, class monitor, etc.). Inform the substitute authority figure of this "special job."

14. Have the substitute authority figure present instructions/directions in a variety of ways (e.g., verbally, written, etc.).

15. Request a substitute authority figure who has the necessary skills to handle problem behavior and special needs students.

16. Make certain that the substitute authority figure is familiar with the behavioral support system used in the classroom (e.g., rules, point system, reinforcers, etc.).

17. If possible, communicate directly with the substitute authority figure to share information which will contribute to the student's success.

18. Choose a student(s) to act as an assistant to the substitute authority figure during the day's activities (e.g., the student(s) provides accurate information about the schedule of activities, behavioral support system, etc.).

19. Provide the substitute authority figure with detailed information on the activities and assignments.

20. Make certain the substitute authority figure follows all procedures indicated by the classroom teacher (e.g., academic activities, behavioral support system, etc.).

21. Have the substitute authority figure provide a written review of the day as feedback for the classroom teacher (e.g., activities completed, student behavior, absences, incidents concerning individual students, etc.).

22. Have special or unique responsibilities performed by other personnel in the building (e.g., administering medication, feeding, toileting, etc.).

23. Have the student record his/her own behavior when a substitute authority figure is in the classroom.

24. Choose a peer to work with the student to model appropriate behavior and to provide information necessary for success for the student.

25. If an aide works in the classroom; have the aide monitor the student's behavior, provide reinforcement, deliver instructions, etc.

26. If there is an aide in the classroom, have the aide work with the student on a one-to-one basis throughout the day.

27. Provide the student with an individualized schedule of daily events. The schedule should be attached to the student's desk or carried with him/her at all times.

28. Instruct the substitute authority figure to interact with the student frequently to provide reinforcement, deliver instructions, provide encouragement, etc.

29. Have the substitute authority figure maintain visibility to and from the student. The substitute authority figure should be able to see the student; the student should be able to see the substitute authority figure. Make eye contact possible at all times.

30. Provide the student with as many high-interest activities as possible.

31. Provide a quiet place for the student to work.

32. Make the student aware of the natural consequences concerning inappropriate behavior in the presence of a substitute authority figure (e.g., removal from the classroom, loss of privileges, etc.).

33. Have a peer deliver instructions to the student.

34. Begin the day or class with an activity which is of high interest to the student.

35. Present activities in the most attractive, interesting manner possible.

36. Do not schedule highly stimulating activities when a substitute authority figure is in the classroom.

37. Structure the environment to reduce the opportunity for inappropriate behavior (e.g., reduce periods of inactivity by having the student actively involved at all times).

38. Provide the substitute authority figure with a seating chart and indicate the student(s) who needs additional supervision.

39. Indicate, for the substitute authority figure, those peers who might be likely to stimulate the student's inappropriate behavior. (It may be necessary to keep the students separated.)

40. Have the substitute authority figure check the student's completed assignments to make certain that work is not carelessly performed.

41. Write a contract with the student or the entire class for reinforcement based on appropriate behavior when a substitute authority figure is present.

42. Have the substitute authority figure maintain mobility to be frequently near the student.

43. Make certain the student receives the necessary information to perform activities (e.g., written information, verbal directions, reminders, etc.).

44. Make certain the substitute authority figure consistently follows the routine established by the classroom teacher (e.g., schedule, delivering instructions, task requirements, reinforcement, negative consequences, etc.).

45. Provide the student with a clearly identified list of consequences for inappropriate behavior in the presence of a substitute authority figure.

46. Have the substitute authority figure help the student begin assignments, check his/her work, provide immediate feedback, etc.

47. Have the student maintain a record of his/her academic performance while a substitute authority figure is in the classroom.

48. Inform the students in advance when it will be necessary for a substitute authority figure to be in the classroom. Establish expectations for behavior and academic performance.

49. Provide the substitute authority figure with instructions for action to be taken if the student becomes abusive or threatening.

50. Teach the student to think before acting (e.g., ask himself/herself "What is happening?" "What am I doing?" "What should I do?" "What will be best for me?").

51. Make certain the student is allowed to voice an opinion in a situation to hear the student's side of the story.

52. Have the student question any directions, explanations, instructions not understood.

53. Evaluate the appropriateness of the task to determine (a) if the task is too easy, (b) if the task is too difficult, and (c) if the length of time scheduled to complete the task is adequate.

54. Communicate with parents (e.g., notes home, phone calls, etc.) to share information concerning the student's progress. The parents may reinforce the student at home for demonstrating appropriate behavior in the presence of a substitute authority figure.

55. Write a contract with the student specifying what behavior is expected (e.g., following the substitute authority figure's directions) and what reinforcement will be made available when the terms of the contract have been met.

56. Reinforce those students in the classroom who demonstrate appropriate behavior in the presence of a substitute authority figure.

57. Establish classroom rules:
- Work on-task.
- Remain in your seat.
- Finish task.
- Meet task expectations.
- Raise your hand.

Review rules often. Reinforce students for following rules.

58. Speak to the student to explain (a) what the student is doing wrong (e.g., not following the substitute authority figure's directions, not following classroom rules, etc.) and (b) what the student should be doing (e.g., following the substitute authority figure's directions, following classroom rules, etc.).

59. Reinforce the student for demonstrating appropriate behavior in the presence of a substitute authority figure: (a) give the student a tangible reward (e.g., classroom privileges, line leading, passing out materials, five minutes free time, etc.) or (b) give the student an intangible reward (e.g., praise, handshake, smile, etc.).

110   Becomes physically aggressive with teachers

Goals:

1. The student will interact appropriately with teachers.

Objectives:

1. The student will refrain from touching the teacher during ___ out of ___ interactions.
2. The student will sit/stand quietly when the teacher discusses the student's behavior with him/her during ___ out of ___ interactions.
3. The student will verbally, rather than physically, express his/her feelings toward the teacher during ___ out of ___ interactions.
4. The student will control his/her anger to the extent of not requiring to be physically restrained by the teacher in ___ out of ___ anger-producing situations.

Interventions:

1. Prevent frustrating or anxiety-producing situations from occurring (e.g., give the student tasks only on his/her ability level, give the student only the number of tasks that can be tolerated in one sitting, reduce social interactions which stimulate the student to become physically aggressive, etc.).

2. Teach the student problem-solving skills: (a) identify the problem, (b) identify goals and objectives, (c) develop strategies, (d) develop a plan for action, and (e) carry out the plan.

3. Provide the student with positive feedback which indicates he/she is successful, important, respected, etc.

4. Structure the environment to prevent opportunities for the student to become physically aggressive toward teachers (e.g., interact frequently with the student to prevent him/her from becoming frustrated).

5. Maintain maximum supervision of the student. As the student demonstrates appropriate behavior, gradually decrease supervision.

6. Maintain visibility to and from the student. The teacher should be able to see the student, and the student should be able to see the teacher. Make eye contact possible at all times.

7. Reduce activities which might be threatening to the student (e.g., announcing test score ranges or test scores aloud, making students read aloud in class, emphasizing the success of particular student(s), etc.).

8. Be mobile to be frequently near the student.

9. Try various groupings to determine the situation in which the student is most successful.

10. Reduce the emphasis on competition and perfection. Repeated failure and frustration may cause outbursts of physical aggression.

11. Make the necessary adjustments in the environment to prevent the student from becoming overstimulated by peers, which in turn would make it necessary for the teacher to intervene.

12. Teach the student alternative ways to deal with situations which make him/her frustrated or angry (e.g., withdrawing, talking, etc.).

13. Facilitate on-task behavior by providing a full schedule of activities. Prevent lag time from occurring when the student would be free to engage in inappropriate behavior.

14. Provide the student with as many high-interest activities as possible to keep him/her from becoming physically aggressive toward teachers.

15. Provide the student with opportunities for social and academic success.

16. Make certain that all school personnel are aware of the student's tendency to become physically aggressive so they may monitor his/her behavior.

17. Avoid arguing with the student (e.g., calmly deliver consequences without reacting to the student's remarks).

18. Provide a quiet place for the student to work independently, away from peer interactions. This is not to be used as punishment but as an opportunity to increase the student's success in his/her environment.

19. Place reinforcement emphasis on academic productivity and accuracy to reduce the likelihood of the student becoming physically aggressive toward teachers (i.e., increased productivity and accuracy will reduce the likelihood of inappropriate behavior).

20. Reduce or remove any stimulus in the environment which leads to the student's physically aggressive behavior (e.g., possessions, competition, teasing, etc.).

21. Make certain the student understands the natural consequences of becoming physically aggressive toward a teacher (e.g., less freedom, more restrictive environment, assault charges, etc.).

22. Prevent the student from receiving too much stimulation (e.g., monitor or supervise student behavior to limit over excitement in physical activities, games, parties, etc.).

23. Limit the student's opportunity to enter areas of the school environment in which he/she is more likely to be physically aggressive.

24. Do not force the student to interact or remain in a group when he/she is physically aggressive (e.g., daily reading group, physical education group, etc.).

25. Always provide the student with behavioral options (e.g., sitting out of an activity, going to a quiet place in the room, performing another activity, etc.).

26. Maintain consistent behavioral expectations and consequences to reduce the likelihood of the student becoming upset by what he/she considers unfair treatment.

27. Limit the student's independent movement in the school environment.

28. Avoid physical contact with the student who is likely to become physically aggressive.

29. Maintain an appropriate physical distance from the student when interacting with him/her to avoid stimulation of aggressive behavior.

30. Use language that is pleasant and calming when speaking with the student to avoid stimulation of aggressive behavior.

31. Deliver directions in a supportive rather than a threatening manner (e.g., "Please finish your math assignment before going to recess." rather than "You had better turn in your math or else!").

32. Do not criticize when correcting the student, be honest yet supportive. Never cause the student to feel negatively about himself/herself.

33. Intervene early when there is a problem to prevent more serious problems from occurring.

34. Be careful to avoid embarrassing the student by giving him/her orders, demands, etc., in front of others.

35. Teach the student appropriate ways to communicate displeasure, anger, frustration, etc.

36. Have the student put himself/herself in someone else's place (e.g., "How would you feel if someone called you dumb or stupid?").

37. Do not force the student to interact with others.

38. Teach the student to "think" before acting (e.g., ask himself/herself "What is happening?" "What am I doing?" "What should I do?" "What will be best for me?").

39. Have the student practice appropriate verbal exchanges which should be made when typical physical exchanges take place (e.g., "Excuse me." "I'm sorry." etc.).

40. Make certain the student is allowed to voice an opinion in a situation to avoid becoming angry or upset.

41. Evaluate the appropriateness of the task to determine (a) if the task is too easy, (b) if the task is too difficult, and (c) if the length of time scheduled to complete the task is adequate.

42. Reinforce those students in the classroom who demonstrate appropriate behavior when interacting with teachers.

43. Remove the student from the group or activity until he/she can demonstrate appropriate behavior and self-control.

44. Write a contract with the student specifying what behavior is expected (e.g., respecting the norms of physical proximity) and what reinforcement will be made available when the terms of the contract have been met.

45. Reinforce the student for demonstrating appropriate behavior based on the length of time the student can be successful. As the student demonstrates success, gradually increase the length of time required for reinforcement.

46. Establish classroom rules:
- Work on-task.
- Remain in your seat.
- Finish task.
- Meet task expectations.
- Raise your hand.

Review rules often. Reinforce students for following rules.

47. Communicate with parents (e.g., notes home, phone calls, etc.) to share information concerning the student's progress. The parents may reinforce the student at home for respecting the norms of physical proximity at school.

48. Speak to the student to explain (a) what the student is doing wrong (e.g., pushing, pulling away, grabbing, etc.) and (b) what the student should be doing (e.g., following rules, interacting in appropriate ways, dealing with anger and frustration in appropriate ways, etc.).

49. Reinforce the student for demonstrating appropriate behavior: (a) give the student a tangible reward (e.g., classroom privileges, line leading, passing out materials, five minutes free time, etc.) or (b) give the student an intangible reward (e.g., praise, handshake, smile, etc.).

111   Behaves inappropriately when others do well or receive praise or attention

Goals:
1. The student will behave appropriately when others do well.
2. The student will behave appropriately when others receive praise or attention.

Objectives:
1. The student will congratulate others when they do well on ___ out of ___ trials.
2. The student will congratulate others when they receive praise or attention on ___ out of ___ trials.
3. The student will clap/cheer, when appropriate for the situation, for others when they do well on ___ out of ___ trials.
4. The student will clap/cheer, when appropriate for the situation, for others when they receive praise or attention on ___ out of ___ trials.
5. The student will make a positive comment when others do well on ___ out of ___ trials.
6. The student will make a positive comment when others receive praise or attention on ___ out of ___ trials.
7. The student will continue to participate in the game/activity when others are doing better than he/she on ___ out of ___ trials.
8. The student will encourage others to do well when competing for an award, prize, etc., on ___ out of ___ trials.
9. The student will demonstrate good sportsmanship by helping his/her team mates, playing fairly, cheering for the opposing team, etc., during ___ out of ___ competitive activities.
10. The student will remove himself/herself from an activity when he/she begins to experience difficulty behaving appropriately during ___ out of ___ competitive activities.
11. The student will shake the opponent's hand and make a positive comment such as "good game," after losing to the opponent on ___ out of ___ trials.

Interventions:

1. Make certain to help the student achieve a level of success in an activity so he/she will do well and receive praise or attention.

2. Make certain that the student is assigned a role in an activity in which he/she can be successful as a participant and enjoy the activity (e.g., banker in *Monopoly*, scorekeeper in a game, teacher assistant, note taker in discussions, etc.).

3. Make certain that some attention is given to the student when others do well or receive praise or attention. As he/she demonstrates appropriate behavior when others do well or receive praise or attention, gradually reduce the attention given to the student.

4. Deliver praise or attention as privately as possible to reduce the likelihood of upsetting any students in the classroom.

5. Reduce the emphasis on competition. Encourage and reinforce participation, team work, good sportsmanship, personal improvement, etc.

6. As the student demonstrates success, gradually increase the degree of difficulty of the task or activity.

7. Make certain that the student succeeds or receives attention often enough to create a balance with those times when other students succeed or receive praise or attention.

8. Make certain that the teacher is a good role model by participating in games, demonstrating good sportsmanship, complimenting others, etc.

9. Establish rules and go over them at the beginning of an activity to reduce the likelihood of misunderstanding.

10. Encourage the student to leave situations which may cause him/her to become upset, angry, embarrassed, etc.

11. Encourage an atmosphere of students helping one another, congratulating each other, finding something about each other to compliment, etc.

12. Have the student take part in activities with students who are appropriate models for behavior when others do well or receive praise or attention.

13. If the student becomes frustrated or upset by the task or activity, remove him/her from the situation, stop the activity, or provide an alternative activity.

14. Make certain that the student understands that an inability to behave appropriately during a game or activity will result in the termination of the activity.

15. Be certain to provide close supervision of the student in tasks and activities to intervene early and provide problem-solving alternatives should inappropriate behaviors occur.

16. Help the student find activities (e.g., reading, creating, peer tutoring, etc.) in which he/she can achieve personal satisfaction and success.

17. Do not require the student to participate in games and activities which may be threatening or cause him/her to demonstrate inappropriate behavior.

18. Make certain the student does not participate in activities with another student(s) who is likely to stimulate inappropriate behavior.

19. Provide the student with several activities throughout the day in which he/she can do well and receive praise and attention.

20. Be aware of the student's strengths and limitations. Have the student participate in activities in which he/she will succeed rather than fail.

21. Have the student engage in games or activities with a younger student with whom he/she will not have a competitive relationship. As the student demonstrates appropriate behavior, gradually have the student participate in games or activities with older, more skilled peers.

22. Call on the student when he/she is most likely to be able to respond correctly (e.g., when discussing something in which the student is interested, when the teacher is certain he/she knows the answer, etc.).

23. Carefully consider the student's age and experience before expecting him/her to behave appropriately when others do well or receive praise or attention.

24. Teach the student to respect others by respecting the student.

25. Encourage the student to refrain from comparing himself/herself to others.

26. Make sure you express your feelings in a socially acceptable way.

27. Do not allow the student to participate if the task or situation is too stimulating.

28. Have the student question any directions, explanations, or instructions not understood.

29. Choose a peer to model behaving appropriately when others do well or receive praise or attention for the student.

30. Evaluate the appropriateness of the task or situation to determine (a) if the task is too easy, (b) if the task is too difficult, and (c) if the length of time scheduled to complete the task is adequate.

31. Communicate with parents (e.g., notes home, phone calls, etc.) to share information concerning the student's progress. The parents may reinforce the student at home for behaving appropriately at school.

32. Write a contract with the student specifying what behavior is expected (e.g., making a positive comment) and what reinforcement will be made available when the terms of the contract have been met.

33. Reinforce the student for behaving appropriately based on the length of time the student can be successful. As the student demonstrates success, gradually increase the length of time required for reinforcement.

34. Reinforce those students in the classroom who behave appropriately when others do well or receive praise or attention.

35. Speak to the student to explain (a) what the student is doing wrong (e.g., getting angry, tantruming, etc.) and (b) what the student should be doing (e.g., making positive comments, continuing to participate appropriately, etc.).

36. Reinforce the student for behaving appropriately when others do well or receive praise or attention: (a) give the student a tangible reward (e.g., classroom privileges, line leading, passing out materials, five minutes free time, etc.) or (b) give the student an intangible reward (e.g., praise, handshake, smile, etc.).

37. Establish a set of standard behavior rules for group games:
- Follow rules of the game.
- Take turns.
- Make positive comments.
- Work as a team member.
- Be a good sport.

Review rules often. Reinforce students for following rules.

38. Praise and recognize equally all members of the class.

112 Verbally or physically threatens other students or teachers

Goals:

1. The student will demonstrate appropriate behavior when angry.
2. The student will demonstrate appropriate behavior when annoyed with others.
3. The student will demonstrate appropriate behavior when upset.

Objectives:

1. The student will be able to settle minor conflicts with others without arguing, yelling, crying, hitting, etc., during ___ out of ___ interactions.
2. The student will tolerate a peer's inappropriate behavior by demonstrating patience and refraining from being verbally or physically aggressive during ___ out of ___ interactions.
3. The student will walk away from a peer or group situation when he/she becomes angry, annoyed, or upset during ___ out of ___ interactions.
4. The student will demonstrate self-control when angered, annoyed, or upset by a peer on ___ out of ___ trials.
5. The student will demonstrate self-control when angered, annoyed, or upset by a teacher on ___ out of ___ trials.
6. The student will continue to demonstrate appropriate behavior and interact with others when angry, annoyed, or upset during ___ out of ___ interactions.

Interventions:

1. Reinforce the student for demonstrating self-control in those situations in which he/she is likely to become angry, annoyed, or upset: (a) give the student a tangible reward (e.g., classroom privileges, line leading, passing out materials, five minutes free time, etc.) or (b) give the student an intangible reward (e.g., praise, handshake, smile, etc.).

2. Speak to the student to explain (a) what he/she is doing wrong (e.g., hitting, arguing, throwing things, etc.) and (b) what he/she should be doing (e.g., moving away from the situation, asking for assistance from the teacher, etc.).

3. Establish classroom rules:
- Work on-task.
- Remain in your seat.
- Finish task.
- Meet task expectations.
- Raise your hand.

Review rules often. Reinforce students for following rules.

4. Reinforce the student for demonstrating self-control based on the length of time he/she can be successful. As the student demonstrates success, gradually increase the length of time required for reinforcement.

5. Reinforce those students in the classroom who demonstrate self-control.

6. Write a contract with the student specifying what behavior is expected (e.g., problem-solving, moving away from the situation, asking for assistance from the teacher, etc.) and what reinforcement will be made available when the terms of the contract have been met.

7. Communicate with the parents (e.g., notes home, phone calls, etc.) to share information concerning the student's progress. The parents may reinforce the student at home for demonstrating self-control at school.

8. Communicate with parents, agencies, or the appropriate parties to inform them of the problem, determine the cause of the problem, and consider possible solutions to the problem.

9. Evaluate the appropriateness of the academic task to determine (a) if the task is too easy, (b) if the task is too difficult, and (c) if the length of time scheduled to complete the task is adequate.

10. Choose a peer to model self-control for the student.

11. Have the student question any directions, explanations, or instructions he/she does not understand.

12. Prevent frustrating or anxiety-producing situations from occurring (e.g., give the student tasks only on his/her ability level, give the student only the number of tasks that he/she can tolerate in one sitting, reduce social interactions which stimulate the student to become physically abusive, etc.).

13. Teach the student problem-solving skills: (a) identify the problem, (b) identify goals and objectives, (c) develop strategies, (d) develop a plan for action, and (e) carry out the plan.

14. Provide the student with positive feedback which indicates that he/she is successful, important, respected, etc.

15. Maintain maximum supervision of the student. The teacher should be able to see the student and the student should be able to see the teacher. Make eye contact possible at all times.

16. Be mobile to be frequently near the student.

17. Reduce activities which might threaten the student (e.g., announcing test score ranges or test scores aloud, making students read aloud in class, emphasizing the success of a particular student or students, etc.).

18. Try various groupings to determine the situation in which the student is most successful.

19. Make the necessary adjustments in the environment to prevent the student from experiencing stress, frustration, and anger.

20. Reduce the emphasis on competition and perfection. Repeated failure and frustration may cause the student to become angry, annoyed, or upset.

21. Teach the student alternative ways to deal with situations which make him/her frustrated, angry, etc., (e.g., withdrawing, talking, etc.).

22. Facilitate on-task behavior by providing a full schedule of daily events. Prevent lag time from occurring when the student would be likely to become involved in activities which would cause him/her to be angry, annoyed, or upset.

23. Maintain supervision so the student is not left alone or allowed to be unattended with other students.

24. Provide the student with as many high-interest activities as possible.

25. Provide the student with opportunities for social and academic successes.

26. Make other personnel aware of the student's tendency to become easily angered, annoyed, or upset.

27. Provide a quiet place for the student to work independently, away from peer interactions. This is not to be used as a form of punishment, but rather as an opportunity to increase the student's success in his/her environment.

28. Place reinforcement emphasis on academic productivity and accuracy to divert the student's attention away from other factors which cause him/her to become angry, annoyed, or upset.

29. Make the student aware of the natural consequences for becoming easily angry, annoyed, or upset (e.g., loss of friendships, injury, more restrictive environment, legal action, etc.).

30. Separate the student from the peer(s) who may be encouraging or stimulating the student to become angry, annoyed, or upset.

31. Do not force the student to interact or remain in a group if he/she is likely to become easily angry, annoyed, or upset.

32. Provide the student with a selection of optional activities to be performed if he/she becomes angry, annoyed, or upset by an assigned task.

33. Maintain consistent expectations.

34. Maintain a consistent daily routine.

35. Remove the student from the group or activity until he/she can demonstrate self-control.

36. Maintain a positive/calm environment (e.g., positive comments, acknowledgment of successes, quiet communications, etc.).

37. Allow flexibility in meeting academic demands when the student becomes angry, annoyed, or upset (e.g., allow more time, modify assignments, provide help with assignments, etc.).

38. Present tasks in the most attractive and interesting manner possible.

39. Make certain to ask the student why he/she becomes easily angered, annoyed, or upset. The student may have the most accurate perception as to why he/she becomes easily angered, annoyed, or upset.

40. Teach the student decision-making steps: (a) think about how others may be influenced, (b) think about consequences, (c) carefully consider the unique situation, (d) think of different courses of action which are possible, and (e) think about what is ultimately best for him/her, etc.

41. Avoid topics, situations, etc., that may cause the student to become easily angered, annoyed, or upset (e.g., divorce, death, unemployment, alcoholism, etc.).

42. Discourage the student from engaging in those activities that cause him/her to become easily angered, annoyed, or upset.

43. Teach the student to verbalize his/her feelings before losing self-control (e.g., "The work is too hard." "Please leave me alone, you're making me angry." etc.).

113 Does not demonstrate appropriate behavior in nonacademic settings

Goal:

1. The student will demonstrate appropriate behavior in nonacademic settings.

Objectives:

1. The student will talk quietly in nonacademic settings on _____ out of _____ trials.
2. The student will walk appropriately in nonacademic settings on _____ out of _____ trials.
3. The student will not make physical contact with others in nonacademic settings on _____ out of _____ trials.
4. The student will follow rules in nonacademic settings with supervision on _____ out of _____ trials.
5. The student will independently follow rules in nonacademic settings on _____ out of _____ trials.
6. The student will take turns in nonacademic settings on _____ out of _____ trials.
7. The student will share materials in nonacademic settings on _____ out of _____ trials.

Interventions:

1. Reinforce the student for staying in an assigned area for the specified time period: (a) give the student a tangible reward (e.g., classroom privileges, line leading, passing out materials, five minutes free time, etc.) or (b) give the student an intangible reward (e.g., praise, handshake, smile, etc.).

2. Speak to the student to explain (a) what he/she is doing wrong (e.g., leaving the assigned area) and (b) what he/she should be doing (e.g., staying in the assigned area for the specified time period).

3. Reinforce those students who demonstrate appropriate behavior in nonacademic settings.

4. Reinforce the student for demonstrating appropriate behavior in nonacademic settings based on the length of time the student can be successful. As the student demonstrates success, gradually increase the length of time required for reinforcement.

5. Write a contract with the student specifying what behavior is expected (e.g., walking in the halls) and what reinforcement will be made available when the terms of the contract have been met.

6. Communicate with parents (e.g., notes home, phone calls, etc.) to share information concerning the student's progress. The parents may reinforce the student at home for demonstrating appropriate behavior in nonacademic settings at school.

7. Evaluate the appropriateness of the assigned activities to determine (a) if the task is too easy, (b) if the task is too difficult, and (c) if the length of time scheduled to complete the task is adequate.

8. Choose a peer to model appropriate behavior in nonacademic settings for the student.

9. Have the student question any directions, explanations, instructions he/she does not understand.

10. Model for the student those behaviors he/she is expected to display in nonacademic settings.

11. Provide the student with a list of rules to be followed in various nonacademic settings.

12. Separate the student from the peer(s) who stimulates the student's inappropriate behavior in nonacademic settings.

13. Have the student be line leader, class monitor, etc., when the class is in nonacademic settings.

14. Have a peer accompany the student in nonacademic settings.

15. Make certain the behavioral demands are appropriate for the student's ability level (e.g., staying in line, waiting a turn, moving with a group, sitting at a table with a group, moving about the building alone, etc.).

16. Make certain the student is actively involved in the environment (e.g., give the student responsibilities, activities, errands to run) to provide purposeful behavior.

17. Inform the other personnel of any behavior problems the student may have so supervision and assistance may be provided.

18. Reinforce the student for following the rules of the nonacademic settings (e.g., hallways, restrooms, cafeteria, school grounds, etc.).

19. Have the student carry a point card at all times so that he/she can be reinforced anywhere in the school environment for demonstrating appropriate behavior.

20. Reinforce the student for moving from one place to another in an appropriate length of time.

21. Reinforce the student for going directly from one location to another.

22. Reinforce the student for taking only the necessary length of time to use the restroom.

23. Be consistent in applying consequences for behavior (i.e., appropriate behavior receives positive consequences while inappropriate behavior receives negative consequences).

24. Reinforce the student for remaining in assigned areas (e.g., free time areas, student lounge, recreational area, etc.)

114   Fights with other students

Goals:
1. The student will interact appropriately with other students.
2. The student will improve his/her ability to resolve conflict situations.

Objectives:
1. The student will refrain from touching other students during ___ out of ___ interactions.
2. The student will be able to settle minor conflicts with peers without becoming physically aggressive during ___ out of ___ interactions.
3. The student will seek teacher assistance when he/she is experiencing difficulty interacting with peers during ___ out of ___ interactions.
4. The student will walk away from peer conflicts during ___ out of ___ interactions.
5. The student will verbally, rather than physically, express his/her feelings toward a peer during ___ out of ___ interactions.
6. The student will remain calm during ___ out of ___ conflict situations.
7. The student will refrain from fighting during ___ out of ___ conflict situations.
8. The student will call upon an arbitrator when involved in a conflicting situation on ___ out of ___ trials.
9. The student will remove himself/herself from a conflict situation by walking away, returning to his/her seat, finding a different activity, etc., on ___ out of ___ trials.
10. The student will attempt to resolve a conflict with a peer(s) by quietly discussing behavioral options, cooperating, etc., on ___ out of ___ trials.

Interventions:

1. Teach the student problem-solving skills: (a) identify the problem, (b) identify goals and objectives, (c) develop strategies, (d) develop a plan of action, and (e) carry out the plan.

2. Provide the student with positive feedback which indicates he/she is successful, important, respected, etc.

3. Structure the environment to reduce opportunities for the student to become physically aggressive toward other students (e.g., seating arrangement, supervision, etc.).

4. Maintain visibility to and from the student. The teacher should be able to see the student and the student should be able to see the teacher. Make eye contact possible at all times.

5. Maintain supervision so the student is not left alone with other students.

6. Reduce activities which might be threatening to the student (e.g., announcing test score ranges or test scores aloud, making students read aloud in class, emphasizing the success of a particular student(s), etc.).

7. Try various groupings to determine the situation in which the student is most likely to succeed socially.

8. Make the necessary adjustments in the environment that will prevent the student from becoming overstimulated by peers.

9. Reduce the emphasis on competition and perfection. Repeated failure and frustration may cause outbursts of physical aggression.

10. Teach the student alternative ways to deal with situations which make him/her feel frustrated or angry (e.g., withdrawing, talking, etc.).

11. Facilitate on-task behavior by providing a full schedule of activities. Prevent lag time from occurring when the student would be free to engage in inappropriate behavior.

12. Be mobile to be frequently near the student.

13. Provide the student with as many high-interest activities as possible to keep him/her from becoming physically aggressive toward other students.

14. Provide the student with opportunities for social and academic success.

15. Make certain that all school personnel are aware of the student's tendency to become physically aggressive so they will monitor the student's behavior.

16. Maintain maximum supervision of the student. As the student demonstrates appropriate behavior, gradually decrease supervision.

17. Provide a quiet place for the student to work independently, away from peer interactions. This is not to be used as a form of punishment but rather as an opportunity to increase the student's success in his/her environment.

18. Place reinforcement emphasis on academic productivity and accuracy to reduce the likelihood of the student becoming physically aggressive (i.e., increased productivity and accuracy will reduce the likelihood of inappropriate behavior).

19. Reduce or remove any stimulus in the environment which leads to the student's physically aggressive behavior (e.g., possessions, competition, teasing, etc.).

20. Make certain the student understands the natural consequences of hurting other students (e.g., less freedom, more restrictive environment, assault charges, etc.).

21. Prevent the student from receiving too much stimulation (e.g., monitor or supervise student behavior to limit overexcitement in physical activities, games, parties, etc.).

22. Limit the student's opportunity to enter areas of the school environment where he/she is more likely to be physically aggressive.

23. Separate the student from the peer(s) who may be encouraging or stimulating the student's inappropriate behavior.

24. Do not force the student to interact or remain in a group when he/she is physically aggressive (e.g., daily reading group, physical education group, etc.).

25. Limit the student's independent movement in the school environment.

26. Intervene early when there is a problem with fighting to prevent more serious problems from occurring.

27. Encourage the student to tell you about problems that occur with other students at school.

28. Make certain there will always be adult supervision where the student will be.

29. Do not force the student to play with other students with whom he/she is not completely comfortable.

30. Make certain the student does not become involved in overstimulating activities.

31. Talk with the student about individual differences, and discuss strengths and weaknesses of individuals the student knows. Stress that the student does not have to do the same things everyone else does.

32. Find a peer to play with the student who will be a good influence (e.g., someone younger, older, of the same gender, of the opposite gender, etc.).

33. Have the student put himself/herself in someone else's place (e.g., "How would you feel if someone called you dumb or stupid?").

34. Make certain the student is not allowed time alone with other students when he/she is upset or angry.

35. Do not force the student to interact with others.

36. Before beginning an activity or game, make certain the student knows the rules, is familiar with the activity or game, and will be compatible with the other individuals who will be playing.

37. Teach the student to ask for things in a positive manner. Teach key words and phrases (e.g., "May I borrow your pencil?" "Do you mind if I play the game with you?" etc.).

38. Do not leave a lot of unstructured time for the student.

39. Teach the student to "think" before acting (e.g., ask himself/herself "What is happening?" "What am I doing?" "What should I do?" "What will be best for me?").

40. Have the student practice appropriate verbal exchanges which should be made when typical physical exchanges take place (e.g., "Excuse me." "I'm sorry." etc.).

41. Make certain the student is allowed to voice an opinion in situations to avoid becoming angry or upset.

42. Talk to the student about ways of handling conflict situations successfully (e.g., walk away from a situation, change to another activity, ask for help, etc.).

43. Prevent frustrating or anxiety-producing situations from occurring (e.g., give the student tasks only on his/her ability level, give the student only the number of tasks that he/she can tolerate in one sitting, reduce social interactions which stimulate the student to become physically aggressive, etc.).

44. Explain to the student that it is natural for conflict situations to occur. What is important is how he/she reacts to the situation.

45. Communicate with parents (e.g., notes home, phone calls, etc.) to share information concerning the student's progress. The parents may reinforce the student at home for respecting the norms of physical proximity at school.

46. Write a contract with the student specifying what behavior is expected (e.g., respecting the norms of physical proximity) and what reinforcement will be made available when the terms of the contract have been met.

47. Remove the student from the group or activity until he/she can demonstrate appropriate behavior and self-control.

48. Reinforce the student for demonstrating appropriate behavior based on the length of time the student can be successful. As the student demonstrates success, gradually increase the length of time required for reinforcement.

49. Reinforce those students in the classroom who demonstrate appropriate behavior when interacting with other students.

50. Establish classroom rules:
- Work on-task.
- Remain in your seat.
- Finish task.
- Meet task expectations.
- Raise your hand.

Review rules often. Reinforce students for following rules.

51. Speak with the student to explain (a) what the student is doing wrong (e.g., scratching, hitting, pulling hair, etc.) and (b) what the student should be doing (e.g., following rules, interacting in appropriate ways, dealing with anger and frustration in appropriate ways, etc.).

52. Reinforce the student for demonstrating appropriate behavior: (a) give the student a tangible reward (e.g., classroom privileges, line leading, passing out materials, five minutes free time, etc.) or (b) give the student an intangible reward (e.g., praise, handshake, smile, etc.).

53. Evaluate the appropriateness of the task to determine (a) if the task is too easy, (b) if the task is too difficult, and (c) if the length of time scheduled to complete the task is adequate.

54. When the student has responded inappropriately to a conflict situation, take time to explore with him/her appropriate solutions which could have been used in dealing with the problem.

115 Continues to engage in a behavior when it is no longer appropriate

Goals:

1. The student will change his/her behavior from one situation to another.
2. The student will demonstrate flexibility in his/her behavior.

Objectives:

1. The student will change his/her behavior from one situation to another on ___ out of ___ trials.
2. The student will demonstrate flexibility in his/her behavior on ___ out of ___ trials.
3. The student will stop an activity when cued by the teacher on ___ out of ___ trials.
4. The student will stop an activity and begin another within ___ minutes. (Gradually increase expectations as the student demonstrates success.)
5. The student will demonstrate behavior appropriate for the situation on ___ out of ___ trials.
6. The student will calm down when he/she enters the building on ___ out of ___ trials.
7. At the end of recess, the student will calm down within ___ minutes and enter the building in a quiet manner.
8. The student will engage in a relaxation activity following a stimulating activity on ___ out of ___ trials.
9. The student will begin a task within ___ minutes. (Gradually increase expectations as the student demonstrates success.)

Interventions:

1. Prevent the student from becoming over-stimulated by an activity. Supervise student behavior to limit overexcitement in physical activities, games, parties, etc.

2. Have the student time activities to monitor personal behavior and accept time limits.

3. Convince the student that work not completed in one sitting can be completed later. Provide the student with ample time to complete earlier assignments to guarantee closure.

4. Provide the student with more than enough time to finish an activity. As the student demonstrates success, decrease the amount of time provided.

5. Structure time limits so the student knows exactly the amount of time there is to work and when he/she must be finished.

6. Allow a transition period between activities so the student can make adjustments in his/her behavior.

7. Employ a signal technique (e.g., turning the lights off and on) to warn that the end of an activity is near.

8. Establish definite time limits and provide the student with this information before the activity begins.

9. Assign the student shorter activities. As the student demonstrates success, gradually increase the length of the activities.

10. Maintain a consistent daily routine.

11. Maintain consistent expectations within the ability level of the student.

12. Establish rules that are to be followed in various parts of the school building (e.g., lunchroom, music room, art room, gymnasium, library, playground, etc.).

13. Allow the student to finish the activity unless it will be disruptive to the schedule.

14. Provide the student with a list of materials needed for each activity (e.g., pencil, paper, textbook, workbook, etc.).

15. Present instructions/directions prior to handing out necessary materials.

16. Collect the student's materials (e.g., pencil, paper, textbook, workbook, etc.) when it is time to change from one situation to another.

17. Provide the student with clearly stated expectations for all situations.

18. Prevent the student from becoming so stimulated by an event or activity that the student cannot control his/her behavior.

19. Identify the expectations of different environments and help the student develop the skills to be successful in those environments.

20. In conjunction with other school personnel, develop as much consistency across the various environments as possible (e.g., rules, criteria for success, behavioral expectations, consequences, etc.).

21. Reduce the student's involvement in activities which prove too stimulating for him/her.

22. Have the student engage in relaxing transitional activities designed to reduce the effects of stimulating activities (e.g., put head on desk, listen to the teacher read a story, put headphones on and listen to relaxing music, etc.).

23. Provide the student with more than enough time to adapt or modify his/her behavior to different situations (e.g., have the student stop recess activities five minutes prior to coming into the building).

24. Communicate clearly to the student when it is time to begin an activity.

25. Schedule activities so the student has more than enough time to finish the activity if he/she works consistently.

26. Communicate clearly to the student when it is time to stop an activity.

27. Evaluate the appropriateness of the task to determine (a) if the task is too easy, (b) if the task is too difficult, and (c) if the length of time scheduled to complete the task is adequate.

28. Reduce the emphasis on competition (e.g., academic or social). Fear of failure may cause the student to fail to adapt or modify his/her behavior to different situations.

29. Have the student begin an activity in a private place (e.g., carrel, "office," quiet study area, etc.) to reduce the difficulty in adapting or modifying his/her behavior to different situations.

30. Allow the student the option of performing the activity at another time (e.g., earlier in the day, later in the day, another day, etc.).

31. Do not allow the student to begin a new activity until he/she has gained self-control.

32. Evaluate the appropriateness of the situation in relation to the student's ability to successfully adapt or modify his/her behavior.

33. Let the student know in advance when changes in his/her schedule will occur (e.g., a change from class time to recess, when reading class will begin, etc.).

34. Explain to the student that he/she should be satisfied with personal best effort rather than insisting on perfection.

35. Choose a peer to work with the student to provide an appropriate model.

36. Communicate with the parents (e.g., notes home, phone calls, etc.) to share information concerning the student's progress. The parents may reinforce the student at home for demonstrating acceptable behavior at school.

37. Have the student question any directions, explanations, and instructions not understood.

38. Provide the student with a schedule of daily events so he/she will know which activity comes next and can prepare for it.

39. Write a contract with the student specifying what behavior is expected (e.g., putting materials away and getting ready for another activity) and what reinforcement will be made available when the terms of the contract have been met.

40. Reinforce the student for demonstrating acceptable behavior based on the length of time the student can be successful. As the student demonstrates success, gradually increase the length of time required for reinforcement.

41. Reinforce those students in the classroom who change their behavior from one situation to another without difficulty.

42. Establish classroom rules:
- Work on-task.
- Remain in your seat.
- Finish task.
- Meet task expectations.
- Raise your hand.

Review rules often. Reinforce students for following rules.

43. Speak to the student to explain (a) what the student is doing wrong (e.g., failing to stop one activity and begin another) and (b) what the student should be doing (e.g., changing from one activity to another).

44. Reinforce the student for changing his/her behavior from one situation to another without difficulty: (a) give the student a tangible reward (e.g., classroom privileges, line leading, passing out materials, five minutes free time, etc.) or (b) give the student an intangible reward (e.g., praise, handshake, smile, etc.).

Reminder: Do not "force" the student to participate in any activity which makes him/her uncomfortable.

116 Does not behave appropriately in the absence of supervision

Goals:

1. The student will behave appropriately in the absence of supervision.

Objectives:

1. The student will wait quietly for an instructor to arrive on _____ out of _____ trials.
2. The student will remain in his/her seat while waiting for an instructor to arrive on _____ out of _____ trials.
3. The student will follow the rules of the classroom while waiting for an instructor to arrive on _____ out of _____ trials.
4. The student will engage in assigned activities while waiting for an instructor to arrive on _____ out of _____ trials.
5. The student will interact quietly with peers while waiting for an instructor to arrive on _____ out of _____ trials.

Interventions:

1. Choose a peer to model appropriate behavior for the student when a supervisor is detained (e.g., stay in seat or assigned area, remain quiet, work on assigned task, etc.).

2. Have the student question any directions, explanations, or instructions not understood.

3. Choose a peer to supervise the student when an instructor is detained.

4. Provide a list of possible activities for the students to participate in when an instructor is detained (e.g., write a letter to a friend, work on assigned tasks, organize work area, look at a magazine, etc.).

5. Along with a directive, provide an incentive statement (e.g., "If you wait quietly, you can have five minutes of free time.").

6. Make sure the student knows when it is acceptable to get others' attention (e.g., in an emergency).

7. Communicate with parents (e.g., notes home, phone calls, etc.) to share information concerning the student's progress. The parents may reinforce the student at home for waiting appropriately for a supervisor.

8. Write a contract with the student specifying what behavior is expected (e.g., stay in seat or assigned area, remain quiet, and work on assigned task) and what reinforcement will be made available when the terms of the contract have been met.

9. Deliver directions in a supportive rather than a threatening manner (e.g., "Please wait quietly." rather than "You had better wait quietly or else!").

10. Reinforce the student for waiting appropriately for a supervisor to arrive based on the length of time the student can be successful. As the student demonstrates success, gradually increase the length of time required for reinforcement.

11. Reinforce those students in the classroom who stay in their seat or assigned area, remain quiet, and work on assigned tasks.

12. Establish classroom rules:
- Work on-task.
- Remain in your seat.
- Finish task.
- Meet task expectations.
- Raise your hand.

Review rules often. Reinforce students for following rules.

13. Speak to the student to explain (a) what the student is doing wrong (e.g., leaving seat, talking, making noises, etc.) and (b) what the student should be doing (e.g., sitting in seat or assigned area, remaining quiet, etc.).

14. Reinforce the student for waiting appropriately for a supervisor to arrive: (a) give the student a tangible reward (e.g., classroom privileges, line leading, passing out materials, five minutes free time, etc.) or (b) give the student an intangible reward (e.g., praise, handshake, smile, etc.).

117 Does not behave in a manner appropriate for the situation

Goals:

1. The student will behave in a manner appropriate for the situation.

Objectives:

1. The student will laugh when appropriate during ___ out of ___ situations.
2. The student will appear alarmed or upset when appropriate during ___ out of ___ situations.
3. The student will show emotion that is appropriate for the situation during ___ out of ___ situations.
4. The student will demonstrate emotion like that of his/her peers during ___ out of ___ situations.
5. The student will cry when appropriate during ___ out of ___ situations.
6. The student will demonstrate anger when appropriate during ___ out of ___ situations.

Interventions:

1. Evaluate the appropriateness of the task to determine (a) if the task is too easy, (b) if the task is too difficult, and (c) if the length of time scheduled to complete the task is adequate.

2. Reduce stimuli which would contribute to unrelated or inappropriate behavior (e.g., testing situations, peers, physical activities, etc.).

3. Interact frequently with the student to maintain involvement.

4. Structure the environment so that time does not permit unrelated or inappropriate behavior from occurring.

5. Give the student responsibilities to keep him/her actively involved in the activity.

6. Modify or adjust situations which cause the student to demonstrate unrelated or inappropriate behavior (e.g., keep the student from becoming overstimulated in activities).

7. Make the necessary adjustments in the environment to prevent the student from experiencing stress, frustration, anger, etc., as much as possible.

8. Reduce distracting stimuli (e.g., place the student in the front row, provide a carrel or quiet place away from distractions, etc.). This is used as a means of reducing distracting stimuli and not as punishment.

9. Choose a peer to model on-task behavior for the student.

10. Interact frequently with the student to maintain his/her attention to the activity (e.g., ask the student questions, ask the student's opinions, stand close to the student, seat the student near the teacher's desk, etc.).

11. Model socially acceptable behavior for the student (e.g., pat on the back, handshake, etc.).

12. Maintain a consistent routine.

13. Make certain that reinforcement is not inadvertently given for the student's inappropriate comments or behaviors (e.g., attending to the student only when he/she demonstrates behaviors which are inappropriate to the situation).

14. Prevent the student from becoming overstimulated by an activity (e.g., monitor or supervise student behavior to limit overstimulation in physical activities, games, parties, etc.).

15. Help the student develop attention-maintaining behaviors (e.g., maintain eye contact, take notes on the subject, ask questions related to the subject, etc.).

16. Try various groupings to determine the situations in which the student demonstrates appropriate behavior.

17. Reduce the emphasis on competition. Repeated failure may result in behaviors which are inappropriate for the situation.

18. Make the student aware of activities or events well in advance so he/she may prepare for them.

19. Remove the student from the group or activity until he/she can demonstrate appropriate behavior and self-control.

20. Do not criticize. When correcting the student, be honest yet supportive. Never cause the student to feel negatively about himself/herself.

21. Intervene early when there is a problem to prevent a more serious problem from occurring.

22. Teach the student to "think" before acting (e.g., ask himself/herself "What is happening?" "What am I doing?" "What should I do?" "What will be best for me?" etc.).

23. Talk to the student about ways of handling situations successfully without conflict (e.g., walk away from the situation, change to another activity, ask for help, etc.).

24. Communicate with parents (e.g., notes home, phone calls, etc.) to share information concerning the student's progress. The parents may reinforce the student at home for demonstrating appropriate behaviors related to situations at school.

25. Write a contract with the student specifying what behavior is expected (e.g., demonstrating appropriate behavior related to the situation) and what reinforcement will be made available when the terms of the contract have been met.

26. Make certain the student does not become involved in overstimulating activities.

27. Deliver a predetermined signal (e.g., hand signal, verbal cue, etc.) when the student begins to display behaviors which are inappropriate for the situation.

28. Reinforce the student for demonstrating appropriate behaviors related to the situation based on the length of time the student can be successful. As the student demonstrates success, gradually increase the length of time required for reinforcement.

29. Reinforce those students in the classroom who demonstrate appropriate behaviors related to the situation.

30. Establish classroom rules:
- Work on-task.
- Remain in your seat.
- Finish task.
- Meet task expectations.
- Raise your hand.

Review rules often. Reinforce students for following rules.

31. Speak with the student to explain (a) what the student is doing wrong (e.g., laughing when a peer gets hurt) and (b) what the student should be doing (e.g., helping the peer).

32. Reinforce the student for demonstrating appropriate behaviors related to the situation: (a) give the student a tangible reward (e.g., classroom privileges, line leading, passing out materials, five minutes free time, etc.) or (b) give the student an intangible reward (e.g., praise, handshake, smile, etc.).

Reminder: Do not "force" the student to participate in any activity he/she finds unpleasant, embarrassing, etc.

118 Does not accept changes in an established routine

Goals:

1. The student will accept change in an established routine.

Objectives:

1. The student will follow changes in an established routine with physical assistance on _____ out of _____ trials.
2. The student will follow changes in an established routine with verbal reminders on _____ out of _____ trials.
3. The student will independently follow changes in an established routine on _____ out of _____ trials.
4. The student will rely on environmental cues to follow changes in an established routine (e.g., class schedule, school schedule, bells, lights turned off and on, clocks) on _____ out of _____ trials.

Interventions:

1. Have the student work near a peer to follow change in an established routine.

2. Provide the student with a schedule of revised daily events which identifies the activities for the day and the times when they will occur.

3. Revisions in the schedule for the day's events should be attached to the student's desk and/or carried with the student throughout the day.

4. Post the revised routine throughout the classroom (e.g., on the student's desk, chalkboard, bulletin board, etc.).

5. Attempt to limit the number of times that changes must occur in the student's routine.

6. Discuss any necessary changes in the student's routine well in advance of the occurrence of the changes.

7. Teach the student to tell time to facilitate his/her ability to accept change in an established routine.

8. Have the student rely on a predetermined signal (e.g., lights turned off and on, hand signal, etc.) to facilitate the ability to accept change in an established routine.

9. Have the student use a timer to remind him/her of changes in an established routine.

10. Reduce distracting stimuli which might cause the student to be unable to accept change in an established routine (e.g., movement, noise, peers, etc.).

11. Model acceptance of change in an established routine.

12. Have the student rely on environmental cues to remind the student when to change activities in his/her revised routine (e.g., other students changing activities, bells, lights, buses arriving, etc.).

13. Have a peer remind the student of changes in routine.

14. Remind the student when it is time to change activities.

15. Have a peer accompany the student to other locations in the building when change in an established routine has occurred.

16. Allow the student an appropriate amount of time to accept changes in an established routine.

17. Explain changes in routine to the student personally.

18. Provide activities similar to those canceled in the student's routine (e.g., if an art activity is canceled due to the art teacher's absence, provide an art activity in the classroom for the student).

19. Provide the student with highly desirable activities to perform when changes in his/her routine are necessary.

20. If change in the student's routine proves too difficult, have the student remain with the established routine (e.g., if an assembly is overstimulating for the student, have the student continue to work in his/her established routine).

21. Initially limit the number/degree of changes in the student's established routine. As the student demonstrates success, gradually increase the number/degree of changes in the routine.

22. Implement environmental changes within the classroom to provide the student with experience in change (e.g., change in seating, instructional delivery, task format, etc.), to help the student accept change in an established routine.

23. Prepare a substitute teacher information packet that includes all information pertaining to the classroom (e.g., student roster, class schedule, class rules, behavior management techniques, class helpers, etc.).

24. Make certain that the student understands that classroom rules and consequences are in effect when a substitute teacher is in the classroom.

25. Indicate the names of several personnel and where they can be located in case the substitute teacher should need some assistance.

26. Inform the substitute teacher of the classroom rules and the consequences if the rules are not followed by the student.

27. Have the student work on practice work (e.g., work that has already been taught to the student and that the student knows how to do) when a substitute teacher is in the classroom to reduce frustration and feelings of failure.

28. Request a substitute teacher who has the necessary skills to handle problem behavior and special needs students.

29. Make certain that the substitute teacher is familiar with the behavioral support system used in the classroom (e.g., rules, point system, reinforcers, etc.).

30. Provide the substitute teacher with detailed information on the activities and assignments.

31. Assign the student specific activities to perform on any day when a substitute teacher may be responsible for the classroom (e.g., assistant to the substitute teacher, errands to run, line leading, class monitor, etc.).

32. Make certain the substitute teacher follows all procedures indicated by the classroom teacher (e.g., academic activities, behavioral support system, etc.).

33. Have special or unique responsibilities performed by other personnel in the building when a substitute teacher is in the classroom (e.g., administering medication, feeding, toileting, etc.).

34. Choose a peer to model appropriate behavior and provide information necessary for success for the student when changes are made in an established routine.

35. If an aide works in the classroom, have the aide monitor the student's behavior; provide reinforcement; deliver instructions; etc.; when a substitute teacher is in the classroom.

36. Provide a quiet place for the student to work.

37. Inform the student in advance when it will be necessary for a substitute teacher to be in the classroom and establish expectations for behavior and academic performance.

38. Let the student know in advance when changes in his/her schedule will occur (e.g., going to P.E. at a different time, going on a field trip, etc.).

39. Teach the student acceptable ways to communicate displeasure, anger, frustration, etc.

40. Have the student question any directions, explanations, instructions not understood concerning the change in an established routine.

41. Choose a peer to model appropriate acceptance of changes in an established routine for the student.

42. Establish classroom rules:
- Work on-task.
- Remain in your seat.
- Finish task.
- Meet task expectations.
- Raise your hand.

Review rules often. Reinforce students for following rules.

43. Write a contract with the student specifying what behavior is expected (e.g., accepting a change in routine) and what reinforcement will be made available when the terms of the contract have been met.

44. Reinforce those students in the classroom who accept changes in an established routine.

45. Reinforce the student for accepting changes in an established routine based on the number of times the student can be successful. As the student demonstrates success, gradually increase the number of times required for reinforcement.

46. Evaluate the appropriateness of the change in routine. Determine if the change is too difficult and if the length of time scheduled is adequate.

47. Communicate with parents (e.g., notes home, phone calls, etc.) to share information concerning the student's progress. The parents may reinforce the student at home for accepting changes in an established routine at school.

48. Speak to the student to explain (a) what the student is doing wrong (e.g., having a tantrum, refusing to accept the change, etc.) and (b) what the student should be doing (e.g., accepting the change in routine).

49. Reinforce the student for accepting changes in an established routine: (a) give the student a tangible reward (e.g., classroom privileges, line leading, passing out materials, five minutes free time, etc.) or (b) give the student an intangible reward (e.g., praise, handshake, smile, etc.).

119   Demonstrates behaviors not related to immediate situations

Goals:

1. The student will behave in a manner appropriate for the situation.

Objectives:

1. The student will laugh when appropriate during ___ out of ___ situations.
2. The student will appear alarmed or upset when appropriate during ___ out of ___ situations.
3. The student will show emotion that is appropriate for the situation during ___ out of ___ situations.
4. The student will demonstrate emotion like that of his/her peers during ___ out of ___ situations.
5. The student will cry when appropriate during ___ out of ___ situations.
6. The student will demonstrate anger when appropriate during ___ out of ___ situations.

Interventions:

1. Reduce stimuli which would contribute to unrelated or inappropriate behavior (e.g., testing situations, peers, physical activities, etc.).

2. Interact frequently with the student to maintain involvement.

3. Structure the environment so time does not permit unrelated or inappropriate behavior.

4. Give the student responsibilities to keep him/her actively involved in the activity.

5. Modify or adjust situations which cause the student to demonstrate unrelated or inappropriate behavior (e.g., keep the student from becoming overstimulated in activities).

6. Make the necessary adjustments in the environment to prevent the student from experiencing stress, frustration, anger, etc., as much as possible.

7. Reduce distracting stimuli (e.g., place the student in the front row, provide a carrel or quiet place away from distractions, etc.). This is used as a means of reducing distracting stimuli and not as a form of punishment.

8. Try various groupings to determine the situations in which the student demonstrates appropriate behavior.

9. Reduce the emphasis on competition. Repeated failure may result in behaviors which are inappropriate for the situation.

10. Interact frequently with the student to maintain his/her attention to the activity (e.g., ask the student questions, ask the student's opinions, stand close to the student, seat the student near the teacher's desk, etc.).

11. Talk to the student about ways of handling situations successfully without conflict (e.g., walk away from the situation, change to another activity, ask for help, etc.).

12. Maintain a consistent routine.

13. Make certain that reinforcement is not inadvertently given for the student's inappropriate comments or behaviors (e.g., attending to the student only when he/she demonstrates behaviors which are inappropriate to the situation).

14. Prevent the student from becoming overstimulated by an activity (e.g., monitor or supervise student behavior to limit overstimulation in physical activities, games, parties, etc.).

15. Help the student develop attention-maintaining behaviors (e.g., maintain eye contact, take notes on the subject, ask questions related to the subject, etc.).

16. Choose a peer to model on-task behavior for the student.

17. Model socially acceptable behavior for the student (e.g., pat on the back, handshake, etc.).

18. Make the student aware of activities or events well in advance so he/she may prepare for them.

19. Remove the student from the group or activity until he/she can demonstrate appropriate behavior and self-control.

20. Do not criticize. When correcting the student, be honest yet supportive. Never cause the student to feel negatively about himself/herself.

21. Intervene early when there is a problem to prevent a more serious problem from occurring.

22. Make certain the student does not become involved in overstimulating activities.

23. Teach the student to "think" before acting (e.g., ask himself/herself "What is happening?" "What am I doing?" "What should I do?" "What will be best for me?" etc.).

24. Evaluate the appropriateness of the task to determine (a) if the task is too easy, (b) if the task is too difficult, and (c) if the length of time scheduled to complete the task is adequate.

25. Communicate with the parents (e.g., notes home, phone calls, etc.) to share information concerning the student's progress. The parents may reinforce the student at home for demonstrating appropriate behaviors related to situations at school.

26. Write a contract with the student specifying what behavior is expected (e.g., demonstrating appropriate behavior related to the situation) and what reinforcement will be made available when the terms of the contract have been met.

27. Deliver a predetermined signal (e.g., hand signal, verbal cue, etc.) when the student begins to display behaviors which are inappropriate for the situation.

28. Reinforce the student for demonstrating appropriate behaviors related to the situation based on the length of time the student can be successful. As the student demonstrates success, gradually increase the length of time required for reinforcement.

29. Reinforce those students in the classroom who demonstrate appropriate behaviors related to the situation.

30. Establish classroom rules:
- Work on-task.
- Remain in your seat.
- Finish task.
- Meet task expectations.
- Raise your hand.

Review rules often. Reinforce students for following rules.

31. Speak with the student to explain (a) what the student is doing wrong (e.g., laughing when a peer gets hurt) and (b) what the student should be doing (e.g., helping the peer).

32. Reinforce the student for demonstrating appropriate behaviors related to the situation: (a) give the student a tangible reward (e.g., classroom privileges, line leading, passing out materials, five minutes free time, etc.) or (b) give the student an intangible reward (e.g., praise, handshake, smile, etc.).

Reminder: Do not "force" the student to participate in any activity he/she finds unpleasant, embarrassing, etc.

120   Talks beyond what is expected or at inappropriate times

Goals:

1. The student will communicate to others in an acceptable manner in the classroom.
2. The student will talk quietly in the classroom.

Objectives:

1. The student will gain permission from the teacher, by raising his/her hand, when he/she needs to speak on _____ out of _____ trials.
2. The student will contribute his/her opinion/answer after being recognized by the teacher on _____ out of _____ trials.
3. The student will wait his/her turn to talk when engaged, or attempting to engage, in interactions with others on _____ out of _____ trials.
4. The student will make comments which are relevant to the situation on _____ out of _____ trials.
5. The student will end what he/she has to say within a reasonable length of time on _____ out of _____ occasions.

Interventions:

1. Communicate with parents (e.g., notes home, phone calls, etc.) to share information concerning the student's appropriate behavior. The parents may reinforce the student at home for talking when appropriate at school.

2. Evaluate the appropriateness of the task to determine (a) if the task is too easy, (b) if the task is too difficult, and (c) if the length of time scheduled to complete the task is adequate.

3. Allow the student to take a break to regroup when he/she is talking excessively.

4. Give adequate opportunities to respond (i.e., enthusiastic students need many opportunities to contribute).

5. Have the student be the leader of a small group activity if he/she possesses mastery of skills or an interest in that area.

6. Deliver a predetermined signal (e.g., hand signal, verbal cue, etc.) if the student begins to talk beyond what is expected or at inappropriate times.

7. Explain to the student that he/she may be trying too hard to fit in and he/she should relax and talk less and at appropriate times.

8. Structure the environment to limit opportunities for inappropriate behaviors (e.g., keep the student engaged in activities, have the student seated near the teacher, etc.).

9. Make certain that reinforcement is not inadvertently given for inappropriate behavior (e.g., talking beyond what is expected or at inappropriate times).

10. Instruct the student to carry a notepad with him/her at all times and to write information down to help him/her remember.

11. Maintain a full schedule of activities. Keeping the student occupied should decrease talking beyond what is expected or at inappropriate times.

12. Educate yourself and others about ADHD to increase understanding and accommodation of interruptive behavior.

13. Reinforce the student for talking an appropriate length of time and at appropriate times in the classroom: (a) give the student a tangible reward (e.g., classroom privileges, line leading, passing out materials, five minutes free time, etc.) or (b) give the student an intangible reward (e.g., praise, handshake, smile, etc.).

14. Speak with the student to explain (a) what he/she is doing wrong (e.g., talking more than is necessary or at inappropriate times) and (b) what he/she should be doing (e.g., keeping comments brief, waiting until it is appropriate to speak, thinking of comments which relate to the situation, etc.).

15. Establish classroom rules:
- Work on-task.
- Work quietly.
- Remain in your seat.
- Finish task.
- Meet task expectations.

Review rules often. Reinforce students for following the rules.

16. Reinforce those students in the classroom who make their comments brief or speak at appropriate times.

17. Reinforce the student for making appropriate comments or speaking at the appropriate time based on the length of time he/she can be successful. As the student demonstrates success, gradually increase the length of time required for reinforcement.

18. Help the student improve concentration skills (e.g., listening to the speaker, taking notes, preparing comments in advance, making comments in the appropriate context, etc.).

19. Educate the student about ADHD and the need to self-monitor behavior.

20. Encourage the student to pause and consider his/her thoughts before speaking.

21. Provide constant, positive reinforcement for appropriate behavior. Ignore as many inappropriate behaviors as possible.

22. Help the student develop an awareness of the consequences of his/her behavior by writing down or talking through problems which may occur due to excessive talking (e.g., perceived as unmannerly, avoided, etc.).

23. Encourage the student to differentiate between spur-of-the-moment and important information that needs to be conveyed.

24. Provide the student with a clearly understood list of consequences for inappropriate behavior.

25. Teach the student to take cues from others (e.g., if he/she is talking and a peer yawns, stop talking; when there is silence in a class, it is not necessary to fill the silence with comments, etc.).

26. Schedule recreational activities at the end of the day. Make participation in these activities dependent upon completion of daily responsibilities and appropriate behavior.

27. Make certain that the student's feelings are considered when it is necessary to deal with his/her inappropriate comments (i.e., handle comments in such a way as to not diminish the student's enthusiasm for participation).

28. Encourage the student to model the behavior of peers who are successful at not interrupting the teacher.

29. Encourage the student to develop an awareness of himself/herself and those around him/her. Have the student periodically step back and ask himself/herself "Am I blurting out answers and dominating the conversation?"

30. Encourage the student to develop an awareness of himself/herself and those around him/her. Have the student periodically step back and ask himself/herself "Am I talking excessively?"

31. Have the student question any directions, explanations, or instructions he/she does not understand prior to beginning an assignment.

32. Deliver directions, explanations, and instructions in a clear, concise manner to reduce the student's need to ask questions.

33. Have the student practice waiting for short periods of time for his/her turn to speak. Gradually increase the length of time required for a turn to speak.

34. Explain to the student the reasons why talking beyond what is expected and at inappropriate times is unacceptable (e.g., impolite, interrupts others, etc.).

35. Avoid seating the student near people with whom he/she may be tempted to converse during lectures, seminars, group projects, etc.

36. Remove the student from the group or activity until he/she can demonstrate appropriate behavior and self-control.

37. Encourage the student to ask himself/herself questions such as "What should I be doing right now?" "Is what I have to say relevant to this topic?" "Is this a good time for me to comment?"

38. Teach the student to redirect himself/herself when talking to others is inappropriate (e.g., make a note to speak to a peer at an appropriate time).

39. Teach the student to monitor his/her impulsivity. Awareness should reduce impulsive behaviors such as talking beyond what is expected or at inappropriate times.

40. Reinforce the student for raising his/her hand to be recognized.

41. Encourage the student to avoid ingesting any substance (e.g., drugs, alcohol, cold remedies, etc.) that might further alter his/her ability to maintain self-control.

42. Make certain that the student is individually supervised if he/she continues to talk beyond what is expected or at inappropriate times.

43. Help the student understand why it is important to wait quietly (e.g., you may not hear what is being said if you are making excessive noise, others will not be able to hear, etc.).

44. Help the student understand the natural consequences of talking excessively (e.g., he/she won't have time to finish his/her other assignments if he/she talks too long on a topic, others will avoid him/ her).

45. Help the student become aware of the times when he/she is most likely to talk beyond what is expected or at inappropriate times (e.g., in a large group of people, when nervous or anxious, etc.) and limit his/her interactions with others during these times.

46. Attempt to provide equal attention to all students in the classroom.

47. Encourage the student to choose play and leisure activities which allow him/her to be highly active and talkative.

48. Teach appropriate social rituals (e.g., say, "Excuse me," before interrupting; wait until someone stops speaking to begin talking, etc.).

49. Help the student identify the situations in which he/she is most likely to talk beyond what is expected or at inappropriate times. After he/she has identified these situations, have him/her think of ways to minimize their occurrences.

50. Teach and practice effective communication skills. These skills include listening, maintaining eye contact, and positive body language.

51. Provide the student with many social and academic successes.

52. Make the necessary adjustments in the environment to prevent the student from experiencing stress, frustration, or anger (e.g., reduce peer pressure, academic failure, teasing, etc.).

53. Maintain visibility to and from the student to keep his/her attention at times when he/she should not talk. The teacher should be able to see the student and the student should be able to see the teacher. Make eye contact possible at all times.

54. Interact frequently with the student to reduce the need for him/her to talk beyond what is expected or at inappropriate times.

55. Assess the appropriateness of the social situation in relation to the student's ability to function successfully.

56. Try various groupings in the classroom to determine the situation in which the student is most able to self-monitor his/her behavior.

57. Have a peer cue the student when he/she talks beyond what is expected (e.g., the person can touch the student on the arm as a signal that the he/she is talking at an inappropriate time).

58. Write a contract with the student specifying what behavior is expected (e.g., making short, appropriate comments and speaking at appropriate times) and what reinforcement will be made available when the terms of the contract have been met.

59. Explain to the student, after telling him/her to stop talking, the reason why he/she should not be talking.

60. Make the student aware of the number of times he/she talks beyond what is expected and at inappropriate times.

61. Teach the student to attend to the source of information by maintaining eye contact, keeping hands free from other materials, and reducing other distractions.

62. Make certain that the student understands the relationship between inappropriate behavior and the consequences which follow (e.g., talking beyond what is expected or at inappropriate times will cause others to not want to be around him/her).

63. Teach the student to recognize when to speak, to know how much to say, and to make appropriate comments (e.g., brief comments, comments within the context of the situation, comments that are a follow-up to what has just been said, etc.).

64. Have the student work in small groups in which he/she would have frequent opportunities to speak. As the student learns to wait longer for his/her turn to speak, gradually increase the size of the group.

121 Climbs on things

Goals:

1. The student will refrain from climbing on things.

Objectives:

1. The student will refrain from climbing on things for ____ minutes at a time. (Gradually increase expectations as the student demonstrates success.)
2. The student will demonstrate behavior appropriate for the situation on ____ out of ____ trials.
3. The student will cease climbing on things when cued by the teacher on ____ out of ____ trials.

Interventions:

1. Immediately remove the student from potentially dangerous situations.

2. When the student has behaved in a dangerous manner, explain what he/she has done wrong (e.g., running in the halls, climbing on the table, etc.) and what he/she should be doing (e.g., walking down the hall, sitting next to the table, etc.).

3. Deliver instructions in a supportive rather than a threatening manner (e.g., "Please sit down." instead of "You had better sit down or else!").

4. Reinforce those students in the classroom who refrain from climbing.

5. Reinforce the student for refraining from climbing based upon the length of time that he/she can be successful. As the student demonstrates success, gradually increase the amount of time required for reinforcement.

6. Reinforce the student for refraining from climbing: (a) give the student a tangible reward (e.g., special privileges, line leading, passing out materials, etc.) or (b) give the student an intangible reward (e.g., praise, handshake, pat on the back, etc.).

7. Remove the student from the group activity until he/she can refrain from engaging in dangerous activities.

8. Provide the student with the most attractive and interesting activities possible.

9. Choose a peer to model refraining from climbing for the student.

10. Interact frequently with the student to prevent the student from climbing on things.

11. Maintain visibility to and from the student. The teacher should be able to see the student and the student should be able to see the teacher. Make eye contact possible at all times.

12. Facilitate appropriate behaviors by providing a full schedule of daily events. Prevent lag time when the student would be more likely to engage in climbing on things.

13. Interact frequently with the student to maintain his/her attention to the activities at hand (e.g., ask the student questions, ask the student's opinion, stand close to the student, seat the student near the teacher, etc.).

14. Maintain supervision at all times and in all parts of the school environment.

15. Prevent the student from becoming overstimulated (i.e., monitor or supervise the student's behavior to limit overexcitement in physical activities, games, parties, etc.).

16. Provide the student with a predetermined signal when he/she begins to climb on things.

17. Make certain that reinforcement is not inadvertently given for inappropriate behavior (e.g., attending to the student only when he/she engages in climbing on things, etc.).

18. Communicate with parents (e.g., notes home, phone calls, etc.) to share information concerning the student's appropriate behavior. The parents may reinforce the student at home for refraining from climbing.

19. Intervene early when there is a problem to prevent more serious problems from occurring.

20. Explain the logical consequences of climbing on things (e.g., hurting himself/herself, injuring other students, losing privileges, damaging property, etc.).

21. Implement logical consequences for students who fail to refrain from climbing on things (e.g., time outs, loss of free-play periods, restricted play opportunities on the playground, etc.).

22. Teach the student to "think" before acting (e.g., ask himself/herself "What is happening?" "What am I doing?" "What should I do?" "What will be best for me?").

23. Evaluate the appropriateness of the task to determine (a) if the task is too easy, (b) if the task is too difficult, and (c) if the length of time scheduled to complete the task is adequate.

24. Model for the student appropriate self-relaxation activities when he/she feels the urge to behave dangerously (e.g., count to three, take three deep breaths, choose a new activity, tell the teacher, etc.).

25. Make certain that the student does not become involved in overstimulating activities.

26. Provide the student with adequate physical outlets throughout the day. This will provide a positive format for excess energy.

122   Lies, denies, exaggerates, distorts the truth

Goals:

1. The student will relate information in an accurate manner.
2. The student will accept responsibility for his/her behavior.
3. The student will tell the truth.

Objectives:

1. The student will relate information in an accurate manner on ___ out of ___ trials.
2. The student will accept responsibility for his/her behavior when confronted by the teacher on ___ out of ___ trials.
3. The student will tell the truth on ___ out of ___ trials.
4. The student will refrain from denying his/her behavior on ___ out of ___ trials.
5. The student will accurately represent information on ___ out of ___ trials.
6. The student will report details in an accurate manner on ___ out of ___ trials.
7. The student will admit to his/her behavior on ___ out of ___ trials.

Interventions:

1. Explain to the student that he/she should be satisfied with personal best effort rather than expecting perfection.

2. Provide the student with many social and academic successes.

3. Provide the student with positive feedback which indicates he/she is successful.

4. Reduce competitiveness in information sharing so the student will not feel compelled to make inaccurate statements about his/her experience.

5. Try various groupings to determine the situation in which the student is most comfortable and does not feel compelled to lie, deny, exaggerate the truth, etc.

6. Provide the student with experiences which can be shared if the absence of such experiences has been causing the student to fabricate information.

7. Reduce or remove punishment for accidents, forgetting, and situations with inadequate evidence. Punishment in these situations often causes students to lie.

8. Treat the student with respect. Talk in an objective manner at all times.

9. Do not punish the student unless you are absolutely sure he/she lied to you.

10. Teach the student that making inaccurate statements does not prevent consequences (e.g., the student has to redo an assignment even though he/she claims the completed assignment was lost).

11. Take no action in situations where conclusive evidence does not exist.

12. Allow natural consequences to occur when the student lies, denies, exaggerates, etc., (e.g., work not completed must be completed, lying to others will cause them not to believe you, etc.).

13. Help the student learn that telling the truth as soon as possible prevents future problems (e.g., admitting that he/she made a mistake, forgot, etc., means that the necessary steps can be taken to correct the situation instead of waiting until the truth is determined in some other way).

14. Help the student to understand that by exaggerating the truth he/she may even come to believe what he/she exaggerates and that exaggerating may become a habit.

15. Teach the student to "think" before acting (e.g., ask himself/herself "What is happening?" "What am I doing?" "What should I do?" "What will be best for me?").

16. Develop a system of shared responsibility (e.g., instead of trying to determine who is guilty, classmates work together to help clean up, return materials, make repairs, etc.).

17. Supervise the student closely to monitor the accuracy of statements made.

18. Avoid making accusations which would increase the probability of the student making inaccurate statements in response. If it is known that the student is responsible, an admission of guilt is not necessary to deal with the situation.

19. Avoid putting the student in a situation in which he/she has the opportunity to lie, deny, exaggerate, etc., (e.g., highly competitive activities, situations with limited supervision, etc.).

20. Communicate with parents (e.g., notes home, phone calls, etc.) to share information concerning the student's progress. The parents may reinforce the student at home for making accurate statements at school.

21. Make certain the student understands that not being honest when confronted will result in more negative consequences than telling the truth. Be certain to be very consistent in this approach.

22. Speak with the student to explain (a) what the student is doing wrong (e.g., lying, denying his/her behavior, etc.) and (b) what the student should be doing (e.g., reporting accurately what has occurred or will occur).

23. Reinforce the student for making accurate statements: (a) give the student a tangible reward (e.g., classroom privileges, line leading, passing out materials, five minutes free time, etc.) or (b) give the student an intangible reward (e.g., praise, handshake, smile, etc.).

24. Attempt to have an open, honest relationship with the student. Encourage the student to tell the truth, and do not use threats to make him/her tell the truth (e.g., "You had better tell the truth or else!").

25. Write a contract with the student specifying what behavior is expected (e.g., making accurate statements) and what reinforcement will be made available when the terms of the contract have been met.

123   Is unpredictable in behavior

Goals:
1. The student will demonstrate behavior that is predictable.
2. The student will respond to situations in a predictable manner.

Objectives:
1. The student will respond consistently to similar situations in the environment on ___out of ___ trials.
2. The student will respond consistently to situations in the environment for ___day(s) at a time.
3. The student will respond consistently to situations in the environment for ___week(s) at a time.
4. The student will respond consistently to situations in the environment for ___month(s) at a time.
5. The student will show emotion that is appropriate to the situation on ___out of ___trials.
6. The student will react in a manner appropriate to the situation on ___out of ___trials.
7. The student will maintain his/her orientation to time and place for ___day(s) at a time.
8. The student will maintain his/her orientation to time and place for ___week(s) at a time.
9. The student will maintain his/her orientation to time and place for ___month(s) at a time.

Interventions:

1. Reduce stimuli which would contribute to unrelated or inappropriate behavior (e.g., testing situations, peers, physical activities, etc.).

2. Modify or adjust situations that cause the student to demonstrate unrelated or inappropriate behavior (e.g., keep the student from becoming overstimulated in activities).

3. Make the necessary adjustments in the environment to prevent the student from experiencing stress, frustration, anger, etc., as much as possible.

4. Reduce distracting stimuli (e.g., place the student in the front row, provide a carrel or quiet place away from distractions, etc.). This is used as a means of reducing distracting stimuli and not as a form or punishment.

5. Try various groupings to determine the situation in which the student demonstrates appropriate behavior.

6. Model socially acceptable behavior for the student (e.g., pat on the back, handshake, etc.).

7. Make certain that reinforcement is not inadvertently given for inappropriate comments or behaviors.

8. Prevent the student from becoming overstimulated by an activity (i.e., monitor or supervise student behavior to limit overstimulation in physical activities, games, parties, etc.).

9. Choose a peer to work with the student to model appropriate behavior.

10. Reduce the emphasis on competition. Repeated failure may result in unpredictable behavior.

11. Make the student aware of activities or events well in advance so he/she may prepare for them.

12. Discuss concerns with other professionals to determine if further investigation is warranted (e.g., abuse or neglect).

13. Explain that concerns or worries, while legitimate, are not unusual for students (e.g., everyone worries about tests, grades, etc.).

14. Provide the student with opportunities for social and academic success.

15. Separate the student from the peer(s) who may be encouraging or stimulating the inappropriate behavior.

16. Provide praise and recognition of appropriate behavior as often as possible.

17. Teach the student to "think" before acting (e.g., ask himself/herself "What is happening?" "What am I doing?" "What should I do?" "What will be best for me?").

18. Do not leave a lot of unstructured time for the student.

19. Structure the environment so time does not permit opportunities for the student to demonstrate inappropriate behavior.

20. Provide the student with alternative approaches to testing (e.g., test the student verbally, make tests shorter, let the student respond verbally, let the student take the test in the resource room, etc.).

21. Avoid discussion of topics sensitive to the student (e.g., divorce, death, unemployment, alcoholism, etc.).

22. Provide as many enjoyable and interesting activities as possible.

23. Provide a consistent routine for the student to facilitate stability.

24. Allow flexibility in meeting academic demands when the student demonstrates sudden or dramatic mood changes (e.g., allow more time, modify assignments, provide help with assignments).

25. Teach the student to recognize sudden or dramatic changes in behavior so he/she may deal with it appropriately.

26. Inform the student in advance when a change at school is going to occur (e.g., change in routine, special events, end of one activity and beginning of another, etc.).

27. Give the student adequate time to make adjustments to activity changes, new situations, etc., (e.g., provide the student with several minutes to move from one activity to another).

28. Prevent the occurrence of specific stimuli that cause the student to demonstrate sudden or dramatic changes in behavior (e.g., demanding situations, interruptions, competition, abrupt changes, etc.).

29. Provide the student with a selection of assignments and require the student to choose a minimum number from the total amount (e.g., present the student with ten academic tasks from which six must be finished that day).

30. Provide the student with a schedule of daily events so the student will know what is expected of him/her.

31. Deliver a predetermined signal (e.g., quiet sign, hand signal, verbal cue, etc.) when the student begins to demonstrate an inappropriate behavior.

32. Provide a pleasant/calm atmosphere which would lessen the possibility of sudden or dramatic changes in behavior.

33. Reduce distracting stimuli (e.g., place the student in the front row, provide a carrel or quiet place away from distractions, etc.). This is used as a means of reducing stimuli and not as punishment.

34. Do not criticize. When correcting the student, be honest yet supportive. Never cause the student to feel negatively about himself/herself.

35. Treat the student with respect. Talk in an objective manner at all times.

36. Intervene early when there is a problem to prevent more serious problems from occurring.

37. Be careful to avoid embarrassing the student by giving him/her orders, demands, etc., in front of others.

38. Teach the student appropriate ways to communicate displeasure, anger, frustration, etc.

39. Encourage the student to use problem-solving skills: (a) identify the problem, (b) identify goals and objectives, (c) develop strategies, (d) develop a plan for action, and (e) carry out the plan.

40. Evaluate the appropriateness of the task to determine (a) if the task is too easy, (b) if the task is too difficult, and (c) if the length of time scheduled to complete the task is adequate.

41. Communicate with parents (e.g., notes home, phone calls, etc.) to share information concerning the student's progress. The parents may reinforce the student at home for demonstrating appropriate behaviors related to situations at school.

42. Write a contract with the student specifying what behavior is expected (e.g., demonstrating appropriate behavior related to the situation) and what reinforcement will be made available when the terms of the contract have been met.

43. Remove the student from the group or activity until he/she can demonstrate appropriate behavior and self-control.

44. Speak with the student to explain (a) what the student is doing wrong and (b) what the student should be doing.

45. Reinforce the student for demonstrating appropriate behavior: (a) give the student a tangible reward (e.g., classroom privileges, line leading, passing out materials, five minutes free time, etc.) or (b) give the student an intangible reward (e.g., praise, handshake, smile, etc.).

46. Establish classroom rules:
- Work on-task.
- Remain in your seat.
- Finish task.
- Meet task expectations.
- Raise your hand.

Review rules often. Reinforce students for following rules.

47. Reinforce the student for demonstrating appropriate behavior related to the situation based on the length of time the student can be successful.

48. Reinforce those students in the classroom who demonstrate appropriate behavior related to the situation.

Reminder: Do not "force" the student to participate in any activity he/she finds unpleasant, embarrassing, etc.

124 Ignores consequences of his/her behavior

Goals:
1. The student will consider consequences of his/her behavior.
2. The student will demonstrate consideration of consequences of his/her behavior.

Objectives:
1. The student will identify appropriate consequences of his/her behavior with the teacher on _____ out of _____ trials.
2. The student will behave in such a way as to demonstrate that he/she considered consequences of his/her behavior on _____ out of _____ trials.
3. The student will refrain from reacting impulsively on _____ out of _____ trials.
4. The student will demonstrate consideration of consequences of his/her behavior on _____ out of _____ trials.
5. The student will demonstrate behaviors that will result in positive consequences on _____ out of _____ trials.

Interventions:

1. Communicate with parents (e.g., notes home, phone calls, etc.) to share information concerning the student's progress. The parents may reinforce the student at home for engaging in appropriate behaviors at school.

2. Inform others who will be working with the student (e.g., teachers, principal, clerks, etc.) about the student's tendency to ignore the consequences of his/her behaviors.

3. Allow natural consequences to occur (e.g., hitting others will result in suspension, stealing will result in being fined, etc.) due to the student's failure to consider the consequences of his/her behavior.

4. Intervene early when there is a problem to prevent a more serious problem from occurring.

5. Talk with the student's family, a school official, a social worker, a mental health worker, etc., about the student's failure to consider the consequences of his/her behavior.

6. Structure the environment to limit opportunities for inappropriate behavior (e.g., keep the student engaged in activities, have the student seated near the teacher, maintain visibility to and from the student, etc.).

7. Educate the student about ADHD and the need to self-monitor behavior.

8. Help the student realize that all behavior has negative or positive consequences. Encourage the student to practice behaviors that will lead to positive consequences.

9. Consider carefully the student's age and ability level before expecting him/her to always think before acting.

10. Remind the student to "stop and think" when he/she begins to do something without thinking first.

11. Teach the student to stop and think about the consequences of his/her behavior before behaving in a certain manner.

12. Encourage the student to pause and consider his/her thoughts before acting on them.

13. Educate yourself and others about ADHD to increase understanding and accommodation of impulsive behavior.

14. Provide constant, positive reinforcement for appropriate behavior. Ignore as many inappropriate behaviors as possible.

15. Reinforce the student for demonstrating appropriate behavior based on the length of time the student can be successful. As the student demonstrates success, gradually increase the length of time required for reinforcement.

16. Help the student develop an awareness of the consequences of his/her behavior by writing down or talking through problems which may occur due to his/her failure to consider the consequences of his/her behavior.

17. Teach the student to "think" before acting (e.g., ask himself/herself "What is happening?" "What am I doing?" "What should I do?" "What will be best for me?").

18. Teach problem-solving skills:
- Identify the problem.
- Identify the goals and objectives.
- Develop a strategy/plan for action.
- Carry out the plan.
- Evaluate the results.

19. Discuss consequences with the student before he/she begins an activity (e.g., cheating in a game will result in the game ending and people not playing again).

20. Immediately stop the student from behaving inappropriately and discuss the consequences of the behavior with him/her.

21. Make the consequence of a behavior obvious by identifying the consequence as it occurs and discussing alternative behavior which would have prevented the particular consequence.

22. Reinforce those students in the classroom who engage in appropriate behavior.

23. Provide the student with a clearly understood list of consequences for inappropriate behavior.

24. Make certain that the student understands the relationship between inappropriate behavior and the consequences which follow.

25. Have the student review the consequences of his/her behavior with someone he/she trusts. Have the student consider different choices he/she could have made and the different outcomes.

26. Have the student make a list of consequences associated with frequently occurring behaviors (e.g., by disrupting others, he/she will be perceived as unmannerly; by behaving aggressively, people will avoid him/her.).

27. Explain to the student when he/she fails to consider the consequences of his/her behavior exactly what he/she did wrong, what he/she should have done, and why.

28. Make certain that consequences are delivered consistently for behavior demonstrated (e.g., appropriate behavior results in positive consequences and inappropriate behavior results in negative consequences).

29. Each time a consequence is delivered, whether it is positive or negative, have the student explain to you why he/she thinks it happened.

30. Provide a learning experience which emphasizes the cause-and-effect relationship between inappropriate behavior and the inevitability of some form of consequence (e.g., both negative and positive behaviors and consequences).

31. Speak with the student to explain (a) what he/she is doing wrong (e.g., taking action before thinking about what he/she is doing) and (b) what he/she should be doing (e.g., considering consequences, thinking about the correct response, considering other persons, etc.).

32. Remove the student from the group or activity until he/she can demonstrate appropriate behavior and self-control.

33. Reinforce the student for engaging in appropriate behavior: (a) give the student a tangible reward (e.g., classroom privileges, passing out materials, five minutes free time, etc.) or (b) give the student an intangible reward (e.g., praise, handshake, smile, etc.).

34. Encourage the student to avoid ingesting any substance (e.g., drugs, alcohol, cold remedies, etc.) that might further alter his/her ability to maintain self-control.

35. Clarify for the student that it is his/her behavior which determines whether consequences are positive or negative.

36. Provide the student with natural consequences for inappropriate behavior (e.g., for disturbing others during group activities, the student should have to leave the activity).

37. Maintain a routine that will minimize erratic or impulsive behavior which may result in negative consequences.

38. Discuss with the student the need to avoid situations in which he/she may engage in risky behavior (e.g., if he/she is more likely to drive fast when his/her friends are in the car, do not drive with friends in the car; abstain from drinking alcohol during parties, etc.).

39. Make certain the student does not become involved in overstimulating activities.

40. Provide the student with many social and academic successes.

41. Be certain to take every opportunity to explain to the student that it is his/her behavior that determines whether consequences are positive or negative.

42. Point out the consequences of other students' behavior as they occur (e.g., take the opportunity to point out that consequences occur for all behavior and for all persons).

43. Prevent the student from becoming over-stimulated by an activity (e.g., frustrated, angry, excited, etc.).

44. Establish classroom rules:
- Work on-task.
- Work quietly.
- Remain in your seat.
- Finish task.
- Meet task expectations.

Review rules often. Reinforce students for following the rules.

45. Have the student list the pros and cons of an action and determine if the pros outweigh the cons before he/she takes action.

46. Consult with a mental health provider about the student's failure to consider the consequences of his/her behavior.

47. Help the student identify the situations in which he/she is most likely to fail to consider the consequences of his/her behavior. After he/she has identified these situations, have him/her think of ways to minimize their occurrences.

48. Supervise the student closely in situations in which he/she is likely to act impulsively and without considering the consequences (e.g., maintain close physical proximity, maintain eye contact, communicate frequently with the student, etc.).

49. Allow the student more decision making opportunities relative to class activities and assignments.

50. Write a contract with the student specifying what behavior is expected (e.g., acting in a deliberate and responsible manner) and what reinforcement will be made available when the terms of the contract have been met.

51. Show an interest in the student (e.g., acknowledge the student, ask the student's opinion, spend time working one-to-one with the student, etc.).

52. Make it possible for the student to earn those things he/she wants or needs so that he/she will not engage in inappropriate behavior to get them (e.g., lying or stealing to get something important to him/her).

53. Make certain the student understands that consequences naturally follow behavior. You do not make the consequence happen; it is his/her behavior that makes the consequence occur.

54. Give the student responsibilities in the classroom (e.g., teacher assistant, peer tutor, group leader, etc.).

55. Avoid competition. Failure may cause the student to ignore the consequences of his/her behavior.

56. Encourage the student to consider the consequences of his/her behavior before engaging in any activity.

57. Deliver natural consequences to help the student learn that his/her behavior determines the consequences which follow (e.g., work not done during work time has to be made up during recreational time, what he/she wastes or destroys has to be replaced by him/her, etc.).

58. Prevent peers from engaging in those behaviors which would cause the student to fail to consider or regard the consequences of his/her behavior (e.g., keep other students from upsetting the student).

59. Do not allow the student to use ADHD as an excuse. Hold the student responsible for his/her actions. However, understand and accept problems that ADHD brings into the student's life while he/she is learning to make accommodations.

125 Does not demonstrate appropriate behavior

Goals:

1. The student will demonstrate appropriate behavior in academic settings.
2. The student will demonstrate appropriate behavior in nonacademic settings.
3. The student will demonstrate appropriate behavior for the immediate environment.

Objectives:

1. The student will follow rules for appropriate behavior before school on ____out of ____days.
2. The student will follow rules for appropriate behavior after school on ____out of ____days.
3. The student will keep hands to his/her side when moving with a group on ____ out of ____ occasions.
4. The student will walk quietly when moving with a group on ____ out of ____ occasions.
5. The student will remain in his/her position in line when moving with a group on ___out of ___occasions.
6. The student will talk quietly in nonacademic settings on ____out of ____occasions.
7. The student will refrain from making physical contact with others in nonacademic settings on ___out of ____ occasions.
8. The student will follow rules in nonacademic settings with supervision on ____out of ____occasions.
9. The student will independently follow rules in nonacademic settings on ____out of ____occasions.
10. The student will take turns on ____ out of ____ occasions.
11. The student will share on ____ out of ____ occasions.
12. The student will work quietly in an academic setting on ____out of ____occasions.
13. The student will remain seated in an academic setting on ____out of ____occasions.
14. The student will follow directions in an academic setting on ____out of ____occasions.
15. The student will adjust verbal behavior to different situations on ____out of ___occasions.
16. The student will adjust physical behavior to different situations on ____out of ___occasions.
17. The student will adjust behavior to the rules of different situations on ____out of ___occasions.
18. The student will adjust behavior to different situations with verbal prompts on ____out of ___occasions.
19. The student will independently adjust behavior to different situations on ____out of ____occasions.

Interventions:

1. Allow a transition period when changing environments so the student can make adjustments in his/her behavior.

2. Speak to the student to explain (a) what he/she is doing wrong (e.g., failing to adapt his/her behavior to the immediate environment) and (b) what he/she should be doing (e.g., adapting his/her behavior to the immediate environment).

3. Reduce the student's involvement in activities which prove too stimulating for him/her.

4. Maintain a consistent daily routine.

5. Maintain consistent expectations within the ability level of the student.

6. Provide the student with clearly stated expectations for all situations.

7. Establish free time rules:
- Find an activity.
- Work or spend time quietly.
- Remain in assigned areas.
- Put materials away when free time is over.

Review rules often. Reinforce students for following rules.

8. Reinforce the student for demonstrating the appropriate behavior for the immediate environment: (a) give the student a tangible reward (e.g., classroom privileges, line leading, passing out materials, five minutes free time, etc.) or (b) give the student an intangible reward (e.g., praise, handshake, smile, etc.).

9. Prevent the student from becoming over stimulated by an activity. Supervise student behavior to limit overexcitement in physical activities, games, parties, etc.

10. Establish classroom rules:
- Work on-task.
- Remain in your seat.
- Finish task.
- Meet task expectations.
- Raise your hand.

Review rules often. Reinforce students for following rules.

11. Reinforce those students in the classroom who demonstrate the appropriate behavior (e.g., walking, sitting, speaking, controlling temper, etc.) for the immediate environment.

12. Reinforce the student for demonstrating acceptable behavior based on the length of time the student can be successful. As the student demonstrates success, gradually increase the length of time required for reinforcement.

13. Write a contract with the student specifying what behavior is expected (e.g., adapting his/her behavior to the immediate environment) and what reinforcement will be made available when the terms of the contract have been met.

14. Communicate with parents (e.g., notes home, phone calls, etc.) to share information concerning the student's progress. The parents may reinforce the student at home for demonstrating appropriate behavior for the immediate environment at school.

15. Evaluate the appropriateness of the task to determine (a) if the task is too easy, (b) if the task is too difficult, and (c) if the length of time scheduled to complete the task is adequate.

16. Have the student question any directions, expectations, instruction he/she does not understand.

17. Choose a peer to model appropriate behavior for the student.

18. Establish definite time limits and provide the student with this information before the student must move to a different environment.

19. Allow the student to finish an activity, unless it will be disruptive to the schedule, before he/she is required to move to a different environment.

20. Provide the student with a list of materials that will be needed when he/she is moving to a different setting (e.g., pencil, paper, textbook, workbook, etc.).

21. Establish rules that are to be followed in various parts of the school building (e.g., lunchroom, music room, art room, gymnasium, library, playground, etc.). Review the rules before entering into the specific environment.

22. Identify the expectations of different environments and help the student develop the skills to be successful in those environments.

23. In conjunction with other school personnel, develop as much consistency across the various environments as possible (e.g., rules, criteria for success, behavioral expectations, consequences, etc.).

24. Have the student engage in relaxing transitional activities designed to reduce the effects of stimulating activities (e.g., put head on desk, listen to the teacher read a story, put headphones on and listen to relaxing music, etc.).

25. Assess the quality and clarity of directions, explanations, and instructions given to the student.

26. Have the student maintain a record (e.g., chart or graph) of his/her behavior in different environments.

27. Maintain mobility to provide assistance to the student if he/she begins to demonstrate inappropriate behavior in his/her immediate environment.

28. Deliver a predetermined signal (e.g., hand signal, verbal cue, etc.) when the student begins to demonstrate inappropriate behavior in his/her immediate environment.

29. Provide the student with a schedule for the day so he/she will know exactly what environments he/she will be in and when it will be necessary to go there.

30. Do not require the student to go to an environment where he/she is unable to demonstrate appropriate behavior (e.g., do not make the student go to an assembly if he/she is not capable of controlling his/her behavior in that environment.).

31. Allow the student the option of completing an activity in a different setting (e.g., allow the student to complete a test in isolation if he/she cannot remain on task in the classroom.).

32. Assess the appropriateness of having the student engage in activities in certain environments in which he/she has difficulty being successful (e.g., if the student cannot demonstrate appropriate behavior in the cafeteria have him/her eat in another room). As he/she demonstrates success for increasing periods of time, gradually integrate the student.

33. Instruct the student in the appropriate behavior for each environment in which he/she is expected to function successfully.

34. Instruct the student in appropriate line behavior (e.g., waiting quietly, refraining from physical contact, moving with the line, etc.).

35. Encourage the student to report problems that occur in various environments (e.g., being bullied, teased by other students, etc.).

36. Make certain the student is aware of the expectations of the activity (e.g., go over rules and directions/instructions often).

37. Make certain the student understands that participating in nonacademic situations is contingent upon appropriate behavior.

38. Teach the student problem-solving skills so he/she may better deal with problems that may occur in various environments (e.g., talking, walking away, calling upon an arbitrator, compromising, etc.).

39. Through observations and interviews with others, determine those characteristics of the student which interfere with appropriate behavior in various environments to determine skills or behaviors the student needs to develop for appropriate behavior.

40. Make certain the student understands that failing to demonstrate appropriate behavior in the immediate environment may result in removal from the activity and/or loss of participation in future activities.

41. Separate the student from the peer(s) who stimulates the student's inappropriate behavior when in specific environments.

42. Give the student the responsibility of helping others in the immediate environment.

43. Allow the student to be present in the immediate environment without requiring active participation. Require more involvement over time.

44. Reduce the emphasis on competition. Fear of failure may cause the student to behave inappropriately.

45. Place the student with peers who will be appropriate role models and are likely to facilitate his/her academic and behavioral success.

46. Intervene early to prevent the student's behavior from becoming inappropriate.

47. Maintain a positive, professional relationship with the student (i.e., an adversarial relationship is likely to result in failure to follow rules).

48. Give the student preferred responsibilities.

49. Provide the student with many social and academic successes.

50. Maintain maximum supervision of the student, gradually decreasing supervision over time.

51. Group the student with peers who are least likely to encourage inappropriate behavior.

52. Prepare the student in advance of the delivery of specific environmental cues for the immediate environment to facilitate the opportunity for appropriate behavior.

53. Role play with the student, various environments which he/she is likely to experience (e.g., move theater, restaurant, library, school assembly, etc.). Demonstrate appropriate behavior for each environment.

54. Before entering a new environment, review rules with the student (e.g., "When we go to the library, we whisper when talking to others." etc.).

55. Model for the student appropriate behavior for different environments (e.g., keeping hands to yourself in the hallway, sitting with your feet on the floor, talking quietly in the lunchroom, etc.).

56. Teach the student strategies to deal with controlling his/her temper in various environments (e.g., stop and count to ten, walk away from the situation, look for a friend, look for a teacher, etc.).

57. Allow natural consequences to occur as a result of the student's failure to demonstrate appropriate behavior in the immediate environment (e.g., being asked to leave the movies for talking out loud, people staring in a restaurant for yelling angrily at the waitress, being fired for sleeping at work, etc.).

126 Needs immediate rewards, reinforcement, or gratification to demonstrate appropriate behavior

Goals:

1. The student will demonstrate the ability to delay rewards/reinforcement.

Objectives:

1. The student will delay rewards/reinforcement for ___ minutes at a time. (Gradually increase expectations as the student demonstrates success.)
2. The student will delay rewards/reinforcement until he/she has successfully completed ___ task(s). (Gradually increase expectations as the student demonstrates success.)
3. The student will delay rewards/reinforcement until the end of the school day on ___ out of ___ trials.
4. The student will delay rewards/reinforcement for ___ week(s). (Gradually increase expectations as the student demonstrates success.)
5. The student will delay rewards/reinforcement for up to ___ months. (Gradually increase expectations as the student demonstrates success.)
6. The student will work for ___ minutes without requiring rewards/reinforcement. (Gradually increase expectations as the student demonstrates success.)
7. The student will complete ___ tasks without requiring rewards/reinforcement. (Gradually increase expectations as the student demonstrates success.)

Interventions:

1. Have the student maintain a chart representing his/her own appropriate behavior so success is recognized.

2. Provide the student with positive feedback which indicates he/she is successful, competent, important, valuable, etc., (e.g., provide social reinforcement in place of tangible reinforcement).

3. Make certain that natural consequences follow appropriate behavior (e.g., recognition from the group for success, compliments, congratulations, etc.).

4. Reduce the emphasis on material rewards and increase the emphasis on intrinsic rewards (e.g., emphasize a job well done, improvement, personal success, etc.).

5. Provide the student with an abundance of tangible reinforcement so it may satisfy his/her need for gratification.

6. Present the task in an attractive and interesting manner with as much success built in as possible (e.g., the task should be inherently reinforcing).

7. Be certain to greet and acknowledge the student as often as possible rather than providing recognition only as a reinforcer.

8. Encourage the student to save tokens, points, etc., over time for delayed reinforcement (e.g., make tangible reinforcement a goal rather than an immediate need).

9. Make certain that reinforcement is not inadvertently given for inappropriate behavior (e.g., responding to the student only when he/she makes errors, responding to the student when he/she misrepresents a need for help, etc.).

10. Interact frequently with the student to replace tangible reinforcement with social reinforcement.

11. Reinforce with tangibles less often as the student experiences more satisfaction with a job well done (i.e., intrinsic satisfaction begins to replace tangibles as reinforcement).

12. Make certain that reinforcement is used as a natural consequence for a job well done or for appropriate behavior.

13. Reinforce those students who can accept extended time periods between reinforcement.

14. Establish classroom rules:
- Work on-task.
- Remain in your seat.
- Finish task.
- Meet task expectations.
- Raise your hand.

Review rules often. Reinforce students for following rules.

15. Speak with the student to explain (a) what the student is doing wrong (e.g., asking for reinforcement as soon as a task is completed) and (b) what the student should be doing (e.g., waiting for reinforcement until the end of the activity or until an established time, saving tokens or points for reinforcement at a later time, etc.).

16. Reinforce the student as often as necessary while gradually increasing the amount of time between reinforcement: (a) give the student a tangible reward (e.g., classroom privileges, line leading, passing out materials, five minutes free time, etc.) or (b) give the student an intangible reward (e.g., praise, handshake, smile, etc.).

17. Provide reinforcement at routine intervals so the student learns that reinforcement is delayed but forthcoming (e.g., free time, end of the day, Friday afternoon, etc.).

18. Do not criticize. When correcting the student, be honest yet supportive. Never cause the student to feel negatively about himself/herself.

19. Evaluate the appropriateness of the task to determine (a) if the task is too easy, (b) if the task is too difficult, and (c) if the length of time scheduled to complete the task is adequate.

20. Communicate with parents (e.g., notes home, phone calls, etc.) to share information concerning the student's progress. The parents may reinforce the student at home for tolerating extended time periods between reinforcement at school.

21. Write a contract with the student specifying what behavior is expected (e.g., working five minutes without asking for reinforcement) and what reinforcement will be available when the terms of the contract have been met.

127 Does not demonstrate the ability to control temper

Goals:

1. The student will interact appropriately with other students.
2. The student will demonstrate appropriate behavior when angry.
3. The student will demonstrate appropriate behavior when annoyed with others.
4. The student will demonstrate appropriate behavior when upset.

Objectives:

1. The student will refrain from touching other students during _____ out of _____ interactions.
2. The student will be able to settle minor conflicts with peers without becoming physically aggressive during _____ out of _____ interactions.
3. The student will seek teacher assistance when he/she is experiencing difficulty interacting with peers during _____ out of _____ interactions.
4. The student will walk away from peer conflicts during _____ out of _____ interactions.
5. The student will verbally, rather than physically, express his/her feelings toward a peer during _____ out of _____ interactions.
6. The student will be able to settle minor conflicts with others without arguing, yelling, crying, hitting, etc., during _____ out of _____ interactions.
7. The student will tolerate a peer's inappropriate behavior by demonstrating patience and refraining from being verbally or physically aggressive during _____ out of _____ interactions.
8. The student will walk away from a peer or group situation when he/she becomes angry, annoyed, or upset during _____ out of _____ interactions.
9. The student will demonstrate self-control when angered, annoyed, or upset by a peer on _____ out of _____ trials.
10. The student will refrain from arguing, using a harsh tone of voice, yelling, etc., during _____ out of _____ interactions.
11. The student will continue to demonstrate appropriate behavior and interact with others when angry, annoyed, or upset during _____ out of _____ interactions.
12. The student will solve problems by withdrawing from conflict situations during _____ out of _____ interactions.
13. The student will solve problems by reasoning in conflict situations during _____ out of _____ interactions.
14. The student will solve problems by apologizing in conflict situations during _____ out of _____ interactions.
15. The student will solve problems by talking in a quiet, controlled manner in conflict situations during _____ out of _____ interactions.
16. The student will solve problems independently in conflict situations during _____ out of _____ interactions.
17. The student will solve problems in conflict situations by allowing others the benefit of the doubt during _____ out of _____ interactions.

Interventions:

1. Teach and encourage the student to use problem-solving skills: (a) identify the problem, (b) identify goals and objectives, (c) develop strategies, (d) develop a plan for action, and (e) carry out the plan.

2. Provide the student with positive feedback which indicates he/she is successful, important, respected, etc.

3. Prevent frustrating or anxiety-producing situations from occurring (e.g., give the student tasks only on his/her ability level, give the student only the number of tasks that can be tolerated in one sitting, reduce social interactions which stimulate the student to become physically abusive, etc.).

4. Maintain maximum supervision of the student. As the student demonstrates self-control, gradually decrease supervision over time.

5. Maintain visibility to and from the student. The teacher should be able to see the student; the student should be able to see the teacher. Make eye contact possible at all times.

6. Be mobile to be frequently near the student.

7. Reduce activities which might threaten the student (e.g., announcing test score ranges or test scores aloud, making students read aloud in class, emphasizing the success of a particular student or students, etc.).

8. Try various groupings to determine the situation in which the student is most successful.

9. Make the necessary adjustments in the environment to prevent the student from experiencing stress, frustration, and anger.

10. Reduce the emphasis on competition and perfection. Repeated failure and frustration may cause the student to become angered, annoyed, or upset.

11. Teach the student alternative ways to deal with situations which make him/her frustrated, angry, etc., (e.g., withdrawing, talking, etc.).

12. Facilitate on-task behavior by providing a full schedule of daily events. Prevent lag time from occurring when the student would be likely to become involved in activities which would cause him/her to be angered, annoyed, or upset.

13. Maintain supervision so the student is not left alone or allowed to be unsupervised with other students.

14. Provide the student with as many high-interest activities as possible.

15. Provide the student with opportunities for social and academic success.

16. Make other personnel aware of the student's tendency to become easily angered, annoyed, or upset.

17. Provide a quiet place for the student to work independently, away from peer interactions. This is not to be used as a form of punishment but as an opportunity to facilitate the student's success in his/her environment.

18. Place reinforcement emphasis on academic productivity and accuracy to divert the student's attention away from others who cause him/her to become angry, annoyed, or upset.

19. Make the student aware of the natural consequences for becoming easily angered, annoyed, or upset (e.g., loss of friendships, injury, more restrictive environment, legal action, etc.).

20. Separate the student from the peer(s) who may be encouraging or stimulating the student to become angry, annoyed, or upset.

21. Do not force the student to interact or remain in a group if he/she is likely to become angry, annoyed, or upset.

22. Provide the student with a selection of optional activities to be performed if he/she becomes angry, annoyed, or upset.

23. Maintain consistent expectations.

24. Maintain a consistent daily routine.

25. Remove the student from the group or activity until he/she can demonstrate self-control.

26. Maintain a positive, calm environment (e.g., positive comments, acknowledgment of successes, quiet communications, etc.).

27. Allow flexibility in meeting academic demands when the student becomes angry, annoyed, or upset (e.g., allow more time; modify assignments; provide help with assignments; etc.).

28. Present tasks in the most attractive, interesting manner possible.

29. Ask the student why he/she becomes easily angered, annoyed, or upset. The student may have the most accurate perception of why he/she becomes easily angered, annoyed, or upset.

30. Teach the student decision-making steps: (a) think about how others may be influenced, (b) think about consequences, (c) carefully consider the unique situation, (d) think of different courses of action which are possible, and (e) think about what is ultimately best for him/her; etc.

31. Avoid topics, situations, etc., that may cause the student to become easily angered, annoyed, or upset (e.g., divorce, death, unemployment, alcoholism, etc.).

32. Discourage the student from participating in those activities that cause him/her to become easily angered, annoyed, or upset.

33. Teach the student to verbalize his/her feelings before losing self-control (e.g., "The work is hard." "Please leave me alone; you're making me angry." etc.).

34. Deliver directions in a supportive rather than a threatening manner (e.g., "Please finish your math assignment before break time." rather than "You had better finish your math or else!").

35. Do not criticize. When correcting the student, be honest yet supportive. Never cause the student to feel negatively about himself/herself.

36. Intervene early when the student becomes angry, annoyed, or upset to prevent more serious problems from occurring.

37. Make certain the student does not become involved in overstimulating activities which cause him/her to become angry, annoyed, or upset.

38. Treat the student with respect. Talk in an objective manner at all times.

39. Be careful to avoid embarrassing the student by giving him/her orders, demands, etc., in front of others.

40. Find a peer to work with the student who would be a good influence (e.g., someone younger, older, of the same gender, of the opposite gender, etc.).

41. Allow the student to attempt something new in private before doing so in front of others.

42. Teach the student acceptable ways to communicate displeasure, anger, frustration, etc.

43. Do not force the student to interact with others.

44. Make sure you express your feelings in a socially acceptable way.

45. Make certain the student is allowed to voice an opinion in a situation to avoid becoming angry or upset.

46. Teach the student to think before acting (e.g., ask himself/herself "What is happening?" "What am I doing?" "What should I do?" "What will be best for me?").

47. Talk to the student about ways of handling situations successfully without conflict (e.g., walk away from a situation; change to another activity; ask for help; etc.).

48. Have the student question any directions, explanations, instructions not understood.

49. Choose a peer to model self-control for the student.

50. Evaluate the appropriateness of the academic task to determine (a) if the task is too easy, (b) if the task is too difficult, and (c) if the length of time scheduled to complete the task is adequate.

51. Communicate with parents, agencies, or the appropriate parties to inform them of the problem, determine the cause of the problem, and consider possible solutions to the problem.

52. Communicate with parents (e.g., notes home, phone calls, etc.) to share information concerning the student's progress. The parents may reinforce the student at home for demonstrating self-control at school.

53. Write a contract with the student specifying what behavior is expected (e.g., problem solving, moving away from the situation, asking for assistance from the teacher, etc.) and what reinforcement will be made available when the terms of the contract have been met.

54. Reinforce the student for demonstrating self-control based on the length of time the student can be successful. As the student demonstrates self-control, gradually increase the length of time required for reinforcement.

55. Establish classroom rules:
- Work on-task.
- Remain in your seat.
- Finish task.
- Meet task expectations.
- Raise your hand.

Review rules often. Reinforce students for following rules.

56. Speak to the student to explain (a) what the student is doing wrong (e.g., hitting, arguing, throwing things, etc.) and (b) what the student should be doing (e.g., moving away from the situation, asking for assistance from the teacher, etc.).

57. Reinforce those students in the classroom who demonstrate self-control.

58. Reinforce the student for demonstrating self-control in those situations in which he/she is likely to become angry, annoyed, or upset: (a) give the student a tangible reward (e.g., classroom privileges, line leading, passing out materials, five minutes free time, etc.) or (b) give the student an intangible reward (e.g., praise, handshake, smile, etc.).

Goals:

1. The student will handle anger, frustration, disappointment, anxiety, etc., in an appropriate manner.
2. The student will demonstrate self-control.
3. The student will not throw temper tantrums.

Objectives:

1. The student will handle anger, frustration, disappointment, anxiety, etc., in an appropriate manner on ___ out of ___ trials.
2. The student will demonstrate self-control when angry, frustrated, disappointed, anxious, etc., on ___ out of ___ trials.
3. The student will not throw temper tantrums when angry, frustrated, disappointed, anxious, etc., on ___ out of ___ trials.
4. The student will demonstrate appropriate ways in which to express his/her anger, frustration, disappointment, anxiety, etc., on ___ out of ___ trials.

Interventions:

1. Assess the situations in which the student throws temper tantrums. Based on these observations, determine ways to prevent situations from stimulating the student to throw temper tantrums.

2. Try various groupings to determine the situation in which the student is most comfortable.

3. Provide the student with many social and academic successes.

4. Take the time to talk with the student so the student realizes that your interest in him/her is genuine.

5. Teach/demonstrate methods for dealing with problems early to prevent problems from becoming overwhelming.

6. Encourage and help the student to make friends (e.g., pair the student with a peer and when that relationship is successful introduce other peers).

7. Explain to the student that feelings of unhappiness are natural, but there is an appropriate length of time for public display of that emotion.

8. When natural consequences occur as a result of the student's throwing temper tantrums, point them out to the student (e.g., peers prefer not to interact with him/her; property is damaged or destroyed, resulting in loss of use or costly replacement; etc.).

9. Provide the student with as many positive interactions as possible (e.g., recognize the student, greet the student, compliment his/her attire, etc.).

10. Provide the student with preferred responsibilities throughout the school environment.

11. Teach and encourage the student to use problem-solving skills: (a) identify the problem, (b) identify goals and objectives, (c) develop strategies, (d) develop a plan for action, and (e) carry out the plan.

12. Make certain that reinforcement is not inadvertently given for inappropriate behavior (i.e., attending to the student only when he/she throws a temper tantrum).

13. Make certain that consequences for both appropriate and inappropriate behavior are consistent.

14. Encourage and assist the student in joining extracurricular activities, clubs, etc.

15. Move the student away from the peer(s) who may be causing his/her unhappiness.

16. Discourage the student from engaging in those activities which cause him/her unhappiness.

17. Provide the student with positive feedback which indicates he/she is successful, competent, important, respected, etc.

18. Identify individuals the student may contact concerning his/her unhappiness (e.g., guidance counselor, school nurse, social worker, school psychologist, etc.).

19. Give the student additional responsibilities (e.g., chores, errands, etc.) to give him/her a feeling of success or accomplishment.

20. Structure the environment so the student does not have time to dwell on real or imagined problems.

21. Help the student identify how he/she wishes things were in the environment and work with the student toward those goals.

22. Teach the student alternative ways to deal with demands, challenges, and pressures of the school-age experience (e.g., deal with problems when they arise, practice self-control at all times, share problems or concerns with others, etc.).

23. Help the student identify when he/she is getting upset so something can be done to help him/her calm down (e.g., walk away, talk about feelings in a socially acceptable way, seek help from an adult, etc.).

24. Teach the student alternative ways to communicate unhappiness (e.g., communicate in writing, verbally, etc.).

25. Avoid topics, situations, etc., which remind the student of unpleasant experiences or problems (e.g., divorce, death, unemployment, alcoholism, etc.).

26. Follow less desirable activities with more desirable activities.

27. Remove the student from the group or activity until he/she can demonstrate appropriate behavior and self-control.

28. Give the student some decision-making power (e.g., seating assignment, order of tasks, daily schedule, etc.).

29. Reduce the emphasis on competition. Repeated failure may cause the student to throw a temper tantrum.

30. Help the student choose activities that do not cause anger, frustration, anxiety, etc.

31. Ignore the student's temper tantrums. Do not let the student have his/her way when crying.

32. Show the student how to control angry feelings when things do not go his/her way (e.g., count to ten, say the alphabet, etc.).

33. Make certain you do not give into the student's temper tantrums because others are present. Maintain consistency at all times.

34. Write a contract with the student specifying what behavior is expected (e.g., dealing with unhappiness in an appropriate manner) and what reinforcement will be made available when the terms of the contract have been met.

35. Provide the student with alternative activities, games, etc., in case activities prove upsetting.

36. Communicate with parents, agencies, or the appropriate parties to inform them of the problem, determine the cause of the problem, and consider possible solutions to the problem.

37. Evaluate the appropriateness of the task to determine (a) if the task is too easy, (b) if the task is too difficult, and (c) if the length of time scheduled to complete the task is adequate.

38. Communicate with parents (e.g., notes home, phone calls, etc.) to share information concerning the student's progress. The parents may reinforce the student at home for dealing with unhappiness in an appropriate manner at school.

39. After telling the student that he/she cannot do or have something, explain the reason.

40. Provide the student with alternative activities to perform in case some activities prove upsetting.

41. Reinforce the student for dealing with unhappiness in an appropriate manner based on the number of times he/she can be successful. As the student demonstrates success, gradually increase the amount of time required for reinforcement.

42. Reinforce those students in the classroom who deal with unhappiness in an appropriate manner.

43. Establish classroom rules:
- Work on-task.
- Remain in your seat.
- Finish task.
- Meet task expectations.
- Raise your hand.

Review rules often. Reinforce students for following rules.

44. Speak with the student to explain (a) that you recognize that he/she is unhappy and (b) appropriate ways to deal with unhappiness.

45. Reinforce the student for dealing with unhappiness in an appropriate manner (e.g., verbally stating his/her unhappiness, problem-solving, etc.): (a) give the student a tangible reward (e.g., classroom privileges, line leading, passing out materials, five minutes free time, etc.) or (b) give the student an intangible reward (e.g., praise, handshake, smile, etc.).

129 Fails to comply with teachers or other school personnel

Goals:

1. The student will follow directives from teachers.
2. The student will follow directives from school personnel.

Objectives:

1. The student will follow through with teacher directives within _____ minutes.
2. The student will follow through with directions given by school personnel within _____ minutes.
3. The student will follow teacher directives when given _____ cues.
4. The student will follow school personnel directives when given _____ cues.
5. The student will stop an activity when told to do so by the teacher on _____ out of _____ trials.
6. The student will stop an activity when told to do so by school personnel on _____ out of _____ trials.

Interventions

1. Communicate with parents (e.g., notes home, phone calls, etc.) to share information concerning the student's progress. The parents may reinforce the student at home for following directives from teachers and other school personnel.

2. Write a contract with the student specifying what behavior is expected (e.g., following teacher directives) and what reinforcement will be made available when the terms of the contract have been met.

3. Structure the environment so the student remains active and involved in appropriate behavior.

4. Maintain visibility to and from the student to keep his/her attention when verbal questions/ directions are being delivered. The teacher should be able to see the student and the student should be able to see the teacher. Make eye contact possible at all times.

5. Give the student responsibilities he/she prefers.

6. Present assignments in the most interesting and attractive manner possible.

7. Maintain maximum supervision of the student. As the student becomes successful at following directives, gradually decrease supervision.

8. Have the student maintain a chart representing the amount of time spent following teacher directives or rules. Reinforcement should be given for increasing acceptable behavior.

9. Choose a peer to model following teacher directives for the student.

10. Interact with the student frequently to determine if directives are being followed.

11. Maintain consistent rules, routine, and general expectations of conduct and procedure.

12. Allow natural consequences to occur (e.g., removed from activities, losing special privileges, accidents occur, detention, etc.) as a result of not following directives from teachers and other school personnel.

13. Limit the student's opportunity to engage in activities in which he/she will not follow directives from teachers and other school personnel (e.g., industrial arts activities, field trips, etc.).

14. Do not allow the student to be unsupervised anywhere in the school environment.

15. Educate yourself and others about ADHD to increase understanding and accommodation of impulsive behavior.

16. Educate the student about ADHD and the need to self-monitor behavior.

17. Provide constant, positive reinforcement for appropriate behavior. Ignore as many inappropriate behaviors as possible.

18. Have the student develop an awareness of the consequences of his/her behavior by writing down or talking through problems which may occur due to his/her inability to comply with school personnel (e.g., may be suspended, fail necessary courses, etc.).

19. Be mobile to be frequently near the student.

20. Provide the student with many social and academic successes.

21. Provide the student with a clearly understood list of consequences for inappropriate behavior.

22. Discuss with the student the consequences of his/her behavior before engaging in any activity.

23. Have the student review the consequences of his/her behavior with someone he/she trusts. Have the student consider different choices he/she could have made and the different outcomes.

24. Reinforce the student for following directives from teachers or other school personnel: (a) give the student a tangible reward (e.g., classroom privileges, passing out materials, five minutes free time, etc.) or (b) give the student an intangible reward (e.g., praise, handshake, smile, etc.).

25. Speak with the student to explain (a) what he/she is doing wrong (e.g., failing to follow directions or observe rules) and (b) what he/she should be doing (e.g., following established guidelines or expectations).

26. Establish classroom rules:
- Work on-task.
- Remain in your seat.
- Finish task.
- Meet task expectations.
- Raise your hand.

Review rules often. Reinforce students for following rules.

27. Reinforce those students in the classroom who follow directives from teachers and other school personnel.

28. Reinforce the student for following the directives of teachers and other school personnel based on the length of time he/she can be successful. As the student demonstrates success, gradually increase the amount of time required for reinforcement.

29. Remove the student from the group or activity until he/she can demonstrate appropriate behavior and self-control.

30. Develop a behavioral plan specifying expectations and consequences. Reinforce the student for complying with directives.

31. Provide the student with positive feedback that indicates he/she is successful.

32. Post rules in various places, including the student's desk.

33. Make sure the student realizes that all behavior has negative or positive consequences. Encourage the student to practice behaviors that will lead to positive consequences.

34. Explain to the student when he/she does not follow a directive exactly what he/she did wrong, what should have been done, and why.

35. Make certain that the student gains your attention when he/she is behaving appropriately, rather than gaining attention through inappropriate behavior.

36. Encourage the student to express his/her feelings. Teach him/her how to talk about his/her feelings in a controlled manner.

37. Refrain from correcting the student in front of his/her peers as much as possible. The student is more likely to talk back if he/she is told to do something, corrected, etc., in front of friends. Speak with the student in private to scold or correct him/her.

38. Teach and encourage the student to use problem-solving skills: (a) identify the problem, (b) identify the goals and objectives, (c) develop a strategy/plan for action, (d) carry out the plan, and (e) evaluate the results.

39. Separate the student from those individuals who encourage him/her to argue and talk back.

40. Encourage the student to avoid ingesting any substance (e.g., drugs, alcohol, cold remedies, etc.) that might further alter his/her ability to maintain self-control.

41. Be consistent. Do not "give in" to the student's arguing one time and expect directives to be followed the next time.

42. Clarify for the student that it is his/her behavior which determines whether consequences are positive or negative.

43. Consider carefully the student's ability level and experience before asking him/her to do something that may be too difficult and may result in arguing.

44. Make sure the student is paying attention when he/she is told to do something. Have the student make eye contact and repeat the information to check for understanding.

45. Encourage the student to ask permission and/or discuss things he/she wants to do well in advance to avoid misunderstandings. This should increase the likelihood of finding solutions to disagreements without arguing.

46. Have the student list the pros and cons of an action and determine if the pros outweigh the cons before he/she takes action.

47. Consult with a mental health provider about the student's failure to comply with school personnel.

48. Deliver directives in a supportive rather than a threatening manner (e.g., "Please take out your textbook," rather than, "You had better take out your book or else!").

49. Teach the student direction-following skills: listen carefully, ask questions, use environmental cues, rely on examples provided, wait until all directions are given before beginning, etc.

50. Maintain a positive, professional relationship with the student (i.e., an adversarial relationship is likely to result in failure to follow directives).

51. Be a consistent authority figure (e.g., be consistent in relationships with students).

52. Provide the student with optional courses of action to prevent total refusal to obey directives from teachers and other school personnel.

53. Take proactive steps to deal with a student's refusal to perform an assignment to prevent contagion in the classroom (e.g., refrain from arguing with the student, place the student at a carrel or other quiet place to work, remove the student from the group or classroom, etc.).

54. Treat the student and others with respect. He/she will learn to treat others with respect by watching you.

55. Model appropriate ways to question someone's decision.

56. Be consistent in expecting the student to follow directives. Do not allow the student to fail to follow directives one time and expect him/her to comply with directives the next time.

57. Explain to the student the reason why he/she cannot do or have something.

58. Do not argue with the student. Arguing with the student conveys to him/her that arguing and not taking "no" for an answer is acceptable.

59. Remove the student immediately from the presence of others when he/she has difficulty following requests or accepting decisions.

60. Do not "give in" to the student when he/she is arguing and demanding. If you do, the student will continue to argue and demand things to get his/her own way.

61. Do not criticize when correcting the student; be honest yet supportive. Never cause the student to feel negatively about himself/herself.

62. Do not give directions to the student from across the room. Go to the student, get his/her undivided attention, and tell him/her what to do.

63. Do not allow the student to use ADHD as an excuse. Hold the student responsible for his/her actions. However, understand and accept problems that ADHD brings into the student's life while he/she is learning to make accommodations.

64. Establish rules (e.g., listen calmly to what others have to say, state your opinion in a kind manner, make appropriate comments, accept directives from authority figures, etc.). These rules should be consistent and followed by everyone in the class. Talk about the rules often.

65. Give simple, specific directions as to what the student is to do.

66. Be consistent with the student when he/she is unable to follow requests or accept decisions. Decide on an appropriate consequence (e.g., after school/lunch detention) and consistently use the consequence every time the student does not comply.

67. Evaluate the appropriateness of the task to determine (a) if the task is too easy, (b) if the task is too difficult, and (c) if the length of time scheduled for the task is adequate.

68. Make certain the student receives the information necessary to perform activities (e.g., written information, verbal directions, reminders, etc.).

69. Deliver directions in a step-by-step sequence.

130 Is preoccupied (as demonstrated with words or pictures) with drugs or alcohol or possesses or uses drugs or alcohol at school

Goals:

1. The student will not take drugs at school.
2. The student will not drink alcohol at school.
3. The student will follow the school's code of conduct.

Objectives:

1. The student will not take drugs at school for ___ out of ___ days per week.
2. The student will not take drugs at school for ___ out of ___ days per month.
3. The student will not take drugs at school for ___ out of ___ days per semester.
4. The student will not drink alcohol at school for ___ out of ___ days per week.
5. The student will not drink alcohol at school for ___ out of ___ days per month.
6. The student will not drink alcohol at school for ___ out of ___ days per semester.
7. The student will be sober at school for ___ out of ___ days per week.
8. The student will be sober at school for ___ out of ___ days per month.
9. The student will be sober at school for ___ out of ___ days per semester.
10. The student will be free from the influence of drugs for ___ out of ___ days per week.
11. The student will be free from the influence of drugs for ___ out of ___ days per month.
12. The student will be free from the influence of drugs for ___ out of ___ days per semester.

Interventions:

1. Communicate with parents (e.g., notes home, phone calls, etc.) to share information concerning the student's progress. The parents may reinforce the student at home for following directives from teachers and other school personnel.

2. Write a contract with the student specifying what behavior is expected (e.g., following teacher directives) and what reinforcement will be made available when the terms of the contract have been met.

3. Structure the environment in such a way that the student remains active and involved in appropriate behavior.

4. Maintain visibility to and from the student to keep his/her attention when verbal questions/ directions are being delivered. The teacher should be able to see the student and the student should be able to see the teacher. Make eye contact possible at all times.

5. Maintain maximum supervision of the student. As the student becomes successful at following directives, gradually decrease supervision.

6. Present assignments in the most interesting and attractive manner possible.

7. Give the student responsibilities he/she prefers.

8. Have the student maintain a chart representing the amount of time spent following teacher directives or rules. Reinforcement should be given for increasing acceptable behavior.

9. Choose a peer to model following teacher directives for the student.

10. Interact with the student frequently to determine if directives are being followed.

11. Maintain consistent rules, routine, and general expectations of conduct and procedure.

12. Allow natural consequences to occur (e.g., removed from activities, losing special privileges, accidents occur, detention, etc.) as a result of not following directives from teachers and other school personnel.

13. Limit the student's opportunity to engage in activities in which he/she will not follow directives from teachers and other school personnel (e.g., industrial arts activities, field trips, etc.).

14. Do not allow the student to be unsupervised anywhere in the school environment.

15. Educate yourself and others about ADHD to increase understanding and accommodation of impulsive behavior.

16. Educate the student about ADHD and the need to self-monitor behavior.

17. Provide constant, positive reinforcement for appropriate behavior. Ignore as many inappropriate behaviors as possible.

18. Have the student develop an awareness of the consequences of his/her behavior by writing down or talking through problems which may occur due to his/her inability to comply with school personnel (e.g., may be suspended, fail necessary courses, etc.).

19. Be mobile to be frequently near the student.

20. Provide the student with many social and academic successes.

21. Provide the student with positive feedback that indicates he/she is successful.

22. Discuss with the student the consequences of his/her behavior before engaging in any activity.

23. Have the student review the consequences of his/her behavior with someone he/she trusts. Have the student consider different choices he/she could have made and the different outcomes.

24. Make sure the student realizes that all behavior has negative or positive consequences. Encourage the student to practice behaviors that will lead to positive consequences.

25. Explain to the student when he/she does not follow a directive exactly what he/she did wrong, what should have been done, and why.

26. Speak with the student to explain (a) what he/she is doing wrong (e.g., failing to follow directions or observe rules) and (b) what he/she should be doing (e.g., following established guidelines or expectations).

27. Establish classroom rules:
- Work on-task.
- Work quietly.
- Remain in your seat.
- Finish task.
- Meet task expectations.

Review rules often. Reinforce students for following the rules.

28. Reinforce those students in the classroom who follow directives from teachers and other school personnel.

29. Reinforce the student for following the directives of teachers and other school personnel based on the length of time he/she can be successful. As the student demonstrates success, gradually increase the amount of time required for reinforcement.

30. Remove the student from the group or activity until he/she can demonstrate appropriate behavior and self-control.

31. Develop a behavioral plan specifying expectations and consequences. Reinforce the student for complying with directives.

32. Provide the student with a clearly understood list of consequences for inappropriate behavior.

33. Post rules in various places, including the student's desk.

34. Reinforce the student for following directives from teachers or other school personnel: (a) give the student a tangible reward (e.g., classroom privileges, passing out materials, five minutes free time, etc.) or (b) give the student an intangible reward (e.g., praise, handshake, smile, etc.).

35. Make certain that the student gains your attention when he/she is behaving appropriately, rather than gaining attention through inappropriate behavior.

36. Encourage the student to express his/her feelings. Teach him/her how to talk about his/her feelings in a controlled manner.

37. Refrain from correcting the student in front of his/her peers as much as possible. The student is more likely to talk back if he/she is told to do something, corrected, etc., in front of friends. Speak with the student in private to scold or correct him/her.

38. Teach and encourage the student to use problem-solving skills: (a) identify the problem, (b) identify the goals and objectives, (c) develop a strategy/plan for action, (d) carry out the plan, and (e) evaluate the results.

39. Separate the student from those individuals who encourage him/her to argue and talk back.

40. Encourage the student to avoid ingesting any substance (e.g., drugs, alcohol, cold remedies, etc.) that might further alter his/her ability to maintain self-control.

41. Be consistent. Do not "give in" to the student's arguing one time and expect directives to be followed the next time.

42. Clarify for the student that it is his/her behavior which determines whether consequences are positive or negative.

43. Consider carefully the student's ability level and experience before asking him/her to do something that may be too difficult and may result in arguing.

44. Make sure the student is paying attention when he/she is told to do something. Have the student make eye contact and repeat the information to check for understanding.

45. Encourage the student to ask permission and/or discuss things he/she wants to do well in advance to avoid misunderstandings. This should increase the likelihood of finding solutions to disagreements without arguing.

46. Have the student list the pros and cons of an action and determine if the pros outweigh the cons before he/she takes action.

47. Consult with a mental health provider about the student's failure to comply with school personnel.

48. Deliver directives in a supportive rather than a threatening manner (e.g., "Please take out your textbook," rather than, "You had better take out your book or else!").

49. Teach the student direction-following skills: listen carefully, ask questions, use environmental cues, rely on examples provided, wait until all directions are given before beginning, etc.

50. Maintain a positive, professional relationship with the student (i.e., an adversarial relationship is likely to result in failure to follow directives).

51. Be a consistent authority figure (e.g., be consistent in relationships with students).

52. Provide the student with optional courses of action to prevent total refusal to obey directives from teachers and other school personnel.

53. Take proactive steps to deal with a student's refusal to perform an assignment to prevent contagion in the classroom (e.g., refrain from arguing with the student, place the student at a carrel or other quiet place to work, remove the student from the group or classroom, etc.).

54. Treat the student and others with respect. He/she will learn to treat others with respect by watching you.

55. Model appropriate ways to question someone's decision.

56. Be consistent in expecting the student to follow directives. Do not allow the student to fail to follow directives one time and expect him/her to comply with directives the next time.

57. Explain to the student the reason why he/she cannot do or have something.

58. Do not argue with the student. Arguing with the student conveys to him/her that arguing and not taking "no" for an answer is acceptable.

59. Establish rules (e.g., listen calmly to what others have to say, state your opinion in a kind manner, make appropriate comments, accept directives from authority figures, etc.). These rules should be consistent and followed by everyone in the class. Talk about the rules often.

60. Give simple, specific directions as to what the student is to do.

61. Do not criticize when correcting the student; be honest yet supportive. Never cause the student to feel negatively about himself/herself.

62. Do not give directions to the student from across the room. Go to the student, get his/her undivided attention, and tell him/her what to do.

63. Do not allow the student to use ADHD as an excuse. Hold the student responsible for his/her actions. However, understand and accept problems that ADHD brings into the student's life while he/she is learning to make accommodations.

64. Remove the student immediately from the presence of others when he/she has difficulty following requests or accepting decisions.

65. Do not "give in" to the student when he/she is arguing and demanding. If you do, the student will continue to argue and demand things to get his/her own way.

66. Be consistent with the student when he/she is unable to follow requests or accept decisions. Decide on an appropriate consequence (e.g., after school/lunch detention) and consistently use the consequence every time the student does not comply.

131 Engages in inappropriate behaviors related to bodily functions

Goals:

1. The student will engage in appropriate behavior related to bodily functions.
2. The student will use school facilities in an appropriate manner.

Objectives:

1. The student will engage in appropriate behaviors related to bodily functions on ___ out of ___ trials.
2. The student will use school facilities in an appropriate manner on ___ out of ___ trials.
3. The student will use acceptable language when referring to bodily functions on ___ out of ___ trials.
4. The student will only make references to bodily functions when appropriate on ___ out of ___ trials.
5. The student will use the toilet appropriately on ___ out of ___ trials.
6. The student will use the urinal appropriately on ___ out of ___ trials.
7. The student will refrain from masturbating for ___ minutes at a time. (Gradually increase expectations as the student demonstrates success.)
8. The student will interact appropriately with others during ___ out of ___ interactions.
9. The student will appropriately perform necessary bodily functions with supervision on ___ out of ___ trials.
10. The student will independently perform necessary bodily functions in an appropriate manner on ___ out of ___ trials.
11. The student will maintain control of bodily functions ___ out of ___ days per week.
12. The student will ask for assistance related to bodily function when necessary on ___ out of ___ trials.

Interventions:

1. Reinforce the student for demonstrating appropriate behavior related to bodily functions: (a) give the student a tangible reward (e.g., classroom privileges, line leading, passing out materials, five minutes free time, etc.) or (b) give the student an intangible reward (e.g., praise, handshake, smile, etc.).

2. Speak to the student to explain (a) what he/she is doing wrong (e.g., urinating on floor, masturbating, etc.) and (b) what he/she should be doing (e.g., demonstrating appropriate social behavior).

3. Reinforce those students in the classroom who demonstrate appropriate social behavior.

4. Reinforce the student for demonstrating appropriate social behavior based on the length of time he/she can be successful. As the student demonstrates success, gradually increase the length of time required for reinforcement.

5. Write a contract with the student specifying what behavior is expected (e.g., talking about topics which are appropriate for social situations) and what reinforcements will be made available when the terms of the contract have been met.

6. Communicate with parents (e.g., notes home, phone calls, etc.) to share information concerning the student's progress. The parents may reinforce the student at home for demonstrating appropriate social behavior at school.

7. Communicate with parents, agencies, or the appropriate parties to inform them of the problem, determine the cause of the problem, and consider possible solutions to the problem.

8. Evaluate the appropriateness of the task to determine (a) if the task is too easy, (b) if the task is too difficult, and (c) if the length of time scheduled to complete the task is adequate.

9. Discuss appropriate social behavior with the student and make certain he/she understands which behaviors are appropriate for public places and which are not.

10. Provide adequate supervision throughout the school environment to prevent the student from talking about bodily functions, masturbating, etc.

11. Make certain that the student is not inadvertently reinforced for participating in inappropriate behavior related to bodily functions (e.g., deal with the problem privately; avoid reacting in a shocked, disgusted or angry manner, etc.).

12. Make certain that natural consequences follow the student's inappropriate behavior related to bodily functions (e.g., others will not want to interact with the student; require the student to clean up urine, feces, etc.).

13. Do not leave the student unsupervised.

14. Remove the student from the group or activity until he/she demonstrates appropriate behavior.

15. Remove the student from the peer or situation which stimulates him/her to engage in inappropriate behavior related to bodily functions.

16. Inform other school personnel to make them aware of the problem.

17. Make certain the student knows how to use restroom facilities appropriately.

18. Provide the student with accurate information regarding bodily functions to answer questions and clear up misunderstandings.

19. Teach the student alternative ways to deal with his/her anger (e.g., talk with the teacher, move away from the situation, talk to other school personnel, etc.).

20. Share concerns with administration and seek referral to an agency for investigation of possible abuse and neglect.

21. Provide the student with a full schedule of daily events to increase active involvement in the environment.

22. Provide the student with a quiet place to work to reduce overstimulation. This is to be used to reduce stimulation and not as a form of punishment.

23. Maintain visibility to and from the student. The teacher should be able to see the student; the student should be able to see the teacher. Make eye contact possible at all times.

24. Choose a peer to model appropriate social behavior for the student.

132 Engages in inappropriate behaviors while seated

Goals:
1. The student will engage in appropriate behaviors while seated.
2. The student will sit appropriately in his/her seat.

Objectives:
1. The student will demonstrate appropriate in-seat behavior by sitting quietly with his/her feet on the floor under the desk, keeping all four legs of the chair in contact with the floor, for _____ minutes at a time. (Gradually increase expectations as the student demonstrates success.)
2. The student will refrain from tipping his/her chair for _____ minutes at a time. (Gradually increase expectations as the student demonstrates success.)
3. The student will refrain from tipping his/her desk while seated for _____ minutes at a time. (Gradually increase expectations as the student demonstrates success.)
4. The student will keep his/her feet on the floor while seated for _____ minutes at a time. (Gradually increase expectations as the student demonstrates success.)
5. The student will sit quietly while seated for _____ minutes at a time. (Gradually increase expectations as the student demonstrates success.)
6. The student will refrain from touching others as they walk by on _____ out of _____ trials.
7. The student will refrain from tapping objects such as a pencil, paper clip, eraser, ruler, etc., for _____ minutes at a time. (Gradually increase expectations as the student demonstrates success.)

Interventions:

1. Communicate with the student's parents (e.g., notes home, phone calls, etc.) to share information concerning the student's progress. The parents may reinforce the student at home for behaving appropriately while seated at school.

2. Intervene early when there is a problem to prevent a more serious problem from occurring.

3. Seat the student next to a peer who behaves appropriately while seated.

4. Maintain a full schedule of activities. Keeping the student engaged in learning should decrease inappropriate behaviors.

5. Choose a peer to model appropriate ways to sit in his/her seat for the student.

6. Provide constant, positive reinforcement for appropriate behavior. Ignore as many inappropriate behaviors as possible.

7. Reinforce the student for behaving appropriately in his/her seat based on the length of time the student can be successful. As the student demonstrates success, gradually increase the length of time required for reinforcement.

8. Reinforce the student for behaving appropriately in his/her seat: (a) give the student a tangible reward (e.g., classroom privileges, passing out materials, five minutes free time, etc.) or (b) give the student an intangible reward (e.g., praise, handshake, smile, etc.).

9. Encourage the student to develop an awareness of himself/herself and those around him/her. Have the student periodically step back and ask himself/herself, "Am I fidgeting and being overactive?"

10. Have the student make a list of consequences associated with frequently occurring behaviors (e.g., by disrupting others, I will be perceived as unmannerly; by behaving aggressively, people will avoid me.).

11. Make certain the student is aware of the natural consequences that may occur from behaving inappropriately while seated (e.g., injury, damaging property, hurting others, etc.).

12. Teach the student to "think" before acting (e.g., ask himself/herself "What is happening?" "What am I doing?" "What should I do?" "What will be best for me?").

13. Place the student in a carrel to reduce distracting stimuli which may cause the student to behave inappropriately while seated.

14. Reinforce those students in the classroom who behave appropriately while seated.

15. Provide the student with a clearly understood list of consequences for inappropriate behavior.

16. Reduce the emphasis on competition. Competitive activities may cause the student to act inappropriately while seated.

17. Assess the degree of task difficulty to determine whether or not the student will require additional information, time, assistance, etc., to avoid becoming frustrated and engaging in inappropriate behaviors while seated.

18. Establish classroom rules:
- Work on-task.
- Work quietly.
- Remain in your seat.
- Finish task.
- Meet task expectations.
- Raise your hand.

Review rules often. Reinforce students for following the rules.

19. Speak to the student to explain (a) what he/she is doing wrong (e.g., tipping chair) and (b) what he/she should be doing (e.g., sitting appropriately in his/her chair).

20. Deliver a predetermined signal (e.g., give a hand signal, ring a bell, etc.) when the student begins to behave inappropriately while seated.

21. Speak with the student to let him/her know exactly what he/she is doing wrong, what he/she should be doing, and what the consequences are for inappropriate behavior.

22. Make certain that the chair or desk the student is assigned is appropriate and/or comfortable for him/her (e.g., the desk is not too high, the chair is not too small, etc.).

23. Enlist different people (e.g., peer, paraprofessional, friend, etc.) to reinforce the student when he/she sits still.

24. Have the student choose a peer who has self-control. Encourage the student to observe that person and try to model the behaviors which contribute to self-control.

25. Seat the student away from peers to reduce the likelihood that the student will behave inappropriately while in his/her seat.

26. Avoid seating the student near people with whom he/she may be tempted to converse during assemblies, seminars, group projects, etc.

27. Provide the student with a specific description of appropriate in-seat behavior (e.g., facing forward, feet on floor, back straight, etc.).

28. Move objects used for tactile stimulation (e.g., pens, paper clips, loose change, etc.) away from the student's reach.

29. Write a contract with the student specifying what behavior is expected (e.g., behaving appropriately while seated) and what reinforcement will be made available when the terms of the contract have been met.

30. Seat the student near the teacher.

31. Explain to the student, after telling him/her to stop talking, the reason why he/she should not be talking.

32. Remove any materials which the student uses to make noise while seated.

33. Do not criticize when correcting the student; be honest yet supportive. Never cause the student to feel negatively about himself/herself.

34. Maintain consistent expectations for the student to sit appropriately in his/her seat.

35. Identify the situations in which the student is most likely to engage in inappropriate behavior while seated. After you have identified these situations, think of ways to minimize their occurrences.

36. Evaluate the necessity of having the student sit facing forward, feet on floor, back straight, etc.

37. Provide activities which are interesting to the student to keep the student on-task and behaving appropriately while seated.

38. Encourage the student to attend to the source of information by maintaining eye contact, keeping hands free from other materials, and reducing other distractions. This should decrease inappropriate behaviors.

39. Model for the student appropriate ways to sit in a chair or at a desk.

40. Reinforce those students in the classroom who sit appropriately in their seats.

41. Implement logical consequences for students who engage in inappropriate behaviors while seated (e.g., the student will have to sit on the floor, stand next to his/her desk to work, sit in a chair without a desk, etc.).

42. Communicate with the student's cooperative work experience/vocational education teacher to choose a job that allows for a high degree of physical movement (e.g., jobs which allow the student to be on his/her feet, move from room to room, have frequent contact with people, and travel from one job site to another, etc.).

43. Have desks and/or chairs that can be fastened to the floor or which are designed to prevent tipping.

44. Place the student in a carrel to reduce distracting stimuli which may cause the student to sit inappropriately in his/her seat.

45. Use natural consequences when the student touches others as they walk by (e.g., move the student to another location in the room, have others walk away from the student, etc.).

46. Evaluate the appropriateness of the task to determine (a) if the task is too easy, (b) if the task is too difficult, and (c) if the length of time scheduled to complete the task is adequate.

47. Allow the student some movement while performing tasks. Monitor and limit the amount of movement.

48. Carefully consider the student's age before expecting him/her to sit quietly for a period of time.

49. Structure the environment so that the student remains active and involved in appropriate behavior.

50. Facilitate on-task behavior by providing a full schedule of activities. Prevent lag time from occurring when the student would be free to engage in inappropriate behavior.

51. Allow the student some movement while listening to instruction from the teacher. Monitor and limit the amount of movement.

133 Makes sexually related comments or engages in inappropriate behavior with sexual overtones

Goals:

1. The student will refrain from making sexually related comments.
2. The student will refrain from engaging in behaviors with sexual overtones.
3. The student will demonstrate appropriate behavior in carrying out his/her social-sexual role at school.

Objectives:

1. The student will make appropriate comments when talking with others during ___out of ___ interactions.
2. The student will make appropriate gestures on ___out of ___trials.
3. The student will refrain from touching others on ___out of ___trials.
4. The student will not expose himself/herself to others on ___out of ___trials.
5. The student will touch himself/herself in appropriate areas on ___out of ___trials.
6. The student will refrain from inappropriately touching himself/herself in public on ___out of ___ trials.
7. The student will remain appropriately clothed on ___out of ___trials.
8. The student will make appropriate comments on ___out of ___trials.

Interventions:

1. Indicate to the student that public displays of sexually related behavior are inappropriate.

2. Supervise the student closely to prevent inappropriate sexually related behaviors from occurring.

3. Structure the environment so that time does not permit the student to engage in inappropriate behavior (e.g., maintain a full schedule of activities).

4. Seat the student close to the teacher to provide more direct supervision.

5. Maintain visibility to and from the student. The teacher should be able to see the student, and the student should be able to see the teacher. Make eye contact possible at all times.

6. Be mobile to be frequently near the student.

7. Do not allow the student to be left alone or unsupervised with other students.

8. Make certain the student understands the natural consequences of his/her inappropriate behavior (e.g., peers will not want to interact with him/her, removal from the group may be necessary, etc.).

9. Model socially acceptable behavior for the student (e.g., pat on the back, appropriate verbal communications, handshake, etc.).

10. Separate the student from the peer(s) who stimulates the inappropriate sexually related behavior.

11. Make certain the student knows exactly which sexually related behaviors are unacceptable at school (e.g., words, gestures, comments, touching, exposing, etc.).

12. Intervene early when there is a problem to prevent more serious problems from occurring.

13. Do not inadvertently reinforce the student for demonstrating sexually related behaviors (e.g., attending to the student only when he/she demonstrates sexually related behaviors, demonstrating shock, etc.).

14. Maintain a professional relationship with students at all times and in all settings, making certain that your behavior does not stimulate sexually related behaviors.

15. Teach the student appropriate ways to communicate displeasure, anger, frustration, etc.

16. Teach the student to "think" before acting (e.g., ask himself/herself "What is happening?" "What am I doing?" "What should I do?" "What will be best for me?").

17. Communicate with parents, agencies, or the appropriate parties to inform them of the problem, determine the cause of the problem, and consider possible solutions to the problem.

18. Establish classroom rules:
- Work on-task.
- Work quietly.
- Remain in your seat.
- Finish task.
- Meet task expectations.
- Raise your hand.

Review rules often. Reinforce students for following the rules.

19. Communicate with the parents (e.g., notes home, phone calls, etc.) to share information concerning the student's progress. The parents may reinforce the student at home for engaging in appropriate behavior at school.

20. Write a contract with the student specifying what behavior is expected (e.g., communicating with others in an appropriate manner) and what reinforcement will be made available when the terms of the contract have been met.

21. Do not force the student to interact with others.

22. Remove the student from the group or activity until he/she can demonstrate appropriate behavior and self-control.

23. Reinforce the student for demonstrating appropriate behavior based on the length of time the student can be successful. As the student demonstrates success, gradually increase the length of time required for reinforcement.

24. Reinforce those students in the classroom who engage in appropriate behavior.

25. Speak with the student to explain (a) what the student is doing wrong (e.g., making sexual references, touching others, making gestures, etc.) and (b) what the student should be doing (e.g., following rules, working on-task, attending to responsibilities, etc.).

26. Reinforce the student for engaging in socially appropriate individual or group behavior: (a) give the student a tangible reward (e.g., classroom privileges, line leading, passing out materials, five minutes free time, etc.) or (b) give the student an intangible reward (e.g., praise, handshake, smile, etc.).

Goals:

1. The student will demonstrate self-control.
2. The student will engage in appropriate behaviors while seated.
3. The student will sit appropriately in his/her seat.
4. The student will demonstrate appropriate behavior when moving with a group.

Objectives:

1. The student will make decisions appropriate to the situation on _____ out of _____ trials.
2. The student will stay in his/her seat for _____ minutes at a time. (Gradually increase expectations as the student demonstrates success.)
3. The student will raise his/her hand to leave his/her seat on _____ out of _____ trials.
4. The student will raise his/her hand to gain the teacher's attention on _____ out of _____ trials.
5. The student will refrain from touching others during _____ out of _____ interactions.
6. The student will demonstrate consideration/regard for others during _____ out of _____ trials.
7. The student will demonstrate appropriate in-seat behavior by sitting quietly with his/her feet on the floor under the desk, keeping all four legs of the chair in contact with the floor, for _____ minutes at a time. (Gradually increase expectations as the student demonstrates success.)
8. The student will refrain from tipping his/her chair for _____ minutes at a time. (Gradually increase expectations as the student demonstrates success.)
9. The student will refrain from tipping his/her desk while seated for _____ minutes at a time. (Gradually increase expectations as the student demonstrates success.)
10. The student will keep his/her feet on the floor while seated for _____ minutes at a time. (Gradually increase expectations as the student demonstrates success.)
11. The student will sit quietly for _____ minutes at a time. (Gradually increase expectations as the student demonstrates success.)
12. The student will demonstrate appropriate behavior when moving with a group on _____ out of _____ trials.
13. The student will stay in line when moving with a group on _____ out of _____ trials.
14. The student will walk quietly when moving with a group on _____ out of _____ trials.
15. The student will keep his/her hands to his/her sides when moving with a group on _____ out of _____ trials.
16. The student will demonstrate appropriate behavior for _____ minutes at a time when moving with a group.
17. The student will walk quietly by the teacher when moving with a group on _____ out of _____ trials.
18. The student will walk quietly by a peer when moving with a group on _____ out of _____ trials.

Interventions:

1. Reduce the opportunity to act impulsively by limiting decision making. As the student demonstrates success, gradually increase opportunities for decision making.

2. Maintain supervision at all times and in all areas of the school environment.

3. Be mobile to be frequently near the student.

4. Provide the student with adequate time to perform activities to reduce his/her impulsive behavior.

5. Assign additional responsibilities to the student (e.g., chores, errands, etc.) to give him/her a feeling of success or accomplishment.

6. Prevent the student from becoming overstimulated by an activity (e.g., monitor or supervise student behavior to limit overexcitement in physical activities, games, parties, etc.).

7. Maintain visibility to and from the student. The teacher should be able to see the student and the student should be able to see the teacher. Make eye contact possible at all times.

8. Provide the student with a routine to be followed when making decisions (e.g., place a list of decision-making strategies on the student's desk).

9. Explain to the student that he/she should be satisfied with personal best effort rather than expecting perfection.

10. Provide the student with clear, simply stated explanations, instructions, and directions so that he/she knows exactly what is expected.

11. Assist the student in beginning each task to reduce impulsive responses.

12. Choose a peer to model deliberate and responsible behavior in academic and social settings for the student.

13. Reduce distracting stimuli (e.g., place the student on the front row, provide a carrel or quiet place away from distractions, etc.). This is used as a means of reducing distracting stimuli and not as a form of punishment.

14. Teach the student decision-making steps: (a) think about how other persons may be influenced, (b) think about consequences, (c) carefully consider the unique situation, (d) think of different courses of action which are possible, and (e) think about what is ultimately best for him/her.

15. Make the student aware of the reasons we all must practice responsibility (e.g., others' rights are not infringed upon, others are not hurt, order is not lost, property is not damaged or destroyed, etc.).

16. Reduce the emphasis on competition. Competition may result in impulsive behavior to win or be first.

17. Emphasize individual success or progress rather than winning or "beating" other students.

18. Deliver a predetermined signal (e.g., hand signal, verbal cue, etc.) when the student begins to demonstrate impulsive behaviors.

19. Make certain the student does not become involved in overstimulating activities on the playground, during P.E., during lunch, etc.

20. Make certain the student has an adequate amount or number of activities scheduled to prevent the likelihood of impulsively engaging in unplanned activities.

21. Assign the student to an area of the classroom where he/she is to remain at any one time.

22. Maintain a consistent daily routine of activities.

23. Make certain the student knows which areas in the classroom are "off limits" to him/her.

24. Do not criticize the student. When correcting the student, be honest yet supportive. Never cause the student to feel negatively about himself/ herself.

25. Intervene early when there is a problem to prevent a more serious problem from occurring.

26. Do not leave a lot of unstructured time for the student.

27. Teach the student to "think" before acting (e.g., ask himself/herself "What is happening?" "What am I doing?" "What should I do?" "What is best for me?").

28. Communicate with parents (e.g., notes home, phone calls, etc.) to share information concerning the student's progress. The parents may reinforce the student at home for acting in a deliberate and responsible manner at school.

29. Write a contract with the student specifying what behavior is expected (e.g., acting in a deliberate and responsible manner) and what reinforcement will be made available when the terms of the contract have been met.

30. Remove the student from the group or activity until he/she can demonstrate appropriate behavior and self-control.

31. Reinforce the student for demonstrating appropriate behavior based on the length of time the student can be successful. As the student demonstrates success, gradually increase the length of time required for reinforcement.

32. Reinforce those students in the classroom who act in a deliberate and responsible manner.

33. Establish classroom rules:
- Work on-task.
- Work quietly.
- Remain in your seat.
- Finish task.
- Meet task expectations.

Review rules often. Reinforce students for following rules.

34. Speak with the student to explain (a) what the student is doing wrong (e.g., taking action before thinking about what he/she is doing) and (b) what the student should be doing (e.g., considering consequences, thinking about the correct response, considering others, etc.).

35. Reinforce the student for acting in a deliberate and responsible manner: (a) give the student a tangible reward (e.g., classroom privileges, line leading, passing out materials, five minutes free time, etc.) or (b) give the student an intangible reward (e.g., praise, handshake, smile, etc.).

36. Separate the student from the peer(s) who stimulates his/her inappropriate behavior when moving with a group.

37. Have the student walk alone, behind the group, beside the teacher, etc., when he/she displays inappropriate behavior when moving with a group.

38. Provide the student with a demonstration of the appropriate way to move with a group.

39. Have the student act as a line leader, line monitor, etc., when moving with a group.

40. Have the students walk in pairs when moving as a group.

41. Clarify for the student that it is his/her behavior which determines consequences (e.g., positive or negative).

42. Provide the student with rules for moving appropriately with a group:
- Walk in the halls.
- Go directly from one area to another.
- Talk quietly in the halls.
- Walk on the right side of the hall.
- Use the appropriate stairway.

Review rules often. Reinforce the student for following rules.

43. Before leaving the classroom, remind the student of the rules for walking in a group (e.g., walk behind the person in front of you, keep hands to yourself, walk quietly, etc.).

44. Choose a peer to model appropriate movement with a group for the student.

45. Reinforce the student for moving appropriately with a group based on the length of time the student can be successful. As the student demonstrates success, gradually increase the length of time required for reinforcement.

46. Reinforce those students who demonstrate appropriate behavior when moving with a group.

47. Make certain that consequences are delivered consistently for behavior demonstrated (e.g., appropriate behavior results in positive consequences and inappropriate behavior results in negative consequences).

48. Provide the student with many social and academic successes.

49. Structure the environment to limit opportunities for inappropriate behavior (e.g., keep the student engaged in activities, have the student seated near the teacher, maintain visibility to and from the student, etc.).

50. Provide the student with a clearly identified list of consequences for inappropriate behavior.

51. Stop the line frequently to assure student success when moving with a group.

52. Provide a learning experience which emphasizes the cause-and-effect relationship between behavior and the inevitability of some form of consequence (e.g., both negative and positive behaviors and consequences).

53. Point out the consequences of other students' behavior as they occur (e.g., take the opportunity to point out that consequences occur for all behavior and for all persons).

54. Supervise the student closely in situations in which he/she is likely to act impulsively (e.g., maintain close physical proximity, maintain eye contact, communicate frequently with the student, etc.).

55. Prevent peers from engaging in those behaviors which would cause the student to fail to consider or regard the consequences of his/her behavior (e.g., keep other students from upsetting the student).

56. Make the consequence of a behavior obvious by identifying the consequence as it occurs and discussing alternative behavior which would have prevented the particular consequence.

57. Allow the student more decision-making opportunities relative to class activities and assignments.

58. Give the student responsibilities in the classroom (e.g., teacher assistant, peer tutor, group leader, etc.).

59. Evaluate the appropriateness of the task in relation to the student's ability to perform the task successfully.

60. Show an interest in the student (e.g., acknowledge the student, ask the student's opinion, spend time working one-on-one with the student, etc.).

61. Inform others who will be working with the student (e.g., teachers, the principal, clerks, etc.) about the student's tendency to ignore consequences of his/her behaviors.

Reminder: Do not confuse impulsive behavior with enthusiasm. Impulsive behavior should be controlled while enthusiasm should be encouraged.

Goals:

1. The student will maintain self-control in stimulating activities.
2. The student will not engage in nervous habits.

Objectives:

1. The student will discontinue engaging in the nervous habit when cued by the teacher on ___ out of ___ trials.
2. The student will temporarily remove himself/herself from a stimulating activity on ___ out of ___ trials.
3. The student will maintain self-control when engaged in ___ out of ___ stimulating activities.
4. The student will refrain from biting his/her fingernails during ___ out of ___ stimulating activities.
5. The student will refrain from twirling his/her hair during ___ out of ___ stimulating activities.
6. The student will refrain from chewing the inside of his/her cheek during ___ out of ___ stimulating activities.
7. The student will refrain from chewing pencils or pens during ___ out of ___ stimulating activities.
8. The student will refrain from spinning/twirling objects during ___ out of ___ stimulating activities.

Interventions:

1. Remove from the environment any object which may be used by the student to engage in nervous habits (e.g., pencils, pens, rubber bands, paperclips, etc.).

2. Prevent the student from becoming overly stimulated by an activity.

3. Try various groupings to determine the situation in which the student is most comfortable.

4. Provide the student with as many social and academic successes as possible.

5. Make the necessary adjustments in the environment to prevent the student from experiencing stress, frustration, anger, etc.

6. Assign a peer tutor to work directly with the student to prevent stress, frustration, anxiety, etc.

7. Interact frequently with the student to maintain his/her involvement in class assignments.

8. Allow the student additional time in which to complete class assignments or homework.

9. Interact frequently with the student to maintain his/her involvement in class assignments.

10. Reduce situations which may contribute to nervous behavior (e.g., testing situations, timed activities, competition, etc.).

11. Reduce the emphasis on competition and perfection.

12. Reduce stimuli which may cause the student to engage in nervous habits (e.g., noise, movement, etc.).

13. Prevent situations in which peers contribute to the student's nervous behaviors.

14. Provide the student with another activity designed to result in productive behavior (e.g., coloring, cutting, using a calculator, working with a peer, etc.).

15. Structure the environment so that time does not allow the student the opportunity to engage in nervous habits.

16. Encourage the student to practice self-control activities designed to allow him/her to gain composure before continuing an activity (e.g., placing hands on desk, sitting with feet on the floor, making eye contact with the instructor, etc.).

17. Provide the student with a high-interest activity which he/she prefers.

18. Provide a calm/pleasant atmosphere.

19. Avoid discussion of topics that are sensitive to the student (e.g., divorce, death, unemployment, alcoholism, etc.).

20. Intervene early when the student begins to engage in nervous habits to prevent more serious problems from occurring.

21. Deliver a predetermined signal (e.g., hand signal, bell ringing, etc.) when the student engages in nervous habits.

22. Evaluate the appropriateness of the task to determine (a) if the task is too easy, (b) if the task is too difficult, and (c) if the length of time scheduled for the task is adequate.

23. Communicate with the parents (e.g., notes home, phone calls, etc.) to share information concerning the student's progress. The parents may reinforce the student at home for demonstrating appropriate behavior at school.

24. Write a contract with the student specifying what behavior is expected (e.g., demonstrating appropriate behavior) and what reinforcement will be made available when the terms of the contract have been met.

25. Remove the student from the group or activity when he/she engages in nervous habits.

26. Reinforce the student for demonstrating appropriate behavior (academic or social) based on the length of time he/she can be successful. As the student demonstrates success, gradually increase the length of time required for reinforcement.

27. Establish classroom rules:
- Work on-task.
- Work quietly.
- Remain in your seat.
- Finish task.
- Meet task expectations.

Review rules often. Reinforce students for following rules.

28. Reinforce those students in the classroom who demonstrate appropriate behavior.

29. Speak with the student to explain (a) what the student is doing wrong (e.g., chewing on pencil, biting nails, twirling objects, etc.) and (b) what the student should be doing (e.g., practicing self-control, working on-task, performing responsibilities, etc.).

30. Reinforce the student for demonstrating appropriate behavior: (a) give the student a tangible reward (e.g., classroom privileges, line leading, passing out materials, five minutes free time, etc.) or (b) give the student an intangible reward (e.g., praise, handshake, smile, etc.).

136   Has forced a sexual encounter with another student or teacher

Goal:

1. The student will develop positive means of self-expression which replaces socially unacceptable sexual attention and/or sexual violence.

Objectives:

1. The student will use positive means of self-expression in social situations across environments on ____ out of ____ trials.
2. The student will refrain from sexual behavior which is socially unacceptable and/or violent for all trials in ____ weeks/months.

Interventions:

1. The student who has forced sexual encounters with others needs additional supports (e.g., counseling) in addition to any behavioral interventions introduced across environments. Advocate for supports to prevent future crisis.

2. Maintain strong communication between home and school (e.g., notes home, phone conversations, conferences, setting up times for informal meetings, etc.). Make certain parents know the student's progress so reinforcement can occur at home as well as at school. Work with parents to develop approaches which can be used at home and school to teach the student how he/she may express himself/herself without resorting to sexual violence.

3. Reinforce those students who are displaying positive social skills and participating in activities rather than attempting forced sexual encounters.

4. Develop a positive relationship with the student so he/she knows you will listen to him/ her during stressful times.

5. Reinforce the student for participating in activities and displaying positive social skills: (a) give the student a tangible reward (e.g., line leading, passing out materials, five minutes free time, etc.) or (b) give the student an intangible reward (e.g., praise, handshake, smile, etc.).

6. To assure safety and well-being, always provide careful monitoring of the student who might attempt sexual violence.

7. Draft a contract with the student which specifies expected behaviors and activity performance, reinforcements for correct attempts and goal/contract completion, and timelines.

8. Provide the student with sexual education which includes measures to teach the student how he/she may be positively involved in the community. Sex education needs to address positive means of sexual and other self-expression to replace violent and/or unacceptable sexual encounters.

9. Help the student understand his/her value as a person and as a group member by (a) working with the student to identify his/her positive attributes and abilities, (b) assuring meaningful, positive reinforcement for positive choice making throughout academic and social activities, and (c) letting the student know you care about him/her by spending time with the student and talking with him/her.

10. Make certain the student is provided with well-monitored opportunities to engage in social and recreational activities for the development of social skills to replace sexually violent behaviors.

11. Through role play, engage the student in exploring the thoughts and feelings of characters on both sides of an argument or conflict so that the student who victimizes learns to attach feelings to other people.

12. Teach all students ways of assuring personal safety across environments. These may include

   (a)   traveling in well-lit, well-trafficked areas;

   (b)   traveling in small groups;

   (c)   knowing how to locate and access help from clerks and persons in authority such as police;

   (d)   knowing basic procedures to take if one becomes lost or separated from a group such as waiting at a predetermined safe place;

   (e)   only talking to unfamiliar persons in the company of the group; and

   (f)   knowing how to say "no," and how to walk/run from an encounter with a stranger or an unwelcome approach.

13. The student who engages in exposing himself/herself may be receiving vicarious reinforcement from others when shock or surprise reactions are expressed. Minimize the amount of such attention the student stands to receive from such behavior.

14. The student who attempts forced sexual encounters may be a victim of sexual or other abuse. Make certain the student receives help through school policy and according to law. Suspected abuse needs to be reported for the sake of the student.

15. The student with a history of sexual violence may not evidence this behavior in all environments. Provide the student with monitoring at all times, but make certain the student is not bearing the burden of stigma for behavior, including behavior no longer evidenced or not evidenced in the current environment. The idea is to help, not to punish.

16. Work with existing supports, such as family and relationship counselors, to complement ongoing efforts for the student who has forced sexual encounters. These supports may provide a valuable resource in the development of coping/replacement skills for sexually violent behavior.

17. Supervise the student closely to prevent inappropriate sexually related behaviors from occurring.

18. Do not allow the student to be left alone or unsupervised with other students.

19. Separate the student from the peer(s) who stimulates the inappropriate sexually related behavior.

20. The student may not acknowledge his/her attempts to force sexual encounters with others. Try the following:

   (a)   Firmly but gently assure consequences for behaviors that hurt others. Remember the idea is to teach, not to punish;

   (b)   Make certain the student has an opportunity to receive reinforcement for his/her positive attempts at scheduled activities and for his/her positive behaviors at all times; and

   (c)   Help the student develop positive replacement skills, such as positive social skills and positive means of self-expression. Make certain these behaviors receive more reinforcement value than what the student may anticipate from vicarious reinforcement for forced sexual attempts.

21. As part of a coping strategy, provide the student opportunities to select and engage in physical activities which are within his/her scope of recreational interests and which are socially acceptable.

22. Coping strategies and/or replacement skills for sexually violent behaviors should not be contingent upon activity or behavioral performance.

23. Provide the student with structured, monitored opportunities for building social skills (e.g., free time to interact with peers and friends after small groups have completed projects, class celebration of birthdays, etc.).

24. Provide anyone identified as a potential victim of sexual violence close monitoring for protection from harm.

25. Indicate to the student that public displays of sexually related behavior are inappropriate.

26. Make certain the student knows exactly which sexually related behaviors are unacceptable at school (e.g., words, gestures, comments, touching, exposing, etc.).

27. Maintain a professional relationship with the student at all times and in all settings, making certain that your behavior does not stimulate sexually related behaviors.

137   Has run away from home overnight

Goals:

1. The student will accept responsibility for his/her problems.
2. The student will attempt to resolve his/her problems.

Objectives:

1. The student will accept responsibility for his/her problems on ___ out of ___ trials.
2. The student will attempt to resolve his/her problems by talking, cooperating, etc., on ___ out of ___ trials.
3. The student will ask for teacher assistance when necessary to help resolve his/her problems on ___ out of ___ trials.

Interventions:

1. Maintain supervision of the student at all times and in all parts of the school.

2. Maintain visibility to and from the student. The teacher should be able to see the student and the student should be able to see the teacher. Make eye contact possible at all times.

3. Provide the student with as many academic and social successes as possible.

4. Record or chart attendance with the student.

5. Give the student a preferred responsibility to be performed at various times throughout the day.

6. Present tasks in the most attractive and interesting manner possible.

7. Interact frequently with the student to maintain involvement in the activity (e.g., ask the student questions, ask the student's opinion, stand close to the student, seat the student near your desk, etc.).

8. Make the necessary adjustments in the environment to prevent the student from experiencing stress, frustration, anger, etc., as much as possible.

9. Inform others (e.g., teachers, aides, lunchroom clerks, etc.) of the student's tendency to run away to avoid problems.

10. Discuss with the student ways to deal with unpleasant experiences which would typically cause him/her to run away (e.g., talk to a teacher, visit with a counselor, etc.).

11. Identify variables in the environment which cause the student to become upset, and reduce or remove those variables.

12. Consider alternative forms of negative consequences if current consequences cause the student to run away. Do not use negative consequences which contribute to a worsening of the situation.

13. Intervene early to prevent the student from becoming upset enough to run away.

14. Provide the student with a quiet place as an alternative to running away. This can be a place where the student elects to go as a form of self-control in place of running away.

15. Identify the student's favorite activities and provide as many of these as possible throughout the day.

16. Do not criticize when correcting the student; be honest yet supportive. Never cause the student to feel negatively about himself/herself.

17. Make certain all school personnel are aware of the student's tendency to run away.

18. Intervene early when there is a problem to prevent more serious problems from occurring.

19. Make certain there will be adult supervision at all times for the student (e.g., during P.E., recess, lunch, etc.).

20. Be careful to avoid embarrassing the student by giving him/her orders, demands, etc., in front of others.

21. Help the student recognize problems that are within his/her ability to deal with and not to worry needlessly about situations over which the student has no control.

22. Teach and encourage the student to use problem-solving skills: (a) identify the problem, (b) identify goals and objectives, (c) develop strategies, (d) develop a plan of action, and (e) carry out the plan.

23. Teach the student to "think" before acting (e.g., ask himself/herself "What is happening?" "What am I doing?" "What should I do?" "What will be best for me?").

24. Make certain the student is allowed to voice an opinion in a situation to avoid becoming angry or upset.

25. Talk to the student about ways of handling situations successfully without conflict (e.g., walk away from a situation, change to another activity, ask for help, etc.).

26. Evaluate the appropriateness of the task to determine (a) if the task is too easy, (b) if the task is too difficult, or (c) if the length of time scheduled to complete the task is adequate.

27. Communicate with parents (e.g., notes home, phone calls, etc.) to share information concerning the student's progress. The parents may reinforce the student at home for dealing with problems in appropriate ways at school.

28. Write a contract with the student specifying what behavior is expected (e.g., asking for help) and what reinforcement will be made available when the terms of the contract have been met.

29. Reinforce the student for dealing with problems in appropriate ways based on the length of time the student can be successful. As the student demonstrates success, gradually increase the length of time required for reinforcement.

30. Reinforce those students in the classroom who deal with problems in appropriate ways.

31. Speak with the student to explain (a) what the student is doing wrong (e.g., running away from situations, running away from home, etc.), and (b) what the student should be doing (e.g., asking for help, practicing problem-solving skills, using self-control, etc.).

32. Reinforce the student for dealing with problems in appropriate ways.

33. Discuss concerns with other professionals to determine if further investigation is warranted (e.g., abuse, neglect, etc.).

34. Teach/demonstrate methods for dealing with problems early to prevent problems from becoming overwhelming.

35. Teach the student acceptable ways to communicate displeasure, anger, frustration, etc.

36. Identify persons the student may contact with worries or concerns (e.g., guidance counselor, school nurse, social worker, school psychologist, etc.).

37. Write a contract with the student and his/her parents that specifies an individual, who is acceptable to both the student and parents, who the student will contact when he/she is upset enough to run away.

38. Treat the student with respect. Talk in an objective manner at all times.

138   Is easily angered, annoyed, or upset

Goals:
1. The student will demonstrate appropriate behavior when angry.
2. The student will demonstrate appropriate behavior when annoyed with others.
3. The student will demonstrate appropriate behavior when upset.

Objectives:
1. The student will be able to settle minor conflicts with others without arguing, yelling, crying, hitting, etc., during _____ out of _____ interactions.
2. The student will tolerate a peer's inappropriate behavior by demonstrating patience and refraining from being verbally or physically aggressive during _____ out of _____ interactions.
3. The student will walk away from a peer or group situation when he/she becomes angry, annoyed, or upset during _____ out of _____ interactions.
4. The student will demonstrate self-control when angered, annoyed, or upset by a peer on _____ out of _____ trials.
5. The student will refrain from arguing, using a harsh tone of voice, yelling, etc., during _____ out of _____ interactions.
6. The student will continue to demonstrate appropriate behavior and interact with others when angry, annoyed, or upset during _____ out of _____ interactions.

Interventions:

1. Allow the student to take a break to re-group when he/she is becoming angry, annoyed, or upset.

2. Teach and encourage the student to use problem-solving skills: (a) identify the problem, (b) identify goals and objectives, (c) develop strategies, (d) develop a plan of action, and (e) carry out the plan.

3. Teach the student decision-making steps: think about how others may be influenced, think about consequences, consider carefully the unique situation, think of different courses of action which are possible, think about what is ultimately best, etc.

4. Maintain a positive/calm environment (e.g., positive comments, acknowledgment of successes, quiet communications, etc.).

5. Look for the warning signs (e.g., arguing, loud voices, etc.) that the student is getting upset or angry. Intervene to change the activity to prevent more serious problems from occurring.

6. Communicate with the student's parents (e.g., notes home, phone calls, etc.) to share information concerning their student's progress. The parents may reinforce the student at home for demonstrating self-control at school.

7. Maintain consistent expectations.

8. Talk with the student's family, a school official, a social worker, etc., about the student's behavior if it is causing him/her to have problems getting along with others.

9. Remove the student immediately from a situation when he/she begins to be angry, annoyed, or upset.

10. Facilitate appropriate behavior by providing a full schedule of daily events. Prevent lag time from occurring when the student would be likely to become involved in activities which would cause him/her to be angry, annoyed, or upset.

11. Evaluate the appropriateness of the academic task to determine (a) if the task is too easy, (b) if the task is too difficult, or (c) if the length of time scheduled to complete the task is adequate.

12. Provide the student with alternative activities, games, etc., in case some activities prove upsetting.

13. Educate yourself and others about ADHD to increase understanding and accommodation of impulsive behavior.

14. Communicate with the student's parents, agencies, or the appropriate parties to inform them of the student's problem, determine the cause of the problem, and consider possible solutions to the problem.

15. Teach behaviors that promote self-control. Allow the student to gain his/her composure before continuing an activity (e.g., placing hands on desk, sitting with feet on the floor, making eye contact with the person who is talking, etc.).

16. Make certain the student is allowed to voice an opinion in a situation to avoid becoming angry or upset.

17. Encourage the student to develop an awareness of himself/herself and those around him/her. Have the student periodically step back and ask himself/herself, "Am I behaving too aggressively?"

18. Reduce the emphasis on competition. Repeated failure and frustration may cause the student to become angry, annoyed, or upset.

19. Educate the student about ADHD and the need to self-monitor behavior.

20. Make certain that all teachers and staff who have contact with the student understand the importance of maintaining consistency in the discipline of the student.

21. Encourage the student to pause and consider his/her thoughts before acting on them.

22. Provide constant, positive reinforcement for appropriate behavior. Ignore as many inappropriate behaviors as possible.

23. Have the student anticipate future tasks/ assignments and develop plans for addressing them.

24. Have the student develop an awareness of the consequences of his/her behavior by writing down or talking through problems which may occur due to his/her inability to adjust his/her behavior to different situations (e.g., perceived as unmannerly, avoided, etc.).

25. Help the student learn to be satisfied with his/her own best effort rather than some arbitrary measure of success. Success is measured individually according to ability level. Progress of any kind is a measure of success.

26. Be mobile to be frequently near the student.

27. Teach the student to "think" before acting (e.g., ask himself/herself "What is happening?" "What am I doing?" "What should I do?" "What will be best for me?").

28. Reinforce those students in the classroom who demonstrate self-control.

29. Provide the student with a clearly understood list of consequences for inappropriate behavior.

30. Remind the student of the consequences of getting angry, annoyed, or upset before going into a store, going to a friend's house, having friends over, etc., to reinforce the need for the student to develop self-monitoring skills.

31. Discuss with the student the consequences of becoming easily angered, annoyed, or upset on the job site (e.g., fired, not viewed as mature enough for the job, loss of respect of co-workers, etc.).

32. Have the student review the consequences of his/her behavior with someone he/she trusts. Have the student consider different choices he/she could have made and the different outcomes.

33. Maintain a consistent daily classroom routine.

34. Allow flexibility in meeting academic demands when the student becomes angry, annoyed, or upset (e.g., allow more time, modify assignments, provide help with assignments, etc.).

35. Choose a peer to model self-control for the student.

36. Assess the degree of task difficulty to determine whether or not the student will require additional information, time, assistance, etc., to avoid becoming frustrated.

37. Discuss the student's behavior with him/her in private rather than in front of others.

38. Schedule recreational activities at the end of the day. Make participation in these activities dependent upon completion of daily responsibilities and appropriate behavior.

39. Delegate assignments on group projects. Equally distribute the work load to reduce frustration for group members.

40. Speak to the student to explain (a) what he/she is doing wrong (e.g., hitting, arguing, throwing things, etc.) and (b) what he/she should be doing (e.g., moving away from the situation, asking for assistance from the teacher, etc.).

41. Provide the student with positive feedback which indicates he/she is successful, important, respected, etc.

42. Provide the student with opportunities for social and academic success.

43. Prevent frustrating or anxiety-producing situations from occurring (e.g., give the student tasks only on his/her ability level, give the student only the number of tasks that can be tolerated in one sitting, reduce social interactions which stimulate the student to become physically abusive, etc.).

44. Teach the student ways to gain self-control (e.g., count to ten, walk away, talk with someone, etc.).

45. Set a good example for the student by dealing in a socially acceptable way with situations that may be upsetting.

46. Remove the student from the group or activity until he/she can demonstrate self-control.

47. Do not let the student have his/her way when he/she gets angry.

48. Consider consulting with a mental health provider about the student's failure to control his/her anger.

49. Have the student ask for help when he/she needs it.

50. Have the student question any directions, explanations, or instructions he/she does not understand.

51. Encourage the student to remove himself/herself from a situation when he/she needs to gain self-control.

52. Encourage the student to ask himself/herself questions to avoid impulsive behavior (e.g., "What should I be doing?" "How do I want to be perceived?").

53. Teach the student to verbalize his/her feelings before losing control (e.g., "I'm getting tired of waiting." "I'm getting bored standing here." etc.).

54. Teach the student to verbalize his/her feelings when he/she becomes frustrated (e.g., "I'm getting frustrated with this project." "I'm feeling pressured to get this task accomplished.").

55. Discourage the student from engaging in those activities that cause him/her to become easily angered, annoyed, or upset.

56. Encourage the student to engage in quiet, calming activities (e.g., listen to music, read, etc.) when feeling frustrated.

57. Involve the student in activities in which he/she can be successful and that will help him/her feel good about himself/herself. Repeated failures result in frustration and impatience.

58. Allow the student to engage in mild exercise such as walking up/downstairs, take a message to the office, etc., when he/she is feeling frustrated.

59. Encourage the student to avoid ingesting any substance (e.g., drugs, alcohol, cold remedies, etc.) that might further alter his/her ability to maintain self-control.

60. Do not assume the student is being treated nicely by others. Peers may be stimulating inappropriate behavior.

61. Clarify for the student that it is his/her behavior which determines whether consequences are positive or negative.

62. Have the student make a list of consequences associated with frequently occurring behaviors (e.g., by disrupting others, I will be perceived as unmannerly; by behaving aggressively, people will avoid me.).

63. Provide the student with as many high-interest activities as possible.

64. Avoid topics, situations, etc., that may cause the student to become easily angered, annoyed, or upset (e.g., divorce, death, unemployment, alcoholism, etc.).

65. Maintain a routine that will minimize erratic or impulsive behavior which may result in negative consequences.

66. Teach the student techniques to monitor and maintain awareness of his/her stress and frustration levels (e.g., for immediate control: stop, count to ten using slow deep breaths, and try to relax. If needed, remove him/herself from the situation.).

67. Make certain the student does not become involved in overstimulating activities which cause him/her to become angry, annoyed, or upset.

68. Do not place an emphasis on perfection. If the student feels he/she must live up to your expectations and cannot do so, he/she may become angry, annoyed, or upset.

69. Closely supervise the student to monitor his/her behavior at all times.

70. Teach the student to verbalize his/her feelings before losing self-control (e.g., "The work is hard." "Please leave me alone; you're making me angry." etc.).

71. Separate the student from the peer that stimulates his/her inappropriate behavior.

72. Have the student list the pros and cons of an action. Encourage the student to determine if the pros outweigh the cons before he/she takes action.

73. Have the student list five qualities of a patient and respectful person. Have the student choose one of those qualities to work on each week for five weeks.

74. Deliver directives in a supportive rather than a threatening manner (e.g., "Please finish your math assignment before going to lunch," rather than, "You had better finish your math or else!").

75. Provide the student with a selection of activities that can be performed if he/she becomes angry, annoyed, or upset.

76. Reinforce the student for demonstrating self-control based on the length of time the student can be successful. As the student demonstrates increased self-control, gradually increase the length of time required for reinforcement.

77. Reinforce the student for demonstrating self-control in those situations in which he/she is likely to become angry, annoyed, or upset: (a) give the student a tangible reward (e.g., classroom privileges, passing out materials, five minutes free time, etc.) or (b) give the student an intangible reward (e.g., praise, handshake, smile, etc.).

78. Reward the student for maintaining self-control in a particular situation (e.g., cafeteria, gym, hallway, etc.).

79. Have the student identify the situations in which he/she is most easily frustrated. After he/she has identified these situations, have him/her think of ways to minimize their occurrences.

80. Allow the student to attempt something new in private before doing so in front of others.

81. Inform individuals who will be spending time with the student (e.g., substitute teachers, coaches, activity sponsors, etc.) about his/her ability to become easily angered, annoyed, or upset.

82. Evaluate the visual and auditory stimuli in the classroom. Determine the amount of stimuli the student can tolerate. Remove extraneous stimuli from the environment.

83. Make certain to ask the student why he/she becomes easily angered, annoyed, or upset. The student may have the most accurate perception as to why he/she becomes easily angered, annoyed, or upset.

84. Write a contract with the student specifying what behavior is expected (e.g., problem solving, moving away from the situation, asking for assistance from the teacher, etc.) and what reinforcement will be made available when the terms of the contract have been met.

85. Maintain maximum supervision of the student. As the student demonstrates self-control, gradually decrease supervision.

86. Monitor the behavior of other students in the class to make certain they are not teasing or otherwise stimulating the student to become angry, annoyed, or upset.

87. Make certain that your comments take the form of constructive criticism rather than criticism that could be perceived as personal, threatening, etc. (e.g., instead of saying, "You always make the same mistake," say, "A better way to do that might be . . .").

88. Treat the student with respect. Talk in an objective manner at all times.

89. Allow the student some movement while performing tasks. Monitor and limit the amount of movement.

90. Analyze daily, weekly, and monthly tasks at school. Determine which tasks stimulate impatience. Organize activities so a pleasurable activity follows one that stimulates impatience.

91. Make certain the student understands that total fairness is impossible. Sometimes people have to do more than others do or do things they do not want to do simply because they have to be done.

92. Make certain the student understands that for appropriate behavior he/she may earn those things which he/she gets angry, annoyed, or upset about. Those things will not be given to him/her but must be earned with appropriate behavior.

93. Encourage the student to realize that all behavior has negative or positive consequences. Encourage the student to practice behaviors that will lead to positive consequences.

94. Teach the student acceptable ways to communicate displeasure, anger, frustration, etc.

95. Make the necessary adjustments in the environment to prevent the student from experiencing stress, frustration, and anger.

96. Maintain visibility to and from the student to keep his/her attention when verbal questions/directions are being delivered. The teacher should be able to see the student and the student should be able to see the teacher. Make eye contact possible at all times.

97. Maintain supervision so the student is not left alone or unsupervised with other students.

98. Make the student aware of the natural consequences for becoming easily angered, annoyed, or upset (e.g., loss of friendships, injury, more restrictive environment, legal action, etc.).

99. Encourage the student to consider the consequences of his/her behavior before engaging in any activity.

100. Reduce activities which might threaten the student (e.g., announcing test score ranges or test scores aloud, making students read aloud in class, emphasizing the success of a particular student or students, etc.).

101. Provide a designated area for the student when he/she becomes frustrated with a situation (e.g., counselor's office, study carrel, resource room, etc.).

102. Help the student to recognize the signs of becoming overexcited. Explain the appropriate action to gain self-control.

103. Be careful to avoid embarrassing the student by giving him/her orders, making demands, etc., in front of others.

104. Make other personnel aware of the student's tendency to become easily angered, annoyed, or upset.

105. Do not criticize when correcting the student; be honest yet supportive. Never cause the student to feel negatively about himself/herself.

106. Have the student identify the situations in which he/she is most likely to fail to consider the consequences

107. Remove the student immediately from the presence of others when he/she gets angered, annoyed, or upset.

108. Provide a quiet place away from peer interactions for the student to work independently. This is not to be used as a form of punishment but as an opportunity to increase the student's success in his/her environment.

109. Explain to the student the reason why he/she cannot have or do something.

110. Try to reduce or prevent things from happening which cause the student to become easily angered, annoyed, or upset.

111. Establish classroom rules:
- Work on-task.
- Work quietly.
- Remain in your seat.
- Finish task.
- Meet task expectations.

Review rules often. Reinforce students for following the rules.

112. Teach the student alternative ways to communicate his/her unhappiness (e.g., talking about a problem, asking for help, etc.).

113. Do not allow the student to use ADHD as an excuse. Hold the student responsible for his/her actions. However, understand and accept problems that ADHD brings into the student's life while he/she is learning to make accommodations.

114. Try various groupings in the classroom to determine the situation in which the student is most successful.

115. Communicate with the student's cooperative work experience/vocational education teacher to ensure reinforcement of appropriate behavior at the student's job site.

116. Do not allow the student to participate in a situation unless he/she can demonstrate self-control.

117. Do not force the student to interact or remain in a group if he/she is likely to become angry, annoyed, or upset.

118. Make certain that the student understands the relationship between inappropriate behavior and the consequences which follow (e.g., being avoided by others, not being able to participate in special activities, etc.).

119. Talk to the student about ways of successfully handling situations without conflict (e.g., walk away from the situation, change to another activity, ask for help, etc.).

120. Teach the student to recognize when he/she is becoming angry, annoyed, or upset and ways in which to deal with his/her feelings.

121. Encourage the student to associate with peers with whom he/she gets along well to prevent him/her from getting angry, annoyed, or upset.

122. Encourage the student to talk with a trusted adult when he/she is angry, annoyed, or upset.

123. Find a peer to work with the student who should be a good influence (e.g., someone younger/ older, of the same/opposite sex, etc.).

124. Be consistent. Try to deal with the student's behavior in a manner that is as fair as possible.

125. Do not force the student to interact with others.

126. Teach the student alternative ways to deal with situations which make him/her frustrated, angry, etc. (e.g., withdrawing, talking, etc.).

139 Makes derogatory or critical remarks about self or other people

Goal:

1. The student will make appropriate comments to other students.
2. The student will demonstrate realistic, objective self-appraisal.
3. The student will improve his/her perception of self.

Objectives:

1. The student will ask for teacher assistance only when necessary on ___ out of ___ trials.
2. The student will attempt ___ out of ___ assigned tasks per day. (Gradually increase expectations as the student demonstrates success.)
3. The student will demonstrate appropriate interaction skills such as sharing, waiting his/her turn, talking in an acceptable manner, and making appropriate gestures during ___ out of ___ interactions with a peer.
4. The student will demonstrate respect for a peer on ___ out of ___ trials.
5. The student will discuss his/her abilities in a realistic manner on ___ out of ___ trials.
6. The student will make an accurate appraisal of his/her performance at the end of each activity on ___ out of ___ trials.
7. The student will make appropriate comments to a peer during ___ out of ___ interactions.
8. The student will make comments that are appropriate to the situation on ___ out of ___ trials.
9. The student will make gestures that are appropriate to the situation on ___ out of ___ trials.
10. The student will make ___ positive comment(s) about himself/herself per day. (Gradually increase expectations as the student demonstrates success.)
11. The student will refrain from arguing with a peer during ___ out of ___ interactions.
12. The student will refrain from calling names during ___ out of ___ interactions with a peer.
13. The student will refrain from cursing during ___ out of ___ interactions with a peer.
14. The student will refrain from making rude comments during ___ out of ___ interactions with a peer.
15. The student will refrain from making self-deprecating remarks such as "I'm stupid," "I'm dumb," "I'm ugly," etc., on ___ out of ___ trials.
16. The student will refrain from using obscenities during ___ out of ___ interactions with a peer.
17. The student will settle minor conflicts with a peer during ___ out of ___ interactions.
18. The student will work for ___ minutes without requiring teacher assistance. (Gradually increase expectations as the student demonstrates success.)

Interventions:

1. Assign a peer to help the student with class assignments, homework, etc.

2. Encourage all students to be complimentary of others' performances.

3. Make certain the student recognizes inappropriate comments (e.g., call attention to the comments when they occur, record each instance, terminate the activity when the comment occurs, etc.).

4. Make certain the student knows which comments will not be tolerated at school.

5. Make certain that positive reinforcement is not inadvertently given for inappropriate language (e.g., attending to the student only when he/she is using profane or obscene language).

6. Make certain the student understands the natural consequences of inappropriate behavior (e.g., peers will choose not to interact with him/her, exclusion from activities, etc.).

7. Avoid discussion of topics that are sensitive to the student (e.g., divorce, unemployment, alcoholism, etc.).

8. Establish classroom rules:

- Work on-task.
- Work quietly.
- Remain in your seat.
- Finish task.
- Meet task expectations.

Review rules often. Reinforce students for following rules.

9. Reduce emphasis on competition and perfection. Repeated failure may result in anger and frustration which may take the form of inappropriate comments.

10. Provide frequent opportunities for the student to meet new people.

11. Interact frequently with the student to monitor language used.

12. Prevent frustrating or anxiety-producing situations from occurring (e.g., give the student tasks only on his/her ability level, give the student only the number of tasks that can be successfully managed in one sitting, reduce social interactions which stimulate the student's use of obscene language, etc.).

13. Emphasize individual success or progress rather than winning or "beating" other students.

14. Emphasize individual differences and that everyone has strengths and weaknesses.

15. Reward others for accepting errors they make.

16. Deliver praise and constructive criticism consistently to all students.

17. Make sure you express your feelings in a socially acceptable manner.

18. Encourage the student to refrain from comparing personal performance to other students' performances, and emphasize giving attention to personal improvement (e.g., maintain records of own progress rather than comparing work to others).

19. Reinforce the student for improvement rather than expecting excellence.

20. Encourage the student to interact with others.

21. Teach and encourage the student to use problem-solving skills: (a) identify the problem, (b) identify goals and objectives, (c) develop strategies, (d) develop a plan for action, and (e) carry out the plan.

22. Prevent the student from becoming overstimulated by an activity (e.g., monitor or supervise student behavior to limit overexcitement).

23. Have the student practice appropriate verbal exchanges which should be made (e.g., "Excuse me." "I'm sorry." etc.).

24. Reduce the stimuli which contribute to the student's arguing, calling names, cursing, etc.

25. Teach the student acceptable ways to communicate displeasure, anger, frustration, etc.

26. Recognize the student often and in various settings (e.g., hallways, cafeteria, etc.).

27. Reinforce the student for accepting errors that he/she makes.

28. Treat the student with respect. Talk in an objective manner at all times.

29. Provide the student with positive feedback which indicates he/she is successful, competent, important, valuable, etc.

30. Teach the student positive ways to interact with other students.

31. Provide the student with as many social and academic successes as possible.

32. Make the necessary adjustments in the environment to prevent the student from experiencing stress, frustration, etc.

33. Encourage the student to refrain from comparing himself/herself to others.

34. Require that the student identify alternative appropriate behaviors following an instance of inappropriate comments (e.g., walking away from the peer, seeking teacher intervention, etc.).

35. Talk with the student about individual differences and discuss strengths and weaknesses of individuals the student knows. Stress that the student does not have to do the same things everyone else does.

36. Act as an appropriate role model by using appropriate language at all times (e.g., use appropriate language to convey disappointment, unhappiness, surprise, etc.).

37. Speak with the student to explain (a) what the student is doing wrong (e.g., being overly critical of himself/herself) and (b) what the student should be doing (e.g., being more constructive in self-criticism when evaluating himself/herself).

38. Provide the student with a quiet place to work. This is used as a means of reducing distracting stimuli and not as a form of punishment.

39. Encourage the student to act as a peer tutor to recognize his/her own strengths and abilities.

40. Teach the student to respect others and their belongings by respecting the student and his/her belongings.

41. Help the student learn those skills necessary to improve his/her personal appearance and hygiene.

42. Call on the student when he/she will most likely be able to answer correctly.

43. Remove the student from the group or activity until he/she can demonstrate appropriate behavior.

44. Make certain the student will have adult supervision at all times (e.g., at P.E., lunch, recess, etc.).

45. Provide the student with the opportunity to work with a peer who will be an appropriate model for interacting with other students.

46. Make certain that your comments take the form of constructive criticism rather than criticism that can be perceived as personal, threatening, etc. (e.g., instead of saying, "You always make that same mistake." say, "A better way to do that might be . . .").

47. Explain to the student that he/she should be happy with personal best effort rather than expecting perfection.

48. Pair the student with a younger or less capable peer to enhance his/her feelings of success or accomplishment.

49. Reinforce the student for communicating in an appropriate manner with other students: (a) give the student a tangible reward (e.g., classroom privileges, line leading, passing out materials, five minutes free time, etc.) or (b) give the student an intangible reward (e.g., praise, handshake, smile, etc.).

50. Teach the student to "think" before acting (e.g., ask himself/herself "What is happening?" "What am I doing?" "What should I do?" "What will be best for me?").

51. Deal with the student in a calm and deliberate manner rather than in a manner that would show evidence of shock and surprise.

52. Make certain the student is allowed to voice an opinion in a situation to avoid becoming angry or upset.

53. Intervene early when the student begins to make inappropriate comments to other students to help prevent the student from losing control.

54. Provide the student with success-oriented tasks. The expectation is that success will result in more positive attitudes and perceptions toward self and environment.

55. Provide the student with a predetermined signal when he/she begins to use inappropriate language.

56. Deliver praise and recognition privately so the student is not aware of the performance of others.

57. Reinforce the student for communicating in an appropriate manner based on the length of time the student can be successful. As the student demonstrates success, gradually increase the length of time required for reinforcement.

58. Separate the student from the student(s) who is the primary stimulus or focus of the inappropriate comments.

59. Reinforce those students in the classroom who communicate in an appropriate manner with other students.

60. Intervene early when there is a problem to prevent more serious problems from occurring.

61. Maintain visibility to and from the student. The teacher should be able to see the student and the student should be able to see the teacher. Make eye contact possible at all times.

62. Deliver a predetermined signal when the student begins to be overly critical of self.

63. Assess the appropriateness of the social situation in relation to the student's ability to function successfully.

64. Do not force the student to interact with other students with whom he/she is not completely comfortable.

65. Provide the student with evidence of his/her ability so he/she might better understand that self-blame/self-criticism is unwarranted.

66. Teach the student appropriate words or phrases to use in situations of anger, stress, frustration, etc.

67. Have the student regularly record his/her own progress to have tangible evidence of success.

68. Reduce activities which might threaten the student (e.g., announcing test score ranges or test scores aloud, making students read aloud in class, emphasizing the success of a particular student or students, etc.).

69. Make cleaning up accidents a group responsibility to convey the idea that we all make mistakes and accidents are common to all of us.

70. Do not criticize when correcting the student; be honest yet supportive. Never cause the student to feel negatively about himself/herself.

71. Facilitate on-task behavior by providing a full schedule of daily events. Prevent lag time from occurring when the student would be free to engage in inappropriate behavior.

72. Evaluate the appropriateness of the task to determine (a) if the task is too easy, (b) if the task is too difficult, and (c) if the length of time scheduled for the task is adequate.

73. Communicate with the parents (e.g., notes home, phone calls, etc.) to share information concerning the student's progress. The parents may reinforce the student at home for communicating in an appropriate manner with other students at school.

74. Write a contract with the student specifying what behavior is expected (e.g., communicating with other students in an appropriate manner, accepting personal best effort, etc.) and what reinforcement will be made available when the terms of the contract have been met.

75. Have the student put himself/herself in the other student's place (e.g., "How would you feel if someone called you dumb or stupid?").

76. Discuss with the student ways he/she could deal with unpleasant experiences which would typically cause him/her to use obscene language (e.g., talk to the teacher, go to a quiet area in the school, talk with a counselor, etc.).

Reminder: Make certain that the self-blame or self-criticism is in fact unwarranted.

140 Makes inappropriate noises

Goals:

1. The student will communicate with others in an acceptable manner in the classroom.
2. The student will work quietly in the classroom.

Objectives:

1. The student will gain permission from the teacher, by raising his/her hand, when he/she needs to talk with a peer on ___ out of ___ trials.
2. The student will contribute his/her opinion/answer after being recognized by the teacher on ___out of ___ trials.
3. The student will wait his/her turn to talk when engaged, or attempting to engage, in interactions with others on ___ out of ___ trials.
4. The student will make comments which are relevant to the situation on ___out of ___trials.
5. The student will refrain from making sounds which are inappropriate for the situation on ___out of ___ trials.
6. The student will make positive comments about others on ___out of ___trials.

Interventions:

1. Remove the student from the group or activity until he/she can demonstrate appropriate behavior and self-control.

2. Write a contract with the student specifying what behavior is expected (e.g., making appropriate comments) and what reinforcement will be made available when the terms of the contract have been met.

3. Communicate with the parents (e.g., notes home, phone calls, etc.) to share information concerning the student's progress. The parents may reinforce the student at home for making appropriate comments at school.

4. Evaluate the appropriateness of the task to determine (a) if the task is too easy, (b) if the task is too long, and (c) if the length of time scheduled for the task is adequate.

5. Make certain that reinforcement is not inadvertently given for inappropriate behavior (e.g., making inappropriate comments or unnecessary noises).

6. Give adequate opportunities to respond (i.e., enthusiastic students need many opportunities to contribute).

7. Provide the student with many social and academic successes.

8. Provide the student with a predetermined signal if he/she begins to make inappropriate comments or unnecessary noises.

9. Explain to the student that he/she may be trying too hard to fit in and that he/she should relax and make more appropriate comments.

10. Structure the environment to limit opportunities for inappropriate behaviors (e.g., keep the student engaged in activities, have the student seated near the teacher, etc.).

11. Give the student responsibilities in the classroom (e.g., running errands, opportunities to help the teacher, etc.).

12. Reduce activities which might threaten the student (e.g., announcing test score ranges or test scores aloud, making students read aloud in class, emphasizing the success of a particular student or students, etc.).

13. Have the student be the leader of a small group activity if he/she possesses mastery of skills or an interest in that area.

14. Make the necessary adjustments in the environment to prevent the student from experiencing stress, frustration or anger (e.g., reduce peer pressure, academic failure, teasing, etc.).

15. Maintain visibility to and from the student. The teacher should be able to see the student and the student should be able to see the teacher. Make eye contact possible at all times.

16. Interact frequently with the student to reduce his/her need to make inappropriate comments or unnecessary noises.

17. Assess the appropriateness of the social situation in relation to the student's ability to function successfully.

18. Try various groupings to determine the situation in which the student is most comfortable.

19. Reinforce the student for raising his/her hand to be recognized.

20. Call on the student when he/she is most likely to be able to respond correctly.

21. Teach the student to recognize and make appropriate comments (e.g., comments within the context of the situation, comments that are a follow-up to what has just been said, etc.).

22. Encourage the student to model the behavior of peers who are successful.

23. Have the student work in small groups in which he/she will have frequent opportunities to speak. As the student learns to wait longer for a turn to speak, gradually increase the size of the group.

24. Make certain that the student's feelings are considered when it is necessary to deal with his/her inappropriate comments (i.e., handle comments so that the student's enthusiasm for participation is not diminished).

25. Help the student improve concentration skills (e.g., listening to the speaker, taking notes, preparing comments in advance, making comments in the appropriate context, etc.).

26. Have the student question any directions, explanations, and instructions not understood.

27. Deliver directions, explanations, and instructions in a clear and concise manner to reduce the student's need to ask questions.

28. Have the student practice waiting for a turn to speak for short periods of time. As the student demonstrates success, gradually increase the length of time required for reinforcement.

29. Explain to the student the reasons why making inappropriate comments and unnecessary noise is not acceptable (e.g., is impolite, might hurt others' feelings, etc.).

30. Attempt to provide equal attention to all students in the classroom.

31. Make the student aware of the number of times he/she makes inappropriate comments and unnecessary noises.

32. Allow natural consequences to occur due to the student making inappropriate comments or unnecessary noises in the classroom (e.g., making noises and inappropriate comments during class time will cause the student to have to make up the work during recreational time).

33. Do not inadvertently reinforce the student's inappropriate behavior by laughing when the student is silly, rude, etc.

34. Make certain the student sees the relationship between his/her behavior and the consequences which may follow (e.g., failing to listen to directions and making distracting noises will cause the student to not understand what to do).

35. Remove the student from the situation until he/she can demonstrate appropriate behavior.

36. Deliver a predetermined signal (e.g., hand signal, bell ringing, etc.) when the student begins to display inappropriate behavior.

37. Make certain the student knows when it is acceptable to interrupt others (e.g., an emergency).

38. Teach the student acceptable ways to communicate displeasure, anger, frustration, etc.

39. Have the student put himself/herself in someone else's place (e.g., "How would you feel if someone called you dumb or stupid?").

40. Reinforce the student for making appropriate comments based on the length of time the student can be successful. As the student demonstrates success, gradually increase the length of time required for reinforcement.

41. Reinforce those students in the classroom who make appropriate comments.

42. Establish classroom rules:
- Work on-task.
- Work quietly.
- Remain in your seat.
- Finish task.
- Meet task expectations.

Review rules often. Reinforce students for following rules.

43. Speak with the student to explain (a) what the student is doing wrong (e.g., making inappropriate comments or unnecessary noises) and (b) what the student should be doing (e.g., waiting until it is appropriate to speak, thinking of comments which relate to the situation, etc.).

44. Reinforce the student for making appropriate comments in the classroom: (a) give the student a tangible reward (e.g., classroom privileges, line leading, passing out materials, five minutes free time, etc.) or (b) give the student an intangible reward (e.g., praise, handshake, smile, etc.).

45. Do not force the student to interact with others.

141 Makes excessive noise

Goal:

1. The student will refrain from making excessive noise.

Objectives:

1. The student will refrain from making excessive noise with reminders for ____ minutes at a time.
2. The student will refrain from making excessive noise without reminders for ____ minutes at a time.

Interventions:

1. Reinforce the student for refraining from making excessive noise: (a) give the student a tangible reward (e.g., classroom privileges, line leading, passing out materials, etc.) or (b) give the student an intangible reward (e.g., praise, handshake, smile, etc.).

2. Speak to the student to explain what he/she is doing wrong (e.g., humming out loud during circle time, etc.), and what he/she should be doing (e.g., listening quietly during circle time and humming during free play time, etc.).

3. Establish classroom rules concerning noise making (e.g., "When inside we work quietly, we can make loud sounds, sing, hum, etc., as much as we want when we are outside."). Review rules often. Reinforce the student for following the rules.

4. Reinforce those students in the classroom who work without making excessive noise.

5. Reinforce the student for refraining from making excessive noise based upon the amount of time that he/she can be successful. As the student demonstrates success, gradually increase the length of time required for reinforcement.

6. Remove the student from the group until he/she can demonstrate appropriate behavior.

7. Communicate with parents (e.g., notes home, phone calls, etc.) to share information concerning the student's appropriate behavior. The parents may reinforce the student at home for refraining from making excessive noise at school.

8. Intervene early to prevent the student's behavior from leading to contagion of other students.

9. Provide the student with adequate opportunities to make joyful noise with his/her voice, instruments, and/or objects.

10. Maintain visibility to and from the student. The teacher should be able to see the student and the student should be able to see the teacher. Make eye contact possible at all times.

11. Facilitate quiet on-task behavior by providing a full schedule of daily events.

12. Reduce stimuli that would contribute to the making of excessive noise.

13. Interact frequently with the student to maintain his/her attention to the activity, and to discourage him/her from making excessive noise.

14. Separate the student from the peer who stimulates inappropriate behavior.

15. Make certain the student sees the relationship between behavior and the consequences that follow (e.g., making excessive noise will cause other students to not want to work with him/her, etc.).

16. Allow natural consequences to occur due to the student's inability to refrain from making excessive noise (e.g., he/she will be removed from circle time for making excessive noise, etc.).

17. Make certain that reinforcement is not inadvertently given for inappropriate behavior (e.g., only attending to the student when he/she makes excessive noise, etc.).

18. Make necessary adjustments in the environment to prevent the student from making excessive noise.

142 Makes inappropriate comments or unnecessary noises in the classroom

Goals:

1. The student will communicate with others in an acceptable manner in the classroom.
2. The student will work quietly in the classroom.

Objectives:

1. The student will gain permission from the teacher, by raising his/her hand, when he/she needs to talk with a peer on _____ out of _____ trials.
2. The student will contribute his/her opinion/answer after being recognized by the teacher on _____ out of _____ trials.
3. The student will wait his/her turn to talk when engaged, or attempting to engage, in interactions with others on _____ out of _____ trials.
4. The student will make comments which are relevant to the situation on _____ out of _____ trials.
5. The student will refrain from making sounds which are inappropriate for the situation on _____ out of _____ trials.
6. The student will make positive comments about others on _____ out of _____ trials.

Interventions:

1. Communicate with the student's parents (e.g., notes home, phone calls, etc.) to share information concerning their student's progress. The parents may reinforce the student at home for making comments when appropriate at school.

2. Allow natural consequences to occur due to the student making unnecessary comments or noises in the classroom (e.g., making noises and inappropriate comments during class time will cause the student to have to make up the work during recreational time).

3. Teach the student behaviors that promote self-control (e.g., placing hands on desk, sitting with feet on the floor, making eye contact with the person who is talking, etc.).

4. Give adequate opportunities to respond (i.e., enthusiastic students need many opportunities to contribute).

5. Instruct the student to carry a notepad with him/her at all times and to write information down to help him/her remember.

6. Encourage the student to recite a mantra to himself/herself when entering a situation where he/she may be tempted to make unnecessary comments or noises (e.g., be quiet, be quiet, be quiet).

7. Structure the environment to limit opportunities for inappropriate behaviors (e.g., keep the student engaged in activities, have the student seated near the teacher, etc.).

8. Educate yourself and others about ADHD to increase understanding and accommodation of interruptive behavior.

9. Encourage the student to develop an awareness of himself/herself and those around him/her. Have the student periodically step back and ask himself/herself, "Am I bothering or disturbing others?"

10. Encourage the student to develop an awareness of himself/herself and those around him/her. Have the student periodically step back and ask himself/herself, "Am I talking too loudly or making unnecessary comments or noises?"

11. Encourage the student to pause and consider his/her thoughts before speaking.

12. Educate the student about ADHD and the need to self-monitor behavior.

13. Teach the student to recognize and make appropriate comments (e.g., comments within the context of the situation, comments that are a follow-up to what has just been said, etc.).

14. Provide constant, positive reinforcement for appropriate behavior. Ignore as many inappropriate behaviors as possible.

15. Reinforce the student for making appropriate comments in the classroom: (a) give the student a tangible reward (e.g., classroom privileges, passing out materials, five minutes free time, etc.) or (b) give the student an intangible reward (e.g., praise, handshake, smile, etc.).

16. Reinforce the student for making appropriate comments based on the length of time the student can be successful. As the student demonstrates success, gradually increase the length of time required for reinforcement.

17. Help the student develop an awareness of the consequences of his/her behavior by writing down or talking through problems which may occur due to disturbing others (e.g., perceived as unmannerly, avoided, etc.).

18. Encourage the student to self-monitor behavior by asking himself/herself questions such as, "What should I be doing right now?" "Is what I have to say relevant to this topic?" "Is this a good time for me to comment?"

19. Reinforce those students in the classroom who make appropriate comments.

20. Try various groupings in the classroom to determine the situation in which the student is most comfortable.

21. Remove the student from the group or activity until he/she can demonstrate appropriate behavior and self-control.

22. Make certain that the student understands the relationship between inappropriate behavior and the consequences which follow (e.g., making unnecessary noise will cause others to not want to be around him/her).

23. Reduce the emphasis on competition. Competitive activities may cause the student to become anxious and excessively noisy.

24. Teach the student to take cues from others (e.g., if he/she blurts out comments with no response from others, stop talking; when there is silence in class, it is not necessary to fill the silence with comments; etc.)

25. Assess the degree of task difficulty to determine whether or not the student will require additional information, time, assistance, etc., to avoid becoming frustrated and making unnecessary comments and noises.

26. Have the student question any directions, explanations, or instructions he/she does not understand.

27. Schedule recreational activities at the end of the day. Make participation in these activities dependent upon completion of daily responsibilities and appropriate classroom behavior.

28. Speak with the student to explain (a) what he/she is doing wrong (e.g., making unnecessary comments or noises) and (b) what he/she should be doing (e.g., waiting until it is appropriate to speak, thinking of comments which relate to the situation, etc.).

29. Make certain that the student's feelings are considered when it is necessary to deal with his/her inappropriate comments (i.e., handle comments so that the student's enthusiasm for participation is not diminished).

30. Have the student practice waiting for a turn to speak for short periods of time. As the student demonstrates success, gradually increase the length of time required for a turn to speak.

31. Provide the student with a clearly understood list of consequences for inappropriate behavior.

32. Explain to the student that he/she may be trying too hard to fit in and that he/she should relax and make more appropriate comments.

33. Have the student put himself/herself in someone else's place (e.g., "How would you feel if someone called you dumb or stupid?").

34. Reinforce the student for raising his/her hand to be recognized.

35. Encourage the student to review his/her thoughts before speaking and make certain his/her thoughts have not already been expressed by someone else, the same question asked, etc.

36. Encourage the student to avoid ingesting any substance (e.g., drugs, alcohol, cold remedies, etc.) that might further alter his/her ability to maintain self-control.

37. Make certain that the student is individually supervised if he/she continues to make unnecessary noise.

38. Help the student understand why it is important to work quietly (e.g., if you are making unnecessary noise you may not hear what is being said, others will not listen to you, etc.).

39. Have the student be the leader of a small group activity if he/she possesses mastery of skills or an interest in that area.

40. Have the student make a list of consequences associated with frequently occurring behaviors (e.g., by disrupting others, I will be perceived as unmannerly; by making unnecessary noises, people will avoid me.).

41. Make certain that reinforcement is not inadvertently given for inappropriate behavior (e.g., making unnecessary comments or noises).

42. Provide the student with a predetermined signal if he/she begins to make inappropriate comments or unnecessary noises.

43. Explain to the student the reasons why making unnecessary comments and noise is not acceptable (e.g., impolite, might hurt others' feelings, etc.).

44. Remove the student from the situation until he/she can demonstrate appropriate behavior.

45. Help the student identify the situations in which he/she is most likely to talk beyond what is expected or at inappropriate times. After he/she has identified these situations, have him/her think of ways to minimize their occurrences.

46. Help the student identify the situations in which he/she is most likely to make unnecessary noise. After he/she has identified these situations, have him/her think of ways to minimize their occurrences.

47. Help the student improve concentration skills (e.g., listening to the speaker, taking notes, preparing comments in advance, making comments in the appropriate context, etc.).

48. Teach and practice effective communication skills. These skills include: listening, maintaining eye contact, and positive body language.

49. Have the student work in small groups in which he/she will have frequent opportunities to speak. As the student learns to wait longer for a turn to speak, gradually increase the size of the group.

50. Provide the student with many social and academic successes.

51. Assess the appropriateness of the social situation in relation to the student's ability to function successfully.

52. Have a peer cue the student when he/she makes unnecessary noise (e.g., the person can touch the student's arm or desk as a signal that he/she is making unnecessary noise).

53. Write a contract with the student specifying what behavior is expected (e.g., making appropriate comments) and what reinforcement will be made available when the terms of the contract have been met.

54. Do not inadvertently reinforce the student's inappropriate behavior by laughing when the student is silly, rude, etc.

55. Evaluate the appropriateness of the task to determine (a) if the task is too easy, (b) if the task is too difficult, and (c) if the length of time scheduled for the task is adequate.

56. Encourage the student to model the behavior of peers who are successful at not interrupting.

57. Explain to the student, after telling him/her to stop talking, the reason why he/she should not be talking.

58. Establish classroom rules:
- Work on-task.
- Work quietly.
- Remain in your seat.
- Finish task.
- Meet task expectations.

Review rules often. Reinforce students for following the rules.

59. Teach the student acceptable ways to communicate displeasure, anger, frustration, etc.

60. Make the student aware of the number of times he/she makes unnecessary comments and noises.

61. Maintain visibility to and from the student to keep his/her attention when verbal questions/directions are being delivered. The teacher should be able to see the student and the student should be able to see the teacher. Make eye contact possible at all times.

62. Attempt to provide equal attention to all students in the classroom.

63. Reduce activities which might threaten the student (e.g., announcing test score ranges or test scores aloud, making students read aloud in class, emphasizing the success of a particular student or students, etc.).

64. Make the necessary adjustments in the environment to prevent the student from experiencing stress, frustration, or anger (e.g., reduce peer pressure, academic failure, teasing, etc.) which may result in unnecessary comments or noises.

65. Teach the student to use techniques such as crossing his/her arms and legs, clinching his/her fists, and webbing his/her hands when making noise is inappropriate.

66. Make certain the student understands the relationship between his/her behavior and the consequences which may follow (e.g., failing to listen to directions and making distracting noises will cause the student to not understand what to do).

67. Reduce the occurrence of activities that you know will stimulate the student to make unnecessary comments.

68. Teach "active listening" skills. Listen to what the other person is saying and respond based on information received.

69. Interact frequently with the student to reduce the need for him/her to make inappropriate comments or unnecessary noises.

143 Moves slowly

Goal:

1. The student will move about his/her environment within mutually understood, predetermined time parameters.

Objective:

1. The student will demonstrate his/her ability to move about the environment within predetermined time parameters for ____ out of ____ trials.

Interventions:

1. Reinforce the student for moving about the environment within specified time limits: (a) give the student a tangible reward (e.g., classroom privileges, line leading, passing out materials, five minutes free time, etc.) or (b) give the student an intangible reward (e.g., praise, handshake, smile, etc.).

2. The student who is taking longer than typically required to move from one activity or location to another may be experiencing other difficulties. Provide the student with time and encouragement to establish rapport, and make certain the student receives options of other supports when needed.

3. Do not let the student's slow movement from one activity or location to another become a means of activity avoidance.

4. Speak with the student to explain (a) what he/she has done wrong (e.g., arriving late for activities) and (b) what he/she should be doing (e.g., arriving for activities within a specified time).

5. Write a contract with the student specifying what behavior is expected (e.g., moving from one location to another within appropriate time limits) and what reinforcement will be available when the terms of the contract have been met.

6. Communicate with parents (e.g., notes home, phone calls, etc.) to share information concerning the student's progress. The parents may reinforce the student at home for timely participation in activities at school.

7. Evaluate the appropriateness of the task to determine (a) if the task is too easy, (b) if the task is too difficult, and (c) if the length of time in which the student is expected to move from one location or activity to the next is reasonable.

8. Reinforce the student for his/her timely, positive participation in activities.

9. Assign a peer to sit/work directly with the student (e.g., in different settings or activities such as art, music, P.E., on the bus, tutoring, group projects, running errands in the building, recess, etc.). Reinforce the peer for his/her timely participation in activities. Reinforce the student when he/she models the peer's behavior.

10. Provide the student with frequent opportunities to feel successful.

11. Make sure the student has the opportunity to be the leader of a small group activity when he/she expresses an interest and/or mastery of the subject. This may help the student become more motivated to participate in a timely manner.

12. Provide the student opportunities for social and academic successes.

13. Provide the student with success-oriented special events or activities (e.g., opportunity to be a charter member of a reading or hobby club, etc.) to develop the student's interests and provide him/her the opportunity for meaningful, timely participation.

14. Adjust expectations to individual strengths and needs. Gradually increase expectations based on student performance.

15. Make certain the student is able to successfully participate (e.g., understands the rules, is familiar with the activity, will be compatible with peers engaged in the activity, etc.).

16. Assign responsibilities related to activities (e.g., being a leader, passing out materials, acting as a peer tutor, etc.) which may enhance the student's desire to participate in a timely manner.

17. The student may appreciate constructive remarks and verbal praise in conversations away from the group and/or in a nonintrusive delivery style typical for an entire group. Loud, open remarks may do more harm than good regarding the promotion of any skills (especially social skills) for the student.

18. Encourage the student to wear a watch and time himself/herself to prevent tardiness.

19. With the student, graph his/her successes at timeliness.

20. Make certain the student understands exactly what is expected of him/her regarding timely behavior. Request that he/she repeat the required steps to the teacher to guarantee understanding.

21. When teaching a student to move from one activity or location to the next in a more timely manner, try the following:
   (a) Establish his/her average time needed to move from one specific activity or location to another (e.g., record the time the student takes to move from this specific activity or location to the next over five to seven days, then divide total time by days observed).
   (b) Establish the time you would like the student to take by observing and timing the same event as you move from this specific activity or location to the next with the class.
   (c) With the student, develop a contract in which the objective to move within his/her best time is clearly stated.
   (d) Reinforce objective completion.
   (e) Gradually increase time demands until these match the time usually taken by the group.

22. The student may have difficulties with other forms of personal organization (e.g., organizing personal belongings and activity materials, etc.). Provide the student with methods and materials to increase organization.

23. With the student, develop a daily schedule to organize his/her day within reasonable time parameters.

144   Performs obsessive or compulsive behaviors

Goals:

1. The student will maintain self-control in stimulating activities.
2. The student will not engage in compulsive behaviors.

Objectives:

1. The student will demonstrate behaviors appropriate to the situation on ___out of ___trials.
2. The student will discontinue engaging in compulsive behaviors when cued by the teacher on ___out of ___ trials.
3. The student will temporarily remove himself/herself from a stimulating activity on ___out of ___ trials.
4. The student will maintain self-control when engaged in ___out of ___stimulating activities.

Interventions:

1. Reduce situations which may contribute to compulsive behavior (e.g., testing situations, timed activities, competition, etc.).

2. Prevent the student from becoming overly stimulated by an activity.

3. Try various groupings to determine the situation in which the student is most comfortable.

4. Provide the student with as many social and academic successes as possible.

5. Make the necessary adjustments in the environment to prevent the student from experiencing stress, frustration, anger, etc.

6. Assign a peer tutor to work directly with the student to prevent stress, frustration, anxiety, etc.

7. Interact frequently with the student to maintain his/her involvement in class assignments.

8. Allow the student additional time in which to complete class assignments or homework.

9. Interact frequently with the student to maintain his/her involvement in class assignments.

10. Remove from the environment any object which may be used by the student to engage in compulsive behaviors (e.g., pencils, pens, rubber bands, paperclips, etc.).

11. Intervene early when the student begins to engage in compulsive behaviors to prevent more serious problems from occurring.

12. Reduce stimuli which may cause the student to engage in compulsive behaviors (e.g., noise, movement, etc.).

13. Prevent situations in which peers contribute to the student's compulsive behaviors.

14. Provide the student with another activity designed to result in productive behavior (e.g., coloring, cutting, using a calculator, working with a peer, etc.).

15. Structure the environment so time does not allow the student the opportunity to engage in compulsive behaviors.

16. Encourage the student to practice self-control activities designed to allow him/her to gain composure before continuing an activity (e.g., placing hands on desk, sitting with feet on floor, making eye contact with the instructor, etc.).

17. Provide the student with a high-interest activity which he/she prefers.

18. Provide a calm/pleasant atmosphere.

19. Avoid discussions of topics that are sensitive to the student (e.g., divorce, death, unemployment, alcoholism, etc.).

20. Reduce the emphasis on competition and perfection.

21. Provide the student with a predetermined signal when he/she engages in compulsive behaviors.

22. Evaluate the appropriateness of the task to determine (a) if the task is too easy, (b) if the task is too difficult, and (c) if the length of time scheduled for the task is adequate.

23. Communicate with the parents (e.g., notes home, phone calls, etc.) to share information concerning the student's progress. The parents may reinforce the student at home for demonstrating appropriate behavior at school.

24. Write a contract with the student specifying what behavior is expected (e.g., demonstrating appropriate behavior) and what reinforcement will be made available when the terms of the contract have been met.

25. Reinforce the student for demonstrating appropriate behavior: (a) give the student a tangible reward (e.g., classroom privileges, line leading, passing out materials, five minutes free time, etc.) or (b) give the student an intangible reward (e.g., praise, handshake, smile, etc.).

26. Establish classroom rules:
- Work on-task.
- Work quietly.
- Remain in your seat.
- Finish task.
- Meet task expectations.

Review rules often. Reinforce students for following rules.

27. Reinforce those students in the classroom who demonstrate appropriate behavior.

28. Speak with the student to explain (a) what the student is doing wrong (e.g., chewing on pencil, biting nails, twirling objects, etc.) and (b) what the student should be doing (e.g., practicing self-control, working on-task, performing responsibilities, etc.).

29. Remove the student from the group or activity when he/she engages in compulsive behaviors.

30. Reinforce the student for demonstrating appropriate behavior (academic or social) based on the length of time he/she can be successful. As the student demonstrates success, gradually increase the length of time required for reinforcement.

145 Perseverates - does the same thing over and over

Goals:

1. The student will improve his/her short-term memory.
2. The student will improve his/her long-term memory.
3. The student will improve his/her understanding of abstract concepts (e.g., spatial relationships, directionality, classifications, generalizations).
4. The student will improve his/her visual memory.
5. The student will improve his/her auditory memory.
6. The student will improve his/her awareness and attention to information and activities in the environment.
7. The student will improve his/her organizational skills.
8. The student will improve his/her skills in logical thinking.

Objectives:

1. The student will discontinue behaviors within ____ minutes of the end of an activity, when instructed to stop, etc., on ____ out of ____ trials.
2. The student will discontinue behaviors at the end of an activity, when instructed to stop, etc., on ____ out of ____ trials.

Interventions:

1. Explain that the student should be satisfied with his/her best effort rather than insist on perfection.

2. Assign the student shorter activities. As the student demonstrates success, gradually increase the length of the activities.

3. Inform the student that work not completed in one sitting can be completed later. Provide the student with ample time to complete earlier assignments to guarantee closure.

4. Provide the student with more than enough time to finish an activity. As the student demonstrates success, gradually decrease the amount of time given to finish an activity.

5. Structure time limits so the student knows exactly how long he/she has to work and when work must be finished.

6. Allow a transition period between activities so the student can make adjustments in his/her behavior.

7. Employ a signal technique (e.g., turning lights off and on) to warn that the end of an activity is near.

8. Establish definite time limits and provide the student with this information before an activity begins.

9. Have the student time activities to monitor his/her own behavior and accept time limits.

10. Maintain a consistent daily routine.

11. Maintain consistent expectations within the ability level of the student.

12. Allow the student to finish the activity unless it will be disruptive to the schedule.

13. Provide the student with a list of materials needed for each activity (e.g., pencil, paper, textbook, workbook, etc.).

14. Present instructions/directions prior to handing out necessary materials.

15. Collect the student's materials (e.g., pencil, paper, textbook, workbook, etc.) when it is time to change from one activity to another.

16. Provide the student with clearly stated expectations for all situations.

17. Provide adequate transition time for the student to finish an activity and get ready for the next activity.

18. Prevent the student from becoming so stimulated by an event or activity that the student cannot control his/her behavior.

19. Identify expectations of different environments and help the student develop the skills to be successful in those environments.

20. In conjunction with other school personnel, develop as much consistency as possible in the school environment (e.g., rules, criteria for success, behavioral expectations, consequences, etc.).

21. Have the student participate in relaxing transitional activities designed to reduce the effects of stimulating activities (e.g., put head on desk, listen to the teacher read a story, put headphones on and listen to relaxing music, etc.).

22. Provide the student with a schedule of daily events so the student knows exactly what is expected for the day.

23. Provide the student with verbal reminders or prompts when he/she perseverates.

24. Provide the student with increased opportunity for help or assistance on academic tasks (e.g., peer tutoring, directions for work sent home, frequent interactions, etc.).

25. Reinforce the student for changing from one activity to another without difficulty: (a) give the student a tangible reward (e.g., classroom privileges, line leading, passing out materials, five minutes free time, etc.) or (b) give the student an intangible reward (e.g., praise, handshake, smile, etc.).

26. Assign a peer to provide an appropriate model for changing from one activity to another.

27. Have the student question any directions, explanations, instructions he/she does not understand.

28. Evaluate the appropriateness of the task to determine (a) if the task is too easy, (b) if the task is too difficult, and (c) if the length of time scheduled to complete the task is adequate.

29. Write a contract with the student specifying what behavior is expected (e.g., put materials away and get ready for another activity) and what reinforcement will be made available when the terms of the contract have been met.

30. Reinforce the student for demonstrating acceptable behavior based on the length of time the student can be successful. As the student demonstrates success, gradually increase the length of time required for reinforcement.

31. Reinforce those students in the classroom who change from one activity to another without difficulty.

32. Establish classroom rules:
- Work on-task.
- Work quietly.
- Remain in your seat.
- Finish task.
- Meet task expectations.

Review rules often. Reinforce students for following rules.

33. Speak to the student to explain (a) what he/she is doing wrong (e.g., failing to stop one activity and begin another) and (b) what he/she should be doing (e.g., changing from one activity to another).

34. Reduce distracting stimuli (noise and motion) around the student (e.g, place the student on the front row, provide a carrel or quiet place away from distractions, etc.). This is used as a means of reducing stimuli and not as a form of punishment.

Goal:

1. The student will engage in positive replacement activities (e.g., positive forms of self-expression) instead of hurting/injuring animals.

Objectives:

1. The student will demonstrate his/her ability to use positive replacement skills instead of hurting/injuring animals on all trials in _____ weeks/months.
2. The student will refrain from hurting/injuring animals on all trials in _____ weeks/months.

Interventions:

1. The student who hurts/injures animals may be in need of additional supports (e.g., counseling, psychiatric evaluation, etc.). Advocate for the student to receive such supports as quickly as possible to prevent future behavioral concerns.

2. Develop strong communication between home and school (e.g., notes home, phone calls, etc.) about behavioral progress and concerns. The student may not hurt/injure animals in one environment, such as school, but may choose to do so at home or in other environments. Work with parents to develop basic approaches to behavioral concerns, such as hurting/injuring animals, and reinforcement strategies to be used across environments.

3. Develop and use a system of tangible rewards (e.g., passing out classroom materials, line leading, five minutes free time, etc.) and intangible rewards (e.g., praise, handshake, smile, etc.) when the student participates in activities and displays positive social skills.

4. Reinforce those students who are displaying positive social skills and who are positively participating in activities rather than trying to hurt animals or others.

5. Draft a contract with the student which specifies expected behaviors and activity performance, reinforcements for correct attempts and goal/contract completion, and timelines.

6. To assure safety and well-being, always provide careful monitoring of the student who attempts to hurt or injure animals.

7. Provide the student with opportunities for self-expression in the classroom.

8. Help the student identify his/her antecedents to behaviors to hurt or injure animals or other maladaptive behaviors. When these antecedents begin to appear, help the student focus upon (a) the ongoing activity, (b) alternative activities, and (c) his/her individualized coping skills for use in stressful situations.

9. The student may not know why he/she attempts to hurt or injure animals, and may not acknowledge participation in such behavior. Since the object is to decrease and hopefully replace this behavior, try the following:

(a) Give the student the "benefit of the doubt" when he/she tells you he/she has not injured an animal. Whether or not the student is being truthful, he/she will probably "stick with his/her story" despite contrary evidence. When other accounts differ with the student's version, explain these differences as impartially as possible.

(b) Firmly but gently assure consequences for behaviors that hurt others, including animals. Consequences need to occur to teach, not to punish.

(c) Make certain the student has the opportunity to receive positive reinforcement for his/her attempts at scheduled activities and for his/her positive behaviors.

(d) Help the student develop positive replacement behaviors (e.g., positive activity participation, social skills for use at home and school, positive forms of self-expression, etc.). Make certain these behaviors receive more reinforcement value than can be obtained by acting out maladaptive behaviors.

10. Before introducing the class to a pet, map out your strategy for a worst case scenario (e.g., the animal gets sick, dies, etc.).

11. Should a pet death occur in your classroom for whatever reason, make certain students are given a chance to grieve and understand death as a natural part of a life cycle.

12. If a student is actively trying to hurt or injure an animal, as quickly and as silently as possible intervene by removing the animal to a safer area. Minimize the amount of reinforcement your "shock reaction" might mean to the student.

13. Help the student develop daily and weekly scheduled activities to reduce his/her opportunities to attempt animal torture.

14. Provide the student with opportunities to identify and describe his/her feelings.

15. Work with support services (e.g., counseling) to develop strategies, reinforcements, and consequences for the student who attempts to hurt or injure animals.

16. It is important to remember that not all behaviors are evidenced across environments. Do not let a stigma prevail about a student because he/she may display positive behaviors in the classroom and may not ever attempt to hurt or injure an animal or another human being at school. The student will still need monitoring and supervision as a preventive measure when background or history indicates the possibility of such behavior exists.

17. Working in cooperation with other support sources in the student's life (e.g., counseling, parents, guardians, direct staff, etc.), develop a small set of positive replacement skills the student can use rather than physical violence. Although some of these skills may be passive in nature (e.g., listening to music, watching TV, etc.), try to make certain the student participates in other activities which would provide a physical tension release (e.g., dancing, roller skating, etc.) in a socially acceptable way.

18. Do not permit activities identified as part of the student's coping strategy to become contingent upon academic or behavioral performance (e.g., a student who is expressing himself/herself in dance should not lose this activity due to a poor choice during the day). The student needs daily opportunities to express himself/herself through choosing among coping skills.

19. Provide the student with structured, monitored opportunities for building social skills (e.g., free time to interact with peers and friends after small groups have completed projects, class celebrations such as birthdays, etc.).

20. The student may not sense an ability to control his/her life. Provide support by

    (a) giving the student experiences in exercising positive choice making and control in his/her life at school (e.g., having activity choices throughout the day; giving the student the opportunity to choose among positive reinforcers; etc.); and

    (b) giving the student ways of expressing his/her feelings that are more positive, acceptable, and productive than hurting (e.g., advocate for counseling time, journal or diary writing, drawing, free time to talk with you that is not contingent upon academic/behavioral performance, etc.).

21. The student who hurts or injures animals may not be able to admit he/she has committed such an act. Accept the student's account of events as his/her version, and share with the student your thoughts, feelings, and observations during a private conversation. When it is obvious a student has hurt an animal, seek support for the student according to school policy and state and federal law.

22. The student who hurts animals may only be doing so privately. Seek and maintain positive parental/guardian involvement to develop approaches to help the student.

23. Help the student build his/her self-esteem:
    (a) Help the student identify his/her positive qualities (e.g., things he/she likes, things he/she can do well, positive social attributes, etc.);
    (b) positively reinforce the student for his/her efforts socially as well as academically; and
    (c) provide a classroom atmosphere in which students can express thoughts/feelings and be accepting of one another.

24. When behavioral consequences affect a student's daily schedule, make certain other scheduled activities, especially those important to coping and/or replacing violent self-expression, occur by modifying plans with the student when he/she returns to activities.

Goal:

1. The student will make physical contact with others when appropriate.

Objectives:

1. The student will interact with others in a physically appropriate manner on ___ out of ___ trials.
2. The student will refrain from making unnecessary contact such as hugging, touching, etc., when interacting with others on ___ out of ___ trials.
3. The student will touch others in only designated areas such as on the arm, shoulder, or hand on ___ out of ___ trials.
4. The student will gain others' attention in an appropriate manner by standing quietly or raising his/her hand until recognized on ___ out of ___ trials.
5. The student will demonstrate acceptable physical contact such as a handshake, pat on the back, "high five," etc., when appropriate on ___ out of ___ trials.

Interventions:

1. Reinforce the student for respecting the norms of physical proximity based on the length of time the student can be successful. As the student demonstrates success, gradually increase the length of time required for reinforcement.

2. Remove the student from the group or activity until the student can demonstrate appropriate behavior and self-control.

3. Write a contract with the student specifying what behavior is expected (e.g., shaking hands rather than hugging) and what reinforcement will be made available when the terms of the contract have been met.

4. Communicate with the parents (e.g., notes home, phone calls, etc.) to share information concerning the student's progress. The parents may reinforce the student at home for respecting the norms of physical proximity at school.

5. Separate the student from the person who is the primary focus of the student's attempts to make frequent physical contact.

6. Reduce the opportunity for the student to engage in inappropriate physical contact (e.g., stand an appropriate distance from the student when interacting).

7. Model socially acceptable physical contact for the student (e.g., handshake, pat on the back, etc.).

8. Provide the student with many social and academic successes.

9. Indicate to the student that public displays of frequent physical contact are inappropriate.

10. When working directly with the student, always be in the presence of others.

11. Provide the student with verbal recognition and reinforcement for social and academic successes.

12. Give the student your full attention when communicating with him/her to prevent the student's need for physical contact.

13. Provide the student with social interaction in place of physical interaction (e.g., call the student by name, speak to the student, praise, congratulate, etc.).

14. Provide the student with high-interest activities (e.g., academic activities which are inherently interesting, activities during free time, etc.).

15. Try various groupings to find a situation in which the student's need for physical attention can be satisfied by socially acceptable interactions (e.g., holding hands while dancing in an extracurricular activity, a hug for an accomplishment, handshake or "high five" in sports, etc.).

16. Make certain the student sees the relationship between his/her behavior and the consequences which may follow (e.g., touching and hugging people all of the time may result in others not wanting to be around him/her).

17. Allow natural consequences to occur as a result of the student's inappropriate behavior (e.g., excessive physical contact may cause people to stay away from the student or may result in pushing, shoving, etc.).

18. Make certain that reinforcement is not inadvertently given for inappropriate behavior (e.g., attending to the student only when he/she makes unnecessary physical contact).

19. Prevent the student from becoming overstimulated by an activity (e.g., monitor or supervise student behavior to limit overexcitement in physical activities, games, parties, etc.).

20. Teach the student appropriate ways to interact with others (e.g., verbal and physical introductions, interactions, etc.).

21. Avoid inadvertently stimulating the student's unnecessary physical contact (e.g., attire, language used, physical proximity, etc.).

22. Acknowledge the student when he/she seeks attention verbally instead of making it necessary for the student to gain attention through physical contact.

23. Find a peer to play with the student who would be a good influence (e.g., someone younger, older, of the same gender, of the opposite gender, etc.).

24. Reinforce those students in the classroom who interact appropriately with other students or teachers.

25. Establish classroom rules:
- Work on-task.
- Work quietly.
- Remain in your seat.
- Finish task.
- Meet task expectations.

Review rules often. Reinforce students for following rules.

26. Speak with the student to explain (a) what the student is doing wrong (e.g., touching, hugging, etc.) and (b) what the student should be doing (e.g., talking, exchanging greetings, etc.). Discuss appropriate ways to seek attention.

27. Reinforce the student for respecting the norms of physical proximity: (a) give the student a tangible reward (e.g., classroom privileges, line leading, passing out materials, five minutes free time, etc.) or (b) give the student an intangible reward (e.g., praise, handshake, smile, etc.).

148 Does not provide relevant verbal responses to conversations, questions, etc.

Goal:

1. The student will give logical and relevant verbal responses to conversations.
2. The student will give logical and relevant verbal responses to questions.

Objectives:

1. The student will demonstrate the ability to tell the speaker, in the student's own words, what the speaker said with ____% accuracy.
2. The student will maintain appropriate eye contact during verbal interactions in ____out of ____trials.
3. The student will respond appropriately to questions which can be answered "yes" or "no" ____% of the time.
4. The student will respond appropriately to questions which begin with the words "what," "who," "when," "where," "how much," "how many," and "why" with ____% accuracy.
5. The student will differentiate between logical and absurd statements in ____out of ____trials.
6. The student will correctly relate what is silly in a sentence containing a verbal absurdity ____% of the time.
7. The student will respond appropriately to questions about a familiar topic in ____out of ____trials.
8. The student will respond appropriately to questions about mixed topics during everyday speaking situations in ____ out of ____trials.
9. The student will demonstrate the ability to infer implied requests from statements (e.g., "It is noisy in here.") with ____% accuracy.

Interventions:

1. Make certain the student's hearing has been recently checked.

2. Evaluate the appropriateness of the task to determine if it is too difficult.

3. Reinforce the student for responding with relevant responses: (a) give the student a tangible reward (e.g., classroom privileges, line leading, passing out materials, five minutes free time, etc.) or (b) give the student an intangible reward (e.g., praise, handshake, smile, etc.).

4. Reinforce other students in the classroom who respond in a relevant manner.

5. Discuss with the student what is expected (e.g., making relevant responses).

6. To detect the student's needs and to provide opportunity for relevant verbal interaction, communicate with the student as often as opportunities permit. Spend time talking with the student on an individual basis and include topics which are of interest to the student.

7. Provide the student with direct eye contact and communicate to him/her that you expect him/her to do the same with you.

8. Allow the student to finish responding before you begin talking. Reinforce other students in the classroom for allowing the student to finish responding before they begin talking.

9. When the student makes an irrelevant response, have him/her rephrase in his/her own words the original question to check for comprehension.

10. Pause often when you speak to encourage the student to participate in conversation.

11. Communicate to the student that he/she is a worthwhile individual.

12. Model appropriate responses.

13. Choose a peer to model relevant responses for the student.

14. Teach the student communication skills (e.g., hand raising, expressing needs in written and/or verbal form, etc.).

15. Provide the student with many academic and social successes.

16. Reduce the emphasis on competition. Failure may cause the student to be reluctant to respond.

17. Have the student practice appropriate verbal interactions with peers and teacher(s).

18. Determine an individual(s) in the school environment with whom the student would most want to converse (e.g., custodian, librarian, resource teacher, principal, older student, etc.). Allow the student to spend time conversing with the individual(s) each day.

19. Pair the student with an outgoing peer who engages in relevant verbal interactions on a frequent basis.

20. Deliver a predetermined signal (e.g., holding up a finger, etc.) to remind the student to give a relevant response.

21. Tape record the student and have him/her listen to the recording to facilitate his/her awareness of times when he/she makes an irrelevant response.

22. When the student makes an inappropriate response, immediately rephrase his/her response to make it relevant/appropriate.

23. Prompt the student to help him/her respond with relevant verbal responses (e.g., Student says, "That thing." Teacher says, "What thing, what is it doing?" etc.).

24. Point out examples of relevant verbal responses as they occur during the day.

25. Make a list of emotions (e.g., sad, scared, happy, etc.) and have the student express them in a sentence.

26. Play word games such as "Twenty Questions," in which you provide clues to clarify questions (e.g., "Is it edible?" "Is it alive?", etc.) and then gradually fade the clues.

27. Create a "feeling box." Place an unseen item in the box and have the student describe what it feels like, while another student tries to guess what it is.

28. Alternating with a peer, have the student take turns adding words in a sentence to create one long sentence. The sentence should be as long as possible without becoming a run-on sentence. Check to ensure that all additions to the sentence are relevant.

29. Place an interesting picture or object on a table and have the student describe it in detail. Provide assistance in formulating relevant responses in these descriptions.

30. Have the student practice being someone else in specific situations (e.g., talking on the telephone, being a cashier in a grocery store, etc.). Make sure all responses are relevant to the situation.

31. Have the student practice taking messages to different persons in the school setting (e.g., librarian, school counselor, principal, etc.) and later actually deliver messages.

32. Have the student practice "echoing" what you or another student says. Teach the student to imitate inflectional patterns and facial expressions as well as to repeat the words.

33. Using "sequence cards" have the student place the cards in the appropriate order and explain the sequence; then have the student tell you what might have happened before or after the provided sequence.

34. Provide the student with a book without words and have him/her narrate the story.

35. Pair the student with a peer and have them take turns being interviewed and interviewing. This may be done with the students acting as themselves or pretending to be another person or a fictitious character.

36. Have the student give answers to "what if" questions (e.g., "What if you were ten feet tall?" "What if dinosaurs still roamed the earth?").

37. Demonstrate acceptable and unacceptable speech (e.g., incomplete thoughts and nondescript terminology such as "thing," "stuff," etc.) and have the student critique each example while making suggestions for improvement.

38. Routinely tape record the student's speech and point out irrelevant comments. With each successive taping reinforce the student as his/her use of relevant responses improves.

39. Provide the student with a topic (e.g., rules to follow when riding your bike) and have him/her make relevant statements about it.

40. Ask the parents to encourage the student's use of relevant responses at home by praising him/her when these are used.

41. Call on the student when he/she is most likely to be able to respond successfully.

42. When the student is required to recall information, remind him/her of the situation in which the material was originally presented (e.g., "Remember yesterday when we talked about..." etc.).

43. Allow the student to speak without being interrupted or hurried.

44. Make a list of attributes which are likely to help a person become a good speaker (e.g., takes his/her time, thinks of what to say before starting, etc.).

45. Ask questions which stimulate language. Avoid those which can be answered by yes/no or a nod of the head (e.g., "What did you do at recess?" rather than "Did you play on the slide?" or "Tell me about your vacation." rather than "Did you stay home over the holidays?" etc.).

46. Have the student role play various situations in which relevant verbal responses are important (e.g., during a job interview).

47. After a field trip or special event, have the student retell the activities which occurred with an emphasis on using relevant responses.

48. Stand directly in front of the student when delivering verbal communication.

49. Encourage verbal output. Increase the student's opportunities to communicate verbally to provide him/her with necessary practice.

50. When engaging in verbal communication be certain to use vocabulary that is within the student's level of comprehension.

51. Explain to the student that he/she may be trying too hard to fit in and that he/she should relax and make more appropriate comments.

52. Assess the appropriateness of the social situation in relation to the student's ability to function successfully.

53. Teach the student to recognize and make appropriate comments (e.g., comments within the context of the situation, comments that are a follow-up to what has just been said, etc.).

54. Make certain that the student's feelings are considered when it is necessary to deal with his/her irrelevant responses (i.e., handle comments in such a way as to not diminish the student's enthusiasm for participation).

55. Deliver a predetermined signal (e.g., clapping hands, turning lights off and on, touching his/her shoulder, calling him/her by name, etc.) before engaging in verbal communication.

56. Make certain the student is attending to the speaker (e.g., making eye contact, hands free of distracting materials, looking at assignment, etc.) before communicating verbally with him/her.

57. Make certain that verbal communications are delivered in a nonthreatening manner (e.g., positive voice, facial expressions, language, etc.).

58. Maintain a consistent format for verbal communications with the student.

59. Seat the student close to the source of the verbal communication to make certain the student understands what is being said or asked.

60. Have the student question any verbal communication he/she does not understand.

61. Encourage the student to use gestures when necessary to clarify his/her message. Gestures may also facilitate recall of vocabulary the student is having difficulty retrieving.

62. Make certain that reinforcement is not inadvertently given for irrelevant responses.

63. Explain to the student the reasons why it is important to listen to others when they talk (e.g., it is impolite not to listen, by not listening he/she might respond with a statement that could hurt feelings, etc.).

64. Rephrase directions, explanations, questions, comments, instructions, etc., to increase the likelihood of the student understanding and providing a relevant response.

149 Avoids any social situation that requires increased interpersonal exchanges

Goal:

1. The student will actively involve himself/herself in social situations which require interpersonal exchanges.

Objectives:

1. The student will passively participate in his/her choice of social situations on ___out of ___trials.
2. The student will actively participate in his/her choice of social situations on ___out of ___trials.

Interventions:

1. Reinforce the student for participating in group activities or special events: (a) give the student a tangible reward (e.g., classroom privileges, line leading, passing out materials, five minutes free time, etc.) or (b) give the student an intangible reward (e.g., praise, handshake, smile, etc.).

2. Provide the student with time and encouragement to establish rapport regardless of his/her lack of verbal response. Any vast change in behavior, such as a student opting total withdrawal after displaying acceptable and typical age appropriate social behaviors, may warrant the need of additional support for the student.

3. Do not force the student to socialize. It is more important to offer opportunities for positive reinforcement from socialization than to demand display of socialization skills.

4. The student who is shy and/or withdraws from socializing needs careful attention to what constitutes positive reinforcement (e.g., a student who receives social praise from his/her instructor or an authority source may decrease socializing behavior due to embarrassment). Through a reinforcer survey and interviews with the student and parents, and observations, develop a list of positive reinforcers specific to that student.

5. Speak with the student to explain (a) what he/she has done correctly (e.g., being present in the room, attempting to interact, etc.) and (b) what he/she might be doing to improve response (e.g., talking, taking turns, playing, sharing, etc.).

6. Establish classroom rules that indicate times when it is acceptable to socialize (e.g., at recess, during class parties, lunchtime, after work is completed at the end of the day, at the beginning of each day before attendance, etc.). Review rules often. Reinforce students for positive social interchanges.

7. Write a contract with the student specifying what behavior is expected (e.g., contributing in group activities) and what reinforcement will be available when the terms of the contract have been met.

8. Communicate with parents (e.g., notes home, phone calls, etc.) to share information concerning the student's progress. The parents may reinforce the student at home for participating in group activities or special events at school.

9. Evaluate the appropriateness of the task to determine (a) if the task is too easy, (b) if the task is too difficult, and (c) if the length of time the student is expected to passively and/or actively socially participate is reasonable.

10. Assign a peer to sit/work directly with the student (e.g., in different settings or activities such as art, music, P.E., on the bus, tutoring, group projects, running errands in the building, recess, etc.). As the student becomes comfortable working with one person, gradually increase the size of the group.

11. Include opportunities for small-group interchanges in social situations (e.g., recess, lunchtime, school parties, dances, etc.).

12. Reinforce others for participating in the group or special activities.

13. Give the student the responsibility of helping another in the group.

14. Ask the student questions that cannot be answered with a yes or no.

15. Call on the student when he/she is more likely to respond successfully (e.g., something of interest to the student, when the teacher is certain the student knows the answer, etc.).

16. Try various groupings to determine the situation in which the student is most comfortable.

17. Encourage friendship building in the classroom (e.g., students may wish to attend extracurricular activities in small groups, etc.).

18. Request the student lead a small group activity if he/she expresses an interest and/or mastery of the subject.

19. Allow passive participation as a social choice across learning activities and environments.

20. Reduce the emphasis on competition. Frequent or continuous failure may result in embarrassment which will cause reluctance to participate.

21. Demonstrate respect for the student's opinions, responses, suggestions, etc.

22. Provide the student with many social and academic successes.

23. Provide the student with positive feedback to indicate he/she is successful.

24. Present tasks in the most attractive, interesting manner possible.

25. Allow the student to choose a special event or activity for the class.

26. Provide the student with success-oriented special events or activities (e.g., opportunity to be a charter member of a reading or hobby club, etc.) to develop the student's interests and provide him/her the opportunity for meaningful social interchanges.

27. Modify situations that cause the student to be reluctant to participate (e.g., degree of difficulty, competition, fear of failure, threat of embarrassment, etc.).

28. Emphasize individual success or progress over winning or "beating" others.

29. Provide the student opportunities for small-group rather than large-group participation.

30. Encourage the student to share things of special interest with others in the class (e.g., special hobbies such as coin collecting, etc.).

31. Choose a peer to model appropriate interactions in classroom activities for the student.

32. Provide the student with the opportunity and encouragement to question directions, explanations, and/or instructions he/she does not understand.

33. Allow the student to interact with peers with whom he/she feels comfortable.

34. Identify peers with whom the student would most prefer to interact and attempt to facilitate interaction.

35. Assign outgoing, nonthreatening peers to help the student participate in classroom activities.

36. Structure the environment so the student has many opportunities to interact with other peers in classroom activities.

37. Assign the student to classroom activities in which he/she is likely to interact successfully with peers.

38. Conduct a sociometric activity to identify peers who would most prefer to interact with the student in classroom activities.

39. Teach the student appropriate ways to interact with others (e.g., share materials, problem solve, take turns, converse, etc.).

40. Supervise classroom activities closely so peers with whom the student interacts do not stimulate inappropriate behavior.

41. Make certain classroom activities and the social atmosphere do not provoke difficulties with desired classroom interactions (e.g., a noisy classroom may overstimulate the student).

42. Teach the student problem-solving skills so he/she is better equipped to manage potential problems (e.g., talking, walking away, calling upon an arbitrator, compromising, etc.).

43. Minimize embarrassment for the student by not placing him/her in humiliating situations (e.g., expecting him/her to participate actively in class discussions after he/she has just experienced failure, etc.).

44. Encourage students to give each other positive feedback for small group contributions and other forms of positive verbal exchange.

45. Use information gained from interviews of other students to identify skills and behaviors students feel important for successful interactions.

46. Have the student practice appropriate interactions with the teacher(s) in classroom activities (e.g., simulations, role play, etc.).

47. Make certain the student has all the materials necessary for the classroom activity.

48. Assign responsibilities related to activities (e.g., being a leader, passing out materials, acting as a peer tutor, etc.) which may enhance the student's opportunities for interaction.

49. Make certain the student knows how to use all the materials for the classroom activity.

50. The student who feels shy or awkward may appreciate constructive remarks and verbal praise in conversations away from the group and/or in a nonintrusive delivery style typical for an entire group. Loud, open remarks do more harm than good regarding the promotion of any skills (especially social skills) for the student.

51. Select nonacademic opportunities that enhance appropriate social interaction during classroom activities for all students (e.g., coloring, board games, model building, etc.).

52. Provide the student with a variety of ways to develop rapport with instructor(s) (e.g., writing notes, talking about concerns privately, etc.).

53. Prior to activities, make certain the student is able to successfully participate (e.g., understands the rules, is familiar with the activity, will be compatible with peers engaged in the activity, etc.).

150 Has difficulty expressing opinions, feelings, and/or emotions

Goals:

1. The student will improve his/her ability to express opinions, feelings, and/or emotions.

Objectives:

1. The student will maintain appropriate eye contact during verbal interactions in _____ our of _____ trials.
2. The student will demonstrate the ability to express feelings through three different modes (e.g., drawing, acting, gesture) _____% of the time.
3. The student will demonstrate the ability to describe the emotion of a pictured character with _____% of accuracy.
4. The student will demonstrate the ability to complete a "what if" statement _____% of the time.
5. The student will demonstrate the ability to report the emotions of the characters in a book, which he/she has read, with _____% of accuracy.
6. The student will demonstrate the ability to correctly complete statements reflecting emotions (e.g., "I am happy when...") _____% of the time.

Interventions:

1. Make certain the student's hearing has recently been checked.

2. Evaluate the appropriateness of the task to determine if (a) the task is too easy, (b) the task is too difficult, and (c) the length of time scheduled for the task is adequate.

3. Reinforce the student for expressing opinions, feelings, and/or emotions: (a) give the student a tangible reward (e.g., classroom privileges, line leading, passing out materials, five minutes free time, etc.) or (b) give the student an intangible reward (e.g., praise, handshake, smile, etc.).

4. Reinforce those students in the classroom who express opinions, feelings, and/or emotions.

5. Model for the student expressing your own opinions, feelings, and/or emotions. Attempt to clearly identify each when you do express them.

6. Each day provide the student with situations which elicit particular emotions and assist the student in expressing those emotions (e.g., "A stranger takes you by the arm in a department store. How do you feel?" "You see smoke coming out of a neighbor's house. Are you happy?" etc.).

7. Provide the student with a list of questions involving opinions, feelings, and/or emotions and assist him/her in answering verbally (e.g., "How do you feel when you an A on a test?" "Do you think recess should be before or after lunch?" "Should people wear seat belts?" etc.).

8. Require the student to explain outcomes, consequences, etc. (e.g., when the student earns a reward or privilege, make certain he/she can explain that the reward was the result of hard work and accomplishment and that he/she should feel proud.).

9. Have the student respond to "what if...?: statements (e.g., "What if it rained for forty days and forty nights?" "What if there were no rules and laws?" etc.) to encourage the expression of opinion and/or feelings.

10. Have the student read stories involving a moral (e.g., *The Tortoise and the Hare, The Boy Who Cried Wolf*, etc.) and state his/her opinions about the outcome of the stories.

11. Have the student read short stories without endings. Assist the student in expressing opinions, feelings, and/or emotions about possible endings to the stories.

12. Show the student pictures of dangerous situations and have him/her explain why they are dangerous (e.g., a child running into the street between parked cars, a child riding a bicycle without using his/her hands, etc.).

13. Use cause-and-effect relationships as they apply to nature and people. Discuss what led to a specific situation in a story or picture, what could happen next, etc.

14. Make certain that the student can verbalize the reason for real-life outcomes of behavior (e.g., why the student had to leave the class line on the way to recess, why he/she earned the privilege of being line leader, etc.).

15. Have the student make up rules and explain why each rule is necessary.

16. Have the student identify appropriate consequences for rules (e.g., consequences for following rules and consequences for not following rules). Have the student explain the choices of consequences he/she identified.

17. Encourage verbal expression in your classroom and listen carefully when the student is trying to express opinions, feelings or emotions about any topic.

18. Provide the student with concrete examples or ways to express opinions, feelings and/or emotions (e.g., speaking, writing, gestures, drawing, etc.)

19. When the student displays anger, take the time to listen and respond not only to what he/she is saying, but also to what the student might be feeling.

20. Provide the student with pictures of people who are happy, sad, angry, etc., and have him/her create stories which are based upon the pictures.

21. Set up a situation in which the student can "role play" various emotions. Provide feedback on how effectively the idea was communicated.

22. Pair the student with a peer who is effective in expressing opinions, feelings, and/or emotions. Have them participate in a simple debate on a current topic of controversy.

23. Have the student take a poll of classmates concerning their feelings about particular TV shows, music groups, movies, foods, etc.

24. Have the student illustrate a story about an event which has emotional overtones. Point out the emotions portrayed or involved in the story.

151   Does not engage in leisure/recreational activities with others

Goals:

1. The student will be involved in recreational activities by himself/herself.
2. The student will participate with others in leisure/recreational activities.

Objectives:

1. Given instruction, the student will participate alone in recreational activities he/she has selected on ____ out of ____ occasions.
2. Given assistance and information, the student will select recreational activities he/she may participate in by himself/herself on ____ out of ____ occasions.
3. Given instruction and assistance, the student will participate with others in leisure/recreational activities on ____ out of ____ occasions.
4. The student will demonstrate his/her ability to participate with others in leisure/recreational activities on ____ out of ____ occasions.
5. The student will participate alone in recreational activities he/she has selected on ____ out of ____ occasions.
6. The student will select recreational activities he/she may participate in by himself/herself on ____ out of ____ occasions.

Interventions:

1. Evaluate the appropriateness of available leisure and recreational activities to determine whether or not the student can be successful with the activity, the length of time scheduled, and the others involved in the activity.

2. Encourage the student's peers to include him/her in leisure/recreational activities.

3. Encourage the student to assist younger peers in leisure/recreational activities.

4. Develop, with the student, a list of high-interest, leisure/recreational activities that require various amounts of time to perform and involve other students.

5. Place leisure/recreational materials (e.g., paper, pencil, glue, crayons, games, etc.) in a location where the student can obtain them on his/her own.

6. Establish centers of high-interest activities at appropriate levels of difficulty for the student and various groups of students for use during leisure/recreational time.

7. Separate the student from the peer(s) who stimulates his/her inappropriate use of leisure/recreational time.

8. Encourage the student to plan with his/her peers the use of leisure/recreational time in advance.

9. Provide sign-up sheets for leisure/recreational activities that involve small groups of students.

10. Give the student an individual schedule to follow so that when an activity is finished he/she knows what to do next.

11. Assign a peer for the student to interact with during leisure/recreational activities.

12. Identify a specified activity for the student to engage in during leisure/recreational time.

13. Have the student act as a peer tutor during leisure/recreational activities.

14. Have the student act as a teacher assistant during leisure/recreational activities.

15. Allow the student to go to other classrooms for specified activities during leisure/recreational time (e.g., typing, home economics, industrial arts, etc.).

16. Provide high-interest, leisure/recreational time activities for completion of assignments (e.g., listening to music, reading, socializing, going to another part of the building, etc.).

17. Provide the student with a list of quiet activities to engage in with other students when he/she finishes assignments early.

18. Find educationally related, leisure/recreational activities for the student to perform (e.g., flash card activities with peers; math, reading, or spelling board games; etc.).

19. Engage in leisure/recreational time activities with the student to model appropriate use of leisure time.

20. Make certain the student is able to successfully engage in the leisure/recreational time activity (e.g., the student understands the rules, the student is familiar with the activity, the student will be compatible with other students engaged in the activity, etc.).

21. Provide supervision of leisure/recreational time activities to monitor the student's willingness to try leisure-time activities that involve other students.

22. Make certain the student is aware of the length of leisure/recreational time available when beginning the leisure-time activity.

23. Make certain the student understands that failing to make appropriate use of leisure/recreational time may result in termination of leisure time and/or loss of future leisure time.

24. Provide the student with frequent short-term leisure/recreational activities with other students so he/she can learn to attempt activities with peers.

25. Give the student a special responsibility during group leisure/recreational time (e.g., headphones, coloring books, reading material, etc.).

26. Provide things that entertain the student during leisure/recreational time (e.g., headphones, coloring books, reading material, etc.).

27. Make certain the student does not become involved in overstimulating activities.

28. Have the student question any directions, explanations, or instructions not understood.

29. Choose a peer to model willingness to try leisure/recreational activities with peers for the student.

30. Communicate with parents (e.g., notes home, phone calls, etc.) to share information concerning the student's progress. The parents may reinforce the student at home for engaging in leisure/recreational activities with peers.

31. Write a contract with the student specifying what behavior is expected (e.g., engaging in leisure/recreational time activities with others, etc.) and what reinforcement will be made available when the terms of the contract have been met.

32. Reinforce the student for making appropriate use of leisure time based on the length of time the student can be successful. As the student demonstrates success, gradually increase the length of time required for reinforcement.

33. Reinforce those students in the classroom who engage in leisure/recreational activities with others.

34. Establish leisure-time rules:
- Find an activity.
- Find someone to work with.
- Remain in assigned areas.
- Put materials away when free time is over.

Review rules often. Reinforce students for following rules.

35. Speak to the student to explain (a) what the student is doing wrong (e.g., working alone) and (b) what he/she should be doing (e.g., participating in an activity with a friend, etc.).

36. Reinforce the student for engaging in leisure/recreational activities with others: (a) give the student a tangible reward (e.g., classroom privileges, line leading, passing out materials, five minutes free time, etc.) or (b) give the student an intangible reward (e.g., praise, handshake, smile, etc.).

37. Involve the student and parents in developing a list of leisure/recreational activities involving others, from which the student makes his/her choices.

38. Per school policy, acquire medical and guardian approvals for physically demanding leisure/recreational activities (e.g., physical activities, team sports, etc.).

39. Expose the student to a variety of group leisure/recreational resources in his/her home community to help the student make informed decisions about leisure/recreational activities that he/she might enjoy.

40. Encourage parental input in developing behavioral and activity expectations in community sites to encourage consistency between home and school.

41. Provide the student choices of two or three group leisure/recreational activities from which to choose.

42. Consider the student's current interests and abilities in skill-building plans for recreation and leisure.

43. Explain to the student that his/her best effort is more important than perfection to help decrease frustration with group leisure/recreational time activity.

44. If the student experiences frustration with a group leisure/recreational activity, modify the activity to meet the student's needs.

45. Teach and emphasize leisure/recreational activity participation as a technique for managing/reducing stress.

46. When possible, observe the student in his/her home and community environment to gather information concerning the student's current leisure/recreational activity decisions.

47. Encourage or reward others for interacting with the student in leisure/recreational activities.

48. Try various groupings to determine the situation in which the student is most comfortable.

49. Have the student choose an ongoing project to work on during free time which will in turn become a regular free-time activity (e.g., puzzle, art project, etc.).

50. Create situations in which the student must interact (e.g., group mural, team sports, etc.).

51. Determine the peer(s) with whom the student would prefer to interact and attempt to facilitate this interaction.

52. Teach the student appropriate ways to interact with another student (e.g., how to greet another student, suggest activities, share materials, problem solve, take turns, converse, etc.).

53. Make certain the interaction is not so stimulating as to make successful interaction with another student difficult.

54. Reduce the emphasis on competition. Failure may cause the student to be reluctant to interact with peers.

55. Find a peer with whom the student is most likely to be able to interact successfully (e.g., a student with similar interests, background, classes, behavior patterns, nonacademic schedule, etc.).

56. Do not force the student to interact with someone with whom his/she is not completely comfortable.

57. Provide organized leisure/recreational activities for the student to participate in before, during, and after school (e.g., board games, softball, four square, tether ball, jump rope, flash cards, etc.).

58. Provide the student with the opportunity to work with a peer who will be an appropriate model for interacting with other students.

59. Assess the appropriateness of the social setting in relation to the student's ability to interact with peers.

60. Provide a quiet, reasonably private area where the student can engage in quiet leisure activities during free time.

61. Teach functional academics that are critical to the process of choosing, locating, and using resources for leisure/recreational activities. (e.g., signing up for activities, getting necessary equipment, etc.).

62. Teach students all phases of selecting and participating in leisure/recreational activities (e.g., making necessary contacts about activities, signing up for activities, gathering necessary equipment, etc.).

63. Determine the student's current ability with a leisure/recreational activity by observing the student's current performance.

64. Teach the student social skills he/she may need to participate in leisure/recreational activities (e.g, team members need to know how to work together, people who are watching a movie in a theater are typically quiet, etc.).

65. Maintain consistent expectations within the ability level of the student.

66. Encourage the student, when possible, to develop leisure/recreational preferences which include physical activity (e.g., exercising, dancing, team sports, roller skating, etc.) and passive entertainment (e.g., watching a baseball game, going to a movie). Acquire medical approval for physically demanding activities.

67. Teach the student to alternate among favorite activities to prevent boredom.

68. Encourage students to budget money, time, and other resources for leisure/recreational activities that are reasonable compared to the demands of other expenses and the parameters of his/her income.

69. Monitor students to assure their continued involvement in selecting and participating in a variety of leisure/recreational activities of their own choosing.

70. Teach students to access locations in the community for chosen leisure/recreational activities (e.g., locate and pay for transportation, give directions to or find the location, etc.).

71. Help the student establish a daily routine which includes a chosen leisure/recreational activity (e.g., dancing, walking, exercising, etc.) and praise him/her for participating in the activity.

72. Encourage the student to try new leisure/recreational activities to stimulate interests and build his/her reference file for future choices. Acquire medical approval for any activities which might represent risk to the student's safety.

Reminder: Do not "force" the student to interact with peers.

152 Does not respond appropriately to environmental social cues

Goal:

1. The student will behave in a manner appropriate for the situation.

Objectives:

1. The student will laugh when appropriate during ___out of ___situations.
2. The student will appear alarmed or upset when appropriate during ___out of ___situations.
3. The student will show emotion that is appropriate for the situation during ___out of ___situations.
4. The student will demonstrate emotion like that of his/her peers during ___out of ___situations.
5. The student will cry when appropriate during ___out of ___situations.
6. The student will demonstrate anger when appropriate during ___out of ___situations.

Interventions:

1. Choose a peer to model appropriate responses to environmental social cues for the student.

2. Have the student question any environmental social cues not understood.

3. Establish environmental social cues that the student is expected to follow (e.g., when it is appropriate to interact, when it is not appropriate to interact, etc.).

4. Provide repeated practice in responding appropriately to environmental social cues.

5. Pair social cues with verbal explanations and immediate reinforcement for appropriate responses.

6. Model appropriate responses to environmental social cues for the student to imitate.

7. To increase success in learning environmental social cues, have the student observe and imitate the responses of peers to environmental social cues (e.g., as the student is learning to interact appropriately when a spectator at a sporting event, the student can imitate the behavior of peers who engage in appropriate behavior when they are spectators at a sporting event).

8. Assign a peer to accompany the student as the student engages in different activities, to act as a model in teaching appropriate responses to environmental social cues.

9. Provide the student with simulation activities in the classroom to teach successful responses to environmental social cues.

10. Reinforce the student for asking the meaning of environmental social cues not understood (e.g., rules, etc.).

11. Provide the student with verbal reminders or prompts when he/she misses environmental social cues.

12. When delivering directions, explanations, and information; be certain to use vocabulary that is within the student's level of comprehension.

13. Evaluate the appropriateness of the environmental social cues the student is expected to follow to determine (a) if the cue is too difficult and (b) if the length of time required to respond to the cue is adequate.

14. Communicate with the parents (e.g., notes home, phone calls, etc.) to share information concerning the student's progress. The parents may reinforce the student at home for responding to environmental social cues at school.

15. Write a contract with the student specifying what behavior is expected (e.g., responding appropriately to social cues) and what reinforcement will be made available when the terms of the contract have been met.

16. Reinforce the student for responding appropriately to environmental social cues based on the number of environmental social cues the student can successfully follow. As the student demonstrates success, gradually increase the number of environmental social cues required for reinforcement.

17. Reinforce those students in the classroom who respond appropriately to environmental social cues.

18. Speak to the student to explain (a) what the student is doing wrong and (b) what the student should be doing.

19. Reinforce the student for responding appropriately to environmental social cues: (a) give the student a tangible reward (e.g., classroom privileges, line leading, passing out materials, five minutes free time, etc.) or (b) give the student an intangible reward (e.g., praise, handshake, smile, etc.).

20. Allow the student to interact with a group of peers with whom he/she feels comfortable to practice appropriate responses to environmental cues.

21. Structure the environment so that the student has many opportunities to interact with other peers in classroom activities.

22. Encourage the student to engage in social situations in which he/she is likely to respond successfully to environmental social cues.

23. Involve the student in extracurricular activities to provide additional opportunities for him/her to practice appropriate responses to environmental social cues.

24. Identify expectations of different environments and help the student develop the skills to be successful in those environments.

25. Point out the natural consequences of failing to respond appropriately to environmental social cues from other students (e.g., other students will avoid him/her, loss of friendships, misunderstandings, etc.).

26. Through interviews with other students and observations, determine those characteristics of the student which interfere with successful interactions in social situations. Use information gained to determine skills or behaviors the student needs to develop for successful interactions.

27. Make certain the academic and social demands of the situation are within the student's ability level.

28. Model for the student appropriate responses to environmental cues in social situations.

29. Make certain that other teachers and school personnel who work with the student know that the student does not respond appropriately to environmental social cues.

30. Have the student practice appropriate responses to environmental social cues with the teacher(s) in classroom activities (e.g., simulations, role playing, etc.).

31. Carefully consider the student's age and experience before expecting him/her to respond appropriately to environmental cues in social situations.

32. Prevent the student from becoming overstimulated by an activity. Supervise student behavior to limit overexcitement in physical activities, games, parties, etc.

33. Maintain consistent expectations within the ability level of the student.

34. Provide the student with clearly stated expectations for all situations.

35. Prevent the student from becoming so stimulated by an event or activity that the student cannot control his/her behavior.

36. Select nonacademic activities designed to provide the student with social situations during which he/she can respond to environmental social cues appropriately.

37. In conjunction with other school personnel, develop as much consistency across the various environments as possible (e.g., rules, criteria for success, behavioral expectations, consequences, etc.).

38. Prepare the student of environmental and social expectations in advance to increase his/her opportunity to successfully respond.

39. Reduce the emphasis on competition (e.g., academic or social). Fear of failure may create anxiety resulting in inappropriate responses to environmental social cues.

40. Explain to the student what he/she has done correctly, what is expected for total correct response, and what he/she can do to improve toward or reach total correct response.

41. Establish cues that the student is expected to follow (e.g., bells; rules, such as standing in line; manners, such as saying "please" and "thank you," etc.).

42. Reinforce the student for adjusting his/her behavior to varying social cues and expectations from one environment or activity to another. As the student demonstrates success, gradually increase the time required for reinforcement.

43. Have the student question any part of the activity or the responses you expect of him/her that the student does not understand.

44. Explain to the student that he/she should be satisfied with his/her best efforts rather than perfection.

45. Identify the expectations of different environments and help the student develop skills needed for success in all environments.

46. Explain the benefits of trying one's best to follow social cues in the community (e.g., a person would be more welcome to return, a person might acquire positive social regard from other people, etc.).

47. Provide the student with social cues commonly found across environments (such as signs to be quiet, signs to wait before being seated, bathroom signs, etc.).

48. Provide the student with more than enough time to adapt or modify his/her behavior to different situations (e.g., have the student stop recess activities five minutes prior to coming into the building).

49. As much as possible, match cues to the student's ability to respond (e.g., visual cues are used for students who cannot hear, auditory cues and symbols are used for students who cannot see, etc.).

50. Make certain attention is not inadvertently given to the student for failing to respond to a social cue (e.g., only responding to the student when he/she demonstrates inappropriate behavior).

51. Make certain explanations regarding how the student should respond to social cues are delivered in a way the student understands. This can be checked by asking the student to repeat the explanation in his/her own words.

52. Demonstrate accepting behavior (e.g., willingness to help, making criticisms constructive and positive, etc.) to encourage the student to socialize and communicate in learning environments.

53. Teach the student to communicate his/her needs in an appropriate manner (e.g., raise hand, use normal tone of voice when speaking, use soft tones of voice when speaking in a restaurant, etc.).

54. Give the student responsibilities in school and community environments which promote his/her ability to socially interact in a positive manner.

55. Make the student responsible for identifying social cues with his/her peers (e.g., saying "please" and "thank you" at lunch and during snack times).

153 Responds inappropriately to praise or recognition from other students or teachers

Goals:

1. The student will respond appropriately to praise.
2. The student will respond appropriately to recognition.

Objectives:

1. The student will respond appropriately when given praise by saying "thank you," smiling, etc., on ___ out of ___ trials.
2. The student will respond appropriately when given recognition by saying "thank you," smiling, etc., on ___ out of ___ trials.
3. The student will respond appropriately when praised by the teacher by saying "thank you," smiling, etc., on ___ out of ___ trials.
4. The student will respond appropriately when recognized by the teacher by saying "thank you," smiling, etc., on ___ out of ___ trials.
5. The student will respond appropriately when praised by a peer by saying "thank you," smiling, etc., on ___ out of ___ trials.
6. The student will respond appropriately when recognized by a peer by saying "thank you," smiling, etc., on ___ out of ___ trials.

Interventions:

1. Model appropriate ways to respond to interactions with other students or teachers.

2. Praise or recognize the student when he/she will most likely be able to demonstrate an appropriate response (e.g., when the student is not being singled out in a group).

3. Praise or recognize the student in private. The public aspect of praise or recognition is often the cause of the inappropriate response.

4. Provide the student with many social and academic successes so he/she may learn how to respond appropriately.

5. Assess the appropriateness of the social situation in relation to the student's ability to function successfully.

6. Distribute praise and recognition equally to all members of the class.

7. Provide praise or recognition for smaller increments of success so that the student may gradually become accustomed to the recognition.

8. Provide praise and recognition as a natural consequence for appropriate behavior.

9. Try various groupings to determine the situation in which the student is most comfortable.

10. Make certain that reinforcement is not inadvertently given for inappropriate behavior (e.g., attending to the student only when he/she responds inappropriately to praise or recognition).

11. Use alternative forms of praise or recognition which are not threatening to the student (e.g., written notes, telephone calls to parents, display of work done well, etc.).

12. Present praise with a matter-of-fact delivery and avoid exaggerated exclamations of success.

13. Use feedback related to performance (e.g., test scores, grades, etc.) in place of praise or recognition. As the student becomes more capable of accepting praise and recognition, gradually deliver verbal praise and recognition.

14. Rather than emphasizing winning or "beating" other students in competition, encourage individual success or progress which may be enjoyed privately rather than publicly.

15. Treat the student with respect. Talk in an objective manner at all times.

16. Maintain trust and confidentiality with the student at all times.

17. Make certain that other teachers and school personnel who work with the student know that the student does not respond appropriately to praise and recognition.

18. Reinforce those students in the classroom who respond appropriately to praise or recognition.

19. Teach the student acceptable ways to communicate displeasure, anger, frustration, etc.

20. Reinforce the student for responding appropriately to praise or recognition: (a) give the student a tangible reward (e.g., classroom privileges, line leading, passing out materials, five minutes free time, etc.) or (b) give the student an intangible reward (e.g., praise, handshake, smile, etc.).

21. Write a contract with the student specifying what behavior is expected (e.g., saying "thank you" when given praise or recognition) and what reinforcement will be made available when the terms of the contract have been met.

22. Reinforce the student for responding appropriately to praise or recognition based on the number of times the student can be successful. As the student demonstrates success, gradually increase the number of times required for reinforcement.

23. Speak with the student to explain (a) what the student is doing wrong (e.g., behaving inappropriately when recognized by others) and (b) what the student should be doing (e.g., saying "thank you," smiling, etc.).

24. Make sure you express your feelings in a socially acceptable way.

25. Communicate with the parents (e.g., notes home, phone calls, etc.) to share information concerning the student's progress. The parents may reinforce the student at home for responding appropriately to praise or recognition at school.

Reminder: Do not punish a student for his/her inability to respond appropriately to praise or recognition.

154 Makes derogatory comments or inappropriate gestures to other students or teachers

Goals:
1. The student will make appropriate comments to other students.
2. The student will make appropriate comments to teachers.

Objectives:
1. The student will make appropriate comments to a peer during ___ out of ___ interactions.
2. The student will settle minor conflicts with a peer during ___ out of ___ interactions.
3. The student will refrain from arguing with a peer during ___ out of ___ interactions.
4. The student will demonstrate appropriate interaction skills such as sharing, waiting his/her turn, talking in an acceptable manner, and making appropriate gestures during ___ out of ___ interactions with a peer.
5. The student will refrain from calling names during ___ out of ___ interactions with peers.
6. The student will refrain from cursing during ___ out of ___ interactions with a peer.
7. The student will refrain from using obscenities during ___ out of ___ interactions with a peer.
8. The student will refrain from making rude comments during ___ out of ___ interactions with a peer.
9. The student will demonstrate respect for a peer on ___ out of ___ trials.
10. The student will make comments that are appropriate to the situation on ___ out of ___ trials.
11. The student will make gestures that are appropriate to the situation on ___ out of ___ trials.
12. The student will make appropriate comments to the teacher in ___ out of ___ interactions.
13. The student will refrain from arguing with the teacher when given a direction, new task, etc., on ___ out of ___ trials.
14. The student will converse with the teacher in a calm tone of voice during ___ out of ___ interactions.
15. The student will verbally express his/her feelings in an appropriate manner when interacting with the teacher on ___ out of ___ trials.
16. The student will use socially acceptable language in public settings on ___ out of ___ trials.

Interventions:

1. Teach the student appropriate ways to communicate displeasure, anger, etc.

2. Reduce the stimuli which contribute to the student's arguing, calling names, cursing, etc.

3. Provide the student with a quiet place to work. This is used as a means of reducing distracting stimuli and not as a form of punishment.

4. Make certain the student understands the natural consequences of inappropriate behavior (e.g., peers/teachers will choose not to interact with him/her, exclusion from activities, etc.).

5. Facilitate on-task behavior by providing a full schedule of daily events. Prevent lag time from occurring when the student would be free to engage in inappropriate behavior.

6. Teach the student problem-solving skills: (a) identify the problem, (b) identify goals and objectives, (c) develop strategies, (d) develop a plan for action, and (e) carry out the plan.

7. Teach the student positive ways to interact with other students/teachers.

8. Make certain the student recognizes inappropriate comments (e.g., call attention to the comments when they occur, record each instance, terminate the activity when the comment occurs, etc.).

9. Interact frequently with the student to monitor language used.

10. Maintain visibility to and from the student. The teacher should be able to see the student and the student should be able to see the teacher. Make eye contact possible at all times.

11. Prevent the student from becoming overstimulated by an activity (e.g., monitor or supervise student behavior to limit overexcitement).

12. Prevent frustrating or anxiety-producing situations from occurring (e.g., give the student tasks only on his/her ability level, give the student only the number of tasks that can be successfully managed in one sitting, reduce social interactions which stimulate the student's use of obscene language, etc.).

13. Reduce activities which might threaten the student (e.g., give the student tasks only on his/her ability level, give the student only the number of tasks that can be successfully managed in one sitting, reduce social interactions which stimulate the student's use of obscene language, etc.).

14. Assess the appropriateness of the social situation in relation to the student's ability to function successfully.

15. Discuss with the student ways he/she could deal with unpleasant experiences which would typically cause him/her to use obscene language (e.g., talk to the teacher, go to a quiet area in the school, talk with a counselor, etc.).

16. Deliver a predetermined signal (e.g., hand signal, verbal cue, etc.) when the student begins to use inappropriate language.

17. Make certain that positive reinforcement is not inadvertently given for inappropriate language (e.g., attending to the student only when he/she is using profane or obscene language).

18. Deal with the student in a calm and deliberate manner rather than in a manner that would show evidence of shock and surprise.

19. Act as an appropriate role model by using appropriate language at all times (e.g., use appropriate language to convey disappointment, unhappiness, surprise, etc.).

20. Evaluate the appropriateness of the task to determine (a) if the task is too difficult and (b) if the length of time scheduled to complete the task is adequate.

21. Make certain the student knows which comments will not be tolerated at school.

22. Avoid discussion of topics that are sensitive to the student (e.g., divorce, unemployment, alcoholism, etc.).

23. Teach the student to respect others and their belongings by respecting the student and his/her belongings.

24. Do not force the student to interact with other students/teachers with whom he/she is not completely comfortable.

25. Encourage the student to interact with others.

26. Provide frequent opportunities for the student to meet new people.

27. Do not force the student to interact with others.

28. Make sure you express your feelings in a socially acceptable manner.

29. Teach the student to "think" before acting (e.g., ask himself/herself "What is happening?" "What am I doing?" "What should I do?" "What will be best for me?").

30. Have the student practice appropriate verbal exchanges which should be made (e.g., "Excuse me." "I'm sorry." etc.).

31. Make certain the student is allowed to voice an opinion in a situation to avoid becoming angry or upset.

32. Teach the student appropriate words or phrases to use in situations of anger, stress, frustration, etc.

33. Remove the student from the group or activity until he/she can demonstrate appropriate behavior.

34. Reinforce those students in the classroom who communicate in an appropriate manner with other students/teachers.

35. Reinforce the student for communicating in an appropriate manner based on the length of time the student can be successful. As the student demonstrates success, gradually increase the length of time required for reinforcement.

36. Establish classroom rules:
- Work on-task.
- Work quietly.
- Remain in your seat.
- Finish task.
- Meet task expectations.

Review rules often. Reinforce students for following rules.

37. Speak with the student to explain (a) what the student is doing wrong (e.g., calling names, arguing, cursing, etc.) and (b) what the student should be doing (e.g., following rules, staying on-task, attending to responsibilities, etc.).

38. Reinforce the student for communicating in an appropriate manner with other students/teachers: (a) give the student a tangible reward (e.g., classroom privileges, line leading, passing out materials, five minutes free time, etc.) or (b) give the student an intangible reward (e.g., praise, handshake, smile, etc.).

39. Provide the student with the opportunity to work with a peer who will be a model for communicating in an appropriate manner.

40. Require that the student identify alternative behaviors following an instance of derogatory comments or inappropriate gestures.

41. Reduce the emphasis on competition. Repeated failure may result in anger and frustration which may take the form of derogatory comments or inappropriate behavior.

42. Modify or adjust situations which may contribute to the student's use of obscene or profane language (e.g., if an assignment causes the student to become upset, modify the assignment to a level at which the student can be successful.

43. Try various groupings to determine the situation in which the student is most successful.

44. Have the student question any directions, explanations, and instructions not understood.

45. Intervene early when inappropriate behavior occurs to prevent the behavior from becoming more serious. Deliberate interventions may prevent future problems.

46. Avoid ignoring the student's inappropriate behavior. Ignored behavior may increase in frequency and may lead to contagion on the part of other students.

47. Develop a routine schedule of activities and tasks for the student so he/she knows what to expect at all times.

48. Evaluate the appropriateness of the task in relation to the student's ability to perform the task.

49. Have the student put himself/herself in someone else's place (e.g., "How would you feel if someone called you dumb or stupid?").

50. Communicate with the parents (e.g., notes home, phone calls, etc.) to share information concerning the student's progress. The parents may reinforce the student at home for communicating in an appropriate manner at school.

51. Write a contract with the student specifying what behavior is expected (e.g., using appropriate language) and what reinforcement will be made available when the terms of the contract have been met.

52. Separate the student from the student(s) who is the primary stimulus or focus of the inappropriate comments.

53. Emphasize individual success or progress rather than winning or "beating" other students.

54. Make certain there will be adult supervision where the student will be (e.g., P.E., lunch, recess, etc.).

55. Avoid arguing with the student.

56. Be consistent in expectations and consequences of behavior.

57. Deliver directions in a supportive rather than threatening manner (e.g., "Please finish your math paper before going to recess." rather than "You had better finish your math paper or else!").

58. Avoid confrontations with the student which lead to inappropriate behavior on the part of the student (e.g., give the student options for alternative tasks, other times to perform assignments, assistance in performing assignments, etc.).

59. Avoid physical contact with the student who is likely to become verbally abusive (e.g., a pat on the back may cause the student to argue, threaten, call names, curse, etc.).

60. Maintain an appropriate physical distance from the student when interacting with him/her to avoid stimulating the student to make inappropriate comments.

61. Use language that is pleasant and calming when speaking with the student to avoid stimulating the student to make inappropriate comments.

62. Do not criticize. When correcting the student, be honest yet supportive. Never cause the student to feel negatively about himself/herself.

63. Treat the student with respect. Talk to the student in an objective and professional manner at all times.

64. Be careful to avoid embarrassing the student by giving him/her orders, demands, etc., in front of others.

65. Make certain that your comments to the student take the form of constructive criticism rather than criticism that can be perceived as personal, threatening, etc. (e.g., instead of saying, "You always make the same mistake." say "A better way to do that might be...").

155 Makes inappropriate comments to teachers

Goal:

1. The student will make appropriate comments to teachers.

Objectives:

1. The student will make appropriate comments to the teacher in ___ out of ___ interactions.
2. The student will refrain from arguing with the teacher when given a direction, new task, etc., on ___ out of ___ trials.
3. The student will converse with the teacher in a calm tone of voice during ___ out of ___ interactions.
4. The student will verbally express his/her feelings in an appropriate manner when interacting with the teacher on ___ out of ___ trials.
5. The student will use socially acceptable language in public settings on ___ out of ___ trials.

Interventions:

1. Teach the student appropriate ways to communicate displeasure, anger, etc.

2. Reduce stimuli which contribute to the student's derogatory comments or inappropriate gestures.

3. Provide the student with a quiet place to work. This is to be used as a means of reducing distracting stimuli and not as punishment.

4. Provide the student with the opportunity to work with a peer who will be a model for communicating in an appropriate manner.

5. Make certain the student understands the natural consequences of his/her inappropriate behavior (e.g., teachers choose not to interact with him/her, exclusion from activities, etc.).

6. Require that the student identify alternative appropriate behaviors following an instance of derogatory comments or inappropriate gestures.

7. Facilitate on-task behavior by providing a full schedule of activities. Prevent lag time from occurring when the student would be free to engage in inappropriate behavior.

8. Reduce the emphasis on competition. Competitive activities may increase the student's anxiety and result in anger and frustration which may take the form of derogatory comments or inappropriate behavior.

9. Emphasize individual success or progress rather than winning or "beating" other students.

10. Modify or adjust situations which contribute to the student's use of obscene or profane language (i.e., if an assignment causes the student to become upset, modify the assignment to a level at which the student can be successful).

11. Interact frequently with the student to monitor language used.

12. Try various groupings to determine the situation in which the student is most successful.

13. Maintain visibility to and from the student. The teacher should be able to see the student, and the student should be able to see the teacher. Make eye contact possible at all times.

14. Prevent frustrating or anxiety-producing situations from occurring (e.g., giving the student tasks only on his/her ability level, give the student only the number of tasks that can be successfully managed in one sitting, reduce social interactions which stimulate the student's use of obscene language, etc.).

15. Reduce activities which might threaten the student (e.g., announcing test score ranges or test scores aloud, making students read aloud in class, emphasizing the success of a particular student(s), etc.).

16. Discuss with the student ways to deal with unpleasant experiences which would typically cause him/her to use obscene language (e.g., talk to the teacher, go to a quiet area in the room, visit a counselor, etc.).

17. Make certain that positive reinforcement is not inadvertently given for inappropriate language (e.g., attending to the student only when he/she is using profane or obscene language).

18. Deliver a predetermined signal (e.g., hand signal, verbal cue, etc.) when the student begins to use inappropriate language.

19. Deal with the student in a calm and deliberate manner rather than in a manner that would show evidence of shock and surprise.

20. Act as an appropriate role model by using appropriate language at all times (e.g., use appropriate language to convey disappointment, unhappiness, surprise, etc.).

21. Teach the student appropriate words or phrases to use in situations of anger, stress, frustration, etc.

22. Have the student question any directions, explanations, or instructions he/she does not understand.

23. Intervene early when inappropriate behavior occurs to prevent the behavior from becoming more serious. Deliberate interventions may prevent future problems.

24. Avoid arguing with the student.

25. Be careful to avoid embarrassing the student by giving him/her orders, demands, etc., in front of others.

26. Treat the student with respect. Talk to the student in an objective and professional manner at all times.

27. Avoid ignoring the student's inappropriate behavior. Ignored behavior may increase in frequency and may lead to contagion on the part of other students.

28. Avoid confrontations with the student which lead to inappropriate behavior on the part of the student (e.g., give the student options for alternative tasks, other times to perform assignments, assistance in performing assignments, etc.).

29. Develop a routine schedule of activities and tasks for the student so he/she knows what to expect at all times.

30. Evaluate the appropriateness of the task in relation to the student's ability to perform the task.

31. Avoid physical contact with the student who is likely to become verbally abusive (e.g., a pat on the back may cause the student to argue, threaten, call names, curse, etc.).

32. Maintain an appropriate physical distance from the student when interacting with him/her to avoid stimulating the student to make inappropriate comments.

33. Use language that is pleasant and calming when speaking with the student to avoid stimulating the student to make inappropriate comments.

34. Do not criticize. When correcting the student, be honest yet supportive. Never cause the student to feel negatively about himself/herself.

35. Deliver directions in a supportive rather than a threatening manner (e.g., "Please finish your math paper before going to recess." rather than "You had better finish your math paper or else!").

36. Treat the student with respect. Talk in an objective manner at all times.

37. Be consistent in expectations and consequences of behavior.

38. Teach the student appropriate ways to communicate displeasure, anger, frustration, etc.

39. Have the student put himself/herself in someone else's place (e.g., "How would you feel if someone called you dumb or stupid?").

40. Make certain that your comments to the student take the form of constructive criticism rather than criticism that can be perceived as personal, threatening, etc., (e.g., instead of saying, "You always make the same mistake." say, "A better way to do that might be...").

41. Reinforce those students in the classroom who communicate in an appropriate manner with teachers.

42. Teach the student to "think" before acting (e.g., ask himself/herself "What is happening?" "What am I doing?" "What should I do?" "What will be best for me?").

43. Make certain the student is allowed to voice an opinion in a situation to avoid becoming angry or upset.

44. Speak with the student to explain (a) what the student is doing wrong (e.g., arguing, threatening, calling names, etc.) and (b) what the student should be doing (e.g., following rules, staying on-task, attending to his/her responsibilities, etc.).

45. Communicate with parents (e.g., notes home, phone calls, etc.) to share information concerning the student's progress. The parents may reinforce the student at home for communicating in an appropriate manner at school.

46. Remove the student from the group or activity until he/she can demonstrate appropriate behavior.

47. Write a contract with the student specifying what behavior is expected (e.g., using appropriate language) and what reinforcement will be made available when the terms of the contract have been met.

48. Reinforce the student for communicating in an appropriate manner based on the length of time the student can be successful. As the student demonstrates success, gradually increase the length of time required for reinforcement.

49. Make sure you express your feelings in a socially acceptable manner.

50. Establish classroom rules:
- Work on-task.
- Work quietly.
- Remain in your seat.
- Finish task.
- Meet task expectations.

Review rules often. Reinforce students for following rules.

51. Evaluate the appropriateness of the task to determine (a) if the task is too easy, (b) if the task is too difficult, and (c) if the length of time scheduled for the task is adequate.

52. Reinforce the student for communicating in an appropriate manner with teachers: (a) give the student a tangible reward (e.g., classroom privileges, line leading, passing out materials, five minutes free time, etc.) or (b) give the student an intangible reward (e.g., praise, handshake, smile, etc.).

156 Does not use verbal skills to maintain positive relationships with others

Goals:

1. The student will improve his/her interpersonal behavior.
2. The student will improve his/her interpersonal behavior in academic settings.
3. The student will improve his/her interpersonal behavior in nonacademic settings.

Objectives:

1. The student will greet others with positive comments on ____ out of ____ occasions.
2. The student will carry on friendly conversations with others on ____ out of ____ occasions.
3. The student will compliment others on ____ out of ____ occasions.
4. The student will ask conversational questions of others on ____ out of ____ occasions.
5. The student will resolve conflict situations with others on ____ out of ____ occasions.
6. The student will initiate conversations with others on ____ out of ____ occasions.
7. The student will respond in a positive manner to conversations initiated by others on ____ out of ____ occasions.

Interventions:

1. Reinforce the student for using communication skills to maintain positive interpersonal relationships with others: (a) give the student a tangible reward (e.g., classroom privileges, line leading, passing out materials, five minutes free time, etc.) or (b) give the student an intangible reward (e.g., praise, handshake, smile, etc.).

2. Speak to the student to explain (a) what he/she is doing wrong (e.g., threatening, teasing, calling names, etc.) and (b) what he/she should be doing (e.g., using acceptable greetings, complimenting, asking conversational questions, etc.).

3. Have the student question any directions, explanations, instructions he/she does not understand.

4. Reinforce the student for using communication skills to maintain positive interpersonal relationships with others based on the number of times the student can be successful. As the student demonstrates success, gradually increase the number of times required for reinforcement.

5. Write a contract with the student specifying what behavior is expected (e.g., asking conversational questions) and what reinforcement will be made available when the terms of the contract have been met.

6. Communicate with parents (e.g., notes home, phone calls, etc.) to share information concerning the student's progress. The parents may reinforce the student at home for using communication skills to maintain positive interpersonal relationships with others at school.

7. Choose a peer to model appropriate use of communication skills to maintain positive interpersonal relationships with others for the student.

8. Provide the student with many opportunities for successful verbal communications with others.

9. Evaluate the appropriateness of expectations for the student to use communication skills to maintain positive interpersonal relationships with others.

10. Teach the student appropriate positive verbal greetings (e.g., "Hi, how are you doing?" "Good to see you." "Haven't seen you in a long time." etc.).

11. Teach the student appropriate positive verbal requests (e.g., "Please pass the paper." "May I please be excused?" "Will you please help me?" etc.).

12. Teach the student appropriate positive ways to verbally indicate disagreement (e.g., "Excuse me, I think I was here first." "Pardon me, I need to get to my locker." "I'm sorry, but I don't think that's correct." etc.).

13. Help the student become aware of his/her tone of voice when greeting, requesting, and/or disagreeing with others by calling attention to voice inflections which are inappropriate for the situation.

14. Teach the student appropriate verbalizations for problem resolution as an alternative to fighting (e.g., "Let's talk about it." "Let's compromise." "Let's see what would be fair for both of us." etc.).

15. Require the student to practice positive verbal communications with a specified number of people throughout the school day.

16. Make certain that all educators interact with the student on a regular basis and use positive verbal communications in speaking to him/her.

17. Require the student to interact with several individuals (e.g., run errands, request materials, etc.) to increase the opportunities for communication with others.

18. Reinforce those students in the classroom who use communication skills to maintain positive interpersonal relationships with others.

19. Identify those with whom the student most often interacts to make certain they model appropriate verbal communications for the student.

20. Teach the student positive social communication skills to maintain positive interpersonal relationships with others (e.g., waiting your turn to speak, asking conversational questions, using an appropriate tone of voice, talking about appropriate subjects with others, making eye contact, nodding your head, etc.).

21. Use role play to demonstrate situations in which the student would need to use positive interactions with others (e.g., interactions with peers at recess, interactions with cafeteria cooks at lunchtime, interaction with P.E. teacher, etc.).

22. Assess the demands of the social situation to determine an appropriate level of expectation for the student's verbal interactions with others.

23. Model for the student appropriate positive verbal greetings, requests, and indications of disagreement.

24. Teach the student appropriate ways to communicate to adults that a problem exists (e.g., "I don't understand the directions." " I was unable to complete my assignment." "I can't find all of my materials." etc.).

25. Teach the student that he/she must respond differently depending on the person to whom he/she is talking (e.g., "What's happening?" is acceptable for a peer but not for the principal). Discuss how age, position, and/or familiarity can change the form of the greeting/closing used.

26. Have the student engage in simulated conversational activities with feedback designed to teach conversational skills (e.g., greetings, closings, questions, topics of conversation, etc.).

27. Have the student practice "echoing" what you or another student say. Teach the student to imitate inflectional patterns and facial expressions as well as to repeat words.

28. Determine an individual(s) in the school environment with whom the student would most want to converse (e.g., custodian, librarian, resource teacher, principal, older student, etc.). Allow the student to spend time conversing with the individual(s) each day.

29. Arrange a private signal (e.g., holding up a finger, a wink, thumbs up, etc.) to remind the student to use positive communication skills with others.

30. Help the student develop social awareness (e.g., people may be embarrassed by what you say, feelings can be hurt by comments, tact is the best policy, remember interactions which have made you feel good and treat others in the same manner, etc.).

157 Does not carry on conversations with peers and adults

Goals:

1. The student will improve his/her production of speech sounds.
2. The student will improve his/her conversational speech.
3. The student will improve the fluency of his/her speech.
4. The student will improve the ability to express himself/herself verbally.
5. The student will improve his/her grammatical speech.

Objectives:

1. The student will respond to conversational questions from peers ____% of the time.
2. The student will respond to conversational questions from adults ____% of the time.
3. The student will participate in conversation with peers ____% of the time he/she is spoken to by a peer.
4. The student will participate in conversation with adults ____% of the time he/she is spoken to by an adult.
5. The student will initiate conversations with peers (identify some criteria such as once a day, three times a day, etc.).
6. The student will initiate conversations with adults (identify some criteria such as once a day, three times a day, etc.).

Interventions:

1. Encourage or reward others for initiating interactions with the student.

2. Give the student the responsibility of tutoring another student.

3. Ask the student to choose another student to work with on a specific assignment. (If the student has difficulty choosing someone, determine the student's preference by other means, such as a class survey.)

4. Be certain to greet or recognize the student as often as possible (e.g., hallways, cafeteria, welcome to class, acknowledge a job well done, etc.).

5. Provide the student with many social and academic successes.

6. Have the student deliver verbal messages to other staff members to increase his/her opportunity to carry on conversations.

7. Interact with the student from a distance, gradually decreasing the distance until close proximity is achieved.

8. Plan for one-to-one teacher-student interactions at various times throughout the school day.

9. Try various groupings to determine the situation in which the student is most comfortable carrying on a conversation with peers and adults.

10. Request that the student be the leader of a small group activity if he/she possesses mastery of skills or has an interest in that area.

11. Have sharing time at school. Encourage the student to talk about anything that interests him/her.

12. Have the student play games which require conversing with others.

13. Allow the student to show visitors and new students around the school.

14. Have the student run errands which will require interactions with teachers, administrators, staff, etc. (e.g., delivering attendance reports to the office, taking messages to other teachers, etc.).

15. Determine an individual(s) in the school environment with whom the student would most want to converse (e.g., custodian, librarian, resource teacher, principal, older student, etc.). Allow the student to spend time with the individual(s) each day.

16. Identify another student who would be willing to spend time each day with the student.

17. Spend time each day talking with the student on an individual basis about his/her friends.

18. Pair the student with an outgoing student who participates in conversation with peers and adults on a frequent basis.

19. Teach the student conversational questions (e.g., "How are you?" "What have you been up to?" "How is it going?" etc.) to use when speaking to peers and adults.

20. Have the student participate in simulated conversational activities with feedback designed to teach conversational skills (e.g., greetings, questions, topics of conversation, etc.).

21. Provide the student with positive feedback which indicates he/she is successful, important, respected, etc.

22. Have the student work with a peer who is nonthreatening (e.g., younger or smaller).

23. Speak to the student to explain (a) what he/she is doing wrong (e.g., failing to converse with peers and adults) and (b) what he/she should be doing (e.g., conversing with peers and adults).

24. Reinforce the student for conversing with peers and adults: (a) give the student a tangible reward (e.g., classroom privileges, line leading, passing out materials, five minutes free time, etc.) or (b) give the student an intangible reward (e.g., praise, handshake, smile, etc.).

25. Assign a peer to sit/work with the student (e.g., in different settings or activities such as art, music, P.E.; on the bus; tutoring; group projects; running errands in the building; free time; etc.) to increase the student's opportunity to participate in conversation.

26. Evaluate the appropriateness of expecting the student to carry on a conversation with peers and adults.

27. Choose a peer to model conversing with peers and adults for the student.

28. Communicate with parents (e.g., notes home, phone calls, etc.) to share information concerning the student's progress. The parents may reinforce the student at home for conversing with peers and adults at school.

29. Reinforce those students in the classroom who converse with peers and adults.

30. Write a contract with the student specifying what behavior is expected (e.g., conversing with peers and adults) and what reinforcement will be made available when the terms of the contract have been met.

31. Reinforce the student for conversing with peers and adults based on the length of time he/she can be successful. As the student demonstrates success, gradually increase the length of time required for reinforcement.

32. Recognize the student's attempts to communicate his/her needs (e.g., facial expressions, gestures, inactivity, self-deprecating comments, etc.).

33. Spend some time talking with the student on an individual basis about his/her interests.

34. Allow the student to be a member of a group without requiring active participation.

158   Does not use communication skills to initiate positive interpersonal relationships with others

Goals:

1. The student will improve his/her interpersonal behavior.
2. The student will improve his/her interpersonal behavior in academic settings.
3. The student will improve his/her interpersonal behavior in nonacademic settings.

Objectives:

1. The student will greet others with positive comments on ____ out of ____ occasions.
2. The student will carry on friendly conversations with others on ____ out of ____ occasions.
3. The student will compliment others on ____ out of ____ occasions.
4. The student will ask conversational questions of others on ____ out of ____ occasions.
5. The student will resolve conflict situations with others on ____ out of ____ occasions.
6. The student will initiate conversations with others on ____ out of ____ occasions.
7. The student will respond in a positive manner to conversations initiated by others on ____ out of ____ occasions.

Interventions:

1. Reinforce the student for using communication skills to initiate positive interpersonal relationships with others: (a) give the student a tangible reward (e.g., classroom privileges, line leading, passing out materials, five minutes free time, etc.) or (b) give the student an intangible reward (e.g., praise, handshake, smile, etc.).

2. Speak to the student to explain (a) what he/she is doing wrong (e.g., threatening, teasing, calling names, etc.) and (b) what he/she should be doing (e.g., using acceptable greetings, complimenting, asking conversational questions, etc.).

3. Evaluate the appropriateness of expectations for the student to use communication skills to initiate positive interpersonal relationships with others.

4. Reinforce the student for using communication skills to initiate positive interpersonal relationships with others based on the number of times the student can be successful. As the student demonstrates success, gradually increase the number of times required for reinforcement.

5. Write a contract with the student specifying what behavior is expected (e.g., initiating a conversation) and what reinforcement will be made available when the terms of the contract have been met.

6. Communicate with parents (e.g., notes home, phone calls, etc.) to share information concerning the student's progress. The parents may reinforce the student at home for using communication skills to initiate positive interpersonal relationships with others at school.

7. Choose a peer to model appropriate use of communication skills to initiate positive interpersonal relationships with others for the student.

8. Have the student question any directions, explanations, or instructions he/she does not understand.

9. Provide the student with many opportunities for successful verbal communications with peers.

10. Teach the student appropriate positive verbal greetings (e.g., "Hi, how are you doing?" "Good to see you." "Haven't seen you in along time." etc.).

11. Teach the student appropriate positive verbal requests (e.g., "Please pass the paper." "May I please be excused?" "Will you please help me?" etc.).

12. Model for the student appropriate positive verbal greetings, requests, and indications of disagreement.

13. Teach the student appropriate verbalizations for problem resolution as an alternative to fighting (e.g., "Let's talk about it." "Let's compromise." "Let's see what would be fair for both of us." etc.).

14. Require the student to practice positive verbal communications with a specified number of peers throughout the school day.

15. Make certain that all educators interact with the student on a regular basis and use positive verbal communication in speaking to him/her.

16. Require the student to interact with several peers (e.g., run errands, request materials, etc.) to increase the opportunities for communication with others.

17. Reinforce those students in the classroom who use communication skills to initiate positive interpersonal relationships with others.

18. Identify the peers with whom the student most often interacts to make certain they model appropriate verbal communications for the student.

19. Assess the appropriateness of the demands of the social situation to determine an appropriate level of expectation for the student's verbal interaction with others.

20. Help the student develop social awareness (e.g., people may be embarrassed by what you say, feelings can be hurt by comments, tact is the best policy, remember interactions which have made you feel good and treat others in the same manner, etc.).

21. Assess the demands of the social situation to determine an appropriate level of expectation for the student's verbal interactions with others.

22. Teach the student skills in initiating positive conversations with others (e.g., asking questions, listening while the other person speaks, making eye contact, nodding head, making comments which relate to what the other person has said, etc.).

23. Help the student become aware of his/her tone of voice when greeting, requesting, and/or disagreeing with others by calling attention to voice inflections which are inappropriate for the situation.

24. Teach the student positive social communication skills to initiate positive interpersonal relationships with others (e.g., waiting your turn to speak, asking conversational questions, using an appropriate tone of voice, talking about appropriate subjects with others, etc.).

159 Does not use communication skills to maintain positive interpersonal relationships with authority figures

Goal:

1. The student will use communication skills to maintain positive interpersonal relationships with authority figures.

Objectives:

1. The student will greet authority figures with positive comments on _____ out of _____ trials.
2. The student will engage in friendly conversations with authority figures on _____ out of _____ trials.
3. The student will ask conversational questions of authority figures on _____ out of _____ trials.
4. The student will resolve conflict situations with authority figures on _____ out of _____ trials.
5. The student will initiate conversations with authority figures on _____ out of _____ trials.
6. The student will respond in a positive manner to conversation initiated by authority figures on _____ out of _____ trials.

Interventions:

1. Reinforce the student for using communication skills to maintain positive interpersonal relationships with authority figures: (a) give the student a tangible reward (e.g., classroom privileges, line leading, passing out materials, five minutes free time, etc.) or (b) give the student an intangible reward (e.g., praise, handshake, smile, etc.).

2. Speak to the student to explain (a) what he/she is doing wrong (e.g., speaking disrespectfully) and (b) what he/she should be doing (e.g., speaking respectfully).

3. Teach the student positive verbal greetings (e.g., "Hi." "How are you doing?" "Good to see you." "Haven't seen you in a long time." etc.).

4. Reinforce the student for using communication skills to maintain positive interpersonal relationships with authority figures based on the number of times the student can be successful. As the student demonstrates success, gradually increase the number of times required for reinforcement.

5. Write a contract with the student specifying what behavior is expected (e.g., speaking respectfully) and what reinforcement will be made available when the terms of the contract have been met.

6. Communicate with parents (e.g., notes home, phone calls, etc.) to share information concerning the student's progress. The parents may reinforce the student at home for using communication skills to maintain positive interpersonal relationships with authority figures at school.

7. Choose a peer to model appropriate use of communication skills to maintain positive interpersonal relationships with authority figures for the student.

8. Evaluate the appropriateness of the expectations for the student to use communication skills to maintain positive interpersonal relationships with authority figures.

9. Provide the student with many successful verbal communications with authority figures.

10. Teach the student positive verbal requests (e.g., "Please pass the paper." "May I be excused?" "Will you please help me?" etc.).

11. Teach the student positive ways to verbally indicate disagreement (e.g., "I'm sorry, but I don't think that's correct." etc.).

12. Teach the student appropriate communication skills for problem resolution (e.g., "Let's talk about it." "Let's compromise." "Let's see what would be fair for both of us." etc.).

13. Require the student to practice positive verbal communications with an identified number of authority figures throughout the school day.

14. Make certain that all educators interact with the student on a regular basis and use positive verbal communication when speaking to him/her.

15. Arrange for the student to interact with several authority figures (e.g., run errands, request materials, etc.) to increase the opportunities for communication with adults.

16. Reinforce those students in the classroom who use communication skills to maintain positive interpersonal relationships with authority figures.

17. Assess the demands of the social situation to determine an appropriate level of expectation for the student's verbal interactions with authority figures.

18. Teach the student appropriate ways to communicate to an authority figure that a problem exists (e.g., "I don't understand the directions." "I was unable to complete my assignment." "I can't find all of my materials." etc.).

19. Model for the student positive verbal greetings, requests, and indications of disagreement.

20. Identify authority figures with whom the student most often interacts to make certain that they model appropriate verbal communications for the student.

21. Teach the student positive social communication skills to maintain positive interpersonal relationships with authority figures (e.g., taking turns to speak, asking conversational questions, using an appropriate tone of voice, discussing appropriate information with authority figures, etc.).

22. Help the student develop social awareness (e.g., people may be embarrassed by what you say, feelings can be hurt by comments you make, tact is the best policy, remember interactions which have made you feel good and treat others in the same manner, etc.).

23. Help the student become aware of his/her tone of voice when greeting, requesting, and/or disagreeing by calling attention to inappropriate voice inflections for the situation.

24. Teach the student skills in maintaining positive conversations with authority figures (e.g., asking questions, listening while the other person speaks, making eye contact, head nodding, making comments which relate to what the other person has said, etc.).

160 Responds inappropriately to constructive criticism or comments from others

Goals:
1. The student will respond appropriately when he/she receives a suggestion.
2. The student will respond appropriately when he/she receives a constructive criticism.

Objectives:
1. The student will correct his/her errors when told to by the teacher on ___ out of ___ trials.
2. The student will change the manner in which he/she performs, talks to others, etc., when given constructive criticism on ___ out of ___ trials.
3. The student will refrain from crying, tantruming, yelling, etc., when he/she receives a suggestion on ___ out of ___ trials.
4. The student will refrain from crying, tantruming, yelling, etc., when he/she receives a constructive criticism on ___ out of ___ trials.
5. The student will respond appropriately to a suggestion by saying "thank you", talking about alternative ways to perform a task, etc., on ___ out of ___ trials.
6. The student will respond appropriately to constructive criticism by discussing alternative ways to behave, perform the task, etc., on ___ out of ___ trials.

Interventions:

1. Reinforce the student for responding in an appropriate manner to constructive criticism based on the number of times the student can be successful. As the student demonstrates success, gradually increase the number of times required for reinforcement.

2. Remove the student from the group or activity until he/she can demonstrate appropriate behavior or self-control.

3. Write a contract with the student specifying what behavior is expected (e.g., responding appropriately to constructive criticism) and what reinforcement will be made available when the terms of the contract have been met.

4. Communicate with the parents (e.g., notes home, phone calls, etc.) to share information concerning the student's progress. The parents may reinforce the student at home for responding in an appropriate manner to constructive criticism at school.

5. Evaluate the appropriateness of the task to determine (a) if the task is too easy, (b) if the task is too difficult, and (c) if the length of time scheduled for the task is adequate.

6. Demonstrate appropriate ways to respond to constructive criticism.

7. Try various groupings to determine the situation in which the student is most comfortable.

8. Provide the student with positive feedback which indicates he/she is successful, competent, important, valuable, etc.

9. Provide the student with many social and academic successes.

10. Assess the appropriateness of the social situation in relation to the student's ability to function successfully.

11. Structure the environment in such a way that the teacher is the only one providing constructive criticism. As the student learns to accept constructive criticism from the teacher, allow input from others.

12. Provide constructive criticism in private.

13. Provide constructive criticism equally to all members of the class.

14. Provide constructive criticism when the student is most likely to demonstrate an appropriate response.

15. Make certain that positive reinforcement is not inadvertently given for inappropriate behavior (e.g., lowering expectations because the student becomes upset when criticism is delivered).

16. Make certain the student receives adequate, positive reinforcement whenever he/she is behaving in an appropriate manner.

17. Assess criticism to make certain it is constructive and positive.

18. Have the student question anything he/she does not understand while performing assignments.

19. Encourage the student to check and correct his/her own work.

20. Explain to the student that constructive criticism is meant to be helpful, not threatening.

21. Reduce the emphasis on competition and perfection. A highly competitive atmosphere or repeated failure may cause the student to react in inappropriate ways to constructive criticism from others.

22. Make the necessary adjustments in the environment to prevent the student from experiencing stress, frustration, anger, etc.

23. Provide the student with academic tasks which can be self-checked.

24. Supervise the student while he/she is performing tasks to monitor quality.

25. Provide the student with clearly stated criteria for acceptable work.

26. Make certain that constructive criticism is tactfully conveyed.

27. Make certain that an offer of assistance is made at the same time constructive criticism is delivered.

28. Require a demonstration of ability rather than having the student perform the entire assignment or activity again (e.g., work a few problems correctly rather than repeating the entire assignment).

29. Choose a peer to model appropriate responses to constructive criticism for the student.

30. Have the student question any directions, explanations, and instructions not understood.

31. Allow natural consequences to occur when the student fails to respond appropriately to constructive criticism (e.g., make highly reinforcing activities contingent upon responding appropriately to redirection in academic and social situations).

32. Make certain that attention is not inadvertently given to the student for failing to respond appropriately to constructive criticism (i.e., remove attention from the student when he/she fails to respond appropriately to redirection in academic and social situations in those instances when attention is reinforcing inappropriate behavior).

33. Provide adequate time for the student to respond appropriately to constructive criticism.

34. Deliver instructions in a clear and concise manner.

35. Assist the student in responding appropriately to constructive criticism (e.g., help the student correct one or two items to get him/her started).

36. Develop subsequent tasks to be performed the next day based on errors the student makes rather than requiring immediate correction of work done incorrectly.

37. Do not criticize when correcting the student; be honest yet supportive. Never cause the student to feel negatively about himself/herself.

38. Intervene early when there is a problem to prevent more serious problems from occurring.

39. Treat the student with respect. Talk in an objective manner at all times.

40. Avoid embarrassing the student by giving him/her orders, demands, etc., in front of others.

41. Make certain that your comments take the form of constructive criticism rather than criticism that can be perceived as personal, threatening, etc. (e.g., instead of saying, "You always make the same mistakes." say, "A better way to do that might be . . .").

42. Reinforce those students in the classroom who respond appropriately to constructive criticism.

43. Establish classroom rules:
- Work on-task.
- Work quietly.
- Remain in your seat.
- Finish task.
- Meet task expectations.

Review rules often. Reinforce students for following rules.

44. Speak with the student to explain (a) what the student is doing wrong (e.g., yelling, cursing, making derogatory comments, crying, etc.) and (b) what the student should be doing (e.g., asking for directions, help, clarification, etc.).

45. Reward others for accepting errors they make.

46. Reinforce the student for responding in an appropriate manner to constructive criticism: (a) give the student a tangible reward (e.g., classroom privileges, line leading, passing out materials, five minutes free time, etc.) or (b) give the student an intangible reward (e.g., praise, hand-shake, smile, etc.).

47. Allow the student to attempt something new in private before doing so in front of others.

48. Provide constructive criticism in a private setting rather than in front of others.

161 Agitates and provokes peers to a level of verbal or physical assault

Goals:

1. The student will demonstrate behaviors that will cause peers to react in a positive manner.
2. The student will refrain from agitating peers.
3. The student will refrain from provoking peers to a level of verbal or physical assault.
4. The student will interact appropriately with peers.

Objectives:

1. The student will interact with others in an appropriate manner during ___out of ___interactions.
2. The student will interact with others in a physically appropriate manner during ___out of ___ interactions.
3. The student will make positive comments when interacting with peers during ___out of ___ interactions.
4. The student will refrain from touching peers during ___out of ___interactions.
5. The student will avoid interacting with peers who are easily agitated and provoked by his/her behavior on ___ out of ___ trials.
6. The student will develop appropriate social interaction skills and use the skills when interacting with others ___% of the time. (Gradually increase expectations as the student demonstrates success.)

Interventions:

1. Teach the student acceptable ways to communicate displeasure, anger, etc.

2. Reduce the stimuli that contribute to the student's derogatory comments or inappropriate gestures.

3. Provide the student with a quiet place to work (e.g., study carrel, "private office," etc.). This is used as a means of reducing distracting stimuli and not as a form of punishment.

4. Provide the student with the opportunity to work with a peer who will be an appropriate model.

5. Separate the student from the peer(s) who is the primary stimulus or focus of the derogatory comments or inappropriate gestures.

6. Make certain the student understands the natural consequences of inappropriate behavior (e.g., peers choosing not to interact with him/her, exclusion from activities, etc.).

7. Require the student to identify alternative appropriate behaviors following an instance of derogatory comments or inappropriate gestures.

8. Facilitate on-task behavior by providing a full schedule of daily events. Prevent lag time from occurring when the student would be free to engage in inappropriate behavior.

9. Reduce the emphasis on competition. Repeated failure may result in anger and frustration that may take the form of derogatory comments or inappropriate gestures.

10. Emphasize individual success or progress rather than winning or "beating" other students.

11. Intervene early when the student begins to agitate or provoke peers.

12. Treat the student with respect. Talk in an objective manner at all times.

13. Remove the student from the classroom if he/she is unable to demonstrate self-control. The student should not be allowed to remain in the classroom and be abusive to peers.

14. Maintain visibility to and from the student. The teacher should be able to see the student and the student should be able to see the teacher. Make eye contact possible at all times.

15. Inform others (e.g., teachers, school personnel, etc.) of the behavior expected of the student so they will encourage appropriate behavior from the student.

16. Remove the student from the group or activity until he/she can demonstrate appropriate behavior.

17. Avoid embarrassing the student by giving him/her orders, demands, etc., in front of others.

18. Have the student put himself/herself in someone else's place (e.g., "How would you feel if someone called you dumb or stupid?").

19. Reinforce those students in the classroom who communicate in an appropriate manner.

20. Encourage the student to use problem-solving skills: (a) identify the problem, (b) identify goals and objectives, (c) develop strategies, (d) develop a plan of action, and (e) carry out the plan.

21. Do not leave a lot of unstructured time for the student.

22. Teach the student to "think" before acting (e.g., ask himself/herself "What is happening?" "What am I doing?" "What should I do?" "What will be best for me?").

23. Make certain the student is allowed to voice an opinion in a situation to avoid becoming angry or upset.

24. Evaluate the appropriateness of the task to determine (a) if the task is too easy, (b) if the task is too difficult, and (c) if the length of time scheduled for the task is adequate.

25. Communicate with parents (e.g., notes home, phone calls, etc.) to share information concerning the student's progress. The parents may reinforce the student at home for demonstrating appropriate behavior at school.

26. Write a contract with the student specifying what behavior is expected (e.g., communicating with peers in a positive manner) and what reinforcement will be made available when the terms of the contract have been met.

27. Make certain there will always be adult supervision where the student will be (e.g., lunch, recess, P.E., etc.).

28. Reinforce the student for communicating in an appropriate manner based on the length of time the student can be successful. As the student demonstrates success, gradually increase the length of time required for reinforcement.

29. Do not force the student to interact with others.

30. Establish classroom rules:
- Work on-task.
- Work quietly.
- Remain in your seat.
- Finish task.
- Meet task expectations.

Review rules often. Reinforce students for following rules.

31. Speak with the student to explain (a) what the student is doing wrong (e.g., calling names, making inappropriate gestures, etc.) and (b) what the student should be doing (e.g., following rules, staying on-task, attending to his/her responsibilities, etc.).

32. Reinforce the student for communicating in an appropriate manner with peers: (a) give the student a tangible reward (e.g., classroom privileges, line leading, passing out materials, five minutes free time, etc.) or (b) give the student an intangible reward (e.g., praise, handshake, smile, etc.).

33. Make certain the student is not allowed time alone with other students when he/she is upset or angry.

34. Avoid discussion of topics that are sensitive to the student (e.g., divorce, unemployment, alcoholism, etc.).

162 Demonstrates inappropriate physical or verbal responses to other students' or teachers' attempts to interact

Goals:

1. The student will respond appropriately to others' attempts to be friendly.
2. The student will respond appropriately to others' attempts to be complimentary.
3. The student will respond appropriately to others' attempts to be sympathetic.
4. The student will respond appropriately to others' attempts to interact with him/her.

Objectives:

1. The student will respond appropriately to others' attempts to be friendly during ___out of ___ interactions.
2. The student will respond appropriately to others' attempts to be complimentary during ___out of ___ interactions.
3. The student will respond appropriately to others' attempts to be sympathetic during ___out of ___ interactions.
4. The student will respond appropriately to others' attempts to interact with him/her on ___out of ___ trials.
5. The student will respond appropriately to others' attempts to interact for ___minutes at a time. (Gradually increase expectations as the student demonstrates success.)
6. The student will be friendly when interacting with others on ___out of ___trials.
7. The student will say "Thank you" when given a compliment on ___out of ___trials.
8. The student will appropriately acknowledge others' attempts to be sympathetic on ___out of ___ trials.
9. The student will appropriately interact with others on ___out of ___ trials.

Interventions:

1. Assess the appropriateness of the social situation in relation to the student's ability to be successful.

2. Assign a peer to sit/work directly with the student (e.g., in different settings or activities such as art, music, P.E., tutoring, group projects, recess, etc.). As the student becomes comfortable working with one other student, gradually increase the size of the group.

3. Provide the student with positive feedback which indicates he/she is important.

4. Provide the student with many social and academic successes.

5. Provide opportunities for appropriate interactions within the classroom (e.g., peer models engaged in appropriate interactions).

6. Try various groupings to determine the situation in which the student is most comfortable.

7. Reduce stimuli which contribute to the student's inappropriate responses to others' attempts to interact.

8. Intervene early to prevent the student from losing self-control.

9. Limit interactions with the peer(s) who is the primary focus of the student's inappropriate responses.

10. Respect the student's right to a reasonable amount of privacy.

11. Allow the student to be a member of a group without requiring active participation.

12. Teach the student social interaction skills (e.g., ways in which to appropriately respond to others' attempts to be friendly, complimentary, sympathetic, etc.).

13. Help the student develop social awareness (e.g., people may be embarrassed by what you say, feelings can be hurt by comments, tact is the best policy, remember interactions which have made you feel good and treat others in the same manner, etc.).

14. Reinforce the student for responding appropriately to others' attempts to be friendly, complimentary, sympathetic, etc.: (a) give the student a tangible reward (e.g., classroom privileges, line leading, passing out materials, five minutes free time, etc.) or (b) give the student an intangible reward (e.g., praise, handshake, smile, etc.).

15. Make certain you express your feelings in a socially acceptable way.

16. Speak to the student to explain (a) what the student is doing wrong (e.g., using inappropriate language, responding negatively, calling names, making inappropriate gestures, etc.) and (b) what the student should be doing (e.g., being positive in response to others).

17. Communicate with the parents (e.g., notes home, phone calls, etc.) to share information concerning the student's progress. The parents may reinforce the student at home for responding appropriately to others' attempts to be friendly, complimentary, sympathetic, etc., at school.

18. Write a contract stating appropriate ways to respond to others and identify what reinforcement will be made available when the terms of the contract have been met.

19. Model appropriate ways to respond to others who are friendly, complimentary, sympathetic, etc.

20. Encourage others to compliment the student.

21. Reinforce other students for responding appropriately to interactions with students or teachers.

22. Treat the student with respect. Talk in an objective manner at all times.

23. Provide the student with frequent opportunities to meet new people.

24. Encourage the student to interact with others.

Goals:

1. The student will interact appropriately with other students.
2. The student will interact appropriately with teachers.

Objectives:

1. The student will refrain from touching other students during ___ out of ___ interactions.
2. The student will be able to settle minor conflicts with peers without becoming physically aggressive during ___ out of ___ interactions.
3. The student will seek teacher assistance when he/she is experiencing difficulty interacting with peers during ___ out of ___ interactions.
4. The student will walk away from peer conflicts during ___ out of ___ interactions.
5. The student will verbally, rather than physically, express his/her feelings toward a peer during ___ out of ___ interactions.
6. The student will refrain from touching the teacher during ___ out of ___ interactions.
7. The student will sit/stand quietly when the teacher discusses the student's behavior with him/her during ___ out of ___ interactions.
8. The student will verbally, rather than physically, express his/her feelings toward the teacher during ___ out of ___ interactions.
9. The student will control his/her anger to the extent of not requiring to be physically restrained by the teacher in ___ out of ___ anger-producing situations.

Interventions:

1. Teach the student problem-solving skills: (a) identify the problem, (b) identify goals and objectives, (c) develop strategies, (d) develop a plan of action, and (e) carry out the plan.

2. Provide the student with positive feedback which indicates he/she is successful, important, respected, etc.

3. Structure the environment to reduce opportunities for the student to become physically aggressive toward other students or teachers (e.g., seating arrangement, supervision, etc.).

4. Teach the student alternative ways to deal with situations which make him/her feel frustrated or angry (e.g., withdrawing, talking, etc.).

5. Be mobile to be frequently near the student.

6. Reduce activities which might be threatening to the student (e.g., announcing test score ranges or test scores aloud, making students read aloud in class, emphasizing the success of a particular student(s), etc.).

7. Try various groupings to determine the situation in which the student is most likely to succeed socially.

8. Make the necessary adjustments in the environment that will prevent the student from becoming overstimulated by peers.

9. Reduce the emphasis on competition and perfection. Repeated failure and frustration may cause outbursts of physical aggression.

10. Maintain visibility to and from the student. The teacher should be able to see the student and the student should be able to see the teacher. Make eye contact possible at all times.

11. Facilitate on-task behavior by providing a full schedule of activities. Prevent lag time from occurring when the student would be free to engage in inappropriate behavior.

12. Maintain supervision so the student is not left alone with other students.

13. Provide the student with as many high-interest activities as possible to keep him/her from becoming physically aggressive toward other students or teachers.

14. Maintain maximum supervision of the student and gradually decrease supervision over time as the student demonstrates appropriate behavior.

15. Make certain that all school personnel are aware of the student's tendency to become physically aggressive so they will monitor the student's behavior.

16. Limit the student's independent movement in the school environment.

17. Provide a quiet place for the student to work independently, away from peer interactions. This is not to be used as a form of punishment but rather as an opportunity to increase the student's success in his/her environment.

18. Place reinforcement emphasis on academic productivity and accuracy to reduce the likelihood of the student becoming physically aggressive (i.e., increased productivity and accuracy will reduce the likelihood of inappropriate behavior).

19. Reduce or remove any stimulus in the environment which leads to the student's physically aggressive behavior (e.g., possessions, competition, teasing, etc.).

20. Make certain the student understands the natural consequences of hurting other students (e.g., less freedom, more restrictive environment, assault charges, etc.).

21. Prevent the student from receiving too much stimulation (e.g., monitor or supervise student behavior to limit overexcitement in physical activities, games, parties, etc.).

22. Limit the student's opportunity to enter areas of the school environment where he/she is more likely to be physically aggressive.

23. Separate the student from the peer(s) who may be encouraging or stimulating the student's inappropriate behavior.

24. Do not force the student to interact or remain in a group when he/she is physically aggressive (e.g., daily reading group, physical education group, etc.).

25. Provide the student with opportunities for social and academic success.

26. Intervene early when there is a problem with fighting to prevent more serious problems from occurring.

27. Encourage the student to tell you about problems that occur with other students at school.

28. Make certain there will always be adult supervision where the student will be.

29. Do not force the student to play with other students with whom he/she is not completely comfortable.

30. Make certain the student does not become involved in overstimulating activities.

31. Talk with the student about individual differences, and discuss strengths and weaknesses of individuals the student knows. Stress that the student does not have to do the same things everyone else does.

32. Find a peer who would be a good influence to play with the student (e.g., someone younger, older, of the same gender, of the opposite gender, etc.).

33. Have the student put himself/herself in someone else's place (e.g., "How would you feel if someone called you dumb or stupid?").

34. Make certain the student is not allowed time alone with other students when he/she is upset or angry.

35. Do not force the student to interact with others.

36. Before beginning an activity or game, make certain the student knows the rules, is familiar with the activity or game, and will be compatible with the other individuals who will be playing.

37. Teach the student to ask for things in a positive manner. Teach key words and phrases (e.g., "May I borrow your pencil?" "Do you mind if I play the game with you?" etc.).

38. Do not leave a lot of unstructured time for the student.

39. Teach the student to "think" before acting (e.g., ask himself/herself "What is happening?" "What am I doing?" "What should I do?" "What will be best for me?").

40. Have the student practice appropriate verbal exchanges which should be made when typical physical exchanges take place (e.g., "Excuse me." "I'm sorry." etc.).

41. Make certain the student is allowed to voice an opinion in situations to avoid becoming angry or upset.

42. Talk to the student about ways of handling conflict situations successfully (e.g., walk away from a situation, change to another activity, ask for help, etc.).

43. Prevent frustrating or anxiety-producing situations from occurring (e.g., give the student tasks only on his/her ability level, give the student only the number of tasks that he/she can tolerate in one sitting, reduce social interactions which stimulate the student to become physically aggressive, etc.).

44. Evaluate the appropriateness of the task to determine (a) if the task is too easy, (b) if the task is too difficult, and (c) if the length of time scheduled to complete the task is adequate.

45. Communicate with parents (e.g., notes home, phone calls, etc.) to share information concerning the student's progress. The parents may reinforce the student at home for respecting the norms of physical proximity at school.

46. Write a contract with the student specifying what behavior is expected (e.g., respecting the norms of physical proximity) and what reinforcement will be made available when the terms of the contract have been met.

47. Remove the student from the group or activity until he/she can demonstrate appropriate behavior and self-control.

48. Reinforce the student for demonstrating appropriate behavior based on the length of time the student can be successful. As the student demonstrates success, gradually increase the length of time required for reinforcement.

49. Reinforce those students in the classroom who demonstrate appropriate behavior when interacting with other students.

50. Establish classroom rules:
- Work on-task.
- Work quietly.
- Remain in your seat.
- Finish task.
- Meet task expectations.

Review rules often. Reinforce students for following rules.

51. Speak with the student to explain (a) what the student is doing wrong (e.g., scratching, hitting, pulling hair, etc.) and (b) what the student should be doing (e.g., following rules, interacting in appropriate ways, dealing with anger and frustration in appropriate ways, etc.).

52. Reinforce the student for demonstrating appropriate behavior: (a) give the student a tangible reward (e.g., classroom privileges, line leading, passing out materials, five minutes free time, etc.) or (b) give the student an intangible reward (e.g., praise, handshake, smile, etc.).

53. Always provide the student with behavioral options (e.g., sitting out of an activity, going to a quiet place in the room, performing another activity, etc.).

54. Avoid arguing with the student (e.g., calmly deliver consequences without reacting to the student's remarks).

55. Maintain consistent behavioral expectations and consequences to reduce the likelihood of the student becoming upset by what he/she considers unfair treatment.

56. Avoid physical contact with the student who is likely to become physically aggressive.

57. Maintain an appropriate physical distance from the student when interacting with him/her to avoid stimulation of aggressive behavior.

58. Teach the student acceptable ways to communicate displeasure, anger, frustration, etc.

59. Deliver directions in a supportive rather than a threatening manner (e.g., "Please finish your math assignment before going to recess." rather than "You had better turn in your math or else!").

60. Do not criticize when correcting the student; be honest yet supportive. Never cause the student to feel negatively about himself/herself.

61. Avoid embarrassing the student by giving him/her orders, demands, etc., in front of others.

62. Use language that is pleasant and calming when speaking with the student to avoid stimulation of aggressive behavior.

63. When working directly with the student, always be in the presence of others.

164   Does not make and keep friends

Goal:

1. The student will make and keep friends.

Objectives:

1. The student will greet peers with positive comments on ____out of ____occasions.
2. The student will carry on friendly conversations with peers on ____out of ____occasions.
3. The student will ask conversational questions of peers on ____out of ____occasions.
4. The student will resolve conflict situations with peers on ____out of ____occasions.
5. The student will initiate conversations with peers on ____out of ____occasions.
6. The student will respond in a positive manner to conversations initiated by peers on ____out of occasions.
7. The student will engage in extracurricular activities with a friend(s) on ____out of ____occasions.
8. The student will initiate activities on ____out of ____occasions.
9. The student will socialize with one or more peers during free time on ____out of ____occasions.
10. The student will demonstrate good sportsmanship in games on ____out of ____occasions.
11. The student will interact with peers in a physically appropriate manner on ____out of ____occasions.
12. The student will demonstrate consideration/regard for his/her peers on ____out of ____occasions.

Interventions:

1. Give the student responsibilities in group situations so peers may view the student in a positive way.

2. Assess the social situation in relation to the student's ability to function successfully (e.g., number of students in the group, behavior of students in the group, etc.).

3. Provide the student with as many academic and social successes as possible so peers may view the student in a more positive way.

4. Encourage the student to further develop any ability or skill he/she may have so peers may view the student in a more positive way.

5. Model appropriate social behavior for the student at all times.

6. Help the student to identify inappropriate behaviors and teach him/her ways to change those behaviors.

7. Reduce the emphasis on competition. Social interactions may be inhibited if the student's abilities are constantly made public and compared to others.

8. Encourage and assist the student in joining extracurricular activities, clubs, etc.

9. Help the student develop friendships by pairing him/her with another student for activities. As the student is socially successful, gradually increase the number of students in the group.

10. Intervene early when there is a problem to prevent more serious problems from occurring.

11. Do not force the student to interact with others with whom he/she is not completely comfortable.

12. Speak with the student to explain that he/she may be trying too hard to fit in and should relax and allow friendships to develop naturally.

13. Do not force the student to interact with others.

14. Communicate with parents (e.g., notes home, phone calls, etc.) to share information concerning the student's progress. The parents may reinforce the student at home for initiating and maintaining friendships with other students at school.

15. Reinforce those students in the classroom who appropriately interact with the student.

16. Reinforce the student for appropriately interacting with other students: (a) give the student a tangible reward (e.g., classroom privileges, line leading, passing out materials, five minutes free time, etc.) or (b) give the student an intangible reward (e.g., praise, handshake, smile, etc.).

17. Try various groupings to determine the situation in which the student is most likely to succeed socially.

18. Make certain the student understands the natural consequences of hurting other students (e.g., less freedom, more restrictive environment, assault charges, etc.).

19. Ask the student to choose a peer to work with on a specific assignment. If the student has difficulty choosing someone, determine the student's preference by other means, such as a class survey.

20. Assign the student to work with one or two peers on a long-term project (e.g., mural, bulletin board, report, etc.).

21. Create situations in which the student must interact (e.g., returning completed assignments to students, proofreading other students' work, etc.).

22. Choose a peer to model appropriate interactions with peers for the student.

23. Determine the peer(s) the student would most prefer to interact with and attempt to facilitate this interaction.

24. Provide ample opportunities for friendships to occur.

25. Structure the environment so the student has many opportunities to interact with peers.

26. Have the student run errands with a peer to facilitate interaction.

27. Conduct a sociometric activity with the class to determine the peer who would most prefer to interact with the student.

28. Teach the student appropriate ways to interact with another student (e.g., how to greet another student, suggest activities, share materials, problem-solve, take turns, converse, etc.).

29. Involve the student in extracurricular activities to encourage interactions with peers.

30. Make certain the student understands the natural consequences of inappropriate behavior (e.g., peers choosing not to interact with him/her, exclusion from activities, etc.).

31. Encourage the student to use problem-solving skills: (a) identify the problem, (b) identify goals and objectives, (c) develop strategies, (d) develop a plan of action, and (e) carry out the plan.

32. Teach the student to "think" before acting (e.g., ask himself/herself "What is happening?" "What am I doing?" "What should I do?" "What will be best for me?").

33. Have the student practice appropriate verbal exchanges which should be made when typical physical exchanges take place (e.g., "Excuse me." "I'm sorry." etc.).

34. Talk to the student about ways of handling conflict situations successfully (e.g., walk away from a situation, change to another activity, ask for help, etc.).

35. Teach the student positive ways to interact with other students.

36. Teach the student to respect others and their belonging by respecting the student and his/her belongings.

37. Talk with the student about choosing friends who are friendly and sincere.

38. Assign an outgoing, nonthreatening peer to help the student interact more appropriately with peers.

39. Help the student develop social awareness (e.g., people may be embarrassed by what you say, feelings can be hurt by comments, tact is the best policy, remember interactions which have made you feel good and treat others in the same manner, etc.).

40. Design group projects (e.g., fund raisers) to create a situation for group cohesiveness and loyalty.

41. Select nonacademic activities designed to enhance appropriate social interaction of the student and peers during classroom activities (e.g., board games, model building, coloring, etc.).

42. Teach the student the difference between friendly teasing, where everyone, including the other person laughs, and teasing that hurts others' feelings.

165 Bothers others who are trying to work, listen, etc.

Goals:

1. The student will communicate with others in an acceptable manner in the classroom.
2. The student will refrain from bothering other students who are trying to work, listen, etc.
3. The student will stay on-task.
4. The student will work quietly in the classroom.

Objectives:

1. The student will ask the teacher's permission prior to interacting with a peer(s) on _____ out of _____ trials.
2. The student will await his/her turn to talk when engaged, or attempting to engage, in interactions with others on _____ out of _____ trials.
3. The student will contribute his/her opinion/answer, after being recognized by the teacher, on _____ out of _____ trials.
4. The student will gain permission from the teacher, by raising his/her hand, when he/she needs to talk with a peer on _____ out of _____ trials.
5. The student will interact with other students during free time, break time, lunch time, etc., on _____ out of _____ trials.
6. The student will interact with other students when appropriate on _____ out of _____ trials.
7. The student will make comments which are relevant to the situation on _____ out of _____ trials.
8. The student will refrain from bothering other students who are trying to work, listen, etc., on _____ out of _____ trials.
9. The student will refrain from making sounds which are inappropriate for the situation on _____ out of _____ trials.
10. The student will remain appropriately seated until given teacher permission to do otherwise on _____ out of _____ trials.
11. The student will stay on-task for _____ minutes at a time. (Gradually increase expectations as the student demonstrates success.)

Interventions:

1. Interact frequently with the student to reduce the need to talk to other students.

2. Allow the student to take a break to regroup when he/she is disturbing others.

3. Arrange for individual assignments when the group setting is overly distracting.

4. Write a contract with the student specifying what behavior is expected (e.g., working quietly) and what reinforcement will be made available when the terms of the contract have been met.

5. Ask the student if he/she needs to talk with you or needs to ask any questions before assigning a task, activity, etc., that will be time consuming.

6. Assess the appropriateness of the social situation in relation to the student's ability to function successfully.

7. Assist the student in identifying the situations in which he/she is most likely to talk beyond what is expected or at inappropriate times. After he/she has identified these situations, have him/her think of ways to minimize their occurrences.

8. Avoid seating the student near people with whom he/she may be tempted to converse during lectures, seminars, group projects, etc.

9. Call on the student when he/she is most likely to be able to respond correctly.

10. Communicate with parents (e.g., notes home, phone calls, etc.) to share information concerning the student's progress. The parents may reinforce the student at home for demonstrating appropriate behavior at school.

11. Consider carefully the student's ability level before expecting him/her not to intrude on others when they are talking, working, reading, etc.

12. Encourage the student to consider the consequences of his/her behavior before engaging in any activity.

13. Deliver directions, explanations, and instructions in a clear and concise manner to reduce the student's need to ask other students for information.

14. Encourage the student to model the behavior of peers who are successful at not talking to others during quiet activity periods.

15. Designate a specific period of time when it is permissible for the student to converse with his/her peers (e.g., each hour on the hour, break time, after completing a task, etc.).

16. Encourage the student to reduce impulsivity to increase work productivity and general happiness.

17. Discuss with the student the need to reduce impulsive behavior to increase work productivity and general happiness.

18. Teach the student to recognize appropriate times to talk to other students (e.g., between activities, during breaks, at recess, etc.).

19. Do not allow the student to use ADHD as an excuse. Hold the student responsible for his/her actions. However, understand and accept problems ADHD brings into the student's life while he/she is learning to make accommodations.

20. Do not leave a lot of unstructured time for the student.

21. Educate the student about ADHD and the need to self-monitor behavior.

22. Educate yourself and others about ADHD to increase understanding and accommodation of impulsive behavior.

23. Educate yourself and others about ADHD to increase understanding and accommodation of excessive talking.

24. Encourage the student to avoid ingesting any substance (e.g., drugs, alcohol, cold remedies, etc.) that might further alter his/her ability to maintain self-control.

25. Create challenges in assigned tasks to increase interest and motivation.

26. Encourage the student to develop an awareness of himself/herself and those around him/her. Have the student periodically step back and ask himself/herself, "Am I bothering others?"

27. Reinforce the student for demonstrating appropriate behavior based on the length of time he/she can be successful. As the student demonstrates success, gradually increase the length of time required for reinforcement.

28. Encourage the student to monitor his/her impulsivity. Awareness should reduce impulsive behaviors.

29. Establish classroom rules:
- Work on-task.
- Work quietly.
- Remain in your seat.
- Finish task.
- Meet task expectations.

Review rules often. Reinforce students for following rules.

30. Evaluate the appropriateness of the task to determine (a) if the task is too easy, (b) if the task is too difficult, and (c) if the length of time scheduled to complete the task is adequate.

31. Explain to the student after telling him/her to stop talking the reason why he/she should not be talking.

32. Reduce distracting stimuli (e.g., place the student on the front row, provide a carrel or "office" away from distractions, etc.). This is used as a means of reducing distracting stimuli and not as a form of punishment.

33. Explain to the student that he/she may be trying too hard to fit in and should relax and wait until more appropriate times to interact.

34. Explain to the student why it is important not to intrude on others. Help him/her understand that it is impolite, that he/she might hurt someone's feelings, etc.

35. Give the student adequate opportunities to speak in the classroom, talk to other students, etc. (i.e., enthusiastic students need many opportunities to contribute).

36. Have all the necessary materials assembled to work on a project, assignment, etc.,to reduce the need to ask for materials.

37. Have the student be the leader of a small group activity if he/she possesses mastery of skills or an interest in that area.

38. Schedule important activities at times when the student is most likely to maintain attention (e.g., one hour after medication, 45 minutes after lunch, first thing in the morning, etc.).

39. Choose a peer to model appropriate behavior for the student.

40. Have the student question any directions, explanations, or instructions before beginning a task to reinforce comprehension and avoid interrupting peers later to ask questions.

41. Have the student review the consequences of his/her behavior with someone he/she trusts. Have the student consider different choices he/she could have made and the different outcomes.

42. Reinforce those students in the classroom who demonstrate appropriate behavior.

43. Have the student work in small groups in which there are frequent opportunities to speak. As the student learns to wait longer for a turn to speak, gradually increase the size of the group.

44. Help the student improve concentration skills (e.g., listening to the speaker, taking notes, preparing comments in advance, making comments in the appropriate context, etc.).

45. Choose a peer who should be a good influence on the student to interact with him/her (e.g., someone younger/older, of the same/opposite gender, etc.).

46. Give the student responsibilities in the classroom (e.g., running errands, opportunities to help the teacher, etc.).

47. Identify the situations in which the student is most likely to bother other students. After you have identified these situations, think of ways to minimize their occurrences.

48. Interact frequently with the student to maintain his/her involvement in the activity (e.g., ask the student questions, ask the student's opinion, stand close to the student, seat the student near the teacher's desk, etc.).

49. After telling the student why he/she should not be talking, explain the reason.

50. Intervene early when there is a problem to prevent a more serious problem from occurring.

51. Maintain visibility to and from the student to keep his/her attention when verbal questions/directions are being delivered. The teacher should be able to see the student and the student should be able to see the teacher. Make eye contact possible at all times.

52. Reinforce those students in the classroom who work quietly.

53. Make certain that the student's feelings are considered when it is necessary to deal with his/her talking to other students (i.e., handle comments in such a way as to not diminish the student's enthusiasm for participation).

54. Teach the student to differentiate between spur-of-the-moment and important information that needs to be conveyed.

55. Make certain the student knows when it is acceptable to interact with other students.

56. Reinforce the student for working quietly based on the length of time the student can be successful. As the student demonstrates success, gradually increase the length of time required for reinforcement.

57. Reduce the emphasis on competition. Competitive activities may cause the student to become anxious and interrupt others.

58. Make sure the student realizes that all behavior has negative or positive consequences. Encourage the student to practice behaviors that will lead to positive consequences.

59. Encourage the student to develop an awareness of the consequences of his/her behavior by writing down or talking through problems which may occur due to interrupting others (e.g., perceived as unmannerly, avoided, etc.).

60. Make the necessary adjustments in the environment to prevent the student from experiencing stress, frustration or anger (e.g., reduce peer pressure, academic failure, teasing, etc.).

61. Provide constant, positive reinforcement for appropriate behavior. Ignore as many inappropriate behaviors as possible.

62. Make certain that reinforcement is not inadvertently given for inappropriate behavior (e.g., making inappropriate comments, talking to others during quiet activity periods, etc.).

63. Provide the student with a clearly understood list of consequences for inappropriate behavior.

64. Have the student make a list of consequences associated with frequently occurring behaviors (e.g., by disrupting others, I will be perceived as unmannerly. By behaving aggressively, people will avoid me.).

65. Deliver a predetermined signal (e.g., hand signal, verbal cue, etc.) if the student begins to talk to other students during quiet activity periods.

66. Deliver a predetermined signal(e.g., hand signal, verbal cue, etc.) when the student begins to display inappropriate behavior.

67. Provide the student with frequent opportunities to participate, share, etc.

68. Seat the student away from those students he/she is most likely to bother.

69. Teach the student to use techniques such as crossing his/her arms and legs, clinching his/her fists, and webbing his/her hands when he/she feels the urge to speak to others during quiet activity periods.

70. Present activities which allow the student to be highly active and talkative.

71. Reinforce the student for demonstrating appropriate behavior: (a) give the student a tangible reward (e.g., classroom privileges, passing out materials, five minutes free time, etc.) or (b) give the student an intangible reward (e.g., praise, handshake, smile, etc.).

72. Reinforce the student for raising his/her hand to be recognized.

73. Provide a full schedule of activities. Prevent lag time from occurring when the student can bother other students.

74. Reinforce the student for working quietly: (a) give the student a tangible reward (e.g., classroom privileges, line leading, passing out materials, five minutes free time, etc.) or (b) give the student an intangible reward (e.g., praise, handshake, smile, etc.).

75. Provide the student with enjoyable activities to perform when he/she completes a task early.

76. Reinforce those students in the classroom who demonstrate on-task behavior.

77. Provide the student with many social and academic successes.

78. Schedule recreational activities at the end of the day. Make participation in these activities dependent upon appropriate behavior during quiet activity periods.

79. Remove the student from the group or activity until he/she can demonstrate appropriate behavior and self-control.

80. Seat the student near the teacher.

81. Speak to the student to explain (a) what he/she is doing wrong (e.g., bothering other students who are trying to work, listen, etc.) and (b) what he/she should be doing (e.g., demonstrating appropriate behavior).

82. Reduce activities which might threaten the student (e.g., announcing test score ranges or test scores aloud, making students read aloud in class, emphasizing the success of a particular student or students, etc.).

83. Structure the environment in such a way as to limit opportunities for talking to other students during quiet activity periods (e.g., keep the student engaged in activities, have the student seated near the teacher, etc.).

84. Teach appropriate social rituals (e.g., say, "Excuse me," before interrupting; wait until someone stops speaking to begin talking, etc.).

85. Try various groupings to determine the situation in which the student is most comfortable.

86. Teach problem-solving skills:
- Identify the problem.
- Identify the goals and objectives.
- Develop a strategy/plan for action.
- Carry out the plan.
- Evaluate the results.

87. Teach the student appropriate ways to communicate his/her needs to others (e.g., waiting a turn, raising his/her hand, etc.).

88. Assess the degree of task difficulty to determine whether or not the student will require additional information, time, assistance, etc., before assigning a task.

89. Make certain that the student understands the relationship between inappropriate behavior and the consequences which follow (e.g., others ignoring him/her, disrupting the learning of others, etc.).

90. Provide students with frequent opportunities to interact with one another (e.g., before and after school, between activities, etc.).

166 Does not demonstrate loyalty to friends and organized groups

Goal:

1. The student will demonstrate loyalty to friends and organized groups.

Objectives:

1. The student will maintain friendships throughout the school term.
2. The student will maintain memberships in groups throughout the school term.
3. The student will maintain a personal friendship throughout the school term.
4. The student will help a friend perform assignments on _____ out of _____ trials.
5. The student will share materials with a friend on _____ out of _____ trials.
6. The student will engage in extracurricular activities with a friend on _____ out of _____ trials.
7. The student will take an active role in chores, work-related activities, etc., on _____ out of _____ trials.
8. The student will contribute information, opinions, etc., during classroom activities on _____ out of _____ trials.
9. The student will initiate an activity with peers in the classroom on _____ out of _____ trials.
10. The student will take responsibility for a classroom activity on _____ out of _____ trials.
11. The student will carry out assigned roles, activities, responsibilities, etc., in the classroom on _____ out of _____ trials.

Interventions:

1. Reinforce the student for participating in group activities or special events, taking responsibility, etc.: (a) give the student a tangible reward (e.g., classroom privileges, line leading, passing out materials, five minutes free time, etc.) or (b) give the student an intangible reward (e.g., praise, handshake, smile, etc.).

2. Speak with the student to explain (a) what he/she is doing wrong (e.g., failing to take part) and (b) what he/she should be doing (e.g., participating, taking turns, playing, sharing, remaining involved in an activity or group, etc.).

3. Design group projects (e.g., fundraisers) to create a situation for group cohesiveness and loyalty.

4. Assign a peer to sit/work directly with the student (e.g., in different settings or activities such as art, music, P.E.; on the bus; tutoring; group projects; running errands in the building; etc.). As the student becomes comfortable working with one other student, gradually increase size of the group. Monitor the student's loyalty to one other student and members of the group as it grows.

5. Write a contract with the student specifying what behavior is expected (e.g., taking part in group activities, being a member of a group, working on a project to its completion, etc.) and what reinforcement will be made available when the terms of the contract have been met.

6. Communicate with parents (e.g., notes home, phone calls, etc.) to share information concerning the student's progress. The parents may reinforce the student at home for participating in group activities, joining a group, maintaining a friendship, etc.

7. Establish classroom rules:
- Work on-task.
- Work quietly.
- Remain in your seat.
- Finish task.
- Meet task expectations.

Review rules often. Reinforce students for following rules.

8. Reinforce students in the classroom for participating in group activities or special events, working with a friend, etc.

9. Encourage or reward others for participation in group or special activities.

10. Give the student the responsibility of helping another student in the group.

11. Give the student responsibilities in a group so others might view him/her in a positive light.

12. Assign the student activities to perform with a friend which will require teamwork and dependence on one another.

13. Have the student join a team or group activity which exists for a specific purpose (e.g., sports, community services, etc.).

14. Try various groupings to determine the situation in which the student is most successful.

15. Have peers invite the student to participate in school activities, extracurricular activities, groups, etc.

16. Request that the student be the leader of a small group activity if he/she possesses mastery or an interest in the activity.

17. Allow the student to be present during group activities without requiring active participation.

18. Reduce the emphasis on competition. Frequent or continuous failure is likely to result in embarrassment which will cause reluctance to participate.

19. Demonstrate respect for the student's opinions, responses, suggestions, etc.

20. Provide the student with many social and academic successes.

21. Provide the student with positive feedback which indicates he/she is successful in interactions with peers, group membership, etc.

22. Present awards for attendance, contributions made to a group, accomplishments in a group, etc.

23. Determine the student's interests. Present activities which require participation based on his/her interests.

24. Allow the student to choose a special event or interesting activity for the class.

25. Provide the student with success-oriented special events or activities so he/she may develop an interest in them.

26. Modify or adjust situations that cause the student to be reluctant to participate (e.g., degree of difficulty, competition, fear of failure, threat of embarrassment, etc.).

27. Emphasize individual satisfaction, success, or progress rather than winning or "beating" other students.

28. Provide the student with opportunities for small group participation as opposed to large group participation to develop close friendships, sharing, mutual dependence, etc.

29. Encourage the student to participate in small groups. As the student demonstrates success, gradually increase size of the group.

30. Encourage the student to share items of special interest with other members of the class.

31. Choose a peer to model appropriate interactions in classroom activities for the student.

32. Allow the student to choose a group of peers with whom he/she feels comfortable.

33. Determine the peers with whom the student would most prefer to interact in classroom activities and attempt to facilitate the interaction.

34. Assign outgoing, nonthreatening peers to help the student participate in classroom activities.

35. Structure the environment so that the student has many opportunities to interact with other peers in classroom activities.

36. Assign the student to classroom activities in which he/she is likely to interact successfully with peers.

37. Conduct a sociometric activity with the class to determine those peers who would most prefer to interact with the student in classroom activities.

38. Teach the student appropriate ways to interact with peers in classroom activities (e.g., share materials, problem solve, take turns, converse, etc.).

39. Supervise classroom activities closely so the peers with whom the student interacts do not stimulate inappropriate behavior.

40. Make certain that the classroom activity is not so stimulating as to make successful interactions with peers difficult.

41. Teach the student appropriate ways to interact with another student (e.g., how to greet another student, suggest activities, share materials, problem solve, take turns, converse, etc.).

42. Limit opportunities for interaction in classroom activities on those occasions in which the student is not likely to be successful (e.g., when the student has experienced academic or social failure prior to the scheduled classroom activity).

43. Select nonacademic activities designed to facilitate appropriate social interaction between the student and peers during classroom activities (e.g., board games, model building, etc.).

44. Through interviews with other students and observations, determine those characteristics of the student which interfere with successful interactions during classroom activities. Use information gained to determine skills or behaviors the student needs to develop for successful interactions.

45. Make certain, beforehand, that the student is able to successfully participate in the classroom activity (e.g., the student understands the rules, is familiar with the activity, will be compatible with peers participating in the activity, etc.).

46. Teach the student problem-solving skills so he/she may better handle problems that may occur in interactions with peers in classroom activities (e.g., talking, walking away, calling upon an arbitrator, compromising, etc.).

47. Have the student work with a peer who is younger or smaller (e.g., choose a peer who would require assistance, be less threatening, etc.).

48. Have the student practice appropriate interactions with the teacher in classroom activities (e.g., simulations, role playing, etc.).

167 Does not demonstrate the ability to resolve conflict situations

Goal:

1. The student will demonstrate the ability to resolve conflict situations.

Objectives:

1. The student will solve problems by withdrawing from conflict situations on _____ out of _____ trials.
2. The student will solve problems by reasoning in conflict situations on _____ out of _____ trials.
3. The student will solve problems by apologizing in conflict situations on _____ out of _____ trials.
4. The student will solve problems by talking in a quiet, controlled manner in conflict situations on _____ out of _____ trials.
5. The student will solve problems independently in conflict situations on _____ out of _____ trials.
6. The student will solve problems in conflict situations by allowing others the benefit of the doubt on _____ out of _____ trials.

Interventions:

1. Reinforce the student for demonstrating the ability to appropriately solve problems in conflict situations: (a) give the student a tangible reward (e.g., classroom privileges, line leading, passing out materials, five minutes free time, etc.) or (b) give the student an intangible reward (e.g., praise, handshake, smile, etc.).

2. Speak to the student to explain (a) what he/she is doing wrong (e.g., fighting, name calling, etc.) and (b) what he/she should be doing (e.g., withdrawing from conflict situations, reasoning, etc.).

3. Teach the student a variety of ways to solve problems in conflict situations (e.g., withdrawing, reasoning, calling upon an arbitrator, apologizing, compromising, allowing others the benefit of the doubt, etc.).

4. Reinforce the student for demonstrating the ability to appropriately solve problems in conflict situations based on the number of times the student can be successful. As the student demonstrates success, gradually increase the number of times required for reinforcement.

5. Write a contract with the student specifying what behavior is expected (e.g., withdrawing from conflict situations, reasoning, etc.) and what reinforcement will be made available when the terms of the contract have been met.

6. Communicate with parents (e.g., notes home, phone calls, etc.) to share information concerning the student's progress. The parents may reinforce the student at home for demonstrating the ability to appropriately solve problems in conflict situations at school.

7. Choose a peer to model appropriately solving problems in conflict situations for the student.

8. Have the student question any directions, explanations, instructions he/she does not understand.

9. Evaluate the student's problem-solving ability and limit his/her exposure to conflict situations at a level with which he/she can participate appropriately.

10. Reinforce those students in the classroom who demonstrate the ability to appropriately solve problems in conflict situations.

11. Model for the student a variety of ways to solve problems in conflict situations (e.g., withdrawing, reasoning, apologizing, compromising, etc.).

12. Provide the student with hypothetical conflict situations and require him/her to suggest appropriate solutions to the situations.

13. Have the student role play ways to solve problems in conflict situations with peers and adults (e.g., withdrawing, reasoning, calling upon an arbitrator, apologizing, compromising, allowing others the benefit of the doubt, etc.).

14. Make certain the student understands that natural consequences may occur if he/she reacts inappropriately in conflict situations (e.g., peers will not want to interact, teachers will have to intervene, etc.)

15. Teach the student to solve problems in conflict situations before the situation becomes too difficult for him/her to solve.

16. Teach the student to avoid becoming involved in conflict situations (e.g., move away from the situation, change his/her behavior, etc.).

17. Explain to the student that it is natural for conflict situations to occur. What is important is how he/she reacts to the situation.

18. Identify typical conflict situations for the student and discuss appropriate solutions to specific situations (e.g., peers taking things from him/her, peers hitting or grabbing, peers not following rules, etc.).

19. If the student has responded inappropriately to a conflict situation, take time to explore with the student appropriate solutions which could have been used in solving the problem.

20. Maintain mobility throughout the classroom to supervise student interactions and intervene in conflict situations in which the student is unable to successfully solve the problems.

168 Responds inappropriately to others' attempts to be friendly, complimentary, sympathetic, etc.

Goals:

1. The student will respond appropriately to others' attempts to be complimentary.
2. The student will respond appropriately to others' attempts to be sympathetic.
3. The student will respond appropriately to others' attempts to interact with him/her.
4. The student will respond appropriately to others' attempts to be friendly.
5. The student will respond appropriately to praise.
6. The student will respond appropriately to recognition.

Objectives:

1. The student will appropriately acknowledge others' attempts to be sympathetic on ___ out of ___ trials.
2. The student will appropriately interact with others on ___ out of ___ trials.
3. The student will be friendly when interacting with others on ___ out of ___ trials.
4. The student will respond appropriately to others' attempts to interact for ___ minutes at a time.
5. The student will respond appropriately to others' attempts to interact with him/her on ___ out of ___ trials.
6. The student will respond appropriately to others' attempts to be complimentary during ___ out of ___ interactions.
7. The student will respond appropriately to others' attempts to be friendly during ___ out of ___ interactions.
8. The student will respond appropriately when praised by a peer by saying "Thank you," smiling, etc., on ___ out of ___ trials.
9. The student will respond appropriately when praised by the teacher by saying "Thank you," smiling, etc., on ___ out of ___ trials.
10. The student will say "Thank you" when given a compliment on ___ out of ___ trials.

Interventions:

1. Allow the student to be a member of a group without requiring active participation.

2. Teach the student social interaction skills (e.g., ways in which to appropriately respond to others' attempts to be friendly, complimentary, sympathetic, etc.).

3. Assign a peer to sit/work directly with the student (e.g., in different settings or activities such as art, music, P.E.; on the bus; tutoring; group projects; running errands in the building; break time; etc.). As the student becomes comfortable working with one other student, gradually increase size of the group.

4. Model demonstrating appropriate ways to respond to others who are friendly, complimentary, sympathetic, etc.

5. Communicate with parents (e.g., notes home, phone calls, etc.) to share information concerning the student's progress. The parents may reinforce the student at home for responding appropriately to praise or recognition at school.

6. Distribute praise and recognition equally to the members of the class.

7. Provide the student with many social and academic successes.

8. Encourage others to compliment the student.

9. Reduce stimuli which contribute to the student's inappropriate responses to others' attempts to interact.

10. Intervene early to prevent the student from losing self-control.

11. Reinforce other students for responding appropriately to interactions with students or teachers.

12. Limit interactions with the peer(s) who is the primary focus of the student's inappropriate responses.

13. Provide the student with frequent opportunities to meet new people.

14. Make certain that reinforcement is not inadvertently given for inappropriate behavior (e.g., attending to the student only when he/she responds inappropriately to praise or recognition).

15. Praise or recognize the student when he/she will most likely be able to demonstrate an appropriate response (e.g., when the student is not being singled out in a group).

16. Encourage the student to interact with others.

17. Make certain you express your feelings in a socially acceptable way.

18. Model appropriate ways to respond to interactions with other students or teachers.

19. Use feedback related to performance (e.g., test scores, grades, etc.) in place of praise or recognition. As the student becomes more capable of accepting praise and recognition, gradually deliver verbal praise and recognition.

20. Reinforce the student for responding appropriately to praise or recognition based on the number of times he/she can be successful. As the student demonstrates success, gradually increase the number of times required for reinforcement.

21. Reinforce those students in the classroom who respond appropriately to praise or recognition.

22. Praise or recognize the student in private. The public aspect of praise or recognition is often the cause of the inappropriate response.

23. Assess the appropriateness of the social situation in relation to the student's ability to be successful.

24. Provide opportunities for appropriate interactions within the classroom (e.g., peer models engaged in appropriate interactions).

25. Treat the student with respect. Talk in an objective manner at all times.

26. Provide praise or recognition for smaller increments of success so that the student may become gradually accustomed to the recognition.

27. Provide the student with positive feedback which indicates he/she is important.

28. Rather than emphasizing winning or "beating" other students in competition, encourage individual success or progress which may be enjoyed privately rather than publicly.

29. Reinforce the student for responding appropriately to others' attempts to be friendly, complimentary, sympathetic, etc.: (a) give the student a tangible reward (e.g., classroom privileges, line leading, passing out materials, five minutes free time, etc.) or (b) give the student an intangible reward (e.g., praise, handshake, smile, etc.).

30. Respect the student's right to a reasonable amount of privacy.

31. Speak with the student to explain (a) what he/she is doing wrong (e.g., using inappropriate language, responding negatively, calling names, making inappropriate gestures, etc.) and (b) what he/she should be doing (e.g., being positive in response to others).

32. Help the student develop social awareness (e.g., people may be embarrassed by what you say, feelings can be hurt by comments, tact is the best policy, remember interactions which have made you feel good and treat others in the same manner, etc.).

33. Present praise with a matter-of-fact delivery and avoid exaggerated exclamations of success.

34. Use alternative forms of praise or recognition which are not threatening to the student (e.g., written notes, telephone calls to parents, display work done well, etc.).

35. Try various groupings to determine the situation in which the student is most comfortable.

36. Provide praise and recognition as a natural consequence for appropriate behavior.

37. Write a contract stating appropriate ways to respond to others and identify what reinforcement will be made available when the terms of the contract have been met.

Reminder: Do not punish a student for his/her inability to respond appropriately to praise or recognition.

169 "Gets back" at others when he/she feels that someone has wronged him/her

Goals:

1. The student will respond to difficult situations, such as perceived hurtful behavior from others, without revenge.
2. The student will practice problem-solving techniques in conflict situations.

Objectives:

1. The student will independently respond to difficult situations without resorting to revenge on ____out of ____ trials.
2. The student will practice problem-solving techniques in conflict situations on ____out of ____trials.

Interventions:

1. Reinforce the student for working through his/her difficulties with others without resorting to revenge: (a) give the student a tangible reward (e.g., line leader status, five minutes free time, classroom privileges, etc.) or (b) give the student an intangible behavior (e.g., praise, handshake, smile, etc.).

2. Write a contract specifying expected behavior (e.g., refraining from hurting others, destroying their property, etc., when he/she feels someone has wronged him/her) and what reinforcement will be available when the terms of the contract have been met.

3. Communicate with parents (e.g., notes home, phone calls, etc.) regarding the student's progress with social and communication skills to replace retributional behavior. Encourage parents to reinforce the student for the use of positive social skills at school, at home, and in community environments.

4. Provide the student with positive role models who do not use revenge to problem solve.

5. The student who expresses and/or acts upon thoughts of revenge may be needing additional services and supports (e.g., counseling).

6. Use role play to explore situations in which someone tries to repay "a wrong with a wrong." Discuss the situation, and arrive at positive alternatives which could occur rather than revenge. Explore the benefits the "wronged person" may realize by choosing positive responses rather than revenge.

7. The student may not know how to actively, positively self-advocate. Provide the student with information and training through problem-solving techniques (e.g., identify the problem, generate positive solutions, implement a solution, evaluate effectiveness of the problem-solving plan, and modify if necessary).

8. Role model problem-solving techniques to replace attempts at revenge.

9. Provide outlets for the student who expresses and/or acts upon thoughts of revenge (e.g., art work, diary writing or self-recording, etc.).

10. Maintain close supervision of the student who expresses or attempts to act upon thoughts of revenge.

11. When a dispute occurs, meet with both parties separately and privately to hear each side of the story. Help each party to identify positive alternatives to problem-solve. Working together, determine a positive course of action which would eliminate the need for revenge by anyone.

12. When working with a student who maintains he/she is being slighted or wronged by another, always listen and respond as objectively as possible. Do not indicate to the student that you think he/she is lying about another, because he/she may then "shut you out" and not meaningfully participate in problem-solving with you.

13. Let the student know you care about his/her thoughts and feelings. When reality is not consistent with the student's thoughts, feelings, or perceptions, introduce the inconsistency by saying something like "I know this is how you think and feel about the situation, but this is what other people saw . . . ."

14. The student who is undergoing personal stress may be more likely to express and/or act upon thoughts of revenge. Provide the student information and instruction on stress-management techniques.

15. The student may not know how to form friendships. Provide the student with closely supervised opportunities to meet others in recreational and social functions.

16. Assist the student in actively implementing his/her reasonable, positive alternative to revenge, but make sure the student
- (a) is calm (e.g., no longer feeling hostile)
- (b) has developed his/her thoughts and plans in the event the positive alternative doesn't work (e.g., will use coping skills and positive forms of self-expression, etc.),
- (c) has developed a "Plan B" which consists of another chosen positive alternative to try, and
- (d) will evaluate the effectiveness of his/her approach with the teacher after this has been attempted.

17. When incidents occur during the course of a day in which someone could have behaved in a revengeful fashion but chose a positive alternative instead, reinforce that student for his/her choice.

18. The student may associate "bad feelings" with "being bad." Encourage the student to instead view himself/herself as good, and to accept feelings. Encourage the student to view the choices he/she makes as either acceptable or unacceptable, poor/good, etc.

19. Avoid inadvertently reinforcing a student for his/her expressed aggressive thoughts, such as thoughts about "paying someone back." Provide the student with more verbal response for positive actions you would like to see again to prevent or discourage the student from expressing and attempting to act upon aggressive thoughts for attention.

20. In the interests of individual and group safety, never assume a student will not carry out expressed plans for revenge. Always provide the student and any potential victims with close monitoring.

21. Encourage the student to think through the idea of "getting back" at others:
- (a) Think about the thoughts and feelings of others (e.g., the person who is the focus of the "get even" reaction, family members and friends of both parties, classmates, school administration, etc.) if revenge occurred;
- (b) think about the potential consequences to himself/herself if revenge occurred;
- (c) identify positive alternatives to revenge;
- (d) identify thoughts/feelings of others should the positive alternative be attempted; and
- (e) identify thoughts/feelings of himself/herself should the positive alternatives be attempted.

22. Provide the student with a clear chain of command he/she and others in the environment need to use to process complaints, grievances, etc. Practice each communication link, and praise the student for resorting to the chain of command.

23. Working with the student, arrive at coping techniques tailored to individual preferences and abilities (e.g., taking two slow, deep breaths; moving to another part of the classroom to calm down; head on table or desk for 20 seconds; etc.).

24. Provide the student the opportunity to communicate with role models from the community who have success stories to relate. Enlist these community heroes in identifying revengeful behavior as damaging and undesirable.

25. Provide positive activities to
- (a) give the student matters of interest to focus upon, think through, and act upon other than revenge,
- (b) give the student opportunities to experience success (this may help decrease stress related to frustration), and
- (c) give the student positive, structured opportunities to work with others to encourage productive teamwork and hopefully render vengeful thoughts/behaviors counterproductive.

26. Provide the student with focus for his/her actions and behaviors by developing with him/her a daily schedule. Reinforce the student for
- (a) initiating schedule development,
- (b) beginning scheduled activities independently,
- (c) following his/her schedule,
- (d) completing scheduled activities, and
- (e) all positive attempts at working on the schedule and on scheduled activities.

27. Provide the student with frequent, natural opportunities to feel successful on a daily basis.

28. Competition may stimulate inappropriate behavior. Allow the student the chance to work in small groups or teams on activities, but structure team learning opportunities so these are not competitive by establishing sincere ways of providing merit for each group's efforts.

29. Once a schedule has been created with student involvement, make certain the student receives assistance to achieve success the first few days. As the student demonstrates success, gradually decrease assistance.

30. The students who is sensitive to failure and who may voice or attempt retribution needs your careful monitoring. Offer positive alternative activities instead of ongoing activities when the student indicates signs of frustration or overstimulation.

31. When providing the student with the opportunity to work with others, try to assure his/her opportunity to complement the group based upon the interests and skills he/she will uniquely contribute. Avoid grouping students totally by ability, and provide small groups structure and monitoring.

170   Is not accepted by other students

Goal:

1. The student will demonstrate behaviors that will be accepted by other students.

Objectives:

1. The student will demonstrate acceptable physical contact such as a handshake, pat on the back, "high five," etc., when appropriate on _____ out of _____ trials.
2. The student will demonstrate consideration/regard for his/her peers on ___ out of ___ trials.
3. The student will demonstrate peer interaction skills by sharing materials, waiting his/her turn, and talking in an acceptable manner on _____ out of _____ trials.
4. The student will develop hygiene skills and manners and use them when interacting with other students on ___ out of ___ trials.
5. The student will develop interaction skills and use them when interacting with a peer(s) during ___ out of ___ interactions.
6. The student will gain others' attention in an appropriate manner by standing quietly or raising his/her hand until recognized on ___ out of ___ trials.
7. The student will interact with other students in a physically appropriate manner on ___ out of ___ trials.
8. The student will show emotion that is appropriate for the situation during ___ out of ___ situations.
9. The student will successfully interact with a peer _____ times per day.
10. The student will successfully interact with a peer ___ times per week.
11. The student will talk to his/her peers in a socially acceptable manner during ___ out of ___ interactions.
12. The student will use a normal tone of voice when talking on _____ out of _____ trials.
13. The student will wait quietly for his/her turn when engaged in activities with peers on ___ out of ___ trials.

Interventions:

1. Allow the student more decision-making opportunities relative to class activities and assignments.

2. Do not force the student to interact with others with whom he/she is not completely comfortable.

3. Assess the social situation in relation to the student's ability to function successfully (e.g., number of students in the group, behavior of students in the group, etc.).

4. Avoid competition. Failure may cause the student to ignore consequences of his/her behavior.

5. Call on the student when he/she can answer successfully.

6. Clarify for the student that it is his/her behavior which determines consequences (e.g., positive or negative).

7. Communicate with parents (e.g., notes home, phone calls, etc.) to share information concerning the student's progress. The parents may reinforce the student at home for appropriately interacting with other students at school.

8. Do not criticize. When correcting the student, be honest yet supportive. Never cause the student to feel negatively about himself/herself.

9. Encourage and assist the student in joining extracurricular activities, clubs, etc.

10. Encourage the student to further develop any ability or skill he/she may have so peers may view the student in a positive way.

11. Allow the student to attempt something new in private before doing it in front of others.

12. Maintain trust and confidentiality with the student at all times.

13. Encourage the student to tell you about problems that occur with peers (e.g., being "bullied," teased by others, etc.).

14. Make the consequence of a behavior obvious by identifying the consequence as it occurs and discussing alternative behavior which would have prevented the particular consequence.

15. Establish classroom rules:
- Work on-task.
- Work quietly.
- Remain in your seat.
- Finish task.
- Meet task expectations.

Review rules often. Reinforce students for following rules.

16. Evaluate the appropriateness of the task to determine (a) if the task is too easy, (b) if the task is too difficult, and (c) if the length of time scheduled to complete the task is adequate.

17. Prevent the student from becoming overstimulated by an activity (e.g., monitor or supervise student behavior to limit overexcitement in physical activities, games, parties, etc.).

18. Do not force the student to interact with others.

19. Deliver a predetermined signal (e.g., hand signal, verbal cue, etc.) when the student begins to exhibit inappropriate behavior(s).

20. Give the student responsibilities in group situations so peers may view the student in a more positive way.

21. Have the student be the leader of a small group activity if he/she possesses mastery of skills or an interest in that area.

22. Reinforce those students in the classroom who appropriately interact with the student.

23. Help the student to identify inappropriate behaviors and teach him/her ways to change those behaviors.

24. Inform others who will be working with the student (e.g., teachers, the principal, clerks, etc.) about the student's tendency to ignore consequences of his/her behaviors.

25. Intervene early when there is a problem to prevent more serious problems from occurring.

26. Provide the student with natural consequences for inappropriate behavior (e.g., for disturbing others during group activities, the student should have to leave the activity).

27. Make certain the student does not become involved in overstimulating activities.

28. Speak with the student to explain that he/she may be trying too hard to fit in and should relax and allow friendships to develop naturally.

29. Model appropriate social behavior for the student at all times.

30. Modify or adjust situations that cause the student to demonstrate behaviors that are different or extreme.

31. Teach the student to be satisfied with his/her own best effort and not insist on perfection.

32. Point out the consequences of other students' behavior as they occur (e.g., take the opportunity to point out that consequences occur for all behavior and for all persons).

33. Give the student the responsibility of tutoring a peer if he/she possesses the necessary skills.

34. Present tasks in the most attractive, interesting manner possible.

35. Prevent peers from engaging in those behaviors which would cause the student to fail to consider or regard consequences of his/her behavior (e.g., keep other students from upsetting the student).

36. Provide a learning experience which emphasizes the cause-and-effect relationship between behavior and the inevitability of some form of consequence (e.g., both negative and positive behaviors and consequences).

37. Reinforce those students in the classroom who participate in appropriate behavior.

38. Provide the student with a clearly identified list of consequences for inappropriate behavior.

39. Maintain maximum supervision of the student's interactions and gradually decrease the amount of supervision over time.

40. Give the student responsibilities in the classroom (e.g., teacher assistant, peer tutor, group leader, etc.).

41. Provide the student with as many academic and social successes as possible so peers may view the student in a more positive way.

42. Reduce the emphasis on competition. Social interactions may be inhibited if the student's abilities are constantly made public and compared to others.

43. Reinforce the student for appropriately interacting with other students: (a) give the student a tangible reward (e.g., classroom privileges, line leading, passing out materials, five minutes free time, etc.) or (b) give the student an intangible reward (e.g., praise, handshake, smile, etc.).

44. Reinforce the student for demonstrating appropriate behavior based on the length of time the student can be successful. As the student demonstrates success, gradually increase the length of time required for reinforcement.

45. Try various groupings to determine the situation in which the student is most comfortable.

46. Remove the student from the group or activity until he/she can demonstrate appropriate behavior and self-control.

47. Use role play to simulate various situations the student might be involved with, and to teach the student how to interact appropriately (e.g., how to have an appropriate conversation at the lunch table, how to ask to play a game with others, etc.).

48. Treat the student with respect. Talk in an objective manner at all times.

49. Show an interest in the student (e.g., acknowledge the student, ask the student's opinion, spend time working one-on-one with the student, etc.).

50. Speak with the student to explain (a) what the student is doing wrong (e.g., taking action before thinking about what he/she is doing) and (b) what the student should be doing (e.g., considering consequences, thinking about the correct response, considering other persons, etc.).

51. Help the student develop a friendship by pairing him/her with another student for activities. As the student demonstrates success, gradually increase the number of students in the group.

52. Structure the environment in such a way as to limit opportunities for inappropriate behavior (e.g., keep the student participating in activities, have the student seated near the teacher, maintain visibility to and from the student, etc.).

53. Supervise the student closely in situations in which he/she is likely to act impulsively (e.g., maintain close physical proximity, maintain eye contact, communicate frequently with the student, etc.).

54. Make certain the student is allowed to voice an opinion in a situation to avoid becoming upset or angry.

55. Write a contract with the student specifying what behavior is expected (e.g., sitting near a student, talking to a student, etc.) and what reinforcement will be made available when the terms of the contract have been met.

56. Teach the student problem-solving skills: (a) identify the problem, (b) identify goals and objectives, (c) develop strategies, (d) develop a plan for action, and (e) carry out the plan.

57. Teach the student to think before acting (e.g., ask himself/herself, "What is happening?" "What am I doing?" "What should I do?" "What will be best for me?").

58. Make certain that consequences are delivered consistently for behavior demonstrated (i.e., appropriate behavior results in positive consequences and inappropriate behavior results in negative consequences).

171 Makes inappropriate comments to other students

Goals:
1. The student will make appropriate comments to other students.
2. The student will make appropriate comments to teachers.

Objectives:
1. The student will converse with the teacher in a calm tone of voice during ___out of ___interactions.
2. The student will demonstrate appropriate interaction skills such as sharing, waiting his/her turn, talking in an acceptable manner, and making appropriate gestures during ___ out of ___ interactions with a peer.
3. The student will demonstrate respect for a peer on ___out of ___trials.
4. The student will make appropriate comments to a peer during ___out of ___interactions.
5. The student will make appropriate comments to the teacher in ___out of ___interactions.
6. The student will make comments that are appropriate to the situation on ___out of ___trials.
7. The student will make gestures that are appropriate to the situation on ___out of ___trials.
8. The student will refrain from arguing with a peer during ___ out of ___ interactions.
9. The student will refrain from arguing with the teacher when given a direction, new task, etc., on ___ out of ___ trials.
10. The student will refrain from calling names during ___out of ___interactions with a peer.
11. The student will refrain from cursing during ___out of ___interactions with a peer.
12. The student will refrain from making rude comments during ___out of ___interactions with a peer.
13. The student will refrain from using obscenities during ___out of ___interactions with a peer.
14. The student will settle minor conflicts with a peer during ___out of ___interactions.
15. The student will use socially acceptable language in public settings on ___out of ___trials.
16. The student will verbally express his/her feelings in an appropriate manner when interacting with the teacher on ___ out of ___ trials.

Interventions:

1. Model using appropriate language at all times (e.g., use appropriate language to convey disappointment, unhappiness, surprise, etc.).

2. Write a contract with the student specifying what behavior is expected (e.g., communicating with other students in an appropriate manner) and what reinforcement will be made available when the terms of the contract have been met.

3. Teach the student to respect others and their belongings by respecting the student and his/her belongings.

4. Avoid arguing with the student.

5. Have the student put himself/herself in the other student's place (e.g., "How would you feel if someone called you dumb or stupid?").

6. Avoid confrontations with the student which lead to inappropriate behavior on the part of the student (e.g., give the student options for alternative tasks, other times to perform assignments, assistance in performing assignments, etc.).

7. Avoid physical contact with the student who is likely to become verbally abusive (e.g., a pat on the back may cause the student to argue, threaten, call names, curse, etc.).

8. Avoid embarrassing the student by giving him/her orders, demands, etc., in front of others.

9. Maintain visibility to and from the student. The teacher should be able to see the student; the student should be able to see the teacher. Make eye contact possible at all times.

10. Communicate with parents (e.g., notes home, phone calls, etc.) to share information concerning the student's progress. The parents may reinforce the student at home for communicating in an appropriate manner with other students at school.

11. Explain to the student why making inappropriate comments and unnecessary noises is not acceptable (e.g., impolite, might hurt others' feelings, etc.).

12. Be consistent in expectations and consequences of behavior.

13. Deliver directions in a supportive rather than a threatening manner (e.g., "Please finish your math paper before going to recess." rather than "You had better finish your math paper or else!").

14. Have the student question any directions, explanations, and instructions not understood.

15. Discuss with the student ways he/she could deal with unpleasant experiences which would typically cause him/her to use obscene language (e.g., talk to the teacher, go to a quiet area in the school, talk with a counselor, etc.).

16. Avoid ignoring the student's inappropriate behavior. Ignored behavior may increase in frequency and may lead to contagion on the part of other students.

17. Do not criticize. When correcting the student, be honest yet supportive. Never cause the student to feel negatively about himself/herself.

18. Emphasize individual success or progress rather than winning or "beating" other students.

19. Establish classroom rules:
- Work on-task.
- Work quietly.
- Remain in your seat.
- Finish task.
- Meet task expectations.

Review rules often. Reinforce students for following rules.

20. Teach the student appropriate ways to communicate displeasure, anger, frustration, etc.

21. Evaluate the appropriateness of the task to determine (a) if the task is too easy, (b) if the task is too difficult, and (c) if the length of time scheduled for the task is adequate.

22. Deal with the student in a calm and deliberate manner rather than in a manner that would show evidence of shock and surprise.

23. Facilitate on-task behavior by providing a full schedule of daily events. Prevent lag time from occurring when the student would be free to engage in inappropriate behavior.

24. Have the student practice appropriate verbal exchanges which should be made (e.g., "Excuse me." "I'm sorry." etc.).

25. Provide the student with the opportunity to work with a peer who will be an appropriate model for interacting with other students.

26. Avoid discussion of topics that are sensitive to the student (e.g., divorce, unemployment, alcoholism, etc.).

27. Interact frequently with the student to monitor language used.

28. Intervene early when the student begins to make inappropriate comments to other students to help prevent the student from losing control.

29. Develop a routine schedule of activities and tasks for the student so he/she knows what to expect at all times.

30. Maintain an appropriate physical distance from the student when interacting with him/her to avoid stimulating the student to make inappropriate comments.

31. Encourage the student to interact with others.

32. Make certain that your comments to the student take the form of constructive criticism rather than criticism that can be perceived as personal, threatening, etc. (e.g., instead of saying, "You always make the same mistake." say, "A better way to do that might be . . .").

33. Make certain the student is allowed to voice an opinion in a situation to avoid becoming angry or upset.

34. Provide the student with a quiet place to work. This is used as a means of reducing distracting stimuli and not as a form of punishment.

35. Make certain the student recognizes inappropriate comments (e.g., call attention to the comments when they occur, record each instance, terminate the activity when the comment occurs, etc.).

36. Reinforce the student for communicating in an appropriate manner with other students: (a) give the student a tangible reward (e.g., classroom privileges, line leading, passing out materials, five minutes free time, etc.) or (b) give the student an intangible reward (e.g., praise, handshake, smile, etc.).

37. Make the student aware of the number of times he/she makes inappropriate comments and unnecessary noises.

38. Teach the student appropriate words or phrases to use in situations of anger, stress, frustration, etc.

39. Modify or adjust situations which contribute to the student's use of obscene or profane language (e.g., if an assignment causes the student to become upset, modify the assignment to a level at which the student can be successful).

40. Prevent frustrating or anxiety producing situations from occurring (e.g., give the student tasks only on his/her ability level, give the student only the number of tasks that he/she can successfully manage in one sitting, reduce social interactions which stimulate the student's use of obscene language, etc.).

41. Provide frequent opportunities for the student to meet new people.

42. Try various groupings to determine the situation in which the student is most successful.

43. Reinforce those students in the classroom who communicate in an appropriate manner with teachers and other students.

44. Deliver a predetermined signal (e.g., hand signal, verbal cue, etc.) when the student begins to use inappropriate language.

45. Make certain that positive reinforcement is not inadvertently given for inappropriate language (e.g., attending to the student only when he/she is using profane or obscene language).

46. Provide the student with the opportunity to work with a peer who will be a model for communicating in an appropriate manner.

47. Do not force the student to interact with other students with whom he/she is not completely comfortable.

48. Reduce stimuli which contribute to the student's derogatory comments, inappropriate gestures, arguing, calling names, cursing, etc.

49. Make certain the student understands the natural consequences of his/her inappropriate behavior (e.g., peers will choose not to interact with him/her, exclusion from activities, etc.).

50. Reduce the emphasis on competition. Repeated failure may result in anger and frustration which may take the form of inappropriate comments.

51. Teach the student problem-solving skills: (a) identify the problem, (b) identify goals and objectives, (c) develop strategies, (d) develop a plan for action, and (e) carry out the plan.

52. Reinforce the student for communicating in an appropriate manner based on the length of time the student can be successful. As the student demonstrates success, gradually increase the length of time required for reinforcement.

53. Remove the student from the group or activity until he/she can demonstrate appropriate behavior.

54. Prevent the student from becoming overstimulated by an activity (i.e., monitor or supervise student behavior to limit overexcitement).

55. Make certain the student knows which comments will not be tolerated at school.

56. Separate the student from the student(s) who is the primary stimulus or focus of the inappropriate comments.

57. Make certain you express your feelings in a socially acceptable manner.

58. Use language that is pleasant and calming when speaking with the student to avoid stimulating the student to make inappropriate comments.

59. Require that the student identify alternative, appropriate behaviors following an instance of inappropriate comments (e.g., walking away from the peer, seeking teacher intervention, etc.).

60. Teach the student positive ways to interact with other students.

61. Teach the student to "think" before acting (e.g., ask himself/herself "What is happening?" "What am I doing?" "What should I do?" "What will be best for me?").

62. Assess the appropriateness of the social situation in relation to the student's ability to function successfully.

63. Treat the student with respect. Talk to the student in an objective and professional manner at all times.

64. Make certain the student will have adult supervision (e.g., at P.E., lunch, break time, etc.).

65. Reduce activities which might threaten the student (e.g., announcing test score ranges or test scores aloud, making students read aloud in class, emphasizing the success of a particular student, etc.).

66. Speak with the student to explain (a) what the student is doing wrong (e.g., arguing, threatening, calling names, etc.) and (b) what the student should be doing (e.g., following rules, staying on-task, attending to his/her responsibilities, etc.).

Goal:

1. The student will make physical contact with others when appropriate.

Objectives:

1. The student will demonstrate acceptable physical contact such as a handshake, pat on the back, "high five," etc., when appropriate on ____ out of ____ trials.
2. The student will gain others' attention in an appropriate manner by standing quietly or raising his/her hand until recognized on _____ out of _____ trials.
3. The student will interact with others in a physically appropriate manner on _____ out of _____ trials.
4. The student will refrain from making unnecessary contact such as hugging, touching, etc., when interacting with others on ____ out of ____ trials.
5. The student will touch others in only designated areas such as the arm, shoulder, or hand on _____ out of _____ trials.

Interventions:

1. Acknowledge the student when he/she seeks attention verbally instead of making it necessary for the student to gain attention through physical contact.

2. Give the student your full attention when communicating with him/her to prevent the student's need for physical contact.

3. Allow natural consequences to occur as a result of the student's inappropriate behavior (e.g., excessive physical contact may cause people to stay away from the student or may result in pushing, shoving, etc.).

4. Encourage faculty/staff members with whom the student interacts to reinforce appropriate physical contact.

5. Avoid inadvertently stimulating the student's unnecessary physical contact (e.g., attire, language used, physical proximity, etc.).

6. Communicate with parents (e.g., notes home, phone calls, etc.) to share information concerning the student's progress. The parents may reinforce the student at home for respecting the norms of physical proximity at school.

7. Explain to the student what kinds of physical contact are appropriate and acceptable on the student's job site.

8. Make certain the student sees the relationship between his/her behavior and the consequences which may follow (e.g., touching and hugging people all of the time may result in others not wanting to be around him/her).

9. Communicate with the student's career exploration/vocational education teacher and employer to provide reinforcement for appropriate physical contact at the job site.

10. Establish classroom rules:
- Work on-task.
- Work quietly.
- Remain in your seat.
- Finish task.
- Meet task expectations.

Review rules often. Reinforce students for following rules.

11. Provide the student with many social and academic successes.

12. Find a peer who would be a good influence to play with the student (e.g., someone younger, older, of the same gender, of the opposite gender, etc.).

13. Speak with the student to explain (a) what the student is doing wrong (e.g., touching, hugging, etc.) and (b) what the student should be doing (e.g., talking, exchanging greetings, etc.). Discuss appropriate ways to seek attention.

14. Model socially acceptable physical contact for the student (e.g., handshake, pat on the back, etc.)

15. Prevent the student from becoming overstimulated by an activity (e.g., monitor or supervise student behavior to limit overexcitement in physical activities, games, parties, etc.).

16. Provide the student with social interaction in place of physical interaction (e.g., call the student by name, speak to the student, praise, congratulate, etc.).

17. Provide the student with verbal recognition and reinforcement for social and academic successes.

18. Reduce the opportunity for the student to engage in inappropriate physical contact (e.g., stand an appropriate distance from the student when interacting).

19. Try various groupings to find a situation in which the student's need for physical attention can be satisfied by socially acceptable interactions (e.g., holding hands while dancing in an extracurricular activity, a hug for an accomplishment, handshake or "high five" in sports, etc.).

20. Teach the student appropriate ways to interact with others (e.g., verbal and physical introductions, interactions, etc.).

21. Use natural consequences when the student touches others as they walk by (e.g., move the student to another location in the room, have others walk away from the student, etc.).

22. Work directly with the student only in the presence of others.

23. Reinforce the student for respecting the norms of physical proximity based on the length of time he/she can be successful. As the student demonstrates success, gradually increase the length of time required for reinforcement.

24. Reinforce those students in the classroom who interact appropriately with other students or teachers.

25. Write a contract with the student specifying what behavior is expected (e.g., shaking hands rather than hugging) and what reinforcement will be made available when the terms of the contract have been met.

26. Remove the student from the group or activity until the student can demonstrate appropriate behavior and self-control.

27. Separate the student from the person who is the primary focus of the student's attempts to gain frequent physical contact.

28. Prevent frustrating or anxiety-producing situations from occurring (e.g., give the student tasks only on his/her ability level, give the student only the number of tasks that can be tolerated in one sitting, reduce social interactions which stimulate the student to become physically abusive, etc.).

29. Indicate to the student that public displays of frequent physical contact are inappropriate. Provide the student with high-interest activities (e.g., academic activities which are inherently interesting, activities during free time, etc.).

30. Make certain that reinforcement is not inadvertently given for inappropriate behavior (e.g., attending to the student only when he/she makes unnecessary physical contact).

31. Encourage faculty/staff members with whom the student interacts to reinforce appropriate physical contact.

32. Reinforce the student for respecting norms of physical proximity: (a) give the student a tangible reward (e.g., classroom privileges, line leading, passing out materials, five minutes free time, etc.) or (b) give the student an intangible reward (e.g., praise, handshake, smile, etc.).

173　Does not respond appropriately to friendly teasing (e.g., joking, name calling, sarcastic remarks, etc.)

Goals:

1. The student will improve his/her interpersonal behavior in academic settings.
2. The student will improve his/her interpersonal behavior in nonacademic settings.
3. The student will improve his/her interpersonal behavior.
4. The student will respond appropriately to friendly teasing.

Objectives:

1. The student will avoid those peers who engage in excessive friendly teasing on ___out of ___trials.
2. The student will discriminate between friendly teasing and unkind, rude remarks on ____out of ____ occasions.
3. The student will joke with peers on _____ out of _____ trials.
4. The student will laugh in response to friendly teasing on ___out of ___trials.
5. The student will respond appropriately to friendly teasing on _____ out of _____ trials.
6. The student will respond to friendly teasing by smiling and laughing on ____out of ___occasions.
7. The student will respond to friendly teasing by joking and/or teasing in return on ____out of ____ occasions.
8. The student will walk away from a peer when he/she has difficulty accepting friendly teasing on ___ out of ___ trials.
9. When teased, the student will tease in return on ___out of ___trials.

Interventions:

1. Model friendly teasing by joking with the students and laughing when they tease you.

2. Speak to the student to explain (a) what he/she is doing wrong (e.g., becoming upset, fighting, etc.) and (b) what he/she should be doing (e.g., laughing, joking in return, etc.).

3. Talk with the student about choosing friends who are friendly and sincere.

4. Allow the student to attempt something new in private before doing so in front of others.

5. Communicate with parents (e.g., notes home, phone calls, etc.) to share information concerning the student's progress. The parents may reinforce the student at home for responding appropriately to friendly teasing at school.

6. Explain to the student that friendly teasing is a positive means by which people demonstrate that they like other people and enjoy their company.

7. Discuss with the student's peers his/her sensitivity and difficulty in dealing with friendly teasing so they may adjust their behavior accordingly.

8. Make certain the student is allowed to voice an opinion in a situation to avoid becoming angry or upset.

9. Teach the student appropriate ways in which to respond to friendly teasing (e.g., laugh, joke in reply, etc.).

10. Discuss with the students those topics which are not appropriate for friendly teasing (e.g., death, disease, handicaps, poverty, etc.).

11. Do not force the student to interact with others with whom the student is not completely comfortable.

12. Help the student recognize the difference between friendly teasing and unkind, rude remarks so the student can accept and appreciate friendly teasing.

13. Choose a peer to model appropriate responses to friendly teasing for the student.

14. Intervene early when there is a problem to prevent more serious problems from occurring.

15. Point out to the student, when he/she is teasing others, that no harm is meant and that the same holds true when others tease him/her.

16. Teach the student acceptable ways to communicate displeasure, anger, frustration, etc.

17. Encourage others to compliment the student.

18. Make sure you express your feelings in a socially acceptable way.

19. Write a contract with the student specifying what behavior is expected (e.g., laughing, joking in return, etc.) and what reinforcement will be made available when the terms of the contract have been met.

20. Help the student learn to deal with teasing which upsets him/her by having the student avoid the teasing, walk away from the situation, move to another location, etc.

21. Help the student understand that if he/she cannot accept friendly teasing, it would be best to avoid those situations where teasing may occur.

22. Reinforce the student for responding appropriately to friendly teasing: (a) give the student a tangible reward (e.g., classroom privileges, line leading, passing out materials, five minutes free time, etc.) or (b) give the student an intangible reward (e.g., praise, handshake, smile, etc.).

23. Reinforce those students in the classroom who respond appropriately to friendly teasing.

24. Evaluate the interaction to determine (a) if the interaction is appropriate, (b) if the timing of the interaction is appropriate, and (c) if the student is able to handle the interaction successfully.

25. Reinforce the student for responding appropriately to friendly teasing based on the number of times he/she can be successful. As the student demonstrates success, gradually increase the number of times required for reinforcement.

26. Treat the student with respect. Talk in an objective manner at all times.

174 Does not respond appropriately to the feelings of others

Goal:

1. The student will respond appropriately to the feelings of others.

Objectives:

1. The student will compliment others when appropriate on ____ out of ____ occasions.
2. The student will express sympathy when appropriate on ____ out of ____ occasions.
3. The student will show concern for others when appropriate on ____ out of ____ occasions.
4. The student will congratulate others when appropriate on ____ out of ____ occasions.
5. The student will praise others when appropriate on ____ out of ____ occasions.
6. The student will offer assistance when appropriate on ____ out of ____ occasions.
7. The student will share with others when appropriate on ____ out of ____ occasions.
8. The student will apologize to others when appropriate on ____ out of ____ occasions.

Interventions:

1. Reinforce the student for interacting appropriately with one other person: (a) give the student a tangible reward (e.g., classroom privileges, line leading, passing out materials, five minutes free time, etc.) or (b) give the student an intangible reward (e.g., praise, handshake, smile, etc.).

2. Speak to the student to explain (a) what he/she is doing wrong (e.g., not sharing materials) and (b) what he/she should be doing (e.g., sharing materials).

3. Establish social rules (e.g., share materials, use a quiet voice in the building, walk indoors, use care in handling materials). Review rules often and reinforce students for following rules.

4. Reinforce those students in the classroom who interact appropriately with one other person.

5. Reinforce the student for interacting appropriately with one other person based on the length of time the student can be successful. As the student demonstrates success, gradually increase the length of time required for reinforcement.

6. Write a contract with the student specifying what behavior is expected (e.g., taking turns, sharing toys and materials) and what reinforcement will be made available when the terms of the contract have been met.

7. Communicate with parents (e.g., notes home, phone calls, etc.) to share information concerning the student's progress. The parents may reinforce the student at home for interacting appropriately with another person at school.

8. Evaluate the expectation for peer interaction to determine if the student can be successful in the interactions and for the expected length of time.

9. Choose a peer to model appropriate interactions with one other person for the student.

10. Have the student question any directions or explanations he/she does not understand.

11. Determine the peer(s) with whom the student would most prefer to interact and attempt to facilitate the interaction.

12. Assign an outgoing, nonthreatening peer to help the student interact more appropriately.

13. Structure the environment so that the student has many opportunities to interact successfully with another person.

14. Assign the student to interact with a younger student (e.g., play areas, cafeteria, hallways, tutoring, etc.).

15. Have the student run errands with another person to facilitate interaction.

16. Assign the student to situations in which he/she is likely to interact successfully with another person.

17. Conduct a sociometric activity with the class to determine the peer who would most prefer to interact with the student.

18. Make certain that the student understands that interacting with another person is contingent upon appropriate behavior.

19. Teach the student appropriate ways to interact with another person (e.g., how to greet another person, suggest activities, share materials, problem-solve, take turns, converse, etc.).

20. Make certain that the student understands that participation with others is contingent upon appropriate behavior.

21. Supervise situations closely so the individual with whom the student interacts does not stimulate the student's inappropriate behavior.

22. Make certain that the situation is not so stimulating as to make successful interactions with another person difficult.

23. Assign an older peer with desirable social skills to interact with the student.

24. Involve the student in extracurricular activities to encourage interactions with others.

25. Reduce the emphasis on competition. Failure may stimulate inappropriate behavior.

26. Teach the student problem-solving skills so he/she may better deal with problems that may occur in interactions with another person (e.g., talking, walking away, calling upon an arbitrator, compromising, etc.).

27. Do not force the student to interact with individuals with whom he/she is not completely comfortable.

28. Structure the activities of the situation according to the need/abilities of the student (e.g., establish rules, limit the stimulation of the activities, limit the length of activities, consider time of day, etc.).

29. Limit opportunities for interaction in situations on those occasions in which the student is not likely to be successful (e.g., the student has experienced academic or social failure prior to the scheduled activity).

30. Select nonacademic activities designed to facilitate appropriate interaction of the student and another person (e.g., board games, model building, coloring, etc.).

31. Through observations and interviews with other students, determine those characteristics of the student which interfere with successful interaction to determine skills or behaviors the student needs to develop for successful interaction.

32. Have the student practice appropriate interactions with the teacher(s).

33. Make certain beforehand that the student is able to successfully engage in the activity (e.g., the student understands the rules, the student is familiar with the activity, the student will be compatible with the other student engaged in the free-time activity, etc.).

34. Make certain that the student understands that failing to interact appropriately during activities may result in removal from the activity and/or loss of participation in future activities.

35. Have the student interact with one other person for short periods of time to facilitate success. As the student demonstrates success, gradually increase the length of time.

36. Intervene early when there is a problem to prevent a more serious problem from occurring.

37. Find a peer with whom the student is most likely to be able to successfully interact (e.g., a student with similar interests, background, classes, behavior patterns, nonacademic schedule, etc.).

175 Responds inappropriately to typical physical exchanges with peers

Goals:
1. The student will improve his/her interpersonal behavior in academic settings.
2. The student will improve his/her interpersonal behavior in nonacademic settings.
3. The student will improve his/her interpersonal behavior.
4. The student will not become upset as a result of typical physical exchanges.
5. The student will respond appropriately to typical physical exchanges with peers.
6. The student will respond appropriately to typical physical exchanges.

Objectives
1. The student will continue working, playing, etc., when typical physical exchanges with other students occur on ___ out of ___ trials.
2. The student will move about the room in an appropriate manner on ___ out of ___ trials.
3. The student will move throughout the halls in an appropriate manner on ___ out of ___ trials.
4. The student will physically respond to physical exchanges by walking away on ____ out of ____ occasions.
5. The student will respond appropriately to typical physical exchanges with other students by saying "Excuse me," moving aside, ignoring, etc., during ___ out of ___ interactions.
6. The student will respond appropriately when accidentally bumped by a peer on ___ out of ___ occasions.
7. The student will respond appropriately when brushed against by a peer on ___ out of ___ occasions.
8. The student will respond appropriately when touched by a peer on ___ out of ___ occasions.
9. The student will respond to physical exchanges by ignoring on ____ out of ____ occasions.
10. The student will respond to physical exchanges by verbalizing an apology ("Excuse me." "I'm sorry.") on ____ out of ____ occasions.

Interventions:

1. Avoid subjecting the student to crowded situations where he/she might feel uncomfortable.

2. Have a peer accompany the student in congested areas of the school to reduce typical physical exchanges and/or intercede should problems occur.

3. Have the student practice appropriate verbal exchanges which should be made when typical physical exchanges take place (e.g., "Excuse me." "I'm sorry." etc.).

4. Communicate with parents (e.g., notes home, phone calls, etc.) to share information concerning the student's progress. The parents may reinforce the student at home for responding appropriately to typical physical exchanges with other students at school.

5. Do not force the student to interact with others.

6. Have the student practice dealing with typical physical exchanges in the classroom (e.g., peers bumping against his/her desk, bumping into others when forming a line, etc.).

7. Point out the natural consequences of failing to respond appropriately to typical physical exchanges with others (e.g., other students will avoid him/her, loss of friendships, loss of opportunity to interact with peers, etc.).

8. Call attention to those times when the student accidentally bumps, touches, or brushes against other students. Help the student realize that those physical exchanges were typical and accidental.

9. Have the student lead the line, walk beside the line, walk at the end of the line, etc., to avoid or reduce typical physical exchanges with other students.

10. Reinforce those students in the classroom who respond appropriately to typical physical exchanges with other students.

11. Have the student walk on the right hand side of the hallways, stairways, etc.

12. Choose a peer to model the appropriate way to respond to typical physical exchanges with other students.

13. Establish classroom rules:
- Work on-task.
- Work quietly.
- Remain in your seat.
- Finish task.
- Meet task expectations.

Review rules often. Reinforce students for following rules.

14. Have the student avoid crowded areas. As the student develops the ability to deal with typical physical exchanges with other students in an appropriate manner, gradually allow the student access to crowded areas.

15. Speak to the student to explain (a) what he/she is doing wrong (e.g., hitting others) and (b) what he/she should be doing (e.g., accepting typical physical exchanges in an appropriate manner).

16. Teach the student to avoid typical physical exchanges by giving others room to pass, taking turns, watching the movement of others around him/her, etc.

17. Intervene early when there is a problem to prevent more serious problems from occurring.

18. Make certain that others are not purposely bumping, touching, or brushing against the student.

19. Practice role playing which involves typical physical exchanges (e.g., being bumped, touched, brushed against, etc.).

20. Teach the student acceptable ways to communicate displeasure, anger, frustration, etc.

21. Reinforce the student for responding appropriately to typical physical exchanges with others: (a) give the student a tangible reward (e.g., classroom privileges, line leading, passing out materials, five minutes free time, etc.) or (b) give the student an intangible reward (e.g., praise, handshake, smile, etc.).

22. Reinforce the student for responding appropriately to typical physical exchanges with others based on the length of time the student can be successful. As the student demonstrates success, gradually increase the length of time required for reinforcement.

23. Write a contract with the student specifying what behavior is expected (e.g., responding appropriately to typical physical exchanges with other students) and what reinforcement will be made available when the terms of the contract have been met.

24. Seat the student away from classroom movement to reduce typical physical exchanges with other students.

25. Teach the student to think before acting (e.g., ask himself/ herself "What is happening?" "What am I doing?" "What should I do?" "What will be best for me?").

26. Make certain the student will have adult supervision (e.g., at P.E., lunch, recess, break time, etc.).

176   Tries to interact with other students but is not accepted by them due to his/her behavior

Goal:

1. The student will demonstrate behaviors that will be accepted by other students.

Objectives:

1. The student will develop interaction skills and use them when interacting with a peer(s) during ___ out of ___ interactions.
2. The student will demonstrate acceptable physical contact such as a handshake, pat on the back, "high five," etc., when appropriate on ___ out of ___ trials.
3. The student will gain others' attention in an appropriate manner by standing quietly or raising his/her hand until recognized on ___ out of ___ trials.
4. The student will use a normal tone of voice when talking on ___ out of ___ trials.
5. The student will interact with other students in a physically appropriate manner on ___ out of ___ trials.
6. The student will develop hygiene skills and manners and use them when interacting with other students on ___ out of ___ trials.
7. The student will talk to his/her peers in a socially acceptable manner during ___ out of ___ interactions.
8. The student will show emotion that is appropriate for the situation during ___ out of ___ situations.
9. The student will wait quietly for his/her turn when engaged in activities with peers on ___ out of ___ trials.
10. The student will demonstrate consideration/regard for his/her peers on ___ out of ___ trials.
11. The student will demonstrate peer interaction skills by sharing materials, waiting his/her turn, and talking in an acceptable manner on ___ out of ___ trials.
12. The student will successfully interact with a peer ___ times per day.
13. The student will successfully interact with a peer ___ times per week.

Interventions:

1. Have the student be the leader of a small group activity if he/she possesses the skills or has an interest in that area.

2. Give the student the responsibility of tutoring a peer if he/she possesses the necessary skills.

3. Deliver a predetermined signal (e.g., hand signal, verbal cue, etc.) when the student begins to exhibit inappropriate behavior(s).

4. Maintain maximum supervision of the student's interaction and gradually decrease the amount of supervision over time.

5. Try various groupings to determine the situation in which the student is most comfortable.

6. Model appropriate social behavior for the student at all times.

7. Give the student responsibilities in group situations so peers may view the student in a more positive way.

8. Assess the social situation in relation to the student's ability to function successfully (e.g., number of students in the group, behavior of students in the group, etc.).

9. Provide the student with as many academic and social successes as possible so peers may view the student in a more positive way.

10. Encourage the student to further develop any ability or skill he/she may have so peers may view the student in a more positive way.

11. Modify or adjust situations that cause the student to demonstrate behaviors that are different or extreme.

12. Help the student to identify inappropriate behaviors and teach him/her ways to change those behaviors.

13. Reduce the emphasis on competition. Social interactions may be inhibited if the student's abilities are constantly made public and compared to others.

14. Teach the student to be satisfied with personal best effort and not to insist on perfection.

15. Encourage and assist the student in joining extracurricular activities, clubs, etc.

16. Help the student develop friendships by pairing him/her with another student for activities. As the student demonstrates success, gradually increase the number of students in the group.

17. Make certain the student is allowed to voice an opinion in a situation to avoid becoming upset or angry.

18. Do not criticize. When correcting the student, be honest yet supportive. Never cause the student to feel negatively about himself/herself.

19. Intervene early when there is a problem to prevent more serious problems from occurring.

20. Encourage the student to tell you about problems that occur with peers (e.g., being "bullied," teased by others, etc.).

21. Do not force the student to interact with others with whom he/she is not completely comfortable.

22. Treat the student with respect. Talk in an objective manner at all times.

23. Maintain trust and confidentiality with the student at all times.

24. Allow the student to attempt something new in private before doing it in front of others.

25. Speak with the student to explain that he/she may be trying too hard to fit in and should relax and allow friendships to develop naturally.

26. Do not force the student to interact with others.

27. Communicate with the parents (e.g., notes home, phone calls, etc.) to share information concerning the student's progress. The parents may reinforce the student at home for appropriately interacting with other students at school.

28. Write a contract with the student specifying what behavior is expected (e.g., sitting near a student, talking to a student, etc.) and what reinforcement will be made available when the terms of the contract have been met.

29. Reinforce those students in the classroom who appropriately interact with the student.

30. Remove the student from the group or activity until he/she can demonstrate appropriate behavior and self-control.

31. Reinforce the student for demonstrating appropriate behavior based on the length of time the student can be successful. As the student demonstrates success, gradually increase the length of time required for reinforcement.

32. Establish classroom rules:
- Work on-task.
- Work quietly.
- Remain in your seat.
- Finish task.
- Meet task expectations.

Review rules often. Reinforce students for following rules.

33. Reinforce the student for appropriately interacting with other students: (a) give the student a tangible reward (e.g., classroom privileges, line leading, passing out materials, five minutes free time, etc.) or (b) give the student an intangible reward (e.g., praise, handshake, smile, etc.).

177 Does not attend successfully unless close to the source of sound

Goals:

1. The student will attend more successfully to specific sounds in the environment.
2. The student will improve his/her awareness and attention to information and activities in the environment.
3. The student will improve listening skills in academic settings.
4. The student will improve listening skills in nonacademic settings.

Objectives:

1. The student will follow one-step verbal directions with _____% accuracy.
2. The student will follow two-step verbal directions with _____% accuracy.
3. The student will follow multi-step verbal directions with _____% accuracy.
4. The student will independently respond appropriately to what is said to him/her with ____% accuracy.
5. The student will independently respond appropriately to what is said to him/her _____% of the time.
6. The student will listen quietly when verbal directions are given _____% of the time.
7. The student will maintain eye contact when information is being communicated _____% of the time.
8. The student will repeat what is said with ____% accuracy.
9. The student will respond appropriately to what is said, with prompting, with ____% accuracy.

Interventions:

1. Interact frequently with the student to help him/her follow directions for an activity.

2. Allow the student to tape record information from lectures and seminars and make notes from these tapes.

3. Avoid placing the student in situations that require listening for an extended period of time such as lectures, seminars, etc. Provide the information for the student through a tape recording or lecture notes.

4. Avoid seating the student near people with whom he/she may be tempted to converse during lectures, assemblies, seminars, projects, etc.

5. Be consistent in expecting the student to listen to and follow directions. Do not allow the student to fail to follow directions one time and expect directions to be followed the next time.

6. Be sure the student has heard what was said by having him/her give acknowledgment (e.g., by saying, "Okay!" "Will do!" etc.).

7. Call the student by name to gain his/her attention prior to delivering directions, explanations, or instructions.

8. Consider carefully the student's age and experience before expecting him/her to be successful in activities that require listening.

9. Deliver verbal questions and directions that involve only one step. As the student demonstrates success, gradually increase the number of concepts or steps.

10. Determine if the student heard a direction by having him/her repeat it.

11. Develop an environment that is quiet and uncluttered (e.g., clean, well-lighted, fresh-smelling, and at a comfortable temperature).

12. Do not criticize when correcting the student; be honest yet supportive. Never cause the student to feel negatively about himself/herself.

13. Do not give directions to the student from across the classroom. Go to the student, get his/her undivided attention, and tell him/her what to do.

14. Encourage the parents to take advantage of dinner and other family-gathering times for their student to converse and practice maintaining attention.

15. Encourage the student to ask for clarification of any directions, explanations, and instructions before beginning a task to enhance comprehension.

16. Instruct the student to ask for clarification if he/she does not understand information given verbally.

17. Encourage the student to develop an awareness of the consequences of his/her behavior by writing down or talking through problems which may occur due to his/her inability to maintain attention (e.g., not focusing on directions may cause misunderstanding of an assignment which could lead to a lower grade and losing a place on the soccer team).

18. Enlist different people (e.g., peer, paraprofessional, counselor, etc.) to help the student improve his/her listening skills.

19. Establish assignment rules (e.g., listen carefully, wait until all verbal directions have been given, ask questions about anything you do not understand, begin the assignment only when you are certain about what you are to do, make certain you have all necessary materials, etc.).

20. Give a signal to gain the student's attention before delivering directions, explanations, or instructions (e.g., clap hands, turn lights off and on, etc.).

21. Let the student know that directions will only be given once and that you will not remind him/her to follow the directions.

22. Give simple, specific directions as to what the student is to do.

23. Interact frequently with the student to help him/her attend to a source of sound.

24. Have the student verbally repeat directions, explanations, and instructions after they have been given to reinforce retention.

25. Have a peer, paraprofessional, friend, etc. cue the student when he/she needs to maintain attention. (e.g., the person can touch the student on the arm when it is time to listen).

26. Have the student's hearing checked if it has not been checked in the past year.

27. Choose a peer to model responding to information from any location in the classroom for the student.

28. Identify the student's preferred learning style and use it consistently to increase the probability of understanding and remaining on-task for longer periods of time.

29. Encourage the student to avoid ingesting any substance (e.g., drugs, alcohol, cold remedies, etc.) that might further alter his/her ability to direct or maintain attention.

30. Instruct the student to ask people to repeat parts of a conversation he/she was unable to follow.

31. Instruct the student to carry a notepad with him/her at all times and to write information down to help him/her remember.

32. Instruct the student to listen for key information when being given directions or receiving information from a distance (e.g., write down main points, ideas, step-by-step instructions, etc.).

33. Instruct the student to maintain attention to the source of information by maintaining eye contact, keeping hands free from other materials, and reducing other distractions.

34. Instruct the student to write down verbal directions and cross each one off as it is completed.

35. Allow natural consequences to occur due to the student's failure to follow verbal directions or attend to information given in public places.

36. Have the student take notes when directions are being given following the "What, How, Materials, and When" format.

37. Establish rules for listening (e.g., listen to directions, ask questions about directions if they are not understood, follow the directions, etc.). These rules should be consistent and followed by everyone in the classroom. Talk about the rules often.

38. Maintain consistency in the manner in which verbal questions are asked and directions are given.

39. Reinforce the student for attending to information presented from any location in the classroom: (a) give the student a tangible reward (e.g., classroom privileges, line leading, passing out materials, five minutes free time, etc.) or (b) give the student an intangible reward (e.g., praise, handshake, smile, etc.).

40. Make certain that directions, explanations, or instructions are delivered loudly enough to be heard by the student.

41. Reduce distracting stimuli (e.g., make certain the classroom is quiet, reduce movement in the classroom, etc.).

42. Make certain that the student has adequate opportunities for repetition of information through different experiences.

43. Reward the student for maintaining eye contact and listening for a specific segment of time (e.g., take a break, visit briefly with a peer, etc.).

44. Make certain the student is attending before delivering directions, explanations or instructions (e.g., maintaining eye contact, hands free of writing materials, looking at the assignment, etc.).

45. Move objects used for tactile stimulation (e.g., pens, paper clips, loose change, etc.) away from the student's reach.

46. Present concepts following the outline of (1) Who, (2) What, (3) Where, (4) When, (5) How, and (6) Why.

47. Present directions, explanations, or instructions as simply and clearly as possible (e.g., "Get your book. Turn to page 29. Do problems 1 through 5.").

48. Stand close to or directly in front of the student when delivering verbal questions and directions.

49. Stop at various points during the presentation of directions, explanations, or instructions to check the student's comprehension of the information given.

50. Present verbal questions and directions in a clear and concise manner.

51. Provide directions on a one-to-one basis before assigning a task.

52. Maintain mobility to provide assistance to the student, frequently be near the student, etc.

53. Make certain that all directions, questions, explanations, and instructions are delivered at an appropriate pace for the student.

54. Reinforce those students who attend to information from any location in the classroom.

55. Remove the student from the situation until he/she can demonstrate self-control and follow directions when he/she has difficulty attending to and following directions in the presence of others (e.g., at an assembly, on a field trip, playing a game with peers, etc.).

56. Maintain visibility to and from the student to keep his/her attention when verbal questions/directions are being delivered. The teacher should be able to see the student and the student should be able to see the teacher. Make eye contact possible at all times.

57. Schedule important activities/assignments/meetings at times when the student is most likely to maintain attention (e.g., one hour after medication, 45 minutes after lunch, first thing in the morning, etc.).

58. Make sure you have the student's undivided attention when you are talking to him/her. Stand close to the student, maintain eye contact, and have him/her repeat the information.

59. Seat the student close to the source of information in the classroom. As the student demonstrates success, gradually move him/her away from the source of information.

60. Present directions following the outline of (1) What, (2) How, (3) Materials, and (4) When.

61. Teach the student direction-following skills (e.g., listen carefully, write down important points, etc.).

62. Teach and practice "active listening" skills. Encourage the student to listen to what another person is saying and respond based on information received.

63. While concepts are presented, have the student listen and takes notes for "Who, What, Where, When, How, and Why."

64. Teach and practice effective communication skills. These skills include: listening, maintaining eye contact, and positive body language.

65. Move the student away from other students who may interfere with his/her ability to attend to directions, explanations, or instructions.

66. Teach the student listening skills (e.g., stop working, clear desk of nonessential materials, attend to the source of information, write down important points, ask for clarification, and wait until all directions are received before beginning).

67. Teach and practice information-gathering skills (e.g., listen carefully, write down important points, ask for clarification, wait until all information is presented before beginning a task, etc.).

68. Write a contract with the student specifying what behavior is expected (e.g., attending to information presented from any location in the classroom) and what reinforcement will be made available when the terms of the contract have been met.

178 Does not direct attention or fails to maintain attention to important sounds in the immediate environment

Goals:

1. The student will improve listening skills in academic settings.
2. The student will improve listening skills in nonacademic settings.
3. The student will attend more successfully to specific sounds in the environment.

Objectives:

1. The student will independently respond appropriately to environmental cues (e.g., bells, signs, etc.) _____% of the time.
2. The student will independently respond appropriately to what is said to him/her with ____% accuracy.
3. The student will listen quietly when verbal directions are given _____% of the time.
4. The student will maintain eye contact when information is being communicated _____% of the time.
5. The student will repeat what is said to him/her with ____% accuracy.
6. The student will respond appropriately to environmental cues (e.g., bells, signs, etc.), when given verbal reminders, _____% of the time.
7. The student will respond appropriately to what is said, with prompting, with ____% accuracy.

Interventions:

1. Intervene when the student has not responded to an environmental sound. Explain exactly what he/she did wrong, what he/she was supposed to do, and why.

2. Be consistent in expecting the student to direct his/her attention to environmental sounds. Do not allow the student to be excused for failure to respond to environmental cues.

3. Consider carefully the student's ability level when expecting him/her to maintain attention to important sounds in the environment.

4. Deliver a predetermined signal (e.g., hand signal, turning lights off and on, etc.) prior to bells ringing, announcements being made, directions being given, etc.

5. Deliver cues in a supportive rather than a threatening manner (e.g., "The bell will ring in two minutes" rather than "Hurry or you will be late!").

6. Deliver directions one step at a time. As the student demonstrates the ability to direct and maintain attention, gradually increase the number of steps.

7. Demonstrate the appropriate way to direct attention to important sounds (e.g., pay attention to intercom announcements, bulletins, etc.).

8. Determine if the student heard an environmental stimuli by asking the student to identify the sound.

9. Encourage the student to develop an awareness of the consequences of his/her behavior by writing down or talking through problems which may occur due to his/her inability to maintain attention (e.g., if I fail to hear the bell ring, I may be last in the lunch line).

10. Do not allow the student to attend school activities unsupervised if the student does not maintain or direct attention to important sounds in the environment.

11. Choose a peer to model directing and maintaining his/her attention to sounds in the immediate environment for the student.

12. Do not criticize when correcting the student; be honest yet supportive. Never cause the student to feel negatively about himself/herself.

13. Evaluate the visual and auditory stimuli in the classroom. Determine the amount of stimuli the student can tolerate. Remove the extraneous stimuli from the environment.

14. Have a peer provide the student with the information not heard.

15. Give a verbal cue (e.g., call the student by name) to gain the student's attention prior to bells ringing, announcements being made, directions being delivered, etc.

16. Give directions in a variety of ways to enhance the student's ability to attend.

17. Have a peer, paraprofessional, counselor, etc. cue the student when he/she has not attended to an important sound in the immediate environment.

18. Have a peer provide the student with a cue to remind him/her of important environmental sounds (e.g., tardy bell, intercom, etc.).

19. Have the student engage in practice activities designed to develop awareness of environmental sounds.

20. Make certain that competing sounds (e.g., talking, movement, noises, etc.) are silenced when directions are being given, public address announcements are being made, etc.

21. Have the student question any directions, explanations, and instructions he/she does not understand.

22. Reduce distracting stimuli in the immediate environment (e.g., place the student on the front row, provide the student with a carrel or "office" space away from distractions, etc.). This is used as a form of reducing distracting stimuli and not as a form of punishment.

23. Have the student take notes when directions are being given following the "What, How, Materials, and When" format.

24. Present directions following the outline of (1) What, (2) How, (3) Materials, and (4) When.

25. Have the student verbally explain the appropriate response to an environmental sound.

26. Have the student verbally repeat information heard.

27. Encourage the student to avoid ingesting any substance (e.g., drugs, alcohol, cold remedies, etc.) that might further alter his/her ability to direct or maintain attention to important sounds in the immediate environment.

28. Increase the volume of auditory indicators (e.g., bells, timers, intercom, etc.).

29. Instruct the student to maintain attention to important sounds by keeping hands free from other materials and reducing other distractions.

30. Familiarize the student with all the sounds in the immediate environment (e.g., bells indicating change in class; microwave sounds; fire, earthquake, tornado alarms; etc.).

31. Allow natural consequences to occur (e.g. arriving late to class because he/she did not hear tardy bell, etc.) due to the student's inability to direct his/her attention to immediate sounds in the environment.

32. Have the student's hearing checked if it has not been checked in the past year.

33. Maintain a consistent format in which auditory information in the immediate environment is delivered (e.g., morning announcements, recess bell, delivering directions, etc.).

34. Have the student participate in practice activities designed to develop listening skills (e.g., following one-, two-, or three-step directions; listening for the main point; etc.).

35. Maintain visibility to and from the student at all times to ensure that he/she is attending.

36. Make certain that all directions, questions, explanations, and instructions are delivered in the most clear and concise manner and at an appropriate pace for the student.

37. Make certain the student is attending (e.g., making eye contact, hands free of materials, etc.) before delivering directions, explanations, and instructions.

38. Stop at various points when delivering directions, public announcements, etc., to ensure that the student is attending.

39. Make certain you direct your attention to environmental sounds when they occur to demonstrate to the student how to respond.

40. Present concepts following the outline of (1) Who, (2) What, (3) Where, (4) When, (5) How, and (6) Why.

41. Teach the student listening skills (e.g., listen carefully, write down important points, ask for clarification, wait until all directions are received before beginning).

42. Reinforce the student for directing and maintaining attention to important sounds in the environment: (a) give the student a tangible reward (e.g., classroom privileges, line leading, passing out materials, five minutes free time, etc.) or (b) give the student an intangible reward (e.g., praise, handshake, smile, etc.).

43. Have the student question any sounds in the environment to which he/she does not know how to respond.

44. Reinforce the student for directing and maintaining his/her attention to important sounds in the immediate environment based on the length of time the student can be successful. As the student demonstrates success, gradually increase the length of time required for reinforcement.

45. Reinforce those students in the classroom who direct and maintain their attention to important sounds in the immediate environment.

46. Seat the student close to the source of important sounds (e.g., public address system, intercom, etc.).

47. Seat the student far enough away from peers to ensure the ability to successfully attend to sounds in the immediate environment.

48. Make certain that directions, public announcements, etc., are delivered in a clear and concise manner (e.g., keep phrases and sentences short).

49. Seat the student next to a peer who directs and maintains attention to sounds in the immediate environment.

50. Stand directly in front of the student when delivering information.

51. Stop at various points during the presentation of information to check the student's comprehension.

52. Provide the student with public announcements, directions, and instructions in written form.

53. Tell the student what to listen for when being given directions, receiving information, etc.

54. Use alternative signals to gain attention (e.g., fire alarm with flashing light, flash class lights for announcements, etc.).

55. Use pictures, diagrams, the chalkboard, and gestures when delivering information.

56. When delivering directions, explanations, and information be certain to use vocabulary that is within the student's level of comprehension.

57. While concepts are presented, have the student listen and takes notes for "Who, What, Where, When, How, and Why."

58. Write a contract with the student. It should be written within his/her ability level and focus on only one behavior at a time. Specify what behavior is expected and what reinforcement will be made available when the terms of the contract have been met.

179 Needs verbal questions and directions frequently repeated

Goals:
1. The student will attend more successfully to specific sounds in the environment.
2. The student will follow directions without requiring repetition, explanations, etc.
3. The student will improve listening skills in academic settings.
4. The student will improve listening skills in nonacademic settings.

Objectives:
1. The student will independently respond appropriately to what is said to him/her with _____% accuracy.
2. The student will listen quietly when verbal directions are given _____% of the time.
3. The student will maintain eye contact when information is being communicated _____% of the time.
4. The student will repeat what is said to him/her with _____% accuracy.
5. The student will respond appropriately to what is said, with prompting, with ____% accuracy.

Interventions:

1. Instruct the student to carry a notepad with him/her at all times and to write information down to help him/her remember.

2. Assess the degree of task difficulty to determine if the student will require additional information, time, assistance, etc. before assigning a task.

3. Deliver verbal questions and directions that involve only one concept or step. As the student demonstrates success, gradually increase the number of concepts or steps.

4. Call the student by name to gain his/her attention prior to delivering verbal questions and directions.

5. Communicate with parents (e.g., notes home, phone calls, etc.) to share information concerning the student's progress. The parents may reinforce the student at home for responding to verbal questions and directions without requiring repetition at school.

6. Demonstrate the appropriate way to listen to verbal questions and directions (e.g., look at the person who is talking, ask questions, etc.).

7. Deliver directions and requests in a supportive rather than a threatening manner (e.g., "Please repeat the directions," rather than, "Tell me what I just said!").

8. Deliver directions, explanations, and information using vocabulary that is within the student's level of comprehension.

9. Deliver information to the student on a one-to-one basis or employ a peer tutor.

10. Deliver verbal directions prior to handing out materials.

11. Avoid placing the student in situations that require listening for an extended period of time such as lectures, seminars, etc. Provide the information for the student through a tape recording or lecture notes.

12. Deliver questions and directions in written form.

13. Demonstrate directions, explanations, and instructions as they are presented verbally (e.g., use the chalkboard to work a problem for the student, begin playing a game with the student, etc.).

14. Consider carefully the student's ability level when expecting him/her to respond to verbal questions and directions.

15. Determine if the student heard what was said by having him/her repeat it.

16. Discuss with the student the consequences of his/her behavior (e.g., if you begin a work assignment before all directions are understood, you may do things incorrectly).

17. Do not accept "forgetting" to listen as an excuse. Make the student accountable for missed information.

18. Encourage the student's parents to take advantage of dinner and other family-gathering times to converse and practice maintaining attention.

19. Do not punish the student for asking questions.

20. Write down important information for the student (e.g., the assembly begins today at 1:40, math test tomorrow, early dismissal on Friday, etc.).

21. Do not talk to the student from across the classroom. Go to the student, get his/her undivided attention, and then speak to him/her.

22. Encourage teachers, coaches, paraprofessionals, school officials, etc. to give the student written directions along with verbal directions.

23. Encourage the student to ask for clarification of any directions, explanations, and instructions before beginning a task to enhance comprehension.

24. Encourage the student to avoid ingesting any substance (e.g., drugs, alcohol, cold remedies, etc.) that might further alter his/her ability to direct or maintain attention.

25. Provide tape-recorded information from lectures and seminars. Develop questions from these tapes for the student.

26. Encourage the student to develop a 30 second definition of his/her goal to help him/her stay on-task and focused (e.g., "I will listen carefully. The better I listen the better I will perform.").

27. Encourage the student to develop an awareness of the consequences of his/her behavior by writing down or talking through problems which may occur due to his/her need to have verbal directions and questions frequently repeated (e.g., not focusing on directions may cause misunderstanding of an assignment which could lead to a lower grade and losing a place on the soccer team).

28. Choose a peer to model good communication skills for the student.

29. Encourage the student to recite a mantra to himself/herself when entering a situation where he/she will receive directions/instructions (e.g., listen carefully, listen carefully, listen carefully).

30. Do not criticize when correcting the student; be honest yet supportive. Never cause the student to feel negatively about himself/herself.

31. Establish classroom rules:
- Stay on-task.
- Work quietly.
- Remain in your seat.
- Finish task.
- Meet task expectations.

Review rules often. Reinforce students for following the rules.

32. Establish rules for listening (e.g., listen to directions, ask questions about directions if they are not understood, follow the directions, etc.). These rules should be consistent and followed by everyone in the classroom. Talk about the rules often.

33. Evaluate the appropriateness of requiring the student to respond to verbal questions and directions without needing repetition.

34. Evaluate the visual and auditory stimuli in the classroom. Determine the amount of stimuli the student can tolerate. Remove the extraneous stimuli from the environment.

35. Give a signal to gain attention prior to delivering directions verbally to the student.

36. Give directions in a very simple, specific manner.

37. Give the student directions to follow with no more than two or three steps (e.g., "Please open your text and turn to page 28."). Directions that involve several steps can be confusing and cause the student to have difficulty following them.

38. Give the student one task to perform at a time. Introduce the next task after the student has followed directions and successfully completed the previous task.

39. Have a peer help the student follow verbal questions and directions.

40. Instruct the student to ask for clarification if he/she does not understand verbal or written directions.

41. Stand close to or directly in front of the student when delivering verbal questions and directions. Encourage the student to maintain written reminders of task sequences.

42. Have the student ask for help when he/she needs it.

43. Teach the student listening skills (e.g., stop working, clear desk of nonessential materials, attend to the source of information, write down important points, ask for clarification, and wait until all directions are received before beginning).

44. Have the student verbally repeat or paraphrase the directions to the teacher.

45. Have the student practice group listening skills (e.g., "Everyone take out a piece of paper. Write your name on the paper. Number your paper from 1 to 20.").

46. Seat the student close to the source of information to enhance his/her ability to maintain attention.

47. Have the student question any directions, explanations, and instructions he/she does not understand.

48. Have the student take notes relative to verbal questions and directions.

49. Encourage the student to develop an awareness of himself/herself and the environment. Instruct the student to periodically, step back and ask himself/herself, "Am I listening and paying attention?" "What is the question?"

50. Have the student take notes when directions are being given following the "What, How, Materials, and When" format.

51. Choose a peer to model responding to verbal questions and directions without requiring repetition for the student.

52. Instruct the student to ask people to repeat parts of a conversation he/she was unable to follow.

53. Instruct the student to maintain attention to the source of information by maintaining eye contact, keeping hands free from other materials, and reducing other distractions.

54. Have the student do those things that need to be done when it is discussed instead of later (e.g., organize needed materials for an assignment to be completed later).

55. Interact frequently with the student to help the student follow directions for an activity.

56. Maintain a consistent manner in which verbal questions and directions are delivered.

57. Maintain mobility to provide assistance to the student.

58. Have the student practice listening skills by taking notes when directions, explanations, and instructions are presented.

59. Maintain visibility to and from the student to keep his/her attention when verbal questions/directions are being delivered. The teacher should be able to see the student and the student should be able to see the teacher. Make eye contact possible at all times.

60. Make certain that all directions, questions, explanations, and instructions are delivered in a clear, concise manner; at an appropriate pace; and loudly enough for the student to hear.

61. Make certain that eye contact is being made between you and the student when delivering verbal questions and directions.

62. Provide questions and directions in written form.

63. Provide opportunities for the student to talk to others on a one-to-one basis. As the student becomes more successful at listening and maintaining attention, gradually include more people in conversations.

64. Make certain that your comments take the form of constructive criticism rather than criticism that could be perceived as personal, threatening, etc. (e.g., instead of saying, "You always make the same mistake," say, "A better way to do that might be . . .").

65. Reduce the number of auditory distractions around the student (e.g., seat the student away from doors, windows, pencil sharpener; move the student to a quiet area, etc.).

66. Make certain the student is attending when you deliver verbal questions and directions (e.g., making eye contact, hands free of writing materials, looking at assignment, etc.).

67. Have a peer, paraprofessional, etc. cue the student when he/she needs to maintain attention (e.g., the person can touch the student on the arm when it is time to listen).

68. Make sure the student is paying attention when he/she is told to do something. Have the student make eye contact and repeat the information to check for understanding.

69. Have the student's hearing checked if it has not been checked in the past year.

70. Present concepts following the outline of (1) Who, (2) What, (3) Where, (4) When, (5) How, and (6) Why.

71. Present verbal questions and directions in a clear and concise manner and at an appropriate pace for the student.

72. Present verbal questions and directions in a variety of ways to increase the probability of understanding (e.g., if the student fails to understand verbal directions, present them in written form).

73. Provide information visually (e.g., written directions, instructions, etc.) to support the information the student receives auditorily.

74. Make certain that the expectations required of the student are appropriate for his/her level of development and ability.

75. Establish assignment rules (e.g., listen to directions, wait until all verbal directions have been given, ask questions about anything not understood, make certain you have all of the necessary materials, and begin the assignment when you are certain about what you are supposed to do, etc.).

76. Provide practice in listening for key information when directions are being given or information is being received (e.g., write down main points, ideas, step-by-step instructions, etc.).

77. Have the student verbally repeat directions, explanations, and instructions after they have been given to reinforce retention.

78. Choose a peer to deliver and/or repeat verbal questions and directions.

79. Provide visual information (e.g., written directions, instructions, etc.) to support the information the student receives auditorily.

80. Reduce distracting stimuli (e.g., place the student on or near the front row, provide a carrel or "office" space away from distractions, etc.). This is used as a form of reducing distracting stimuli and not as a form of punishment.

81. Make it pleasant and positive for the student to ask questions about things not understood. Reinforce the student by assisting, congratulating, praising, etc.

82. Reduce distractions to enhance the student's ability to listen and follow directions.

83. Make instructions meaningful to the student. Attempt to relate instructions to past experiences.

84. Reinforce the student for responding to verbal questions and directions without requiring frequent repetition: (a) give the student a tangible reward (e.g., classroom privileges, line leading, passing out materials, five minutes free time, etc.) or (b) give the student an intangible reward (e.g., praise, handshake, smile, etc.).

85. Reinforce those students in the classroom who respond to verbal questions and directions without requiring repetition.

86. Write down verbal directions. Instruct the student to cross each step off as it is completed.

87. Reward other students for listening, following directions, and answering verbal questions.

88. Provide directions/instructions that will accommodate different learning styles (e.g., visual, auditory, etc.).

89. Make a written list of procedures the student is to follow (e.g., how to label papers, format for mathematic assignments, etc.).

90. Reward the student for maintaining eye contact and listening for a specific segment of time (e.g., take a break, visit briefly with a peer, etc.).

91. Schedule important activities/assignments/lectures at times when the student is most likely to maintain attention (e.g., one hour after medication, 45 minutes after lunch, first thing in the morning, etc.).

92. Use pictures, diagrams, the chalkboard, and gestures when delivering information.

93. Speak to the student to explain (a) what he/she is doing wrong (e.g., needing verbal questions and directions repeated) and (b) what he/she should be doing (e.g., responding to verbal questions and directions without requiring repetition).

94. Tell the student what to listen for when being given directions, receiving information, etc.

95. Tape record the assignments and allow the student to listen to directions/instructions as often as necessary.

96. Teach and practice "active listening" skills. Instruct the student to listen to what another person is saying and respond based on information received.

97. Teach and practice effective communication skills. These skills include: listening, maintaining eye contact, and positive body language.

98. Tell the student that verbal questions and directions will be given only once.

99. Provide directions/instructions on a one-to-one basis before assigning a task.

100. Reinforce the student for responding to verbal questions and directions without requiring repetition based on the number of times the student can be successful. As the student demonstrates success, gradually increase the number of times required for reinforcement.

101. Teach the student direction-following skills (e.g., listen carefully, write down steps, etc.).

102. Stop at various points during the presentation of directions, explanations, or instructions to check the student's comprehension of the information given.

103. Use a timer to help the student know how much time he/she has to follow through with directions.

104. While concepts are presented, have the student listen and takes notes for "Who, What, Where, When, How, and Why."

105. Write a contract with the student specifying what behavior is expected (e.g., following directions with one cue) and what reinforcement will be made available when the terms of the contract have been met.

Goal:

1. The student will follow verbal directions.

Objectives:

1. The student will complete one step of the verbal direction before going on to the next step on _____ out of _____ trials.
2. The student will demonstrate the ability to follow verbal directions by listening carefully and completing the task with _____ % accuracy.
3. The student will follow _____ out of _____ verbal directions.
4. The student will follow one-step verbal directions on ___ out of ___ trials. (Gradually increase expectations as the student demonstrates success.)
5. The student will follow verbal directions with teacher assistance on _____ out of _____ trials.
6. The student will independently follow verbal directions on _____ out of _____ trials.
7. The student will listen to verbal directions on his/her ability level and follow them in correct sequential order on ___ out of ___ trials.

Interventions:

1. Maintain visibility to and from the student. The teacher should be able to see the student, and the student should be able to see the teacher. Make eye contact possible at all times when giving verbal directions.

2. Assess the quality and clarity of verbal directions, explanations, and instructions given to the student.

3. Assign a peer to work with the student to help him/her follow verbal directions.

4. Deliver directions, explanations, and information using vocabulary that is within the student's level of comprehension.

5. Avoid placing the student in situations that require listening for an extended period of time such as lectures, seminars, etc. Provide the information for the student through a tape recording or lecture notes.

6. Be consistent in expecting the student to listen to and follow directions. Do not allow the student to fail to follow directions one time and expect directions to be followed the next time.

7. Be sure the student has heard what was said by having him/her give acknowledgment (e.g., by saying, "Okay!" "Will do!" etc.).

8. Clarify for the student that it is his/her behavior which determines whether consequences are positive or negative.

9. Communicate clearly to the student when it is time to listen to verbal directions.

10. Assist the student in performing his/her responsibilities. Gradually decrease the assistance and require the student to independently assume more responsibility as he/she demonstrates success following verbal directions.

11. Deliver a predetermined signal (e.g., clapping hands, turning lights off and on, etc.) before giving verbal directions.

12. Communicate with parents (e.g., notes home, phone calls, etc.) to share information concerning the student's progress. The parents may reinforce the student at home for following verbal directions at school.

13. Demonstrate directions, explanations, and instructions as they are presented verbally (e.g., use the chalkboard to work a problem for the student, begin playing a game with the student, etc.).

14. Demonstrate the steps of verbal directions as they are delivered to enhance the likelihood that the student will follow the directions accurately.

15. Develop direction-following assignments/activities (e.g., informal activities designed to have the student carry out verbal directions in steps with increasing degrees of difficulty).

16. Evaluate the visual and auditory stimuli in the environment. Determine the amount of stimuli the student can tolerate. Remove the extraneous stimuli from the environment.

17. Do not criticize when correcting the student; be honest yet supportive. Never cause the student to feel negatively about himself/herself.

18. Do not give directions to the student from across the classroom. Go to the student, get his/her undivided attention, and tell the student what he/she is to do. As the student's ability to follow verbal directions increases, gradually increase the distance of communication.

19. Give verbal directions before handing out materials.

20. Give the student short directions, explanations, and instructions to follow. As the student demonstrates success, gradually increase the length of the directions, explanations, and instructions.

21. Encourage the student to develop an awareness of the consequences of his/her behavior by writing down or talking through problems which may occur due to his/her need to have verbal directions and questions frequently repeated (e.g., If you do not focus on the directions, you may not complete assignments correctly. Then, you may not pass the class and earn the credit needed for graduation.).

22. Encourage the student to recite a mantra to himself/herself when entering a situation where the student will receive directions/instructions (e.g., listen carefully, listen carefully, listen carefully).

23. Establish classroom rules:
- Work on-task.
- Work quietly.
- Remain in your seat.
- Finish task.
- Meet task expectations.

Review rules often. Reinforce students for following rules.

24. Establish rules for listening to and following directions (e.g., listen when someone is giving directions, ask questions about directions if they are not understood, etc.). These rules should be consistent and followed by everyone in the class. Talk about the rules often.

25. Evaluate the appropriateness of the task to determine (a) if the task is too easy, (b) if the task is too difficult, and (c) if the length of time scheduled to complete the task is adequate.

26. Facilitate the student's ability to follow verbal directions by communicating with the student's cooperative work experience/vocational education teacher to provide appropriate strategies and interventions at the student's job site.

27. Follow a less desirable task with a highly desirable task. Make the following of verbal directions and completion of the first task necessary to perform the second task.

28. Give directions in a variety of ways to increase the probability of understanding (e.g., if the student fails to understand verbal directions, present them in written form).

29. Give the student one task to perform at a time. Introduce the next task only when the student has successfully completed the previous task.

30. Encourage the student to avoid ingesting any substance (e.g., drugs, alcohol, cold remedies, etc.) that might further alter his/her ability to listen to or follow verbal directions.

31. Encourage the student to ask for clarification of any directions, explanations, and instructions before beginning a task to enhance comprehension.

32. Have a designated person be the only individual to deliver verbal directions to the student.

33. Have a peer help the student with any verbal directions he/she does not understand.

34. Instruct the student to periodically, step back and ask himself/herself, "Am I on-task and paying attention?" "What should I be doing now?"

35. Have the student attend to the source of information by maintaining eye contact, keeping hands free from other materials, and reducing other distractions.

36. Require that assignments done incorrectly, for any reason, be redone.

37. Have the student maintain a record (e.g., chart or graph) of his/her performance in following verbal directions.

38. Reduce verbal directions to steps (e.g., give the student each additional step after completion of the previous step).

39. Have the student practice group listening skills (e.g., "Everyone take out a piece of paper. Write your name on the paper. Number your paper from 1 to 20.").

40. Make certain the student is attending (e.g., making eye contact, hands free of writing materials, looking at assignment, etc.) before verbal directions are given.

41. Have the student question any verbal directions, explanations, and instructions he/she does not understand.

42. Provide constant, positive reinforcement for appropriate behavior. Ignore as many inappropriate behaviors as possible.

43. Have the student tape record directions, explanations, and instructions. Allow him/her to replay information as often as needed.

44. Have the student's hearing checked if it has not been checked in the past year.

45. Make certain that the student understands the relationship between inappropriate behavior and the consequences which follow (e.g., failing to listen to and follow directions during football practice may result in being benched for a game).

46. Have the student verbally repeat directions, explanations, and instructions after they have been given to reinforce retention.

47. Let the student know that directions will only be given once and that you will not remind him/her to follow the directions.

48. Maintain consistency in the format of verbal directions.

49. Allow natural consequences to occur (e.g., school or class detention, missed assignment, etc.) due to the student's failure to listen to and follow directions.

50. Make certain that all directions, questions, explanations, and instructions are delivered in a clear, concise manner; at an appropriate pace; and loudly enough for the student to hear.

51. Present directions in both written and verbal form.

52. Make certain that verbal directions are delivered in a supportive rather than threatening manner (e.g., "Will you please . . ." or "You need . . ." rather than "You better . . ." or "If you don't . . .").

53. Make certain the student achieves success when following verbal directions.

54. Make certain the student has all the materials needed to perform the assignment/activity.

55. Have the student practice verbal direction-following on nonacademic tasks (e.g., recipes, games, etc.).

56. Provide alternatives for the traditional format of presenting verbal directions (e.g., tape record directions, summarize directions, directions given by peers, etc.).

57. Have the student repeat directions or give an interpretation after receiving verbal directions.

58. Make certain the student knows that you expect him/her to listen to you (e.g., by saying, "William, it is important that you listen carefully to what I have to say. The book report is due on Monday.").

59. Interact frequently with the student to help him/her follow verbal directions for the activity.

60. Make instructions meaningful to the student. Attempt to relate instructions to past experiences.

61. Choose a peer to model appropriate listening to and following of verbal directions for the student.

62. Make sure the student is paying attention when he/she is told to do something. Have the student make eye contact and repeat the information to check for understanding.

63. Prevent the student from becoming overstimulated by an activity (e.g., frustrated, angry, etc.).

64. Provide clearly stated verbal directions (e.g., make the directions as simple and concrete as possible).

65. Make certain that verbal directions are given at the level at which the student can be successful (e.g., two-step or three-step directions are not given to students who can only successfully follow one-step directions).

66. Provide directions on a one-to-one basis before assigning a task.

67. Provide supplemental directions/instructions in the student's preferred learning style (e.g., visual, auditory, etc.).

68. Work the first problem or problems with the student to make certain that he/she follows the verbal directions accurately.

69. Provide the student with a written copy of verbal directions.

70. Speak to the student to explain (a) what he/she is doing wrong (e.g., ignoring verbal directions) and (b) what he/she should be doing (e.g., listening to and following through when given verbal directions).

71. Reduce distracting stimuli to increase the student's ability to follow verbal directions (e.g., place the student on the front row, provide a carrel or "office" space away from distractions, etc.). This is used as a means of reducing distracting stimuli and not as a form of punishment.

72. Make certain that verbal directions are delivered in a nonthreatening manner (e.g., positive voice, facial expression, language used, etc.).

73. Reduce the emphasis on competition. Competitive activities may cause the student to hurry to begin the task without verbal directions.

74. Reduce the emphasis on early completion. Hurrying to complete assignments may cause the student to fail to follow directions.

75. Reinforce the student for following verbal directions: (a) give the student a tangible reward (e.g., classroom privileges, line leading, passing out materials, five minutes free time, etc.) or (b) give the student an intangible reward (e.g., praise, handshake, smile, etc.).

76. Have the student carry out one step of the verbal directions at a time, checking with the teacher to make certain that each step is successfully followed before attempting the next.

77. Reinforce the student for following verbal directions based on the length of time he/she can be successful. As the student demonstrates success, gradually increase the length of time required for reinforcement.

78. Reinforce those students in the classroom who follow verbal directions.

79. Require the student to wait until the teacher gives him/her a signal to begin a task (e.g., give a hand signal, ring a bell, etc.).

80. Teach the student skills for following verbal directions (e.g., listen carefully, write down important points, use environmental cues, wait until all directions are received before beginning, etc.).

81. Reward the student for maintaining eye contact and listening for a specific segment of time (e.g., take a break, visit briefly with a peer, etc.).

82. Structure the environment to provide the student with increased opportunities for help or assistance on academic tasks (e.g., peer tutoring, directions for work sent home, frequent interactions, etc.).

83. Stand next to the student when giving verbal directions.

84. Tape record directions for the student to listen to and replay as necessary.

85. Teach and have the student practice listening for key information when he/she is being given directions or receiving information (e.g., write down main points, ideas, step-by-step instructions, etc.).

86. Teach and practice effective communication skills. These skills include: listening, maintaining eye contact, and positive body language.

87. Work through the steps of the verbal directions as they are delivered to make certain the student follows the directions accurately.

88. Teach and provide practice in information-gathering skills (e.g., listen carefully, write down important points, ask for clarification, wait until all information is presented before beginning a task, etc.).

89. Teach the student listening skills (e.g., stop working, clear desk of nonessential materials, attend to the source of information, write down important points, ask for clarification, and wait until all directions are received before beginning).

90. Seat the student close to the source of the verbal directions (e.g., teacher, aide, peer, etc.).

91. Provide the student with a predetermined signal when he/she is not following verbal directions (e.g., lights turned off and on, hand signals, etc.).

92. Seat the student far enough away from peers to ensure increased opportunities for attending to verbal directions.

93. Provide the student with a clearly understood list of consequences for inappropriate behavior.

94. When delivering directions, explanations, and information, be certain to use vocabulary that is within the student's level of comprehension.

95. Write a contract with the student specifying what behavior is expected (e.g., following verbal directions) and what reinforcement will be made available when the terms of the contract have been met.

96. Teach and provide practice in "active listening" skills. Have the student listen to what another person is saying and respond based on information received.

97. Write down verbal directions. Instruct the student to cross each step off as it is completed.

Goals:
1. The student will attend to what other students say.
2. The student will improve listening skills in nonacademic settings.

Objectives:
1. The student will listen quietly when other students are speaking on _____ out of _____ occasions.
2. The student will maintain eye contact when other students are speaking on _____ out of _____ occasions.
3. The student will repeat what other students have said with _____% accuracy.
4. The student will respond appropriately to what other students say on _____ out of _____ occasions.

Interventions:

1. Instruct the student to maintain attention to the source of information by maintaining eye contact, keeping hands free from other materials, and reducing other distractions.

2. Do not force the student to interact with someone when he/she is not completely comfortable.

3. Allow the student to work with a peer and teacher. The first student will dictate a short paragraph to be typed by the teacher and will also compose a comprehension question. The second student, after listening to the process, will read the story verbally and point out the answer. Then student roles can be reversed.

4. Be consistent in expecting the student to listen to what others are saying. Do not provide missed information if the student fails to listen.

5. Consider carefully the student's ability level and experience when expecting him/her to be a good listener. Have the student's hearing checked if it has not been checked in the past year.

6. Demonstrate the appropriate way to listen by listening to the student when he/she talks.

7. Encourage the student to develop a 30 second definition of his/her goal to help stay on-task and focused on the speaker (e.g., "I will listen carefully. The better I focus and stay on-task, the better I will listen.").

8. Determine if the student heard what was said by having him/her repeat it.

9. Develop the student's awareness of the consequences of his/her behavior by writing down or talking through problems which may occur due to his/her inability to maintain attention (e.g., not focusing on directions may cause misunderstanding of an assignment which could lead to a lower grade and losing a place on the soccer team).

10. Do not criticize when correcting the student; be honest yet supportive. Never cause the student to feel negatively about himself/herself.

11. Allow the student some movement while listening to other students. Monitor and limit the amount of movement.

12. Do not ignore the student when he/she wants to tell you something. When you ignore the student, he/she learns that it is acceptable to be inattentive.

13. Encourage parents to take advantage of dinner and other family-gathering times to converse and practice maintaining attention.

14. Encourage the student to develop an awareness of himself/herself and those around him/her. Instruct the student to periodically step back and ask himself/herself, "Am I on-task and paying attention?" "What should I be doing now?"

15. Encourage the student to interact with others.

16. Make certain the student is near the students who are speaking.

17. Enlist different people (e.g., peers, para-professionals, counselors, etc.) to help the student maintain attention to conversations.

18. Establish rules for listening (e.g., listen when others are talking, ask questions if you do not understand, etc.). These rules should be consistent and followed by everyone in the class. Talk about the rules often.

19. Evaluate the visual and auditory stimuli in the classroom. Determine the amount of stimuli the student can tolerate. Remove the extraneous stimuli from the environment.

20. Teach and have the student practice listening for key information when he/she is being given directions or receiving information (e.g., write down main points, ideas, step-by-step instructions, etc.).

21. Have a peer, paraprofessional, student, etc. cue the student when he/she needs to maintain attention (e.g., the person can touch the student on the arm when it is time to listen).

22. Have other students call the student by name before speaking to him/her.

23. Write a contract with the student. It should be written within his/her ability level and focus on only one behavior at a time. Specify what behavior is expected and what reinforcement will be made available when the terms of the contract have been met.

24. Have other students stand directly in front of the student when speaking to him/her so the student will be more likely to listen to what others are saying.

25. Provide opportunities for the student to talk to others on a one-to-one basis. As the student becomes more successful at listening and maintaining attention, gradually include more people in conversations.

26. Reduce the emphasis on competition in the classroom. Competition may cause the student to become excited or distracted and fail to listen to what other students are saying.

27. Have the student silently repeat information just heard from other students to help in remembering important information.

28. Identify a classmate who has good communication skills. Encourage the student to observe that classmate and try to model his/her behaviors which promote good communication.

29. Instruct the student to ask for clarification if he/she does not understand information given verbally.

30. Instruct the student to ask people to repeat parts of a conversation he/she was unable to follow.

31. Allow natural consequences to occur (e.g., miss information, miss a school activity, etc.) due to the student failing to listen to others.

32. Instruct the student's peers to preface statements with the student's name to gain his/her attention before speaking.

33. Make certain that competing sounds (e.g., talking, noises, motion in the classroom, etc.) are silenced when other students are talking, to enhance the student's ability to listen to what others are saying.

34. Encourage the student to recite a mantra to himself/herself when entering a situation where he/she will receive directions/instructions (e.g., listen carefully, listen carefully, listen carefully).

35. Make certain that other students speak clearly and concisely when speaking to the student.

36. Have the student repeat or paraphrase what other students have said to him/her to determine what the student heard.

37. Provide group settings that are quiet, well-lighted, and at a comfortable temperature.

38. Talk to the student before beginning an activity and remind him/her of the importance of listening to others.

39. Have the student practice listening to what other students are saying (e.g., following simple instructions, sharing information, etc.).

40. Reduce the number of visual distractions in the classroom when listening is required (e.g., move the student's work area away from windows, doors, etc.).

41. Teach and practice information-gathering skills (e.g., listen carefully, write down important points, ask for clarification, wait until all information is presented before beginning a task, etc.).

42. Reduce the occurrence of situations that may contribute to difficulty maintaining attention (e.g., timed activities, competition, long meetings, etc.).

43. Provide the student with frequent opportunities to meet new people.

44. Reinforce the students in the classroom who listen to what other students are saying.

45. Remove the student from the situation when he/she has difficulty listening to others (e.g., at a school assembly, at a school play, when a guest speaker is present, etc.) until he/she can demonstrate self-control and listen to what others are saying.

46. Schedule opportunities for peer interaction at times when the student is most likely to maintain attention (e.g., one hour after medication, 45 minutes after lunch, first thing in the morning, etc.).

47. Teach the student to respect others and what they are saying by respecting the student and what he/she says.

48. Instruct the student to sit close to the source of information to increase his/her ability to maintain attention.

49. Make certain the student is attending to what other students are saying (e.g., making eye contact, stopping other activities, responding appropriately, etc.).

50. Talk to the student before going to an activity (e.g., assembly, school play, field trip, etc.) and remind the student of the importance of listening to what others are saying.

51. Teach "active listening" skills. Provide opportunities for the student to listen to what another person is saying and respond based on information received.

52. Teach and practice effective communication skills. These skills include: listening, maintaining eye contact, and positive body language.

53. Reinforce the student for listening (e.g., making eye contact, putting aside materials, answering the students, etc.) to what is said to him/her by other students: (a) give the student a tangible reward (e.g., classroom privileges, passing out materials, five minutes free time, etc.) or (b) give the student an intangible reward (e.g., praise, handshake, smile, etc.).

54. Teach the student listening skills (e.g., stop working, clear desk of nonessential materials, attend to the source of information, write down important points, ask for clarification, and wait until all directions are received before beginning).

55. Reinforce the student for listening to what other students are saying based on the length of time the student can be successful. As the student demonstrates success, gradually increase the number of times or length of time required to listen.

56. Treat the student with respect. Talk in an objective manner at all times.

57. Speak to the student to explain (a) what he/she is doing wrong (e.g., failing to listen to what other students are saying) and (b) what he/she should be doing (e.g., listening to other students when they speak to him/her, listening to other students when they speak to a group, etc.).

182 Is unsuccessful in activities requiring listening

Goals:

1. The student will attend more successfully to specific sounds in the environment.
2. The student will improve listening skills in academic settings.
3. The student will improve listening skills in nonacademic settings.

Objectives:

1. The student will follow one-step verbal directions with ____% accuracy.
2. The student will follow two-step verbal directions with ____% accuracy
3. The student will follow multi-step verbal directions with ____% accuracy.
4. The student will independently respond appropriately to what is said with ____% accuracy.
5. The student will listen quietly when verbal directions are given ____% of the time.
6. The student will maintain eye contact when information is being communicated ____% of the time.
7. The student will quietly listen when verbal directions are given ____% of the time.
8. The student will repeat what is said with ____% accuracy.
9. The student will respond appropriately to what is said, with prompting, with ____% accuracy.

Interventions:

1. Have the student tape record directions, explanations, and instructions so that he/she may apply information as often as needed.

2. Allow the student to tape record information from lectures and seminars and make notes from these tapes.

3. Deliver a predetermined signal (e.g., hand signal, turning off and on lights, etc.) prior to bells ringing, announcements being made, etc.

4. Ask the student for immediate repetition of directions.

5. Avoid placing the student in situations which require listening for an extended period of time such as lectures, seminars, etc. Provide supplemental information through a tape recording or lecture notes.

6. Avoid seating the student near people with whom he/she may be tempted to converse during lectures, guest speakers, group projects, etc.

7. Be consistent in expecting the student to listen. Hold the student accountable for not listening to important information.

8. Call the student by name prior to bells ringing, announcements being made, directions being given, etc.

9. Consider carefully the student's ability level and experience before expecting the student to be successful in activities that require listening.

10. Reduce the number of visual distractions around the student (e.g., move the student's work area away from windows, doors, computer area, etc.).

11. Arrange for individual assignments when the group setting is overly distracting.

12. Deliver directions to the student individually.

13. Make certain that competing sounds (e.g., talking, movement, noises, etc.) are silenced when directions are being given, public address announcements are being made, etc.

14. Deliver directives in a supportive rather than a threatening manner (e.g., "Please repeat the directions given," rather than, "Tell me what I just said!").

15. Deliver information slowly to the student.

16. Deliver verbal directions prior to handing out materials.

17. Demonstrate appropriate listening behavior (e.g., sit up straight, eyes on speaker, etc.).

18. Demonstrate directions, explanations, and instructions as they are presented verbally (e.g., use the chalkboard to work a problem for the student, begin playing a game with the student, etc.).

19. Allow natural consequences to occur (e.g., miss assignments, miss information regarding a school event, etc.) due to the student's failure to follow directions.

20. Provide activities designed to teach listening skills.

21. Develop an environment that is quiet and uncluttered (e.g., clean, well-lighted, fresh-smelling, and at a comfortable temperature).

22. Talk to the student before beginning an activity and remind him/her of the importance of listening to others.

23. Give the student directions to follow with no more than two or three steps (e.g., "Please open your text and turn to page 28."). Directions that involve several steps can be confusing and cause the student to have difficulty following them.

24. Do not criticize when correcting the student; be honest yet supportive. Never cause the student to feel negatively about himself/herself.

25. Deliver information in a variety of ways (e.g., pictures, diagrams, gestures, etc.) to enhance the student's ability to attend.

26. Do not give directions to the student from across the room. Go to the student, get his/her undivided attention, and tell the student what he/she is to do.

27. Encourage the student to ask for clarification of any directions, explanations, and instructions before beginning a task to enhance comprehension.

28. Have the student ask for help when he/she needs it.

29. Encourage the student to develop an awareness of himself/herself and the environment. Instruct the student to periodically step back and ask himself/herself, "Am I listening and paying attention?" "What should I be doing now?"

30. Encourage the student to develop an awareness of the consequences of his/her behavior by writing down or talking through problems which may occur due to his/her inability to listen for sustained periods of time (e.g., not focusing on directions may cause misunderstanding of an assignment which could lead to a lower grade and losing a place on the soccer team).

31. Encourage the student to recite a mantra to himself/herself when entering a situation where he/she will receive directions/instructions (e.g., listen carefully, listen carefully, listen carefully).

32. Establish rules for listening (e.g., listen to directions, ask questions about directions if they are not understood, follow the directions, etc.). These rules should be consistent and followed by everyone in the class. Talk about the rules often.

33. Teach the student listening skills (e.g., listen carefully, write down important points, ask for clarification, wait until all directions are received before beginning).

34. Evaluate the difficulty level of information to which the student is expected to listen (e.g., information communicated on the student's ability level).

35. Give directions in a variety of ways to enhance the student's ability to attend.

36. Have a peer, paraprofessional, etc. cue the student when he/she is not listening (e.g., the person can touch the student's arm as a signal that he/she is not focused on the speaker).

37. Evaluate the visual and auditory stimuli in the classroom. Determine the amount of stimuli the student can tolerate. Remove the extraneous stimuli from the environment.

38. Have a peer provide the information the student does not hear.

39. Have the student engage in practice activities designed to develop his/her listening skills (e.g., following one-, two-, or three-step directions; listening for the main point; etc.).

40. Choose a peer to model good listening skills for the student.

41. Have the student practice group listening skills (e.g., "Everyone take out a piece of paper. Write your name on the paper. Number your paper from 1 to 20.").

42. Make certain that your comments take the form of constructive criticism rather than criticism that could be perceived as personal, threatening, etc. (e.g., instead of saying, "You always make the same mistake," say, "A better way to do that might be . . .").

43. Have the student practice listening to what other students are saying (e.g., following simple instructions, sharing information, etc.).

44. Ask the student to repeat parts of a conversation as the discussion is taking place.

45. Have the student question any directions, explanations, and instructions he/she does not understand.

46. Provide the student with public announcements, directions, and instructions in written form while presenting them verbally.

47. Have the student silently repeat information just heard to help him/her remember the important facts.

48. Have the student take notes when directions are being given following the "What, How, Materials, and When" format.

49. Allow the student to occasionally take assignments home when the class setting is overly distracting.

50. Have the student's hearing checked if it has not been checked in the past year.

51. Have the student verbally repeat directions, explanations, and instructions after they have been given to reinforce retention.

52. Identify the student's most efficient learning mode and use it consistently to increase the probability of understanding (e.g., if the student fails to understand directions or information verbally, present it in written form).

53. Instruct the student to maintain attention to the source of information by maintaining eye contact, keeping hands free from other materials, and reducing other distractions.

54. Interact frequently with the student. Make certain that eye contact is being made to ensure that the student is attending.

55. Let the student know that directions will only be given once and that you will not remind him/her to follow the directions.

56. Maintain visibility to and from the student at all times to ensure he/she is attending.

57. Write a contract with the student specifying what behavior is expected (e.g., listening to directions, explanations, and instructions) and what reinforcement will be made available when the terms of the contract have been met.

58. Make certain the student is attending (e.g., making eye contact, hands free of writing materials, etc.) before delivering directions, explanations, and instructions.

59. Make certain the student understands that if he/she does not listen to and follow directions when working in a group, participating in activities, etc. others will not want to work with him/her.

60. Make certain the student's hearing has been checked recently.

61. Make sure the student is paying attention when he/she is given direction. Have the student make eye contact and repeat the information to check for understanding.

62. Play games designed to teach listening skills (e.g., *Simon Says*, *Red Light-Green Light*, *Mother May I?*, etc.).

63. Instruct the student to carry a notepad with him/her at all times and to write information down to help him/her remember.

64. Have the student participate in practice activities designed to develop his/her listening skills (e.g., following one-, two-, or three-step directions; listening for the main point; etc.).

65. Present directions following the outline of (1) What, (2) How, (3) Materials, and (4) When.

66. Present one concept at a time. Make certain the student understands each concept before presenting the next.

67. Provide directions on a one-to-one basis.

68. Speak to the student when he/she does not listen to explain (a) what he/she is doing wrong (e.g., not listening to directions, explanations, and instructions) and (b) what he/she should be doing (e.g., listening to directions, explanations, and instructions) and why.

69. Have the student practice listening skills by taking notes when directions, explanations, and instructions are presented.

70. Present directions, explanations, and instructions as simply and clearly as possible (e.g., "Get your book. Turn to page 29. Do problems 1 through 5.").

71. Provide the student with public announcements, directions, and instructions in written form.

72. Reduce distracting stimuli in the immediate environment (e.g., place the student on or near the front row, provide the student with a carrel or "office" space away from distractions, etc.). This is used as a form of reducing distracting stimuli and not as a form of punishment.

73. Reduce visual and auditory stimuli in and around the classroom which interfere with the student's ability to listen successfully (e.g., close the classroom door and windows, draw the shades, etc.).

74. Reinforce the student for listening: (a) give the student a tangible reward (e.g., classroom privileges, five minutes free time, etc.) or (b) give the student an intangible reward (e.g., praise, handshake, smile, etc.).

75. Reinforce those students in the classroom who listen to directions, explanations, and instructions.

76. Teach information-gathering skills (e.g., listen carefully, write down important points, ask for clarification, wait until all information is presented before beginning a task, etc.).

77. Rephrase directions, explanations, and instructions to increase the likelihood of the student understanding what is being presented.

78. Reward the student for listening. Possible rewards include verbal praise (e.g., "You did a great job listening to every step of the directions!" "You were able to tell me five details." etc.).

79. Schedule important activities/assignments/lectures at times when the student is most likely to maintain attention (e.g., one hour after medication, 45 minutes after lunch, first thing in the morning, etc.).

80. Seat the student close to the source of directions, explanations, and instructions to increase his/her ability to maintain attention.

81. Present concepts following the outline of (1) Who, (2) What, (3) Where, (4) When, (5) How, and (6) Why.

82. Teach the student direction-following skills (e.g., stop doing other things, listen carefully, write down important points, wait until all directions are given, question any directions not understood, etc.).

83. Stand directly in front of the student when delivering directions, explanations, and instructions.

84. Stop at various points when delivering directions, public announcements, etc. to ensure that the student is attending.

85. Teach and have the student practice how to listen for key information when he/she is being given directions or receiving information (e.g., write down main points, ideas, step-by-step instructions, etc.).

86. Evaluate the level of information presented to the student to determine if the information is presented at a level the student can understand.

87. Remove the student from the situation until he/she can demonstrate self-control and follow directions when he/she has difficulty listening and following directions in the presence of others (e.g., at an assembly, when a guest speaker is present, etc.).

88. Use pictures, diagrams, and gestures when delivering information.

89. Use multiple modalities (e.g., auditory, visual, tactile, etc.) when presenting directions, explanations, and instructional content. Determine which modality is stronger and utilize the results.

90. While concepts are presented, have the student listen and takes notes for "Who, What, Where, When, How, and Why."

91. Teach the student when to ask questions, how to ask questions, and what types of questions obtain what types of information.

92. Deliver directions, explanations, and information using vocabulary that is within the student's level of comprehension.

93. Have the student repeat or paraphrase information given to determine if the student heard what was said.

183   Requires eye contact to listen successfully

Goals:

1. The student will attend more successfully to specific sounds in the environment.
2. The student will improve his/her awareness and attention to information and activities in the environment.
3. The student will improve listening skills in academic settings.
4. The student will improve listening skills in nonacademic settings.

Objectives:

1. The student will be able to repeat what is said to him/her with _____% accuracy.
2. The student will independently respond appropriately to what is said to him/her with _____% accuracy.
3. The student will listen quietly, when verbal directions are given, _____% of the time.
4. The student will maintain eye contact, when information is being communicated, _____% of the time.
5. The student will respond appropriately to what is said, with prompting, with _____% accuracy.
6. The student will respond appropriately to what is said, with prompting, _____% of the time.

Interventions:

1. Make certain that the student is seated close enough to make eye contact with and hear the teacher when information is being delivered.

2. Encourage the student to ask for clarification of any directions, explanations, and instructions before beginning a task to enhance comprehension.

3. Avoid placing the student in situations that require listening for an extended period of time such as lectures, seminars, assemblies, etc. Provide the information for the student through a tape recording or lecture notes.

4. Call the student by name to gain his/her attention prior to delivering information.

5. Deliver information in a clear, concise manner.

6. Make certain information is delivered loudly enough to be heard by the student.

7. Deliver information to the student on a one-to-one basis. As the student demonstrates the ability to listen successfully, gradually include more students in the group with him/her.

8. Determine which stimuli in the environment interfere with the student's ability to listen successfully. Reduce or remove those stimuli from the environment.

9. Encourage the parents to take advantage of dinner and other family-gathering times for their child to converse and practice maintaining eye contact.

10. Teach the student listening skills (e.g., stop working, clear desk of nonessential materials, attend to the source of information, write down important points, ask for clarification, and wait until all directions are received before beginning).

11. Encourage the student to ask people to repeat parts of a conversation he/she was unable to follow.

12. Deliver a predetermined signal to the student (e.g., hand signal, turn lights off and on, etc.) prior to delivering information.

13. Make certain the student is not engaged in activities that interfere with directions, explanations, and instructions (e.g., looking at other materials, putting away materials, talking to others, etc.).

14. Choose a peer to model good attending skills for the student.

15. Reinforce the student for listening based on the length of time the student can be successful. As the student demonstrates success, gradually increase the length of time required for reinforcement.

16. Encourage the student to recite a mantra to himself/herself when entering a situation where he/she will receive directions/instructions (e.g., maintain eye contact, maintain eye contact, maintain eye contact).

17. Enlist different people (e.g., peer, paraprofessional, counselor, friend, etc.) to help the student maintain eye contact.

18. Evaluate the difficulty level of information presented to the student. Determine if the information is presented at a level the student can understand.

19. Deliver information in both verbal and written form.

20. Have a peer, paraprofessional, friend, etc. cue the student when he/she needs to maintain eye contact (e.g., the person can touch the student on the arm when it is time to attend to a speaker).

21. Reinforce the student for listening based on the length of time the student can be successful. As the student demonstrates success, gradually increase the length of time required for reinforcement.

22. Have the student verbally repeat directions, explanations, and instructions after they have been given to reinforce retention.

23. Have the student take notes when directions are being given following the "What, How, Materials, and When" format.

24. Have the student take notes when information is verbally presented.

25. While concepts are presented, have the student listen and takes notes for "Who, What, Where, When, How, and Why."

26. Have the student's hearing checked if it has not been checked in the past year.

27. Present directions following the outline of (1) What, (2) How, (3) Materials, and (4) When.

28. Instruct the student to maintain attention to the source of information by maintaining eye contact, keeping hands free from other materials, and reducing other distractions.

29. Maintain a consistent format in which information is verbally presented.

30. Maintain visibility to and from the student at all times to ensure that the student is attending.

31. Allow natural consequences to occur as a result of the student's failure to listen (e.g., the inability to respond correctly, a failing grade, etc.).

32. Evaluate the visual and auditory stimuli in the classroom. Determine the amount of stimuli the student can tolerate. Remove the extraneous stimuli from the environment.

33. Make the subject matter meaningful to the student (e.g., explain the purpose of an assignment, relate the subject matter to the student's environment, etc.).

34. Move objects used for tactile stimulation (e.g., pens, paper clips, loose change, etc.) away from the student's reach.

35. Have the student question any directions, explanations, or instructions he/she does not understand.

36. Encourage the student to develop an awareness of himself/herself and the environment. Instruct the student to periodically step back and ask himself/herself, "Am I maintaining eye contact?" "What should I be doing now?"

37. Schedule important activities/assignments/ lectures at times when the student is most likely to maintain attention (e.g., one hour after medication, 45 minutes after lunch, first thing in the morning, etc.). Tell the student what to listen for when given directions or receiving information, etc.

38. Present concepts following the outline of (1) Who, (2) What, (3) Where, (4) When, (5) How, and (6) Why.

39. Provide opportunities for the student to talk to others on a one-to-one basis. As the student becomes more successful at maintaining attention and eye contact, gradually include more people in conversations.

40. Reduce visual and auditory stimuli in and around the classroom which interfere with the student's ability to listen successfully (e.g., close the classroom door and windows, draw the shades, etc.).

41. Stop at various points during the presentation of information to check the student's comprehension.

42. Reinforce the student for attending to the source of information. Continuous eye contact is not necessary for reinforcement.

43. Teach and practice information-gathering skills (e.g., listen carefully, write down important points, ask for clarification, wait until all information is presented before beginning a task, etc.).

44. Reinforce the student for maintaining eye contact: (a) give the student a tangible reward (e.g., classroom privileges, five minutes free time, etc.) or (b) give the student an intangible reward (e.g., praise, handshake, smile, etc.).

45. Provide directions on a one-to-one basis before assigning a task.

46. Reinforce those students in the classroom who focus visual attention on the speaker.

47. Remove distracting stimuli in the student's immediate environment (e.g., books, writing materials, personal property, etc.).

48. Require the student to repeat or paraphrase information heard to determine successful listening.

49. Seat the student close to the source of information in the classroom. As the student demonstrates success, gradually move the him/her farther away from the source of information.

50. Speak to the student to explain (a) what he/she is doing wrong (e.g., failing to listen to directions, explanations, and instructions) and (b) what the student should be doing (e.g., listening to directions, explanations, and instructions).

51. Reinforce those students in the classroom who listen to directions, explanations, and instructions.

52. Teach and practice "active listening" skills. Instruct the student to listen to what another person is saying and respond based on information received.

53. Reinforce the student for listening: (a) give the student a tangible reward (e.g., classroom privileges, line leading, passing out materials, five minutes free time, etc.) or (b) give the student an intangible reward (e.g., praise, handshake, smile, etc.).

54. Teach and practice effective communication skills. These skills include: listening, maintaining eye contact, and positive body language.

55. Tell the student what to listen for when being given directions, receiving information, etc.

56. Use multiple modalities (e.g., auditory, visual, tactile, etc.) when presenting directions, explanations, and instructional content. Determine which modality is stronger and utilize the results.

57. Verbally present information that is necessary for the student to know to perform a task successfully.

58. Encourage the student to develop an awareness of the consequences of his/her behavior by writing down or talking through problems which may occur due to his/her inability to maintain attention (e.g., not focusing on directions may cause misunderstanding of an assignment which could lead to a lower grade and losing a place on the soccer team).

59. Maintain eye contact when delivering information to the student. As the student demonstrates the ability to listen successfully, gradually decrease the amount of eye contact.

60. Write a contract with the student specifying what behavior is expected (e.g., listening to directions, maintaining eye contact) and what reinforcement will be made available when the terms of the contract have been met.

61. Stop at various points during the presentation of information to ensure the student is attending and maintaining eye contact.

184   Does not demonstrate initiative in the absence of directions

Goal:

1. The student will demonstrate initiative in the absence of directions.

Objectives:

1. The student will attempt to perform a given assignment before asking for teacher assistance on _____ out of _____ trials.
2. The student will read necessary directions, instructions, explanations, etc., before asking for teacher assistance on _____ out of _____ trials.
3. The student will independently complete _____ out of _____ assignments per school day.
4. The student will ask for teacher assistance only when necessary when performing assignments on _____ out of _____ trials.
5. The student will work for _____ minutes without requiring assistance from the teacher on _____ out of _____ trials.
6. The student will continue working on parts of the assignment while waiting for assistance from an instructor.

Interventions:

1. Reinforce the student for taking action rather than remaining inactive: (a) give the student a tangible reward (e.g., classroom privileges, line leading, passing out materials, five minutes free time, etc.) or (b) give the student an intangible reward (e.g., praise, handshake, smile, etc.).

2. Reinforce the student for performing assignments independently.

3. Speak to the student to explain (a) what he/she is doing wrong (e.g., sitting and waiting, doing nothing, etc.) and (b) what he/she should be doing (e.g., beginning an activity, asking for assistance, finding something else to do, etc.).

4. Establish classroom rules:
- Work on-task.
- Work quietly.
- Remain in your seat.
- Finish task.
- Meet task expectations.

Review rules often. Reinforce students for following rules.

5. Reinforce those students in the classroom who find things to do, remain productive, ask for assistance, etc.

6. Reinforce the student for finding something to do based on the number of times he/she can be successful. As the student demonstrates success, gradually increase the number of times required for reinforcement.

7. Write a contract with the student specifying what behavior is expected (e.g., remaining productive with tasks, alternative assignments, etc.) and what reinforcement will be made available when the terms of the contract have been met.

8. Communicate with parents (e.g., notes home, phone calls, etc.) to share information concerning the student's progress. The parents may reinforce the student at home for remaining active, seeking direction, working on-tasks, etc., at school.

9. Choose a peer to model remaining productive and involved for the student.

10. Encourage the student to question any directions, explanations, instructions he/she does not understand.

11. Evaluate the appropriateness of expecting the student to remain actively involved for extended periods of time.

12. Maintain mobility throughout the classroom to determine the student's needs.

13. Offer the student assistance frequently throughout the day.

14. Make certain that directions, explanations, and instructions are delivered on the student's ability level.

15. Structure the environment so the student is not required to rely on others for information about assignments (e.g., make certain the student's tasks are on his/her ability level; make certain instructions are clear; maintain frequent interactions with the student to ensure his/her success).

16. To detect the student's needs, communicate with the student as often as opportunities permit.

17. Demonstrate accepting behavior (e.g., willingness to help others, making criticisms constructive and positive, demonstrating confidentiality in personal matters, etc.).

18. Communicate to the student an interest in his/her needs.

19. Communicate to the student that he/she is a worthwhile individual.

20. Call on the student often to encourage communication.

21. Teach the student communication skills (e.g., hand raising, expressing needs in written and/or verbal forms, etc.).

22. Encourage communication skills in the classroom.

23. Allow the student additional time to complete assignments when working independently.

24. Encourage the student to communicate his/her needs to other personnel in the educational environment (e.g., school counselor, school psychologist, principal, etc.).

25. Communicate with parents, agencies, or the appropriate parties to inform them of the problem, determine the cause of the problem, and consider possible solutions to the problem.

26. Teach the student to communicate his/her needs in an appropriate manner (e.g., raise hand, use a normal tone of voice when speaking, verbally express problems, etc.).

27. Recognize the student's attempts to communicate his/her needs (e.g., facial expressions, gestures, inactivity, self-deprecating comments, etc.).

28. Have the student interact with a peer to encourage him/her to communicate his/her needs to others. As the student demonstrates success in communicating his/her needs to others, gradually increase the number of peers with whom the student interacts.

29. Pair the student with a non-threatening peer, a peer with similar interests and ability level, etc.

30. Give the student responsibilities in the classroom to increase the probability of more involvement and activity (e.g., passing out materials, collecting lunch money, collecting schoolwork, etc.).

31. Give the student responsibilities in the classroom that require communication (e.g., peer tutor, group leader, teacher assistant, etc.).

32. Present the task in the most interesting manner possible.

33. Have the student keep a chart or graph representing the number of assignments he/she completes independently and the amount of time spent working on the assignments.

34. Assess the degree of task difficulty in comparison with the student's ability to perform the task.

35. Assign the student shorter tasks (e.g., modify a 20-problem math activity to 4 activities of 5 problems each, to be done at various times during the day). As the student demonstrates success, gradually increase the number of problems.

36. Reduce distracting stimuli (e.g., place the student in the front row, provide a carrel or quiet place away from distractions, etc.). This is to be used as a means of reducing distracting stimuli and not as a form of punishment.

37. Encourage the student to ask for clarification of directions for assignments.

38. Provide the student with step-by-step written directions for performing assignments.

39. Allow the student to perform alternative assignments. Gradually introduce more components of the assignment until those assignments are routinely performed.

40. Choose a peer from whom the student may seek assistance.

41. Maintain consistent expectations. Keep expectations within the ability level of the student.

42. Maintain a consistent daily routine.

43. Work a few problems with the student on an assignment to serve as a model and help the student begin a task.

44. Reinforce the student for beginning, working on, and completing assignments.

45. Attempt to provide assistance immediately. Gradually increase the length of time the student must wait for assistance when the teacher is helping another student, instructing, etc.

46. Encourage the student to go to the next problem, go to another part of the assignment, begin a new assignment, etc., when waiting for assistance from an instructor.

47. Explain to the student that work not done during work time will have to be done during other times (e.g., break time, recreational time, after school, etc.).

48. Establish alternative activities for the student to perform when waiting for assistance from an instructor (e.g., check work already completed; look at a magazine; organize work area; begin another task; etc.).

185 Tries to avoid situations, assignments, responsibilities

Goals:

1. The student will respond appropriately to situations, assignments, or responsibilities in the classroom.
2. The student will attempt new situations in the classroom.
3. The student will attempt new assignments in the classroom.
4. The student will accept responsibilities in the classroom.

Objectives:

1. The student will refrain from making somatic complaints to avoid situations, assignments, or responsibilities on ___ out of ___ trials.
2. The student will complain of physical discomfort when appropriate in ___ out of ___ trials.
3. The student will attempt new situations in the classroom on ___ out of ___ trials.
4. The student will attempt new assignments on ___ out of ___ trials.
5. The student will accept responsibilities in the classroom on ___ out of ___ trials.
6. The student does not ask to use the restroom, go to his/her locker, go to the office, etc., to avoid situations in the classroom on ___ out of ___ trials.
7. The student does not ask to use the restroom, go to his/her locker, go to the office, etc., to avoid assignments in the classroom on ___ out of ___ trials.
8. The student does not ask to use the restroom, go to his/her locker, go to the office, etc., to avoid accepting responsibilities in the classroom on ___ out of ___ trials.

Interventions:

1. Choose a peer to model appropriate participation, performance of assignments, or acceptance of responsibilities for the student.

2. Have the student question any directions, explanations, or instructions not understood.

3. Give the student assignments and responsibilities he/she will enjoy performing (e.g., teacher assistant, line leading, chores in the classroom, etc.). As the student demonstrates success, gradually introduce less desirable assignments and responsibilities.

4. Follow a less desirable activity with a more desirable activity, requiring the student to complete the first to perform the second.

5. Make certain the student understands that leaving the classroom may only be done at regularly scheduled intervals (e.g., during recess, break time, lunch, class changes, etc.).

6. Provide the student with many academic and social successes.

7. Assess the appropriateness of the social setting in relation to the student's ability to function successfully (i.e., do not place the student with peers who are threatening to him/her).

8. Program alternative activities for the student to perform or engage in if he/she has difficulty performing assigned activities. As the student demonstrates success, gradually remove the alternative activities.

9. Allow the student to leave the classroom to get materials from his/her locker, use the restroom, go to the nurse's office, go to the counselor's office, etc., after assignments are completed or responsibilities are performed.

10. Provide the student with positive feedback that indicates he/she is successful, competent, important, valuable, etc.

11. Have the student record and chart his/her own appropriate behavior (e.g., participating in classroom activities, performing assignments, taking responsibilities, etc.).

12. Make certain that reinforcement is not inadvertently given for complaints of physical discomfort (e.g., allowing the student to leave the room, avoid assignments, leave school, etc.).

13. Seek student input in planning the curriculum, extracurricular activities, etc.

14. Reduce the emphasis on competition. Competitive activities may increase the student's anxiety and reduce the student's ability to remember information.

15. Provide the student with a selection of assignments and require the student to choose a minimum number from the total amount (e.g., present the student with ten academic tasks from which six must be finished each day).

16. Explain to the student that work not done during work time must be done during other times (e.g., recreational time, break time, after school, etc.).

17. Give the student a preferred responsibility to be performed at various times throughout the day.

18. Present assignments and responsibilities in the most attractive and interesting manner possible.

19. Interact frequently with the student to maintain his/her involvement in assignments, responsibilities, etc.

20. Make the necessary adjustments in the environment to prevent the student from experiencing stress, frustration, anger, etc., as much as possible.

21. Allow the student to attempt something new in private before doing so in front of others.

22. Identify variables in the environment which cause the student to avoid situations, assignments, or responsibilities; reduce or remove these variables from the environment.

23. Vary the student's assignments and responsibilities so the student does not get tired of doing the same things.

24. Limit the number of assignments and responsibilities for which the student is responsible. As the student demonstrates the ability to get things done on time, gradually increase the number of chores.

25. Make certain the student has all the necessary materials to get assignments and responsibilities done on time.

26. Do not accept excuses. The student must understand that, regardless of the reasons, it is necessary that he/she take responsibility for not turning in a math assignment, losing pencils, etc.

27. Carefully consider those things the student may be trying to avoid. If something unpleasant is causing the student to pretend to be sick, do all you can to change the situation.

28. Give the student a special job for assignments (e.g., collecting math papers, passing out materials, sharpening pencils, etc.) to do when the student completes his/her work.

29. Deliver directions in a supportive rather than threatening manner (e.g., "Please turn in your math paper." rather than "You had better turn in your math paper or else!").

30. Sit down with the student and discuss a list of assignments, responsibilities, etc., that he/she needs to do.

31. Assist the student in performing responsibilities. As the student demonstrates success, gradually require the him/her to independently assume more responsibility.

32. Schedule the student's work and responsibilities around highly enjoyable activities (e.g., the student may go to recess after the math assignment is finished).

33. Go with the student or have someone else accompany the student to those things he/she may be trying to avoid. Gradually decrease the length of time you or someone else stays with the student.

34. Make positive comments about school and the importance of school.

35. Reinforce those students in the classroom who are participating, performing assignments, or taking responsibilities.

36. Evaluate the appropriateness of the task to determine (a) if the task is too difficult and (b) if the length of time scheduled to complete the task is adequate.

37. Communicate with parents, agencies, or the appropriate parties to inform them of the problem, determine the cause of the problem, and consider possible solutions to the problem.

38. Communicate with parents (e.g., notes home, phone calls, etc.) to share information concerning the student's progress. The parents may reinforce the student at home for appropriate behavior at school.

39. Write a contract with the student specifying what behavior is expected (e.g., participating, performing assignments, or taking responsibilities) and what reinforcement will be made available when the terms of the contract have been met.

40. Reinforce the student for participating, performing assignments, or taking responsibilities based on the length of time the student can be successful. As the student demonstrates success, gradually increase the length of time required for reinforcement.

41. Set aside time each day for everyone in the classroom to care for belongings.

42. Speak to the student to explain (a) what he/she is doing wrong (e.g., complaining, asking to leave the room, etc.) and (b) what he/she should be doing (e.g., reporting legitimate discomfort or needs).

43. Establish classroom rules:
- Work on-task.
- Work quietly.
- Remain in your seat.
- Finish task.
- Meet task expectations.

Review rules often. Reinforce students for following rules.

44. Determine if physical discomfort is being used as an excuse to avoid situations and is not the result of a medical problem, neglect, or abuse.

45. Reinforce the student for participating, performing assignments, or taking responsibilities: (a) give the student a tangible reward (e.g., classroom privileges, line leading, passing out materials, five minutes free time, etc.) or (b) give the student an intangible reward (e.g., praise, handshake, smile, etc.).

Reminder: Do not "force" the student to participate in any activity.

186 Is not willing to try new leisure time activities

Goal:
1. The student will try new leisure time activities.

Objectives:
1. The student will use leisure time to find an activity, interact quietly with a peer(s), follow directions, etc. on ____ out of ____ trials.
2. The student will independently engage in a new activity for ____minutes during leisure time.
3. The student will engage in a new activity with a peer for ____minutes during leisure time.
4. The student will engage in a new activity with a teacher for ____minutes during leisure time.

Interventions:

1. Evaluate the appropriateness of leisure-time activities to determine whether or not the student can be successful with the activity and the length of time scheduled.

2. Encourage the student's peers to include him/her in new leisure-time activities.

3. Encourage the student to assist younger peer in new leisure-time activities.

4. Develop, with the student, a list of high-interest, leisure-time activities that require various amounts of time to perform.

5. Place leisure-time materials (e.g., paper, pencil, glue, crayons, games, etc.) in a location where the student can obtain them on his/her own.

6. Establish centers of high-interest activities at appropriate levels of difficulty for the student's use during leisure time.

7. Provide a quiet, reasonably private area where the student can do nothing during leisure-time activities.

8. Separate the student from the peer(s) who stimulates his/her inappropriate use of leisure time.

9. Encourage the student to plan the use of leisure time in advance.

10. Provide sign-up sheets for new leisure-time activities.

11. Give the student an individual schedule to follow so that when an activity is finished he/she knows what to do next.

12. Assign a peer for the student to interact with during new leisure-time activities.

13. Identify a specified new activity for the student to engage in during leisure time.

14. Have the student act as a peer tutor during new leisure-time activities.

15. Have the student act as a teacher assistant during new leisure-time activities.

16. Allow the student to go to other classrooms for specified activities during leisure time (e.g., typing, home economics, industrial arts, etc.).

17. Provide high-interest, leisure-time activities for completion of assignments (e.g., listening to music, reading, socializing, going to another part of the building, etc.).

18. Provide the student with a list of quiet activities to engage in when he/she finishes assignments early.

19. Find educationally related, leisure-time activities for the student to perform (e.g., flash card activities with peers; math, reading, or spelling board games; etc.).

20. Engage in leisure-time activities with the student to model appropriate use of leisure time.

21. Make certain the student is able to successfully engage in the leisure-time activity (e.g., the student understands the rules, the student is familiar with the activity, the student will be compatible with other students engaged in the activity, etc.).

22. Provide supervision of new leisure-time activities to monitor the student's willingness to try new leisure-time activities.

23. Make certain the student is aware of the length of leisure time available when beginning the leisure-time activity.

24. Make certain the student understands that failing to make appropriate use of leisure time may result in termination of leisure time and/or loss of future leisure time.

25. Provide the student frequently with new short-term leisure-time activities so he/she can learn to attempt new activities.

26. Give the student a special responsibility during leisure time (e.g., headphones, coloring books, reading material, etc.).

27. Provide things that entertain the student during leisure time (e.g., headphones, coloring books, reading material, etc.).

28. Make certain the student does not become involved in overstimulating activities.

29. Reinforce the student for attempting new leisure-time activities: (a) give the student a tangible reward (e.g., classroom privileges, line leading, passing out materials, five minutes free time, etc.) or (b) give the student an intangible reward (e.g., praise, handshake, smile, etc.).

30. Communicate with parents (e.g., notes home, phone calls, etc.) to share information concerning the student's progress. The parents may reinforce the student at home for attempting new leisure-time activities at school.

31. Write a contract with the student specifying what behavior is expected (e.g., trying new activities, appropriate use of leisure time, etc.) and what reinforcement will be made available when the terms of the contract have been met.

32. Reinforce the student for making appropriate use of leisure time based on the length of time the student can be successful. As the student demonstrates success, gradually increase the length of time required.

33. Reinforce those students in the classroom who attempt new leisure-time activities.

34. Establish leisure-time rules:
- Find an activity.
- Spend time quietly.
- Remain in assigned areas.
- Put materials away when free time is over.

Review rules often. Reinforce students for following rules.

35. Speak to the student to explain (a) what the student is doing wrong (e.g., doing nothing, refusing to attempt new activities, etc.) and (b) what he/she should be doing (e.g., participating in a new activity, observing a new activity, etc.).

36. Have the student question any directions, explanations, or instructions not understood.

37. Choose a peer to model willingness to try new leisure-type activities for the student.

187 Indicates that he/she does not care or is not concerned about performance, grades, report cards, graduating, consequences of behavior, etc.

Goals:

1. The student will demonstrate an interest in graduating from high school.
2. The student will demonstrate concern about his/her classroom performance.
3. The student will demonstrate consideration of consequences of his/her behavior.

Objectives:

1. The student will attend ___ out of ___ classes per month.
2. The student will attend ___ out of ___ classes per semester.
3. The student will attend ___ out of ___ classes per week.
4. The student will be on time to ___ out of ___ classes per semester.
5. The student will be on time to ___ out of ___ classes per month.
6. The student will be on time to ___ out of ___ classes per week.
7. The student will demonstrate an interest in graduating from high school by talking about graduation, making plans for college or future employment, etc., on ___ out of ___ trials.
8. The student will demonstrate behaviors that will result in positive consequences on ___ out of ___ trials.
9. The student will demonstrate concern about his/her classroom performance on ___ out of ___ trials.
10. The student will demonstrate consideration of consequences of his/her behavior on ___ out of ___ trials.
11. The student will demonstrate pride in his/her classroom performance by making positive comments, displaying his/her work for others to view, asking to take on new responsibilities, etc., on ___ out of ___ trials.
12. The student will perform academic tasks designed to meet his/her level of functioning with ___% accuracy. (Gradually increase expectations as the student demonstrates success.)

Interventions:

1. Communicate with parents, agencies, or the appropriate parties to inform them of the problem, determine the cause of the problem, and consider possible solutions to the problem.

2. Avoid competition. Failure may cause the student to lose interest or not participate in school activities.

3. Call on the student when he/she can answer successfully.

4. Communicate with parents (e.g., notes home, phone calls, etc.) to share information concerning the student's progress. The parents may reinforce the student at home for showing an interest and participating in school activities.

5. Allow the student more decision-making opportunities relative to class activities and assignments.

6. Determine the student's preferred activities, interests, etc., and incorporate them into his/her daily schedule, program, etc., at various points throughout the day.

7. Establish classroom rules:
- Work on-task.
- Work quietly.
- Remain in your seat.
- Finish task.
- Meet task expectations.

Review rules often. Reinforce students for following rules.

8. Evaluate the appropriateness of the task in relation to the student's ability to perform the task successfully.

9. Evaluate the appropriateness of the task to determine (a) if the task is too easy, (b) if the task is too difficult, and (c) if the length of time scheduled to complete the task is adequate.

10. Give the student responsibilities in the classroom (e.g., teacher assistant, peer tutor, group leader, etc.).

11. Help the student to develop self-confidence and satisfaction in personal self-worth and successes by pointing out strengths, emphasizing positive aspects, etc.

12. Inform others who will be working with the student (e.g., teachers, principals, clerks, etc.) about the student's tendency to ignore consequences of his/her behavior.

13. Intervene early when there is a problem to prevent more serious problems from occurring.

14. Make certain the student does not become involved in overstimulating activities.

15. Present tasks in the most attractive and interesting manner possible.

16. Provide a full schedule of daily events to keep the student actively involved.

17. Reinforce those students in the classroom who show an interest and participate in school activities.

18. Provide the student with as many academic and social successes as possible.

19. Reinforce the student for showing an interest and participating in school activities based on the length of time he/she can be successful. As the student demonstrates success, gradually increase the length of time required for reinforcement.

20. Reinforce the student for showing an interest and participating in school activities: (a) give the student a tangible reward (e.g., classroom privileges, line leading, passing out materials, five minutes free time, etc.) or (b) give the student an intangible reward (e.g., praise, handshake, smile, etc.).

21. Provide the student with "real-life" experiences from the environment. Have individuals from the work force (e.g., mechanic, draftsman, secretary, etc.) visit the class to relate the importance of schoolwork to work experiences that involve, math, reading, writing, etc.

22. Show an interest in the student (e.g., acknowledge the student, ask the student's opinion, spend time working one-on-one with the student, etc.).

23. Speak with the student to explain (a) what he/she is doing wrong (e.g., failing to show an interest and participate in school activities) and (b) what he/she should be doing (e.g., showing an interest and participating in school activities).

24. Teach the student to "think" before acting (e.g., ask himself/herself, "What is happening?" "What am I doing?" "What should I do?" "What will be best for me?").

25. Write a contract with the student specifying what behavior is expected (e.g., showing an interest and participating in school activities) and what reinforcement will be made available when the terms of the contract have been met.

188 Is not motivated by rewards

Goal:

1. The student will be motivated by rewards at school.

Objectives:

1. The student will identify something he/she enjoys doing when asked by the teacher on ___ out of ___ occasions.
2. The student will identify something he/she would like to earn when asked by the teacher on ___ out of ___ occasions.
3. The student will identify a reinforcer he/she will work toward earning on ___ out of ___ trials.
4. The student will earn ___ identified reinforcer(s) per day.
5. The student will earn ___ identified reinforcer(s) per week.

Interventions:

1. Conduct a reinforcer survey with the student to determine his/her reinforcer preferences.

2. Communicate with parents to determine what the student finds reinforcing at home.

3. Present tasks in the most attractive, interesting manner possible.

4. Write a contract with the student so he/she can earn reinforcement at home for appropriate behavior at school.

5. Make certain that the student can be successful at school to earn reinforcement.

6. Provide a wide variety of reinforcers for the student at school (e.g., eating lunch with the teacher, one-to-one time with the teacher, principal's assistant, assistant to the custodian, extra time in a favorite class, etc.).

7. Make an agreement with the parents so enjoyable activities at home (e.g., watching television, riding bike, visiting with friends, etc.) are contingent upon appropriate behavior at school.

8. Communicate with parents, agencies, or the appropriate parties to inform them of the problem, determine the cause of the problem, and consider possible solutions to the problem.

9. Provide reinforcers that are social in nature (e.g., extracurricular activities, clubs, community organizations such as 4-H, scouting, YMCA, YWCA, etc.).

10. Help the student develop an interest in a hobby which can be used as a reinforcer at school (e.g., stamp collecting, rock collecting, model building, photography, art, reading, sewing, cooking, etc.).

189   Is not persistent in seeking success

Goal:

1. The student will be persistent in seeking success.

Objectives:

1. The student will remain on-task until the task is completed on _____ out of _____ trials.
2. The student will remain on-task for the required amount of time with supervision on _____ out of _____ trials.
3. The student will independently remain on-task for the required amount of time on _____ out of _____ trials.
4. The student will rely on environmental cues (e.g., timers, clocks, bells, other students) to remain on-task for the required amount of time on _____ out of _____ trials.
5. The student will ask for clarification of directions or instructions not understood on _____ out of _____ trials.

Interventions:

1. Reinforce the student for remaining on-task for the required amount of time: (a) give the student a tangible reward (e.g., classroom privileges, line leading, passing out materials, five minutes free time, etc.) or (b) give the student an intangible reward (e.g., praise, handshake, smile, etc.).

2. Speak to the student to explain (a) what he/she is doing wrong (e.g., failing to attend to a task) and (b) what he/she should be doing (e.g., looking at the task, watching the teacher when directions are given, remaining on-task, etc.).

3. Establish classroom rules:
- Work on-task.
- Work quietly.
- Remain in your seat.
- Finish task.
- Meet task expectations.

Review rules often. Reinforce students for following rules.

4. Reinforce those students in the classroom who remain on-task for the required amount of time.

5. Reinforce the student for staying on-task based on the length of time the student can be successful. As the student demonstrates success, gradually increase the length of time required for reinforcement.

6. Write a contract with the student specifying what behavior is expected (e.g., establish a reasonable length of time to stay on-task) and what reinforcement will be made available when the terms of the contract have been met.

7. Communicate with parents (e.g., notes home, phone calls, etc.) to share information concerning the student's progress. The parents may reinforce the student at home for remaining on-task for the specified amount of time at school.

8. Choose a peer to model appropriate on-task behavior for the student.

9. Evaluate the appropriateness of a task to determine (a) if the task is too easy, (b) if the task is too difficult, and (c) if the length of time scheduled to complete the task is adequate.

10. Have the student question any directions, explanations, instructions he/she does not understand.

11. Assign the student shorter tasks but more of them (e.g., modify a 20-problem math activity to 4 activities of 5 problems each, to be done at various times during the day). As the student demonstrates success, gradually increase the number of problems.

12. Present the task in the most attractive, interesting manner possible.

13. Reduce distracting stimuli (e.g., place the student on the front row, provide a carrel or "office" space away from distractions). This is used as a means of reducing distracting stimuli and not as a form of punishment.

14. Interact frequently with the student to involve him/her in the activity (e.g., ask the student questions; ask the student's opinions; stand close to the student; seat the student near the teacher's desk; etc.).

15. Maintain visibility to and from the student. The teacher should be able to see the student and the student should be able to see the teacher. Make eye contact possible at all times.

16. Assess the appropriateness of the degree of difficulty of academic tasks in comparison to the student's ability.

17. Have the student maintain a chart representing the amount of time spent on-task.

18. Provide the student with a timer he/she may use to increase units of time during which he/she maintains attention (i.e., have the student work on the activity until the timer goes off).

19. Have the student work with a tutor to maintain his/her attention to tasks.

20. Deliver a predetermined signal (e.g., hand clap, verbal cue, etc.) when the student begins to display off-task behavior.

21. Structure the environment to reduce the opportunity for off-task behavior (e.g., reduce lag time by providing the student with enough activities to maintain productivity).

22. Create a quiet area in the classroom where absolute silence must be observed.

23. Provide the student with a selection of assignments and require him/her to choose a minimum number from the total (e.g., present the student with 10 academic tasks from which he/she must finish 6 that day).

24. Make certain only those materials necessary for performing the task are on the student's desk (e.g., pencil, textbook, paper, etc.). Additional materials may distract the student (e.g., crayons, library book, etc.).

25. Make certain the student has all the materials necessary to perform the task (e.g., pencil, textbook, flash cards, paper, etc.).

26. Make certain the student has enough work area to perform the task.

27. Position the student's desk or work area so that he/she is not visually distracted by others (e.g., turn the student's desk away from other students, etc.).

28. Reduce distracting stimuli which could interfere with the student's ability to remain on-task (e.g., provide enough room to move without physical contact, keep noise level to a minimum, keep movement in the environment to a minimum, etc.).

29. Make certain the student understands the instructions/directions for the task (e.g., present instructions in a variety of ways, have the student verbalize what he/she is to do to perform the activity, etc.).

30. Help the student learn to be satisfied with his/her own best effort rather than some arbitrary measure of success. Success is measured individually according to ability levels, and progress of any kind is a measure of success.

31. Place the student with peers who will be appropriate role models and are likely to facilitate his/her academic and behavioral success.

32. Schedule highly desirable activities contingent upon the student staying on-task a required amount of time (i.e., staying on-task for a required amount of time earns the student the opportunity to participate in a desirable activity).

33. Reduce the emphasis on competition. Repeated failure may cause the student to remove himself/herself from competition by not remaining on-task.

34. Establish initial expectations for staying on-task based on the length of time the student can be successful. As the student demonstrates success, gradually increase the length of time required for reinforcement.

35. Have the student chart his/her own record of on-task behavior. Reinforce the student for increasing the amount of time spent on-task.

36. Consider individual needs of the student which may be interfering with his/her on-task behavior (e.g., hunger, need for rest, comfort level, etc.). Intervene to correct the situation or change the expectations.

37. Remove any peer from the immediate environment who may be interfering with the student's ability to remain on-task.

38. Minimize stimulation which interferes with the student's ability to remain on-task (e.g., maintain a routine schedule of events, schedule special activities for the end of the day, etc.).

39. Have the student communicate with appropriate personnel (e.g., counselor, nurse, administrator, etc.) about concerns (e.g., home, peer, personal problems, etc.) which interfere with his/her ability to stay on-task.

40. Provide flexibility in scheduling so the student may perform alternative activities which result in more successful on-task behavior.

41. Allow the student to choose the place in the classroom where he/she can best demonstrate on-task behavior.

42. Provide the student with a list of assignments for the day and allow the student to choose the order of the activities. The student may be in the best position to identify the order of tasks he/she will be able to perform successfully.

43. Provide the student with adequate transition time between activities to increase on-task behavior after activities have begun (e.g., after break time, lunch, special activities, etc.).

44. Provide the student with alternative ways to perform an assignment and allow the student to choose the most desirable.

45. Provide the student with assistance for those activities which he/she has the most difficulty attending to for the required amount of time.

46. Make certain that natural consequences occur as a result of the student's inability to remain on-task (e.g., work not done during work time must be done during other times such as break time, after school, etc.).

47. Provide the student with earphones, ear plugs, etc., if reduced sound will facilitate his/her ability to remain on-task.

48. Allow the student to take assignments/tasks to other areas of the school where he/she is most likely to be able to demonstrate on-task behavior (e.g., library, study hall, learning center, etc.).

49. Allow the student to leave the task and return to it at a later time when he/she can be more successful remaining on-task.

190   Is not willing to assume extra responsibilities, tasks, etc.

Goal:

1. The student will be willing to assume extra responsibilities, tasks, etc.

Objectives:

1. The student will attempt extra responsibilities, tasks, etc., with physical assistance on _____ out of _____ trials.
2. The student will attempt extra responsibilities, tasks, etc., with verbal prompts on _____ out of _____ trials.
3. The student will independently attempt extra responsibilities, tasks, etc., on _____ out of _____ trials.
4. The student will attempt extra responsibilities, tasks, etc., within _____ (indicate a given time period).
5. The student will attempt extra responsibilities, tasks, etc., with peer assistance on _____ out of _____ trials.

Interventions:

1. Reinforce the student for assuming extra responsibilities, tasks, etc.: (a) give the student a tangible reward (e.g., classroom privileges, line leading, passing out materials, five minutes free time, etc.) or (b) give the student an intangible reward (e.g., praise, handshake, smile, etc.).

2. Speak with the student to explain (a) what he/she is doing wrong (e.g., failing to assume extra responsibilities) and (b) what he/she should be doing (e.g., asking for assistance or clarification, following directions, starting on time, etc.).

3. Reinforce those students in the classroom who assume extra responsibilities, tasks, etc.

4. Reinforce the student for assuming extra responsibilities, tasks, etc., within the length of time the student can be successful. Gradually decrease the amount of time to begin the task to be reinforced.

5. Write a contract with the student specifying what behavior is expected (e.g., assuming extra responsibilities, tasks, etc.) and what reinforcement will be made available once the terms of the contract have been met.

6. Communicate with parents (e.g., notes home, phone calls, etc.) to share information. The parents may reinforce the student at home for assuming extra responsibilities, tasks, etc., at school.

7. Evaluate the appropriateness of the task to determine (a) if the task is too easy, (b) if the task is too difficult, and (c) if the length of time scheduled to complete the task is adequate.

8. Have the student question any directions, explanations, and instructions he/she does not understand.

9. Teach the student skills in following directions.

10. Assess the quality and clarity of directions, explanations, and instructions given to the student.

11. Assign a peer or volunteer to help the student assume an extra responsibility.

12. Structure the environment to provide the student with increased opportunity for help or assistance.

13. Reduce distracting stimuli (e.g., place the student on the front row, provide a carrel or "office" space away from distractions, etc.). This is used as a means of reducing distracting stimuli and not as a form of punishment.

14. Have the student maintain a record (e.g., chart or graph) of his/her performance in assuming new responsibilities/tasks.

15. Communicate clearly to the student when it is time to begin an assignment.

16. Present the task in the most interesting, attractive manner possible.

17. Maintain mobility to provide assistance for the student.

18. Give directions in a variety of ways to increase the probability of understanding (e.g., if the student fails to understand verbal directions, present them in written form to facilitate understanding).

19. Reduce the emphasis on competition (e.g., academic or social). Fear of failure may cause the student to refuse to assume an extra responsibility/task.

20. Have the student attempt the new responsibility/task in a private place (e.g., carrel, "office," quiet study area, etc.) to reduce the fear of public failure.

21. Tell the student that directions will only be given once.

22. Allow the student to perform extra responsibilities/tasks in a variety of places in the building (e.g., resource room, library, learning center, etc.).

23. Provide the student with a sample of the assignment or activity which has been partially completed by a peer or the teacher (e.g., book reports, projects).

24. Do not require the student to complete the extra responsibility/task in one sitting.

25. Allow the student the option of performing the extra responsibility/task at another time (e.g., earlier in the day, later, on another day).

26. Make certain that the student has all the materials he/she needs to perform the extra responsibility/task.

27. Have the student explain to the teacher what he/she thinks he/she should do to perform the extra responsibility/task.

28. Have the student time his/her activities to monitor his/her own behavior and accept time limits.

29. Structure time units so the student knows exactly how long he/she has to work and when he/she must be finished.

30. Provide the student with more than enough time to finish an activity. As the student demonstrates success, decrease the amount of time provided to finish an activity.

31. Have the student repeat the directions verbally to the teacher.

32. Give a signal (e.g., clapping hands, turning lights off and on, etc.) before giving verbal directions.

33. Deliver a predetermined signal (e.g., turning lights off and on, hand signals, etc.) when the student is not beginning a task.

34. Provide the student with the opportunity to perform the extra responsibility/task in a variety of ways (e.g., on tape, with a calculator, verbally, etc.).

35. Rewrite directions at a lower reading level.

36. Deliver simple, verbal directions.

37. Help the student with the first few items on a task. Gradually reduce the amount of assistance over time.

38. Follow a less desirable task with a highly desirable task; make completion of the first necessary to perform the second.

39. Provide the student with a schedule of activities so he/she knows exactly what and how much there is to do in a day.

40. Prevent the student from becoming overstimulated by an activity (e.g., frustrated, angry, etc.).

41. Specify exactly what is to be done for the completion of a task (e.g., make definite starting and stopping points, identify a minimum requirement, etc.).

42. Require the student to begin each assignment within a specified period of time (e.g., three minutes, five minutes, etc.).

43. Provide the student with shorter tasks given more frequently.

44. Provide the student with a selection of assignments, requiring him/her to choose a minimum number from the total (e.g., present the student with 10 academic tasks from which he/she must finish 6 that day).

45. Provide the student with a certain number of problems to do on the assignment, requiring him/her to choose a minimum number from the total (e.g., present the student with 10 math problems from which he/she must complete 7).

46. Start with a single problem and add more problems to the task over time.

47. Provide the student with self-checking materials so he/she may check work privately reducing the fear of public failure.

48. Have the student practice a new skill (e.g., jumping rope, dribbling a basketball) alone, with a peer, or the teacher, before the entire group attempts the activity.

49. Deliver directions/instructions before handing out materials.

50. Explain to the student that work not done during work time will have to be made up at other times (e.g., break time, before school, after school, lunch time).

Goal:

1. The student will be awake during school time.

Objective:

1. The student will be awake for the school day on ____ out of ____ trials.

Interventions:

1. Reinforce the student for positively participating in activities without sleeping: (a) give the student a tangible reward (e.g., classroom privileges, line leading, passing out materials, five minutes free time, etc.) or (b) give the student an intangible reward (e.g., praise, handshake, smile, etc.).

2. Provide the student with time and encouragement to establish rapport. Any vast change in behavior, such as falling asleep in class, withdrawn behavior, and/or other behavior changes after the student has displayed acceptable and typical age appropriate social behaviors, may warrant the need of additional support.

3. Write a contract with the student specifying what behavior is expected (e.g., contributing in group activities, active individual participation) and what reinforcement will be available when the terms of the contract have been met.

4. Communicate with parents (e.g., notes home, phone calls, etc.) to share information concerning the student's progress with staying awake during school. The parents may reinforce the student at home for staying awake during school.

5. Involve parents when possible in the development of approaches to the problem. Intervention plans might include a daily structure which encompasses the student's life beyond the classroom (e.g., when the student typically goes to bed and awakens).

6. Determine whether the student falls asleep at certain times of the day, during specific activities, etc. Incorporate this information in the body of plans and/or daily schedules developed to address sleeping in school.

7. Allow natural consequences to occur for incompleted work due to sleeping (e.g., except for meals, the student needs to complete work before going on to other activities).

8. Develop a daily activity schedule with the student that incorporates his/her interests. It may help to follow low-interest activities with high-interest activities.

9. When developing an intervention strategy for sleeping in school that requires parental and student involvement during after-school hours, make certain the plan is
(a) easily implemented (e.g., consequences and reinforcements are reasonable; parents and student agree to the plan; the plan does not place extraordinary time and financial demands upon the family); and
(b) nonpunitive (e.g., to be equipped to succeed, parents and student need to be involved in a positive relationship).

10. Focus the approach to student sleepiness in school on desired replacement behavior. Rather than providing encouragement for the student to remain awake or punishment for sleeping, positively reinforce the student for participating in activities.

11. With student and parental involvement, develop a daily schedule that provides structured time for activities before bedtime (e.g., homework, chores, etc.) so the student develops a healthy, daily routine.

12. Help the student define and achieve short-term goals and objectives when assisting him/her to develop alert behavior in school.

13. With the student, develop a small graph to chart progress on short-term goals and objectives.

14. With the student, determine what he/she can do when the urge to sleep occurs in school (e.g., get a drink of water, stretch, review progress chart for inspiration, review schedule for motivation, read a magazine when activities are completed, etc.).

15. Make sure the student receives more attention from instructor and peer sources when he/she is actively participating in activities rather than sleeping.

16. Do not prohibit the student from engaging in preferred activities because he/she went to sleep. Instead, following completion of work as scheduled, assure activity participation.

17. The student may feel failure from an inability to meet a hallmark of perfection. Encourage the student to view individual effort as more important.

18. The student may not feel he/she has been given the opportunity to make self-governing choices. Assist the student to identify choices he/she may make within realistic parameters (e.g., age, situation, etc.).

19. Structure the environment so the student has many opportunities to succeed.

20. Let the student know you value his/her thoughts and opinions. When the student expresses concern about his/her tendency to sleep in school, establish with him/her those positive steps he/she may choose right now.

21. Encourage or reinforce others for participation in class activities.

22. Give the student the responsibility of helping another in the group.

23. Encourage friendship building in the classroom (e.g., students may wish to attend extracurricular activities in small groups, etc.). The opportunity to work with friends on projects may motivate the student to become more alert.

24. Request the student lead a small-group activity if he/she expresses an interest and/or mastery of the subject.

25. Make certain the student has opportunities to benefit from active participation.

26. Increase activity time and expectations based upon student success.

27. Make certain the student understands what is expected of him/her for successful activity participation.

28. Provide the student with positive feedback to indicate he/she is successfully meeting activity expectations.

29. Present tasks in the most attractive and interesting manner possible.

30. Provide the student with success-oriented special events or activities (e.g., opportunity to be a charter member of a reading or hobby club, etc.) to develop the student's interests and afford him/her the opportunity for meaningful participation.

31. Assign outgoing, nonthreatening peers to help the student participate in classroom activities.

32. Make certain the student has the opportunity to learn how he/she is appreciated individually regardless of his/her sleeping behavior.

33. Encourage students to give each other positive feedback for small group contributions and other forms of positive verbal exchange.

34. Provide the student with a variety of ways to develop rapport with instructor(s) (e.g., writing notes, talking about concerns privately, etc.).

35. Build positive self-concept among students by including the following approaches:
(a) Offer opportunities for students to work together noncompetitively on class projects;
(b) Identify and compliment each student's unique contribution to group work when this will be perceived by the student as positive reinforcement;
(c) Organize time to speak with students individually.

36. Do not force the student to participate. Encourage the student to develop and work toward his/her goals to remain alert during activities.

37. The student may not be aware of his/her personal strengths at school. Develop a list of the student's strong points. Use this list as a source for goal, objective, and activity development.

38. Investigate the student's eating habits and the amount of rest he/she is getting outside of school.

39. Have the parents reinforce the student at home for a balanced program of nutrition, rest, and exercise.

192 Does not take appropriate care of personal property

Goal:

1. The student will be responsible for appropriate care of personal property.

Objectives:

1. The student will take appropriate care of personal property with supervision on _____ out of _____ trials.
2. The student will independently take appropriate care of personal property at all times.
3. The student will keep personal property organized in the designated locations at all times.
4. The student will use personal property for its designated purpose at all times.
5. The student will maintain personal property in good working condition at all times.
6. The student will maintain cleanliness of personal property at all times.
7. The student will replace personal property when necessary at all times.
8. The student will use personal property conservatively at all times.

Interventions:

1. Reinforce the student for appropriate care of personal property: (a) give the student a tangible reward (e.g., classroom privileges, line leading, passing out materials, five minutes free time, etc.) or (b) give the student an intangible reward (e.g., praise, handshake, smile, etc.).

2. Communicate with parents (e.g., notes home, phone calls, etc.) to share information concerning the student's progress. The parents may reinforce the student at home for organization and appropriate use of materials at school.

3. Establish classroom rules:
- Work on-task.
- Work quietly.
- Remain in your seat.
- Finish task.
- Meet task expectations.

Review rules often. Reinforce students for following rules.

4. Reinforce the student for appropriate care of personal property based on the length of time the student can be successful. As the student demonstrates success, gradually increase the length of time required for reinforcement.

5. Write a contract with the student specifying what behavior is expected (e.g., organization and appropriate use of materials) and what reinforcement will be made available when the terms of the contract have been met.

6. Speak to the student to explain (a) what he/she is doing wrong (e.g., failing to maintain organization or use materials appropriately) and (b) what he/she should be doing (e.g., keeping inside of desk organized, organizing materials on top of desk, using materials as instructed, etc.).

7. Provide the student with additional work space (e.g., a larger desk or table at which to work).

8. Assign a peer to work directly with the student to serve as a model for appropriate use and organization of materials.

9. Provide time at the beginning of each day for the student to organize his/her materials.

10. Provide time at various points throughout the day for the student to organize his/her materials (e.g., before school, break time, or lunch; at the end of the day).

11. Evaluate the appropriateness of the task to determine (a) if the task is too easy, (b) if the task is too difficult, and (c) if the length of time scheduled to complete the task is adequate.

12. Provide storage space for materials the student is not using.

13. Reduce distracting stimuli (e.g., place the student on the front row, provide a carrel or quiet place away from distractions, etc.). This is used as a means of reducing distracting stimuli and not as a form of punishment.

14. Interact frequently with the student to encourage organizational skills or appropriate use of materials.

15. Assign the student organizational responsibilities in the classroom (e.g., equipment, software materials, etc.).

16. Limit the student's use of materials (e.g., provide only necessary materials to the student).

17. Act as a model for organization and appropriate use of work materials (e.g., putting materials away before getting more out, having a place for all materials, maintaining an organized desk area, following a schedule for the day, etc.).

18. Provide adequate transition time between activities for the student to organize himself/herself.

19. Establish a routine to be followed for organization and appropriate use of work materials (e.g., provide the routine for the student in written form or verbally review often).

20. Provide adequate time for the completion of activities.

21. Supervise the student while he/she is performing schoolwork to monitor appropriate care of materials.

22. Allow natural consequences to occur as the result of the student's inability to organize or use materials appropriately (e.g., materials not maintained appropriately will be lost or not usable).

23. Assess the quality and clarity of directions, explanations, and instructions given to the student.

24. Assist the student in beginning each task to reduce impulsive behavior.

25. Provide the student with structure for all academic activities (e.g., specific directions, routine format for tasks, time units, etc.).

26. Give the student a checklist of materials necessary for each activity.

27. Minimize materials needed.

28. Provide an organizer inside the student's desk for materials.

29. Provide the student with an organizational checklist (e.g., routine activities and steps to follow).

30. Teach the student appropriate care of personal property (e.g., sharpening pencils, keeping books free of marks and tears, etc.).

31. Make certain that all personal property is labeled with the student's name.

32. Point out to the student that loaning personal property to other students does not reduce his/her responsibility for the property.

33. Provide reminders (e.g., list of property or materials) to help the student maintain and care for personal property.

34. Teach the student how to conserve rather than waste materials (e.g., amount of glue, paper, tape, etc., to use; putting lids, caps, and tops on such materials as markers, pens, bottles, jars, cans; etc.).

35. Teach the student appropriate ways to deal with anger and frustration rather than destroying personal property and school materials (e.g., pencils, pens, workbooks, notebooks, textbooks, etc.).

36. Teach the student to maintain care of personal property and school materials (e.g., keep property with him/her, know where property is at all times, secure property in locker, leave valuable property at home, etc.).

37. Provide the student with an appropriate place to store/secure personal property (e.g., desk, locker, closet, etc.) and require the student to store all property when not in use.

38. Teach the student that failure to care for personal property will result in the loss of freedom to retain property (e.g., if the student cannot care for property, the teacher(s) will store all property).

39. Limit the student's freedom to take property from school if he/she is unable to remember to return the items.

40. Provide the student with verbal reminders of personal property or materials needed for each activity.

41. Limit the student's opportunity to use school materials if he/she is unable to care for his/her own personal property.

42. Make certain that failure to have necessary materials results in loss of the opportunity to participate in activities or a failing grade for that day's activity.

43. Reduce the number of materials for which the student is responsible. As the student demonstrates appropriate care of property, increase the number of materials for which the student is responsible.

44. Teach the student safety rules in the handling of personal property and materials (e.g., pencils; scissors; compass; science, industrial arts, and home economic materials; etc.).

45. Teach the student the appropriate use of personal property and materials (e.g., scissors; pencils; compass; rulers; and science, industrial arts, and home economic materials; etc.).

46. Require that lost or damaged property be replaced by the student. If the student cannot replace the property, restitution can be made by working at school.

47. Make certain that the student is not inadvertently reinforced for losing or damaging property (e.g., replace lost property with used or damaged materials, copies of materials, etc., rather than new materials).

193 Demonstrates confusion

Goals:

1. The student will improve his/her short-term memory.
2. The student will improve his/her long-term memory.
3. The student will improve his/her understanding of abstract concepts (e.g., spatial relationships, directionality, classifications, generalizations).
4. The student will improve his/her visual memory.
5. The student will improve his/her auditory memory.
6. The student will improve his/her awareness and attention to information and activities in the environment.
7. The student will improve his/her organizational skills.
8. The student will improve his/her skills in logical thinking.

Objectives:

1. The student will find locations in the building, materials, etc., with verbal cues and directions _____% of the time.
2. The student will use environmental cues (e.g., signs, labels, room numbers, etc.) to find locations in the building, materials, etc., _____% of the time.
3. The student will independently find locations in the building, materials, etc., _____% of the time.

Interventions:

1. Make certain the student's vision has been checked recently.

2. Make certain that all directions, explanations, and instructions are delivered in the most clear and concise manner.

3. Teach the student direction-following skills (e.g., stop doing other things; listen to what is being said; do not begin until all information is delivered; question any directions, explanations, and instructions you do not understand).

4. Teach the student to rely on environmental cues when moving about the school and related areas (e.g., look for signs, room numbers, familiar surroundings, etc.).

5. Make certain the student knows how to ask questions, ask for directions, etc.

6. Teach the student a basic survival/directional word vocabulary (e.g., *ladies, gentlemen, push, pull, left, right,* etc.).

7. Have the student verbally repeat/paraphrase instructions and information given so that the instructor can provide a means of clarification and redirection of the given information.

8. Have the student practice finding various locations in the building before or after school or during classes when few other students are in the halls.

9. Have the student practice finding locations in the building by following verbal directions, written directions, directions from teachers or other students, etc.

10. Have the student follow a schedule of daily events as he/she moves from place to place in the school.

11. Pair the student with a classmate who has a similar class schedule to have a peer who can direct the student if he/she gets lost or confused.

12. Have the student learn to use a floor plan to find specific rooms, hallways, and areas while following his/her daily class or work schedule.

13. Make certain the student has designated instructors or peers who act as a source of information within the school.

14. Have a peer accompany the student to locations in the building until the student develops familiarity with his/her surroundings.

15. Make certain the student has been provided with an adequate orientation to all areas of the school environment he/she will be using.

16. Have the student practice problem-solving skills if he/she should become lost or confused in the school environment (e.g., ask directions, return to where you started, look for familiar surroundings, read signs, etc.).

17. Make certain the school environment is conducive to finding locations the student uses (e.g., posting signs, posting directions, color-coding pods and similar areas, etc.).

18. Before leaving the classroom have the student review directions to locate certain points throughout the building (e.g., have the student repeat directions back to you, have the student look at a map, etc.).

19. When giving the student directions to certain points throughout the building, use landmarks such as the drinking fountain, restroom, lunchroom, etc. (e.g., "Go to the room that is just past the lunchroom." "The bathroom is on the left side of the drinking fountain." etc.).

20. When delivering directions, explanations, and information, be sure to use vocabulary that is within the student's level of comprehension.

21. Make certain the student is attending when directions are being given (e.g., eye contact is being made, hands are free of materials, etc.).

22. Reduce or remove those stimuli from the environment which are distracting to the student and interfering with his/her ability to listen successfully.

23. Have the student act as a peer tutor to teach another student a concept he/she has mastered. This can serve as reinforcement for the student.

24. Use pictures, diagrams, the chalkboard, and gestures when delivering information.

25. Call on the student when he/she is most likely to be able to respond successfully.

26. Provide the student with shorter tasks, but more of them, throughout the day (e.g., four assignments of five problems each rather than one assignment of 20 problems).

27. Review, on a daily basis, those skills, concepts, tasks, etc., which have been previously introduced.

28. Give the student one task to perform at a time. Introduce the next task only when the student has successfully completed the previous task.

29. Stop at various points during the presentation of information to check the student's comprehension.

30. Make certain the student is attending to the source of information (e.g., eye contact is being made, hands are free of materials, student is looking at the assignment, etc.).

31. Provide the student with environmental cues and prompts designed to facilitate his/her success in the classroom (e.g., posted rules, schedule of daily events, steps for performing a task, etc.).

32. Reduce the amount of information on a page if it causes visual distractions for the student (e.g., have less print to read, have fewer problems, isolate information that is presented to the student).

33. Assign the student shorter tasks. As the student demonstrates success, gradually increase the length of tasks.

34. Identify the student's most efficient learning mode and use it consistently to increase the probability of understanding (e.g., if the student fails to understand directions or information verbally, present it in written form; if the student has difficulty understanding written information or directions, present it verbally).

35. Make certain that verbal directions are delivered in a nonthreatening and supportive manner (e.g., positive voice, facial expressions and language such as "Will you please..." or "You need..." rather than "You better..." or "If you don't...").

36. Make certain the student has mastery of concepts at one level before introducing a new skill level.

37. When delivering directions, explanations, and information, be certain to use vocabulary that is within the student's level of comprehension.

38. Deliver information to the student on a one-to-one basis or employ a peer tutor.

194   Does not organize responsibilities

Goal:

1. The student will be organized.

Objectives:

1. The student will use available time to work on assignments, perform responsibilities, read, etc., with reminders on _____ out of _____ trials.
2. The student will independently use available time to work on assignments, perform responsibilities, read, etc., on _____ out of _____ trials.
3. The student will prioritize and complete assignments with verbal prompts _____ out of _____ trials.
4. The student will independently prioritize and complete assignments on _____ out of _____ trials.
5. The student will put materials where they belong, with reminders, on _____ out of _____ trials.
6. The student will independently put materials where they belong on _____ out of _____ trials.

Interventions:

1. Have the student question any directions, explanations, or instructions he/she does not understand.

2. Assign a peer to accompany the student to specified activities to make certain the student has the necessary materials.

3. Provide the student with a list of necessary materials for each activity of the day.

4. Provide the student with verbal reminders of materials required for each activity.

5. Provide time at the beginning of each day for the student to organize materials.

6. Provide time at various points throughout the day for the student to organize materials (e.g., before school, during break time, at lunch, at the end of the day, etc.).

7. Provide storage space for materials when not in use.

8. Act as a model for being organized/prepared for specified activities.

9. Make certain that work not completed because necessary materials were not brought to the specified activity must be completed during recreational or break time.

10. Have the student chart the number of times he/she is organized/prepared for specified activities.

11. Remind the student at the end of the day what materials are required for specified activities for the next day (e.g., note sent home, verbal reminder, etc.).

12. Have the student establish a routine to follow before attending class (e.g., check which activity is next, determine what materials are necessary, collect materials, etc.).

13. Have the student leave necessary materials at specified activity areas.

14. Provide the student with a container in which to carry necessary materials for specified activities (e.g., backpack, book bag, briefcase, etc.).

15. Provide adequate transition time between activities for the student to organize materials.

16. Establish a routine to be followed for organization and appropriate use of work materials. Provide the routine for the student in written form or verbally review often.

17. Provide adequate time for the completion of activities.

18. Assess the quality and clarity of directions, explanations, and instructions given to the student.

19. Provide the student with structure for all academic activities (e.g., specific directions, routine format for tasks, time units, etc.).

20. Minimize materials that the student needs to keep inside his/her desk.

21. Provide an organizer inside the student's desk for materials.

22. Provide the student with an organizational checklist (e.g., routine activities, materials needed, and steps to follow).

23. Make certain that all personal property is labeled with the student's name.

24. Teach the student how to conserve rather than waste materials (e.g., amount of glue, paper, tape, etc., to use; putting lids, caps, tops on such materials as markers, pens, bottles, jars, cans, etc.).

25. Teach the student to maintain care of personal property and school materials (e.g., keep property with him/her, know where property is at all times, secure property in lockers, leave valuable property at home, etc.).

26. Provide the student with an appropriate place to store/secure personal property (e.g., desk, locker, closet, etc.) and require the student to store all property when not in use.

27. Limit the student's freedom to take school or personal property from school if the student is unable to remember to return such items.

28. Reduce the number of materials for which the student is responsible. As the student demonstrates appropriate use of materials, increase the number of materials for which the student is responsible.

29. Require that lost or damaged property be replaced by the student. If the student cannot replace the property, restitution can be made by working at school.

30. Make certain that the student is not inadvertently reinforced for losing materials. Provide the student with used materials, copies of the materials, etc., rather than new materials if the student fails to care for the materials in an appropriate manner.

31. Provide the student with more work space (e.g., a larger desk or table at which to work).

32. Reduce distracting stimuli (e.g., place the student on the front row, provide a carrel or quiet place away from distractions, etc.). This is used as a means of reducing distracting stimuli and not as a form of punishment.

33. Interact frequently with the student to prompt organizational skills and appropriate use of materials.

34. Assign the student organizational responsibilities in the classroom (e.g., equipment, software materials, etc.).

35. Supervise the student while he/she is performing schoolwork to monitor quality.

36. Act as a model for organization and appropriate use of work materials (e.g., putting materials away before getting others out, having a place for all materials, maintaining an organized desk area, following a schedule for the day, etc.).

37. Have the student maintain an assignment notebook which indicates those materials needed for each activity.

38. Provide the student with a schedule of daily events so the student knows exactly what and how much there is to do in a day.

39. Allow natural consequences to occur as the result of the student's inability to organize or use materials appropriately (e.g., work not done during work time must be made up during recreational time, materials not maintained must be replaced, etc.).

40. Assist the student in beginning each task to reduce impulsive behavior.

41. Provide the student with structure for all academic activities (e.g., specific directions, routine format for tasks, time units, etc.).

42. Provide a coded organizational system (e.g., notebook, folders, etc.).

43. Teach the student to prioritize assignments (e.g., according to importance, length, etc.).

44. Provide adequate time for completion of activities.

45. Develop monthly calendars to keep track of important events, due dates, assignments, etc.

46. Give the student one task to perform at a time. Introduce the next task only when the student has successfully completed the previous task in an organized way.

47. Assign the student fewer tasks. As the student demonstrates success in organizing academic activities, gradually increase the number of tasks over time.

48. Require that assignments done incorrectly, for any reason, be redone.

49. Provide the student with clearly stated criteria for acceptable work (e.g., neatness, etc.).

50. Provide the student with only those materials he/she needs to complete an assignment (e.g., pencil, paper, dictionary, handwriting sample, etc.). Be certain that the student has only these necessary materials on his/her desk.

51. Choose a peer to model being organized/prepared for specified activities for the student.

52. Evaluate the appropriateness of the task to determine (a) if the task is too easy, (b) if the task is too difficult, and (c) if the length of time scheduled to complete the task is adequate.

53. Communicate with parents (e.g., notes home, phone calls, etc.) to share information concerning the student's progress. The parents may reinforce the student at home for being organized/prepared for specified activities at school.

54. Write a contract with the student specifying what behavior is expected (e.g., having necessary materials for specified activities) and what reinforcement will be made available when the terms of the contract have been met.

55. Reinforce the student for being organized/prepared for specified activities based on the number of times the student can be successful. As the student demonstrates success, gradually increase the number of times required for reinforcement.

56. Reinforce those students in the classroom who are organized/prepared for specified activities.

57. Establish classroom rules:
- Have necessary materials.
- Work on-task.
- Work quietly.
- Remain in your seat.
- Finish task.
- Meet task expectations.

Review rules often. Reinforce students for following rules.

58. Speak to the student to explain (a) what the student is doing wrong (e.g., failing to bring necessary materials for specified activities) and (b) what the student should be doing (e.g., having necessary materials for specified activities).

59. Reinforce the student for being organized/prepared for specified activities: (a) give the student a tangible reward (e.g., classroom privileges, line leading, passing out materials, five minutes free time, etc.) or (b) give the student an intangible reward (e.g., praise, handshake, smile, etc.).

195   Does not prepare for assigned activities or daily routines

Goals:
1. The student will be prepared for school assignments.
2. The student will be prepared for assigned activities.

Objectives:
1. The student will be prepared for assigned activities by reading the assigned material for ___ out of ____ activities.
2. The student will complete his/her assigned tasks such as book reports, projects, etc., by the due date on ___ out of ___ trials.
3. The student will complete his/her homework prior to coming to the assigned activity on ___ out of ____ trials.
4. The student will correctly answer questions covering the assigned reading material on ___ out of ____ trials.
5. The student will read necessary information prior to coming to the assigned activity on _____ out of _____ trials.
6. The student will study and perform classroom quizzes with _____% accuracy. (Gradually increase expectations as the student demonstrates success.)
7. The student will study and perform classroom tests with _____% accuracy. (Gradually increase expectations as the student demonstrates success.)
8. The student will study for _____ out of _____ quizzes.
9. The student will study for _____ out of _____ tests.

Interventions:

1. Have the student verbally repeat the school assignment to reinforce the student's awareness of the assignment.

2. Allow natural consequences to occur (e.g., receiving low grades, being excluded from extra-curricular activities, not earning course credit, etc.) due to the student's failure to complete his/her school assignments.

3. Encourage the student to develop an awareness of the consequences of his/her behavior by writing down or talking through problems which may occur due to his/her inability to complete assignments (e.g., if you do not return the assignment to school, you are in danger of failing the class then you may not get the credit you need for graduation).

4. Allow natural consequences to occur for failure to turn in homework assignments (e.g., students who do not finish their homework do not get to participate in more desirable activities).

5. Allow the student to perform a highly desirable task when assignments have been turned in.

6. Provide the student with adequate time at school to prepare for assigned activities (e.g., supervised study time).

7. Have the student make it a habit to periodically review notes, daily calendar of events, or tasks that need to be completed.

8. Allow the student to perform alternative homework assignments. Gradually introduce more components of the regular homework assignment until the assignments are routinely performed and returned to school.

9. Arrange with the student's parents to pick up homework each day if the student has difficulty "remembering" to take it home.

10. Ask the student why he/she is unprepared for assigned activities. The student may have the most accurate perception.

11. Have the student chart his/her completed assignments.

12. Assess the quality and clarity of directions, explanations, and instructions given to the student.

13. Assign a peer to accompany the student to specified activities to make certain the student has the necessary materials.

14. Have the student find a method of organization that works best for him/her (e.g., daily list, weekly list, etc.) and use that method consistently. Delete accomplished tasks to keep an up-to-date list.

15. Assign a peer to help the student with homework.

16. Assign a peer tutor to work with the student to prepare for assigned activities.

17. Assign short-term tasks that can be quickly and accurately completed. As the student demonstrates success, gradually increase the length of assignments.

18. Assign small amounts of homework initially, gradually increasing the amount as the student demonstrates success (e.g., one or two problems may be sufficient to begin the homework process).

19. Assist the student in performing his/her school assignments. As the student demonstrates success, gradually decrease the assistance and require the student to independently assume more responsibility.

20. At the end of the day, remind the student when materials are required for specified activities for the next day (e.g., send a note home, give a verbal reminder, etc.).

21. Chart homework assignments completed.

22. Communicate with parents (e.g., notes home, phone calls, etc.) to share information concerning the student's progress. The parents may reinforce the student at home for being prepared for assigned activities at school.

23. Communicate with parents or guardians to inform them of the student's homework assignments and what they can do to help him/her prepare for assigned activities.

24. Consider carefully the student's ability level when expecting him/her to be able to study for a specific amount of time.

25. Create a learning center at school, open the last hour of each school day, where professional educators are available to help with homework.

26. Deliver directions verbally and in written format to increase the probability of the student's understanding of school assignments.

27. Allow natural consequences to occur when the student is unprepared for assigned activities (e.g., the student will fail a test or quiz, work not done during work time must be completed during recreational time, etc.).

28. Deliver reinforcement for any and all measures of improvement.

29. Develop a contract with the student and his/her parents requiring that homework be done before more desirable activities take place at home (e.g., playing, watching television, going out for the evening, etc.).

30. Do not use homework as a punishment (i.e., homework should not be assigned as a consequence for inappropriate behavior at school).

31. Assign a peer to help the student review information needed to successfully complete a school assignment.

32. Encourage the parents to provide the student with a quiet, comfortable place and adequate time to study and prepare for school assignments.

33. Encourage the parents to set aside quiet time each night when the family turns off the TV, radio, etc.; to read, do homework, write letters, etc.

34. Encourage the student to put completed homework assignments in a designated place to be taken to school (e.g., in front of the door, at the bottom of the stairs, etc.).

35. Establish a time line for completing a school assignment. Expect the student to meet each deadline to complete the project on time.

36. Have the student leave necessary materials at specified activity areas.

37. Establish school assignment rules:
- Stay on-task.
- Work quietly.
- Finish task.
- Meet task expectations.
- Turn in task.

Review rules often. Reinforce students for following the rules.

38. Make certain the student has mastered the concepts presented at school. All homework should be a form of practice for what has been learned at school.

39. Evaluate the appropriateness of the assignment to determine (a) if the task is too easy, (b) if the task is too difficult, and (c) if the length of time scheduled to complete the task is adequate.

40. Find a tutor (e.g., a volunteer in the community, peer, etc.) to help the student complete his/her school assignments.

41. Find a tutor (e.g., peer, volunteer, etc.) to work with the student at home.

42. Assess the appropriateness of assigning the student homework if his/her ability level or circumstances at home make it impossible for him/her to complete and return the assignments.

43. Follow a less desirable task with a more desirable task. Make completion of the first necessary to perform the second.

44. Give directions in a variety of ways to increase the probability of understanding (e.g., if the student fails to understand verbal directions, present them in written form).

45. Have the student anticipate future tasks/ assignments and develop plans for addressing them.

46. Have the student develop a checklist/chart to follow which will allow him/her to self-monitor all assignments.

47. Have the student establish a routine to follow before coming to class (e.g., check which activity is next, determine what materials are necessary, collect materials, etc.)

48. Assess the degree of task difficulty to determine whether or not the student will require additional information, time, assistance, etc., before beginning a task.

49. Have the student keep a chart/graph of the number of assignments turned in to the teacher.

50. Act as a model for being prepared for assigned activities.

51. Have the student question any directions, explanations, and instructions not understood.

52. Choose a peer to model turning in school assignments for the student.

53. Develop a school/home assignment sheet to be reviewed and signed by the parents each evening. Communicate with the parents and student to establish clear expectations and positive consequences for completing and returning the assignment sheet.

54. Have the student time activities to monitor personal behavior and accept time limits.

55. Choose a peer to model being prepared for assigned activities for the student.

56. Have the student set a timer to complete assignments in a reasonable period of time.

57. Provide the student with a written list of assignments to be performed each day and have him/her check each assignment as it is completed.

58. Identify the materials the student consistently fails to take home. Provide a set of those materials for the student to keep at home.

59. Maintain consistent expectations within the ability level of the student.

60. Maintain consistency in assigning homework (i.e., assign the same amount of homework each day).

61. Reinforce those students who complete their assignments at school during the time provided.

62. Make certain that failure to be prepared for assigned activities results in loss of the opportunity to participate in activities or a failing grade for that day's activity.

63. Have the student establish a routine and utilize a weekly schedule. Have the student develop a checklist/chart for daily school assignments to be completed.

64. Make certain that homework is designed to provide drill activities rather than introduce new information.

65. Provide the student with a book bag, backpack, etc., to take homework assignments and materials to and from home.

66. Make certain the student is not required to learn more information than he/she is capable of learning at any one time.

67. Identify resource personnel from whom the student may receive additional assistance (e.g., librarian, special education teacher, other personnel with expertise or time to help, etc.).

68. Make certain the student understands that assignments not completed and turned in on time must still be completed and turned in late.

69. Provide the student with written directions to follow in preparing for all assigned activities.

70. Make positive comments about school and the importance of completing assignments.

71. Schedule the student's time at school so homework will not be absolutely necessary if he/she takes advantage of the school time provided to complete assignments.

72. Make sure the student has all the materials necessary to complete school assignments (e.g., pencils, paper, erasers, etc.).

73. Meet with the student's parents to discuss with them appropriate ways to help their child with school assignments.

74. Minimize materials needed.

75. Introduce the student to other resource persons who may be of help in doing homework (e.g., other teachers, the librarian, etc.).

76. Present assignments/tasks in the most attractive and interesting manner possible.

77. Provide individual assistance to the student to help him/her prepare for assigned activities (e.g., time set aside during the day, study hall, after school, etc.).

78. Provide the student with a list of necessary materials for each activity of the day.

79. Provide the student with structure for all academic activities (e.g., specific directions, routine format for tasks, time units, etc.).

80. Make certain that the student understands the relationship between inappropriate behavior and the consequences which follow (e.g., forgetting to complete his/her school assignments will result in a low grade).

81. Provide the student with verbal reminders of materials required for each activity.

82. Provide time at school for homework completion when the student cannot be successful in performing assignments at home.

83. Reduce the number/length of assignments. As the student demonstrates success, gradually increase the number/length of assignments.

84. Provide time each day for the student to organize his/her materials (e.g., before school, break time, at lunch, at the end of the day, etc.).

85. Repeat directions to increase the student's probability of understanding.

86. Work a few problems of the school assignment with the student to serve as a model and start the student on the assignment.

87. Speak to the student to explain (a) what he/she is doing wrong (e.g., not turning in assignments) and (b) what he/she should be doing (e.g., completing homework/school assignments and returning them to school).

88. Reinforce those students in the classroom who are prepared for assigned activities.

89. Review on a daily basis, those skills, concepts, tasks, etc., which have been previously introduced.

90. Send home explanations each day so the student's parents may help their child with his/her school assignments if necessary.

91. Write a contract with the student specifying what behavior is expected (e.g., studying for tests or quizzes) and what reinforcement will be made available when the terms of the contract have been met.

92. Send homework assignments and materials home with someone other than the student (e.g., brother, sister, neighbor, etc.).

93. Set aside time at the end of the day for the student to complete unfinished assignments.

94. Set up a homework system for the student (e.g., two days a week work with drill flash cards, three days a week work on book work sent home, etc.). This will add some variety to homework.

95. Reinforce the student for being prepared for assigned activities: (a) give the student a tangible reward (e.g., classroom privileges, line leading, passing out materials, five minutes free time, etc.) or (b) give the student an intangible reward (e.g., praise, handshake, smile, etc.).

96. Specify exactly what is to be done for the completion of assignments (e.g., make definite starting and topping points, determine a minimum requirement, etc.).

97. Take proactive steps to deal with a student's refusal to perform a school assignment to prevent contagion in the classroom (e.g., refrain from arguing with the student, place the student in a carrel or other quiet place to work, remove the student from the group or classroom, etc.).

98. Reinforce the student for being prepared for assigned activities based on the number of times he/she can be successful. As the student demonstrates success, gradually increase the number of times required for reinforcement.

99. Teach the student time-management skills. Have the student make a daily plan and follow it. Encourage the student to avoid becoming distracted by events, impulses, and moods.

100. Send home only one homework assignment at a time. As the student demonstrates success completing assignments at home, gradually increase the number of homework assignments sent home.

Goals:
1. The student will improve his/her short-term memory.
2. The student will improve his/her long-term memory.
3. The student will improve his/her understanding of abstract concepts (e.g., spatial relationships, directionality, classifications, generalizations).
4. The student will improve his/her visual memory.
5. The student will improve his/her auditory memory.
6. The student will improve his/her awareness and attention to information and activities in the environment.
7. The student will improve his/her organizational skills.
8. The student will improve his/her skills in logical thinking.

Objectives:
1. The student will use available time to work on assignments, perform responsibilities, read, etc., with prompting, on _____ out of _____ occasions.
2. The student will independently use available time to work on assignments, perform responsibilities, read, etc., on _____ out of _____ occasions.
3. The student will prioritize and complete assignments, with verbal prompts, on _____ out of _____ occasions.
4. The student will independently prioritize and complete assignments on _____ out of _____ occasions.
5. The student will put materials where they belong, with reminders, on _____ out of _____ occasions.
6. The student will independently put materials where they belong on _____ out of _____ occasions.

Interventions:

1. Teach the student time management skills (e.g., determine amount of time needed per subject, set aside specific study time daily, etc.).

2. Provide an organizer inside the student's locker and desk for materials.

3. Evaluate the appropriateness of the student's assignment to determine (a) if the task is too easy, (b) if the task is too difficult, and (c) if the length of time scheduled to complete the task is adequate.

4. Provide time at the beginning of each day to help the student organize his/her materials, time, etc.

5. Provide the student with more work space to help him/her be more organized (e.g., a larger desk or table at which to work).

6. Provide storage space for materials when not in use.

7. Reduce distracting stimuli (e.g., place the student on the front row; provide a carrel or quiet place away from distractions; etc.). This is used as a means of reducing distracting stimuli and not as a form of punishment.

8. Interact frequently with the student to prompt organizational skills and appropriate use of materials.

9. Assign the student organizational responsibilities in the classroom (e.g., equipment, software materials, etc.).

10. Communicate with parents (e.g., notes home, phone calls, etc.) to share information concerning the student's progress. The parents may reinforce the student at home for organization of his/her school assignments, materials, time, etc.

11. Have the student maintain a record of his/her performances on assignments, activities, etc.

12. Act as a model for organization of time and materials, performing assignments, etc. (e.g., putting materials away before getting others out, having a place for all materials, following a schedule for the day, using time wisely, etc.).

13. Minimize the amount of materials the student will need for assignments.

14. Allow natural consequences to occur as the result of the student's inability to organize time or materials, complete assignments, etc. (e.g., work not done during work time must be made up during recreational time).

15. Provide an organizational notebook/folder for loose-leaf papers (e.g., math assignments, spelling lists, etc.).

16. Provide a color-coded organizational system (e.g., notebook dividers, folders, etc.).

17. Teach the student to prioritize assignments (e.g., according to importance, length, etc.).

18. Provide the student with adequate transition time between activities so that he/she can organize himself/herself.

19. Establish a daily routine to be followed for organization and appropriate use of work materials (e.g., provide the routine for the student in written form or verbally review the routine often).

20. Provide adequate time for completion of activities.

21. Require the student to organize his/her work at regular intervals. (It is recommended that this be done at least three times per day or more often as necessary.)

22. Assist the student in beginning each task to reduce impulsive/disorganized behavior.

23. Provide shelving, containers, organizers, etc., for the student's personal possessions. Label the storage areas and require the student to keep possessions organized.

24. Provide the student with an organizational checklist (e.g., routine activities and steps to follow).

25. Develop monthly calendars for the student to keep track of important events, due dates, assignments, etc.

26. Instruct the student to prioritize assignments according to due dates, grade value, length, etc.

27. Have the student use an assignment sheet to list homework assignments for the following day, week, etc.

28. Provide the student with an outline of reading material, lectures, etc. Make certain the student follows the outline, makes notes on the outline, etc.

29. Give the student one task to perform at a time. Introduce the next task only when the student has successfully completed the previous task.

30. Reinforce the student for beginning, staying, and completing the assignments.

31. Communicate clearly with the student the amount of time he/she has to complete the assignment and the exact time the assignment must be completed. The student may want to use a timer to complete tasks within a specified time period.

32. Specify exactly what is to be done for the completion of a task (e.g., indicate definite starting and stopping points, indicate a minimum requirement, etc.).

33. Make certain the student is not required to learn more information than he/she is capable of learning at any one time.

34. Reduce the amount of information on a page if it is causing visual distractions for the student (e.g., less print to read, fewer problems, isolate information that is presented to the student).

35. Assign the student fewer tasks. As the student demonstrates success, gradually increase the number of tasks over time.

36. Provide the student with structure for all academic activities (e.g., specific directions, routine format for tasks, time units, etc.).

37. Limit the use of those things which the student uses carelessly.

38. Set aside time each day for everyone in the room to care for personal property.

39. Assign a peer to work directly with the student to serve as a model for appropriate organization of time, materials, etc.

40. Write a contract with the student specifying what behavior is expected (e.g., completing assignments, having correct materials for class, organizing materials, etc.) and what reinforcement will be made available when the terms of the contract have been met.

41. Present directions following the outline of (1) What, (2) How, (3) Materials, and (4) When.

42. Have the student maintain an assignment notebook for all school-related activities.

43. Provide the student with a schedule of daily events so he/she knows exactly what and how much there is to do throughout the day, week, etc.

44. Reinforce the student for demonstrating organizational behavior based on the length of time he/she can be successful. As the student demonstrates success, gradually increase the length of time required for reinforcement.

45. Establish classroom rules:
- Work on-task.
- Work quietly.
- Remain in your seat.
- Finish task.
- Meet task expectations.

Review rules often. Reinforce students for following rules.

46. Speak with the student to explain (a) what he/she is doing wrong (e.g., failing to organize time, assignments, materials, etc.) and (b) what he/she should be doing (e.g., organizing desk or materials, completing assignments, etc.).

47. Reinforce the student for organization and appropriate use of time and work materials: (a) give the student a tangible reward (e.g., classroom privileges, line leading, passing out materials, five minutes free time, etc.) or (b) give the student an intangible reward (e.g., praise, handshake, smile, etc.).

48. Provide the student with a daily checklist of the supplies needed for each activity, assignment, class, etc.

49. Have the student take notes when directions are being given following the "What, How, Materials, and When" format.

50. While concepts are presented, have the student listen and take notes for "Who, What, Where, When, How, and Why."

51. Present concepts following the outline of (1) Who, (2) What, (3) Where, (4) When, (5) How, and (6) Why.

Goal:

1. The student will follow necessary steps involved with activities.

Objectives:

1. The student will follow appropriate steps in activities with reminders on ____ out of ____ trials.
2. The student will follow appropriate steps in activities without reminders on ____ out of ____ trials.
3. The student will prepare for daily routines with reminders on ____ out of ____ trials.
4. The student will prepare for daily routines without reminders on ____ out of ____ trials.

Interventions:

1. Reinforce the student for following necessary steps: (a) give the student a tangible reward (e.g., classroom privileges, line leading, passing out materials, etc.) or (b) give the student an intangible reward (e.g., praise, handshake, smile, etc.).

2. Speak with the student to explain (a) what he/she is doing wrong (e.g., not being prepared for going outside, etc.) and (b) what he/she should be doing (e.g., putting materials away, getting jacket and gloves on to prepare to go outside, etc.).

3. Interact frequently with the student to encourage appropriate preparation behaviors.

4. Reinforce those students in the classroom who follow necessary steps.

5. Reinforce the student for following necessary steps based on the length of time he/she can be successful. As the student demonstrates success, gradually increase the length of time required for reinforcement as the student demonstrates success.

6. Communicate with parents (e.g., notes home, telephone calls, etc.) to share information concerning the student's appropriate behavior. The parents may reinforce the student at home for following necessary steps.

7. Evaluate the appropriateness of the task to determine (a) if the task is too easy, (b) if the task is too difficult, and (c) if the length of time scheduled for the task is adequate.

8. Provide a classroom environment that is well organized and labeled with pictures and words.

9. Demonstrate the steps necessary for daily routines as often as the student needs until he/she can follow the steps independently.

10. Work alongside the student offering assistance as he/she prepares for daily routines. As the student demonstrates success, gradually reduce the assistance that you provide.

11. Be certain to provide adequate time between activities to allow the student the opportunity to get prepared.

12. Reduce stimuli which would contribute to the student's inability to appropriately prepare for daily routines.

13. Choose a peer to model appropriate behavior (e.g., preparing for going outside by putting materials away and getting jacket on, etc.) when preparing for daily routines for the student.

14. Be consistent when expecting the student to follow necessary steps. Do not allow him/her to be unprepared for activities, and then expect him/her to be prepared for the next activity.

15. Deliver instructions, directions, and explanations in clear and simple language. Have the student question any of these he/she does not understand prior to beginning activities.

16. Make certain that the student understands the relationship between behaviors and consequences (e.g., failing to prepare for going outside during the time given results in less time to play outside, etc.).

17. Allow natural consequences to occur as a result of the student failing to follow necessary steps (e.g., the student will not get to choose his/her seat at lunch because he/she was not ready when it was time to sit down for lunch, etc.).

18. Do not allow the student to proceed with daily routines until he/she has completed necessary steps in the activity.

19. Establish a regular daily routine for the classroom. Adhere to this routine as closely as possible to help the student prepare for daily routines.

20. Set aside time daily for all students in the classroom to organize personal items and prepare for the daily activities.

21. Provide a cubby or other appropriate personal space for the student to store and organize personal items.

22. Provide the student with a written and illustrated list of activities (and related steps) for which he/she is responsible. The student can check off each item he/she completes, observing his/her own success.

23. Pace the daily schedule to provide periods of time that are of interest to the student throughout the day.

24. Establish a rule (e.g., take your time and follow directions, etc.). This rule should be reviewed often and reinforced for all students.

198   Fails to make appropriate use of study time

Goal:

1. The student will make appropriate use of study time.

Objectives:

1. The student will begin assignments during study time on _____ out of _____ occasions.
2. The student will continue working on assignments during study time on _____ out of _____ occasions.
3. The student will complete assignments during study time on _____ out of _____ occasions.
4. The student will independently find school-related activities to engage in during study time on _____ out of _____ occasions.

Interventions:

1. Interact frequently with the student to help him/her make appropriate use of study time.

2. Deliver directions verbally to increase the probability of the student's understanding of class assignments.

3. Allow the student the option of performing assignments during another study time (e.g., earlier in the day, later, on another day, or at home).

4. Allow the student to work with a peer who uses study time appropriately.

5. Along with a directive, provide an incentive statement (e.g., "If you make appropriate use of study time, you may have free time." etc.).

6. Assess the degree of task difficulty in relation to the student's ability to perform the task.

7. Encourage the student to define his/her goals. Have the student develop specific strategies to achieve his/her goals then follow through on those strategies.

8. Assess the degree of task difficulty to determine whether or not the student will require additional information, time, assistance, etc., before beginning a task.

9. Assess the quality and clarity of directions, explanations, and instructions given to the student.

10. Assign a peer to help the student with class assignments during study time.

11. Allow the student additional time to complete class assignments.

12. Assign short-term projects that can be quickly completed.

13. Assign the student shorter tasks (e.g., modify a 20-problem math activity to 4 activities of 5 problems each, to be done at various times during the day). As the student demonstrates success, gradually increase the number of problems over time.

14. Chart those assignments with the student that have been completed during study time.

15. Communicate clearly with the student the length of time he/she has to complete an assignment and when the assignment is due. The student may want to use a timer to complete the tasks within the given period of time.

16. Allow the student to perform alternative assignments during study time. Gradually introduce more components of the regular assignments until those assignments are routinely performed.

17. Communicate with parents (e.g., notes home, phone calls, etc.) to share information concerning the student's progress. The parents may reinforce the student at home for completing assignments at school.

18. Encourage the student to be self-determining by identifying tasks and completing assignments independently.

19. Encourage the student to develop a 30 second definition of his/her goal to help him/her stay on-task and focused (e.g., study five vocabulary terms before taking a break).

20. Have the student use a timer to complete the tasks within a given period of time.

21. Encourage the student to develop an awareness of the consequences of his/her behavior by writing down or talking through problems which may occur due to his/her procrastination (e.g., incomplete assignments, low test scores, lack of credit).

22. Encourage the student to manage his/her daily performance as if he/she were self-employed. This should increase his/her motivation to use study time effectively and fulfill his/her responsibilities.

23. Encourage the student to reward himself/herself (e.g., take a ten minute break, speak briefly with a relative, telephone a friend, etc.) for completing an assignment within the amount of time allotted.

24. Establish assignment rules (e.g., listen to directions, wait until all directions have been given, ask questions about anything you do not understand, make certain you have all necessary materials, begin assignments only when you are certain about what you are supposed to do, etc.).

25. Establish classroom rules:
- Stay on-task.
- Work quietly.
- Remain in your seat.
- Finish task.
- Meet task requirements.

Review rules often. Reinforce students for following the rules.

26. Have the student keep a chart or graph representing the number of class assignments completed during study time.

27. Evaluate the appropriateness of the task to determine (a) if the task is too easy, (b) if the task is too difficult, and (c) if the length of time scheduled to complete the task is adequate.

28. Explain to the student that work not done during study time will have to be done during other times (e.g., break time, recreational time, after school, etc.).

29. Follow a less desirable task with a highly desirable task. Make the following of verbal directions and completion of the first task necessary to perform the second task.

30. Give directions in a variety of ways to increase the probability of understanding (e.g., if the student fails to understand verbal directions, present them in written form).

31. Have reference materials readily available in the classroom (e.g., dictionary, thesaurus, list of frequently misspelled words, etc.).

32. Have the student anticipate future tasks/assignments and develop plans for addressing them.

33. Have the student ask for help when he/she needs it.

34. Have the student ask for immediate clarification of the directions.

35. Have the student assemble all the materials necessary to work on a project, assignment, etc., to reduce the need to search for materials.

36. Have the student complete assignments in a private place (e.g., carrel, "office," quiet study area, etc.) to reduce the anxiety of public failure.

37. Have the student develop a checklist/chart to follow which will allow him/her to complete specific assignments during study time.

38. Have the student explain to the teacher what should be done to perform the assignments.

39. Establish times when it is permissible for the student to be out of his/her seat (e.g., leave his/her seat only to get a book, to ask a question of the study supervisor, etc.).

40. Have the student list five qualities of a productive worker. Have the student choose one of those qualities to work on each week for five weeks.

41. Maintain visibility to and from the student to make certain the student is attending. The teacher should be able to see the student and the student should be able to see the teacher. Make eye contact possible at all times.

42. Have the student organize assignments by breaking them into small segments. Set deadlines and provide the student with a reward after completing each segment of the assignment.

43. Interact frequently with the student to maintain his/her involvement with class assignments (e.g., ask the student questions, ask the student's opinion, stand in close proximity to the student, seat the student near the teacher's desk, etc.).

44. Have the student prioritize tasks by importance (e.g., task A must be done today, task B can be done today, and task C can wait until tomorrow).

45. Supervise the student during study time to maintain on-task behavior.

46. Take proactive steps to deal with a student's refusal to perform an assignment to prevent contagion in the classroom (e.g., refrain from arguing with the student, place the student at a carrel or other quiet place to work, remove the student from the group or classroom, etc.).

47. Have the student question any directions, explanations, and instructions not understood.

48. Provide the student with a schedule of daily events so he/she knows exactly what and how much there is to do in a day.

49. Have the student repeat the directions verbally to the teacher.

50. Choose a classmate to model appropriate use of study time for the student.

51. Maintain sample letters, reports, forms, etc., as references for written communication.

52. Choose a peer to model appropriate completion of assignments for the student.

53. Designate a specific period of time when it is permissible for the student to converse with his/her peers (e.g., the last 5 minutes of study time, after completing a task, etc.).

54. Encourage the student to ask for clarification of the directions for classroom assignments to be completed during study time.

55. Interact frequently with the student to help him/her follow directions for the assignments.

56. Allow the student access to pencils, pens, etc., only after directions have been given.

57. Maintain consistency in daily routine.

58. Maintain consistency of expectations while keeping expectations within the ability level of the student.

59. Make certain that the student is attending to the teacher when directions are given (e.g., making eye contact, hands free of writing materials, looking at assignment, etc.).

60. Make certain that your comments take the form of constructive criticism rather than criticism that could be perceived as personal, threatening, etc. (e.g., instead of saying, "You always make the same mistake," say, "A better way to do that might be . . .").

61. Make certain the student achieves success when following directions.

62. Make certain the student has assignments to work on during study time.

63. Make certain the student understands the natural consequences of failing to complete assignments during study time (e.g., students who do not finish their work will not be allowed to do more desirable activities).

64. Have the student time his/her assignments to monitor personal behavior and accept time limits.

65. Provide an incentive statement along with a directive (e.g., "If you make appropriate use of study time, you may have free time.").

66. Structure time units so the student knows exactly how much time is available to work and when work should be finished.

67. Provide study guides with questions presented in sequential order to facilitate attention to the reading material presented in the student's content area textbooks (e.g., American history, biology, health, etc.).

68. Reinforce the student for attempting and completing assignments based on the amount of work the student successfully completes. As the student demonstrates success, gradually increase the amount of work required for reinforcement.

69. Provide the student with more than enough time to finish an activity and decrease the amount of time as the student demonstrates success.

70. Work a few problems of the assignment with the student to serve as a model and help the student begin a task prior to independent study time.

71. Provide the student with shorter tasks given more frequently.

72. Provide the student with step-by-step written directions for doing assignments during study time.

73. Provide the student with the opportunity to perform assignments/activities in a variety of ways (e.g., on tape, with a calculator, verbally, etc.).

74. Reduce directions to steps (e.g., give the student each additional step after completion of the previous step).

75. Reduce distracting stimuli (e.g., place the student in the front row, provide a carrel or quiet place away from distractions). This is used as a means of reducing stimuli and not as a form of punishment.

76. Reduce the emphasis on early completion. Hurrying to complete assignments may cause the student to fail to follow directions.

77. Provide clearly stated directions in written or verbal form (i.e., make the directions as simple and concrete as possible).

78. Reinforce the student for attempting and completing class assignments during study time: (a) give the student a tangible reward (e.g., classroom privileges, line leading, passing out materials, five minutes free time, etc.) or (b) give the student an intangible reward (e.g., praise, handshake, smile, etc.).

79. Reinforce the student for beginning, staying on, and completing assignments during study time.

80. Present one assignment at a time. As each assignment is completed, deliver reinforcement along with the presentation of the next assignment.

81. Prevent the student from becoming overstimulated by an activity (e.g., frustrated, angry, excited, etc.).

82. Provide alternatives for the traditional format of directions (e.g., tape record directions, summarize directions, directions given by peers, etc.).

83. Reinforce those students in the classroom who attempt and complete assignments during study time.

84. Move objects used for tactile stimulation (e.g., pens, paper clips, loose change, etc.) away from the student's reach.

85. Practice direction-following skills on nonacademic tasks.

86. Present assignments in the most attractive and interesting manner possible.

87. Repeat directions to increase the probability of understanding.

88. Require the student to begin each assignment within a specified period of time (e.g., three minutes, five minutes, etc.).

89. Set time limits so that the student knows exactly how much time is available to work and when work should be finished.

90. Structure the environment in such a way as to provide the student with increased opportunities for help or assistance.

91. Provide the student with a selection of assignments and require him/her to choose a minimum number from the total amount (e.g., present the student with three academic tasks from which two must be completed during study time).

92. Teach the student time-management skills. Have the student make a daily plan and follow it. Encourage the student to avoid becoming distracted by events, impulses, and moods.

93. Rewrite directions at a lower reading level.

94. With the student, chart those assignments that have been completed in a given period of time.

95. Speak with the student to explain (a) what he/she is doing wrong (e.g., not working during study time) and (b) what he/she should be doing (e.g., completing assignments during study time, studying, etc.).

96. Use a timer to help the student know how much time he/she has to study.

97. Reduce emphasis on academic and social competition. Fear of failure may cause the student to not want to complete assignments in a given period of time.

98. Specify exactly what is to be done for the completion of an assignment (e.g., indicate definite starting and stopping points, indicate the minimum requirements, etc.).

99. Structure the environment in such a way as to reduce distracting stimuli (e.g., place the student on or near the front row, provide a carrel or quiet place away from distractions, etc.). This is to be used as a means of reducing distracting stimuli and not as a form of punishment.

100. Write a contract with the student specifying what behavior is expected (e.g., working on class assignments during study time) and what reinforcement will be made available when the terms of the contract have been met.

199 Is disorganized to the point of not having necessary materials, losing materials, failing to find materials, etc.

Goals:

1. The student will have necessary materials for specified activities.
2. The student will improve his/her organizational skills related to assignments.

Objectives:

1. The student will be organized and prepared to work within _____ minutes of the beginning of class.
2. The student will bring necessary materials to specified activities with verbal prompts on _____ out of _____ trials.
3. The student will carry his/her materials and assignments to and from activities in a book bag/backpack to prevent loss on ___ out of ___ trials.
4. The student will have the necessary materials for assigned activities on _____ out of _____ trials.
5. The student will independently remember necessary materials for specified activities on _____ out of _____ trials.
6. The student will maintain necessary materials at designated locations for specified activities on _____ out of _____ trials.
7. The student will organize his/her materials at the beginning and end of each assigned task on _____ out of _____ trials.
8. The student will place his/her completed work in a specified location (folder, "mailbox," etc.) on _____ out of _____ trials.
9. The student will prioritize and complete assignments with the help of the teacher on ___ out of ___ opportunities.
10. The student will rely on environmental cues (e.g., lists, rules) to help him/her remember necessary materials for specified activities on _____ out of _____ trials.
11. The student will return materials to their specified locations on ___ out of ___ trials.

Interventions:

1. Have the student's cooperative work experience/vocational education teacher provide the student with organizational interventions to assist the student in maintaining organization at his/her job site.

2. Act as a model for organization and appropriate use of work materials (e.g., putting materials away before getting others out, having a place for all materials, maintaining an organized desk area, following a schedule for the day, etc.).

3. Allow natural consequences to occur (e.g., work not done during work time must be made up during recreational time, materials not maintained will be lost or not serviceable, etc.) as the result of the student's inability to organize or use materials appropriately.

4. Allow the student to finish an activity unless it will be disruptive to the schedule.

5. Assess the quality and clarity of directions, explanations, and instructions given to the student.

6. Assign a peer to work with the student on specified activities to make certain the student has the materials necessary to do the activity.

7. Encourage the student to develop a habit of asking himself/herself, "Do I have everything?" before leaving the house each morning.

8. Have the student leave necessary materials at specified activity areas.

9. Assist the student in finding a method of organization that works best for him/her (e.g., subject folders, tabbed binder, checklist, etc.).

10. Communicate with parents (e.g., notes home, phone calls, etc.) to share information concerning the student's progress. The parents may reinforce the student at home for being organized/prepared for specified activities at school.

11. Develop monthly calendars to keep track of important events, due dates, assignments, etc.

12. Do not accept excuses. The student must understand that, regardless of the reasons, it is necessary that he/she takes responsibility for not turning in a math assignment, losing pencils, etc.

13. Have the student chart the number of times he/she is organized/prepared for specified activities.

14. Encourage the student to develop an awareness of himself/herself and the environment. Instruct the student to step back and ask himself/herself, "What materials do I need to complete this assignment?" "Have I put my assignment in the correct folder?"

15. Have the student list five qualities of an organized person. Have the student choose one of those qualities to work on each week for five weeks.

16. Encourage the student to keep necessary materials for specified activities together (e.g., gym clothes in a gym bag in the car, backpack with all school-related materials by the door, etc.).

17. Reduce distracting stimuli (e.g., place the student on the front row, provide a carrel or quiet place away from distractions, etc.). This is used as a means of reducing distracting stimuli and not as punishment.

18. Encourage the student to manage his/her daily performance as if he/she were self-employed. This should increase his/her motivation to be organized and fulfill his/her responsibilities.

19. Encourage the student to put items that should be taken to work/school in a designated place (e.g., in front of the door, at the bottom of the stairs, etc.).

20. Enlist different people (e.g., counselor, paraprofessional, peer, etc.) to help the student maintain organization of assignments, materials, etc., at school.

21. Provide the student with an appropriate place to store/secure personal property (e.g., desk, locker, closet, etc.). Require the student to store all property when not in use.

22. Establish a routine to be followed for organization and appropriate use of work materials. Provide the routine for the student in written form and verbally review it often.

23. Assign the student organizational responsibilities in the classroom (e.g., equipment, software materials, etc.).

24. Establish classroom rules:
- Have necessary materials.
- Work on-task.
- Work quietly.
- Remain in your seat.
- Finish task.
- Meet task expectations.

Review rules often. Reinforce students for following rules.

25. Evaluate the appropriateness of the task to determine (a) if the task is too easy, (b) if the task is too difficult, and (c) if the length of time scheduled to complete the task is adequate.

26. Assist the student in organizing materials. As the student demonstrates success, gradually decrease the assistance and require the student to independently assume more responsibility for organization.

27. Give the student one task to perform at a time. Introduce the next task after the student has successfully completed the previous task in an organized way.

28. Have the student assemble all the materials necessary to work on a project, assignment, etc., to reduce the need to search for materials.

29. Make the student aware that work not completed because necessary materials were not brought to the specified activity will need to be completed during recreational or break time.

30. Have the student discard items/paperwork that have no future use.

31. Reduce the number of materials for which the student is responsible. As the student demonstrates appropriate use of materials, increase the number of materials for which the student is responsible.

32. Do not give the student additional materials if he/she fails to appropriately care for materials.

33. Have the student establish a routine to follow before coming to class (e.g., check which activity is next, determine what materials are necessary, collect materials, etc.).

34. Have the student choose a peer, friend, etc., who displays the ability to organize an assignment prior to beginning it. Have the student observe that person and try to model the behaviors which allow him/her to organize assignments.

35. Have the student label all personal property with his/her name.

36. Encourage the student to develop an awareness of the consequences of his/her behavior by writing down or talking through problems which may occur due to disorganization (e.g., missed assignments, incomplete projects, misplaced textbooks, etc.).

37. Have the student list and assemble all clothing and materials needed for his/her cooperative work experience or vocational training class. Encourage the student to review the list each evening.

38. Have the student list necessary tasks and materials required on his/her job site.

39. Make certain that failure to have necessary materials results in loss of opportunity to participate in activities or a failing grade for that day's activity (e.g., art, home economics, industrial arts, physical education, etc.).

40. Have the student develop a list of materials necessary for each class (e.g., band instrument, gym clothes, calculator, etc.).

41. Have the student organize major projects/assignments by breaking them into small segments. Set deadlines and provide the student with a reward after completing each segment of the assignment.

42. Have the student perform one task or step of a major project at a time.

43. Have the student question any directions, expectations, instructions he/she does not understand.

44. Act as a model for being organized/prepared for specified activities.

45. Choose a peer to model being organized/prepared for specified activities for the student.

46. Instruct the student to carry important items in a backpack or binder.

47. Have the student establish a routine and utilize a weekly schedule. Have the student develop an organizational checklist/chart for daily assignments to be completed.

48. Interact frequently with the student to prompt organizational skills and appropriate use of materials.

49. Have the student establish a routine to follow before changing activities (e.g., put away materials, assemble materials for the next activity, make a list of what materials need to be replenished, etc.).

50. Limit the student's freedom to borrow school property if he/she is unable to remember to return borrowed items.

51. Limit the student's use of materials (i.e., provide the student with only those materials necessary at any given time).

52. Make certain that all personal property is labeled with the student's name.

53. Have the student organize his/her book bag everyday before going home. Place paperwork in folders, prioritize the next day's assignments, and update his/her organizational calendar.

54. Make certain the student understands that he/she must replace things which are lost.

55. Minimize materials needed for specified activities.

56. Monitor the student's performance in activities or tasks to make certain the student begins, works on, and completes an assignment in a timely manner so that he/she can go to the next activity in his/her routine.

57. Provide a color coded organizational system (e.g., notebook, folders, etc.).

58. Teach the student to maintain care of personal property and school materials (e.g., keep property with him/her, know where property is at all times, secure property in lockers, leave valuable property at home, etc.).

59. Provide adequate time for completion of activities.

60. Provide an organizer for materials inside the student's desk.

61. Require that lost or damaged property be replaced by the student. If the student cannot replace the property, restitution can be made by working at school.

62. Provide the student with a container in which to carry necessary materials for specified activities (e.g., backpack, book bag, briefcase, etc.).

63. Provide the student with a list of necessary materials for each activity of the day.

64. Remind the student at the end of the class period of materials required for specified activities the next day (e.g., note sent home, verbal reminder, etc.).

65. Provide the student with a schedule of daily events so that he/she knows exactly what and how much there is to do in a day.

66. Assign the student shorter tasks. As the student demonstrates success in organizing academic activities, gradually increase the number over time.

67. Assist the student in beginning each task to reduce impulsive behavior.

68. Provide the student with an organizational checklist (e.g., routine activities, materials needed, and steps to follow).

69. Provide the student with clearly stated criteria for acceptable work (e.g., neatness, etc.).

70. Reinforce those students in the classroom who are organized/prepared for specified activities.

71. Provide the student with more work space (e.g., a larger desk or table at which to work).

72. Provide the student with only those materials he/she needs to complete an assignment (e.g., pencil, paper, dictionary, handwriting sample, etc.). Be certain that the student has only these necessary materials on his/her desk.

73. Minimize materials needed to be kept inside the student's desk.

74. Provide the student with structure for all academic activities (e.g., specific directions, routine format for tasks, time units, etc.).

75. Have the student maintain an assignment notebook which indicates those materials needed for each class.

76. Provide time at various points throughout the day for the student to organize his/her materials (e.g., before school, beginning of class period, break time, recess, lunch, end of the day, etc.).

77. Make certain that the student is not inadvertently reinforced for losing materials. Provide the student with used materials, copies of the materials, etc., rather than new materials if he/she fails to care for the materials in an appropriate manner.

78. Set aside time each week for the student to organize his/her locker.

79. Speak to the student to explain (a) what he/she is doing wrong (e.g., failing to bring necessary materials for specified activities) and (b) what he/she should be doing (e.g., having necessary materials for specified activities).

80. Require that assignments done incorrectly, for any reason, be redone.

81. Have the student develop monthly calendars to keep track of important events, due dates, assignments, etc.

82. Supervise the student while he/she is performing school work to monitor quality.

83. Provide storage space for materials the student is not using.

84. Provide adequate transition time between activities for the student to organize his/her materials.

85. Teach the student time-management skills. Have the student make a daily plan and follow it. Encourage the student to avoid becoming distracted by events, impulses, and moods.

86. Provide the student with verbal reminders of necessary materials required for each activity.

87. Teach the student to prioritize assignments (e.g., according to importance, length, etc.).

88. Reinforce the student for having necessary materials for specified activities: (a) give the student a tangible reward (e.g., classroom privileges, line leading, passing out materials, five minutes free time, etc.) or (b) give the student an intangible reward (e.g., praise, handshake, smile, etc.).

89. Teach the student how to conserve rather than waste materials (e.g., amount of glue, paper, tape, etc., to use; putting lids, caps, tops on such materials as markers, pens, bottles, jars, cans, etc.).

90. Write a contract with the student specifying what behavior is expected (e.g., having necessary materials for specified activities) and what reinforcement will be made available when the terms of the contract have been met.

91. Have the student develop and maintain one list of things to do to organize and focus on what needs to be accomplished for a specific task, day, etc.

200 Does not make appropriate use of free time

Goals:

1. The student will improve his/her independent behavior in nonacademic settings.
2. The student will improve his/her independent behavior in academic settings.
3. The student will improve his/her independent behavior inside the classroom.
4. The student will improve his/her independent behavior outside the classroom.
5. The student will improve his/her independent behavior.
6. The student will make appropriate use of free time.

Objectives:

1. The student will be actively involved in an activity during free time on _____ out of _____ trials.
2. The student will remain in assigned areas during free time on _____ out of _____ trials.
3. The student will socialize with one or more peers during free time on _____ out of _____ trials.
4. The student will use free time to complete homework assignments on _____ out of _____ trials.
5. The student will use free time to complete unfinished assignments on _____ out of _____ trials.
6. The student will use free time to work ahead on assignments on _____ out of _____ trials.
7. The student will work independently during free time on _____ out of _____ trials.
8. The student will work quietly during free time on _____ out of _____ trials.

Interventions:

1. Make certain that assignments are scheduled to minimize free time.

2. Assign a peer for the student to interact with during free time.

3. Communicate with parents (e.g., notes home, phone calls, etc.) to share information concerning the student's progress. The parents may reinforce the student at home for making appropriate use of free time at school.

4. Develop, with the student, a list of high-interest free time activities that require various amounts of time to perform.

5. Do not leave a lot of unstructured time for the student.

6. Encourage the student to assist younger peers in free time activities.

7. Encourage the student to plan the use of free time in advance.

8. Encourage the student's peers to include him/her in free time activities.

9. Establish centers of high-interest activities at appropriate levels of difficulty for the student's use during free time.

10. Establish free time rules:
- Find an activity.
- Spend time quietly.
- Remain in assigned areas.
- Put materials away when free time is over.

Review rules often. Reinforce students for following rules.

11. Evaluate the appropriateness of free time activities to determine whether or not the student can be successful with the activity and the length of time scheduled.

12. Find educationally related free time activities for the student to perform (e.g., flash card activities with peers; math, reading, or spelling board games; etc.).

13. Give the student a special responsibility during free time (e.g., grading papers, straightening books, feeding pets, etc.).

14. Provide a quiet, reasonable private area where the student can do nothing during free time.

15. Give the student an individual schedule to follow so that when an activity is finished he/she knows what to do next.

16. Have the student act as a peer tutor during free time.

17. Have the student act as a teacher assistant during free time.

18. Have the student begin an ongoing project during free time that will be a regular free time activity.

19. Have the student question any directions, explanations, or instructions not understood.

20. Choose a peer to model appropriate use of free time for the student.

21. Identify a specific activity for the student to participate in during free time.

22. Intervene early when there is a problem to prevent more serious problems from occurring.

23. Allow the student to go to other classrooms for specified activities during free time (e.g., typing, home economics, industrial arts, etc.).

24. Make certain that free time is contingent upon academic productivity and accuracy (e.g., the student must finish three activities with 80 percent accuracy before participating in free time).

25. Make certain that the free time activity does not overstimulate and cause the student to demonstrate inappropriate behavior.

26. Make certain the student does not become involved in overstimulating activities.

27. Make certain the student is able to successfully engage in the free time activity (e.g., the student understands the rules, the student is familiar with the activity, the student will be compatible with other students engaged in the activity, etc.).

28. Make certain the student understands that failing to make appropriate use of free time may result in termination of free time and/or loss of opportunity to earn free time.

29. Separate the student from the peer(s) who stimulates the student's inappropriate use of free time.

30. Reinforce the student for making appropriate use of free time: (a) give the student a tangible reward (e.g., classroom privileges, line leading, passing out materials, five minutes free time, etc.) or (b) give the student an intangible reward (e.g., praise, handshake, smile, etc.).

31. Make certain the student understands that failure to conclude activities and return to assignments may result in the loss of opportunity to earn free time.

32. Participate in free time activities with the student to model appropriate use of free time.

33. Place free time materials (e.g., paper, pencil, glue, crayons, games, etc.) in a location where the student can access them on his/her own.

34. Provide high interest free time activities for completion of assignments (e.g., listening to music, reading, socializing, going to another part of the building, etc.).

35. Provide sign-up sheets for free time activities.

36. Provide supervision of free time activities to monitor the student's appropriate use of free time.

37. Provide the student with a list of quiet activities to participate in when he/she finishes assignments early.

38. Provide the student with frequent short-term, free time activities so he/she can learn to finish free time projects at another time and be willing to go back to assignments.

39. Provide items of interest for the student during free time (e.g., headphones, coloring books, reading material, etc.).

40. Reinforce the student for making appropriate use of free time based on the length of time the student can be successful. As the student demonstrates success, gradually increase the length of time required for reinforcement.

41. Make certain the student is aware of the length of free time available when beginning an activity.

42. Reinforce those students in the classroom who make appropriate use of free time.

43. Speak to the student to explain (a) what the student is doing wrong (e.g., talking loudly, getting out of seat, etc.) and (b) what he/she should be doing (e.g., talking quietly, sitting quietly, etc.).

44. Write a contract with the student specifying what behavior is expected (e.g., talking quietly, sitting quietly, studying, etc.) and what reinforcement will be made available when the terms of the contract have been met.

201 Does not use time outside of class appropriately

Goal:

1. The student will use time outside of class appropriately.

Objectives:

1. The student will work independently during free time on _____ out of _____ trials.
2. The student will socialize with one or more peers during free time on _____ out of _____ trials.
3. The student will work quietly during free time on _____ out of _____ trials.
4. The student will remain in assigned areas during free time on _____ out of _____ trials.
5. The student will use free time to complete unfinished assignments on _____ out of _____ trials.
6. The student will use free time to work ahead on assignments on _____ out of _____ trials.
7. The student will use free time to complete homework assignments on _____ out of _____ trials.
8. The student will be actively involved in an activity during free time on _____ out of _____ trials.

Interventions:

1. Reinforce the student for making appropriate use of free time: (a) give the student a tangible reward (e.g., classroom privileges, line leading, passing out materials, five minutes free time, etc.) or (b) give the student an intangible reward (e.g., praise, handshake, smile, etc.).

2. Speak to the student to explain (a) what he/she is doing wrong (e.g., talking loudly, leaving seat) and (b) what he/she should be doing (e.g., talking quietly, sitting quietly).

3. Establish free time rules:
- Find an activity.
- Work or spend the time quietly.
- Remain in assigned areas.
- Put materials away when free time is over.

Review rules often. Reinforce students for following rules.

4. Reinforce those students in the classroom who make appropriate use of free time.

5. Reinforce the student for making appropriate use of free time based on the length of time the student can be successful. As the student demonstrates success, gradually increase the length of time required for reinforcement.

6. Write a contract with the student specifying what behavior is expected (e.g., talking quietly, sitting quietly, studying, etc.) and what reinforcement will be made available when the terms of the contract have been met.

7. Communicate with parents (e.g., notes home, phone calls, etc.) to share information concerning the student's progress. The parents may reinforce the student at home for making appropriate use of free time at school.

8. Choose a peer to model appropriate use of free time for the student.

9. Have the student question any directions, explanations, instructions he/she does not understand.

10. Evaluate the appropriateness of free time to determine whether or not the student can be successful with the length of time available.

11. Encourage the student's peers to include him/her in free time activities.

12. Encourage the student to assist younger peers in free time activities.

13. Develop, with the student, a list of high-interest free time activities that require various lengths of time.

14. Place free time materials (e.g., paper, pencil, glue, crayons, games, etc.) in a location where the student can access them on his/her own.

15. Establish centers of high-interest activities at appropriate levels of difficulty for use at free time.

16. Provide a quiet, private area to remain inactive during free time.

17. Separate the student from the peer(s) who stimulates the student's inappropriate use of free time.

18. Encourage the student to plan his/her use of free time in advance.

19. Provide sign-up sheets for free time activities.

20. Give the student an individual schedule to follow so that when an activity is finished he/she knows what to do next.

21. Assign a peer for the student to interact with during free time.

22. Identify a specified activity for the student to participate in during free time.

23. Have the student act as a peer tutor during free time.

24. Have the student act as a teacher assistant during free time.

25. Allow the student to go to other classrooms for specified activities during free time (e.g., typing, home economics, industrial arts, etc.).

26. Have the student begin an ongoing project to work on during free time which will then be a regular free time activity.

27. Provide supervision of free time activities to monitor the student's appropriate use of free time.

28. Make certain that assignments are scheduled in such a way as to minimize the student running out of assignments in which to participate.

29. Provide high-interest free time activities for completion of assignments (e.g., listening to music, reading, socializing, going to another part of the building, etc.).

30. Provide the student with a list of quiet activities to participate in when he/she finishes assignments early.

31. Find educationally related free time activities for the student to perform (e.g., flash card activities with peers; math, reading, or spelling board games, etc.).

32. Participate in free time activities with the student to model appropriate use of free time.

33. Make certain that the free time activity does not overstimulate and cause the student to demonstrate inappropriate behavior.

34. Make certain the student is able to successfully participate in the free time activity (e.g., the student understands the rules, the student is familiar with the activity, the student will be compatible with other students participating in the free time activity, etc.).

35. Make certain that free time is contingent upon academic productivity and accuracy (e.g., the student must finish three activities with 80 percent accuracy before participating in free time).

36. Make certain the student is aware of the length of free time available when beginning the free time activity.

37. Make certain the student understands that failing to make appropriate use of free time may result in termination of free time and/or loss of the opportunity to earn free time.

38. Make certain the student understands that failure to conclude free time activities and return to assignments may result in loss of the opportunity to earn free time.

39. Provide the student with frequent short-term free time activities so he/she can learn to finish free time projects at another time and be willing to return to assignments.

202 Does not care for personal appearance

Goals:
1. The student will care for his/her personal appearance.
2. The student will improve his/her hygiene skills.

Objectives:
1. The student will come to class with his/her hair combed ___ out of ___ classes per week.
2. The student will come to class free of offending odors on ___ out of ___ trials.
3. The student will wear clothing to school that is clean, properly fitted, and free of tears and holes on ___ out of ___ trials.
4. The student will wash his/her hands after using the restroom, eating, playing outside, etc., on ___ out of ___ trials.
5. The student will blow his/her nose in an appropriate manner on ___ out of ___ trials.
6. The student will wear clothing that matches in color and style on ___ out of ___ trials.

Interventions:

Note: Evidence of inappropriate care for personal appearance would include such things as dirt on body and under fingernails, dirty hair, body odor, unbrushed teeth, offensive breath, failure to use a handkerchief appropriately, and toileting accidents.

1. Choose a peer to model appropriate hygiene (e.g., wearing clean clothing, washing hair, cleaning fingernails, etc.) for the student.

2. Have the student question any hygiene expectations not understood.

3. Establish hygiene rules:
- Bathe regularly.
- Brush teeth.
- Wash hair.
- Launder clothing after wearing.
- Clean and trim nails.
- Maintain personal cleanliness after using restroom.
- Use a handkerchief.

Review rules often. Reinforce students for following rules.

4. Evaluate the demands of the responsibility on the student for personal hygiene to determine if the expectations are too high. If expectations are too difficult for the student, assistance should be provided.

5. Have the student keep a change of clean clothing at school.

6. Provide the student with training in the use of personal grooming and related materials (e.g., washcloth, soap, shampoo, toothbrush, toothpaste, hairbrush, comb, nail clippers, toilet paper, handkerchief, etc.).

7. Allow the student to attend to personal hygiene needs at school if the opportunity is not available elsewhere (e.g., launder clothing, bathe, wash hair, etc.).

8. Maintain personal hygiene materials at school for the student's use.

9. Provide a comprehensive unit of information and instruction on personal hygiene. The unit should include health and appearance aspects. Classroom visitors can include a dentist, nurse, doctor, cosmetologist, etc.

10. Communicate with parents, agencies, or the appropriate parties to inform them of the problem, determine the cause of the problem, and consider possible solutions to the problem.

11. Require the student to maintain a daily routine of grooming and attending to personal hygiene at school.

12. Designate one adult in the educational environment to work directly with the student to help him/her care for personal appearance.

13. As part of instruction on interviewing and job placement, emphasize the importance of personal hygiene and grooming (e.g., have a representative of business or industry visit the class to make a presentation on the importance of personal appearance).

14. Provide the student with a checklist of personal hygiene activities and have the student complete the checklist daily.

15. Provide visual reminders of personal hygiene in appropriate locations (e.g., picture of washing hands and brushing teeth at sink, picture of deodorant in restroom, etc.).

16. Teach the student to launder clothing.

17. Reinforce the student for gradually improving personal hygiene over time rather than expecting total mastery of personal hygiene skills immediately.

18. Make certain that all communications with the student concerning personal hygiene are conducted in a private manner.

19. Provide the student with scheduled times during the day to attend to personal hygiene needs.

20. Allow the student to arrive early at school to care for his/her personal appearance.

21. Do not criticize when correcting the student; be honest yet supportive. Never cause the student to feel badly about himself/herself.

22. Communicate with parents (e.g., notes home, phone calls, etc.) to share information concerning the student's progress. The parents may reinforce the student at home for caring for personal appearance.

23. Write a contract with the student specifying what behavior is expected (e.g., wearing clean clothing, washing hair, cleaning fingernails, etc.) and what reinforcement will be made available when the terms of the contract have been met.

24. Reinforce the student for caring for personal appearance based on the length of time the student can be successful. As the student demonstrates success, gradually increase the length of time required for reinforcement.

25. Reinforce those students in the classroom who care for their personal appearance.

26. Speak to the student to explain (a) what the student is doing wrong (e.g., wearing dirty clothing, failing to wash hair or clean fingernails, etc.) and (b) what the student should be doing (e.g., wearing clean clothing, washing hair, cleaning fingernails, etc.).

27. Reinforce the student for caring for personal appearance: (a) give the student a tangible reward (e.g., classroom privileges, line leading, passing out materials, five minutes free time, etc.) or (b) give the student an intangible reward (e.g., praise, handshake, smile, etc.).

28. Carefully consider the student's age and experience before expecting him/her to care for personal hygiene independently.

29. Make certain that the student sees the relationship between his/her behavior and the consequences which follow (e.g., offending others, being avoided by others, not being able to participate in special activities, etc.).

30. Set an example for the student by caring about your personal appearance (e.g., combing your hair, bathing daily, etc.).

31. Encourage the student to take a home economics class, a health class, etc., to learn the importance of personal hygiene.

32. Make certain that the student understands that others might "make fun" if the student does not comb hair, zip pants, tie shoes, etc.

33. Compliment the student for being neat, clean, etc.

34. Set aside time to practice hair combing, putting on make-up, shaving, using deodorant, etc.

35. Stress to the student the social importance of brushing teeth, washing hair, bathing, etc. Not only is inadequate hygiene offensive, but other children can be cruel.

36. Provide the student with instruction on fastening articles of clothing.

37. Teach the student how to fasten articles of clothing when buttons are missing, zippers are broken, etc. (e.g., sewing a button back in place, using a safety pin, etc.).

38. Guide the student's hands through the activity of zipping, buttoning, and snapping his/her own clothing.

39. Help the student learn those skills necessary to improve his/her personal appearance and hygiene.

40. Provide the student with verbal reminders to fasten his/her articles of clothing.

41. If the student is incapable of fastening articles of clothing, they should be fastened for the student.

42. Reinforce the student for gradually improving his/her ability to fasten articles of clothing over time rather than expecting total mastery immediately.

43. Reinforce the student at regular intervals throughout the day for having articles of clothing fastened.

44. Provide the student with time to practice fastening his/her articles of clothing. (The clothing needs to be on the student during practice.)

45. Have the student practice fastening articles of clothing with oversized zippers, buttons, and snaps. As the student demonstrates success, gradually reduce the size of the fasteners.

46. Place visual reminders to fasten articles of clothing inside of restrooms and on the classroom door (e.g., pictures of zipping, buttoning, and snapping).

47. Provide the student with a checklist of articles of clothing to fasten (e.g., shirt, pants, shoes, coat, etc.). Have the student complete the checklist routinely throughout the day.

48. Place a full-length mirror in the classroom for the student to make certain that all of his/her articles of clothing are fastened.

49. Be careful to avoid embarrassing the student by asking him/her to fasten articles of clothing in front of peers.

203 Does not demonstrate appropriate grooming habits

Goal:

1. The student will demonstrate appropriate grooming habits.

Objectives:

1. The student will demonstrate appropriate grooming habits by combing his/her hair ____% of the time.
2. The student will demonstrate appropriate grooming habits by bathing every ____.
3. The student will demonstrate appropriate grooming habits by wearing clean clothes ____% of the time.
4. The student will demonstrate appropriate grooming habits by wearing clothes that are of an appropriate size on ____ out of ____ occasions.
5. The student will demonstrate appropriate grooming habits by wearing clothing that is coordinated by color and/or pattern on ____ out of ____ occasions.
6. The student will clean his/her fingernails daily.
7. The student will keep his/her hair clean.
8 The student will brush his/her teeth daily.
9. The student will demonstrate appropriate grooming skills with physical assistance on ____ out of ____ occasions.
10. The student will demonstrate appropriate grooming skills with verbal reminders on ____ out of ____ occasions.
11. The student will demonstrate appropriate grooming skills independently on ____ out of ____ occasions.

Interventions:

1. Choose a peer to model appropriate grooming habits (e.g., wearing clean clothing, washing hair, cleaning fingernails, etc.) for the student.

2. Have the student question any grooming expectations not understood.

3. Establish grooming rules:
- Bathe regularly.
- Brush teeth.
- Comb or brush hair.
- Launder clothing after wearing.
- Clean and trim nails.
- Wear clothes that fit.
- Wear clothes that coordinate.

Review rules often. Reinforce students for following the rules.

4. Evaluate the demands on the student to be responsible for grooming to determine if the expectations are too high. If expectations are too difficult for the student, assistance should be provided.

5. Communicate with parents, agencies, or the appropriate parties to inform them of the problem, determine the cause of the problem, and consider possible solutions to the problem.

6. Provide the student with training in the use of personal grooming and related materials (e.g., washcloth, soap, shampoo, toothbrush, toothpaste, hairbrush, comb, nail clippers, toilet paper, handkerchief, etc.).

7. Allow the student to attend to grooming needs at school if the opportunity is not available elsewhere (e.g., launder clothing, bathe, wash hair, etc.).

8. Maintain grooming materials at school for the students to use.

9. Provide a comprehensive unit of information and instruction on personal hygiene and grooming. The unit should include health and appearance aspects. Classroom visitors can include a dentist, nurse, doctor, cosmetologist, etc.

10. Designate one adult in the educational environment to work directly with the student to help him/her with grooming skills.

11. Require the student to maintain a daily routine of grooming and attending to personal hygiene at school.

12. Have the student keep a change of clean clothing at school.

13. As part of instruction on interviewing and job placement, emphasize the importance of personal hygiene and grooming (e.g., have a representative of business or industry visit the class to make a presentation on the importance of personal appearance).

14. Provide the student with a checklist of grooming activities and have the student complete the checklist daily.

15. Provide visual reminders of grooming habits in appropriate locations (e.g., picture of washing hands and brushing teeth at sink, picture of deodorant in restroom, etc.).

16. Teach the student to launder clothing.

17. Reinforce the student for gradually improving grooming skills over time rather than expecting total mastery of grooming skills immediately.

18. Make certain that all communications with the student concerning grooming are conducted in a private manner.

19. Provide the student with scheduled times during the day to attend to grooming needs.

20. Encourage the student to take a home economics class, a health class, etc., in school to learn the importance of appropriate grooming habits.

21. Do not criticize when correcting the student, be honest yet supportive. Never cause the student to feel badly about himself/herself.

22. Communicate with parents (e.g., notes home, phone calls, etc.) to share information concerning the student's progress. The parents may reinforce the student at home for demonstrating appropriate grooming habits.

23. Write a contract with the student specifying what behavior is expected (e.g., wearing clean clothing, washing hair, cleaning fingernails, etc.) and what reinforcement will be made available when the terms of the contract have been met.

24. Reinforce the student for demonstrating appropriate grooming habits based on the length of time the student can be successful. As the student demonstrates success, gradually increase the length of time required for reinforcement.

25. Reinforce those students in the classroom who demonstrate appropriate grooming habits.

26. Speak to the student to explain (a) what the student is doing wrong (e.g., wearing dirty clothing, failing to wash hair or clean fingernails, etc.) and (b) what the student should be doing (e.g., wearing clean clothing, washing hair, cleaning fingernails, etc.).

27. Reinforce the student for demonstrating appropriate grooming habits: (a) give the student a tangible reward (e.g., classroom privileges, line leading, passing out materials, five minutes free time, etc.) or (b) give the student an intangible reward (e.g., praise, handshake, smile, etc.).

28. Carefully consider the student's age and experience before expecting him/her to demonstrate appropriate grooming habits independently.

29. Make certain that the student sees the relationship between his/her behavior and the consequences which follow (e.g., offending others, being avoided by others, not being able to participate in special activities, etc.).

30. Set an example for the student by caring about your personal appearance (e.g., combing your hair, bathing daily, etc.).

31. Allow the student to arrive early at school to care for his/her personal appearance.

32. Make certain the student understands that others might make fun of him/her if the student does not comb hair, zip pants, tie shoes, etc.

33. Compliment the student for being neat, clean, etc.

34. Set aside time to practice hair combing, putting on makeup, shaving, using deodorant, etc.

35. Stress to the student the social importance of brushing teeth, washing hair, bathing, etc. Not only is inadequate personal care offensive, but other children can be cruel.

204   Does not demonstrate appropriate hygiene

Goals:
1. The student will increase his/her ability to care for personal needs.
2. The student will improve his/her self-help skills.
3. The student will demonstrate appropriate hygiene.

Objectives:
1. The student will wear clean clothing on ____ out of ____ occasions.
2. The student will clean his/her fingernails daily.
3. The student will keep his/her hair clean.
4. The student will bathe regularly.
5. The student will brush his/her teeth daily.
6. The student will maintain personal hygiene while using the restroom facilities.
7. The student will use a handkerchief when necessary.
8. The student will demonstrate hygiene skills with physical assistance on ____ out of ____ occasions.
9. The student will demonstrate hygiene skills with verbal reminders on ____ out of ____ occasions.
10. The student will independently demonstrate hygiene skills on ____ out of ____ occasions.

Interventions:

1. Reinforce the student for demonstrating appropriate hygiene: (a) give the student a tangible reward (e.g., classroom privileges, line leading, passing out materials, five minutes of free time, etc.) or (b) give the student an intangible reward (e.g., praise, handshake, smile, etc.).

2. Speak to the student to explain (a) what he/she is doing wrong (e.g., wearing dirty clothing, failing to wash hair or clean fingernails, etc.) and (b) what he/she should be doing (e.g., wearing clean clothing, washing hair, cleaning fingernails, etc.).

3. Choose a peer to model appropriate hygiene (e.g., wearing clean clothing, washing hair, cleaning fingernails, etc.) for the student.

4. Reinforce the student for demonstrating appropriate hygiene based on the length of time the student can be successful. As the student demonstrates success, gradually increase the length of time required for reinforcement.

5. Write a contract with the student specifying what behavior is expected (e.g., wearing clean clothing, washing hair, cleaning fingernails, etc.) and what reinforcement will be made available when the terms of the contract have been met.

6. Communicate with parents (e.g., notes home, phone calls, etc.) to share information concerning the student's progress. The parents may reinforce the student at home for demonstrating appropriate hygiene at school.

7. Reinforce those students in the classroom who demonstrate appropriate hygiene.

8. Have the student question any hygiene expectation he/she does not understand.

9. Establish hygiene rules:
- Bathe regularly.
- Brush teeth.
- Wash hair.
- Launder clothing after wearing.
- Clean and trim nails.
- Maintain personal cleanliness after using restroom.
- Use a handkerchief.

Review rules often. Reinforce students for following rules.

10. Evaluate the demands on the student to be responsible for his/her own hygiene to determine if the expectations are too high. If expectations are too difficult for the student, assistance will need to be provided.

11. Designate one adult in the educational environment to work directly with the student to help him/her improve personal hygiene.

12. Provide the student with a checklist of personal hygiene activities and have the student complete the checklist daily.

13. Allow the student to attend to personal hygiene needs at school if the opportunity is not available elsewhere (e.g., launder clothing, bathe, wash hair, etc.).

14. Maintain personal hygiene materials at school for the student's use.

15. Provide a comprehensive unit of information and instruction on personal hygiene. The unit should include health and appearance components. Classroom visitors can include a dentist, nurse, doctor, cosmetologist, etc.

16. Communicate with parents, agencies, or the appropriate parties, to inform them of the problem, determine the cause of the problem, and consider possible solutions to the problem.

17. Require the student to maintain at school a daily routine of grooming and attending to personal hygiene.

18. Have the student keep a change of clean clothing at school.

19. As part of instruction on interviewing and job placement, emphasize the importance of personal hygiene and grooming (e.g., have a representative of business or industry visit the class to make a presentation on the importance of personal appearance).

20. Provide the student with training in the use of personal grooming and related materials (e.g., washcloth, soap, shampoo, toothbrush, toothpaste, hairbrush, comb, nail clippers, toilet paper, handkerchief, etc.).

21. Provide visual reminders of personal hygiene in appropriate locations (e.g., picture of hand washing and brushing teeth at sink, picture of deodorant in restroom, etc.).

22. Teach the student to launder clothing.

23. Reinforce the student for gradually improving personal hygiene over time rather than expecting total mastery of personal hygiene skills immediately.

24. Make certain all communications with the student concerning personal hygiene are conducted in a private manner.

25. Provide the student with scheduled times during the day to attend to personal hygiene needs.

26. Allow the student to arrive early at school to care for his/her personal hygiene.

205   Does not demonstrate appropriate mealtime behavior

Goals:

1. The student will increase his/her ability to care for personal needs.
2. The student will improve his/her self-help skills.
3. The student will demonstrate appropriate mealtime behavior.

Objectives:

1. The student will wait quietly when in the cafeteria serving line on ____ out of ____ occasions.
2. The student will move through the cafeteria serving line without making physical contact with other students on ____ out of ____ occasions.
3. The student will use a knife to cut food during mealtime on ____ out of ____ occasions.
4. The student will use a spoon to eat soup, ice cream, etc., during mealtime on ____ out of ___ occasions.
5. The student will use a fork to eat food during mealtime on ____ out of ____ occasions.
6. The student will use a straw to drink liquids during mealtime on ____ out of ____ occasions.
7. The student will drink liquids without spilling during mealtime on ____ out of ____ occasions.
8. The student will use a napkin to wipe his/her mouth during mealtime on ____ out of ____ occasions.
9. The student will talk quietly during mealtime on ____ out of ____ occasions.
10. The student will dispose of trash when finished eating on ____ out of ____ occasions.
11. The student will eat food in small bites on ____ out of ____ occasions.
12. The student will remain seated during mealtime on ____ out of ____ occasions.
13. The student will chew food with his/her mouth closed on ____ out of ____ occasions.
14. The student will clean up spills during mealtime with a napkin or cloth on ____ out of ____ occasions.
15. The student will only eat the food on his/her tray during mealtime on ____ out of ____ occasions.
16. The student will ask for assistance when necessary during mealtime on ____ out of ____ occasions.
17. The student will finish eating within the designated mealtime on ____ out of ____ occasions.
18. The student will wait with his/her group until dismissed from the cafeteria after mealtime on ___ out of ____ occasions.

Interventions:

1. Reinforce the student for demonstrating appropriate mealtime behaviors: (a) give the student a tangible reward (e.g., classroom privileges, line leading, passing out materials, five minutes free time, etc.) or (b) give the student an intangible reward (e.g., praise, handshake, smile, etc.).

2. Speak to the student to explain (a) what he/she is doing wrong (e.g., eating with his/her fingers) and (b) what he/she should be doing (e.g., using a fork).

3. Reinforce those students who demonstrate appropriate mealtime behaviors.

4. Reinforce the student for demonstrating appropriate mealtime behaviors based on the length of time the student can be successful. As the student demonstrates success, gradually increase the length of time required for reinforcement.

5. Write a contract with the student specifying what behavior is expected (e.g., disposing of his/her food in the trash can) and what reinforcement will be made available when the terms of the contract have been met.

6. Communicate with parents (e.g., notes home, phone calls, etc.) to share information concerning the student's progress. The parents may reinforce the student at home for demonstrating appropriate mealtime behaviors at school.

7. Evaluate the appropriateness of the task to determine (a) if the task is too easy, (b) if the task is too difficult, and (c) if the length of time scheduled to complete the task is adequate.

8. Choose a peer to model appropriate mealtime behaviors for the student.

9. Have the student question any directions, expectations, instructions he/she does not understand.

10. Provide the student with a list of clearly defined mealtime behavioral expectations (e.g., rules for the cafeteria serving line, sitting at tables, remaining seated, use of utensils, disposing of trash, etc.).

11. Reinforce other students for demonstrating appropriate mealtime behaviors.

12. Assess the appropriateness of the student eating with a group of peers. If necessary, have the student eat with one peer and gradually increase the size of the group as the student experiences success.

13. Instruct the student in the appropriate use of eating utensils in both simulation and actual eating situations.

14. Instruct the student in appropriate mealtime conversation (e.g., topics to discuss, asking conversational questions, speaking quietly, etc.).

15. Instruct the student in appropriate mealtime etiquette (e.g., speaking with an empty mouth, eating with mouth closed, chewing quietly, etc.).

16. Instruct the student in selecting an appropriate amount of food, eating an appropriate amount of food, taking appropriately sized bites, etc.

17. Instruct the student in appropriate clean-up activities upon completion of eating (e.g., disposing of trash, putting trays and tableware in appropriate locations, washing hands, etc.).

18. Instruct the student in the appropriate use of napkins (e.g., keep on lap, wipe mouth, clean up spills, etc.).

19. Instruct the student in appropriate line behavior (e.g., waiting quietly, refraining from physical contact, moving with the line, etc.).

20. Make certain the student sits appropriately while eating (e.g., sits close to the table, sits upright, leans forward, etc.).

21. Instruct the student in appropriate behavior when finishing a meal early (e.g., making conversation, remaining in his/her seat, excusing himself/herself, etc.).

22. Instruct the student in appropriate ways to get seconds or additional food (e.g., asking for seconds, going through the cafeteria line a second time, purchasing seconds, etc.).

23. Remove the student from eating with his/her peers if he/she cannot demonstrate appropriate mealtime behaviors.

24. Teach the student appropriate ways to drink liquids (e.g., opening milk cartons and juice containers, using a straw, pouring into a glass, drinking from a glass, etc.).

25. Teach the student appropriate ways to respond to food he/she does not want (e.g., sample everything at least once, leave the food on the plate, offer extra portions to others, etc.).

26. Instruct the student in appropriate ways to clean up spills (e.g., ask for assistance, use paper towels and napkins, etc.).

27. Instruct the student in appropriate ways to clean clothing when accidents occur during mealtime (e.g., immediately go to the restroom, use paper towels and napkins, etc.).

Goals:

1. The student will increase his/her ability to care for personal needs.
2. The student will improve his/her self-help skills.

Objectives:

1. The student will take care of his/her toileting needs with supervision on ____ out of ____ occasions.
2. The student will independently take care of his/her toileting needs on ____ out of ____ occasions.
3. The student will take care of toileting needs when necessary on ____ out of ____ occasions.
4. The student will use the correct restroom facility on ____ out of ____ occasions.
5. The student will use the restroom facilities (toilet, sink, towel and soap dispensers) for which they are designed on ____ out of ____ occasions.
6. The student will engage in necessary hygiene activities (use toilet paper, wash hands) after using the restroom on ____ out of ____ occasions.
7. The student will leave the restroom appropriately dressed on ____ out of ____ occasions.
8. The student will use the restroom within a designated length of time on ____ out of ____ occasions.

Interventions:

1. Reinforce the student for toileting himself/herself appropriately: (a) give the student a tangible reward (e.g., classroom privileges, line leading, passing out materials, five minutes free time, etc.) or (b) give the student an intangible reward (e.g., praise, handshake, smile, etc.).

2. Speak to the student to explain (a) what he/she is doing wrong (e.g., failing to inform someone of his/her need to use the restroom or appropriately waiting his/her turn to use the restroom) and (b) what he/she should be doing (e.g., independently identifying the correct facility and returning to the classroom when he/she has finished using the restroom).

3. Establish restroom rules:
- Get the teacher's permission to use the restroom.
- Behave appropriately in the restroom.
- Return to the classroom when finished using the restroom.

Review rules often. Reinforce students for following rules.

4. Have the student inform someone of his/her need to use the restroom in enough time to avoid an accident.

5. Write a contract with the student specifying what behavior is expected (e.g., informing someone of his/her need to use the restroom) and what reinforcement will be made available when the terms of the contract have been met.

6. Communicate with parents (e.g., notes home, phone calls, etc.) to share information concerning the student's progress. The parents may reinforce the student at home for appropriately taking care of his/her toileting needs at school.

7. Choose a peer to model appropriate toileting activities (e.g., asking permission to use the restroom, taking advantage of scheduled restroom breaks, washing hands, leaving the restroom appropriately dressed, etc.) for the student.

8. Have the student question any directions, explanations, and instructions he/she does not understand.

9. Reinforce those students in the classroom who appropriately attend to their toileting needs.

10. Make certain that the student can independently find and use the restroom.

11. Demonstrate to the student how to appropriately dry his/her hands (e.g., using paper or cloth dispensers, using an appropriate number of paper towels, using an air dryer, etc.).

12. Instruct the student in the proper use of toilet paper (e.g., use enough toilet paper, deposit the toilet paper in the toilet, etc.).

13. Have the student flush the toilet after each use.

14. Demonstrate to the student and make certain that he/she leaves the restroom appropriately dressed (e.g., position underwear, pants, shirt; and zips, snaps, and buckles clothing).

15. Have the student return from the restroom after toileting.

16. Provide the student with the opportunity to use the restroom at appropriate intervals (e.g., before school, recess, lunch, restroom breaks, etc.).

17. Reinforce the student for returning from the restroom in an appropriate amount of time.

18. Have the student demonstrate to a peer how to use the restroom properly (e.g., securing door, flushing toilet, etc.).

19. Require the student to independently identify the correct restroom facility (e.g., boys, girls, men, women, etc.).

20. Instruct the student on the proper closing and securing of the stall doors in the restroom (e.g., latch, bolt lock, etc.).

21. Require the student to wait his/her turn when using the restroom.

22. Have the male student practice using different facilities for toileting (e.g., toilet, various types of urinals, etc.).

23. Demonstrate appropriate restroom behavior for the student (e.g., wait quietly, leave the restroom when finished, respect others' privacy, etc.).

24. Require the student to report any problems relating to the restroom facility (e.g., malfunctioning of toilets; empty towel, soap, and toilet paper dispensers; inappropriate behavior of other students; etc.).

25. Reinforce the student for displaying all behaviors that relate to taking care of his/her toileting needs in an appropriate manner.

207 Absent or tardy without legitimate reason (i.e., unexcused)

Goals:

1. The student will improve his/her attendance at school.
2. The student will improve his/her attendance in class.
3. The student will improve his/her punctuality.

Objectives:

1. The student will attend ___ out of ___ school days per week. (Gradually increase expectations as the student demonstrates success.)
2. The student will attend ___ out of ___ school days per month. (Gradually increase expectations as the student demonstrates success.)
3. The student will attend ___ out of ___ class periods per week. (Gradually increase expectations as the student demonstrates success.)
4. The student will attend ___ out of ___ class periods per month. (Gradually increase expectations as the student demonstrates success.)
5. The student will be on time to school on ___ out of ___ days per week. (Gradually increase expectations as the student demonstrates success.)
6. The student will be on time to school on ___ out of ___ days per month. (Gradually increase expectations as the student demonstrates success.)
7. The student will be on time to class on ___ out of ___ class periods per day. (Gradually increase expectations as the student demonstrates success.)
8. The student will be on time to class on ___ out of ___ class periods per week. (Gradually increase expectations as the student demonstrates success.)
9. The student will be on time to (specified activity) on ___ out of ___ days per week. (Gradually increase expectations as the student demonstrates success.)
10. The student will be on time to (specified activity) on ___ out of ___ days per month. (Gradually increase expectations as the student demonstrates success.)

Interventions:

1. Determine why the student is not arriving at activities at the specified times.

2. Make certain that the student's daily schedule follows an established routine.

3. Limit the number of interruptions in the student's schedule.

4. Make certain the student has adequate time to get to an activity.

5. Make certain that the student knows how to get from one activity to another.

6. Use a timer to help the student get to activities at specified times.

7. Provide the student with verbal cues when it is time to change activities (e.g., "It is time for the red group to have reading." "Now it is time for the red group to put away materials and move to the next activity." etc.).

8. Provide the student with a schedule of daily events so he/she will know which activities to attend and at what times.

9. Ask the student the reason for not attending school or arriving at activities at the specified times. The student may have the most accurate perception as to why he/she is absent/tardy.

10. Help the student understand that it is permissible to leave work unfinished and return to it at a later time.

11. Determine if there are aspects of activities that the student dislikes. Remove, reduce, or modify the unpleasant aspects of activities to encourage the student to be on time for and participate in activities.

12. Make certain that the student is successful in school-related activities. The student will be more likely to be present/prompt if he/she experiences success.

13. Make the student a leader of the activity or group.

14. Make certain the student has all necessary materials for activities.

15. Give the student a preferred responsibility to be performed at the beginning of each activity.

16. Make certain that other students do not make it unpleasant for the student to attend activities.

17. Give the student a schedule of daily events to be signed by each teacher to document promptness.

18. Have the student document personal attendance at the end of each activity.

19. Make certain the student is appropriately placed according to ability level in those classes in which he/she is enrolled (e.g., the class is not too difficulty, the class is not too easy).

20. Do not force the student to interact with others or do things that make him/her uncomfortable and would cause the student to want to be absent/tardy.

21. Begin each day with a fun activity which will cause the student to want to attend and be on time for class.

22. Choose a peer to model arriving at an activity at the specified time for the student.

23. Communicate with the parents (e.g., notes home, phone calls, etc.) to share information concerning the student's progress. The parents may reinforce the student at home for school attendance/promptness.

24. Reinforce the student for coming to an activity within a given period of time. As the student becomes more successful at being punctual, gradually reduce the length of time the student has to come to an activity.

25. Reinforce those students in the classroom who come to an activity at the specified time.

26. Establish classroom rules:
- Work on-task.
- Work quietly.
- Remain in your seat.
- Finish task.
- Meet task expectations.

Review rules often. Reinforce students for following rules.

27. Communicate with parents, agencies, or the appropriate parties to inform them of the problem, determine the cause of the problem, and consider possible solutions to the problem.

28. Record or chart attendance/promptness with the student.

29. Begin the day or class with a success-oriented activity which is likely to be highly reinforcing for the student.

30. Give the student a preferred responsibility to be performed at the beginning of each day or each class (e.g., feeding the classroom pet, helping to get the classroom ready for the day, etc.).

31. Reinforce the student for getting on the bus or leaving home on time.

32. Assess the degree of task difficulty in comparison with the student's ability to perform the task successfully.

33. Provide the student with as many high-interest activities as possible.

34. Involve the student in extracurricular activities.

35. Provide the student with many social and academic successes.

36. Provide the student with academic activities presented in the most attractive and interesting manner possible.

37. Require the student's attendance to be documented by his/her teachers (e.g., have teachers sign an attendance card).

38. Interact with the student in a positive manner frequently throughout the day.

39. Collect anecdotal information on the student's absences/tardies. If a trend can be determined, remove the student from the situation, modify the situation, or help the student develop the skills to be more successful in the situation.

40. Have the parent bring the student to school.

41. Have a responsible peer accompany the student to school/activities.

42. Establish a time for the student to leave his/her home in the morning.

43. Require that time spent away from class/school be made up at recess, during lunch, or after school.

44. Have the student document personal attendance at the end of each school day (e.g., have the student maintain a record of attendance in the library, office, etc., and fill in the data at the end of each day).

45. Reduce the emphasis on competition. Repeated failure may cause the student to be tardy or absent to avoid competitive situations.

46. Provide the student with the option of going to the special education resource room when he/she would otherwise not attend school and work toward a goal of increased attendance in regular classes.

47. Make certain the student and parents are aware of the laws involving attendance in school.

48. Evaluate the appropriateness of the task to determine (a) if the task is too easy, (b) if the task is too difficult, and (c) if the length of time scheduled to complete the task is adequate.

49. Write a contract with the student specifying what behavior is expected (e.g., being in attendance, coming to school/class on time), and what reinforcement will be made available when the terms of the contract have been met.

50. Reinforce those students who come to school/class.

51. Speak with the student to explain (a) what the student is doing wrong (e.g., being absent from school/class, coming late to an activity) and (b) what the student should be doing (e.g., being in attendance, coming to an activity at the specified time).

52. Reinforce the student for coming to school/class or coming to an activity at the specified time: (a) give the student a tangible reward (e.g., classroom privileges, line leading, passing out materials, five minutes free time, etc.) or (b) give the student an intangible reward (e.g., praise, handshake, smile, etc.).

53. Schedule time in the special education resource room at the beginning, middle, and end of each day to support attendance.

54. Help the student develop friendships which may encourage his/her attendance in school/class.

55. Maintain open communication with the student's family to make certain that the student is leaving for school at the designated time.

208 Brings inappropriate or illegal materials to school

Goals:
1. The student will bring appropriate materials to school.
2. The student will bring legal materials to school.
3. The student will follow the school's code of conduct.

Objectives:
1. The student will bring appropriate materials to school ___out of ___days per week.
2. The student will bring appropriate materials to school ___out of ___days per month.
3. The student will bring appropriate materials to school ___out of ___days per semester.
4. The student will bring legal materials to school ___out of ___days per week.
5. The student will bring legal materials to school ___out of ___days per month.
6. The student will bring legal materials to school ___out of ___days per semester.
7. The student will refrain from bringing magazines to school ___out of ___days per week.
8. The student will refrain from bringing magazines to school ___out of ___days per month.
9. The student will refrain from bringing magazines to school ___out of ___days per semester.
10. The student will refrain from bringing weapons to school ___out of ___days per week.
11. The student will refrain from bringing weapons to school ___out of ___days per month.
12. The student will refrain from bringing weapons to school ___out of ___days per semester.
13. The student will refrain from bringing drugs to school ___out of ___days per week.
14. The student will refrain from bringing drugs to school ___out of ___days per month.
15. The student will refrain from bringing drugs to school ___out of ___days per semester.
16. The student will refrain from bringing alcohol to school ___out of ___days per week.
17. The student will refrain from bringing alcohol to school ___out of ___days per month.
18. The student will refrain from bringing alcohol to school ___out of ___days per semester.
19. The student will arrive at school sober ___out of ___days per week.
20. The student will arrive at school sober ___out of ___days per month.
21. The student will arrive at school sober ___out of ___days per semester.
22. The student will be free from the influence of drugs ___out of ___days per week.
23. The student will be free from the influence of drugs ___out of ___days per month.
24. The student will be free from the influence of drugs ___out of ___days per semester.
25. The student will not consume drugs or alcohol at school ___out of ___days per week.
26. The student will not consume drugs or alcohol at school ___out of ___days per month.
27. The student will not consume drugs or alcohol at school ___out of ___days per semester.
28. The student will not possess drugs or alcohol at school ___out of ___days per week.
29. The student will not possess drugs or alcohol at school ___out of ___days per month.
30. The student will not possess drugs or alcohol at school ___out of ___days per semester.

Interventions:

1. Reinforce the student for demonstrating appropriate behavior: (a) give the student a tangible reward (e.g., classroom privileges, line leading, passing out materials, five minutes free time, etc.) or (b) give the student an intangible reward (e.g., praise, handshake, smile, etc.).

2. Speak with the student to explain (a) what he/she is doing wrong (e.g., bringing inappropriate or illegal materials to school) and (b) what he/she should be doing (e.g., following an established code of conduct, following rules, taking care of responsibilities, etc.).

3. Establish classroom rules:
- Work on-task.
- Work quietly.
- Remain in your seat.
- Finish task.
- Meet task expectations.

Review rules often. Reinforce students for following rules.

4. Reinforce those students in the classroom who demonstrate appropriate behavior.

5. Reinforce the student for demonstrating appropriate behavior based on the length of time he/she can be successful. As the student demonstrates success, gradually increase the length of time required for reinforcement.

6. Remove the student from the group or activity until he/she can demonstrate appropriate behavior and self-control.

7. Write a contract with the student specifying what behavior is expected (e.g., not bringing alcohol to school) and what reinforcement will be made available when the terms of the contract have been met.

8. Communicate with parents (e.g., notes home, phone calls, etc.) to share information concerning the student's progress. The parents may reinforce the student at home for demonstrating appropriate behavior at school.

9. Encourage the student's parents to be positive and supportive with the student as opposed to being negative and threatening.

10. Provide a drug information program for the individual student, the class, or the student body.

11. Provide information on penalties for possession or use of alcohol and drugs at school.

12. Involve the student in extracurricular activities to help him/her develop appropriate interests.

13. Identify individuals the student may contact with his/her concerns (e.g., guidance counselor, school nurse, social worker, school psychologist, etc.).

14. Share concerns with the administration and seek referral to an agency for investigation of alcohol or drug abuse.

15. Encourage the student to become involved in athletic or extracurricular activities.

16. Assign the student activities which would require interactions with a respected role model (e.g., older student, high school student, college student, community leader, someone held in esteem, etc.).

17. Provide the student with intelligent, accurate information concerning drugs and alcohol rather than sensationalized scare tactic information.

18. Provide many opportunities for social and academic success.

19. Encourage the student to excel in a particular area of interest (e.g., provide information for the student; provide personal and professional support; sponsor the student; etc.).

20. Maintain frequent contact with the student during school hours (e.g., follow up on details of earlier communications; maintain a direction for conversation; etc.).

21. Lead and direct the student. Do not lecture and make demands.

22. Maintain anecdotal records of the student's behavior to check patterns or changes in behavior.

23. When natural consequences from peers occur (e.g., criticism, loss of friendship, etc.) as the result of the use of drugs or alcohol at school bring the consequences to the attention of the student.

24. Communicate with parents, agencies, or the appropriate parties to inform them of the problem, determine the cause of the problem, and consider possible solutions to the problem.

25. Act as a resource for parents by providing information on agencies, counseling programs, etc.

26. Teach the student to be satisfied with his/her best effort rather than perfection.

27. Reduce the emphasis on competition and help the student realize that success is individually defined.

28. Be willing to take the time to listen, share, and talk with the student.

29. Increase your own professional knowledge of laws and treatment concerning drug or alcohol use and abuse.

30. Provide appropriate reading material (e.g., magazines, novels, etc.) at school, which is of interest to the student, so that he/she will not bring inappropriate reading material to school.

31. Maintain adequate supervision at all times and in all areas of the school (e.g., hallways, bathrooms, between classes, before and after school, school grounds, etc.).

32. Teach the student alternative ways to deal with demands, challenges, and pressures of the school-age experience (e.g., deal with problems when they arise, practice self-control at all times, share problems or concerns with others, etc.).

209 Does not come to or is not ready for an activity at the specified time

Goals:

1. The student will be ready for an activity at the specified time.
2. The student will be ready for an activity at the specified time in academic settings.
3. The student will be ready for an activity at the specified time in nonacademic settings.
4. The student will be ready for an activity at the specified time outside the classroom.
5. The student will be ready for an activity at the specified time in the classroom.

Objectives:

1. The student will be ready for an activity at the specified time with verbal reminders on ____out of ____ occasions.
2. The student will be ready for activity at the specified time with physical assistance on ____out of ____ occasions.
3. The student will independently get ready for an activity at the specified time on ____out of ____ occasions.
4. The student will rely on environmental cues (e.g., clocks, bells, lights, other students coming to the activity) to get ready for an activity at the specified time on ____out of ____occasions.
5. The student will be ready for an activity within a given period of time on ____out of ____occasions.
6. The student will be ready for an activity on time on ____out of ____occasions.

Interventions:

1. Reinforce the student for being ready for an activity at the specified time: (a) give the student a tangible reward (e.g., classroom privileges, line leading, passing out materials, five minutes free time, etc.) or (b) give the student an intangible reward (e.g., praise, handshake, smile, etc.).

2. Speak to the student to explain (a) what he/she is doing wrong (e.g., coming late/early to an activity) and (b) what he/she should be doing (e.g., coming to an activity at the specified time).

3. Establish classroom rules:
- Come to class on time.
- Work on-task.
- Work quietly.
- Remain in your seat.
- Finish task.
- Meet task expectations.

Review rules often. Reinforce students for following rules.

4. Choose a peer to model being ready for an activity at the specified time for the student.

5. Reinforce the student for coming to an activity within a given period of time. As the student becomes more successful in being punctual, gradually reduce the length of time the student has to come to an activity.

6. Write a contract with the student specifying what behavior is expected (e.g., coming to class on time, having necessary materials, etc.) and what reinforcement will be made available when the terms of the contract have been met.

7. Communicate with parents (e.g., notes home, phone calls, etc.) to share information concerning the student's progress. The parents may reinforce the student at home for being ready for activities at the specified time at school.

8. Evaluate the appropriateness of the task to determine (a) if the task is too easy, (b) if the task is too difficult, and (c) if the length of time scheduled to complete the task is adequate.

9. Give the student a specific responsibility to be performed at the beginning of each activity to encourage him/her to be on time.

10. Have a peer accompany the student to activities.

11. Make certain that the student's daily schedule follows an established routine.

12. Limit the number of interruptions in the student's schedule.

13. Make certain the student has adequate time to get to an activity.

14. Make certain that the student knows how to get from one activity to another.

15. Use a timer to help the student get to activities at specified times.

16. Reinforce those students in the classroom who are ready for an activity at the specified time.

17. Provide the student with verbal cues when it is time to change activities (e.g., "It is time for the red group to have reading." "Now it is time for the red group to put away materials and move to the next activity." etc.).

18. Determine why the student is not ready for activities at the specified times.

19. Ask the student why he/she is not ready for activities at the specified times. The student may have the most accurate perception as to why he/she is not ready for activities at the specified times.

20. Help the student understand that it is permissible to leave work unfinished and return to it at a later time.

21. Determine if there are aspects of activities that the student dislikes. Remove, reduce, or modify the unpleasant aspects of activities to encourage the student to be ready for and participate in activities.

22. Make the student responsible for time missed (e.g., if the student misses five minutes of an activity, he/she must make up the time during recess, lunch, or other desired activities).

23. Provide the student with a schedule of daily events so that he/she will know which activities to attend and their times.

24. Make certain that the student is successful in school-related and social activities. The student will be more likely to be ready for activities in which he/she experiences success.

25. Give the student a schedule of classes that must be signed by every instructor to document his/her promptness.

26. Make certain that other students do not make it unpleasant for the student to attend activities.

27. Make certain the student has all necessary materials for activities.

28. Record or chart promptness with the student.

29. Begin activities with a task that is highly reinforcing to the student.

30. Assess appropriateness of the degree of difficulty of tasks in comparison with the student's ability.

31. Provide the student with as many high-interest activities as possible.

32. Provide the student academic activities in the most attractive manner possible.

33. Make the student a leader of the activity or group.

34. Collect anecdotal information on the student's tardy behavior. If a trend can be determined, remove the student from the situation and/or help the student be prompt.

35. Have the student document his/her attendance at the end of each activity.

36. Make certain the student is appropriately placed according to his/her ability level in those classes in which he/she is enrolled.

37. Reduce the emphasis on competition. Repeated failure may cause the student to avoid being on time for activities which are competitive.

38. Teach the student how to use a calender to acknowledge upcoming activities that are not part of the daily routine (e.g., Tuesday at 12:00-Field trip to the Zoo, etc.).

39. Deliver directions in a supportive rather than a threatening manner (e.g., "Please come to your reading group now." rather than "You had better come to your reading group or else!" etc.).

40. Give the student a special responsibility before the group meets (e.g., sharpening pencils, arranging chairs, passing out books, etc.).

41. Use a timer to help the student know how much time he/she has to follow through with directions.

42. Treat the student with respect. Talk in an objective manner at all times.

43. Be careful to avoid embarrassing the student by giving him/her orders, demands, etc., in front of others.

44. Make certain the student knows how to tell time and has an understanding of his/her daily routine.

45. Provide the student with a schedule of events for the day to keep at his/her desk. Make notes of any special materials needed for an activity.

46. Make certain the student has a working watch or clock available to encourage his/her promptness to an activity.

47. Along with a directive, provide an incentive statement (e.g., "When you come to your reading group, you may pass out the books." "Please come to your reading group early to help arrange the chairs." etc.).

48. Teach the student to use a pocket calender to record specific times, places and activities that need to be remembered.

49. Teach the student organizational skills (e.g., before leaving the classroom, make certain materials are put away; take all necessary materials along; arrive five minutes early; etc.).

50. Allow natural consequences to occur as a result of the student's inability to be ready for an activity at the specified time (e.g., miss an assembly, miss the bus, late for class, etc.).

210 Does not conform to the requirements of various situations

Goal:

1. The student will conform to the requirements of various situations.

Objectives:

1. The student will follow ____ out of ____ verbal directions.
2. The student will follow through with directions given by school personnel within ____ minutes. (Gradually increase expectations as the student demonstrates success.)
3. The student will stop an activity when told to do so by school personnel on ____ out of ____ trials.
4. The student will behave in such a way as to demonstrate that he/she considered the consequences of his/her behavior on ____ out of ____ trials.
5. The student will follow school rules on ____ out of ____ trials.
6. The student will demonstrate behavior appropriate for the situation on ____ out of ____ trials.
7. The student will follow the rules of the classroom on ____ out of ____ trials.
8. The student will demonstrate appropriate care and handling of others property on ____ out of ____ trials.
9. The student will stay in an assigned area for the specified time period on ____ out of ____ trials.
10. The student will demonstrate appropriate behavior on the school grounds before and after school on ____ out of ____ trials.
11. The student will demonstrate appropriate behavior on the school bus on ____ out of ____ trials.
12. The student will demonstrate appropriate behavior walking to and from school on ____ out of ____ trials.
13. The student will independently follow rules in nonacademic settings on ____ out of ____ occasions.
14. The student will walk in the halls when moving from one location to another on ____ out of ____ trials.
15. The student will refrain from throwing food in the cafeteria on ____ out of ____ trials.
16. The student will keep his/her food on his/her plate on ____ out of ____ trials.
17. The student will work quietly in the library on ____ out of ____ trials.
18. The student will talk quietly with a peer when in the library on ____ out of ____ trials.
19. The student will handle school property with care on ____ out of ____ trials.
20. The student will walk quietly through the halls on ____ out of ____ trials.
21. The student will interact appropriately with his/her peers during lunch, recess, break time, etc., on ____ out of ____ trials.

Interventions:

1. Reinforce the student for conforming to the requirements of various situations: (a) give the student a tangible reward (e.g., classroom privileges, line leading, passing out materials, five minutes free time, etc.) or (b) give the student an intangible reward (e.g., praise, handshake, smile, etc.).

2. Speak to the student to explain (a) what he/she is doing wrong (e.g., failing to conform to the requirements of various situations) and (b) what he/she should be doing (e.g., conforming to the requirements of various situations).

3. Establish classroom rules:
- Walk in halls.
- Arrive to class on time.
- Respect the privacy of others.
- Talk quietly in the halls.

Review rules often. Reinforce students for following rules.

4. Reinforce those students in the classroom who conform to the requirements of various situations (e.g., going to and from school, in the cafeteria, etc.).

5. Reinforce the student for conforming to the requirements of various situations based on the number of times he/she can be successful. As the student demonstrates success, gradually increase the number of times required for reinforcement.

6. Write a contract with the student specifying what behavior is expected (e.g., walking in halls, sitting quietly on the bus, etc.) and what reinforcement will be made available when the terms of the contract have been met.

7. Communicate with parents (e.g., notes home, phone calls, etc.) to share information concerning the student's progress. The parents may reinforce the student at home for conforming to the requirements of various situations (e.g., rules, regulation, expectations, laws).

8. Evaluate the appropriateness of the task to determine (a) if the task is too easy, (b) if the task is too difficult, and (c) if the length of time scheduled to complete the task is adequate.

9. Have the student question any directions, explanations, instructions he/she does not understand.

10. Structure the environment so that the student remains active and involved.

11. Maintain visibility to and from the student. The teacher should be able to see the student and the student should be able to see the teacher. Make eye contact possible at all times.

12. Maintain maximum supervision of the student and gradually decrease supervision as the student is able to conform to the requirements of various situations.

13. Have the student maintain a chart representing the amount of time spent conforming to rules, regulations, expectations, etc., with reinforcement for increasing acceptable behavior.

14. Practice mobility to be frequently near the student.

15. Provide the student with many social and academic successes.

16. Provide the student with positive feedback that indicates he/she is successful.

17. Post rules and regulation in various places, including on the student's desk, in the hallways, etc.

18. Be a consistent authority figure (e.g., be consistent in relationships with students).

19. Provide the student with optional courses of action to prevent total refusal to conform to rules, regulations, expectations, laws, etc. (e.g., return to the classroom).

20. Intervene early to prevent the student's behavior from leading to contagion for other students.

21. Require the student to verbalize the rules, regulations, expectation, etc., at designated times throughout the day (e.g., before school, recess, lunch, at the end of the day, etc.).

22. Choose a peer to model conforming to school rules, regulations, expectations, etc.

23. Interact with the student frequently to determine if school rules are being followed.

24. Make certain that all educators maintain consistent enforcement of school rules and regulations.

25. Have the student question any rules, regulations, expectations, etc., he/she does not understand.

26. Provide the student with a list of school rules and/or behavior expectations to carry at all times in the school environment.

27. Help the student identify specific school rules he/she has difficulty following and make these rules goals for behavior improvement.

28. Separate the student from the peer(s) who stimulates his/her inappropriate behavior.

29. Make certain that rules and behavior expectations are consistent throughout the school and classrooms.

30. Model for the student those behaviors he/she is expected to display in the school environment.

31. Have a peer accompany the student in nonacademic settings.

32. Make certain the behavioral demands are appropriate for the student's ability level (e.g., staying in line, waiting a turn, moving with a group, sitting at a table with a group, moving about the building alone, etc.).

33. Make certain the student is actively involved in the environment (e.g., give the student responsibilities, activities, and errands to run to provide purposeful behavior).

34. Reinforce the student for moving from one place to another in an appropriate length of time.

35. Have the student carry a point card at all times so that he/she can be reinforced anywhere in the school environment for conforming to rules, regulations, expectations, laws, etc.

36. Inform other school personnel of any behavior problems the student may have so supervision and assistance may be provided.

37. Reduce the emphasis on competition. Competitive situations may cause the student to disregard the requirements of various situations.

38. Be consistent in applying consequences for behavior (e.g., appropriate behavior receives positive consequences, while inappropriate behavior receives negative consequences).

39. Reinforce the student for remaining in assigned areas (e.g., play areas, student lounge, recreational area, etc.).

40. Use related consequences for the student's inappropriate behavior (e.g., running in the halls results in having to walk with an adult, throwing food in the cafeteria results in having to sit next to an adult when eating, disruption in the library requires additional adult supervision, etc.).

41. Choose a peer to model appropriate behavior in various situations for the student.

42. Assign a peer to accompany the student in various situations to monitor and encourage appropriate behavior.

43. Accompany the student in various situations to teach the student appropriate behavior (e.g., using sidewalks, crossing at crosswalks, going directly to class, walking in the hallway, remaining seated while eating in the cafeteria, etc.).

44. Assign the student responsibilities to perform in various situations (e.g., act as the bus driver's assistant to monitor behavior, run office errands, pick up trash on the school grounds, etc.).

45. Reinforce the student for going directly from one location to another.

Goal:

1. The student will demonstrate positive, replacement behaviors instead of deliberately starting fires.

Objectives:

1. The student will demonstrate positive, replacement behaviors rather than deliberately setting fires for all possible trials in ____ weeks/months.
2. The student will refrain from deliberately setting fires for all possible trials in ____ weeks/months.

Interventions:

1. Reinforce the student for demonstrating appropriate behaviors instead of setting fires: (a) give the student a tangible reward (e.g., classroom privileges, line leading, passing out material, five minutes free time, etc.) or (b) give the student an intangible reward (e.g., praise, handshake, smile, etc.).

2. Reinforce those students who chose a positive alternative instead of behaving in an inappropriate or violent manner.

3. Communicate with parents (e.g., notes home, phone calls, etc.) regarding the student's progress with social and communication skills to replace fire setting behavior. The parents may reinforce the student for the use of positive social skills at school, at home, and in community environments.

4. Provide the student with positive role models who use problem-solving techniques to resolve problems.

5. The student who thinks about and/or deliberately sets fires may need additional services and supports (e.g., counseling).

6. Provide outlets for the student who thinks about or deliberately sets fires (e.g., art work, diary writing or self-recording, etc.).

7. Provide close monitoring to protect all concerned.

8. Let the student know you care about his/her thoughts and feelings.

9. Provide information and instruction on stress-management techniques.

10. Develop coping techniques for the student tailored to his/her preferences and abilities (e.g., taking two slow, deep breaths; removing himself/herself to another part of the classroom to calm down; placing head on table or desk for 20 seconds, etc.). Rehearse use of these skills to provide replacement activity for deliberate fire setting.

11. Provide the student with a clear chain of command he/she and others in the environment need to use to process complaints, grievances, etc. Rehearse each communication link, and praise the student for resorting to chain of command.

12. Develop a contract with the student that specifies positive behaviors to replace deliberate fire setting, and the positive reinforcements a student may obtain by meeting contract terms.

13. The student may associate "bad feelings" with "being bad." Encourage the student to view himself/herself as good, and to accept feelings. Encourage the student to view the choices he/she makes as either acceptable or unacceptable, poor/good, etc.

14. In the interests of individual and group safety, never assume a student will not carry out expressed plans to deliberately set fires. Always provide the student and any potential victims close monitoring.

15. Do not indirectly reinforce a student for his/her expressed aggressive thoughts, such as thoughts about deliberately setting fires. Provide the student with more verbal response for positive actions you would like to see again to prevent or discourage the student from expressing and attempting to act upon aggressive thoughts for attention.

16. Encourage the student to think through the consequences of setting fires:

- (a) Think about the thoughts and feelings of others (e.g., family members, friends, classmates, school administration, etc.) if revenge occurred;
- (b) think about the potential consequences to himself/herself if revenge occurred;
- (c) identify positive alternatives to revenge;
- (d) identify thoughts/feelings of others should the positive alternative be attempted; and
- (e) identify his/her thoughts/feelings should the positive alternatives be attempted.

17. Assist the student in actively implementing his/her reasonable, positive alternative to deliberate fire setting, but make sure the student

- (a) is calm (e.g., no longer feeling hostile);
- (b) has developed his/her thoughts and plans in the event the positive alternative doesn't work (e.g., will use coping skills and positive forms of self-expression, etc.);
- (c) has developed a "Plan B" which consists of another chosen positive alternative to try; and
- (d) will evaluate the effectiveness of his/her approach with the teacher after this has been attempted.

18. Provide positive activities to

- (a) give the student matters of interest to focus upon, think through, and act upon other than fire setting;
- (b) give the student opportunities to experience success (this may help decrease stress related to frustration); and
- (c) give the student positive, structured opportunities to work with others to encourage productive teamwork and hopefully render vengeful thoughts/behaviors counterproductive.

19. Provide the student with focus for his/her actions/behaviors by developing with him/her a daily schedule. Reinforce the student for

- (a) initiating schedule development;
- (b) beginning scheduled activities independently;
- (c) following his/her schedule;
- (d) completing scheduled activities; and
- (e) all positive attempts at working on the schedule and on scheduled activities.

20. Students who think about and/or attempt deliberate fire setting may need opportunities for teamwork, but may overreact to competitive activities. Allow the student the chance to work in small groups or teams on activities, but structure team learning opportunities so these are not competitive by establishing sincere ways of providing merit for each group's efforts.

21. The student prone to such negative reactions as fire setting may also be prone to feelings of failure. Provide the student with frequent, natural opportunities to feel successful on a daily basis.

22. Provide positive alternative activities instead of ongoing activities when the student indicates signs of frustration or overstimulation to prevent problems from occurring.

23. Review existing information about students who deliberately attempt to set fires to determine whether or not the behavior is an attempt to communicate a need for attention. If so, design behavioral approaches to include frequent opportunities for the student to receive attention when he/she is following class rules and is positively attempting scheduled activities.

24. Establish mutual eye contact and positive communication with the student. Make certain he/she is seated close to the teacher for monitoring and communication.

25. Know the student's antecedents or signals of stress, frustration, and difficult feelings and provide him/her with additional structure at these times.

26. Continuity between home and school can be critical to intervention/prevention of deliberate fire setting. Work with parents and support sources (e.g., psychological counseling, psychiatric counseling, etc.) to establish continuity.

27. Because fire setting might be vicariously reinforcing (e.g., the student might enjoy the appearance of fire trucks, the "break" in the day, the damage the fire causes, the explosion of noise and confusion often caused by a fire, etc.), make certain the student has frequent opportunities to seek and gain attention for positive behaviors and participation in activities.

28. While close monitoring and supervision is always recommended, the student who deliberately sets fires in one environment may not necessarily do so in another. Look for differences between environments (e.g., types of activities, structure, consequences in each environment, etc.) for ideas to prevent/decrease risk of fire setting.

29. Provide the student with a well-structured day full of positive activity choices. Active participation in positive choices can be counterproductive to fire setting and other undesirable behaviors.

30. Consequences need to be immediate, nonpunitive, and delivered in a low key, private manner. Otherwise, the student who deliberately sets fires for attention may receive vicarious reinforcement.

31. Provide the student with structured celebrations (e.g., well-monitored free activity time, well-monitored small group outings, etc.) for actively engaging in positive activities rather than fire setting.

212 Destroys school, teachers', or other students' property

Goals:
1. The student will take proper care of school property.
2. The student will care for school property in a responsible manner.
3. The student will take proper care of other students' property.
4. The student will care for other students' property in a responsible manner.

Objectives:
1. The student will return school property to a designated location in the same or better condition on ___ out of ___ trials.
2. The student will return other students' property in the same or better condition on ___ out of ___ trials.
3. The student will care for school property in a responsible manner on ___ out of ___ trials.
4. The student will care for other students' property in a responsible manner on ___ out of ___ trials.
5. The student will demonstrate appropriate care and handling of school property on ___ out of ___ trials.
6. The student will demonstrate appropriate care and handling of other students' property on ___ out of ___ trials.
7. The student will refrain from defacing school property on ___ out of ___ trials.
8. The student will refrain from defacing other students' property on ___ out of ___ trials.
9. The student will refrain from damaging school property on ___ out of ___ trials.
10. The student will refrain from damaging other students' property on ___ out of ___ trials.
11. The student will refrain from vandalizing school property on ___ out of ___ trials.
12. The student will refrain from vandalizing other students' property on ___ out of ___ trials.

Interventions:

1. Provide time at the beginning of each day to help the student organize the materials that will be used throughout the day.

2. Provide the student with adequate work space (e.g., a large desk or table at which to work).

3. Provide storage space for materials the student is not using at any particular time.

4. Reduce distracting stimuli (e.g., place the student on the front row, provide a carrel or quiet place away from distractions, etc.). Overstimulation may cause the student to misuse others' property.

5. Interact frequently with the student to prompt organizational skills and appropriate use of materials.

6. Assign the student organizational responsibilities in the classroom (e.g., equipment, software materials, etc.).

7. Limit the student's use of materials (e.g., provide the student with only those materials necessary at any given time).

8. Model organization and appropriate use of work materials (e.g., putting materials away before getting other materials out, having a place for all materials, maintaining an organized desk area, following a schedule for the day, etc.).

9. Provide adequate time for the completion of activities. Inadequate time for completion of activities may result in the student's misuse of others' property.

10. Allow natural consequences to occur as the result of the student's inability to appropriately care for and handle others' property (e.g., property not maintained appropriately may be lost or not usable).

11. Assess the quality and clarity of directions, explanations, and instructions given to the student concerning the care and handling of others' property.

12. Assist the student in beginning each task to reduce impulsive behavior.

13. Provide the student with structure for all academic activities (e.g., specific directions, routine format for tasks, time units, etc.).

14. Give the student a checklist of materials necessary for each activity.

15. Minimize materials needed.

16. Provide an organizer for materials inside the student's desk.

17. Teach the student appropriate care and handling of others' property (e.g., sharpening borrowed pencils, keeping books free of marks and tears, etc.).

18. Make certain that all personal property is labeled with the student's name.

19. Point out to the student that borrowing personal property from others does not reduce his/her responsibility for the property.

20. Teach the student how to conserve rather than waste materials (e.g., amount of glue, tape, etc., to use; putting lids, caps, and tops on such materials as markers, pens, bottles, jars, cans; etc.).

21. Teach the student appropriate ways to deal with anger and frustration rather than destroying others' property (e.g., pencils, pens, workbooks, notebooks, textbooks, etc.).

22. Teach the student to maintain property belonging to others (e.g., keep property with him/her, know where property is at all times, secure property in locker, etc.).

23. Provide the student with an appropriate place to store/secure others' property (e.g., desk, locker, closet, etc.) and require the student to store all property when not in use.

24. Teach the student that the failure to care for others' property will result in the loss of freedom to use others' property.

25. Provide reminders (e.g., a list of property or materials) to help the student maintain and care for school property.

26. Limit the student's freedom to take property from school if he/she is unable to remember to return the items.

27. Limit the student's opportunities to use others' property if the student is unable to care for his/her own personal property.

28. Reduce the number of materials for which the student is responsible. As the student demonstrates appropriate care of property, gradually increase the number.

29. Teach the student safety rules in the care and handling of others' property and materials (e.g., pencils, scissors, compass; biology, industrial arts and home economics materials; etc.).

30. Require that lost or damaged property be replaced by the student. If the student cannot replace the property, restitution can be made by working at school.

31. Make certain the student is not inadvertently reinforced for losing or damaging property by providing him/her with new materials. Provide the student with used or damaged materials, copies of the materials, etc., rather than new materials.

32. Teach the student rules for the care and handling of others' property (e.g., always ask to use others' property, treat the property with care, inform the teacher if the property becomes damaged, return the property in the same or better condition, etc.).

33. Do not permit peers to allow the student to use their property if he/she is not able to care for it properly.

34. Remove others' property from the student if he/she is unable to appropriately care for and handle the property.

35. Maintain mobility throughout the classroom to supervise the student's care and handling of others' property.

36. Remove the student from the group or activity until he/she can demonstrate appropriate behavior and self-control.

37. Structure the environment to reduce free or unplanned time which is likely to contribute to the student's inappropriate behavior.

38. Maintain visibility to and from the student. The teacher should be able to see the student and the student should be able to see the teacher. Make eye contact possible at all times.

39. Make the necessary adjustments in the environment to prevent the student from experiencing stress, frustration, anger, etc., as much as possible.

40. Prevent the student from becoming overstimulated by an activity.

41. Make the student responsible for specific materials (e.g., tape recorder, overhead projector, microscope, etc.) in the school environment to facilitate a sense of responsibility and obligation to use the materials with care.

42. Teach the student to respect others and their belongings by respecting the student's belongings.

43. Make certain the student is always under adult supervision.

44. Make certain the student is aware of local and federal laws regarding the destruction of others' property.

45. Require the student to replace damaged items when he/she destroys others' property.

46. Teach the student to "think" before acting (e.g., ask himself/herself "What is happening?" "What am I doing?" "What should I do?" "What will be best for me?").

47. Have the student question any directions, explanations, and instructions not understood.

48. Talk to the student about ways of handling situations successfully without conflict (e.g., walk away from a situation, change to another activity, ask for help, etc.).

49. Choose a peer to model appropriate care and handling of others' property for the student.

50. Evaluate the appropriateness of the task to determine (a) if the task is too easy, (b) if the task is too difficult, and (c) if the length of time scheduled to complete the task is adequate.

51. Communicate with parents (e.g., notes home, phone calls, etc.) to share information concerning the student's progress. The parents may reinforce the student at home for demonstrating appropriate care and handling of others' property at school.

52. Write a contract with the student specifying what behavior is expected (e.g., putting property away, returning property, etc.) and what reinforcement will be made available when the terms of the contract have been met.

53. Reinforce the student for demonstrating appropriate care and handling of others' property based on the length of time the student can be successful. As the student demonstrates success, gradually increase the length of time required for reinforcement.

54. Reinforce those students in the classroom who demonstrate appropriate care and handling of others' property.

55. Establish classroom rules:
- Work on-task.
- Work quietly.
- Remain in your seat.
- Finish task.
- Meet task expectations.

Review rules often. Reinforce students for following rules.

56. Reinforce the student for demonstrating appropriate care and handling of others' property: (a) give the student a tangible reward (e.g., classroom privileges, line leading, passing out materials, five minutes free time, etc.) or (b) give the student an intangible reward (e.g., praise, handshake, smile, etc.).

57. Speak to the student to explain (a) what the student is doing wrong (e.g., defacing property, destroying property, etc.) and (b) what the student should be doing (e.g., putting property away, returning property, etc.).

213 Does not demonstrate appropriate care and handling of others' property

Goal:

1. The student will demonstrate appropriate care and handling of others' property.

Objectives:

1. The student will appropriately care for and handle peers' property on _____ out of _____ trials.
2. The student will return peers' property in the same or better condition on _____ out of _____ trials.
3. The student will use peers' property in designated areas on _____ out of _____ trials.
4. The student will appropriately care for and handle peers' property with supervision on _____ out of _____ trials.
5. The student will appropriately care for and handle school property on _____ out of _____ trials.
6. The student will return school property in the same or better condition to the appropriate location on _____ out of _____ trials.
7. The student will use school property in designated areas on _____ out of _____ trials.
8. The student will care for and handle school property with supervision on _____ out of _____ trials.
9. The student will use others' property conservatively on _____ out of _____ trials.

Interventions:

1. Reinforce the student for demonstrating appropriate care and handling of others' property: (a) give the student a tangible reward (e.g., classroom privileges, line leading, passing out materials, five minutes free time, etc.) or (b) give the student an intangible reward (e.g., praise, handshake, smile, etc.).

2. Speak to the student to explain (a) what he/she is doing wrong (e.g., losing property, destroying property, etc.) and (b) what he/she should be doing (e.g., putting property away, returning property, etc.).

3. Establish classroom rules:
- Work on-task.
- Work quietly.
- Remain in your seat.
- Finish task.
- Meet task expectations.

Review rules often. Reinforce students for following rules.

4. Write a contract with the student specifying what behavior is expected (e.g., putting property away, returning property, etc.) and what reinforcement will be made available when the terms of the contract have been met.

5. Reinforce the student for demonstrating appropriate care and handling of others' property based on the length of time the student can be successful. As the student demonstrates success, gradually increase the length of time required for reinforcement.

6. Reinforce those students in the classroom who demonstrate appropriate care and handling of others' property.

7. Communicate with parents (e.g., notes home, phone calls, etc.) to share information concerning the student's progress. The parents may reinforce the student at home for demonstrating appropriate care and handling of others' property at school.

8. Choose a peer to model appropriate care and handling of others' property for the student.

9. Have the student question any directions, explanations, instructions he/she does not understand.

10. Provide time at the beginning of each day to help the student organize the materials he/she will use throughout the day.

11. Provide time at various points throughout the day to help the student organize materials he/she will use throughout the day (e.g., before school, break time, or lunch; end of the day; etc.).

12. Provide the student with structure for all academic activities (e.g., specific directions, routine format for tasks, time units, etc.).

13. Provide storage space for materials the student is not using.

14. Reduce distracting stimuli (e.g., place the student on the front row, provide a carrel or quiet place away from distractions, etc.). Overstimulation may cause the student to misuse others' property.

15. Interact frequently with the student to prompt organizational skills and appropriate use of materials.

16. Assign the student organizational responsibilities in the classroom (e.g., equipment, software, materials, etc.).

17. Limit the student's use of materials (e.g., provide only necessary materials to the student).

18. Model organization and appropriate use of work materials (e.g., putting materials away before getting out other materials, having a place for all materials, maintaining an organized desk area, following a schedule for the day, etc.).

19. Provide adequate time for the completion of activities. Inadequate time for completion of activities may result in the student's misuse of others' property.

20. Establish a routine to be followed for organization and appropriate use of work materials.

21. Require the student to organize his/her work area at regular intervals.

22. Allow natural consequences to occur as the result of the student's inability to appropriately care for and handle others' property (e.g., property not maintained appropriately may be lost or not usable).

23. Teach the student that failure to care for others' property will result in the loss of freedom to use others' property.

24. Assist the student in beginning each task to reduce impulsive behavior.

25. Provide the student with adequate work space (e.g., a large desk or table at which to work).

26. Give the student a checklist of materials necessary for each activity.

27. Minimize the amount of materials needed.

28. Provide an organizer inside the student's desk for materials.

29. Provide the student with an organizational checklist (e.g., routine activities and materials needed).

30. Teach the student appropriate care and handling of others' property (e.g., sharpening pencils, keeping books free of marks and tears, etc.).

31. Make certain that all personal property is labeled with the students' names.

32. Point out to the student that borrowing personal property from others does not reduce his/her responsibility for the property.

33. Teach the student how to conserve rather than waste materials (e.g., amount of glue, paper, tape, etc., to use; putting lids, caps, and tops on such materials as markers, pens, bottles, jars, cans, etc.).

34. Teach the student appropriate ways to deal with anger and frustration rather than destroying property belonging to others (e.g., pencils, pens, workbooks, notebooks, textbooks, etc.).

35. Teach the student to maintain property belonging to others (e.g., keep property with him/her, know where property is at all times, secure property in locker, etc.).

36. Provide the student with an appropriate place to store/secure others' property (e.g., desk, locker, closet, etc.). Require the student to store all property when not in use.

37. Assess the quality and clarity of directions, explanations, and instructions given to the student for use in the care and handling of others' property.

38. Provide reminders (e.g., a list of property or materials) to help the student maintain and care for school property.

39. Limit the student's freedom to take property from school if he/she is unable to remember to return such items.

40. Limit the student's opportunity to use others' property if he/she is unable to care for his/her own personal property.

41. Do not permit peers to allow the student to use their property if he/she is not able to care for it properly.

42. Teach the student safety rules in the care and handling of others' property and materials (e.g., pencils; scissors; compass; science, industrial arts, and home economics materials; etc.).

43. Require that lost or damaged property be replaced by the student. If the student cannot replace the property, restitution can be made by working at school.

44. Remove others' property from the student if he/she is unable to appropriately care for and handle the property.

45. Teach the student rules for the care and handling of others' property (e.g., always ask to use others' property; treat the property with care; inform the teacher if the property becomes damaged; return the property in the same or better condition than when it was borrowed; etc.).

46. Maintain mobility throughout the classroom to supervise the student's care and handling of others' property.

47. Make certain the student is not inadvertently reinforced for losing or damaging property (e.g. replace lost property with used or damaged materials, copies of the materials, etc., rather than new materials).

48. Reduce the number of materials for which the student is responsible. As the student demonstrates appropriate care of property, increase the number of materials for which the student is responsible.

49. Provide adequate transition time between activities for the student to organize himself/herself.

50. Permit the student to use only the amount of property that he/she can care for and handle appropriately. As the student demonstrates success, gradually increase the amount of property.

214 Does not demonstrate appropriate use of school-related materials

Goal:

1. The student will demonstrate appropriate use of school-related materials.

Objectives:

1. The student will use school-related materials for their designated purposes on _____ out of _____ trials.
2. The student will use school-related materials according to accepted procedures on _____ out of _____ trials.
3. The student will use school-related materials with supervision on _____ out of _____ trials.
4. The student will independently use school-related materials on _____ out of _____ trials.
5. The student will return school-related materials in the same or better condition on _____ out of _____ trials.

Interventions:

1. Reinforce the student for demonstrating appropriate use of school-related materials: (a) give the student a tangible reward (e.g., classroom privileges, line leading, passing out materials, five minutes free time, etc.) or (b) give the student an intangible reward (e.g., praise, handshake, smile, etc.).

2. Speak to the student to explain (a) what he/she is doing wrong (e.g., failing to use school-related materials appropriately) and (b) what he/she should be doing (e.g., using materials as directed).

3. Establish classroom rules:
- Work on-task.
- Work quietly.
- Remain in your seat.
- Finish task.
- Meet task expectations.

Review rules often. Reinforce students for following rules.

4. Provide time at the beginning of each day to help the student organize his/her school-related materials.

5. Reinforce the student for using school-related materials appropriately based on the length of time the student can be successful. As the student demonstrates success, gradually increase the length of time required for reinforcement.

6. Write a contract with the student specifying what behavior is expected (e.g., appropriate use of school-related materials) and what reinforcement will be made available when the terms of the contract have been met.

7. Communicate with parents (e.g., notes home, phone calls, etc.) to share information concerning the student's progress. The parents may reinforce the student at home for using school-related materials appropriately at school.

8. Evaluate the appropriateness of the task to determine (a) if the task is too easy, (b) if the task is too difficult, and (c) if the length of time scheduled to complete the task is adequate.

9. Choose a peer to model appropriate use of school-related materials for the student.

10. Have the student question any directions, explanations, instructions he/she does not understand.

11. Reinforce those students in the classroom who use school-related materials appropriately.

12. Provide time at various points throughout the day to help the student organize his/her school-related materials (e.g., before school, break time, or lunch; end of the day; etc.).

13. Provide the student with adequate work space (e.g., a larger desk or table at which to work).

14. Provide storage space for school-related materials the student is not using.

15. Reduce distracting stimuli (e.g., place the student on the front row; provide a carrel or quiet place away from distractions; etc.). This is used as a means of reducing distracting stimuli and not as a form of punishment.

16. Interact frequently with the student to prompt organizational skills and appropriate use of school-related materials.

17. Assign the student organizational responsibilities in the classroom (e.g., equipment, software, materials, etc.).

18. Limit the student's use of school-related materials (e.g., provide only necessary school-related materials to the student).

19. Model organization and appropriate use of school-related materials (e.g., putting materials away before getting out other materials, having a place for all materials, maintaining an organized desk area, following a schedule for the day, etc.).

20. Provide adequate transition time between activities for the student to organize himself/herself.

21. Establish a routine to be followed for organization and appropriate use of school-related materials.

22. Provide adequate time for the completion of activities.

23. Require the student to organize his/her work area at regular intervals. It is recommended that this be done at least three times per day or more often if necessary.

24. Supervise the student while he/she is performing schoolwork to monitor quality.

25. Allow natural consequences to occur as the result of the student's inability to organize or use school-related materials appropriately (e.g., materials not maintained appropriately may be lost or not usable).

26. Assess the quality and clarity of directions, explanations, and instructions given to the student.

27. Assist the student in beginning each task to reduce impulsive behavior.

28. Provide the student with structure for all academic activities (e.g., specific directions; routine format for tasks, time units, etc.).

29. Give the student a checklist of school-related materials necessary for each activity.

30. Minimize the amount of school-related materials needed.

31. Provide an organizer inside the student's desk for school-related materials.

32. Provide the student with an organizational checklist (e.g., routine activities and steps to follow).

33. Teach the student appropriate care of school-related materials (e.g., sharpening pencils, keeping books free of marks and tears, etc.).

34. Make certain that all of the student's school-related materials are labeled with his/her name.

35. Point out to the student that loaning his/her school-related materials to other students does not reduce his/her responsibility for the materials.

36. Teach the student to conserve rather than waste school-related materials (e.g., amount of glue, paper, tape, etc., to use; putting lids, caps, and tops on such materials as markers, pens, bottles, jars, cans, etc.).

37. Teach the student appropriate ways to deal with anger and frustration rather than destroying school-related materials.

38. Teach the student to maintain school-related materials (e.g., keep materials with him/her, know where materials are at all times, secure materials in lockers, etc.).

39. Provide the student with an appropriate place to store/secure school-related materials (e.g., desk, locker, closet, etc.). Require the student to store all materials not in use.

40. Explain to the student that failure to care for school-related materials will result in the loss of their use.

41. Provide reminders (e.g., a list of school-related materials) to help the student maintain and care for school-related materials.

42. Limit the student's freedom to take school-related materials from school if he/she is unable to return such items.

43. Teach the student the appropriate use of school-related materials (e.g., scissors; pencils; compass; rulers; science, industrial arts, and home economics materials; etc.).

44. Provide the student with verbal reminders of school-related materials needed for each activity.

45. Make certain that failure to have necessary school-related materials results in the loss of the opportunity to participate in activities or a failing grade for that day's activity.

46. Reduce the number of school-related materials for which the student is responsible. As the student demonstrates appropriate care of materials, increase the number of materials for which the student is responsible.

47. Teach the student safety rules in the handling of school-related materials (e.g., pencils; scissors; compass; science, industrial arts, and home economics materials; etc.).

48. Require that lost or damaged school-related materials be replaced by the student. If the student cannot replace the property, restitution can be made by working at school.

49. Make certain the student is not inadvertently reinforced for losing or damaging school-related materials (e.g., replace lost materials with used or damaged materials, copies of the materials, etc., rather than new materials).

50. Limit the student's opportunity to use school-related materials if he/she is unable to care for his/her own personal property.

215 Is not honest

Goals:

1. The student will relate information in an accurate manner.
2. The student will accept responsibility for his/her behavior.
3. The student will tell the truth.
4. The student will independently perform his/her assignments.
5. The student will not cheat.
6. The student will not take things that belong to others.

Objectives:

1. The student will relate information in an accurate manner on _____ out of _____ trials.
2. The student will accept responsibility for his/her behavior when confronted by a teacher on _____ out of _____ trials.
3. The student will tell the truth on _____ out of _____ trials.
4. The student will refrain from denying his/her behavior on _____ out of _____ trials.
5. The student will accurately represent information on _____ out of _____ trials.
6. The student will report details in an accurate manner on _____ out of _____ trials.
7. The student will admit to his/her behavior on _____ out of _____ trials.
8. The student will independently perform his/her assignments on _____ out of _____ trials.
9. The student will refrain from cheating on _____ out of _____ tasks.
10. The student will independently perform _____ out of _____ tasks.
11. The student will refrain from copying other students' work on _____ out of _____ trials.
12. The student will refrain from using notes during _____ out of _____ tests or quizzes.
13. The student will independently perform _____ out of _____ homework assignments.
14. The student will ask for teacher assistance when necessary on _____ out of _____ trials.
15. The student will refrain from stealing on _____ out of _____ trials.
16. The student will refrain from forcibly taking things from others on _____ out of _____ trials.
17. The student will ask the owner's permission before using materials, possessions, etc., on _____ out of _____ trials.
18. The student will ask the user's permission before using materials, equipment, etc., on _____ out of _____ trials.
19. The student will ask to use materials, will ask to share materials, and will return materials in the same or better condition on _____ out of _____ trials.
20. The student will ask to borrow materials, equipment, possessions, etc., before taking them on _____ out of _____ trials.

Interventions:

1. Reinforce the student for making accurate statements, being honest, doing his her own work, etc.: (a) give the student a tangible reward (e.g., classroom privileges, line leading, passing out materials, five minutes free time, etc.) or (b) give the student an intangible reward (e.g., praise, handshake, smile, etc.).

2. Speak with the student to explain (a) what he/she is doing wrong (e.g., lying, cheating, stealing, denying his/her behavior, etc.) and (b) what he/she should be doing (e.g., reporting accurately what has occurred or will occur; asking to use things; borrowing, sharing, and returning things; doing his/her own work; etc.)

3. Write a contract with the student specifying what behavior is expected (e.g., making accurate statements, not taking things which belong to others, doing his/her own work, etc.) and what reinforcement will be made available when the terms of the contract have been met.

4. Communicate with parents (e.g., notes home, phone calls, etc.) to share information concerning the student's progress. The parents may reinforce the student at home for making accurate statements at school, for appropriate use or consideration of others' belongings at school, for doing his/her own work at school, etc.

5. Avoid putting the student in a situation in which he/she has the opportunity to lie, deny, exaggerate, cheat, steal, etc. (e.g., highly competitive activities, situations with limited supervision, etc.).

6. Avoid making accusations which would increase the probability of the student responding with inaccurate statements. If it is known that the student is responsible, an admission of guilt is not necessary to deal with the situation.

7. Supervise the student closely to monitor the accuracy of statements made by him/her.

8. Explain to the student that he/she should be satisfied with his/her own best effort rather than perfection.

9. Provide the student with many social and academic successes.

10. Provide the student with positive feedback which indicates he/she is successful.

11. Reduce competitiveness in information sharing so the student will not feel compelled to make inaccurate statements about his/her experiences.

12. Try various groupings to determine the situation in which the student is most comfortable and does not feel compelled to lie, deny, exaggerate the truth, etc.

13. Provide the student with experiences which can be shared if the absence of such experiences has been causing the student to fabricate information.

14. Reduce or remove punishment for accidents, forgetting, and situations with inadequate evidence. Punishment in these situations often causes students to lie.

15. Develop a system of shared responsibility (e.g., instead of trying to determine who is guilty; classmates work together to help clean up, return materials, make repairs, etc.).

16. Teach the student that making inaccurate statements does not prevent consequences (e.g., the student has to redo a task even though he/she claims the task was completed and lost).

17. Take no action in situations where conclusive evidence does not exist.

18. Help the student learn that telling the truth as soon as possible prevents future problems (e.g., admitting that he/she made a mistake, forgot, etc., so the necessary steps can be taken to correct the situation instead of waiting until the truth is determined in some other way).

19. Reduce the opportunity to steal by restricting students from bringing unnecessary items to school.

20. Allow natural consequences to occur when the student lies, denies, exaggerates, etc. (e.g., work not completed must be completed, lying to others will cause them not to believe you, etc.).

21. Establish classroom rules:
- Work on-task.
- Work quietly.
- Remain in your seat.
- Finish task.
- Meet task expectations.

Review rules often. Reinforce students for following rules.

22. Reinforce those students in the classroom who demonstrate appropriate behavior in reference to others' belongings, who tell the truth, who do their own work, etc.

23. Reinforce the student for demonstrating appropriate behavior based on the length of time he/she can be successful. As the student demonstrates success, gradually increase the length of time required for reinforcement.

24. Remove the student from the group or activity until he/she can demonstrate appropriate behavior and self-control.

25. Structure the environment so that time does not permit inappropriate behavior.

26. Teach the student the concept of borrowing by loaning and requiring the return of those items the student has been taking from others.

27. Identify those things the student has been taking from others and provide the student with those items as reinforcers for appropriate behavior.

28. Evaluate the appropriateness of a task to determine (a) if the task is too easy, (b) if the task is too difficult, and (c) if the length of time scheduled to complete the task is adequate.

29. Choose a peer to model performing his/her own work for the student.

30. Review information prior to administering tests and quizzes to better prepare the student.

31. Reduce the emphasis on test and quiz scores by grading the student's daily performance.

32. Maintain mobility to be frequently near the student when he/she takes tests and quizzes or performs daily assignments.

33. Reduce the emphasis on competition. Fear of failure may cause the student to resort to cheating or copying others' work to be successful.

34. Seat the student away from others if he/she is prone to cheating and/or copying others' work.

35. Seat the student near the teacher when he/she takes tests and quizzes.

36. Make certain that other students do not allow the student to look at their work when taking tests and quizzes and while performing assignments.

37. Make certain the student is aware of the consequences for cheating and/or copying others' work (e.g., assignments will be taken away, failing grades will be recorded, etc.).

38. Arrange to have a peer help the student study for tests and quizzes and perform daily assignments.

39. Evaluate the level of difficulty in relation to the student's ability to perform the task.

40. Make certain the student understands the natural consequences of stealing (e.g., the student must make restitution for taking things which belong to others).

41. Make certain the student knows that he/she can ask questions when taking tests and quizzes or performing assigned activities.

42. Communicate with parents or guardians so they may help the student study for tests and quizzes (e.g., send home directions, explanations, and instructions relating to content covered on tests and quizzes, material to review, etc.).

43. Have the student take tests and quizzes elsewhere in the building under the individual supervision of a supervisor (e.g., library, resource room, counselor's office, etc.).

44. Check the student for obvious attempts to cheat prior to taking a test or quiz (e.g., "cheat sheet," answers written on hands and cuffs, etc.).

45. Help the student understand that self-improvement is more important than getting the highest grade in the class, making all A's, being the first one to complete an assignment, etc., by reinforcing and grading on the basis of self-improvement.

46. Maintain visibility to and from the student. The teacher should be able to see the student; the student should be able to see the teacher. Make eye contact possible at all times.

47. Supervise the student to monitor behavior.

48. Encourage all students to monitor their own belongings.

49. Make certain the student has the necessary school-related items (e.g., pencil, ruler, paper, etc.).

50. Label all property brought to school by students and teachers with a permanent marker.

51. Secure all school items of value (e.g., cassette tapes, lab materials, industrial arts and home economics supplies, etc.).

52. Make certain the student understands all directions, explanations, and instructions prior to taking tests and quizzes and performing assignments.

53. Communicate with the student's family to establish procedures whereby the student may earn those things he/she would otherwise take.

54. Teach the student to share (e.g., schedule activities daily which require sharing).

55. Have the student question any directions, explanations, instructions he/she does not understand.

56. Deal with the taking of belongings privately rather than publicly.

57. Provide multiples of the items which are being taken to have enough for all or most students to use (e.g., pencils, erasers, rulers, etc.).

58. Help the student build or create a prized possession to satisfy his/her need for ownership (e.g., this can be done in art, home economics, industrial arts, etc.).

Goals:

1. The student will relate information in an accurate manner.
2. The student will accept responsibility for his/her behavior.
3. The student will tell the truth.

Objectives:

1. The student will relate information in an accurate manner on ____ out of ____ trials.
2. The student will accept responsibility for his/her behavior when confronted by the teacher on ____ out of ____ trials.
3. The student will tell the truth on ____ out of ____ trials.
4. The student will refrain from denying his/her behavior on ____ out of ____ trials.
5. The student will accurately represent information on ____ out of ____ trials.
6. The student will report details in an accurate manner on ____ out of ____ trials.
7. The student will admit to his/her behavior on ____ out of ____ trials.

Interventions:

1. Explain to the student that he/she should be satisfied with personal best effort rather than expecting perfection.

2. Provide the student with many social and academic successes.

3. Provide the student with positive feedback which indicates he/she is successful.

4. Reduce competitiveness in information sharing so the student will not feel compelled to make inaccurate statements about his/her experience.

5. Try various groupings to determine the situation in which the student is most comfortable and does not feel compelled to lie, deny, exaggerate, distort the truth, etc.

6. Provide the student with experiences which can be shared if the absence of such experiences has been causing the student to fabricate information.

7. Reduce or remove punishment for accidents, forgetting, and situations with inadequate evidence. Punishment in these situations often causes students to lie.

8. Develop a system of shared responsibility (e.g., instead of trying to determine who is guilty, classmates work together to help clean up, return materials, make repairs, etc.).

9. Teach the student that making inaccurate statements does not prevent consequences (e.g., the student has to redo an assignment even though he/she claims the completed assignment was lost).

10. Take no action in situations where conclusive evidence does not exist.

11. Allow natural consequences to occur when the student lies, denies, exaggerates, etc. (e.g., work not completed must be completed, lying to others will cause them not to believe you, etc.).

12. Help the student learn that telling the truth as soon as possible prevents future problems (e.g., admitting that he/she made a mistake, forgot, etc., so the necessary steps can be taken to correct the situation instead of waiting until the truth is determined in some other way).

13. Treat the student with respect. Talk in an objective manner at all times.

14. Do not punish the student unless you are absolutely sure he/she lied to you.

15. Help the student to understand that by exaggerating the truth he/she may even come to believe what he/she exaggerates and that exaggerating may become a habit.

16. Reinforce the student for making accurate statements: (a) give the student a tangible reward (e.g., classroom privileges, line leading, passing out materials, five minutes free time, etc.) or (b) give the student an intangible reward (e.g., praise, handshake, smile, etc.).

17. Avoid making accusations which would increase the probability of the student making inaccurate statements in response. If it is known that the student is responsible, an admission of guilt is not necessary to deal with the situation.

18. Avoid putting the student in a situation in which he/she has the opportunity to lie, deny, exaggerate, etc. (e.g., highly competitive activities, situations with limited supervision, etc.).

19. Communicate with parents (e.g., notes home, phone calls, etc.) to share information concerning the student's progress. The parents may reinforce the student at home for making accurate statements at school.

20. Write a contract with the student specifying what behavior is expected (e.g., making accurate statements) and what reinforcement will be made available when the terms of the contract have been met.

21. Speak with the student to explain (a) what the student is doing wrong (e.g., lying, denying his/her behavior, etc.) and (b) what the student should be doing (e.g., reporting accurately what has occurred or will occur).

22. Teach the student to "think" before acting (e.g., ask himself/herself "What is happening?" "What am I doing?" "What should I do?" "What will be best for me?").

23. Supervise the student closely to monitor the accuracy of statements made.

217   Does not consider the consequences of his/her behavior

Goals:
1. The student will consider consequences of his/her behavior.
2. The student will demonstrate consideration of consequences of his/her behavior.

Objectives:
1. The student will identify appropriate consequences of his/her behavior with the teacher on ___out of ___ trials.
2. The student will behave in such a way as to demonstrate that he/she considered consequences of his/her behavior on ___ out of ___ trials.
3. The student will refrain from reacting impulsively on ___out of ___trials.
4. The student will demonstrate behaviors that will result in positive consequences on ___out of ___ trials.

Interventions:

1. Make certain that consequences are delivered consistently for behavior demonstrated (e.g., appropriate behavior results in positive consequences and inappropriate behavior results in negative consequences).

2. Provide the student with many social and academic successes.

3. Structure the environment to limit opportunities for inappropriate behavior (e.g., keep the student engaged in activities, have the student seated near the teacher, maintain visibility to and from the student, etc.).

4. Prevent the student from becoming overstimulated by an activity (e.g., monitor or supervise student behavior to limit overexcitement in physical activities, games, parties, etc.).

5. Provide the student with natural consequences for inappropriate behavior (e.g., for disturbing others during group activities, the student should have to leave the activity).

6. Provide the student with a clearly identified list of consequences for inappropriate behavior.

7. Prevent peers from engaging in those behaviors which would cause the student to fail to consider or regard the consequences of his/her behavior (e.g., keep other students from upsetting the student).

8. Clarify for the student that it is his/her behavior which determines consequences (e.g., positive or negative).

9. Provide a learning experience which emphasizes the cause-and-effect relationship between behavior and the inevitability of some form of consequence (e.g., both negative and positive behaviors and consequences).

10. Point out the consequences of other students' behavior as they occur (e.g., take the opportunity to point out that consequences occur for all behavior and for all persons).

11. Call on the student when he/she can answer successfully.

12. Supervise the student closely in situations in which he/she is likely to act impulsively (e.g., maintain close physical proximity, maintain eye contact, communicate frequently with the student, etc.).

13. Teach the student problem-solving skills: (a) identify the problem, (b) identify goals and objectives, (c) develop strategies, (d) develop a plan of action, and (e) carry out the plan.

14. Make the consequence of a behavior obvious by identifying the consequence as it occurs and discussing alternative behavior which would have prevented the particular consequence.

15. Allow the student more decision-making opportunities relative to class activities and assignments.

16. Present tasks in the most attractive and interesting manner possible.

17. Give the student responsibilities in the classroom (e.g., teacher assistant, peer tutor, group leader, etc.).

18. Evaluate the appropriateness of the task in relation to the student's ability to perform the task successfully.

19. Show an interest in the student (e.g., acknowledge the student, ask the student's opinion, spend time working one-on-one with the student, etc.).

20. Intervene early when there is a problem to prevent more serious problems from occurring.

21. Inform others who will be working with the student (e.g., teachers, the principal, clerks, etc.) about the student's tendency to ignore consequences of his/her behaviors.

22. Make certain the student does not become involved in overstimulating activities.

23. Teach the student to "think" before acting (e.g., ask himself/herself "What is happening?" "What am I doing?" "What should I do?" "What will be best for me?").

24. Evaluate the appropriateness of the task to determine (a) if the task is too easy, (b) if the task is too difficult, and (c) if the length of time scheduled to complete the task is adequate.

25. Communicate with the parents (e.g., notes home, phone calls, etc.) to share information concerning the student's progress. The parents may reinforce the student at home for engaging in appropriate behaviors at school.

26. Avoid competition. Failure may cause the student to ignore consequences of his/her behavior.

27. Write a contract with the student specifying what behavior is expected (e.g., acting in a deliberate and responsible manner) and what reinforcement will be made available when the terms of the contract have been met.

28. Remove the student from the group or activity until he/she can demonstrate appropriate behavior and self-control.

29. Reinforce the student for demonstrating appropriate behavior based on the length of time the student can be successful. As the student demonstrates success, gradually increase the length of time required for reinforcement.

30. Reinforce those students in the classroom who engage in appropriate behavior.

31. Establish classroom rules:
- Work on-task.
- Work quietly.
- Remain in your seat.
- Finish task.
- Meet task expectations.

Review rules often. Reinforce students for following rules.

32. Speak with the student to explain (a) what the student is doing wrong (e.g., taking action before thinking about what he/she is doing) and (b) what the student should be doing (e.g., considering consequences, thinking about the correct response, considering other persons, etc.).

33. Reinforce the student for engaging in appropriate behavior: (a) give the student a tangible reward (e.g., classroom privileges, line leading, passing out materials, five minutes free time, etc.) or (b) give the student an intangible reward (e.g., praise, handshake, smile, etc.).

218 Does not follow classroom rules

Goal:

1. The student will follow the rules of the classroom.

Objectives:

1. The student will follow the rules of the classroom on ___ out of ___ trials.
2. The student will talk only after being given permission on ___ out of ___ trials.
3. The student will ask to leave his/her seat before doing so on ___ out of ___ trials.
4. The student will immediately respond to redirection on ___ out of ___ trials.
5. The student will follow the rules of the classroom with ___ reminders.
6. The student will independently follow the rules of the classroom on ___ out of ___ trials.
7. The student will follow classroom rules when interacting with peers during group activities, free time, etc., on ___ out of ___ trials.
8. The student will handle classroom materials and equipment with care on ___ out of ___ trials.
9. The student will walk quietly in the classroom on ___ out of ___ trials.
10. The student will complete ___ out of ___ assigned tasks per day.

Interventions:

1. Structure the environment so that the student remains active and involved while demonstrating acceptable behavior.

2. Maintain visibility to and from the student. The teacher should be able to see the student, and the student should be able to see the teacher. Make eye contact possible at all times.

3. Be a consistent authority figure (e.g., be consistent in relationships with students).

4. Present tasks in the most interesting and attractive manner possible.

5. Have the student maintain a chart representing the amount of time spent following classroom rules, with reinforcement for increasing acceptable behavior.

6. Practice mobility to be frequently near the student.

7. Provide the student with many social and academic successes.

8. Provide the student with positive feedback that indicates he/she is successful.

9. Post rules in various places, including on the student's desk.

10. Make certain the student receives the information necessary to perform activities (e.g., written information, verbal directions, reminders, etc.).

11. Teach the student direction-following skills.

12. Maintain a positive and professional relationship with the student (e.g., an adversarial relationship is likely to result in failure to follow directions).

13. Give the student preferred responsibilities.

14. Provide the student with optional courses of action to prevent total refusal to obey teacher directives.

15. Intervene early to prevent the student's behavior from leading to contagion of other students.

16. Have the student question any directions, explanations, or instructions not understood.

17. Require the student to verbalize the classroom rules at designated times throughout the day (e.g., before school, during recess, at break time, at lunch, at the end of the day, etc.).

18. Deliver directions in a step-by-step sequence.

19. Choose a peer to model following the rules of the classroom for the student.

20. Interact with the student frequently to determine if directives are being followed.

21. Maintain consistent rules, routine, and general expectations of conduct and procedure.

22. Remove the student from the group or activity until he/she can demonstrate acceptable behavior and self-control.

23. Help the student identify specific rules he/she has difficulty following and make these areas goals for behavior improvement.

24. Separate the student from the peer(s) who stimulates his/her inappropriate behavior.

25. Make certain that rules and behavior expectations are consistent throughout the school and classrooms.

26. Along with a directive, provide an incentive statement (e.g., "When you finish your math, you may go outside to play." or, "You may have free time after you finish your work.").

27. Intervene early when there is a problem to prevent more serious problems from occurring.

28. Before beginning a new activity, make sure the student knows the classroom rules.

29. Teach the student to "think" before acting (e.g., ask himself/herself, "What is happening?" "What am I doing?" "What should I do?" "What will be best for me?").

30. Evaluate the appropriateness of the assigned task to determine (a) if the task is too easy, (b) if the task is too difficult, and (c) if the length of time scheduled to complete the task is adequate.

31. Communicate with parents (e.g., notes home, phone calls, etc.) to share information concerning the student's progress. The parents may reinforce the student at home for following the rules of the classroom.

32. Write a contract with the student specifying what behavior is expected (e.g., following classroom rules) and what reinforcement will be made available when the terms of the contract have been met.

33. Provide the student with a list of rules and/or behavior expectations.

34. Reinforce the student for following the rules of the classroom based on the length of time the student can be successful. As the student demonstrates success, gradually increase the length of time required for reinforcement.

35. Reinforce those students who follow the rules of the classroom.

36. Establish classroom rules:
- Work on-task.
- Work quietly.
- Remain in your seat.
- Finish task.
- Meet task expectations.

Review rules often. Reinforce students for following rules.

37. Speak with the student to explain (a) what the student is doing wrong (e.g., failing to follow classroom rules) and (b) what the student should be doing (e.g., following the rules of the classroom).

38. Reinforce the student for following the rules of the classroom: (a) give the student a tangible reward (e.g., classroom privileges, line leading, passing out materials, five minutes free time, etc.) or (b) give the student an intangible reward (e.g., praise, handshake, smile, etc.).

219 Does not follow the rules of games

Goal:

1. The student will follow the rules of games.

Objectives:

1. The student will take turns in group games on _____ out of _____ occasions.
2. The student will interact with peers in group games, with supervision, on _____ out of _____ occasions.
3. The student will interact without supervision, with peers, in group games on _____ out of _____ occasions.
4. The student will follow existing rules of group games, with verbal prompts, on _____ out of _____ occasions.
5. The student will independently follow existing rules of group games on _____ out of _____ occasions.
6. The student will share materials in group games on _____ out of _____ occasions.

Interventions:

1. Communicate with the student's parents (e.g., notes home, phone calls, etc.) to share information concerning their child's appropriate behavior. The parents may reinforce the student at home for following the rules of games at school.

2. Involve the student in extracurricular activities to encourage interaction with peers in games.

3. Reduce the emphasis on competition. Failure may stimulate inappropriate behavior in games.

4. Play games with the student and help him/her do well so there is no need to cheat.

5. Interview and observe other students to determine which skills or behaviors the student needs to develop to enable him/her to follow rules during games.

6. Consider carefully the student's age and ability level before expecting him/her to play fairly.

7. Reinforce the student for demonstrating appropriate behavior in games: (a) give the student a tangible reward (e.g., classroom privileges, passing out materials, five minutes free time, etc.) or (b) give the student an intangible reward (e.g., praise, handshake, smile, etc.).

8. Choose a peer to model following rules of games for the student.

9. Establish a set of standard behavior rules for games (e.g., follow the rules of the game, take turns, make positive comments, work as a team member, be a good sport, etc.). Review rules often. Reinforce students for following the rules.

10. Set a good example for the student. Make sure that you play by the rules, wait your turn, share materials, and do not argue with others when playing competitive games.

11. Reinforce those students in the classroom who follow the rules of games.

12. Limit the student's participation in competitive activities.

13. Deal with the student's behavior consistently each time he/she has a problem following rules (e.g., remove the student from the situation when he/she cheats and do not allow him/her to return, etc.).

14. Have the student question any directions, explanations, or instructions for games he/she does not understand.

15. Evaluate the expectations for participation in games to determine if the student can be successful in the interaction for the expected length of time.

16. Remove the student immediately from games if he/she is unable to demonstrate appropriate behavior.

17. Have the student engage in a game activity with one peer. As the student demonstrates success, gradually increase the size of the group.

18. Determine the peers with whom the student would most prefer to interact in games and attempt to facilitate success.

19. Speak to the student to explain (a) what he/she is doing wrong (e.g., failing to follow rules, cheating, etc.) and (b) what he/she should be doing (e.g., following rules, playing fairly, etc.).

20. Explain to the student when he/she has trouble following rules exactly what he/she is doing wrong, what he/she is supposed to be doing, and why. For example: You see the student cheating while playing a game. Stop the game and say, "William, you are cheating. You need to play fairly if you want to continue playing."

21. Be a model for participating for enjoyment rather than always needing to "win" or "beat" someone else.

22. Teach the student to ask for help, stop playing, etc., when he/she feels like not following the rules.

23. Have the student engage in games of short duration. As the student demonstrates success, gradually increase the duration of games.

24. Establish rules for playing competitive games (e.g., play by the rules, wait your turn, share materials, do not fight, etc.). These rules should be consistent and followed by everyone in the class. Talk about the rules often.

25. Reduce the student's need to not play fairly by helping him/her improve his/her skills in activities in which he/she has not followed the rules.

26. Allow the student to choose a group of peers with whom he/she feels comfortable.

27. Assign the student to games in which he/she is likely to interact successfully with peers.

28. Conduct a sociometric activity with the class to determine those peers who would most prefer to interact with the student in games.

29. Make certain that the student demonstrates appropriate behavior in nonacademic situations prior to placing him/her with peers for games.

30. Encourage the student to participate in activities, sports, etc., for self-improvement rather than "winning" or "beating" someone else (e.g., trying to improve his/her own batting average or defensive skills rather than being disappointed if his/her team does not win).

31. Encourage the student to engage in less competitive activities (e.g., reading, clubs, scouting, student council, etc.).

32. Teach the student problem-solving skills so he/she may better deal with problems that may occur in interactions with peers in games (e.g., talking, walking away, calling upon an arbitrator, compromising, etc.).

33. Teach the student appropriate ways in which to deal with his/her anger, frustrations, etc., so he/she does not feel the need to cheat.

34. Discourage the student from participating in activities where other people cheat to win.

35. Assign outgoing, nonthreatening peers to interact with the student in games.

36. Structure the environment so that the student has many opportunities to participate with peers in games.

37. Assign the student to interact with younger peers in games.

38. Have the student practice appropriate interactions with the teacher(s) in games.

39. Make certain before beginning a game or competitive activity that the student is able to successfully participate in the game (e.g., the student understands the rules, is familiar with the game, will be compatible with the other individuals playing the game, etc.).

40. Make certain that the student understands that failing to interact appropriately with peers during games may result in termination of the game and/or loss of future opportunities to participate in games.

41. Increase supervision when the student is involved in competitive situations to help prevent him/her from not following rules.

42. Make sure that activities are not so difficult as to make cheating necessary to win, to be a member of the team, to participate, etc.

43. Make certain that games are not so stimulating as to make successful interactions with peers difficult.

44. Assign older peers with desirable social skills to interact with the student in games.

45. Do not put an emphasis on winning. If the student feels that winning is the most important thing, he/she may resort to not following rules to win.

46. Encourage the student to participate in more individualized sports (e.g., aerobics, swimming, track and field, golf, etc.).

47. Make sure that others follow rules when they play competitive activities with the student.

48. Have the student study, practice, simulate, etc., the rules for group games before participating.

49. Write a contract with the student specifying what behavior is expected (e.g., following the rules of games) and what reinforcement will be made available when the terms of the contract have been met.

50. Play the game with the student before he/she engages in the game with peers to model appropriate behavior, determine the student's ability to play the game, determine the student's ability to follow behavior rules, etc.

51. Make certain that all teachers, substitutes, etc., know that the student has a tendency to not follow the rules when playing games.

52. Make certain the student understands that not following rules in competitive activities may result in others not wanting to interact, play, compete, etc., with him/her again.

53. Supervise games closely so the peers with whom the student interacts do not stimulate inappropriate behavior.

54. Attempt to facilitate interaction between the student and a peer(s) (e.g., a student with similar interest, background, classes, behavior patterns, nonacademic schedule, etc.) with whom the student may successfully follow the rules of a game.

55. Structure games according to the needs/ abilities of the student (e.g., establish rules, limit the stimulation of the activities, limit the length of the game, consider the time of day, etc.).

56. Limit opportunities for interaction in games on those occasions in which the student is not likely to be successful (e.g., the student has experienced academic or social failure prior to the scheduled game).

57. Select games designed to facilitate appropriate interaction between the student and his/her peers.

58. Teach problem-solving skills:
- Identify the problem.
- Identify the goals and objectives.
- Develop a strategy/plan for action.
- Carry out the plan.
- Evaluate the results.

59. Allow the student to choose the game which he/she will play with peers.

60. Have the student verbally explain the rules of the game prior to allowing the student to interact with peers.

61. Reinforce the student for following the rules of games based on the length of time the student can be successful. As the student demonstrates success, gradually increase the length of time required for reinforcement.

62. Put the emphasis on personal improvement, getting along, sharing, and having fun when playing competitive activities.

63. Assess the degree of difficulty to determine whether or not the student will require additional explanation before playing a game.

64. Evaluate the appropriateness of games to determine if the games are too difficult and if the length of time scheduled to complete the games is adequate.

65. Deal with the student's inability to follow rules privately rather than publicly.

66. Teach the student necessary skills to successfully participate in particular games (e.g., volleyball, basketball, football, baseball, etc.).

67. Encourage the student to interact with less competitive friends (e.g, older/younger friends, opposite gender, etc.).

68. Do not allow the student to cheat. Immediately correct him/her when he/she begins to cheat.

69. Make certain that the student understands that interacting with peers in group games is contingent upon following the rules.

70. Teach the student appropriate ways to interact with peers in group games (e.g., suggest activities, share materials, problem solve, take turns, follow game rules, etc.).

71. Make certain that the student understands the relationship between inappropriate behavior and the consequences which follow (e.g., others not wanting to play with him/her, making others angry, not being allowed to play, etc.).

72. Do not take action unless you know for certain that the student is not playing fairly.

73. Encourage the student to take up a hobby. Assist him/her in successfully developing the hobby.

74. Discuss with the student the intrinsic value of good sportsmanship, personal improvement, finishing a season, etc., if he/she does not win awards (e.g., trophies, plaques, certificates, etc.) in competitive activities.

75. Encourage the student and others to engage in activities where winning is not a high priority.

220 Does not follow rules

Goal:

1. The student will follow school rules.

Objectives:

1. The student will follow school rules on _____ out of _____ trials.
2. The student will walk in the halls when moving from one location to another on _____ out of _____ trials.
3. The student will refrain from throwing food in the cafeteria on _____ out of _____ trials.
4. The student will keep his/her food on his/her plate on _____ out of _____ trials.
5. The student will work quietly in the library on _____ out of _____ trials.
6. The student will talk quietly with a peer when in the library on _____ out of _____ trials.
7. The student will handle school property with care on _____ out of _____ trials.
8. The student will walk quietly through the halls on _____ out of _____ trials.
9. The student will interact appropriately with his/her peers during lunch, recess, break time, etc., on _____ out of _____ trials.

Interventions:

1. Be a consistent authority figure (e.g., be consistent in relationships with students).

2. Communicate with the student's parents (e.g., notes home, phone calls, etc.) to share information concerning their child's progress. The parents may reinforce the student at home for following school rules.

3. Choose a peer to model following school rules for the student.

4. Structure the environment so that the student remains active and involved.

5. Intervene early when there is a problem to prevent a more serious problem from occurring.

6. Consult with the school psychologist about the student's failure to consider the consequences of his/her behavior.

7. Make certain the student is actively involved in the environment (i.e., give the student responsibilities, activities, and errands to run to provide purposeful behavior).

8. Educate yourself and others about ADHD to increase understanding and accommodation of impulsive behavior.

9. Encourage the student to develop an awareness of the consequences of his/her behavior by writing down or talking through problems which may occur due to his/her inability to adjust his/her behavior to different situations (e.g., perceived as unmannerly, avoided, etc.).

10. Educate the student about ADHD and the need for developing skills to self-monitor behavior.

11. Encourage the student to pause and consider his/her thoughts before acting on them.

12. Provide constant, positive reinforcement for appropriate behavior. Ignore as many inappropriate behaviors as possible.

13. Have the student make a list of consequences associated with frequently occurring behaviors (e.g., by disrupting others, I will be perceived as unmannerly. By behaving aggressively, people will avoid me.).

14. Teach the student to "think" before acting (e.g., ask himself/herself "What is happening?" "What am I doing?" "What should I do?" "What will be best for me?").

15. Make certain that rules and behavior expectations are consistent in the classroom and throughout the school.

16. Inform other personnel of any behavior problem that the student may have so that supervision and assistance may be provided.

17. Model for the student those behaviors he/she is expected to display in the school environment.

18. Have the student maintain a chart representing the amount of time spent following school rules. Reinforcement should be given for increasing acceptable behavior.

19. Reinforce those students in the classroom who follow school rules.

20. Provide the student with a clearly understood list of consequences for inappropriate behavior.

21. Teach problem-solving skills:
- Identify the problem.
- Identify the goals and objectives.
- Develop a strategy/plan for action.
- Carry out the plan.
- Evaluate the results.

22. Reduce the emphasis on competition. Competitive activities may cause the student to act inappropriately.

23. Enforce consistently the rules and consequences contained in the school discipline plan.

24. Have the student review the consequences of his/her behavior. Have the student consider different choices he/she could have made and the different outcomes.

25. Provide the student with optional courses of action to prevent total refusal to obey school rules (e.g., may return to the classroom).

26. Have the student question any directions, explanations, or instructions he/she does not understand.

27. Reinforce the student for going directly from one location to another.

28. Speak to the student to explain (a) what he/she is doing wrong (e.g., failing to follow school rules) and (b) what he/she should be doing (e.g., following school rules).

29. Hold the student accountable for failing to follow school rules.

30. Provide the student with positive feedback that indicates he/she is successful.

31. Be consistent in applying consequences for behavior (e.g., appropriate behavior receives positive consequences while inappropriate behavior receives negative consequences).

32. Reinforce the student for moving from one place to another in an appropriate length of time.

33. Teach the student ways to gain self-control (e.g., count to ten, walk away, talk with someone, etc.).

34. Encourage the student to play games, sports, etc., with friends who do not encourage him/her to disregard school rules.

35. Reinforce the student for remaining in assigned areas (e.g., student lounge, recreational area, assembly, etc.).

36. Clarify for the student that it is his/her behavior which determines whether consequences are positive or negative.

37. Provide the student with a list of school rules and/or behavior expectations to carry with him/her at all times in the school environment.

38. Make certain that all educators who work with the student consistently enforce school rules.

39. Make sure the student knows the rules before beginning a new activity.

40. Maintain a routine that will minimize erratic or impulsive behavior which may result in negative consequences.

41. Practice mobility to be frequently near the student.

42. Separate the student from the peer that stimulates his/her inappropriate behavior.

43. Post school rules in various places, including on the student's desk, in the hallways, etc.

44. Explain verbally the school discipline plan and consequences to the student on a one-to-one basis.

45. Have the student carry a point card at all times so that he/she can be reinforced anywhere in the school environment for following rules.

46. Have the student list the pros and cons of an action. Have the student consider if the pros outweigh the cons before he/she takes action.

47. Discuss with the student the role and benefit of rules outside the school setting (e.g., job site, social situation, recreational activities, etc.).

48. Reinforce the student for following school rules based on the length of time the student can be successful. As the student demonstrates success, gradually increase the length of time required for reinforcement.

49. Reinforce the student for following school rules: (a) give the student a tangible reward (e.g., classroom privileges, passing out materials, five minutes free time, etc.) or (b) give the student an intangible reward (e.g., praise, handshake, smile, etc.).

50. Help the student identify specific school rules he/she has difficulty following and make these rules into goals for behavior improvement.

51. Have the student question any school rules he/she does not understand.

52. Have the student and his/her parents sign a copy of the school discipline plan and consequences for failing to follow school rules.

53. Have the student identify the situations in which he/she is most likely to fail to consider the consequences of his/her behavior. After he/she has identified these situations, have him/her think of ways to minimize their occurrences.

54. Provide the student with many social and academic successes.

55. Maintain maximum supervision of the student. As the student is able to successfully follow school rules, gradually decrease supervision.

56. Have a peer accompany the student in nonacademic settings.

57. Write a contract with the student specifying what behavior is expected and what reinforcement will be made available when the terms of the contract have been met.

58. Use related consequences for the student's inappropriate behavior (e.g., running in the halls results in having to walk with an adult, throwing food in the cafeteria results in having to sit next to an adult when eating, disruption in the library requires additional adult supervision, etc.).

59. Intervene early to prevent the student's behavior from leading to contagion of other students.

60. Encourage the student to realize that all behavior has negative or positive consequences. Discuss with the student behaviors that will lead to positive consequences.

61. Have the student verbally repeat the school discipline plan and consequences.

62. Require the student to verbalize the school rules at designated times throughout the day (e.g., before school, during recess, at lunch, at the end of the day, etc.).

63. Maintain visibility to and from the student. The teacher should be able to see the student and the student should be able to see the teacher. Make eye contact possible at all times.

64. Do not allow the student to use ADHD as an excuse. Hold the student responsible for his/her actions. However, understand and accept problems that ADHD brings into the student's life while he/she is learning to make accommodations.

65. Interact with the student frequently to determine if school rules are being followed.

66. Make certain that the student understands the relationship between inappropriate behavior and the consequences which follow (e.g., lunch detention, suspension, after school detention, etc.).

67. Establish school rules:
- Walk in halls.
- Arrive for class on time.
- Respect the privacy of others.
- Talk quietly in the halls.

Review rules often. Reinforce students for following the rules.

221 Does not play or work quietly

Goals:

1. The student will communicate with others in an acceptable manner in the classroom.
2. The student will work quietly in the classroom.

Objectives:

1. The student will gain permission from the teacher, by raising his/her hand, when he/she needs to talk with a peer on _____ out of _____ trials.
2. The student will contribute his/her opinion/answer after being recognized by the teacher on _____ out of _____ trials.
3. The student will wait his/her turn to talk when engaged, or attempting to engage, in interactions with others on _____ out of _____ trials.
4. The student will make comments which are relevant to the situation on _____ out of _____ trials.
5. The student will refrain from making sounds which are inappropriate for the situation on _____ out of _____ trials.
6. The student will make positive comments about others on _____ out of _____ trials.

Interventions:

1. Remove the student from the group or activity until he/she can demonstrate appropriate behavior and self-control.

2. Write a contract with the student specifying what behavior is expected (e.g., making appropriate comments) and what reinforcement will be made available when the terms of the contract have been met.

3. Communicate with the parents (e.g., notes home, phone calls, etc.) to share information concerning the student's progress. The parents may reinforce the student at home for making appropriate comments at school.

4. Evaluate the appropriateness of the task to determine (a) if the task is too long and (b) if the length of time scheduled for the task is adequate.

5. Make certain that reinforcement is not inadvertently given for inappropriate behavior (e.g., making inappropriate comments or unnecessary noises).

6. Give adequate opportunities to respond (i.e., enthusiastic students need many opportunities to contribute).

7. Have the student be the leader of a small group activity if he/she possesses mastery of skills or an interest in that area.

8. Provide the student with a predetermined signal if he/she begins to make inappropriate comments or unnecessary noises.

9. Explain to the student that he/she may be trying too hard to fit in and that he/she should relax and make more appropriate comments.

10. Structure the environment to limit opportunities for inappropriate behaviors (e.g., keep the student engaged in activities, have the student seated near the teacher, etc.).

11. Give the student responsibilities in the classroom (e.g., running errands, opportunities to help the teacher, etc.).

12. Reduce activities which might threaten the student (e.g., announcing test score ranges or test scores aloud, making students read aloud in class, emphasizing the success of a particular student or students, etc.).

13. Provide the student with many social and academic successes.

14. Make the necessary adjustments in the environment to prevent the student from experiencing stress, frustration or anger (e.g., reduce peer pressure, academic failure, teasing, etc.).

15. Maintain visibility to and from the student. The teacher should be able to see the student and the student should be able to see the teacher. Make eye contact possible at all times.

16. Interact frequently with the student to reduce his/her need to make inappropriate comments or unnecessary noises.

17. Assess the appropriateness of the social situation in relation to the student's ability to function successfully.

18. Try various groupings to determine the situation in which the student is most comfortable.

19. Reinforce the student for raising his/her hand to be recognized.

20. Call on the student when he/she is most likely to be able to respond correctly.

21. Teach the student to recognize and make appropriate comments (e.g., comments within the context of the situation, comments that are a follow-up to what has just been said, etc.).

22. Do not inadvertently reinforce the student's inappropriate behavior by laughing when the student is silly, rude, etc.

23. Have the student work in small groups in which he/she will have frequent opportunities to speak. As the student learns to wait longer for a turn to speak, gradually increase the size of the group.

24. Make certain that the student's feelings are considered when it is necessary to deal with his/her inappropriate comments (i.e., handle comments in such a way as to not diminish the student's enthusiasm for participation).

25. Help the student improve concentration skills (e.g., listening to the speaker, taking notes, preparing comments in advance, making comments in the appropriate context, etc.).

26. Have the student question any directions, explanations, and instructions not understood.

27. Deliver directions, explanations, and instructions in a clear and concise manner to reduce the student's need to ask questions.

28. Have the student practice waiting for a turn to speak for short periods of time. As the student demonstrates success, gradually increase the length of time required for reinforcement.

29. Explain to the student the reasons why making inappropriate comments and unnecessary noise is not acceptable (e.g., is impolite, might hurt others' feelings, etc.).

30. Attempt to provide equal attention to all students in the classroom.

31. Make the student aware of the number of times he/she makes inappropriate comments and unnecessary noises.

32. Allow natural consequences to occur due to the student making inappropriate comments or unnecessary noises in the classroom (e.g., making noises and inappropriate comments during class time will cause the student to have to make up the work during recreational time).

33. Encourage the student to model the behavior of peers who are successful.

34. Make certain the student sees the relationship between his/her behavior and the consequences which may follow (e.g., failing to listen to directions and making distracting noises will cause the student to not understand what to do).

35. Remove the student from the situation until he/she can demonstrate appropriate behavior.

36. Deliver a predetermined signal when the student begins to display inappropriate behavior.

37. Make certain the student knows when it is acceptable to interrupt others (e.g., an emergency).

38. Teach the student acceptable ways to communicate displeasure, anger, frustration, etc.

39. Have the student put himself/herself in someone else's place (e.g., "How would you feel if someone called you dumb or stupid?").

40. Reinforce the student for making appropriate comments based on the length of time the student can be successful. As the student demonstrates success, gradually increase the length of time required for reinforcement.

41. Reinforce those students in the classroom who make appropriate comments.

42. Establish classroom rules:
- Work on-task.
- Work quietly.
- Remain in your seat.
- Finish task.
- Meet task expectations.

Review rules often. Reinforce students for following rules.

43. Speak with the student to explain (a) what the student is doing wrong (e.g., making inappropriate comments or unnecessary noises) and (b) what the student should be doing (e.g., waiting until it is appropriate to speak, thinking of comments which relate to the situation, etc.).

44. Reinforce the student for making appropriate comments in the classroom: (a) give the student a tangible reward (e.g., classroom privileges, line leading, passing out materials, five minutes free time, etc.) or (b) give the student an intangible reward (e.g., praise, handshake, smile, etc.).

45. Separate the student from the peers who may be encouraging or stimulating the inappropriate behavior.

46. Avoid ignoring the student's inappropriate behavior. Ignored behavior may increase in frequency and may lead to contagion on the part of other students.

47. Do not force the student to interact with others.

222　Does not stay in an assigned area for the specified time period

Goal:

1. The student will stay in an assigned area for the specified time period.

Objectives:

1. The student will follow the rules of assigned areas on _____ out of _____ trials.
2. The student will remain in an assigned area for the specified time period with assistance (physical barriers, boundary markings, verbal reminders) on _____ out of _____ trials.
3. The student will independently remain in an assigned area unsupervised for the specified time period on _____ out of _____ trials.
4. The student will rely on environmental cues (e.g., clocks and bells) to remain in an assigned area for the specified time period on _____ out of _____ trials.
5. The student will remain in an assigned area with supervision for the specified time period on _____ out of _____ trials.

Interventions:

1. Reinforce the student for staying in an assigned area for the specified time period: (a) give the student a tangible reward (e.g., classroom privileges, line leading, passing out materials, five minutes free time, etc.) or (b) give the student an intangible reward (e.g., praise, handshake, smile, etc.).

2. Speak to the student to explain (a) what he/she is doing wrong (e.g., leaving the assigned area) and (b) what he/she should be doing (e.g., staying in the assigned area for the specified time period).

3. Establish classroom rules:
- Work on-task.
- Work quietly.
- Remain in your seat.
- Finish task.
- Meet task expectations.

Review rules often. Reinforce students for following rules.

4. Evaluate the appropriateness of the task to determine (a) if the task is too easy, (b) if the task is too difficult, and (c) if the length of time scheduled to complete the task is adequate.

5. Reinforce the student for staying in an assigned area for the specified time period based on the length of time the student can be successful. As the student demonstrates success, gradually increase the length of time required for reinforcement.

6. Write a contract with the student specifying what behavior is expected (e.g., staying in an assigned area for the specified time period) and what reinforcement will be made available when the terms of the contract have been met.

7. Communicate with parents (e.g., notes home, phone calls, etc.) to share information concerning the student's progress. The parents may reinforce the student at home for staying in an assigned area at school for the specified time period.

8. Reinforce those students in the classroom who stay in an assigned area for the specified time period.

9. Choose a peer to model staying in an assigned area for the specified time period for the student.

10. Have the student question any directions, explanations, instructions he/she does not understand.

11. Evaluate the appropriateness of requiring the student to stay in an assigned area for the specified time period.

12. Establish rules for the school grounds (e.g., remain in assigned areas, share school equipment, use appropriate language, use school property with care, etc.).

13. Have the student question any rules for the school grounds he/she does not understand.

14. Separate the student from the peer(s) who stimulates his/her inappropriate behavior in assigned areas.

15. Have the student carry a point card with him/her at all times so that he/she can be reinforced for staying in assigned areas in the building and on the school grounds.

16. Inform other school personnel of any behavior problems the student may have so that supervision and assistance may be provided in the assigned areas before, during, and after school.

17. Be consistent in applying consequences for behavior (i.e., appropriate behavior receives positive consequences while negative behavior receives negative consequences).

18. Provide organized activities in which to participate in assigned areas before, during, and after school (e.g., board games, softball, computer games, puzzles, checkers, flash cards, etc.).

19. Identify a specified area of the school grounds to be used as a "time-out" area when the student demonstrates inappropriate behavior on the school grounds.

20. Have the student take responsibility for a younger student in assigned areas.

21. Make certain the student knows where he/she is expected to be at all times.

22. Require the student to remain in assigned areas for short periods of time. As the student demonstrates success, gradually increase the length of time.

23. Make certain the student knows the location of all assigned areas.

24. Make certain the behavioral demands are appropriate for the student's abilities (e.g., ability to find locations of assigned areas, ability to tell time, ability to interact with peers appropriately, etc.).

25. Make certain the student is actively involved in an activity in the assigned area to facilitate his/her ability to stay in the assigned area for the specified time period.

26. Assign the student a responsibility to perform in an assigned area to keep him/her actively involved (e.g., supervision of others, responsibility for materials, group leader, etc.).

27. Provide the student with a timer to help him/her remain in the assigned area for the specified time period.

28. Post a clock showing the times the student should enter and leave an assigned area (e.g., one clock face indicates time to enter, another clock face indicates time to leave, etc.).

29. Have the student carry a hall pass on which teachers will indicate arrival and departure times of assigned areas.

30. Deliver a predetermined signal (e.g., ring a bell, turn lights off and on, etc.) to indicate when to enter and leave assigned areas.

31. Set up physical barriers or boundary markings to help the student remain in an assigned area.

32. Identify areas that are off limits with signs such as "Danger," "Keep Out," etc.

33. Provide adequate supervision in assigned areas. As the student demonstrates success, gradually reduce the amount of supervision.

34. Provide the student with many opportunities for social and academic success in assigned areas.

35. Require time spent away from an assigned area to be made up during break time, lunch, free time, etc.

36. Assign a peer to remain in an assigned area with the student for the specified time period.

37. Make certain the student is able to tell time to increase the probability that he/she will know how long to remain in assigned areas.

38. Reduce stimuli in the assigned area which would cause the student to be unable to remain in the assigned area for the specified time period.

39. Reinforce the student for remaining in assigned areas (e.g., free time areas, student lounge, recreational areas, etc.).

40. Teach the student ways to deal with stimuli or problems in assigned areas which may cause the student to leave the area (e.g., talk to a teacher, move to a quiet place in the assigned area, avoid confrontations, etc.).

223 Steals or forcibly takes things from other students, teachers, the school building, etc.

Goal:

1. The student will not grab things away from others.
2. The student will not take things that belong to others.

Objectives:

1. The student will refrain from forcibly taking things from others on _____ out of _____ trials.
2. The student will ask the owner's permission before using materials, possessions, etc., on _____ out of _____ trials.
3. The student will ask the user's permission before using materials, equipment, etc., on _____ out of _____ trials.
4. The student will ask to use materials, will share materials, and will return materials in the same or better condition on _____ out of _____ trials.
5. The student will ask to borrow materials, equipment, possessions, etc., before taking them on _____ out of _____ trials.

Interventions:

1. Communicate with the student's parents (e.g., notes home, phone calls, etc.) to share information concerning their child's appropriate behavior. The parents may reinforce the student at home for appropriate use or consideration of others' belongings at school.

2. Intervene early when there is a problem to prevent a more serious problem from occurring.

3. Educate yourself and others about ADHD to increase understanding and accommodation of impulsive behavior.

4. Encourage the student to develop an awareness of the consequences of his/her behavior by writing down or talking through problems which may occur due to his/her impulsivity (e.g., perceived as unmannerly, avoided, etc.).

5. Encourage the student to develop an awareness of himself/herself and those around him/her. Have the student periodically step back and ask himself/herself, "Am I behaving impulsively?"

6. Educate the student about ADHD and the need for developing skills to self-monitor behavior.

7. Provide constant, positive reinforcement for appropriate behavior. Ignore as many inappropriate behaviors as possible.

8. Reinforce the student for demonstrating appropriate behavior: (a) give the student a tangible reward (e.g., classroom privileges, passing out materials, five minutes free time, etc.) or (b) give the student an intangible reward (e.g., praise, handshake, smile, etc.).

9. Reinforce the student for demonstrating appropriate behavior based on the length of time the student can be successful. As the student demonstrates success, gradually increase the length of time required for reinforcement.

10. Establish rules (e.g., be friendly, ask permission to borrow things, share, etc.). These rules should be consistent and followed by everyone in the class. Talk about the rules often.

11. Show the student how to ask permission to use something and how to react if he/she is told "no."

12. Arrange for the student to be involved in many activities with other students to help him/her learn the skills necessary to interact appropriately with them.

13. Teach the student to "think" before acting (e.g., ask himself/herself "What is happening?" "What am I doing?" "What should I do?" "What will be best for me?" etc.).

14. Deal with the grabbing of belongings privately rather than publicly.

15. Reinforce those students in the classroom who demonstrate appropriate behavior in reference to others' belongings.

16. Provide the student with a clearly understood list of consequences for inappropriate behavior.

17. Help the student build or create a prized possession to satisfy the need for ownership (e.g., this can be done in art, home economics, industrial arts, etc.).

18. Make certain that the student does not get away with taking things from others by having him/her immediately return what he/she takes forcefully.

19. Speak with the student to explain (a) what he/she is doing wrong (e.g., grabbing things from others) and (b) what he/she should be doing (e.g., asking to use things, borrowing, sharing, returning, etc.).

20. Teach the student to ask for things in a positive manner. Teach key words and phrases (e.g., "May I borrow your pencil?" "Do you mind if I listen to your CD player?" etc.).

21. Remove the student from the group or activity until he/she can demonstrate appropriate behavior and self-control.

22. Identify those things the student has been grabbing from others and provide the student with those items as reinforcers for appropriate behavior.

23. Encourage the student to ask himself/herself questions to avoid impulsive behavior (e.g., "What should I be doing?" "How do I want to be perceived?").

24. Encourage the student to self-monitor his/her impulsivity. Awareness should reduce impulsive behaviors.

25. Teach the student to handle his/her anger, frustration, disappointment, etc., by walking away from the situation, talking with an adult, etc.

26. Encourage the student to verbalize his/her feelings before losing control (e.g., "I'm starting to act impulsively. I need to walk away from this situation.").

27. Choose a peer who will be a good influence to engage in activities with the student (e.g., someone younger/older, of the same/opposite gender, etc.).

28. Remove the student immediately from interacting with others when he/she begins to take things in a forceful manner.

29. Do not assume the student is being treated nicely by others. Peers may be stimulating inappropriate behavior.

30. Use a permanent marker to label all property brought to school by students and teachers.

31. Have the student make a list of consequences associated with grabbing things away from others (e.g., break something, hurt someone, embarrass self or others, etc.).

32. Make certain other students do not take things forcefully from the student. That may result in him/her attempting to forcefully take things from others.

33. Teach the student the concept of borrowing by loaning and requiring the return of those things the student has been taking from others.

34. Teach the student to respect others and their belongings by respecting the student's belongings.

35. Increase supervision (e.g., by teacher, peer, paraprofessional, etc.) of the student and those activities in which he/she is likely to forcefully take things from others.

36. Have the student identify the situations in which he/she is likely to act impulsively. After he/she has identified these situations, have him/her think of ways to minimize their occurrences.

37. Write a contract with the student specifying what behavior is expected (e.g., not grabbing things away from others) and what reinforcement will be made available when the terms of the contract have been met.

38. Make certain the student understands that things he/she breaks, destroys, etc., when taking things forcefully will be replaced by him/her.

39. Make certain the student understands the natural consequences of inappropriate behavior (e.g., the student must make restitution for taking things which belong to others).

40. Teach the student the concept of borrowing by allowing the student to borrow things from you and requiring him/her to ask permission before doing so.

41. Encourage the student to consider the consequences of his/her behavior before engaging in any activity.

42. Encourage all students to monitor their own belongings.

43. Reduce the opportunity to take things from other students by restricting students from bringing unnecessary items to school.

44. Give the student suggestions of things to do (e.g., count to 10, say the alphabet to himself/herself, walk away from the situation and then return, etc.) to avoid taking things from others in a forceful manner.

45. Communicate with the student's family to establish procedures whereby the student may earn those things he/she would otherwise take from other students.

46. Teach the student acceptable ways to communicate displeasure, anger, frustration, etc.

47. Supervise the student to monitor behavior.

48. Do not allow the student to use ADHD as an excuse. Hold the student responsible for his/her actions. However, understand and accept problems that ADHD brings into the student's life while he/she is learning to make accommodations.

49. Do not allow the student to participate in activities with those students with whom he/she has trouble getting along.

50. Become aware of the times when the student is most impulsive (e.g., in a large group of people, when he/she is angry, etc.) and limit his/her interactions with others during these times.

51. Be consistent. Deal with the student and his/her behavior in a manner that is as consistent as possible by reacting in the same manner each time, using the same consequences, etc.

Goal:

1. The student will demonstrate responsible behavior instead of stealing.

Objectives:

1. The student will demonstrate his/her ability to perform responsible replacement behaviors (e.g., completing/submitting his/her original homework instead of forging; buying rather than stealing clothing; etc.) instead of stealing on ____ out of ____ trials.
2. The student will refrain from stealing on all possible trials for ____ consecutive weeks/months.

Interventions:

1. Reinforce the student for behaving responsibly and not stealing by: (a) give the student a tangible reward (e.g., classroom privileges, line leading, passing out materials, five minutes free time, etc.) or (b) give the student an intangible reward (e.g., praise, handshake, smile, etc.).

2. Define what has been done correctly and what the student needs to do to replace theft and deceitful behaviors with positive, alternative behaviors (e.g., completing/submitting original homework instead of forging; relying upon himself/herself rather than cheating during exams; etc.).

3. Establish classroom rules and reinforce the student for following rules. Give positive, replacement behaviors more preferred attention than the undesired behavior can earn.

4. Reinforce those students who are choosing honesty rather than theft or deceit.

5. Write a contract specifying expected behavior (e.g., making positive decisions in the best interests of himself/herself and others, opting for honest actions rather than theft or deceit, etc.) and reinforcements that will be made available when the terms of the contract have been met.

6. Communicate with the student's parents (e.g., notes home, phone calls, etc.) to share information concerning the student's progress. The parents may reinforce the student at home for appropriate behavior at school.

7. Evaluate the situation and/or task in terms of relative ease or difficulty for the student.

8. Always supervise the student who does not consider the consequences of inappropriate, risky, and/or abusive behavior such as theft or deceit.

9. Establish nonverbal communication with the student, including reciprocal eye contact. Opportunity for eye contact needs to be available at all times.

10. Maintain mobility so your physical presence near the student is possible throughout the day.

11. Give the student additional responsibilities (e.g., chores, errands, etc.) so he/she can realize success and feelings of accomplishment through positive, purposeful behavior. This will decrease the impulse to cheat for attention.

12. Prevent the student from becoming overstimulated by an activity (e.g., monitor/supervise the student's behavior during physical activities, games, parties, etc.).

13. Provide adequate time to perform activities to prevent any need the student may feel to cheat.

14. Provide the student with clear, simply stated explanations, instructions, and directions so expectations can be readily understood and followed.

15. Assist the student to begin tasks carefully and thoughtfully.

16. Identify and seek the involvement of a peer who exercises honesty instead of deceit in his/her daily affairs for the student to model.

17. Be a consistent, positive authority figure.

18. Consistently act upon the student's antecedent behaviors (e.g., increased restlessness, marked changes in moods, etc.). At these times, intervention can include
(a) redirection to focus on the daily routine and the positive reinforcements the student can decide to earn;
(b) alternatives to the daily routine to lower frustration with the understanding that a return to daily activities needs to and will occur; and
(c) modification of activities to reduce frustration and/or overstimulation.
Providing early intervention may reduce the frequency of stealing and deceitful behavior.

19. Make certain the student receives and understands information for performing requested activities through written and verbal information (e.g., directions, reminders, etc.).

20. Maintain a positive, professional relationship with the student. Adverse relationships may increase the student's perceived need or desire to steal and behave deceitfully.

21. Deliver directions in a step-by-step sequence. Rehearse these with the student, and reinforce him/her for thinking through each before work on a task begins.

22. Encourage the student to communicate thoughts and concerns rather than resorting to forms of cheating.

23. Do not allow the student to be unsupervised anywhere.

24. Provide the student with a "pro and con" list of consequences that occur due to choices the student decides upon.

25. Provide learning experiences that emphasize cause-and-effect links between behaviors and consequences.

26. The student may not have a positive sense of ownership. Provide an opportunity to achieve a sense of ownership by
(a) making purchases for articles of clothing and other socially desirable items through paid work (when age appropriate);
(b) encouraging/praising the student for keeping his/her possessions and clothing clean and in good repair (e.g., being able to earn reinforcement for having a clean desk or locker, etc.);
(c) providing age appropriate tangible reinforcement linked with positive social reinforcement (e.g., praise, etc.); and
(d) helping the student to build or create a prize possession.

27. The student who steals or behaves deceitfully may only feel the behavior is wrong if caught. Encourage the student to value the principle of honesty by giving it high reinforcement value in the classroom.

28. Structure the environment to reduce opportunities for stealing (e.g., seating the student in the front of the classroom for careful monitoring, providing the student ways of safely storing items that are needed at school, etc.).

29. Make certain the student knows that everyone makes mistakes to decrease fear of failure.

30. Provide extremely close supervision at times when the student's likelihood of stealing increases.

31. Prevent peers from stimulating the student's inappropriate behavior.

32. Make the consequences of stealing obvious by identifying the consequence as it occurs and discussing alternatives which would have prevented a particular consequence.

33. Provide the student with frequent opportunities for success (e.g., calling on the student when he/she can answer successfully, etc.).

34. Give the student structured opportunities to receive naturally occurring consequences for his/her choices.

35. Increase the number and duration of situations requiring the student's demonstration of positive, replacement skills instead of stealing based on the following:

(a) The student's current attempts at making positive, informed decisions for himself/herself.

(b) The student's current ability to productively manage environmental stress (e.g., the student may make positive decisions during a situation or task in one environment but may not in another due to fear of social embarrassment, noise levels, etc.).

(c) The student's current ability to productively manage task related stress (e.g., the length of time and number of steps required for successful task completion may be frustrating or stressful to the student).

36. Avoid competition. Failure may cause the student to ignore consequences of his/her behavior, and cheat or steal to look like a winner or fit in.

37. Show an interest in the student (e.g., acknowledge the student, ask for the student's opinion, work one-on-one with the student).

38. Through role play, rehearse positive alternatives to behaving/reacting impulsively to challenging situations.

39. Teach the student to respect others and their belongings by respecting the student and his/her belongings.

40. Assist the student to develop a system or approach to situational problem solving tailored to the student's unique abilities and his/her likes/dislikes (e.g., the student may ask himself/herself a few questions to identify the problem and decide upon a positive action).

41. Help the student identify his/her antecedents to stealing or deceit. For every antecedent identified, help the student develop positive, alternative actions he/she may take toward problem solving.

42. Offer the student opportunities for creative self-expression (e.g., sculpting, gymnastics, writing, drawing, dancing, acting, etc.). Activities need to be viewed as an avenue of self-expression rather than a way to reinforce, reward, or earn grades.

43. Introduce and maintain positive, consistent class management which incorporates an opportunity to think through consequences before decisions are made.

44. Help the student review his/her decisions to determine whether improvements can be made. When improvements are needed, help the student identify and practice positive alternatives. Reinforce the student's attempts at one of these positive alternatives.

45. Insist upon reciprocity in teacher-student relationships (e.g., trust can be viewed as something not freely given or expected, it is earned; the student will need to know what is expected to earn the teacher's trust).

46. Maintain consistent behavioral expectations across environments.

47. Provide students and parents information about stress, ways to reduce and/or manage stress.

48. Establish positive communication with the student, and help assure the student receives any needed support (e.g., counseling) to build self-esteem and interpersonal relationships.

49. When a student's patterns of behavior indicate that he/she will steal or be deceitful with no regard for the consequences of his/her choices, assure this student receives the support and monitoring needed across environments in the interests of the student and his/her community.

50. Incorporate into definitions of socially desirable behavior stopping and thinking through impulses rather than stealing.

51. When a student requires reassurance before beginning a new task, remind him/her of past accomplishments. Reinforce positive attempts, and rehearse the fact that sincere, positive effort is always more important than perfection. This may help provide the student support to honestly try rather than cheat.

52. Make certain the student receives more attention for appropriate behavior than he/she would receive for cheating or deceitful behavior.

53. The student may deny any wrong doing to avoid embarrassment and negative consequences. When the student's version of what occurred differs from what was witnessed, describe both versions to the student for his/her reference without accusing. (The student may stop listening during a direct confrontation. It is most important that he/she calms, and associates his/her behavior with consequences.)

54. Make certain consequences for stealing and being deceitful do not stigmatize the student. Nonpunitive consequences might include environmental restitution (e.g., replacing/returning stolen items).

55. Communicate with the student's family to establish procedures whereby the student may earn those things he/she would otherwise take from other students.

56. Encourage all students to monitor their own belongings.

57. Reduce the opportunity to steal by restricting students from bringing unnecessary items to school.

58. Make certain the student is aware of local and federal laws regarding stealing.

225 Has been arrested for breaking and entering into a house, building, or car

Goal:

1. The student will choose positive skills and behaviors rather than breaking and entering.

Objectives:

1. The student will demonstrate his/her ability to use positive, adaptive skills instead of breaking and entering on _____ out of _____ trials.
2. The student will demonstrate his/her ability to access his/her support system during stressful times instead of breaking and entering on _____ out of _____ trials.
3. The student will refrain from breaking and entering following training on all trials in _____ consecutive weeks/months.

Interventions:

1. Reinforce the student for behaving responsibly and not breaking and entering by: (a) give the student a tangible reward (e.g., classroom privileges, line leading, passing out materials, five minutes free time, etc.) or (b) give the student an intangible reward (e.g., praise, handshake, smile, etc.).

2. Define what has been done correctly and what the student needs to do to productively replace breaking and entering behaviors with positive, alternative behaviors (e.g., spending money the student has earned on items he/she needs/wants; developing positive leisure, recreational, and social skills instead of breaking and entering when bored; etc.).

3. Establish classroom rules. Rehearse rules and reinforce rule-abiding behavior frequently. (Give positive, replacement behaviors more preferred attention than the undesired behavior can earn.)

4. Reinforce those students who are choosing positive, adaptive behaviors rather than breaking and entering.

5. Give the student additional responsibilities (e.g., chores, errands, etc.) so he/she can realize success and feelings of accomplishment through positive, purposeful behavior. This may decrease the impulse to break and enter for purposes of gaining attention.

6. Communicate with parents (e.g., notes home, phone calls, etc.) regarding the student's progress. The parents may reinforce the student at home for choosing to use positive, adaptive behaviors instead of breaking and entering.

7. As the student successfully makes informed decisions, gradually increase opportunities for informed decision making.

8. Supervise the student who does not consider the consequences of inappropriate, risky, and/or abusive behavior such as breaking and entering.

9. Establish nonverbal communication with the student, including reciprocal eye contact. Opportunity for eye contact needs to be available at all times.

10. Maintain mobility so your physical presence near the student is possible throughout the day.

11. Write a contract specifying expected behavior (e.g., making positive decisions in the best interests of himself/herself and others; opting to use positive, adaptive behaviors instead of breaking and entering; etc.) and reinforcements which will be made available when the terms of the contract have been met.

12. The student who is involved in breaking and entering may also be involved in destructive gangs and/or be involved in other forms of anti-social, destructive behavior. The student and family members will need community support beyond the scope of the classroom. However, the following may prove helpful:

(a) Encourage the student to develop thoughts, opinions, and positive alternatives to try in challenging situations specific to local communities. Identify, develop, and rehearse positive actions to try in role-play situations.

(b) Help the student locate and communicate with support sources in the local community. These may be formal support sources (e.g., police, counseling, etc.) and/or informal (e.g., concerned neighbors, friends, neighborhood watch programs, business persons, etc.). Listen to the student carefully (e.g., he/she may not want to contact police for fear of gang retribution) and develop support sources with him/her.

(c) Provide the class with a tangible list of local heroes in the community who do not break the law.

(d) Adopt part of the community with the class for clean-up, gardening, etc., to instill a sense of neighborhood pride and membership.

13. Provide the student with clear, simply stated explanations, instructions, and directions so expectations for behaviors that are positive and adaptive can be readily understood and followed.

14. Identify and seek the involvement of a peer who exercises positive, adaptive skills in his/her daily affairs for the student to model.

15. Maintain a positive, professional relationship with the student. Adverse relationships may increase the student's perceived need or desire to break and enter.

16. Be a consistent, positive authority figure.

17. Observe and consistently act upon the student's antecedent behaviors (e.g., increased restlessness, marked changes in moods, etc.). At these times, intervention can include

(a) redirection to focus on the daily routine and the positive reinforcements the student can decide to earn;

(b) alternatives to the daily routine to lower frustration with the understanding that a return to daily activities needs to and will occur; and

(c) modification of activities to reduce frustration and/or overstimulation.

18. Encourage the student to communicate thoughts and concerns to you rather than resorting to breaking and entering.

19. Do not allow the student to be unsupervised anywhere.

20. Through role play, provide the student positive ways of "walking away" from socially challenging situations in which others may try to persuade the student to break and enter.

21. Provide the student with opportunities to learn and practice positive social skills.

22. Provide the student with a "pro and con" list of consequences that occur due to choices the student decides upon (e.g., the consequence of purchasing items with money earned and budgeted for shopping is more rewarding than the consequence of breaking and entering).

23. Provide learning experiences which emphasize cause-and-effect links between behaviors such as breaking and entering and consequences.

24. Increase the student's opportunity for success on a daily basis.

25. Provide the student with an opportunity to achieve a sense of ownership by

(a) making purchases for articles of clothing and other socially desirable items through paid work (when age appropriate);

(b) encouraging/praising the student for keeping his/her possessions and clothing clean and in good repair (e.g., being able to earn reinforcement for having a clean desk or locker, etc.); and

(c) providing age-appropriate tangible reinforcement linked with positive social reinforcement (e.g., praise, etc.).

26. Teach the student how to create and achieve positive, personal goals and objectives. Help the student identify a short-term goal which can be attained via completion of a few objectives in a brief period of time (e.g., within a week or two). Goals should be chosen based upon the student's learning style and personal preferences. As the student achieves success, gradually increase the goals, time between reinforcement and type of reinforcement.

27. Incorporate the student's positive, personal goals into a contract format. Celebrate completed contracts as part of the reinforcement strategy.

28. Encourage the student to value the principles of honesty and respect for other's property by giving these high reinforcement value in the classroom.

29. Structure the environment to reduce opportunities for stealing and/or intruding upon other's property (e.g., seating the student up front for careful monitoring, providing students ways of safely storing items such as jackets, etc.).

30. Make certain the student knows that everyone makes mistakes to decrease fear of failure.

31. Provide extremely close supervision at times when the student's likelihood of breaking and entering increases.

32. Prevent peers from provoking the student into breaking and entering.

33. Make the consequences of breaking and entering obvious by identifying the consequence as it occurs and discussing alternatives which would have prevented a particular consequence.

34. Provide frequent opportunities for success (e.g., calling on the student at times when he/she may experience the success inherent to a correct answer, etc.).

35. Avoid competition. Failure may cause the student to ignore consequences of his/her behavior, and break and enter and/or steal to look like a winner or fit in.

36. Show an interest in the student (e.g., acknowledge the student, ask for the student's opinion, work one-on-one with the student).

37. Give the student structured opportunities to receive naturally occurring consequences for his/her choices. For example, in a classroom, breaking and entering someone's desk or locker might result in consequences as specified in school policy; refraining from such behavior should result in naturally occurring social privileges and regard.

38. Increase the number and duration of situations requiring the student's demonstration of positive, replacement skills instead of stealing or breaking and entering based on the following:
(a) The student's current attempts at making positive, informed decisions for himself/herself.
(b) The student's current ability to productively manage environmental stress (e.g., the student may make positive decisions during a situation or task in one environment but may not in another due to fear of social embarrassment, noise levels, etc.).
(c) The student's current ability to productively manage task-related stress (e.g., the length of time and number of steps required for successful task completion may be frustrating or stressful to the student).

39. Maintain consistent behavioral expectations across environments.

40. Teach the student to respect others and their belongings by respecting the student and his/her belongings.

41. Assist the student to develop a system or approach to situational problem solving tailored to the student's abilities and his/her likes/dislikes (e.g., the student may ask himself/herself a few questions to identify the problem and decide upon a positive action).

42. Help the student identify his/her antecedents to breaking and entering. For every antecedent identified, help the student develop positive, alternative actions he/she may take toward problem solving.

43. Offer the student opportunities for creative self-expression (e.g., sculpting, gymnastics, writing, drawing, dancing, acting, etc.). Activities need to be viewed as an avenue of self-expression rather than a way to reinforce, reward, or earn grades.

44. Introduce and maintain positive, consistent class management which incorporates an opportunity to think through consequences before decisions are made.

45. Help the student review his/her decisions to determine whether improvements can be made. When improvements are needed, help the student identify and practice positive alternatives. Find a way to positively reinforce the student's attempts at one of the positive alternatives.

46. Insist upon reciprocity in teacher-student relationships (e.g., Trust can be viewed as something not freely given or expected, it is earned. The student will need to know what is expected to earn the teacher's trust).

47. Help the student think through his/her impulses to steal or be deceitful in terms of how these may affect his/her social and work relationships.

48. Through role play, rehearse positive alternatives to behaving/reacting impulsively to challenging situations.

49. Provide students and parents with information about stress, including positive alternatives to reduce and/or manage stress.

50. Establish positive communication with the student, and help assure he/she receives any needed support (e.g., counseling) to build self-esteem and interpersonal relationships.

51. The student who is involved in law-breaking behaviors may be involved in substance abuse, and/or may have other severe emotional and/or behavioral concerns. Advocate for the student to receive support (e.g., counseling, medical attention, etc.) to address emotional/behavioral concerns and/or addiction.

52. Incorporate into definitions of socially desirable behavior stopping and thinking through impulses rather than breaking and entering.

53. Make certain the student receives more attention for appropriate behavior than he/she would receive for breaking and entering.

54. The student may deny any wrongdoing to avoid embarrassment and negative consequences. When the student's version of what occurred differs from what was witnessed, describe both versions to the student for his/her reference without accusing. (The student may stop listening during a direct confrontation. It is most important that he/she calms, and associates his/her behavior with consequences.)

55. Make certain consequences for breaking and entering do not stigmatize the student. Nonpunitive consequences might include environmental restitution (e.g., replacing/returning stolen items).

56. When a student's patterns of behavior indicate that he/she will break and enter with no regard for the consequences of his/her choices, make certain the student receives support and monitoring across environments in the interests of the student and his/her community.

57. Assist the student in developing a structured approach to his/her daily and weekly activities to help prevent boredom and encourage positive goal achievement. Incorporate reinforcement strategies for the daily/weekly activities the student attempts and completes.

Goals:

1. The student will move about the classroom only when necessary.
2. The student will demonstrate body movements appropriate to the situation.

Objectives:

1. The student will leave his/her seat only when given permission by the teacher on _____ out of _____ trials.
2. The student will move about the classroom only when given permission by the teacher on _____ out of _____ trials.
3. The student will go directly to a specific location and immediately return to his/her seat when given permission by the teacher on _____ out of _____ trials.

Interventions:

1. Communicate with the student's parents (e.g., notes home, phone calls, etc.) to share information concerning their child's appropriate behavior. The parents may reinforce the student at home for staying in his/her seat at school.

2. Allow the student to take a break while working on monotonous assignments to relieve restlessness and improve concentration.

3. Encourage the student to recite a mantra to himself/herself when entering a situation where he/she has to sit for an extended period of time (e.g., be still, be still, be still).

4. Have the student chart the length of time he/she is able to remain in his/her seat.

5. Make sure the student knows when it is acceptable to leave his/her seat (e.g., in an emergency).

6. Require the student to have all the necessary materials assembled prior to beginning a project, assignment, etc., to reduce the need to leave his/her seat.

7. Provide constant, positive reinforcement for appropriate behavior. Ignore as many inappropriate behaviors as possible.

8. Have the student question any directions, explanations, or instructions he/she does not understand.

9. Allow some time for movement between assignments if the student appears to need a break.

10. Try various groupings in the classroom to determine the situation in which the student is most comfortable and remains seated without constant supervision.

11. Make the necessary adjustments in the environment to prevent the student from experiencing stress, frustration, anger, etc., as much as possible, to decrease the student's tendency to leave his/her seat.

12. Reinforce those students in the classroom who stay in their seat, ask permission to leave their seat, etc.

13. Reinforce the student for staying in his/her seat based on the length of time he/she can be successful. As the student demonstrates success, gradually increase the length of time required for reinforcement.

14. Remove the student from the group or activity until he/she can stay in his/her seat.

15. Provide the student with a clearly understood list of consequences for inappropriate behavior.

16. Reduce the emphasis on competition. Competitive activities may cause the student to become overstimulated and leave his/her seat.

17. Choose a peer to model staying in his/her seat for the student.

18. Schedule short activities for the student to perform while seated. As the student demonstrates success staying in his/her seat, gradually increase the length of the activities.

19. Give the student frequent opportunities to leave his/her seat for appropriate reasons (e.g., getting materials, running errands, assisting the teacher, etc.).

20. Speak with the student to explain (a) what he/she is doing wrong (e.g., leaving seat without permission, etc.) and (b) what he/she should be doing (e.g., remaining in his/her seat, asking permission to leave seat, etc.).

21. Establish classroom rules:
- Work on-task.
- Work quietly.
- Remain in your seat.
- Finish task.
- Meet task expectations.

Review rules often. Reinforce students for following the rules.

22. Make certain that the expectation for the student to remain seated is appropriate for his/her level of development and ability.

23. Encourage the student to remind himself/herself to wait when he/she feels the urge to get out of his/her seat (e.g., "Stop. Count to ten.").

24. Encourage the student to self-monitor his/her behavior to decrease the need for teacher intervention to remain seated.

25. Interact frequently with the student to maintain his/her attention to the activity (e.g., ask the student questions, ask the student's opinions, stand close to the student, seat the student near the teacher's desk, etc.).

26. Remind the student when needed to remain in his/her seat.

27. Reinforce the student for staying in his/her seat: (a) give the student a tangible reward (e.g., classroom privileges, five minutes free time, etc.) or (b) give the student an intangible reward (e.g., praise, handshake, smile, etc.).

28. Encourage the student to participate in high energy activities after school that allow him/her to release excess energy (e.g., racquetball, soccer, etc.).

29. Provide the student with frequent opportunities to participate, take a turn, etc., to keep him/her involved in an activity.

30. Prevent the student from becoming overstimulated by an activity (e.g., frustrated, angry, excited, etc.).

31. Seat the student near the teacher.

32. Separate the student from the peer who stimulates his/her inappropriate behavior.

33. Provide the student with the most attractive and interesting activities possible.

34. Provide the student with a calm, quiet environment in which to work.

35. Establish times when it is permissible for the student to be out of his/her seat (e.g., leave his/her seat only to get a book, only after obtaining permission, etc.).

36. Provide the student with a predetermined signal when he/she begins to leave his/her seat.

37. Make certain that reinforcement is not inadvertently given for inappropriate behavior (e.g., attending to the student only when he/she leaves his/her seat).

38. Be proactive. Work with the school counselor to design a schedule conducive to the student's success (e.g., physical education scheduled the last period of the day, intersperse electives which allow greater freedom of movement with classes requiring extended periods of concentration, etc.).

39. Avoid placing the student in situations that require sitting for an extended period of time such as lectures, seminars, assemblies, etc. Provide the information for the student through a tape recording or lecture notes.

40. Evaluate the visual and auditory stimuli in the classroom. Determine the amount of stimuli the student can tolerate. Remove extraneous stimuli from the environment.

41. Interact frequently with the student to prevent the student from leaving his/her seat.

42. Evaluate the appropriateness of tasks to determine (a) if the tasks are too easy, (b) if the tasks are too difficult, and (c) if the length of time scheduled for the tasks is adequate.

43. Be consistent in expecting the student to stay seated. Do not allow him/her to get up and walk around one time and expect him/her to remain seated the next time.

44. Discuss your concerns regarding the student's attention span and inability to remain seated with his/her family, a school official, etc., if it is interfering with his/her progress at school.

45. Have the student perform one task or assignment at a time. Give the student the opportunity for movement between activities.

46. Teach the student to use techniques such as crossing his/her arms and legs, clinching his/her fists, and webbing his/her hands when he/she feels the urge to leave his/her seat.

47. Identify the situations in which the student is most likely to engage in inappropriate behavior and fail to remain seated. After you have identified these situations, think of ways to minimize their occurrences.

48. Write a contract with the student specifying what behavior is expected (e.g., staying in his/her seat) and what reinforcement will be made available when the terms of the contract have been met.

49. Maintain visibility to and from the student to keep his/her attention when verbal questions/directions are being delivered. The teacher should be able to see the student and the student should be able to see the teacher. Make eye contact possible at all times.

50. Facilitate on-task behavior by providing a full schedule of daily events. Prevent lag time when the student would be free to leave his/her seat.

51. Communicate with the student's cooperative work experience/vocational education teacher to place the student on a job site allowing a high degree of physical movement.

52. Limit the amount of time you expect the student to be seated to perform tasks and assignments. Do not initially give him/her things to do that take more than 10-15 minutes to complete.

Goal:

1. The student will resolve his/her differences in ways which preclude using weapons.

Objectives:

1. The student will demonstrate ability to use positive means of conflict resolution that preclude use of weapons for all trials in _____ weeks/months.
2. The student will refrain from fighting behavior for all trials in _____ weeks/months.
3. The student will refrain from using weapons for all trials in _____ weeks/months.

Interventions:

1. Reinforce the student for working through his/her difficulties with others without resorting to violence (such as fighting with weapons): (a) give the student a tangible reward (e.g., classroom privileges, line leading, passing out materials, five minutes free time, etc.) or (b) give the student an intangible reward (e.g., praise, handshake, smile, etc.).

2. Develop with the student a contract which specifies positive behaviors to replace attempts at retributional behavior, and the positive reinforcements a student may obtain by meeting contract terms.

3. Communicate with parents (e.g., notes home, phone calls, etc.) regarding the student's progress with social and communication skills to replace fighting with weapons. The parents may reinforce the student for the use of positive social skills at school, at home, and in community environments.

4. Develop positive alternatives to violent responses such as fighting with weapons. Provide the student with positive role models who do not use retributional behavior to problem solve, and give the student positive problem-solving approaches.

5. The student who expresses and/or acts upon thoughts of fighting with weapons may need additional services and supports (e.g., counseling).

6. When working with someone who maintains he/she is being slighted or wronged by another, always listen and respond as objectively as possible. Do not indicate to the student that you think he/she is lying about another, because he/she may then "shut you out" and not meaningfully invest in problem solving with you.

7. Provide the student with information concerning problem-solving techniques (e.g., identify the problem, generate positive solutions, implement a solution, evaluate effectiveness of the problem-solving plan, and modify if necessary).

8. Model using problem-solving techniques to replace attempts at fighting.

9. Provide outlets for the student who expresses and/or acts upon thoughts of fighting with weapons (e.g., art work, diary writing or self-recording, etc.).

10. Provide the student who expresses or attempts to act upon violent thoughts and persons who are the focus of potentially vengeful behavior close monitoring to prevent harm.

11. When a dispute occurs, meet with both parties separately and privately to hear each side of the story. Help each party to identify positive alternatives instead of fighting.

12. Use role play to explore situations in which someone tries to repay "a wrong with a wrong." Discuss the situation, and arrive at positive alternatives which could occur rather than fighting with weapons. Explore the benefits the "wronged person" may realize by choosing positive responses.

13. Let the student know you care about his/her thoughts and feelings.

14. Provide the student with information and instruction on stress-management techniques.

15. Working with the student, arrive at coping techniques tailored to individual preferences and abilities (e.g., taking two slow, deep breaths; self-timing out to another part of the classroom to calm; head on table or desk for 20 seconds, etc.). Rehearse use of these skills to replace attempted violence.

16. Provide the student with a clear chain of command he/she and others in the environment need to use to process complaints, grievances, etc. Rehearse each communication link, and praise the student for resorting to the chain of command.

17. Provide the student with closely supervised opportunities to meet others in recreational and social functions. Social skills may be among the student's replacement skills for retributional behaviors.

18. Provide the student with the opportunity to communicate with role models from the community who have success stories to relate. Enlist these community heroes in identifying retributional behavior as damaging and undesirable.

19. Reinforce those students who chose a positive alternative instead of behaving in an inappropriate or violent manner.

20. The student may associate "bad feelings" with "being bad." Encourage the student to view himself/herself as good, and to accept feelings. Encourage the student to view the choices he/she makes as either acceptable or unacceptable, poor/good, etc.

21. In the interests of individual and group safety, never assume a student will not carry out expressed plans for violence (e.g., fighting with a weapon). Always provide the student and any potential victims close monitoring.

22. Do not indirectly reinforce a student for his/her expressed aggressive thoughts, such as thoughts about "paying someone back." Provide the student with more verbal response for positive actions you would like to see again to prevent or discourage the student from expressing and attempting to act upon aggressive thoughts for attention.

23. Encourage the student to
- (a) think about the thoughts and feelings of others if revenge occurred (e.g., the person who is the focus of the "get even" reaction, family members and friends of both parties, classmates, school administration, etc.);
- (b) think about the potential consequences to self;
- (c) identify positive alternatives to revenge;
- (d) identify thoughts/feelings of others should the positive alternative be attempted; and
- (e) identify thoughts/feelings of himself/herself should the positive alternatives be attempted.

24. Assist the student to actively implement his/her reasonable, positive alternatives to fighting, but make sure the student
- (a) is calm (e.g., no longer feeling hostile);
- (b) has developed his/her thoughts and plans in the event the positive alternative does not work (e.g., will use coping skills and positive forms of self-expression, etc.);
- (c) has developed a "Plan B" which consists of another positive alternative to try; and
- (d) will evaluate the effectiveness of his/her approach with the teacher after this has been attempted.

25. Provide the student with positive activities to
- (a) give the student matters of interest to focus upon, think through, and act upon other than violence;
- (b) give the student opportunities to experience success (this may help decrease stress related to frustration); and
- (c) give the student positive, structured opportunities to work with others to encourage productive teamwork and render violent thoughts/behaviors counterproductive.

26. Provide the student with focus for his/her actions/behaviors by developing with him/her a daily schedule. Reinforce students for
- (a) initiating schedule development;
- (b) beginning scheduled activities independently;
- (c) following his/her schedule;
- (d) completing scheduled activities; and
- (e) all positive attempts at working on the schedule and on scheduled activities.

27. Once a schedule has been created with student involvement, make certain the student receives assistance from you to realize success the first few (e.g., one to three) days. As the student demonstrates success, gradually decrease assistance.

28. Provide reinforcement linked to successful completion of scheduled activities.

29. The student may need opportunities for teamwork, but may overreact to competitive activities. Provide the student the chance to work in small groups or teams on activities, but structure team learning opportunities so these are not competitive by establishing sincere ways of providing merit for each group's efforts.

30. The student who fights with weapons may have already experienced some form of consequence from the legal system, and may have resultant negative (or positive) social status. Help the student define himself/herself as successful in terms of positive accomplishments in school.

31. Provide positive alternative activities instead of ongoing activities when the student indicates signs of frustration or overstimulation to prevent problems from occurring.

32. When providing the student with the opportunity to work in a group, consider his/her interests and skills.

33. Provide the student with frequent, natural opportunities to feel successful on a daily basis. Plan to provide additional encouragement for the student to begin and complete new activities which may seem threatening to him/her.

34. Provide the student with coping strategies which include physical activities for tension release.

35. Work with other service providers (e.g., social workers, counselors, etc.) to provide the student with coping/replacement skills to use rather than fighting with weapons. Reinforce the student's use of these skills.

36. Coping skills and activities need not be contingent upon activity and behavioral performance.

37. Provide structured, monitored opportunities for building social skills.

38. Provide any person who has been identified as a potential victim of violence close monitoring to prevent harm.

39. Teach all students ways of safely traveling across community environments.

40. Intervene early when there is a problem with fighting to prevent more serious problems from occurring.

228   Is not dependable

Goals:
1. The student will improve his/her punctuality.
2. The student will demonstrate behavior that is predictable.
3. The student will respond to situations in a predictable manner.

Objectives:
1. The student will be on time to school on ____ out of ____ days per week.
2. The student will be on time to school on ____ out of ____ days per month.
3. The student will be on time to class on ____ out of ____ class periods per day.
4. The student will be on time to class on ____ out of ____ class periods per week.
5. The student will be on time to (specified activity) on ____ out of ____ days per week.
6. The student will be on time to (specified activity) on ____ out of ____ days per month.
7. The student will respond consistently to similar situations in the environment on ____ out of ____ trials.
8. The student will respond consistently to situations in the environment for ____ day(s) at a time.
9. The student will respond consistently to situations in the environment for ____ week(s) at a time.
10. The student will respond consistently to situations in the environment for ____ month(s) at a time.
11. The student will show emotion that is appropriate to the situation on ____ out of ____ trials.
12. The student will react in a manner appropriate to the situation on ____ out of ____ trials.
13. The student will maintain his/her orientation to time and place for ____ day(s) at a time.
14. The student will maintain his/her orientation to time and place for ____ week(s) at a time.
15. The student will maintain his/her orientation to time and place for ____ month(s) at a time.

Interventions:

1. Reinforce the student for being on time, prepared, ready to work, etc.: (a) give the student a tangible reward (e.g., classroom privileges, line leading, passing out materials, five minutes free time, etc.) or (b) give the student an intangible reward (e.g., praise, handshake, smile, etc.).

2. Speak with the student to explain (a) what he/she is doing wrong (e.g., failing to be on time, prepared, ready to work, etc.) and (b) what he/she should be doing (e.g., being on time, prepared, ready to work, etc.).

3. Establish classroom rules:
- Work on-task.
- Work quietly.
- Remain in your seat.
- Finish task.
- Meet task expectations.

Review rules often. Reinforce students for following the rules.

4. Reinforce those students in the classroom who are on time, prepared, ready to work, etc.

5. Reinforce the student for being on time, prepared, ready to work, etc., based on the length of time he/she can be successful. As the student demonstrates success, gradually increase the length of time required for reinforcement.

6. Write a contract with the student specifying what behavior is expected (e.g., being on time, prepared, ready to work, etc.) and what reinforcement will be made available when the terms of the contract have been met.

7. Communicate with the parents (e.g., notes home, phone calls, etc.) to share information concerning the student's progress. The parents may reinforce the student at home for being on time, prepared, ready to work, etc., at school.

8. Evaluate the appropriateness of the task to determine (a) if the assignments are too easy, (b) if the assignments are too difficult, and (c) if the length of time scheduled for assignments is adequate.

9. Reduce stimuli which would contribute to failing to be on time, prepared, ready to work, etc. (e.g., testing situations, peers, physical activities, etc.).

10. Modify or adjust situations that cause the student to fail to be on time, prepared, ready to work, etc.

11. Make the necessary adjustments in the environment to prevent the student from experiencing stress, frustration, anger, etc., as much as possible.

12. Reduce distracting stimuli (e.g., place the student in the front row, provide a carrel or quiet place away from distractions, etc.). This is used as a means of reducing distracting stimuli and not as a form of punishment.

13. Try various groupings to determine the situation in which the student is most likely to be on time, prepared, ready to work, etc.

14. Make certain that reinforcement is not inadvertently given for failure to be on time, prepared, ready to work, etc.

15. Prevent the student from becoming overstimulated by an activity (e.g., monitor or supervise student behavior to limit overstimulation in physical activities, games, parties, etc.).

16. Assign a peer to work with the student to model being on time, prepared, ready to work, etc.

17. Reduce the emphasis on competition. Repeated failure may result in inappropriate behaviors.

18. Make the student aware of activities or events well in advance so he/she may prepare for them.

19. Explain that failing to be on time, prepared, ready to work, etc., is not unusual for students; but that continued failure to be on time, prepared, ready to work etc., is self-defeating.

20. Provide the student with opportunities for social and academic success.

21. Separate the student from the peer(s) who may be contributing to or stimulating the inappropriate behavior.

22. Provide praise and recognition for being on time, prepared, ready to work, etc., as often as possible.

23. Structure the environment so the schedule does not permit opportunities for the student to fail to be on time, prepared, ready to work, etc.

24. Avoid discussion of topics sensitive to the student (e.g., divorce, death, unemployment, alcoholism, etc.).

25. Provide as many enjoyable and interesting activities as possible so the student will want to be on time, prepared, ready to work, etc.

26. Provide a consistent routine for the student to facilitate dependability.

27. Allow flexibility in meeting academic demands when the student demonstrates sudden or dramatic mood changes (e.g., allow more time, modify assignments, provide help with assignments).

28. Teach the student to recognize changes in his/her behavior so he/she may deal with them appropriately.

29. Inform the student in advance when a change at school is going to occur (e.g., change in routine, special events, end of one activity and beginning of another, etc.) so he/she can prepare and make the necessary adjustments in advance.

30. Give the student adequate time to make adjustments to activity changes, situations, etc. (e.g., provide the student with several minutes to move from one activity to another).

31. Prevent the occurrence of specific stimuli that cause the student to fail to be on time, prepared, ready to work, etc. (e.g., demanding situations, interruptions, competition, abrupt changes, etc.).

32. Provide the student with a predetermined signal (e.g., quiet sign, hand signal, verbal cue, etc.) when he/she begins to demonstrate an inappropriate behavior.

33. Provide a pleasant/calm atmosphere which would lessen the possibility of the student failing to be on time, prepared, ready to work, etc.

34. Provide the student with a schedule of daily events so he/she will know what is expected of him/her.

35. Provide the student with a selection of assignments and require him/her to choose a minimum number from the total amount (e.g., present the student with ten academic tasks from which he/she must finish six that day).

Reminder: Do not "force" the student to participate in any activity he/she finds unpleasant, embarrassing, etc.

229 Does not take care of personal property

Goals:

1. The student will improve his/her care of personal property behavior.
2. The student will improve his/her care of personal property behavior in academic settings.
3. The student will improve his/her care of personal property behavior in nonacademic settings.
4. The student will improve his/her care of personal property behavior outside the classroom.
5. The student will improve his/her care of personal property behavior in the classroom.

Objectives:

1. The student will take care of personal property with supervision on _____ out of _____ occasions.
2. The student will independently take care of personal property on ____ out of ____ occasions.
3. The student will keep personal property organized in the designated locations on ____ out of ____ occasions.
4. The student will use personal property for its designated purpose on ____ out of ____ occasions.
5. The student will maintain personal property in good working condition on ____ out of ____ occasions.
6. The student will maintain cleanliness of personal property on ____ out of ____ occasions.
7. The student will replace personal property when necessary on ____ out of ____ occasions.
8. The student will use personal property conservatively on ____ out of ____ occasions.

Interventions:

1. Reinforce the student for appropriate care of personal property: (a) give the student a tangible reward (e.g., classroom privileges, line leading, passing out materials, five minutes free time, etc.) or (b) give the student an intangible reward (e.g., praise, handshake, smile, etc.).

2. Speak to the student to explain (a) what he/she is doing wrong (e.g., failing to maintain organization or use materials appropriately) and (b) what he/she should be doing (e.g., keeping inside of desk organized, organizing materials on top of desk, using materials as instructed, etc.).

3. Establish classroom rules:
- Work on-task.
- Work quietly.
- Remain in your seat.
- Finish task.
- Meet task expectations.

Review rules often. Reinforce students for following rules.

4. Reinforce the student for appropriate care of personal property based on the length of time the student can be successful. As the student demonstrates success, gradually increase the length of time required for reinforcement.

5. Write a contract with the student specifying what behavior is expected (e.g., organization and appropriate use of materials) and what reinforcement will be made available when the terms of the contract have been met.

6. Communicate with parents (e.g., notes home, phone calls, etc.) to share information concerning the student's progress. The parents may reinforce the student at home for organization and appropriate use of materials at school.

7. Provide the student with additional work space (e.g., a larger desk or table at which to work).

8. Assign a peer to work directly with the student to serve as a model for appropriate use and organization of materials.

9. Provide time at the beginning of each day for the student to organize his/her materials.

10. Provide time at various points throughout the day for the student to organize his/her materials (e.g., before school, recess, or lunch; at the end of the day).

11. Evaluate the appropriateness of the task to determine (a) if the task is too easy; (b) if the task is too difficult; and (c) if the length of time scheduled to complete the task is adequate.

12. Minimize materials needed.

13. Reduce distracting stimuli (e.g., place the student on the front row, provide a carrel or quiet place away from distractions, etc.). This is used as a means of reducing distracting stimuli and not as a form of punishment.

14. Interact frequently with the student to encourage organizational skills or appropriate use of materials.

15. Assign the student organizational responsibilities in the classroom (e.g., equipment, software materials, etc.).

16. Limit the student's use of materials (i.e., provide the student with only those materials necessary at any given time).

17. Model organization and appropriate use of work materials (e.g., putting materials away before getting more out, having a place for all materials, maintaining an organized desk area, following a schedule for the day, etc.).

18. Provide adequate transition time between activities for the student to organize himself/herself.

19. Establish a routine to be followed for organization and appropriate use of work materials (e.g., provide the routine for the student in written form or verbally review often).

20. Provide adequate time for the completion of activities.

21. Supervise the student while he/she is performing schoolwork to monitor appropriate care of materials.

22. Allow natural consequences to occur as the result of the student's inability to organize or use materials appropriately (e.g., materials not maintained appropriately may be lost or not usable).

23. Assess the quality and clarity of directions, explanations, and instructions given to the student.

24. Assist the student in beginning each task to reduce impulsive behavior.

25. Provide the student with structure for all academic activities (e.g., specified directions, routine format for tasks, time units, etc.).

26. Give the student a checklist of materials necessary for each activity.

27. Provide storage space for materials the student is not using at any particular time.

28. Provide an organizer for materials inside the student's desk.

29. Provide the student with an organizational checklist (e.g., sharpening pencils, keeping books free of marks and tears, etc.).

30. Teach the student appropriate care of personal property (e.g., sharpening pencils, keeping books free of marks and tears, etc.).

31. Make certain that all personal property is labeled with the student's name.

32. Point out to the student that loaning personal property to other students does not reduce his/her responsibility for the property.

33. Teach the student how to conserve rather than waste materials (e.g., amount of glue, paper, tape, etc., to use; putting lids, caps, and tops on such materials as markers, pens, bottles, jars, cans; etc.).

34. Teach the student appropriate ways to deal with anger and frustration rather than destroying personal property and school materials (e.g., pencils, pens, workbooks, notebooks, textbooks, etc.).

35. Teach the student to maintain care of personal property and school materials (e.g., keep property with him/her, know where property is at all times, secure property in locker, leave valuable property at home, etc.).

36. Provide the student with a cubby, an extra desk, laundry basket, etc., for his/her materials to be kept away from where the student is working. Require the student to retrieve those materials needed for a specified activity. As the student demonstrates responsibility for materials, gradually allow the student to keep materials at his/her desk.

37. Provide reminders (e.g., list of property or materials) to help the student maintain and care for personal property.

38. Limit the student's freedom to take property from school if he/she is unable to remember to return the items.

39. Provide the student with verbal reminders of personal property or materials needed for each activity.

40. Limit the student's opportunity to use school materials if he/she is unable to care for his/her own personal property.

41. Make certain that failure to have necessary materials results in loss of opportunity to participate in activities or a failing grade for that day's activity.

42. Reduce the number of materials for which the student is responsible. As the student demonstrates appropriate care of property, gradually increase the number.

43. Provide the student with an appropriate place to store/secure personal property (e.g., desk, locker, closet, etc.) and require that the student store all property when not in use.

44. Teach the student that failure to care for personal property will result in the loss of freedom to maintain property (e.g., if the student cannot care for property the teacher(s) will hold all property).

45. Provide reminders (e.g. list of property or materials to help the student maintain and care for personal property).

46. Provide the student with a picture example or written list of how to hang a coat on a hook, where to put gloves, how to care for lunch box after using, etc.

47. List reminders by the restroom door of steps to follow before leaving the restroom (e.g., button shirt, tuck shirt in, snap and zip pants, wash hands, etc.).

48. Provide the student with a container in which to carry necessary materials to/from school, etc. (e.g., backpack, book bag, briefcase, etc.).

49. Review with the student how to care for personal property (e.g., practice with the student how to rinse out a lunch box, how to put crayons back in a box, how to tuck gloves and hat in a pocket and hang up a coat on a hook, etc.).

230 Stays out at night despite parental prohibitions

Goal:

1. The student will stay out at night only with parental permission.

Objectives:

1. The student will be home at the established hour of ____ on ____ out of ____ occasions.
2. The student will telephone parents to get permission to stay out later than planned on ____ out of ____ occasions.
3. The student will make certain his/her parents know where he/she is, when away from home, on ____ out of ____ trials.

Interventions:

1. Reinforce the student for behaving responsibly and not staying out late at night by: (a) give the student a tangible reward (e.g., classroom privileges, line leading, passing out materials, five minutes free time, etc.) or (b) give the student an intangible reward (e.g., praise, handshake, smile, etc.).

2. Define what has been done correctly and what the student needs to do to productively replace irresponsible behaviors with positive, alternative behaviors.

3. Establish classroom rules. Rehearse rules and reinforce rule-abiding behavior frequently. (Give positive, replacement behaviors more preferred attention than the undesired behavior can earn.)

4. Reinforce those students who are choosing positive, adaptive behaviors rather than staying out late at night.

5. Write a contract specifying expected behavior (e.g., making positive decisions in the best interests of himself/herself and others; opting to use positive, adaptive behaviors instead of irresponsible behaviors; etc.) and reinforcements which will be made available when the terms of the contract have been met.

6. As the student successfully makes informed decisions, gradually increase opportunities for informed decision making.

7. Supervise the student who does not consider the consequences of inappropriate, risky, and/or abusive behavior such as staying out at night despite parental prohibition.

8. Establish nonverbal communication with the student, including reciprocal eye contact. Opportunity for eye contact needs to be available at all times.

9. Maintain mobility so your physical presence near the student is possible throughout the day.

10. Give the student additional responsibilities (e.g., chores, errands, etc.) so he/she can realize success and feelings of accomplishment through positive, purposeful behavior. This may decrease the impulse to stay out at night for purposes of gaining attention.

11. Provide the student with clear, simply stated explanations, instructions, and directions so expectations for behaviors that are positive and adaptive can be readily understood and followed.

12. Identify and seek the involvement of a peer who exercises positive, adaptive skills in his/her daily affairs for the student to model.

13. Maintain a positive, professional relationship with the student. Adverse relationships may increase the student's irresponsible behavior.

14. Be a consistent, positive authority figure.

15. Encourage the student to communicate his/her thoughts and concerns to others.

16. Do not allow the student to be unsupervised anywhere.

17. Provide the student with opportunities to learn and practice positive social skills.

18. Provide the student with a "pro and con" list of consequences that occur due to choices the student decides upon.

19. Provide learning experiences which emphasize cause and effect links between behaviors such as staying out all night against parents' rules.

20. Increase the student's opportunity for success on a daily basis.

21. Teach the student how to create and achieve positive, personal goals and objectives. Help the student identify a short-term goal which can be attained via completion of a few objectives in a brief period of time (e.g., within a week or two). Goals should be chosen based upon the student's learning style and personal preferences. As the student achieves success, gradually increase the goals, time between reinforcement and type of reinforcement.

22. Incorporate the student's positive, personal goals into a contract format. Celebrate completed contracts as part of the reinforcement strategy.

23. Prevent peers from provoking the student into staying out at night.

24. Make the consequences of staying out at night obvious by identifying the consequence as it occurs and discussing alternatives which would have prevented a particular consequence.

25. Provide the student frequent opportunities for success (e.g., calling on the student at times when he/she may experience the success inherent to a correct answer, etc.).

26. Show an interest in the student (e.g., acknowledge the student, ask for the student's opinion, work one-on-one with the student).

27. Give the student structured opportunities to receive naturally occurring consequences for his/her choices.

28. Maintain consistent behavioral expectations across environments.

29. Assist the student to develop a system or approach to situational problem solving tailored to the student's abilities and his/her likes/dislikes (e.g., the student may ask himself/herself a few questions to identify the problem and decide upon a positive action).

30. Help the student identify his/her antecedents to staying out at night. For every antecedent identified, help the student develop positive, alternative actions he/she may take toward problem solving.

31. Offer the student opportunities for creative self-expression (e.g., sculpting, gymnastics, writing, drawing, dancing, acting, etc.). Activities need to be viewed as an avenue of self-expression rather than a way to reinforce, reward, or earn grades.

32. Introduce and maintain positive, consistent class management which incorporates an opportunity to think through consequences before decisions are made.

33. Help the student review his/her decisions to determine whether improvements can be made. When improvements are needed, help the student identify and practice positive alternatives. Find a way to positively reinforce the student's attempts at one of the positive alternatives.

34. Insist upon reciprocity in teacher-student relationships. For example, trust can be viewed as something not freely given or expected, it is earned. The student will need to know what is expected to earn the teacher's trust.

35. Help the student think through his/her impulses to stay out at night in terms of how these may affect his/her social and work relationships.

36. Through role play, rehearse positive alternatives to behaving/reacting impulsively to challenging situations.

37. Provide students and parents with information about stress, including positive alternatives to reduce and/or manage stress.

38. Establish positive communication with the student, and help assure he/she receives any needed support (e.g., counseling) to build self-esteem and interpersonal relationships.

39. Make certain the student receives more attention for appropriate behavior than he/she would receive for staying out at night.

40. Teach the student to "think" before acting (e.g., ask himself/herself "What is happening?" "What am I doing?" "What should I do?" "What will be best for me?").

41. Write a contract with the student and his/her parents specifying that the student will call them when he/she wants to stay out later so they can discuss the situation and reach a compromise.

42. Assist the student in developing a structured approach to his/her daily and weekly activities to help prevent boredom and to encourage positive goal achievement. Incorporate reinforcement strategies for the daily/weekly activities the student attempts and completes.

43. Continuity between home and school can be critical to intervention/prevention of staying out at night despite parental prohibition. Work with parents and support sources (e.g., psychological counseling, psychiatric counseling, etc.) to establish continuity.

44. Students who stay out at night may be involved in substance abuse, and/or may have other severe emotional and/or behavioral concerns. Advocate for these students to receive support (e.g., counseling, medical attention, etc.) to address emotional/behavioral concerns and/or addiction.

231 Does not take responsibility for his/her own actions

Goals:

1. The student will consider consequences of his/her own actions.
2. The student will demonstrate consideration of consequences of his/her own actions.

Objectives:

1. The student will identify appropriate consequences of his/her own actions with the teacher on _____ out of _____ trials.
2. The student will behave in such a way as to demonstrate that he/she considered consequences of his/her own actions on _____ out of _____ trials.
3. The student will refrain from reacting impulsively on _____ out of _____ trials.
4. The student will demonstrate consideration of consequences of his/her own actions on _____ out of _____ trials.
5. The student will demonstrate actions that will result in positive consequences on _____ out of _____ trials.

Interventions:

1. Make certain that consequences are delivered consistently for behavior demonstrated (i.e., appropriate behavior results in positive consequences and inappropriate behavior results in negative consequences).

2. Provide the student with many social and academic successes.

3. Point out the consequences of other students' behavior as they occur (e.g., take the opportunity to point out that consequences occur for all behavior and for all persons).

4. Prevent the student from becoming overstimulated by an activity (e.g., monitor or supervise student behavior to limit overexcitement in physical activities, games, parties, etc.).

5. Provide the student with natural consequences for inappropriate behavior (e.g., for disturbing others during group activities, the student should have to leave the activity).

6. Provide the student with a clearly identified list of consequences for inappropriate behavior.

7. Teach the student problem-solving skills: (a) identify the problem; (b) identify goals and objectives; (c) develop strategies; (d) develop a plan for action; and (e) carry out the plan.

8. Clarify for the student that it is his/her behavior which determines consequences (e.g., positive or negative).

9. Provide a learning experience which emphasizes the cause-and-effect relationship between behavior and the inevitability of some form of consequence (e.g., both negative and positive behaviors and consequences).

10. Structure the environment to limit opportunities for inappropriate behavior (e.g., keep the student participating in activities; have the student seated near the teacher; maintain visibility to and from the student, etc.).

11. Call on the student when he/she can answer successfully.

12. Supervise the student closely in situations in which he/she is likely to act impulsively (e.g., maintain close physical proximity; maintain eye contact; communicate frequently with the student; etc.).

13. Prevent peers from engaging in those behaviors which would cause the student to fail to consider or regard consequences of his/her behavior (e.g., keep other students from upsetting the student).

14. Make the consequence of a behavior obvious by identifying the consequence as it occurs and discussing alternative behavior which would have prevented the particular consequence.

15. Avoid competition. Failure may cause the student to ignore consequences of his/her behavior.

16. Allow the student more decision-making opportunities relative to class activities and assignments.

17. Present tasks in the most attractive, interesting manner possible.

18. Give the student responsibilities in the classroom (e.g., teacher assistant, peer tutor, group leader, etc.).

19. Evaluate the appropriateness of the task in relation to the student's ability to perform the task successfully.

20. Show an interest in the student (e.g., acknowledge the student, ask the student's opinion, spend time working one-on-one with the student, etc.).

21. Intervene early when there is a problem to prevent more serious problems from occurring.

22. Inform others who will be working with the student (e.g., teachers, the principal, clerks, etc.) about the student's tendency to ignore consequences of his/her behaviors.

23. Make certain the student does not become involved in overstimulating activities.

24. Teach the student to think before acting (e.g., ask himself/herself, "What is happening?" "What am I doing?" "What should I do?" "What will be best for me?").

25. Evaluate the appropriateness of the task to determine (a) if the task is too easy, (b) if the task is too difficult, and (c) if the length of time scheduled to complete the task is adequate.

26. Communicate with parents (e.g., notes home, phone calls, etc.) to share information concerning the student's progress. The parents may reinforce the student at home for engaging in appropriate behaviors at school.

27. Write a contract with the student specifying what behavior is expected (e.g., acting in a deliberate and responsible manner) and what reinforcement will be made available when the terms of the contract have been met.

28. Remove the student from the group or activity until he/she can demonstrate appropriate behavior and self-control.

29. Reinforce the student for demonstrating appropriate behavior based on the length of time the student can be successful. As the student demonstrates success, gradually increase the length of time required for reinforcement.

30. Reinforce those students in the classroom who participate in appropriate behavior.

31. Establish classroom rules:
- Work on-task.
- Work quietly.
- Remain in your seat.
- Finish task.
- Meet task expectations.

Review rules often. Reinforce students for following the rules.

32. Speak with the student to explain (a) what the student is doing wrong (e.g., taking action before thinking about what he/she is doing) and (b) what the student should be doing (e.g., considering consequences, thinking about the correct response, considering other persons, etc.).

33. Reinforce the student for engaging in appropriate behavior: (a) give the student a tangible reward (e.g., classroom privileges, line leading, passing out materials, five minutes free time, etc.) or (b) give the student an intangible reward (e.g., praise, handshake, smile, etc.).

Goals:
1. The student will make appropriate comments to other students.
2. The student will express thoughts and feelings without using obscene or profane language.

Objectives:
1. The student will make appropriate comments to a peer during ___out of ___interactions.
2. The student will settle minor conflicts with a peer during ___out of ___interactions.
3. The student will refrain from arguing with a peer during ___out of ___interactions.
4. The student will demonstrate appropriate interaction skills such as sharing, waiting his/her turn, talking in an acceptable manner, and making appropriate gestures during ___out of ___interactions with a peer.
5. The student will refrain from calling names during ___out of ___interactions with a peer.
6. The student will refrain from cursing during ___out of ___interactions with a peer.
7. The student will refrain from using obscenities during ___out of ___interactions with a peer.
8. The student will refrain from making rude comments during ___out of ___interactions with a peer.
9. The student will demonstrate respect for a peer on ___out of ___trials.
10. The student will make comments that are appropriate to the situation on ___out of ___trials.
11. The student will make gestures that are appropriate to the situation on ___out of ___trials.
12. The student will express his/her thoughts and feelings without using obscene/profane language on ___ out of ___ trials.

Interventions:

1. Immediately remove the student from interacting with others when cursing.

2. Make certain that you do not curse. If you curse, the student will learn to do the same.

3. Establish a rule (e.g., no cursing). This rule should be consistent and followed by everyone in the school environment. Talk about the rule often.

4. Reward other students in the classroom for not cursing.

5. When the student curses, explain exactly what he/she is doing wrong, what should be done and why. For example: You hear the student cursing at another student. Go to the student and say, "William, you are cursing at Kim. You need to use appropriate language when you are angry at someone or you will offend him/her."

6. Allow natural consequences to occur as a result of the student's cursing (e.g., not being able to participate in special activities, being removed from interacting with others, being avoided by others who do not curse, etc.).

7. Make certain that the student sees the relationship between his/her behavior and the consequences which follow (e.g., being removed from activities).

8. Talk to the student in the manner in which you want him/her to talk to you. Treat the student with respect and do not curse at him/her.

9. Teach the student acceptable ways to express anger, frustration, anxiety, etc.

10. Be consistent when the student curses. Decide on an appropriate consequence for cursing (e.g., sitting in a certain chair for five minutes) and use it every time the student curses.

11. Separate the student from those individuals who encourage or stimulate him/her to curse.

12. Make certain that others with whom the student associates do not use inappropriate language.

13. Separate the student from the peer(s) who stimulate inappropriate language.

14. Inform other teachers, school personnel, etc., of the student's use of inappropriate language to make certain they follow through with discipline.

15. Remind the student of the consequences of swearing before participating in activities.

16. Separate the student from other peers who curse.

17. Avoid those situations which are likely to stimulate the student's swearing (e.g., highly competitive activities, extreme disappointment, quarreling with other students, etc.).

18. Teach the student to recognize when he/she is becoming upset or angry and ways, other than cursing, to express feelings.

19. Do not allow the student to participate in a situation unless he/she can demonstrate self-control.

20. Provide the student with a place to go when he/she gets upset or angry (e.g., a quiet chair, a room, a corner, etc.).

21. Make certain you deal in a socially acceptable way with situations that may be upsetting.

22. Teach the student to verbalize feelings before losing control (e.g., "The work is too hard." "Please leave me alone, you're making me angry.").

23. Monitor the behavior of others to make certain they are not teasing or otherwise stimulating the student to become upset or angry.

24. Teach the student ways to deal with conflict situations (e.g., talking, reasoning, asking an adult to intervene, walking away, etc.).

25. Look for the warning signs (e.g., arguing, loud voices, etc.) that the student is getting upset or angry and intervene to change the activity.

26. Make certain you approach the student with words and phrases that offer support rather than stimulating antagonism, anger, etc.

27. Repeat rules and expectations before activities occur which might result in the student becoming upset or angry.

28. Make certain to intervene early when the student does curse, before cursing becomes an established part of his/her speech.

29. Make certain the student knows the consequences of cursing that will be delivered in your class (e.g., loss of privileges, loss of opportunity to associate with those with whom he curses, loss of freedom to be left alone with friends, etc.).

30. Make certain the student understands that other teachers will not stand for cursing, the student should expect to be embarrassed, may be prevented from interacting with others.

31. Reduce the emphasis on competition. Highly competitive activities may cause the student to become upset, angry, frustrated, etc., and curse.

32. Do not inadvertently reinforce the student's cursing by laughing, smiling, ignoring, etc.

33. Prevent the student from becoming frustrated to the extent that cursing results. Intervene to help the student in those situations which may result in frustration and cursing.

34. If highly competitive activities contribute to the student's cursing, either reduce the student's involvement in those activities, or make certain the student understands that cursing will result in loss of opportunities to participate in those activities.

35. Point out to the student successful persons who actively participate in a variety of activities without cursing.

36. Make certain the student is taught those words which are socially appropriate to use in place of cursing (e.g., "dang," "shoot," "darn," "heck," etc.).

37. Cursing is not a behavior that should be ignored. By ignoring the student's cursing, you send the message that it is acceptable.

38. Discuss with the student ways to deal with unpleasant experiences which would typically cause him/her to use obscene language (e.g., talk to the teacher, go to a quiet area in the room, visit a counselor, etc.).

39. Model using appropriate language at all times (e.g., use appropriate language to convey disappointment, unhappiness, surprise, etc.).

40. Deal with the student in a calm and deliberate manner rather than in a manner that would show evidence of shock and surprise.

41. Modify or adjust situations which contribute to the student's use of obscene or profane language (e.g., if an assignment causes the student to become upset, modify the assignment to a level at which the student can be successful).

42. Make certain the student has frequent, positive opportunities to define self-expression without using obscene/profane language.

43. Reinforce the student for behaving responsibly and not using obscene/profane language for self-expression by: (a) give the student a tangible reward (e.g., classroom privileges, line leading, passing out materials, five minutes free time, etc.) or (b) give the student an intangible reward (e.g., praise, handshake, smile, etc.).

44. Define what has been done correctly and what the student needs to do to improve upon his/her ability to communicate without obscene/profane language.

45. Make certain those who are expressing thoughts and feelings without resorting to obscene/profane language are positively reinforced.

46. Deliver your response and consequences to the use of obscene/profane language in a low key manner because the student may be using this kind of language to elicit shock/surprise responses from those sharing the environment.

47. Teach the student to recognize when he/she feels the need to use obscene/profane language and ways to deal with it (e.g., counting to 10, moving to a different location in the classroom, reading, etc.). Give the student structured practice at using coping skills which could be adapted to life beyond the classroom.

48. Write a contract specifying expected behavior (e.g., taking the time to express thoughts/ feelings without use of obscene/profane language) and what reinforcement will be made available when the terms of the contract have been met.

49. Communicate with the student's parents (e.g., notes home, phone calls, etc.) to share information concerning the student's progress. The parents may reinforce students at home for using positive communication techniques at school.

50. Supervise the student who does not consider the consequences of using obscene/profane language.

51. Provide the student with models of the behavioral choices you expect of him/her during times of frustration or stress to preclude use of obscene/profane language.

52. Interact frequently with the student to monitor language used.

53. Try to prevent task-related stress so student frustration and temptation to use obscene/profane language is decreased by (a) providing clear task expectations and assuring these are understood by the student before he/she receives task materials and before he/she is expected to begin the task, (b) providing the student ample time for task completion, (c) providing the student frequent opportunities for communication to encourage his/her positive self-expression throughout the day, and (d) making certain tasks are appropriate for the student's age and ability.

54. Encourage the student to express thoughts and feelings carefully and thoughtfully. Praise the student for self-expression without using obscene/profane language.

55. Deliver consequences in a nonthreatening, calm manner.

56. Make certain the student knows the following:
- You are confident that he/she can communicate thoughts/feelings without using obscene/profane language.
- The student will have many more opportunities to earn positive reinforcement by communicating thoughts/feelings without using obscene/profane language.

57. Provide peer role models who express thoughts and feelings without resorting to obscene/profane language.

58. Be a consistent, positive authority figure.

59. Consistently act upon the student's antecedent behaviors (e.g., increased restlessness, marked changes in moods, etc.) to teach positive forms of self-expression. He/she can then have the opportunity to identify and describe thoughts, feelings, and/or problems before the situation escalates.

60. Provide learning experiences which emphasize cause and effect links between behavior (e.g., use of obscene/profane language to express one's thoughts and feelings) and consequences (e.g., loss of others' respect, lost communication because the obscene/profane language overshadowed the message, etc.).

61. Structure the environment to encourage opportunities for self-expression without obscene/profane language (e.g., seating the student in front of the classroom for careful monitoring and to prevent task and communication related frustration, etc.).

62. Teach the student ways of working through problems to decrease frustration and stress-related behavior. These include (a) problem identification, (b) goal/objective development, (c) strategy development, (d) plan development, (e) plan implementation, and (f) evaluation of plan effectiveness.

63. Prevent peers from provoking the student into reactive, verbal responses.

64. Show an interest in the student (e.g., acknowledge the student, ask for the student's opinion, work one-on-one with the student).

65. Help the student focus upon positive attempts to communicate thoughts and feelings without use of obscene/profane language. He/ she needs to be able to recognize successes and errors for improvement in self-expression.

66. Help the student identify his/her own unique set of antecedents to the use of obscene/profane language. For every antecedent identified, help the student develop positive, alternative actions he/she may take toward problem solving.

67. Offer the student opportunities for creative self-expression (e.g., sculpting, gymnastics, writing, drawing, dancing, acting, etc.). Activities need to be viewed as an avenue of self-expression rather than a way to reinforce, reward, or earn grades.

68. Introduce and maintain positive, consistent class management which incorporates an opportunity to think through consequences before decisions are made.

69. Provide students and parents information about stress. Include positive alternatives to reduce and/or manage stress.

70. Advocate for supports and services to rule out and/or provide for organic or physical concerns such as Tourette's Disorder according to individual need.

71. The student who is experiencing emotional or behavior disturbances may respond to stressful situations with abusive or profane language. Advocate for support and service.

72. Observe the student for changes in behavior. A student who does not typically use obscene/profane language but has begun to do so may be experiencing other concerns (e.g., personal crisis, substance abuse, etc.).

73. When teaching the student to express thoughts and feelings without using obscene/profane language, provide functional lessons (e.g., interviewing for a job, attempting an introduction to a new person, etc.) so the student can assign practical value to this skill.

74. Address and correct the use of obscene/profane language by talking one-on-one with the student instead of confronting the student in large groups. Do this to minimize embarrassment and decrease the chances a student may have for vicarious reinforcement (e.g., approving statements and actions of peers for using obscene/profane language, etc.).

75. Teach the student self-reinforcement techniques for positive self-expression (e.g., going to a movie or out to eat after a week of communicating without obscene/profane language, etc.).

76. Encourage the student to view himself/herself positively. Make certain the student understands the use of obscene/profane language represents a poor choice, but he/she is a "good" person. This may help reduce potential crisis situations in which use of obscene/profane language is an antecedent to other undesirable behaviors (e.g., attempts to hurt himself/herself or others, etc.).

Reminder: The student will repeat what he/she hears.

233   Does not use supplies or operate equipment and machinery safely

Goal:

1. The student will use supplies or operate equipment and machinery safely.

Objectives:

1. The student will use supplies or operate equipment and machinery for their designated purposes on _____ out of _____ trials.
2. The student will use supplies or operate equipment and machinery according to accepted procedures on _____ out of _____ trials.
3. The student will use supplies or operate equipment and machinery safely with supervision on _____ out of _____ trials.
4. The student will independently use supplies or operate equipment and machinery safely on _____ out of _____ trials.
5. The student will return supplies, equipment, and machinery in the same or better condition on _____ out of _____ trials.

Interventions:

1. Provide time at the beginning of each day to help the student organize his/her school-related supplies.

2. Provide time at various points throughout the day to help the student organize school-related supplies (e.g., before school, during break time, during lunch, end of the day, etc.).

3. Establish a routine to be followed for organization and safe use of school-related supplies, equipment, and machinery.

4. Reduce distracting stimuli (e.g., place the student on the front row, provide a carrel or quiet place away from distractions, etc.). This is a means of reducing distracting stimuli and not a form of punishment.

5. Interact frequently with the student to prompt organizational skills and safe use of school-related supplies and equipment.

6. Assign the student organizational responsibilities in the classroom (e.g., equipment, software, materials, etc.).

7. Limit the student's use of school-related supplies (e.g., provide the student with only those school-related supplies necessary for an activity).

8. Model organization and safe use of school-related supplies (e.g., putting materials away before getting others out, having a place for all supplies, maintaining an organized desk area, following safety rules, etc.).

9. Provide adequate transition time between activities for the student to organize himself/herself.

10. Provide the student with adequate work space (e.g., larger desk or table at which to work).

11. Provide adequate time for the completion of activities.

12. Require the student to organize his/her work area at regular intervals. (It is recommended that this be done at least three times per day or more often if necessary.)

13. Supervise the student while he/she is using supplies or operating equipment and machinery to monitor safety.

14. Assess the quality and clarity of directions, explanations, and instructions given to the student.

15. Assist the student in beginning each task to reduce impulsive behavior.

16. Provide the student with structure for all academic activities (e.g., specific directions, routine format for tasks, time units, etc.).

17. Minimize school-related supplies necessary for each activity.

18. Provide an organizer inside the student's desk for school-related supplies.

19. Provide the student with an organizational and safety checklist (e.g., routine steps to follow).

20. Point out to the student that loaning his/her school-related supplies to other students does not reduce personal responsibility for the supplies.

21. Have the student question any directions, explanations, or instructions not understood.

22. Teach the student to maintain school-related supplies (e.g., keep supplies with him/her, know where supplies are at all times, secure supplies in his/her locker, etc.).

23. Provide the student with an appropriate place to store/secure supplies (e.g., desk, locker, closet, etc.) and require him/her to store all supplies when not in use.

24. Explain to the student that failure to safely care for school-related supplies will result in the loss of freedom to use the supplies.

25. Provide reminders (e.g., a list of school-related supplies) to help the student maintain and safely care for school-related supplies.

26. Limit the student's freedom to take school-related supplies and equipment from school if he/she is unable to use such items safely.

27. Limit the student's opportunity to use school-related supplies if the student is unable to safely care for personal property.

28. Make certain that failure to safely use school-related supplies and equipment results in the loss of the opportunity to participate in activities or a failing grade for that day's activity.

29. Reduce the number of school-related supplies and equipment for which the student is responsible. As the student demonstrates safe use of supplies and equipment, increase the number of supplies and equipment for which the student is responsible.

30. Teach the student safety rules in the handling of school-related supplies and equipment (e.g., pencils; scissors; compass; biology, industrial arts, and home economics supplies and equipment; etc.).

31. Teach the student appropriate use of school-related supplies and equipment (e.g., scissors; pencils; compass; rulers; biology, industrial arts, and home economics supplies and equipment; etc.).

32. Do not give the student additional supplies and equipment if he/she is not able to safely use what he/she already possesses.

33. Teach the student appropriate ways to deal with anger and frustration rather than destroying school-related supplies.

34. Choose a peer to model safe use of school-related supplies and equipment for the student.

35. Evaluate the appropriateness of the task to determine (a) if the task is too easy, (b) if the task is too difficult, and (c) if the length of time scheduled to complete the task is adequate.

36. Communicate with parents (e.g., notes home, phone calls, etc.) to share information concerning the student's progress. The parents may reinforce the student at home for using school-related supplies, equipment, and machinery safely at school.

37. Write a contract with the student specifying what behavior is expected (e.g., safe use of school-related supplies) and what reinforcement will be made available when the terms of the contract have been met.

38. Reinforce those students in the classroom who use school-related supplies, equipment, and machinery safely.

39. Teach the student appropriate care of school-related supplies, equipment, and machinery (e.g., sharpening pencils, keeping books free of marks and tears, etc.).

40. Establish classroom rules:
- Work on-task.
- Remain in your seat.
- Finish task.
- Meet task expectations.
- Raise your hand.

Review rules often. Reinforce students for following rules.

41. Speak to the student to explain (a) what the student is doing wrong (e.g., failing to use school-related supplies, equipment, and machinery safely) and (b) what the student should be doing (e.g., using school-related supplies, equipment, and machinery as directed).

42. Reinforce the student for demonstrating safe use of school-related supplies, equipment, and machinery: (a) give the student a tangible reward (e.g., classroom privileges, line leading, passing out materials, five minutes free time, etc.) or (b) give the student an intangible reward (e.g., praise, handshake, smile, etc.).

43. Make certain the student is not inadvertently reinforced for losing or damaging school-related supplies, equipment, and machinery (e.g., replace lost supplies with used or damaged supplies, rather than new supplies).

44. Allow natural consequences to occur as the result of the student's inability to organize or use school-related supplies appropriately (e.g., supplies not maintained appropriately will be lost or not usable, etc.).

45. Give the student a checklist of school-related materials necessary for each activity.

46. Reinforce the student for using school-related supplies safely based on the length of time the student can be successful. As the student demonstrates success, gradually increase the length of time required for reinforcement.

47. Make certain that all of the student's school-related supplies are labeled with his/her name.

48. Teach the student to conserve rather than waste school-related supplies (e.g., amount of glue, paper, tape, etc., to use; putting lids, caps, and tops on such materials as markers, pens, bottles, jars, cans; etc.).

49. Require that lost or damaged school-related supplies, equipment, and machinery be replaced by the student. (If the student cannot replace the property, restitution can be made by working at school.)

50. Provide storage space for school-related supplies the student is not using.

Goal:

1. The student will participate in extracurricular activities.

Objectives:

1. The student will participate in _____ out of _____ extracurricular activities per month.
2. The student will demonstrate an interest in extracurricular activities by asking about the events, talking about the events, helping prepare for the events, etc., in _____ out of _____ special events.
3. The student will passively participate in an extracurricular activity by sitting/standing quietly, walking with the group, watching others play games, etc., during _____ out of _____ events.
4. The student will actively participate in an extracurricular activity by having a role in the activity, producing the activity, decorating the room, performing in the assembly, etc., during _____ out of _____ events.

Interventions:

1. Reinforce the student for participating in group activities or special events: (a) give the student a tangible reward (e.g., classroom privileges, line leading, passing out materials, five minutes free time, etc.) or (b) give the student an intangible reward (e.g., praise, handshake, smile, etc.).

2. Speak to the student to explain (a) what he/she is doing wrong, (e.g., failing to take part) and (b) what he/she should be doing (e.g., talking, taking turns, playing, sharing, etc.).

3. Establish classroom rules:
- Work on-task.
- Remain in your seat.
- Finish task.
- Meet task expectations.
- Raise your hand.

Review rules often. Reinforce students for following the rules.

4. Reinforce other students in the classroom for participating in group activities or special events.

5. Write a contract with the student specifying what behavior is expected (e.g., taking part in group activities) and what reinforcement will be made available when the terms of the contract have been met.

6. Try various groupings to determine the situation in which the student is most successful.

7. Have peers invite the student to participate in school or extracurricular activities.

8. Evaluate the appropriateness of the task to determine (a) if the task is too easy, (b) if the task is too difficult, and (c) if the length of time scheduled for the task is adequate.

9. Assign a peer to sit/work directly with the student (e.g., in different settings or activities such as art, music, P.E., on the bus, tutoring, group projects, running errands in the building, break time, etc.). As the student becomes comfortable working with one other student, gradually increase the size of the group.

10. Encourage or reward others for participation in the group for special activities.

11. Give the student the responsibility of helping another student in the group.

12. Give the student responsibilities in a group so they might view him/her in a positive light.

13. Ask the student questions that cannot be answered yes or no.

14. Call on the student when he/she is most likely to be able to respond successfully (e.g., something in which the student is interested, when the teacher is certain the student knows the answer, etc.).

15. Communicate with parents (e.g., notes home, phone calls, etc.) to share information concerning the student's progress. The parents may reinforce the student at home for participating in group activities or special events at school.

16. Request that the student be the leader of a small group activity if he/she possesses mastery or an interest in the activity.

17. Allow the student to be present during group activities without requiring active participation.

18. Reduce the emphasis on competition. Frequent or continuous failure is likely to result in embarrassment which will cause reluctance to participate.

19. Demonstrate respect for the student's opinions, responses, suggestions, etc.

20. Provide the student with many social and academic successes.

21. Provide the student with positive feedback which indicates he/she is successful.

22. Present tasks in the most attractive, interesting manner possible.

23. Determine the student's interests. Present activities which require participation based on his/her interests.

24. Allow the student to choose a special event or interesting activity for the class.

25. Provide the student with success-oriented special events or activities so he/she may develop an interest in them.

26. Modify or adjust situations that cause the student to be reluctant to participate (e.g., degree of difficulty, competition, fear of failure, threat of embarrassment, etc.).

27. Emphasize individual success or progress rather than winning or "beating" other students.

28. Provide the student with opportunities for small group participation as opposed to large group participation.

29. Encourage the student to participate in small groups. As the student demonstrates success, gradually increase the size of the group.

30. Encourage the student to share items of special interest with other members of the class.

31. Choose a peer to model appropriate interactions in classroom activities for the student.

32. Have the student question any directions, explanations, instructions he/she does not understand.

33. Allow the student to choose a group of peers with whom he/she feels comfortable.

34. Determine the peers with whom the student would prefer to interact and attempt to facilitate the interaction.

35. Assign outgoing, nonthreatening peers to help the student participate in classroom activities.

36. Structure the environment so that the student has many opportunities to interact with peers in classroom activities.

37. Assign the student to classroom activities in which he/she is likely to interact successfully with peers.

38. Conduct a sociometric activity with the class to determine those peers who would most prefer to interact with the student in classroom activities.

39. Make certain that the student understands that interacting with peers in classroom activities is contingent upon appropriate behavior.

40. Teach the student appropriate ways to interact with peers in classroom activities (e.g., share materials, problem solve, take turns, converse, etc.).

41. Supervise classroom activities closely so that the peers with whom the student interacts do not stimulate inappropriate behavior.

42. Make certain that the classroom activity is not so stimulating as to make successful interactions with peers difficult.

43. Teach the student problem-solving skills so he/she may better handle problems that may occur in interactions with peers in classroom activities (e.g., talking, walking away, calling upon an arbitrator, compromising, etc.).

44. Limit opportunities for interaction in classroom activities on those occasions in which the student is not likely to be successful (e.g., the student has experienced academic or social failure prior to the scheduled classroom activity).

45. Select nonacademic activities designed to facilitate appropriate social interaction of the student and peers during classroom activities (e.g., board games, model building, etc.).

46. Through interviews with other students and observations, determine those characteristics of the student which interfere with successful interactions during classroom activities. Use information gained to determine skills or behaviors the student needs to develop for successful interactions.

47. Make certain the student knows how to use all materials for the activity.

48. Make certain, beforehand, that the student is able to successfully participate in the activity (e.g., the student understands the rules, is familiar with the activity, will be compatible with peers participating in the activity, etc.).

49. Make certain the student has the necessary materials for the activity.

50. Assign the student responsibilities to perform during activities to facilitate peer interaction (e.g. being a leader, passing out materials, acting as a peer tutor, etc.).

51. Have the student practice appropriate interactions with the teacher(s) in classroom activities (e.g., simulations, role playing, etc.).

Reminder: Do not "force" the student to take part in any activity or special event.

Goals:

1. The student will refrain from bothering other students who are trying to work, listen, etc.
2. The student will stay on-task.

Objectives:

1. The student will refrain from interrupting other students who are trying to work, listen, etc., on _____ out of _____ trials.
2. The student will stay on-task for _____ minutes at a time. (Gradually increase expectations as the student demonstrates success.)
3. The student will interact with other students when appropriate on _____ out of _____ trials.
4. The student will interact with other students during free time, break time, lunch time, etc., on _____ out of _____ trials.
5. The student will ask the teacher's permission prior to interacting with a peer(s) on _____ out of _____ trials.
6. The student will remain appropriately seated until given teacher permission to do otherwise on _____ out of _____ trials.

Interventions:

1. Communicate with the student's parents (e.g., notes home, phone calls, etc.) to share information concerning the student's appropriate behavior. The parents may reinforce the student at home for not interrupting other students at school.

2. Encourage the student to recite a mantra to himself/herself when entering a situation where he/she may be inclined to interrupt (e.g., do not interrupt, do not interrupt, do not interrupt).

3. Instruct the student to carry a notepad with him/her at all times and to write information down to help him/her remember.

4. Educate yourself and others about ADHD to increase understanding and accommodation of interruptive behavior.

5. Help the student realize that all behavior has negative or positive consequences. Encourage the student to practice behaviors that will lead to positive consequences.

6. Encourage the student to develop an awareness of himself/herself and those around him/her. Have the student periodically step back and ask himself/herself, "Am I interrupting others?"

7. Encourage the student to develop an awareness of the consequences of his/her behavior by writing down or talking through problems which may occur due to interrupting others (e.g., perceived as unmannerly, avoided, etc.).

8. Consider carefully the student's age and ability level before expecting him/her not to interrupt others when they are talking, working, reading, etc.

9. Educate the student about ADHD and the need to self-monitor behavior.

10. Provide constant, positive reinforcement for appropriate behavior. Ignore as many inappropriate behaviors as possible.

11. Reinforce the student for demonstrating appropriate behavior: (a) give the student a tangible reward (e.g., classroom privileges, passing out materials, five minutes free time, etc.) or (b) give the student an intangible reward (e.g., praise, handshake, smile, etc.).

12. Reinforce the student for demonstrating appropriate behavior (e.g., waiting for a turn to speak, working quietly, etc.) based on the length of time the student can be successful. As the student demonstrates success, gradually increase the length of time required for reinforcement.

13. Choose a peer to model appropriate behavior for the student.

14. Encourage the student to become aware of the times when he/she is most impulsive and likely to interrupt others (e.g., in a large group of people, when he/she is angry, etc.) and limit his/her interactions with others during these times.

15. Talk to the student before beginning an activity and remind him/her of the importance of listening to others.

16. Reinforce those students in the classroom who wait their turn to speak, do not interrupt others, work quietly, etc.

17. Provide the student with a clearly understood list of consequences for inappropriate behavior.

18. Reduce the emphasis on competition. Competitive activities may cause the student to become anxious and interrupt others.

19. Teach the student to take cues from others (e.g., if he/she begins to interrupt a peer and that person continues to talk, realize that he/she is interrupting and stop talking; when there is silence in a class, it is not necessary to fill the silence with comments, etc.).

20. Have the student question any directions, explanations, or instructions before beginning a task to reinforce comprehension and avoid interrupting peers later to ask questions.

21. Speak to the student to explain (a) what he/she is doing wrong (e.g., interrupting other students who are trying to work, listen, etc.) and (b) what he/she should be doing (e.g., waiting for a turn to speak, working quietly, etc.).

22. Remove the student from the group or activity until he/she can demonstrate appropriate behavior and self-control.

23. Teach the student to ask himself/herself questions such as, "What should I be doing right now?" "Is what I have to say relevant to this topic?" "Is this a good time for me to comment?"

24. Encourage the student to remind himself/herself to wait when he/she feels the urge to interrupt (e.g., "Stop. Count to ten.").

25. Teach the student to use techniques such as crossing his/her arms and legs, clinching his/her fists, and webbing his/her hands when he/she feels the urge to interrupt.

26. Explain to the student the importance of treating people as he/she wants to be treated (e.g., people will not interrupt you if you do not interrupt them).

27. Interact frequently with the student to maintain his/her involvement in the activity (e.g., ask the student questions, ask the student's opinion, stand close to the student, seat the student near the teacher's desk, etc.).

28. Explain to the student why it is important not to interrupt others. Help him/her understand that it is impolite, that he/she might hurt someone's feelings, etc.

29. Have the student make a list of consequences associated with frequently occurring behaviors (e.g., By disrupting others, he/she will be perceived as unmannerly. By behaving aggressively, people will avoid him/her.).

30. Explain to the student the need to reduce impulsive behavior to increase work productivity and general happiness.

31. Make sure that you do not interrupt others. If you interrupt others, the student will continue to do so.

32. Establish rules for conversing with others (e.g., wait your turn to talk, stand quietly by the person with whom you want to talk until you are noticed, excuse yourself when you interrupt others, etc.). These rules should be consistent and followed by everyone in the class. Talk about the rules often.

33. Have the student choose a peer who does not interrupt others. Encourage the student to observe that person and try to model the behaviors which allow him/her to be patient.

34. Deliver a predetermined signal (e.g. hand signal, verbal cue, etc.) when the student begins to display inappropriate behaviors.

35. Reinforce consistently the class rules regarding talking aloud during quiet activity periods.

36. Teach appropriate social rituals (e.g., say, "Excuse me," before interrupting; wait until someone stops speaking to begin talking, etc.).

37. Have the student identify the situations in which he/she is most likely to interrupt. After he/she has identified these situations, have him/her think of ways to minimize their occurrences.

38. Teach and practice effective communication skills. These skills include: listening, maintaining eye contact, and positive body language.

39. Establish classroom rules:
- Work on-task.
- Remain in your seat.
- Finish task.
- Meet task expectations.
- Raise your hand.

Review rules often. Reinforce students for following the rules.

40. Have a peer cue the student when he/she is interrupting others (e.g., the peer can touch the student's arm or desk as a signal that he/she is interrupting).

41. Be consistent in expecting the student to behave appropriately. Do not allow the student to interrupt one time and expect him/her not to interrupt the next time.

42. Write a contract with the student specifying what behavior is expected (e.g., waiting for a turn to speak, working quietly, etc.) and what reinforcement will be made available when the terms of the contract have been met.

43. Treat the student with respect. Talk in an objective manner at all times.

44. Explain to the student when he/she interrupts that you are talking now and he/she may talk to you in a few moments.

45. Do not criticize when correcting the student; be honest yet supportive. Never cause the student to feel negatively about himself/herself.

46. Maintain visibility to and from the student to keep his/her attention when verbal questions/ directions are being delivered. The teacher should be able to see the student and the student should be able to see the teacher. Make eye contact possible at all times.

47. Seat the student away from those students he/she is most likely to bother.

48. Teach the student appropriate ways to communicate needs to others (e.g., waiting a turn, raising his/her hand, etc.).

49. Do not allow the student to use ADHD as an excuse. Hold the student responsible for his/her actions. However, understand and accept problems ADHD brings into the student's life while he/she is learning to make accommodations.

50. Provide students with frequent opportunities to interact with one another (e.g., before and after school, between activities, etc.).

51. Give the student frequent opportunities to join in conversations with others by allowing him/her time to talk, asking him/her to restate an experience, etc.

52. Make certain that the student understands the relationship between inappropriate behavior and the consequences which follow (e.g., others ignoring him/her, hurting others' feelings, etc.).

53. Show the student the appropriate way to get someone's attention without interrupting.

54. Do not interrupt the student when he/she is doing something, talking to someone, etc.

55. Make sure the student knows when it is acceptable to interrupt others (e.g., in an emergency).

56. Seat the student near the teacher.

Goals:
1. The student will refrain from bothering other students who are trying to work, listen, etc.
2. The student will stay on-task.

Objectives:
1. The student will refrain from bothering other students who are trying to work, listen, etc., on ___ out of ___ trials.
2. The student will stay on-task for ___ minutes at a time. (Gradually increase expectations as the student demonstrates success.)
3. The student will interact with other students when appropriate on ___ out of ___ trials.
4. The student will interact with other students during free time, break time, lunch time, etc., on ___ out of ___ trials.
5. The student will ask the teacher's permission prior to interacting with a peer(s) on ___ out of ___ trials.
6. The student will remain appropriately seated until given teacher permission to do otherwise on ___ out of ___ trials.

Interventions:

1. Reduce distracting stimuli (e.g., place the student on the front row, provide a carrel or "office" away from distractions, etc.). This is used as a means of reducing distracting stimuli and not as a form of punishment.

2. Interact frequently with the student to maintain his/her involvement in the activity (e.g., ask the student questions, ask the student's opinion, stand close to the student, seat the student near the teacher's desk, etc.).

3. Maintain visibility to and from the student. The teacher should be able to see the student and the student should be able to see the teacher. Make eye contact possible at all times.

4. Assess the degree of task difficulty in relation to the student's ability to perform the task successfully.

5. Provide a full schedule of activities. Prevent lag time from occurring when the student can bother other students.

6. Choose a peer who would be a good influence to interact with the student (e.g., someone younger, older, of the same gender, of the opposite gender, etc.).

7. Teach the student appropriate ways to communicate needs to others (e.g., waiting a turn, raising his/her hand, etc.).

8. Provide the student with enjoyable activities to perform when he/she completes a task early.

9. Seat the student near the teacher.

10. Provide the student with frequent opportunities to participate, share, etc.

11. Provide students with frequent opportunities to interact with one another (e.g., before and after school, between activities, etc.).

12. Seat the student away from those students he/she is most likely to bother.

13. Intervene early when there is a problem to prevent a more serious problem from occurring.

14. Teach the student to respect others and their belongings by respecting the student and his/her belongings.

15. Remove the student from the group or activity until he/she can demonstrate appropriate behavior and self-control.

16. Make certain the student knows when it is acceptable to interrupt others (e.g., an emergency).

17. Reinforce those students in the classroom who demonstrate on-task behavior.

18. Have the student question any directions, explanations, and instructions not understood.

19. Choose a peer to model appropriate behavior for the student.

20. Evaluate the appropriateness of the task to determine (a) if the task is too easy, (b) if the task is too difficult, and (c) if the length of time scheduled to complete the task is adequate.

21. Communicate with the parents (e.g., notes home, phone calls, etc.) to share information concerning the student's progress. The parents may reinforce the student at home for demonstrating appropriate behavior at school.

22. Reinforce the student for demonstrating appropriate behavior: (a) give the student a tangible reward (e.g., classroom privileges, line leading, passing out materials, five minutes free time, etc.) or (b) give the student an intangible reward (e.g., praise, handshake, smile, etc.).

23. Reinforce the student for demonstrating appropriate behavior based on the length of time the student can be successful. As the student demonstrates success, gradually increase the length of time required for reinforcement.

24. Reinforce those students in the classroom who demonstrate appropriate behavior.

25. Establish classroom rules:
- Work on-task.
- Work quietly.
- Remain in your seat.
- Finish task.
- Meet task expectations.

Review rules often. Reinforce students for following rules.

26. Speak to the student to explain (a) what the student is doing wrong (e.g., bothering other students who are trying to work, listen, etc.) and (b) what the student should be doing (e.g., demonstrating appropriate behavior).

27. Write a contract with the student specifying what behavior is expected (e.g., demonstrating appropriate behavior) and what reinforcement will be made available when the terms of the contract have been met.

237　Does not interact appropriately with one other person

Goals:

1. The student will improve his/her interpersonal behavior.
2. The student will improve his/her interpersonal behavior in academic settings.
3. The student will improve his/her interpersonal behavior in nonacademic settings.

Objectives:

1. The student will follow directions given by a peer in a tutoring situation on ____ out of ____ occasions.
2. The student will share materials with one other person in an academic situation on ____ out of ____ occasions.
3. The student will work quietly with one other person in an academic situation on ____ out of ____ occasions.
4. The student will take turns with one other person in an academic situation on ____ out of ____ occasions.
5. The student will verbally participate with one other person in an academic situation on ____ out of ____ occasions.
6. The student will physically participate with one other person in an academic situation on ____ out of ____ occasions.
7. The student will take turns with one other person in a nonacademic situation on ____ out of ____ occasions.
8. The student will interact successfully with one other person in nonacademic situations with supervision on ____ out of ____ occasions.
9. The student will interact successfully with one other person without supervision in nonacademic situations on ____ out of ____ occasions.
10. The student will share materials with one other person in nonacademic situations on ____ out of ____ occasions.
11. The student will communicate successfully with one other person in nonacademic situations on ____ out of ____ occasions.

Interventions:

1. Reinforce the student for interacting appropriately with one other person: (a) give the student a tangible reward (e.g., classroom privileges, line leading, passing out materials, five minutes free time, etc.) or (b) give the student an intangible reward (e.g., praise, handshake, smile, etc.).

2. Speak to the student to explain (a) what he/she is doing wrong (e.g., not sharing materials) and (b) what he/she should be doing (e.g., sharing materials).

3. Write a contract with the student specifying what behavior is expected (e.g., taking turns, sharing toys and materials) and what reinforcement will be made available when the terms of the contract have been met.

4. Reinforce those students in the classroom who interact appropriately with one other person.

5. Reinforce the student for interacting appropriately with one other person based on the length of time the student can be successful. As the student demonstrates success, gradually increase the length of time required for reinforcement.

6. Establish social rules:
- Share materials.
- Use a quiet voice in the building.
- Walk indoors.
- Use care in handling materials.

Review rules often. Reinforce students for following rules.

7. Communicate with parents (e.g., notes home, phone calls, etc.) to share information concerning the student's progress. The parents may reinforce the student at home for interacting appropriately with another person at school.

8. Evaluate the expectation for peer interaction to determine if the student can be successful in the interactions and for the expected length of time.

9. Choose a peer to model appropriate interactions with one other person for the student.

10. Have the student question any directions or explanations he/she does not understand.

11. Determine the peer(s) with whom the student would most prefer to interact and attempt to facilitate the interaction.

12. Assign an outgoing, nonthreatening peer to help the student interact more appropriately.

13. Structure the environment so that the student has many opportunities to interact successfully with another person.

14. Assign the student to interact with a younger student (e.g., play areas, cafeteria, hallways, tutoring, etc.).

15. Have the student run errands with another person to facilitate interaction.

16. Assign the student to situations in which he/she is likely to interact successfully with another person.

17. Conduct a sociometric activity with the class to determine the peer who would most prefer to interact with the student.

18. Make certain that the student understands that interacting with another person is contingent upon appropriate behavior.

19. Teach the student appropriate ways to interact with another person (e.g., how to greet another person, suggest activities, share materials, problem-solve, take turns, converse, etc.).

20. Make certain that the student understands that participation with others is contingent upon appropriate behavior.

21. Supervise situations closely so the individual with whom the student interacts does not stimulate the student's inappropriate behavior.

22. Make certain that the situation is not so stimulating as to make successful interactions with another person difficult.

23. Assign an older peer with desirable social skills to interact with the student.

24. Involve the student in extracurricular activities to encourage interactions with others.

25. Reduce the emphasis on competition. Failure may stimulate inappropriate behavior.

26. Teach the student problem-solving skills so he/she may better deal with problems that may occur in interactions with another person (e.g., talking, walking away, calling upon an arbitrator, compromising, etc.).

27. Find a peer with whom the student is most likely to be able to successfully interact (e.g., a student with similar interests, background, classes, behavior patterns, nonacademic schedule, etc.).

28. Structure the activities of the situation according to the need/abilities of the student (e.g., establish rules, limit the stimulation of the activities, limit the length of activities, consider time of day, etc.).

29. Limit opportunities for interaction on those occasions when the student is not likely to be successful (e.g., the student has experienced academic or social failure prior to the scheduled activity).

30. Select nonacademic activities designed to enhance appropriate interaction of the student and another person (e.g., board games, model building, coloring, etc.).

31. Through observations and interviews with other students, determine those characteristics of the student which interfere with successful interaction to determine skills or behaviors the student needs to develop for successful interaction.

32. Have the student practice appropriate interactions with the teacher(s).

33. Make certain beforehand that the student is able to successfully engage in the activity (e.g., the student understands the rules, the student is familiar with the activity, the student will be compatible with the other student engaged in the free time activity, etc.).

34. Do not force the student to interact with individuals with whom he/she is not completely comfortable.

35. Have the student interact with one other person for short periods of time to enhance success. As the student experiences success, gradually increase the length of time.

36. Intervene early when there is a problem to prevent a more serious problem from occurring.

37. Make certain that the student understands that failing to interact appropriately during activities may result in removal from the activity and/or loss of participation in future activities.

Goals:

1. The student will make contact with others when appropriate.
2. The student will answer only when called upon.
3. The student will communicate with others in an acceptable manner in the classroom.
4. The student will refrain from bothering other students who are trying to work, listen, etc.
5. The student will stay on-task.
6. The student will work quietly in the classroom.

Objectives

1. The student will demonstrate acceptable physical contact such as a handshake, pat on the back, "high five," etc., when appropriate on ____ out of ____ trials.
2. The student will gain others' attention in an appropriate manner by standing quietly or raising his/her hand until recognized on ____ out of ____ trials.
3. The student will interact with others in a physically appropriate manner on ____ out of ____ trials.
4. The student will refrain from making unnecessary contact such as hugging, talking, touching, etc., when attempting to interact with others on ____ out of ____ trials.
5. The student will ask the teacher's permission prior to interacting with a peer(s) on _____ out of _____ trials.
6. The student will await his/her turn to talk when engaged, or attempting to engage, in interactions with the teacher on _____ out of _____ trials.
7. The student will await his/her turn to talk when engaged, or attempting to engage, in interactions with others on _____ out of _____ trials.
8. The student will contribute his/her opinion/answer after being recognized by the teacher on _____ out of _____ trials.
9. The student will gain permission from the teacher, by raising his/her hand, when he/she needs to talk with a peer on _____ out of _____ trials.
10. The student will interact with other students during free time, break time, lunch time, etc., on _____ out of _____ trials.
11. The student will interact with other students when appropriate on _____ out of _____ trials.
12. The student will make comments to the teacher which are relevant to the situation on _____ out of _____ trials.
13. The student will refrain from interrupting other students who are trying to work, listen, etc., on _____ out of _____ trials.
14. The student will refrain from making sounds which are inappropriate for the situation on _____ out of _____ trials.
15. The student will remain appropriately seated until given teacher permission to do otherwise on _____ out of _____ trials.
16. The student will stay on-task for _____ minutes at a time. (Gradually increase expectations as the student demonstrates success.)

Interventions:

1. Prevent the student from becoming over-stimulated by an activity (e.g., monitor or supervise the student's behavior to limit overexcitement in physical activities, games, parties, etc.).

2. Reinforce the student for demonstrating appropriate behavior (e.g., waiting for a turn to speak, working quietly, etc.) based on the length of time the student can be successful. As the student demonstrates success, gradually increase the length of time required for reinforcement.

3. Allow natural consequences to occur as a result of the student's inappropriate behavior (e.g., excessive physical contact may cause people to stay away from the student or may result in pushing, shoving, etc.).

4. Reduce the opportunity for the student to engage in inappropriate physical contact (e.g., stand an appropriate distance from the student when interacting).

5. Attempt to provide equal attention to all students in the classroom.

6. Avoid inadvertently stimulating the student's unnecessary physical contact (e.g., attire, language used, physical proximity, etc.).

7. Have the student question any directions, explanations, and instructions not understood.

8. Communicate with parents (e.g., notes home, phone calls, etc.) to share information concerning the student's appropriate behavior. The parents may reinforce the student at home for waiting his/her turn to speak at school.

9. Deliver directions, explanations, and instructions in a clear and concise manner to reduce the student's need to ask questions.

10. Provide the student with many social and academic successes.

11. Encourage the student to model the behavior of peers who are successful.

12. Establish classroom rules:
- Work on-task.
- Work quietly.
- Remain in your seat.
- Finish task.
- Meet task expectations.

Review rules often. Reinforce students for following rules.

13. Treat the student with respect. Talk in an objective manner at all times.

14. Provide the student with frequent opportunities to participate, share, etc.

15. Reinforce those students in the classroom who interact appropriately with other students or teachers.

16. Reinforce the student for raising his/her hand to be recognized.

17. Acknowledge the student when he/she seeks attention verbally instead of making it necessary for the student to gain attention through physical contact.

18. Give the student responsibilities in the classroom (e.g., running errands, opportunities to help the teacher, etc.).

19. Provide students with frequent opportunities to interact with one another (e.g., before and after school, between activities, etc.).

20. Deliver a predetermined signal (e.g., hand signal, verbal cue, etc.) when the student begins to display inappropriate behaviors.

21. Provide the student with high-interest activities (e.g., academic activities which are inherently interesting, activities during free time, etc.).

22. Seat the student near the teacher.

23. Help the student improve concentration skills (e.g., listening to the speaker, taking notes, preparing comments in advance, making comments in the appropriate context, etc.).

24. Make the necessary adjustments in the environment to prevent the student from experiencing stress, frustration, or anger (e.g., reduce peer pressure, academic failure, teasing, etc.).

25. Reinforce the student for respecting the norms of physical proximity: (a) give the student a tangible reward (e.g., classroom privileges, line leading, passing out materials, etc.) or (b) give the student an intangible reward (e.g., praise, handshake, smile, etc.).

26. Model socially acceptable physical contact for the student (e.g., handshake, pat on the back, etc.).

27. Make certain that reinforcement is not inadvertently given for inappropriate behavior (e.g., interrupting others, making inappropriate comments, talking to others during quiet activity periods, etc.).

28. Reinforce those students in the classroom who demonstrate on-task behavior.

29. Make certain the student sees the relationship between his/her behavior and the consequences which may follow (e.g., touching and hugging people all of the time may result in others not wanting to be around him/her).

30. Provide the student with verbal recognition and reinforcement for social and academic successes.

31. Speak to the student to explain (a) what the student is doing wrong (e.g., interrupting other students who are trying to work, listen, etc.) and (b) what the student should be doing (e.g., waiting for a turn to speak, working quietly, etc.).

32. Reinforce the student for working quietly: (a) give the student a tangible reward (e.g., classroom privileges, line leading, passing out materials, five minutes free time, etc.) or (b) give the student an intangible reward (e.g., praise, handshake, smile, etc.).

33. Reduce activities which might cause the student to interrupt or talk out (e.g., announcing test score ranges or test scores aloud, emphasizing the success of a particular student or students, etc.).

34. Choose a peer to model appropriate behavior for the student.

35. Remove the student from the group or activity until he/she can demonstrate appropriate behavior and self-control.

36. Teach the student to recognize appropriate times to talk to other students (e.g., between activities, during breaks, at recess, etc.).

37. Seat the student away from those students he/she is most likely to bother.

38. Reduce distracting stimuli (e.g., place the student on the front row, provide a carrel or "office" away from distractions, etc.). This is used as a means of reducing distracting stimuli and not as a form of punishment.

39. Make certain that the student's feelings are considered when it is necessary to deal with his/her interruptions (i.e., handle comments in such a way as to not diminish the student's enthusiasm for participation).

40. Explain to the student that he/she may be trying too hard to fit in and should relax and wait until more appropriate times to interact.

41. Write a contract with the student specifying what behavior is expected (e.g., waiting for a turn to speak, working quietly, etc.) and what reinforcement will be made available when the terms of the contract have been met.

42. Explain to the student why it is inappropriate to interrupt the teacher (e.g., impolite, unfair to other students, others cannot hear what the teacher is saying, etc.).

43. Make certain the student knows when it is acceptable to interrupt others (e.g., in an emergency).

44. Try various groupings to determine the situation in which the student is most comfortable.

45. Reinforce the student for respecting the norms of physical proximity based on the length of time the student can be successful. As the student demonstrates success, gradually increase the length of time required for reinforcement.

46. Interact frequently with the student to reduce the need to interrupt the teacher or talk to other students.

47. Try various groupings to find a situation in which the student's need for physical attention can be satisfied by socially acceptable interactions (e.g., holding hands while dancing in an extracurricular activity, a hug for an accomplishment, handshake or "high five" in sports, etc.).

48. Reinforce those students in the classroom who wait their turn to speak, work quietly, etc.

49. Acknowledge the student's presence and/or need to talk with you (e.g., by saying, "Just a minute;" putting your arm around the student; smiling and nodding your head; etc.).

50. Explain to the student the reason why he/she should not be talking.

51. Maintain visibility to and from the student. The teacher should be able to see the student and the student should be able to see the teacher. Make eye contact possible at all times.

52. Have the student be the leader of a small group activity if he/she possesses mastery of skills or an interest in that area.

53. Reinforce the student for waiting for a turn to speak: (a) give the student a tangible reward (e.g., classroom privileges, line leading, passing out materials, five minutes free time, etc.) or (b) give the student an intangible reward (e.g., praise, handshake, smile, etc.).

54. Find a peer who would be a good influence to play with the student (e.g., someone younger, older, of the same gender, of the opposite gender, etc.).

55. Provide a full schedule of activities. Prevent lag time from occurring when the student can bother other students.

56. Give the student adequate opportunities to speak in the classroom, talk to other students, etc. (i.e., enthusiastic students need many opportunities to contribute).

57. Provide the student with enjoyable activities to perform when he/she completes a task early.

58. Teach the student to recognize the appropriate time to speak (e.g., when the teacher has finished speaking, after raising his/her hand, to make comments within the context of the situation, to make comments that are a follow-up to what has just been said, etc.).

59. Make the student aware of the number of times he/she interrupts the teacher.

60. Evaluate the appropriateness of the task to determine (a) if the task is too easy, (b) if the task is too difficult, and (c) if the length of time scheduled to complete the task is adequate.

61. Provide the student with social interaction in place of physical interaction (e.g., call the student by name, speak to the student, praise, congratulate, etc.).

62. Structure the environment to limit opportunities for interrupting the teacher or talking to other students during quiet activity periods (e.g., keep the student engaged in activities, have the student seated near the teacher, etc.).

63. Deliver a predetermined signal (e.g. hand signal, bell ringing, etc.) if the student begins to interrupt the teacher or talk to other students during quiet activity periods.

64. Talk to the student before beginning an activity and remind him/her of the importance of listening and not interrupting.

65. Do not criticize when correcting the student, be honest yet supportive. Never cause the student to feel negatively about himself/herself.

66. Have the student work in small groups in which there are frequent opportunities to speak. As the student learns to wait longer for a turn to speak, gradually increase the size of the group.

67. Call on the student when he/she is most likely to be able to respond correctly.

68. Have the student practice waiting for short periods of time for a turn to speak. As the student demonstrates success, gradually increase the length of time required for reinforcement.

69. Assess the appropriateness of the social situation in relation to the student's ability to function successfully.

70. Interact frequently with the student to maintain his/her involvement in the activity (e.g., ask the student questions, ask the student's opinion, stand close to the student, seat the student near the teacher's desk, etc.).

71. Teach the student appropriate ways to communicate needs to others (e.g., waiting a turn, raising his/her hand, etc.).

Goal:

1. The student will increase his/her interactions with peers.

Objectives:

1. The student will verbally respond to ___ out of ___ questions asked by a peer.
2. The student will interact with a peer for ___ minutes at a time.
3. The student will engage in parallel play with a peer for ___ minutes at a time.
4. The student will share materials with a peer during ___ out of ___ interactions.
5. The student will demonstrate appropriate peer interaction skills by sharing materials, waiting his/her turn, and talking in an acceptable manner on ___ out of ___ trials.
6. The student will interact with a peer ___ times per day. (Gradually increase expectations as the student demonstrates success.)
7. The student will initiate ___ interaction(s) with a peer per day. (Gradually increase expectations as the student demonstrates success.)
8. The student will make eye contact with a peer when interacting on ___ out of ___ trials.

Interventions:

1. Assign a peer to sit/work directly with the student (e.g., in different settings or activities such as art, music, P.E., on the bus, tutoring, group projects, running errands in the building, recess, etc.). As the student becomes comfortable working with another student, gradually increase the size of the group.

2. Encourage or reward others for interacting with the student.

3. Give the student the responsibility of acting as a teacher's aide for an activity (e.g., holding up flash cards, demonstrating the use of equipment, etc.).

4. Give the student the responsibility of tutoring a peer.

5. Ask the student to choose a peer to work with on a specific assignment. If the student has difficulty choosing someone, determine the student's preference by other means such as a class survey.

6. Choose a peer to model appropriate interactions with peers for the student.

7. Try various groupings to determine the situation in which the student is most comfortable.

8. Assess the appropriateness of the social setting in relation to the student's ability to interact with peers.

9. Provide the student with many social and academic successes.

10. Assign the student to work with one or two peers on a long-term project (e.g., mural, bulletin board, report, etc.).

11. Create situations in which the student must interact (e.g., returning completed assignments to students, proofreading other students' work, etc.).

12. Have the student work with a peer who is younger or smaller (e.g., choose a peer who would be the least threatening).

13. Establish social rules:
- Share materials.
- Use a quiet voice in the building.
- Walk indoors.
- Use care in handling materials.

Review rules often. Reinforce students for following rules.

14. Request that the student be the leader of a small group activity if he/she possesses mastery of skills or an interest in that area.

15. Determine the peer(s) with whom the student would prefer to interact and attempt to facilitate this interaction.

16. Assign an outgoing, nonthreatening peer to help the student interact more appropriately with peers.

17. Structure the environment so that the student has many opportunities to interact with peers.

18. Have the student run errands with a peer to facilitate interaction.

19. Conduct a sociometric activity with the class to determine the peer who would most prefer to interact with the student.

20. Make certain the student understands that interacting with a peer is contingent upon appropriate interactions.

21. Teach the student appropriate ways to interact with another student (e.g., how to greet another student, suggest activities, share materials, problem solve, take turns, converse, etc.).

22. Supervise interaction closely so the peer with whom the student interacts does not stimulate the student's inappropriate behavior.

23. Make certain that the interaction is not so stimulating as to make successful interaction with another student difficult.

24. Involve the student in extracurricular activities to encourage interactions with peers.

25. Assign an older peer with desirable social skills to interact with the student (e.g., in the play area, cafeteria, hallways, etc.).

26. Reduce the emphasis on competition. Failure may cause the student to be reluctant to interact with peers.

27. Teach the student problem-solving skills so he/she may better deal with problems that occur in interactions with another peer (e.g., talking, walking away, calling upon an arbitrator, compromising, etc.).

28. Find a peer with whom the student is most likely to be able to interact successfully (e.g., a student with similar interests, background, classes, behavior patterns, nonacademic schedule, etc.).

29. Structure the interaction according to the needs/abilities of the student (e.g., establish rules, limit the stimulation of the activity, limit the length of the activity, consider time of day, etc.).

30. Limit opportunities for interaction on those occasions when the student is not likely to be successful (e.g., when the student has experienced academic or social failure prior to the scheduled nonacademic activity).

31. Select nonacademic activities designed to facilitate appropriate interaction of the student and a peer (e.g., board games, model building, coloring, etc.).

32. Through interviews with other students and observations, determine those characteristics of the student which interfere with successful interactions to determine skills or behaviors the student needs to develop.

33. Have the student practice appropriate interactions with the teacher(s).

34. Make certain the student understands that failing to interact appropriately with a peer may result in removal from the activity and/or loss of participation in future activities.

35. Encourage the student to interact with others.

36. Have the student interact with a peer for short periods of time to enhance success. As the student demonstrates success, gradually increase the length of time.

37. Do not force the student to interact with someone with whom he/she is not completely comfortable.

38. Communicate with parents (e.g., notes home, phone calls, etc.) to share information concerning the student's progress. The parents may reinforce the student at home for interacting with peers at school.

39. Write a contract with the student specifying what behavior is expected (e.g., sitting near another student, talking to another student, etc.) and what reinforcement will be made available when the terms of the contract have been met.

40. Reinforce the student for interacting with peers based on the length of time he/she can be successful. As the student demonstrates success, gradually increase the length of time required for reinforcement.

41. Have peers invite the student to participate in school or extracurricular activities.

42. Facilitate the development of friendships with peers (e.g., assign activities for the student involving peers, give the student and a peer joint responsibilities, etc.).

43. Speak with the student to explain (a) what he/she is doing wrong (e.g., not talking, sharing, etc.) and (b) what he/she should be doing (e.g., talking, sharing, etc.).

44. Reinforce the student for interacting with peers: (a) give the student a tangible reward (e.g., classroom privileges, line leading, passing out materials, five minutes free time, etc.) or (b) give the student an intangible reward (e.g., praise, handshake, smile, etc.).

45. Provide organized activities for the student to participate in before, during, and after school (e.g., board games, softball, four square, tether ball, jump rope, flash cards, etc.).

46. Provide the student with the opportunity to work with a peer who will be an appropriate model for interacting with other students.

47. Encourage the student's peers to include him/her in free time activities.

48. Reinforce those students in the classroom who interact appropriately with peers.

49. Establish classroom rules:
- Work on-task.
- Work quietly.
- Remain in your seat.
- Finish task.
- Meet task expectations.

Review rules often. Reinforce students for following rules.

50. Encourage the student to become involved in athletic activities.

Reminder: Do not "force" the student to interact with peers.

240   Does not display the appropriate social interaction with strangers, acquaintances, close friends, family, etc.

Goals:

1. The student will improve his/her interpersonal behavior in academic situations.
2. The student will improve his/her interpersonal behavior in nonacademic situations.

Objectives:

1. The student will share materials on ____out of ____occasions.
2. The student will take turns with one other student ____out of ____occasions.
3. The student will wait his/her turn in a group situation on ____out of ____occasions.
4. The student will communicate successfully with one other student in a social situation on ____ out of ____ occasions.
5. The student will communicate successfully in a group social situation on ____out of ____occasions.
6. The student will greet others appropriately on ____out of ____occasions.
7. The student will maintain the appropriate distance from others in a social situation on ____out of ____ occasions.
8. The student will ask conversational questions in a social situation on ____out of ____occasions.
9. The student shake hands when appropriate on ____out of ____occasions.
10. The student will hug others only when appropriate on ____out of ____occasions.
11. The student will verbally respond to ___ out of ___questions asked by a peer.
12. The student will interact with a peer for ___minutes at a time.
13. The student will engage in parallel play with a peer for ___minutes at a time.
14. The student will share materials with a peer during ___out of ___interactions.
15. The student will demonstrate appropriate peer interaction skills by sharing materials, waiting his/her turn, and talking in an acceptable manner on ___out of ___trials.
16. The student will interact with a peer ___times per day. (Gradually increase expectations as the student demonstrates success.)
17. The student will initiate ___interaction(s) with a peer per day. (Gradually increase expectations as the student demonstrates success.)
18. The student will make eye contact with a peer when interacting on ___out of ___trials.
19. The student will verbally respond to ___out of ___questions asked by the teacher.
20. The student will make eye contact with the teacher when spoken to on ___out of ___trials.
21. The student will make eye contact with the teacher when speaking on ___out of ___trials.
22. The student will maintain eye contact with the teacher for ___minutes during a conversation.
23. The student will seek assistance from the teacher when necessary on ___out of ___trials.
24. The student will interact with the teacher ___times per day. (Gradually increase expectations as the student demonstrates success.)
25. The student will initiate ___interaction(s) with the teacher per day. (Gradually increase expectations as the student demonstrates success.)
26. The student will interact for ___minutes per day with the teacher. (Gradually increase expectations as the student demonstrates success.)

Interventions:

1. Reinforce the student for demonstrating appropriate social interaction skills: (a) give the student a tangible reward (e.g., classroom privileges, line leading, passing out materials, five minutes free time, etc.) or (b) give the student an intangible reward (e.g., praise, handshake, smile etc.).

2. Speak to the student to explain (a) what he/she is doing wrong (e.g., hugging strangers, responding rudely to greetings, etc.) and (b) what he/she should be doing (e.g., shaking hands when greeting an acquaintance, asking conversational questions, etc.).

3. Provide the student with many opportunities to demonstrate appropriate social interaction skills.

4. Reinforce the student for demonstrating appropriate social interaction skills based on the number of times the student can be successful. As the student demonstrates success, gradually increase the number of times required for reinforcement.

5. Write a contract with the student specifying what behavior is expected (e.g., asking conversational questions) and what reinforcement will be made available when the terms of the contract have been met.

6. Communicate with parents (e.g., notes home, phone calls, etc.) to share information concerning the student's progress. The parents may reinforce the student at home for demonstrating appropriate social interaction skills at school.

7. Choose a peer to model appropriate social interaction skills (e.g., maintaining appropriate distance from others, greeting others appropriately, etc.) for the student.

8. Have the student question any directions, explanations, and instructions he/she does not understand.

9. Evaluate the appropriateness of expectations for the student to demonstrate appropriate social interaction skills.

10. Teach the student appropriate positive verbal greetings (e.g., "Hi, how are you doing?" "Good to see you." "Haven't seen you in a long time." etc.).

11. Teach the student appropriate positive verbal requests (e.g., "Please pass the paper." "May I please be excused?" "Will you please help me?" etc.).

12. Teach the student appropriate positive ways to verbally indicate disagreement (e.g., "Excuse me, I think I was here first." "Pardon me, I need to get to my locker." "I'm sorry, but I don't think that's correct." etc.).

13. Model for the student appropriate positive verbal greetings, requests, and indications of disagreement.

14. Require the student to practice social interaction skills with a specified number of peers throughout the school day.

15. Make certain that all educators interact with the student on a regular basis and use positive verbal communication in speaking to him/her.

16. Require the student to interact with several peers (e.g., run errands, request materials, etc.) in social interaction.

17. Reinforce those students in the classroom who demonstrate appropriate social interaction skills.

18. Choose peers with whom the student most often interacts to model appropriate social interaction skills.

19. Teach the student positive social communication skills to help develop appropriate social interaction skills (e.g., waiting your turn to speak, asking conversational questions, using an appropriate tone of voice, talking about appropriate subjects with others, etc.).

20. Help the student develop social awareness (e.g., an acquaintance may be uncomfortable if hugged by someone he/she does not know well, it is not acceptable to reveal personal information to someone you have just met, etc.).

21. Assess the demands of the social situation to determine an appropriate level of expectation for the student's social interaction skills.

22. Teach the student skills in interacting socially with others (e.g., asking questions, listening while the other person speaks, making eye contact, nodding head, making comments which relate to what the other person has said, etc.).

23. Help the student become aware of his/her tone of voice when greeting, requesting, and/or disagreeing with others by calling attention to voice inflections which are inappropriate for the situation.

24. Teach the student appropriate ways to communicate displeasure, anger, etc.

25. Reduce the stimuli which contribute to the student's arguing, calling names, cursing, etc.

26. Treat the student with respect. Talk in an objective manner at all times.

27. Make certain the student understands the natural consequences of inappropriate social interactions (e.g., others will choose not to interact with him/her, exclusion from activities, etc.).

28. Require that the student identify alternative appropriate behaviors following an instance of inappropriate social interactions (e.g., shaking hands rather than hugging, asking/answering conversational questions, seeking teacher intervention, etc.).

29. Teach the student problem-solving skills: (a) identify the problem; (b) identify goals and objectives; (c) develop strategies; (d) develop a plan for action; and (e) carry out the plan.

30. Teach the student positive ways to interact with others.

31. Make certain the student recognizes inappropriate social interactions (e.g., call attention to the comments when they occur, record each instance, terminate the activity when the comment occurs, etc.).

32. Interact frequently with the student to monitor his/her social interactions.

33. Make certain that positive reinforcement is not inadvertently given for inappropriate social interactions (e.g., attending to the student only when he/she has demonstrated inappropriate social interactions).

34. Teach the student appropriate words or phrases to use in situations of anger, stress, frustration, etc.

35. Do not force the student to interact with other students with whom he/she is not completely comfortable.

36. Provide the student with the opportunity to work with a peer who will be an appropriate model for social interactions.

37. Encourage the student to interact with others.

38. Provide frequent opportunities for the student to meet new people.

39. Do not force the student to interact with others.

40. Teach the student to think before acting (e.g., ask himself/herself "What is happening?" "What am I doing?" "What should I do?" "What will be best for me?").

41. Have the student practice appropriate verbal exchanges which should be made (e.g., "Excuse me." "I'm sorry." etc.).

42. Role play various situations with the student to model appropriate social interactions (e.g., appropriate greetings, closings, conversations, etc.).

43. Discuss inappropriate social interactions privately with the student rather than in front of a group. Encourage the student to think of more appropriate ways to have handled the situation.

44. Provide the student with verbal reminders before entering a social situation (e.g., "Remember to shake hands when being introduced." "Say excuse me when you need to leave a conversation." etc.).

Goal:

1. The student will increase his/her interactions with teachers.

Objectives:

1. The student will verbally respond to ___ out of ___ questions asked by the teacher.
2. The student will make eye contact with the teacher when spoken to on ___ out of ___ trials.
3. The student will make eye contact with the teacher when speaking on ___ out of ___ trials.
4. The student will maintain eye contact with the teacher for ___ minutes during a conversation.
5. The student will seek assistance from the teacher when necessary on ___ out of ___ trials.
6. The student will interact with the teacher ___ times per day. (Gradually increase expectations as the student demonstrates success.)
7. The student will initiate ___ interaction(s) with the teacher per day. (Gradually increase expectations as the student demonstrates success.)
8. The student will interact for ___ minutes per day with the teacher. (Gradually increase expectations as the student demonstrates success.)

Interventions:

1. Give the student the responsibility of acting as a teacher's assistant for an activity (e.g., holding up flash cards, demonstrating the use of equipment, etc.).

2. Give the student the responsibility of tutoring another student.

3. Be certain to greet or recognize the student as often as possible (e.g., greet in the hallways or cafeteria, welcome to class, acknowledge a job well done, call the student by name, etc.).

4. Request that the student be the leader of a small group activity if he/she possesses mastery of skills or an interest in that area.

5. Have the student run errands which will require interactions with teachers (e.g., delivering attendance reports, taking messages to other teachers, etc.).

6. Interact with the student from a distance, gradually decreasing the distance until a close proximity is achieved.

7. Make certain that directions, explanations, and instructions are delivered on the student's ability level.

8. Use an alternative form of communication (e.g., puppet).

9. Provide the student with many social and academic successes.

10. Create situations in which the student must interact (e.g., handing completed assignments to the teacher, delivering a message to a teacher, etc.).

11. Choose a peer to model appropriate interaction with teachers for the student.

12. Encourage the student to question any directions, explanations, and instructions not understood.

13. Evaluate the appropriateness of expecting the student to communicate needs to teachers.

14. Maintain mobility throughout the classroom to determine the student's needs.

15. Offer the student assistance frequently throughout the day.

16. Arrange for one-to-one, teacher/student interactions.

17. Structure the environment so the student is not required to communicate all needs to teachers (e.g., make certain the student's tasks are on his/her ability level, be sure instructions are clear, and maintain frequent interactions with the student to ensure success).

18. To detect the student's needs, communicate with the student as often as opportunities permit.

19. Model for the student appropriate positive verbal greetings, requests, and indications of disagreement.

20. Communicate to the student that he/she is a worthwhile individual.

21. Call on the student often to encourage communication.

22. Teach the student communication skills (e.g., hand raising, expressing needs in written and/or verbal form, etc.).

23. Encourage the student to communicate needs to other personnel in the educational environment (e.g., school counselor, school psychologist, principal, etc.).

24. Communicate with parents, agencies, or the appropriate parties to inform them of the problem, determine the cause of the problem, and consider possible solutions to the problem.

25. Recognize the student's attempts to communicate needs (e.g., facial expressions, gestures, inactivity, self-depreciating comments, etc.).

26. Teach the student appropriate positive verbal greetings (e.g., "Hi." "How are you doing?" "Good to see you." "Haven't seen you in a long time." etc.).

27. Teach the student appropriate positive verbal requests (e.g., "Please pass the paper." "May I be excused?" "Will you please help me?" etc.).

28. Teach the student appropriate positive ways to verbally indicate disagreement (e.g., "Excuse me." "I'm sorry, but I don't think that's correct." etc.).

29. Demonstrate accepting behavior and interest in the student's needs (e.g., willingness to help others, making criticisms constructive and positive, demonstrating confidentiality in personal matters, etc.).

30. Teach the student appropriate verbalization for problem resolution as an alternative (e.g., "Let's talk about it." "Let's compromise." "Let's see what would be fair for both of us." etc.).

31. Require the student to practice positive verbal communications with an identified number of teachers throughout the school day.

32. Make certain that all teachers interact with the student on a regular basis and use positive verbal communications when speaking to him/her.

33. Require the student to interact with several adults (e.g., run errands, request materials, etc.) to increase the opportunities for communication with adults.

34. Teach the student appropriate ways to communicate to teachers that a problem exists (e.g., "I don't understand the directions." "I couldn't complete my assignment." "I can't find all of my materials." etc.).

35. Identify teachers with whom the student most often interacts to make certain that they model appropriate verbal communications for the student.

36. Spend some time each day talking with the student on an individual basis about his/her interests.

37. Teach the student skills in maintaining positive conversations with teachers (e.g., asking questions, listening while the other person speaks, making eye contact, head nodding, making comments which relate to what the other person has said, etc.).

38. Help the student become aware of his/her tone of voice when greeting, requesting, and/or disagreeing by calling attention to inappropriate voice inflections for the situation.

39. Determine an individual(s) in the school environment with whom the student would most want to converse (e.g., custodian, librarian, resource teacher, principal, older student, etc.). Allow the student to spend time with the individual(s) each day.

40. Reinforce those students in the classroom who interact appropriately with teachers.

41. Deliver directions in a supportive rather than a threatening manner (e.g., "Please finish your math paper before going to recess." rather than "You had better finish your math paper or else!").

42. Do not criticize. When correcting the student, be honest yet supportive. Never cause the student to feel negatively about himself/herself.

43. Treat the student with respect. Talk in an objective manner at all times.

44. Be careful to avoid embarrassing the student by giving him/her orders, demands, etc., in front of others.

45. Have the student practice appropriate interactions with the teacher(s) in classroom activities (e.g., simulations, role playing, etc.).

46. Spend individual time with the student. Do not give more attention to students who are more outgoing.

47. Communicate with parents (e.g., notes home, phone calls, etc.) to share information concerning the student's progress. The parents may reinforce the student at home for interacting with teachers at school.

48. Do not force the student to interact.

49. Write a contract with the student specifying what behavior is expected (e.g., sitting near the teacher, talking to the teacher, etc.) and what reinforcement will be made available when the terms of the contract have been met.

50. Reinforce the student for interacting with teachers based on the length of time the student can be successful. As the student demonstrates success, gradually increase the length of time required for reinforcement.

51. Pair the student with an outgoing student who engages in conversation with teachers on a frequent basis.

52. Establish classroom rules:
- Work on-task.
- Work quietly.
- Remain in your seat.
- Finish task.
- Meet task expectations.

Review rules often. Reinforce students for following rules.

53. Speak with the student to explain (a) what the student is doing wrong (e.g., not talking, not making eye contact, etc.) and (b) what the student should be doing (e.g., talking, looking at the teacher, etc.).

54. Reinforce the student for interacting with teachers: (a) give the student a tangible reward (e.g., classroom privileges, line leading, passing out materials, five minutes free time, etc.) or (b) give the student an intangible reward (e.g., praise, handshake, smile, etc.).

55. Maintain trust and confidentiality with the student at all times.

Reminder: Do not "force" the student to interact with teachers.

242 Does not adjust or has difficulty adjusting behavior to the expectations of different situations

Goals:

1. The student will change his/her behavior from one situation to another.
2. The student will demonstrate flexibility in his/her behavior.
3. The student will improve his/her independent behavior.
4. The student will improve his/her independent behavior in academic settings.
5. The student will improve his/her independent behavior in nonacademic settings.

Objectives:

1. At the end of recess, the student will calm down within _____ minutes and enter the building in a quiet manner.
2. The student will adjust behavior to different situations with verbal prompts on ____ out of ____ occasions.
3. The student will adjust behavior to the rules of different situations on ____ out of ____ occasions.
4. The student will adjust physical behavior to different situations on ____ out of ____ occasions.
5. The student will adjust verbal behavior to different situations on ____ out of ____ occasions.
6. The student will begin a task within ____ minutes.
7. The student will calm down when he/she enters the building on ____ out of ____ trials.
8. The student will change his/her behavior from one situation to another on _____ out of _____ trials.
9. The student will demonstrate behavior appropriate for the situation on ____ out of ____ trials.
10. The student will demonstrate flexibility in his/her behavior on _____ out of _____ trials.
11. The student will engage in a relaxation activity following a stimulating activity on _____ out of _____ trials.
12. The student will independently adjust behavior to different situations on ____ out of ____ occasions.
13. The student will stop an activity and begin another within ___ minutes.
14. The student will stop an activity when cued by the teacher on _____ out of _____ trials.

Interventions:

1. Allow a transition period between activities so the student can make adjustments in his/her behavior.

2. Teach the student some ways to settle down when he/she gets overly excited (e.g., count to ten, say the alphabet, sit in a chair, leave the situation, etc.).

3. Use reminders to prepare the student well in advance (e.g., homeroom, 30 minutes, etc.) for such activities as guest speakers, assemblies, field trip, etc.

4. Do not allow the student to begin a new activity until he/she has gained self-control.

5. Write a contract with the student specifying what behavior is expected (e.g., stopping a behavior when it is no longer acceptable) and what reinforcement will be made available when the terms of the contract have been met.

6. Allow the student the option of performing the activity at another time (e.g., earlier/later in the day, on another day, or at home).

7. Communicate clearly to the student when it is time to begin a new activity and the expectations for the student's behavior.

8. Encourage the student to pause and consider his/her thoughts before acting on them.

9. Be proactive. Work with the school counselor to schedule the student's classes to facilitate adjustment from high activity to low activity classes.

10. Collect the student's materials (e.g., pencil, paper, textbook, workbook, etc.) when it is time to change from one situation to another.

11. Educate yourself and others about ADHD to increase understanding and accommodation of behaviors.

12. Communicate clearly to the student when it is time to stop an activity and prepare for a new activity or situation.

13. Deliver directions/instructions before handing out materials.

14. Communicate clearly to the student when it is time to stop an activity.

15. Encourage the student to avoid ingesting any substance (e.g., drugs, alcohol, cold remedies, etc.) that might further alter his/her ability to maintain self-control.

16. Communicate with parents (e.g., notes home, phone calls, etc.) to share information concerning the student's progress. The parents may reinforce the student at home for adjusting his/her behavior to the expectations of different situations at school.

17. Give directions in a variety of ways to increase the probability of understanding (e.g., if the student fails to understand verbal directions, present them in written form).

18. Establish classroom rules:
- Work on-task.
- Remain in your seat.
- Finish task.
- Meet task expectations.
- Raise your hand.

Review rules often. Reinforce students for following the rules.

19. Encourage the student to self-monitor himself/herself. Encourage the student to take a break to regroup when he/she is acting inappropriately.

20. Convince the student that work not completed in one sitting can be completed later. Provide the student ample time to complete earlier assignments to guarantee closure.

21. Have the student develop an awareness of the consequences of his/her behavior by writing down or talking through problems which may occur due to his/her inability to adjust his/her behavior to different situations (e.g., perceived as unmannerly, avoided, etc.).

22. Encourage the student to develop an awareness of himself/herself and those around him/her. Have the student periodically step back and ask himself/herself "Am I behaving appropriately?"

23. Evaluate the appropriateness of the situation in relation to the student's ability to successfully adapt or modify his/her behavior.

24. Develop, in conjunction with other school personnel, as much consistency across the various environments as possible (e.g., rules, criteria for success, behavioral expectations, consequences, etc.).

25. Do not allow the student to participate in activities that cause him/her to become so excited that he/she cannot settle down.

26. Educate the student about ADHD and the need to self-monitor behavior.

27. Employ a signal technique (e.g., turning the lights off and on) to warn that the end of an activity is near and it is time to finish and put materials away.

28. Encourage the student to consider the consequences of his/her behavior before engaging in any activity.

29. Communicate clearly to the student when it is time to start an activity.

30. Provide the student with a clearly understood list of consequences for inappropriate behavior.

31. Have the student repeat the directions verbally to the teacher.

32. Establish rules that are to be followed in various parts of the school building (e.g., lunchroom, music room, art room, gymnasium, library, etc.).

33. Evaluate the appropriateness of the task to determine (a) if the task is too easy, (b) if the task is too difficult, and (c) if the length of time scheduled to complete the task is adequate.

34. Assign a peer to sit/work directly with the student (e.g., in different settings such as art, music, physical education, on the bus; or different activities such as tutoring, group projects, running errands in the building, recess, etc.).

35. Explain to the student that he/she should be satisfied with his/her best effort rather than insist on perfection.

36. Consider carefully the student's age and maturity level before expecting him/her to follow a routine without becoming excited.

37. Give the student a special signal when he/she is not settling down (e.g., a secret word, a hand signal, etc.).

38. Reinforce the student for adjusting his/her behavior to the expectations of different situations based on the length of time the student can be successful. As the student demonstrates success, gradually increase the length of time required for reinforcement.

39. Explain to the student when he/she cannot calm down exactly what he/she is doing wrong, what he/she is supposed to be doing, and why.

40. Follow a less desirable task with a highly desirable task, making the completion of the first task necessary to perform the second task.

41. Give a signal (e.g., clapping hands, turning lights off and on, etc.) to indicate the beginning of a new activity.

42. Have the student begin an activity in a private place (e.g., carrel, "office", quiet study area, etc.) to reduce his/her difficulty in adapting or modifying his/her behavior to different situations.

43. Assign a peer to work with the student to provide an appropriate model for adjusting his/her behavior.

44. Have the student question any directions, explanations, or instructions he/she does not understand.

45. Establish definite time limits and provide the student with this information before the activity begins.

46. Communicate with the student's cooperative work experience/vocational education teacher to provide interventions appropriate for the student's job site.

47. Identify the expectations of different environments and help the student develop the skills to be successful in those environments (e.g., working on assignments for extended periods of time, working in a large group, waiting a turn, waiting for attention, etc.).

48. Make certain that the student understands the relationship between inappropriate behavior and the consequences which follow (e.g., not being allowed to attend field trips, being avoided by friends, missing out on special activities, etc.).

49. Provide the student with more than enough time to adapt or modify his/her behavior to different situations (e.g., have the student stop recess activities five minutes prior to coming into the building).

50. Have the student time his/her activities to monitor his/her own behavior and accept time limits.

51. Reduce the student's involvement in activities which prove too stimulating (e.g., if some recess activities prove too stimulating, the student should be directed to less stimulating activities).

52. State clearly the manner in which you expect the student to act before going on a field trip or entering a new situation (e.g., assembly, special activity etc.).

53. Maintain consistent expectations within the ability level of the student.

54. Limit the number of changes in the student's established routine. As the student demonstrates success, gradually increase the number of changes in the routine.

55. Maintain a routine that will minimize erratic or impulsive behavior which may result in negative consequences.

56. Have the student explain what he/she thinks should be done to perform the activity/assignment.

57. Choose a peer to model appropriate adjustment of his/her behavior to the expectations of different situations for the student.

58. Let the student know in advance when changes in his/her schedule will occur (e.g., a change from class time to recess, when reading class will begin, etc.).

59. Maintain a consistent daily routine.

60. Have the student identify the situations in which he/she does not adjust his/her behavior. After identifying these situations, have the student think of ways to minimize their occurrences

61. Allow the student to finish an activity unless it will be disruptive to the schedule.

62. Have the student maintain a record (e.g., chart or graph) of his/her performance in adjusting his/her behavior to expectations of different situations.

63. Help the student with the first few items on a task and gradually reduce the amount of help over time.

64. In conjunction with other school personnel, develop as much consistency across different environments as possible (e.g., rules, criteria for individual success, behavioral expectations, consequences, etc.).

65. Supervise the student to prevent him/her from getting too excited to settle down.

66. Prevent the student from becoming so stimulated by an event or activity that he/she cannot control his/her behavior.

67. Increase supervision (e.g., by teacher, peer, paraprofessional, etc.) of the student when he/she is involved in activities that tend to overexcite him/her to facilitate the student's ability to adjust behavior to different situations.

68. Have the student engage in relaxing transitional activities designed to reduce the effects of stimulating activities (e.g., put head on desk, put headphones on and listen to relaxing music, etc.).]

69. Have the student engage in another activity until he/she can settle down and gain control of his/her behavior.

70. Provide constant, positive reinforcement for appropriate behavior. Ignore as many inappropriate behaviors as possible.

71. Reinforce those students in the classroom who adjust their behavior to the expectations of different situations.

72. Structure time limits so the student knows exactly how long he/she has to work and when he/she must be finished.

73. Schedule recreational activities at the end of the day. Make participation in these activities dependent upon completion of daily responsibilities and the demonstration of appropriate behavior.

74. Make certain that the student has all the materials he/she needs to perform the assignment/activity.

75. Present the task in the most interesting and attractive manner possible.

76. Make certain the student is aware of the expectations of the activity (e.g., go over rules and directions/instructions often).

77. Provide a transition activity between tasks (e.g., class stretch, five minutes conversation time, etc.).

78. Provide adequate transition time for the student to finish an activity and get ready for the next activity.

79. Provide the student with a list of materials needed for each activity (e.g., pencil, paper, textbook, workbook, etc.).

80. Reward the student for behaving appropriately in a specific situation (e.g., guest speaker, field trip, etc.). Try to give the student as much structure and "sameness" in his/her school day as possible.

81. Schedule activities so the student has more than enough time to finish the activity if he/she works consistently.

82. Deliver a predetermined signal (e.g., turning lights off and on, hand signals, etc.) when the student is not beginning a task.

83. Provide the student with the opportunity to perform the assignment/activity in a variety of ways (e.g., on tape, with a calculator, verbally, etc.).

84. Provide the student with a schedule of activities so he/she knows exactly what and how much there is to do in a day.

85. Assign the student shorter activities. As the student demonstrates success, gradually increase the length of the activities.

86. Be consistent in expecting the student to adjust his/her behavior to a different situation (e.g., give only one reminder before removing the student from the group, allow five minutes for the student to adjust behavior, etc.).

87. Provide the student with a schedule of daily events so he/she will know which activity comes next and can prepare for it.

88. Provide the student with established time limits before an activity begins.

89. Speak to the student to explain (a) what he/she is doing wrong (e.g., behaving inappropriately in a situation) and (b) what he/she should be doing (e.g., adjusting behavior to the situation).

90. Provide the student with more than enough time to finish an activity. Decrease the time provided as the student demonstrates success.

91. Teach problem-solving skills:
- Identify the problem.
- Identify the goals and objectives.
- Develop a strategy/plan for action.
- Carry out the plan.
- Evaluate the results.

92. Teach the student behaviors that promote self-control and allow him/her to gain his/her composure before continuing an activity (e.g., placing hands on desk, sitting with feet on the floor, making eye contact with the person who is talking, etc.).

93. Reduce emphasis on academic and/or social competition. Fear of failure may cause the student to not want to change from a desirable task to a less desirable task.

94. Provide the student with clearly stated expectations for al situations (e.g., rules, schedules, directions, etc.).

95. Reinforce the student for adjusting his/her behavior to the expectations of different situations: (a) give the student a tangible reward (e.g., classroom privileges, line leading, passing out materials, five minutes free time, etc.) or (b) give the student an intangible reward (e.g., praise, handshake, smile, etc.).

96. Remove the student immediately from an activity when he/she becomes too excited and cannot calm down.

243 Does not adjust behavior to the expectations of community situations

Goals:

1. The student will improve his/her independent behavior in community settings.
2. The student will adjust behavior to the expectations of community situations.

Objectives:

1. The student will adjust verbal behavior to different situations in the community on ____out of ____ occasions.
2. The student will adjust physical behavior to different situations in the community on ____out of ____ occasions.
3. The student will adjust behavior to the rules of different community situations on ____out of ____ occasions.
4. The student will independently adjust behavior to different situations on ____out of ____ occasions.
5. The student will demonstrate behavior which typifies basic social manners expected in community settings on ____ out of ____ occasions.
6. The student will demonstrate flexibility in his/her behavior on ____out of ____trials.
7. The student will demonstrate behavior appropriate for the situation on ____out of ____trials.

Interventions:

1. Reinforce the student for adjusting his/her behavior to the expectations of different community situations: (a) give the student a tangible reward (e.g., classroom privileges, line leading, passing out materials, five minutes free time, etc.) or (b) give the student an intangible reward (e.g., praise, handshake, smile, etc.).

2. Speak to the student to explain (a) what he/she is doing wrong (e.g., failing to stand in line) and (b) what he/she should be doing (e.g., standing in line appropriately).

3. Reinforce those students in the classroom who adjust their behavior to the expectations of different community situations.

4. Reinforce the student for adjusting his/her behavior to the expectations of different community situations based on the length of time the student can be successful. As the student demonstrates success, gradually increase the length of time required for reinforcement.

5. Write a contract with the student specifying what behavior is expected (e.g., engaging in appropriate social interaction with a stranger) and what reinforcement will be made available when the terms of the contract have been met.

6. Communicate with parents (e.g., notes home, phone calls, etc.) to share information concerning the student's progress. The parents may reinforce the student at home for adjusting his/her behavior to the expectations of different community situations.

7. Evaluate the appropriateness of the task to determine (a) if the task is too easy, (b) if the task is too difficult, and (c) if the length of time scheduled to complete the task is adequate.

8. Choose a peer to model appropriate adjustment of his/her behavior to the expectations of different community situations for the student.

9. Have the student question any directions, explanations, and instructions he/she does not understand.

10. Explain to the student that he/she should be satisfied with his/her best effort rather than insist on perfection.

11. Prevent the student from becoming overstimulated by an activity (e.g., monitor or supervise student behavior to limit overexcitement in physical activities, on field trips, etc.).

12. Model socially acceptable behavior in community situations for the student (e.g., standing in line to buy tickets at the movie theater).

13. Employ a signal technique (e.g., turning the lights off and on) to warn that the student needs to adjust his/her behavior to the expectation of the community situation.

14. Maintain consistent expectations within the ability level demonstrated by the student.

15. Maintain a consistent daily routine.

16. Have the student maintain a record (e.g., chart or graph) of his/her performance in adjusting his/her behavior to expectations of different community situations.

17. Give directions in a variety of ways to increase the probability of understanding (e.g., if the student fails to understand verbal directions, present them in written form).

18. Reduce emphasis on competition. Fear of failure or anxiety may cause the student to have difficulty adjusting his/her behavior to the community situation.

19. Make certain the student is aware of the expectations of the activity in the community (e.g., go over rules and expectations often).

20. Provide the student with clearly stated expectations for all situations (e.g., rules, schedules, directions, etc.).

21. Establish rules that are to be followed in various parts of the community (e.g., library, mall, fast food restaurant, movie theater, museum, etc.).

22. In conjunction with other school personnel, develop as much consistency across different environments as possible (e.g., rules, criteria for individual success, behavioral expectations, consequences, etc.).

23. Identify the expectations of different environments and help the student develop the skills to be successful in those environments (e.g., working/reading quietly in a library, speaking in a conversational voice in a fast food restaurant, standing in line at a movie theater, etc.).

24. Reduce the student's involvement in activities which prove too stimulating (e.g., if some community activities prove too stimulating, the student should be directed to less stimulating activities until he/she is capable of handling those which are more stimulating).

25. Have the student time his/her activities to monitor his/her own behavior and accept time limits.

26. Talk to the student about ways of handling different community situations successfully (e.g., how to interact with a stranger).

27. Teach the student to "think" before acting (e.g., ask himself/herself "What is happening?" "What am I doing?" "What should I do?" "What will be best for me?").

28. Make certain that all students get equal opportunities to participate in activities in community situations (e.g., students take turns, everyone has an equal opportunity to be first, etc.).

29. Allow natural consequences to occur when the student fails to adjust his/her behavior to the expectations of different community situations (e.g., those who are not able to remain quiet in the library may not be allowed to go the next time).

30. Do not criticize the student. When correcting the student be honest yet supportive. Never cause the student to feel negatively about himself/herself.

31. Make the student aware of activities which will take place in community situations well in advance so he/she may prepare for them.

32. Provide praise and recognition of appropriate behavior as often as possible.

33. Be careful to avoid embarrassing the student by giving him/her orders, demands, etc., in front of others.

34. Reinforce the student for adjusting behavior to current expectations in different situations: (a) give the student a tangible reward (e.g., classroom privileges, line leading, passing out materials, five minutes free time, etc.) or (b) give the student an intangible reward (e.g., praise, handshake, smile, etc.).

35. Speak to the student to explain (a) what he/she is doing correctly, (b) what is expected of him/her for total correct response, and (c) what he/she can be doing to improve or reach this correct response.

36. Establish classroom rules:
- Work on-task.
- Work quietly.
- Remain in your seat.
- Finish task.
- Meet task expectations.

Review rules often. Reinforce students for following rules.

37. Reinforce those students in the classroom who adjust their behavior to the expectations of different situations.

38. Discuss general social expectations required during participation in community based activities with students, and share this information with parents. Encourage parents to rehearse and reinforce these community based expectations with their children.

39. Provide the student opportunities to become oriented to areas of the community in which he/she will be participating in activities by first visiting those areas in small groups.

40. Explain to the student the benefits of best efforts of behavior adjustment in community settings (e.g., acquiring positive social regard of other people, being welcome to return to that area of the community, etc.).

41. Role play community activity expectations with the student to reduce the anxiety of failure in public places.

42. Based upon community observation, establish for instructional reference a brief list of behaviors which can and can not be tolerated during community based activities.

43. Identify the expectations of different environments and help the student develop skills needed for success in those environments.

44. Allow a transition period between activities so the student has time to adjust behaviors to meet new expectations. During transition, provide the student opportunities to rehearse his/her upcoming expectations.

45. Assign the student shorter activities in the community and gradually increase the length of activities based on student success.

46. Have the student engage in relaxing transitional activities designed to reduce the effects of more stimulating activities (e.g., putting on headphones and listening to relaxing music).

47. Have the student maintain a record (e.g., chart or graph) of performance in adjusting behavior to expectations in different community situations.

48. Structure time limits so the student knows exactly how long he/she will be sitting in a movie, standing in line, etc.

244　Does not adjust his/her behavior to the demands of the social situation

Goal:

1. The student will demonstrate the ability to adjust his/her behavior to the demands of the social situation.

Objectives:

1. The student will adjust verbal behavior to different social situations on ____out of ____occasions.
2. The student will adjust physical behavior to different social situations on ____out of ____occasions.
3. The student will adjust behavior to the rules of different social situations on ____out of ____occasions.
4. The student will adjust behavior to different social situations with verbal prompts on ____out of ____ occasions.
5. The student will independently adjust behavior to different social situations on ____out of ____ occasions.
6. The student will solve problems in conflict situations on ____out of ____occasions.
7. The student will make decisions appropriate to the situation on ____out of ____trials.
8. The student will demonstrate consideration/regard for others on ____out of ____trials.
9. The student will maintain self-control when redirected in a social situation on ____out of ____trials.
10. The student will demonstrate flexibility in his/her behavior on ____out of ____trials.

Interventions:

1. Prevent the student from becoming over-stimulated by an activity. Supervise student behavior to limit overexcitement in physical activities, games, parties, etc.

2. Provide the student with clearly stated expectations for all situations.

3. Prevent the student from becoming so stimulated by an event or activity that the student cannot control his/her behavior.

4. Identify the expectations of different environments and help the student develop the skills to be successful in those environments.

5. In conjunction with other school personnel, develop as much consistency across the various environments as possible (e.g., rules, criteria for success, behavioral expectations, consequences, etc.).

6. Reduce the student's involvement in activities which prove too stimulating for him/her.

7. Have the student engage in relaxing transitional activities designed to reduce the effects of stimulating activities (e.g., put head on desk, listen to the teacher read a story, put headphones on and listen to relaxing music, etc.).

8. Reduce the emphasis on academic and/or social competition. Fear of failure may cause the student to fail to adapt or modify his/her behavior to different social situations.

9. Evaluate the appropriateness of the social situation in relation to the student's ability to successfully adapt or modify his/her behavior.

10. Evaluate the appropriateness of the task to determine (a) if the task is too easy, (b) if the task is too difficult, and (c) if the length of time scheduled to complete the task is adequate.

11. Write a contract with the student specifying what behavior is expected (e.g., compromising to reasonable demands) and what reinforcement will be made available when the terms of the contract have been met.

12. Reinforce those students in the classroom who adjust their behavior from one social situation to another without difficulty.

13. Speak to the student to explain (a) what the student is doing wrong (e.g., failing to be flexible to changing social situations) and (b) what the student should be doing (e.g., adjusting his/her behavior to the demands of social situations).

14. Reinforce the student for adjusting his/her behavior to the demands of the social situation without difficulty: (a) give the student a tangible reward (e.g., classroom privileges, line leading, passing out materials, five minutes free time, etc.) or (b) give the student an intangible reward (e.g., praise, handshake, smile, etc.).

15. Reinforce those students in the classroom who adjust their behavior to the expectations of different situations.

16. Reinforce the student for adjusting his/her behavior to the expectations of different social situations based on the length of time the student can be successful. As the student demonstrates success, gradually increase the length of time required for reinforcement.

17. Communicate with parents (e.g., notes home, phone calls, etc.) to share information concerning the student's progress. The parents may reinforce the student at home for adjusting his/her behavior to the expectations of different social situations at school.

18. Choose a peer to model appropriate adjustment of his/her behavior to the expectations of different social situations for the student.

19. Allow a transition period between activities so the student can make adjustments in his/her behavior.

20. Maintain consistent expectations within the ability level demonstrated by the student.

21. Maintain a consistent daily routine.

22. Have the student maintain a record (e.g., chart or graph) of his/her performance in adjusting his/her behavior to expectations of different social situations.

23. Communicate to the student that he/she is a worthwhile individual.

24. Do not criticize the student. When correcting the student, be honest yet supportive. Never cause the student to feel negatively about himself/herself.

25. Pair the student with a peer who demonstrates the ability to adjust his/her behavior to the demands of social situations.

26. Provide opportunities for interactions within the classroom to allow the student to practice adjusting his/her behavior to the demands of various social situations.

27. Assess the appropriateness of the social situation in relation to the student's ability to be successful.

28. Experiment with various groupings to determine the situation in which the student is most comfortable in adjusting his/her behavior to the demands of various social situations.

29. Teach the student social interaction skills (e.g., ways to respond to changing social situations). Be specific about ways of reacting to certain situations.

30. Teach the student appropriate verbal and non-verbal responses to common everyday situations.

31. Have the student engage in simulated social activities with feedback designed to improve behavioral responses to various social situations.

32. Allow natural consequences to occur so the student can learn that persons who adjust behavior to the demands of the social situation are more successful than those who are inflexible in their behavior (e.g., if you are never willing to compromise to acceptable demands, others may avoid being in social situations with you).

33. Provide the opportunity for the student to experience many social and academic successes.

34. Intervene early when there is a problem to prevent a more serious problem from occurring.

35. Teach the student to "think" before acting (e.g., ask himself/herself "What is happening?" "What am I doing?" "What should I do?" "What is best for me?").

36. Teach the student acceptable ways to communicate displeasure, anger, frustration, etc.

37. In conjunction with other school personnel, develop as much consistency across different environments as possible (e.g., rules, criteria for individual success, behavioral expectations, consequences, etc.).

38. Make certain the student is aware of the different expectations in different social situations (e.g., rules, schedules, directions, etc.).

245 Makes up excuses to avoid social situations or activities that are new or different for him/her

Goal:

1. The student will participate in classroom activities or special events.

Objectives:

1. The student will participate in ___ out of ___ new activities each week.
2. The student will participate in ___ out of ___ special events per month.
3. The student will demonstrate an interest in new activities by asking about the activities, talking about the activities, helping prepare for the activities, etc., in ___ out of ___ activities.
4. The student will demonstrate an interest in special events by asking about the events, talking about the events, helping prepare for the events, etc., in ___ out of ___ special events.
5. The student will passively participate in a new activity or social situation during ___ out of ___ activities.
6. The student will actively participate in a new activity or social situation during ___ out of ___ activities.
7. The student will passively participate in a special event by sitting/standing quietly, walking with the group, watching others play games, etc., during ___ out of ___ events.
8. The student will actively participate in a special event by having a role in the play, producing the play, decorating the room, performing in the assembly, etc., during ___ out of ___ events.

Interventions:

1. Reinforce the student for participating in social situations or activities that are new or different: (a) give the student a tangible reward (e.g., classroom privileges, line leading, passing out materials, five minutes free time, etc.) or (b) give the student an intangible reward (e.g., praise, handshake, smile, etc.).

2. Speak to the student to explain (a) what the student is doing wrong (e.g., avoiding new or different social situations or activities) and (b) what the student should be doing (e.g., participating in new or different social situations or activities).

3. Reinforce other students who participate in new or different social situations or activities.

4. Reinforce the student for participating in new or different social situations or activities based on the number of times the student can be successful. As the student demonstrates success, gradually increase the number of times required for reinforcement.

5. Write a contract with the student specifying what behavior is expected (e.g., participating in new or different social situations or activities) and what reinforcement will be made available when the terms of the contract have been met.

6. Make positive comments about participating in new or different social situations or activities.

7. Do not force the student to attend new or different social situations or activities.

8. Provide the student with as many social and academic successes as possible.

9. Encourage and assist the student in joining extracurricular activities, clubs, etc.

10. Choose a peer to model participation in new or different social situations or activities for the student.

11. Carefully consider those activities in which the student does not want to participate. If something unpleasant is causing the student to not participate, do all you can to change the situation.

12. Have a peer (e.g., a close friend) accompany the student to those activities in which he/she does not want to participate. As the student demonstrates success, gradually decrease the length of time the peer stays with the student.

13. Make certain that the activities planned for the student are those in which he/she can be most successful.

14. Make certain the student feels as comfortable as possible about his/her appearance. Compliment the student on his/her personal appearance and encourage or reinforce others for complimenting the student.

15. Make certain that the student's peers will be accepting, reassuring, etc., in social situations or activities that are new or different.

16. Make certain the student is familiar with the peers with whom he/she will participate in the activity or social situation.

17. Make certain the student is compatible with the peers who will be engaging in the activity or social situation.

18. Reduce the emphasis on competition. Competitive activities or social situations may cause the student to be uncomfortable.

19. Make certain the student has a schedule of all activities so he/she knows what to expect at all times.

20. Simulate or practice any new or different activity or social situation with the student before the actual activity takes place.

21. Have the student choose peers with whom he/she will participate in any activity or situation that is new or different for him/her.

22. Make certain the student has permission to leave any social situation or activity when he/she is uncomfortable.

23. Have the student's peers share their feelings about being uncomfortable in social situations or activities that were new or different.

246   Does not interact appropriately with a peer(s) in nonacademic situations

Goal:

1. The student will interact appropriately with a peer(s) in nonacademic situations.

Objectives:

1. The student will take turns with one other student in nonacademic situations on _____ out of _____ trials.
2. The student will interact appropriately with one other student in nonacademic situations with supervision on _____ out of _____ trials.
3. The student will interact appropriately without supervision with one other student in nonacademic situations on _____ out of _____ trials.
4. The student will share materials with one other student in nonacademic situations on _____ out of _____ trials.
5. The student will communicate appropriately with one other student in nonacademic situations on _____ out of _____ trials.

Interventions:

1. Reinforce the student for interacting appropriately with one other student in nonacademic situations: (a) give the student a tangible reward (e.g., classroom privileges, line leading, passing out materials, five minutes free time, etc.) or (b) give the student an intangible reward (e.g., praise, handshake, smile, etc.).

2. Speak to the student to explain (a) what he/she is doing wrong (e.g., not sharing materials) and (b) what he/she should be doing (e.g., sharing materials).

3. Establish social rules:
   - Share materials.
   - Use a quiet voice in the building.
   - Walk indoors.
   - Use care in handling materials.
   Review rules often. Reinforce students for following rules.

4. Reinforce those students in the classroom who interact appropriately with one other student in nonacademic situations.

5. Reinforce the student for interacting appropriately with one other student in nonacademic situations based on the length of time the student can be successful. As the student demonstrates success, gradually increase the length of time required for reinforcement.

6. Write a contract with the student specifying what behavior is expected (e.g., sharing materials) and what reinforcement will be made available when the terms of the contract have been met.

7. Communicate with parents (e.g., notes home, phone calls, etc.) to share information concerning the student's progress. The parents may reinforce the student at home for interacting appropriately with one other student in nonacademic situations at school.

8. Evaluate the expectations for peer interactions to determine if the student can be successful in the interactions and for the expected length of time.

9. Choose a peer to model appropriate interactions with one other student in nonacademic situations for the student.

10. Have the student question any directions or expectations he/she does not understand.

11. Determine the peer(s) with whom the student would most prefer to interact in nonacademic situations and attempt to facilitate the interaction.

12. Assign an outgoing, nonthreatening peer to help the student interact more appropriately.

13. Structure the environment so that the student has many opportunities to interact with another student in nonacademic situations.

14. Assign the student to interact with a younger student in nonacademic situations (e.g., free time areas, cafeteria, hallways, etc.).

15. Have the student run errands with a peer to facilitate interaction.

16. Assign the student to nonacademic situations in which he/she is likely to interact successfully with another student.

17. Conduct a sociometric activity with the class to determine the peer who would most prefer to interact with the student in nonacademic situations.

18. Make certain that the student understands that interacting with a peer in nonacademic situations is contingent upon appropriate behavior.

19. Teach the student appropriate ways to interact with another student in nonacademic situations (e.g., how to greet another student, suggest activities, share materials, problem solve, take turns, converse, etc.).

20. Make certain that the student understands that participation in nonacademic situations is contingent upon appropriate behavior.

21. Supervise nonacademic situations closely so the peer with whom the student interacts does not stimulate the student's inappropriate behavior.

22. Make certain that the nonacademic situation is not so stimulating as to make successful interactions with another student difficult.

23. Assign an older peer with positive social skills to interact with the student in nonacademic situations (e.g., free time area, cafeteria, hallways, etc.).

24. Involve the student in extracurricular activities to encourage interactions with a peer in nonacademic situations.

25. Reduce the emphasis on competition. Failure may stimulate inappropriate behavior in nonacademic situations.

26. Teach the student problem solving skills so he/she may better handle problems that may occur in interactions with another student in nonacademic situations (e.g., talking, walking away, calling upon an arbitrator, compromise, etc.).

27. Find a peer with whom the student is most likely to be able to successfully interact in nonacademic situations (e.g., a student with similar interests, background, classes; behavior patterns; nonacademic schedule; etc.).

28. Structure the activities of the nonacademic situation according to the needs/abilities of the student (e.g., establish rules; limit the stimulation of the activities; limit the length of the activities; consider time of day; etc.).

29. Limit opportunities for interaction in nonacademic situations on those occasions in which the student is not likely to be successful (e.g., the student has experienced academic or social failure prior to the scheduled nonacademic activity).

30. Select nonacademic activities designed to facilitate appropriate interaction of the student and a peer (e.g., board games, model building, etc.).

31. Through observations and interviews with other students, determine those characteristics of the student which interfere with successful interaction during nonacademic situations. Determine the skills or behaviors the student needs to develop for successful interaction.

32. Have the student practice appropriate interactions with the teacher(s) in nonacademic situations.

33. Make certain beforehand that the student is able to successfully participate in the nonacademic activity (e.g., the student understands the rules; the student is familiar with the activity; the student will be compatible with the other student participating in the free time activity; etc.).

34. Make certain that the student understands that failing to interact appropriately with a peer during nonacademic activities may result in removal from the activity and or loss of participation in future activities.

35. Have the student interact with a peer for short periods of time to facilitate success. As the student experiences success, gradually increase the length of time.

247 Does not demonstrate the ability to determine the appropriate duration of interaction for the situation

Goal:

1. The student will demonstrate the ability to determine the appropriate duration of interaction for the situation.

Objectives:

1. The student will engage in social interactions for the appropriate length of time on ____ out of ____ occasions.
2. The student will engage in greeting-type interactions for a short duration on ____ out of ____ occasions.
3. The student will engage in conversational-type interactions for several minutes on ____ out of ____ occasions.

Interventions:

1. Make certain the student's hearing has recently been checked.

2. Reinforce the student for determining the appropriate duration for interaction: (a) give the student a tangible reward (e.g., classroom privileges, line leading, passing out materials, five minutes free time, etc.) or (b) give the student an intangible reward (e.g., praise, handshake, smile, etc.).

3. Reinforce other students in the classroom when they demonstrate the ability to determine the appropriate duration of interaction for the situation.

4. Be sure to act as an appropriate model for determining the appropriate duration of interaction for the situation.

5. Speak with the student to explain that he/she is not demonstrating the ability to determine the appropriate duration of interaction for the situation.

6. Choose a peer to model appropriate duration of interaction for the situation for the student.

7. Communicate to the student that he/she is a worthwhile individual.

8. Provide the student with many academic and social successes.

9. Determine an individual(s) in the school environment with whom the student would most want to converse (e.g., custodian, librarian, resource teacher, principal, older student, etc.). Allow the student to spend time conversing with the individual(s) each day. Make sure these people model appropriate duration of interaction for the situation.

10. Pair the student with an outgoing student who demonstrates the ability to determine the appropriate duration of interaction for the situation.

11. Provide opportunities for interactions within the classroom to allow the student to practice determining the appropriate duration of interaction for the situation (e.g., peer models engaged in interactions of the appropriate duration).

12. Assess the appropriateness of the social situation in relation to the student's ability to be successful.

13. Be certain to greet or recognize the student as often as possible (e.g., in the hallways or cafeteria, welcome to class, acknowledge a job well done, etc.). Encourage him/her to recognize you in return.

14. Have the student run errands which will require verbal interactions with other students, teachers, administrators, etc.

15. Experiment with various groupings to determine the situation in which the student is most comfortable initiating and maintaining conversations with peers and adults.

16. Teach the student social interaction skills (e.g., ways in which to appropriately respond to others when first seeing them or when leaving them, how to ask and answer conversational questions, etc.). Be specific about phrases which are appropriate to use and situations in which you would use them.

17. Teach the student conversational phrases (e.g., "How are you?" "I'm fine." "How's it going?" "See you later." etc.) to use when engaging in a conversation.

18. Teach the student conversational rules (e.g., explain that it is appropriate to say "hello" when you are seeing someone for the first time during the day, but not when it's only been five minutes since the last encounter).

19. Teach the student appropriate verbal and nonverbal responses to common everyday situations.

20. Have the student engage in simulated conversational activities with feedback designed to teach verbal communication skills (e.g., greetings, closings, questions, topic maintenance, etc.).

21. Create a communication unit for the entire classroom which includes the basic rules of verbal communication in various situations.

22. Prompt the student to help him/her utilize greetings/closings more appropriately (e.g., Teacher says, "How are you?" Student says nothing. Teacher says, "I'm fine today. How are you?").

23. Teach the student to be aware of "listener response" to determine if the interaction is of appropriate duration.

24. Set up fictitious situations in the classroom (e.g., restaurant, gas station, grocery store, etc.) and have the students in the class role play "working" in each situation. Have them change roles often and emphasize appropriate duration of interaction in various situations.

25. Pair the student with a peer and have them take turns being interviewed and interviewing. This may be done with the students acting as themselves or pretending to be fictitious characters. Emphasize appropriate duration of the interaction in various situations.

26. Have a sharing time at school. Encourage the student to talk about anything of interest to him/her while emphasizing appropriate duration of the interaction.

27. Allow the student to speak without being interrupted or hurried.

28. Reduce the emphasis on competition. Competitive activities may cause the student to become anxious and engage in interactions of inappropriate duration for the situation.

29. Teach the student that the appropriate duration of interaction depends upon the person to whom he/she is talking (e.g., a greeting to a close friend would probably be more extended than when greeting an acquaintance). Discuss how age, position and/or familiarity can change the duration of interaction.

30. Create situations in which the student must interact (e.g., returning completed assignments to students, proofreading other students' work, etc.).

31. Structure the environment so the student has many opportunities to interact with peers.

32. Make sure the interaction is not so stimulating as to make successful interaction with another student difficult.

33. Have the student interact with a peer for short periods of time to enhance success. As the student demonstrates success, gradually increase the length of time.

34. Communicate with parents (e.g., notes home, phone calls, etc.) to share information concerning the student's progress. The parents may reinforce the student at home for demonstrating the ability to determine the appropriate duration for the situation at school.

248   Does not engage in a variety of leisure and recreational interests

Goal:

1. The student will engage in a variety of leisure and recreational interests.

Objectives:

1. The student will participate in ____ out of ____ leisure or recreational activities each week.
2. The student will participate in ____ out of ____ leisure or recreational activities each month.
3. The student will demonstrate an interest in leisure or recreational activities by asking about the activities, talking about the activities, participating in the activities, etc. in ____ out of ____ activities.
4. The student will demonstrate an interest in leisure or recreational activities by asking about the events, talking about the events, helping prepare for the events, etc. in ____ out of ____ special events.
5. The student will passively participate in leisure or recreational activities by sitting/standing quietly, walking with the group, watching others participate etc. during ____ out of ____ events.
6. The student will actively participate in leisure or recreational activities by having a role in the play, attending a club meeting, decorating the room, participating in a sports activity, etc. during ____ out of ____ events.

Interventions:

1. Evaluate the appropriateness of available leisure and recreational activities to determine whether or not the student can be successful with the activity and the length of time scheduled.

2. Develop, with the student, a list of high-interest leisure and recreational activities that require various amounts of time to perform.

3. Place materials to be used for leisure and recreational activities (e.g., paper, pencil, glue, crayons, games, equipment, books, etc.) in a location where the student can obtain them on his/her own.

4. Establish centers of high-interest leisure and recreational activities at appropriate levels of difficulty for the student's use during free time.

5. Provide a quiet, reasonably private area where the student can engage in quiet leisure activities during free time.

6. Provide things that entertain the student during free time (e.g., headphones, coloring books, reading material, etc.).

7. Provide sign-up sheets for leisure and recreational activities.

8. Have the student choose an ongoing project to work on during free time which will in turn become a regular free time activity.

9. Provide the student with a list of quiet activities to engage in when he/she finishes assignments early.

10. Make certain the student is able to successfully engage in the free time activity (e.g., the student understands the rules, the student is familiar with the activity, the student will be compatible with other students engaged in the activity, etc.).

11. Encourage the student to plan the use of free time in advance.

12. Have the student question any directions, explanations, or instructions not understood.

13. Choose a peer to model self-initiation of leisure and recreational activities for the student.

14. Communicate with parents (e.g., notes home, phone calls, etc.) to share information concerning the student's progress. The parents may reinforce the student at home for self-initiating leisure and recreational activities at school.

15. Write a contract with the student specifying what behavior is expected (e.g., choosing an activity in which to engage, beginning an activity, etc.) and what reinforcement will be made available when the terms of the contract have been met.

16. Reinforce those students in the classroom who self-initiate leisure and recreational activities.

17. Establish free time rules:
- Find an activity.
- Spend time quietly.
- Remain in assigned areas.
- Put materials away when free time is over.

Review rules often. Reinforce students for following rules.

18. Speak to the student to explain (a) what the student is doing wrong (e.g., sitting idly, allowing others to choose activities for him/her, etc.) and (b) what he/she should be doing (e.g., choosing an activity, beginning an activity independently, etc.).

19. Reinforce the student for self-initiating a leisure or recreational activity: (a) give the student a tangible reward (e.g., classroom privileges, line leading, passing out materials, five minutes free time, etc.) or (b) give the student an intangible reward (e.g., praise, handshake, smile, etc.).

20. Expose the student to a variety of leisure/recreational resources in his/her home, school, and community to help the student make informed decisions about leisure/recreational activities available.

21. When possible, observe the student in his/her home and community environment to gather information concerning the student's current leisure/recreational activity decisions.

22. Provide the student assistance and support as needed to follow through with activity plans he/she has initiated.

23. Provide the student a small list of leisure/recreational activities which are well liked and familiar to him/her. Reinforce the student for initiating selection of an activity.

24. Encourage parental input in developing behavioral and activity expectations in community sites to encourage consistency between home and school.

25. Explain to the student that his/her best effort is more important than perfection to help decrease frustration with the task.

26. If a student experiences frustration with his/her choice of leisure/recreational activity, modify the activity to meet the student's needs.

27. Prevent the student from becoming overstimulated by an activity (e.g., monitor or supervise student behavior to limit overexcitement in physical activities). Help the student develop one or two coping strategies to use in community settings to prevent overexcitement (e.g., counting to ten, walking away, talking to a teacher, etc.).

28. Assure the student can or will communicate his/her leisure/recreational interests to you to facilitate the student's participation in the process of choosing and engaging in leisure/recreational activities.

29. As much as possible, assure the student's leisure/recreational interests are given priority in activity decisions.

30. Incidentally teach functional academics that are critical to the process of choosing, locating, and using resources for leisure/recreational activities (e.g., signing up for activities, getting necessary equipment, etc.).

31. Teach students all phases of selecting and participating in leisure/recreational activities (e.g., making necessary contacts about activities, signing up for activities, gathering necessary equipment, etc.).

32. Determine the student's current ability with a leisure/recreational activity by observing the student's current performance.

33. Incidentally teach the student social skills he/she may need to participate in leisure/recreational activity (e.g, team members need to know how to work together, people who are watching a movie in a theater are typically quiet, etc.)

34. Maintain consistent expectations within the ability of the student.

35. Give directions in a variety of different ways to increase the probability of understanding (e.g., if the student does not understand verbal instructions, present them in writing).

36. Encourage the student, when possible, to develop leisure/recreational preferences which include physical activity (e.g., exercising, dancing, team sports, roller skating, etc.) and passive entertainment (e.g., watching a baseball game, going to a movie). Acquire medical approval for physically demanding activities.

37. Help the student establish a daily routine which includes a chosen leisure/recreational activity (e.g., dancing, walking, exercising, etc.) and praise him/her for participating in the activity.

38. Encourage the student to try new leisure/recreational activities to stimulate interests and build his/her reference file for future choices. Acquire medical approval for any activities which might represent risk to the student's safety.

39. Teach the student to alternate among favorite activities to prevent boredom.

40. Teach students to access locations in the community for chosen leisure/recreational activities (e.g., locate and pay for transportation, give directions to or find the location, etc.).

41. Incidentally teach and emphasize leisure/recreational activity participation as a technique for managing/reducing stress.

42. Monitor students to assure their continued involvement in selecting and participating in a variety of leisure/recreational activities of their own choosing.

43. Teach students to budget money, time, and other resources for leisure/recreational activities that are realistic in comparison to the demands of other expenses and the parameters of his/her income.

249   Fails to demonstrate a sense of humor when appropriate

Goals:
1. The student will smile.
2. The student will laugh.
3. The student will demonstrate happiness.

Objectives:
1. The student will smile when appropriate on ___ out of ___ trials.
2. The student will laugh when appropriate on ___ out of ___ trials.
3. The student will demonstrate happiness when appropriate on ___ out of ___ trials.
4. The student will demonstrate happiness by smiling, laughing, joking with peers, etc., on ___ out of ___ trials.
5. The student will laugh or smile when humorous events or activities take place on ___ out of ___ trials.

Interventions:

1. Present tasks in the most attractive and interesting manner possible.

2. Determine those activities the student prefers and provide them often.

3. Have peers invite the student to participate in school and extracurricular activities.

4. Make every attempt to create a positive atmosphere in the classroom (e.g., cooperative group activities, positive motivation strategies, positive communications, etc.).

5. Provide the student with as many social and academic successes as possible.

6. Include the student in classroom/group activities (e.g., invite the student to join a group, assign the student a part or responsibility in an activity, etc.).

7. Indicate a need for the student's involvement in an activity (e.g., the student is a part of the class/activities, is valued and needed, etc.).

8. Include fun and enjoyable activities as a part of the daily curriculum.

9. Encourage the student to interact with others.

10. Reduce or discontinue competitive activities. Repeated failure reduces enjoyment of the activity.

11. Avoid discussions of topics sensitive to the student (e.g., divorce, death, unemployment, alcoholism, etc.).

12. Be certain to greet or recognize the student as often as possible (e.g., greet in hallways or in the cafeteria, welcome to class, acknowledge a job well done, etc.).

13. Call attention to the student's accomplishments (e.g., publicly or privately, depending on which is most appropriate).

14. Interact frequently with the student.

15. Try various groupings to determine the situation in which the student is most comfortable.

16. Make certain that interactions with the student are natural and not contrived.

17. Help the student develop a friendship by assigning him/her to work with a peer on an activity, project, etc.

18. Do not force the student to interact with others.

19. Provide the student with frequent opportunities to meet new people.

20. Speak to the student to explain (a) that you recognize he/she is unhappy and (b) appropriate ways to deal with unhappiness.

21. Reinforce those students in the classroom who deal with unhappiness in an appropriate manner.

22. Take time to talk with the student in order for the student to realize that the teacher's interest in him/her is genuine.

23. Make certain that reinforcement is not inadvertently given when the student does not smile, laugh, or demonstrate happiness (e.g., attending to the student only when he/she demonstrates unhappiness).

24. Discourage the student from engaging in those activities which cause him/her unhappiness.

25. Give the student additional responsibilities (e.g., chores, errands, etc.) to give him/her a feeling of success or accomplishment.

26. Help the student identify things he/she wishes were in the environment and work with the student toward these goals.

27. Treat the student with respect. Talk in an objective manner at all times.

28. Allow the student to attempt something new in private before doing so in front of others.

29. Have the student complete a reinforcer survey to determine his/her interests, his/her favorite activities, what is rewarding to the student, etc.; and use the information obtained to create a pleasant atmosphere at school for the student.

30. Make sure you express your feelings in a socially acceptable way.

31. Evaluate the appropriateness of the task to determine (a) if the task is too easy, (b) if the task is too difficult, and (c) if the length of time scheduled to complete the task is adequate.

32. Communicate with parents, agencies, or the appropriate parties to inform them of the problem, determine the cause of the problem, and consider possible solutions to the problem.

33. Reinforce those students in the classroom who engage in classroom activities or special events.

34. Encourage the student to engage in classroom activities or special events.

35. Reinforce the student for demonstrating happiness when appropriate: (a) give the student a tangible reward (e.g., classroom privileges, line leading, passing out materials, five minutes free time, etc.) or (b) give the student an intangible reward (e.g., praise, handshake, smile, etc.).

250 Does not find necessary locations in the community

Goals:

1. The student will find necessary locations in the community with assistance.
2. The student will independently find necessary locations in the community.

Objectives:

1. The student will find necessary locations in the community when given verbal directions on ____ out of ____ occasions.
2. The student will find necessary locations in the community when given written directions on ____ out of ____ occasions.
3. The student will find necessary locations in the community independently on ____ out of ____ occasions.
4. The student will verbally request directions when in need of assistance in finding necessary locations in the community on ____ out of ____ occasions.
5. The student will find necessary locations in the community by relying upon environmental cues such as building numbers and signs on ____ out of ____ occasions.

Interventions:

1. Reinforce the student for demonstrating the ability to find necessary locations in the community: (a) give the student a tangible reward (e.g., classroom privileges, line leading, passing out materials, five minutes free time, etc.) or (b) give the student an intangible reward (e.g., praise, handshake, smile, etc.).

2. Limit the number of locations the student is required to find on his/her own. Gradually increase the number of locations the student is required to find on his/her own.

3. Write a contract with the student specifying what behavior is expected (e.g., going to and from the restroom in a reasonable amount of time) and what reinforcement will be made available when the terms of the contract have been met.

4. Communicate with parents (e.g., notes home, phone calls, etc.) to share information concerning the student's progress. The parents may reinforce the student at home for finding necessary locations in the community.

5. Have the student run errands to specific locations in the building for practice in finding locations in the community.

6. Inform other personnel that the student has difficulty finding locations in the community so assistance and supervision may be provided.

7. Have a peer accompany the student as he/she attempts to find locations in the community.

8. Make certain the behavior demands are appropriate for the student's abilities (e.g., finding locations alone, finding locations with many students around, etc.).

9. Take the student on a personal tour of locations in the community.

10. Reinforce those students in the classroom who demonstrate the ability to find necessary locations in the community.

11. Develop clear, concise, written directions or a map for the student to use to find locations in the community.

12. Evaluate the appropriateness of the task to determine (a) if the task is too easy, (b) if the task is too difficult, and (c) if the length of time scheduled to complete the task is adequate.

13. Choose a peer to model the ability to find necessary locations in the community for the student.

14. Have the student question any directions, explanations, instructions he/she does not understand.

15. Teach the student to ask for directions when he/she has difficulty finding locations in the community.

16. Be consistent in applying consequences for behavior (i.e., appropriate behavior receives positive consequences while inappropriate behavior receives negative consequences).

17. Have the student identify landmarks throughout the community which help him/her find necessary locations in the community.

18. Have the student carry a map of locations in the community.

19. Have the student develop his/her own directions for finding locations in the community.

20. Encourage the student to keep maps of how to reach each location that he/she visits (e.g., map to the library, map to the grocery store, etc.).

21. Have the student move from one location to another with a group of students until he/she develops the ability to find the locations independently.

22. Explain to the student what he/she has done correctly, what is expected for total correct response, and what he/she can be doing to improve toward or reach total correct response.

23. Encourage the parents' input in developing community access activity expectations in community sites to encourage consistency between home and school.

24. Explain to the student that his/her best effort is more important than perfection to help decrease frustration with the community access task.

25. Use existing community maps at community sites to teach map skills.

26. If the student has difficulty following written directions or a map, tape record directions for the student to follow.

27. Highlight with a marker, colored pencil, etc. a map with the most direct route for the student to follow in getting around the community.

28. If the student is uncertain about where he/she is going in the community, make certain that he/she is accompanied by someone who knows the way. As the student demonstrates success, gradually allow him/her to take community trips alone.

29. Teach map skills in the classroom.

30. Make certain the student has all the necessary items in case that he/she were to get lost in the community (e.g., phone numbers of someone to call for help, change for a pay phone, identification card, etc.).

31. Identify regular routes the student is required to use to find locations in the community.

251 Does not initiate activities appropriate for the situation

Goal:

1. The student will initiate activities appropriate for the situation.

Objectives:

1. The student will independently clean up his/her area at the end of the day on ____ out of ____ occasions.
2. The student will clean up his/her area after a verbal cue at the end of the day on ____ out of ____ occasions.
3. The student will begin an appropriate free time activity after receiving a verbal cue on ____ out of ____ occasions.
4. The student will independently begin an appropriate free time activity on ____ out of ____ occasions.
5. The student will prepare necessary materials for a scheduled activity with a verbal prompt on ____ out of ____ occasions.
6. The student will independently prepare materials for a scheduled activity on ____ out of ____ occasions.
7. The student will rely on environmental cues (e.g., bells, timers, clocks, other students, etc.) to change from one activity to another on ____ out of ____ trials.
8. The student will ask for assistance when necessary on ____ out of ____ trials.
9. The student will use available time to work on assignments, perform responsibilities, read, etc. on ____ out of ____ trials.
10. The student will prioritize and complete assignments on ____ out of ____ trials.
11. The student will put materials where they belong on ____ out of ____ trials.
12. The student will continue working on parts of an assignment while waiting on assistance from an instructor on ____ out of ____ trials.

Interventions:

1. Reinforce the student for initiating activities appropriate to the situation: (a) give a tangible reward (e.g., classroom privileges, line leading, passing out materials, five minutes free time, etc.) or (b) give the student an intangible reward (e.g., praise, handshake, smile, etc.).

2. Reinforce those students in the classroom who initiate activities appropriate to the situation.

3. Carefully consider the age and ability of the student when considering his/her ability to initiate activities appropriate to the situation.

4. Allow natural consequences to occur as a result of the student's initiating activities appropriate to the situation (e.g., finishing assignments during free time at school will result in having no homework).

5. Do not criticize when correcting the student; be honest yet supportive. Never cause the student to feel negatively about himself/herself.

6. Communicate with parents (e.g., notes home, phone calls, etc.) to share information concerning the student's progress. The parents may reinforce the student at home for initiating activities appropriate for the situation at school.

7. Choose a peer to model initiating activities appropriate to the situation for the student.

8. Encourage the student to question any directions, explanations, and instructions not understood.

9. Evaluate the appropriateness of expecting the student to initiate activities appropriate for the situation.

10. Maintain mobility throughout the classroom to determine the student's needs.

11. Make certain the student has the necessary materials to complete assignments/activities.

12. Give the student responsibilities in the classroom to increase the probability of his/her initiating activities appropriate to the situation (e.g., passing out materials, watering plants, collecting schoolwork, etc.).

13. Give the student responsibilities in the classroom that require self-initiation (e.g., peer tutor, group leader, teacher assistant, etc.).

14. Have the student keep a chart or graph representing the number of appropriate assignments/ activities which he/she initiated.

15. Assess the degree of task difficulty in comparison with the student's ability to perform the task.

16. Assign the student shorter tasks (e.g., modifying a 20-problem math activity to 4 activities of 5 problems each, to be done at various times during the day). As the student demonstrates success in initiating assignments/activities, gradually increase the length of the task.

17. Present tasks in the most interesting manner possible.

18. Reduce distracting stimuli (e.g., place the student in the front row, provide a carrel or quiet place away from distractions, etc.). This is to be used as a means of reducing stimuli and not as a form of punishment.

19. Encourage the student to ask for clarification of directions for assignments.

20. Together with the student, develop a list of personal interest/hobbies that can be done during free time (e.g., putting a puzzle together, reading, painting, etc.). Remind the student that when he/she is finished with academic work, he/she may engage in the specified activity.

21. Give the student verbal prompts (e.g., clean up work area when finished, find something to do after assignment is finished, etc.). As the student begins to initiate activities appropriate to the setting, gradually decrease the amount of prompting.

22. Establish classroom rules and work rules that involve cleaning up the work area after work is complete.

23. Provide the student with step-by-step written directions for assignments.

24. Explain to the student that work not done during work time will have to be done during other times (e.g., break time, recreational time, after school, etc.).

25. Maintain consistent expectations within the ability level of the student.

26. Maintain a consistent daily routine.

27. Reinforce the student for beginning, working on, and completing assignments.

28. Provide the student with a selection of responsibilities and require him/her to choose a minimum number of tasks to perform independently (e.g., present the student with 10 academic tasks from which six must be finished that day).

29. Reinforce the student for performing tasks/ activities independently.

30. Speak to the student to explain (a) what the student is doing wrong (e.g., waiting to be told to perform activities) and (b) what the student should be doing (e.g., initiating appropriate activities/ tasks for the situation).

31. Make certain that directions, explanations, and instructions are delivered on the student's ability level.

32. Structure the environment so the student is not required to rely on others for information about assignments (e.g., make certain the student's tasks are on his/her ability level, be sure that instructions are clear, and maintain frequent interactions with the student to ensure success).

33. To detect the student's needs, communicate with the student as often as opportunities permit.

34. Communicate to the student that he/she is a worthwhile individual.

35. Teach the student communication skills (e.g., hand raising, expressing needs in written and/or verbal form, etc.).

36. Encourage communication skills in the classroom.

37. Encourage the student to communicate needs to other personnel in the educational environment (e.g., school counselor, school psychologist, principal, etc.).

38. Provide time at the beginning of each day for the student to organize materials.

39. Provide time at various points throughout the day for the student to organize materials (e.g., before school, during recess, at lunch, at the end of the day, etc.).

40. Assess the quality and clarity of directions, explanations, and instructions given to the student.

41. Provide the student with structure for all academic activities (e.g., specific directions, routine format for tasks, time units, etc.).

42. Provide the student with an organizational checklist (e.g., routine activities, materials needed, and steps to follow).

43. Teach the student to prioritize assignments/ activities (e.g., according to importance, length, etc.).

44. Develop monthly calendars to keep track of important events, due dates, assignments, etc.

45. Provide the student with a list of daily tasks, weekly tasks, etc. (e.g., journal entry each afternoon, literature group always meets on Thursday, etc.).

46. Establish alternative activities for the student to perform when waiting for assistance from an instructor (e.g., check work already completed, color, look at a magazine, organize work area, begin another task, etc.).

252   Does not respond appropriately to redirection in social situations

Goal:

1. The student will respond appropriately to redirection in social situations.

Objectives:

1. The student will be quiet when told to do so on _____ out of _____ trials.
2. The student will return to his/her seat when told to do so on _____ out of _____ trials.
3. The student will cease interaction with others when told to do so on _____ out of _____ trials.
4. The student will respond immediately to redirection in social situations on _____ out of _____ trials.

Interventions:

1. Reinforce the student for responding appropriately to redirection in social situations: (a) give the student a tangible reward (e.g., classroom privileges, line leading, passing out materials, five minutes free time, etc.) or (b) give the student an intangible reward (e.g., praise, handshake, smile, etc.).

2. Speak to the student to explain (a) what he/she is doing wrong (e.g., responding inappropriately to redirection) and (b) what he/she should be doing (e.g., responding appropriately to redirection).

3. Establish classroom rules:
- Work on-task.
- Work quietly.
- Remain in your seat.
- Finish task.
- Meet task expectations.

Review rules often. Reinforce students for following rules.

4. Evaluate the appropriateness of the task to determine if (a) the task is too easy, (b) the task is too difficult, and (c) the length of time scheduled to complete the task is adequate.

5. Reinforce the student for responding appropriately to redirection within a given period of time based on the length of time the student can be successful. As the student demonstrates success, gradually increase the amount of time required for reinforcement.

6. Write a contract specifying what behavior is expected (e.g., returning to seat when told to do so) and what reinforcement will be made available when the terms of the contract have been met.

7. Communicate with parents (e.g., notes home, phone calls, etc.) to share information concerning the student's progress. The parents may reinforce the student at home for responding appropriately to redirection in academic and social situations at school.

8. Reinforce those students in the classroom who respond appropriately to redirection in academic and social situations.

9. Choose a peer to model responding appropriately to redirection in academic and social situations for the student.

10. Have the student question any directions, explanations, or instructions he/she does not understand.

11. Allow natural consequences to occur when the student fails to respond appropriately to redirection in academic and social situations (e.g., make highly reinforcing activities contingent upon responding appropriately to redirection in academic and social situations).

12. Remove the student from the activity if he/she fails to respond appropriately to redirection in academic and social situations.

13. Make certain that attention is not inadvertently given to the student for failing to respond appropriately to redirection in academic and social situations (i.e., remove attention from the student in those instances when attention is reinforcing inappropriate behavior).

14. Provide adequate time for the student to respond appropriately to redirection in academic and social situations.

15. Make certain that redirection in academic and social situations is delivered in the most positive manner possible.

16. Develop subsequent tasks based on errors the student makes rather than requiring an immediate correction of work done incorrectly.

17. Deliver instructions in a clear and concise manner.

18. Assist the student in responding appropriately to redirection in academic situations (e.g., help the student correct one or two items to get him/her started).

19. Deliver redirection to the student as privately as possible.

III. Forms

CONTRACT

I, _____ ,

HEREBY DECLARE THAT I WILL _____

_____

_____

THIS JOB WILL BE CONSIDERED SUCCESSFUL _____

_____

NAME _____

FOR THE SUCCESSFUL COMPLETION OF THE ABOVE JOB

YOU MAY _____

_____

DATE SIGNED _____

DATE COMPLETED _____

_____
(SIGNED)

Outline Form

SUBJECT: _____

Topic: _____

	General	**Specific**
Who:		
What:		
Where:		
When:		
How:		
Why:		
Vocabulary:		

Outline Form (Alternative)

SUBJECT: _____

Topic: _____

	General	**Specific**
What:		
Why:		
How:		
Vocabulary:		
Example:		

Mapping Form

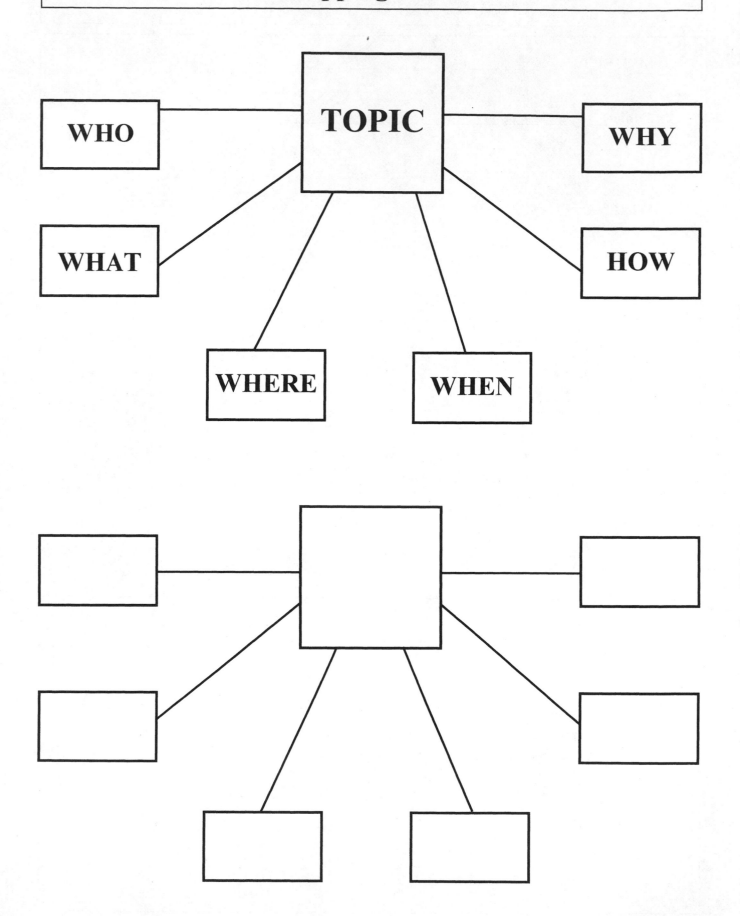

Double-Column Form

SUBJECT: _____

Who

What

Where

When

How

Why

Assignment Form

Subject: _____

	General	Specific
What:		
How:		
Materials:		
When:		

Subject: _____

	General	Specific
What:		
How:		
Materials:		
When:		

Assignment Sheet

ASSIGNMENT SHEET

DATE _____

SUBJECT	ASSIGNMENT	DUE DATE	TEACHER INITIALS

Comments:

_____
PARENT SIGNATURE

ASSIGNMENT SHEET

DATE _____

SUBJECT	ASSIGNMENT	DUE DATE	TEACHER INITIALS

Comments:

_____
PARENT SIGNATURE

2-Week Project Outline

DAY 1   **Determine the exact assignment**
- Identify due date

DAY 2-4   **Project preparation**
- Read assigned materials
- Research related materials
- Gather necessary materials

DAY 5   **Summarize reading material**
- Answer: Who, What, Where, When, How, Why

DAY 6   **Preliminary project construction**
- Make sketches, determine scale, make revisions

DAY 7-11   **Project construction**
- Lay out all materials
- Prepare materials to scale
- Draw/color
- Cut
- Glue
- Paint

DAY 12   **Touch up work**
- Label, check that all items are secure, etc.

DAY 13   **Write paragraph from summary (Day 5)**

DAY 14   **Turn in!**

Test-Taking Skills

1. Survey entire test for the kinds of items that are included (e.g., true-false, multiple- choice, fill-in-the-blank, etc.).

2. Read all directions.

3. Underline or circle all key words or phrases in the directions (e.g., locate, write, choose the best answer, identify the main idea, etc.).

4. Do not answer any items until the directions are thoroughly understood (i.e., ask the teacher for clarification if directions are not thoroughly understood).

5. Respond to all items for which the answer is known; skip remaining items to answer later.

6. For those items which are difficult to answer, underline the key words (e.g., who, what, where, when, how, why) and then respond.

7. For those items still not understood, ask the teacher for clarification.

8. Go back and check all answers for accuracy (e.g., followed directions, proper use of math operations, no careless errors).

ADDITIONAL SUGGESTIONS

- In order for a statement to be true, all of the statement must be true (e.g., note words such as all, never, always, etc.).

- When matching, first answer items that are known. Cross off answers that are used; then go back to remaining items and make the best choice.

- Some items may provide clues or reminders for items that could not be answered the first time through the test.

- When writing an essay answer, construct the answer around Who, What, Where, When, How, and Why.

- On multiple-choice items, read all choices before responding. If any of the choices look new or different, they are probably not the correct answer.

- If a true-false item looks new or different, it is probably false.

Studying for a Test

1. Identify the information to be covered on the test.

2. Identify and collect all necessary materials (e.g., textbook, notebook, etc.).

3. Identify major topics.

4. Under each topic, identify major headings.

5. Under each heading, use the Outline Form to identify Who, What, Where, When, How, and Why or underline/highlight.

6. Make study aids such as flash cards. (See Appendix.)

7. Memorize information using the Outline Form and/or mnemonic strategies.

ADDITIONAL SUGGESTIONS

● Study with a friend.

● Write practice questions from the Outline Form and answer the questions.

● If study questions are provided, answer all questions.

● Make certain that all information in the summary is thoroughly understood.

Flash Card Study Aid

Questions   Topic:_____

Who:

What:

Where:

When:

How:

Why:

Questions   Topic:_____

Who:

What:

Where:

When:

How:

Why:

Fiction Frame

TITLE: _____

AUTHOR: _____

This story takes place _____. An important character in this story

is _____ who _____.

A problem occurs when _____

_____.

Next, _____

_____.

The problem is solved when _____

_____

_____.

At the end of the story, _____

_____

_____.

Parent Letter Sample

Dear Parents:

Your child will be bringing home an assignment sheet each day. This assignment sheet will indicate the assignments that are to be completed at home and when they are due.

Please check for this sheet every day in order to monitor homework completion. After all assignments are completed, please sign the sheet and return it to school with your child. Thank you for your support.

Sincerely,

Note Taking

- Outline Form
  (e.g., Who, What, Where, When, How, Why)

- Mapping Form
  (e.g., Who, What, Where, When, How, Why)

- Double-Column Form
  (e.g., Who, What, Where, When, How, Why)

- Assignment Form
  (e.g., What, How, Materials, When)

- Assignment Sheet

- 2-Week Project Outline

Selected Abbreviations and Symbols

ab.	about		$	money
addn.	addition		mo.	month
&	and		natl.	national
bk.	book		no.	number
bldg.	building		#	number
cap.	capital		oz.	ounce
c/o	in care of		p., pg.	page
cm	centimeter		pd.	paid
cent.	century		par.	paragraph
ch., chap.	chapter		pop.	population
co.	company		lb.	pound
cont.	continent		Pres.	president
cont.	continued		qt.	quart
corp.	corporation		rd.	road
dept.	department		rep.	representative
dict.	dictionary		Rev.	Reverend
educ.	education		sch.	school
enc.	encyclopedia		sc.	science
Eng.	English		sig.	signature
fig.	figure		s.s.	social studies
geog.	geography		sp.	spelling
gov., govt.	government		sq.	square
g	gram		subj.	subject
ht., hgt.	height		subt.	subtraction
hist.	history		syn.	synonym
ill., illus.	illustration		temp.	temporary
in.	inch		T	ton
intro.	introduction		treas.	treasurer
lab.	laboratory		US, USA	United States of America
lang.	language		univ.	university
lat.	latitude		v.	verb
leg.	legislature		vs.	versus
lib.	library		VP	vice president
liq.	liquid		wk.	week
max.	maximum		wt.	weight
meas.	measure		w/	with
mi.	mile		yd.	yard
min.	minute		yr.	year
misc.	miscellaneous			

The above list only serves as an example. The student should further develop his/her own list.

References:

Cormier, R.A. (1995). *Error-free writing: A lifetime guide to flawless business writing.* Englewood Cliffs, NJ: Prentice-Hall.

University of Chicago Press. (1982). *The chicago manual of style* (13th ed.). Chicago: Author.

New York Public Library Staff & Paul Fargis, Editor. (1998). *The new york public library™ desk reference* (3rd ed.). New York: Author.

Typical Methods of Modifying Academic Tasks

- Reduce the number of problems on a page (e.g., five problems to a page; the student may be required to do four pages of 5 problems on each page throughout the day if necessary).

- Use a highlight marker to identify key words, phrases, or sentences for the student to read.

- Remove pages from workbooks or reading material and present these to the student one at a time rather than allowing the student to become anxious with workbooks or texts.

- Outline reading material for the student at his/her reading level, emphasizing main ideas.

- Tape record material for the student to listen to as he/she reads along.

- Read tests/quizzes aloud for the student.

- Tape record tests/quizzes for the student.

- Make a bright construction paper border for the student to place around reading material in order to maintain his/her attention to the task.

- Make a reading window from construction paper which the student places over sentences or paragraphs in order to maintain attention.

- Provide manipulative objects for the student to use in solving math problems.

- Rearrange problems on a page (e.g., if crowded, create more space between the problems).

- Use graph paper for math problems, handwriting, etc.

- Rewrite directions at an appropriate reading level.

- Tape record directions.

- Have peers deliver directions or explanations.

- Allow more time to take tests or quizzes.

Preventing Behavior Problems

- Determine reinforcer preferences.

- Determine academic ability levels.

- Determine social interaction skills.

- Determine ability to remain on-task.

- Determine group behavior.

- Monitor and limit contemporary determinants of inappropriate behavior such as having to wait, task length, task difficulty, peer involvement, etc.

- Base seating arrangements on behavior.

- Base group involvement on behavior.

- Maintain teacher mobility in the classroom.

- Maintain teacher/student contact: visual, verbal, and physical.

- Use criteria for expectations based on observed behavior and performance.

- Use shaping, fading, and imitation procedures to gradually change behavior.

- Maintain variety in reinforcers.

- Use the *Premack Principle* in arranging the schedule (i.e., a more desirable task can be used to reinforce the completion of a less desirable task).

- Use curriculum as reinforcement.

- Use rules, point cards, and schedules of daily events as discriminative stimuli.

- Use contracting to individualize, specify expected behavior, and identify reinforcers.

- Arrange seating so all students have visibility to and from the teacher, and the teacher can scan the entire class.

- Maintain a full schedule of activities.

- Use language that is positive and firm, not demeaning, insulting, or harassing.

- Intervene early when any form of conflict occurs.

- Do not ignore behavior as an excuse for not intervening.

- Use time-out to help the student resolve problem behavior.

- Use removal to prevent contagion, destruction of property, and danger to others.

- Communicate and coordinate with other teachers.

- Communicate with home to prevent students playing one adult against another.

Reinforcer Survey

Name: _____ Age: _____ Date: _____

1. **The things I like to do after school are** _____
    _____

2. **If I had ten dollars I would** _____
    _____

3. **My favorite TV programs are** _____
    _____

4. **My favorite game at school is** _____
    _____

5. **My best friends are** _____
    _____

6. **My favorite time of day is** _____
    _____

7. **My favorite toys are** _____
    _____

8. **My favorite CD is** _____
    _____

9. **My favorite subject at school is** _____
    _____

10. **I like to read books about** _____
    _____

11. **The places I like to go in town are** _____
    _____

12. **My favorite foods are** _____
    _____

13. **My favorite inside activities are** _____
    _____

14. **My favorite outside activities are** _____
    _____

15. **My hobbies are** _____
    _____

16. **My favorite animals are** _____
    _____

17. **The three things I like to do most are** _____
    _____

The Reinforcer Survey may be given to one student or a group of students. If the students cannot read, the survey is read to them. If they cannot write their answers, the answers are given verbally.

A List of Reinforcers Identified by Elementary-Age Students

1. Listen to the radio
2. Free time
3. Watch favorite TV program
4. Talk to best friend
5. Listen to favorite tapes, CDs
6. Read a book
7. Candy
8. Play sports - baseball, kickball, soccer, hockey
9. Ride a bike
10. Do something fun with best friend
11. Go to the zoo
12. Build a model plane or car
13. Go to the arcade and play video games
14. Camping trip
15. Play with pets
16. Go to a fast-food restaurant
17. Pop popcorn
18. Go to a movie
19. Play in the gym
20. Play outside
21. Help clean up classroom
22. Play with puppets
23. Play with dolls and a dollhouse
24. Ice cream
25. Cookies
26. Go shopping at a grocery store
27. Tacos
28. Hamburgers and french fries
29. Pizza
30. Money
31. Trade cards (sports, magic, etc.)
32. Parties
33. Teacher's helper
34. Field trips
35. Eat lunch outside on a nice day
36. Recess
37. Student-of-the-week
38. Honor roll
39. Buy sodas
40. Work on puzzles
41. Write on the board
42. Gumball machine
43. Race cars
44. Use colored markers
45. Roller skating
46. Puppet show
47. Water slide
48. Stickers
49. Pencils
50. Use the computer
51. Fly model airplanes
52. Visit the principal

A List of Reinforcers Identified by Secondary-Age Students

1. Free time

   - Doing nothing

   - Reading magazines (from home or library)

   - Reading newspapers

   - Writing a letter (to a rock star, favorite author, politician, probation officer, friend)

   - Peer tutoring (your class or another one)

   - Listen to CDs or tapes (from class, library, home)

   - Visit library

   - Work on a hobby

   - See a movie

   - Draw - Paint - Create

2. Acting as teacher assistant (any length of time)

3. Acting as principal assistant (any length of time)

4. Have class outside

5. Field trip

6. Go to a movie

7. Have a soda

8. Have an afternoon for a sports activity (some students play and some watch)

9. Play a game (Bingo, cards, board games)

10. Use a camera (take pictures and have them developed)

11. Play trivia games

12. Time off from school

13. Coach's assistant (any length of time)

14. Picnic lunch

15. Run errands

16. Extra time in high interest areas (shop, art, P.E.)

17. Do clerical work in building (use copy machine, run office errands)

18. Library assistant (any length of time)

19. Custodian's assistant (any length of time)

20. Watch TV

21. Earn a model airplane or car

22. Use a computer

23. Attend a sports event

24. Food or treat coupons

25. Iron-on decals

Reinforcer Menu

REINFORCER MENU

Reinforcer	Points Needed
Delivering Messages	15
Feeding Pets	20
Carrying Wastebasket	20
Passing out Materials	20
Peer Tutoring	25
Leading the Class Line	25
Using a Computer	25
Working with Clay	30
Using Colored Markers	30
Using Colored Chalk	30
Operating Audio-Visual Equipment	30
Playing a Board Game	35

CLASS REINFORCER MENU

Reinforcer	Points Needed
Tape Songs	15
Lunch Outdoors	20
Class Visitor	25
Put on a Play	25
See a Movie	30
Write and Mail Letters	30
Field Trip	30
Take Class Pictures	30
Have Adults in for Lunch	30
Pop Popcorn	35

The Reinforcer Menu is compiled from information gathered by having a student or students respond to the Reinforcer Survey.

Point Card

TIME	DAYS OF WEEK				
	M	T	W	T	F
8:00 - 8:50					
9:00 - 9:50					
10:00 - 10:50					
11:00 - 11:20					
11:30 - 12:20					
12:30 - 1:20					
1:30 - 2:20					
2:30 - 3:20					

Name: _____

     This is a Point Card for secondary level students and may be used in special or regular education classes. Teachers assign points, give checks, or sign initials for appropriate behavior demonstrated by the student while in the classroom. These points are relative to rules of the classroom, expected behavior, a contract developed with the student, etc. A 3 x 5 inch index card is easily kept in a shirt pocket and small enough to reduce embarrassment for students who would prefer to keep their behavioral support program confidential.

Point Record

ACADEMIC POINTS

Monday

1	2	3	4	5	6	7	8	9	10	11	12	13	14

Tuesday

1	2	3	4	5	6	7	8	9	10	11	12	13	14

Wednesday

1	2	3	4	5	6	7	8	9	10	11	12	13	14

Thursday

1	2	3	4	5	6	7	8	9	10	11	12	13	14

Friday

1	2	3	4	5	6	7	8	9	10	11	12	13	14

SOCIAL POINTS

Monday

Tuesday

Wednesday

Thursday

Friday

   The Point Record is for recording Academic Points, top section, for each task completed with criteria met; and Social Points, bottom section, for demonstrating appropriate behavior in and around the classroom. The Point Record is kept with the student at all times, wherever he/she may be, in order that points may be given for following any school rules.

Rules for School Environments

GENERAL SOCIAL RULES....

- BE QUIET.
- REMAIN IN YOUR SEAT.
- WORK ON ASSIGNED TASK.
- RAISE YOUR HAND.

HALLWAY RULES....

- WALK IN THE HALL.
- WALK IN A LINE.
- WALK ON THE RIGHT.
- WALK QUIETLY.

CAFETERIA RULES....

- BE QUIET IN THE CAFETERIA LINE.
- WALK TO YOUR TABLE.
- TALK QUIETLY.
- REMAIN SEATED.

OUTDOOR RULES....

- TAKE PART IN SOME ACTIVITY.
- TAKE TURNS.
- BE FRIENDLY.
- LINE UP WHEN IT IS TIME.

ACADEMIC RULES....

- FINISH ONE TASK.
- MEET THE CRITERIA
  TO EARN 5 POINTS.

These rules, except for perhaps the outdoor rules, are applicable to all grade levels and have been used in public schools for general behavioral expectations.

Student Conference Report

Student's Name: _____ Grade Level: _____ Date: _____

School Personnel Involved and Titles: _____

_____

———···•··———

Initiation of Conference:

Regularly Scheduled Conference ☐   Teacher Initiation ☐   Other Personnel Initiation ☐

Student Initiation ☐   Parent Initiation ☐

———···•··———

Nature of Communication:

Information Sharing ☐   Progress Update ☐   Problem Identification ☐   Other ☐

———···•··———

Conference Summary (Attach Copies of Written Communications):

_____

_____

_____

_____

———···•··———

Expectations Based on Conference:

_____

_____

_____

———···•··———

Signatures of Conference Participants:

_____

_____

_____

_____

———···•··———

The Student Conference Report is used for recording conferences held with the student to identify problems, concerns, progress, etc.

Parent Communication Form

Student's Name: _____ Grade Level: _____ Date: _____

Teacher's Name: _____ Class: _____

Parent(s): _____

Other School Personnel: _____

Type of Communication:

Parent Visit to School ☐   Teacher Visit to Home ☐   Out-of-School Location ☐

Letter ☐   Note ☐   Telephone Call ☐   Other ☐

Initiation of Communication:

School Scheduled Meeting ☐   Teacher Initiation ☐   Parent Initiation ☐   Other ☐

Nature of Communication:

Information Sharing ☐   Progress Update ☐   Problem Identification ☐   Other ☐

Communication Summary (Attach Copies of Written Communications):

_____

_____

_____

_____

Expectations for Further Communication:

_____

_____

_____

Signatures of Participants (If Communication Made in Person):

_____

_____

The Parent Communication Form is a record of communication made with parents in person, by telephone, or by notes or letters.

Schedule of Daily Events

SCHEDULE OF DAILY EVENTS

NAME: _____

	#1	#2	#3	#4	#5	#6	#7	#8	#9	#10
Monday										
Tuesday										
Wednesday										
Thursday										
Friday										

SCHEDULE OF DAILY EVENTS

NAME: _____

	#1	#2	#3	#4	#5	#6	#7	#8	#9	#10
Tuesday										

Each individual student's Schedule of Daily Events is developed for him/her and attached to his/her desk for a week at a time or for one day at a time. This schedule identifies each activity/task the student is assigned for the day, and the schedule is filled in by the teacher one day at a time. Students tend to know what they are to do next when the schedule is provided, and teachers can expect fewer interruptions for directions when students refer to their schedules.